December 28, 1992

To Dad,

May all of your future birthdays be happy and fulfilling. May your thirst for knowledge always continue.

Love,

Allison
&
Family

PRINCIPLES *And* PRACTICES

OF · THE RESTORED GOSPEL

VICTOR L. LUDLOW

Deseret Book Company
Salt Lake City, Utah

Library of Congress Cataloging-in-Publication Data

Ludlow, Victor L.
  Principles and practices of the restored gospel / Victor L. Ludlow.
    p. cm.
  Includes bibliographical references and index.
  ISBN 0-87579-649-4
  1. The Church of Jesus Christ of Latter-day Saints—Doctrines.
2. Mormon Church—Doctrines. I. Title.
BX8635.2.L83   1992
230'.9332—dc20   92-29955
                                                          CIP

Printed in the United States of America

10 9 8 7 6 5 4 3 2 1

CONTENTS

PART 5

CHRIST'S KINGDOM ON EARTH 499

KEY TO ABBREVIATIONS IN NOTES

AHD	Morris, William, ed. *The American Heritage Dictionary of the English Language.* New York: American Heritage Publishing Company, 1969.
BD	Bible Dictionary. In LDS edition of the King James Version.
BP	Nibley, Hugh. "Beyond Politics." In *Nibley on the Timely and the Timeless.* Religious Studies Monograph Series, Volume One. Provo, Utah: BYU Religious Studies Center, 1978, 279–305.
CA	*Deseret News 1991–92 Church Almanac.* Salt Lake City: Deseret News, 1990.
CN	*Church News.* Various weeks.
CR	Conference Reports. Salt Lake City: The Church of Jesus Christ of Latter-day Saints. Various months and years.
DBY	Widtsoe, John A., comp. *Discourses of Brigham Young.* Salt Lake City: Deseret Book Company, 1954.
DS	Smith, Joseph Fielding. *Doctrines of Salvation.* 3 vols. Bruce R. McConkie, comp. Salt Lake City: Bookcraft, 1954–56.
EM	Ludlow, Daniel H., gen. ed. *Encyclopedia of Mormonism.* 5 vols. New York: Macmillan Publishing Company, 1992.
FPM	Kimball, Spencer W. *Faith Precedes the Miracle.* Salt Lake City: Deseret Book Company, 1972.
GD	Smith, Joseph F. *Gospel Doctrine.* Salt Lake City: Deseret Book Company, 1939.
GHI	*General Handbook of Instructions.* Salt Lake City: The Church of Jesus Christ of Latter-day Saints. Various years.
GP	*Gospel Principles.* Salt Lake City: The Church of Jesus Christ of Latter-day Saints, 1979.
HC	*History of The Church of Jesus Christ of Latter-day Saints.* 7 vols., index. Salt Lake City: Deseret Book Company, 1951–83.
HSIH	Highway Safety Issues Hearings before the Subcommittee on Surface Transportation of the Committee on Public Works and Transportation, House of Representatives, One Hundredth Congress, Second Session, March 15, March 23, May 3, 1988.
IE	*Improvement Era.* Various months.
ISBE	Geoffrey W. Bromiley, gen. ed. *International Standard Bible Encyclopedia.* 4 vols. Grand Rapids: Eerdmans, 1986.

JD	*Journal of Discourses.* 26 vols. Liverpool: 1854–86.
LF	Joseph Smith. *Lectures on Faith.* Salt Lake City: Deseret Book Company, 1985.
MD	McConkie, Bruce R. *Mormon Doctrine.* 2nd ed. Salt Lake City: Bookcraft, 1966.
MF	Kimball, Spencer W. *The Miracle of Forgiveness.* Salt Lake City: Bookcraft, 1969.
MM	McConkie, Bruce R. *The Millennial Messiah.* Salt Lake City: Deseret Book Company, 1982.
MPLH	*Melchizedek Priesthood Leadership Handbook.* Salt Lake City: The Church of Jesus Christ of Latter-day Saints, 1990.
NWAF	McConkie, Bruce R. *A New Witness for the Articles of Faith.* Salt Lake City: Deseret Book Company, 1985.
STH	Centers for Disease Control, Center for Health Promotion and Education, Office on Smoking and Health. *Smoking, Tobacco and Health. A Fact Book.* Rockville, Maryland: U.S. Department of Health and Human Services, Public Health Service, 1987.
SY	*BYU Speeches of the Year.* Provo: Brigham Young University Press. Various years.
TC	Maxwell, Neal A. *A Time to Choose.* Salt Lake City: Deseret Book Company, 1972.
TETB	Benson, Ezra Taft. *The Teachings of Ezra Taft Benson.* Salt Lake City: Bookcraft, 1988.
TG	Topical Guide. In the LDS edition of the King James Version.
TPJS	Smith, Joseph Fielding, comp. *Teachings of the Prophet Joseph Smith.* Salt Lake City: Deseret Book Company, 1938.
TSWK	Kimball, Spencer W. *The Teachings of Spencer W. Kimball.* Edward L. Kimball, ed. Salt Lake City: Bookcraft, 1982.
UA	Goodman, Susan. "Understanding Alcohol." *Current Health* 2, no. 14 (Nov. 1987): 3–6.
WNTCD	*Webster's New Twentieth Century Dictionary of the English Language,* Unabridged. 2nd ed. New York: Simon and Schuster, 1979.
WSRH	*Welfare Services Resource Handbook.* Salt Lake City: The Church of Jesus Christ of Latter-day Saints, 1984.

ACKNOWLEDGMENTS

Foremost, I appreciate the promptings and inspirations of the Spirit, which motivated this work. As readers ponder the messages of this book, they should open themselves to their own spiritual promptings so that this book can enrich their spiritual understanding.

I am thankful for the love and support of my wife, V-Ann, and our children over the past several years of research and writing. Jason, Jared, Sharryl, Shawnda, Daniel, and David have been patient, and many of the messages of this book are directed to them.

I thank special friends in Boston during my Harvard and Brandeis years of graduate school for the genesis of *Principles and Practices of the Restored Gospel.* Fred and Carol, James and JoAnn, and Jim and Sue — our many hours of gospel discussion planted seeds of need in my mind. This work is their fruit, and its words are dedicated to them.

I have also received help in research, secretarial work, and editing, much of which was made available through the BYU Religious Studies Center. My former secretary, Patty Smith, has provided much assistance. Students and helpers Susan, Michele, Janiel, Janet, Adam, Kristina, Keith, Jana, Mike, Ellen, and others have aided with researching, editing, and polishing this manuscript over the past six years. The publishing staff of Deseret Book, especially Richard Tice, have provided valuable help.

In the end, however, I alone am responsible for the contents. I have learned more than I could ever write in these pages. I also know that in ten years I will have learned much more and thus will probably want to add and change parts of this book—this is the risk and the reward of serious study. Nevertheless, read on, and let us share this learning experience together.

INTRODUCTION

After decades of teaching religion topics on three continents in at least three languages, the beauty and power of the restored gospel message of Jesus Christ continues to amaze and inspire me. To help teach others, both in classroom settings as a professor of theology at Brigham Young University and during informal discussions with friends and neighbors, I have often felt the need for a clear, correct, and complete guide to Latter-day Saint teachings and practices. The principles of the restored gospel are rich with eternal value, like a heavenly treasure chest waiting to be opened, and they need to find place in our hearts. As we reach for and strive to understand God's inspired teachings, we naturally desire to live by them and to help others do the same. Although the gospel truths are worth studying, their greater value lies in learning how to apply them in our own lives. Indeed, Latter-day Saint beliefs are something precious to live by.

In explaining the importance of living the gospel, President Ezra Taft Benson has distinguished between the doctrines and practices of a religion: "Theology is not religion, although the terms are used loosely and often as if they were completely interchangeable in meaning. Both are important. Theology is a science—religion is an art. The sciences stress the acquisition of knowledge while the concern of the arts is mainly the development of specific skills. 'The difference between theology and religion is much like the difference between knowing and doing.' Theology represents what we know and say regarding God—our beliefs. Religion is what we do about it—the way we live our beliefs."[1] Thus, this book, *Principles and Practices of the Restored Gospel,* is about both theology and religion. It will present the major LDS beliefs and teachings about the restored gospel of Jesus Christ, and it will also emphasize the application and living of those principles. In particular, this book will concentrate on the principal truths that lead toward the path of eternal life and salvation.

TRUTHS OF SALVATION

In the normal course of life, we have a variety of priorities we must establish. Foremost among them should be a study and application of the gospel teachings of Jesus Christ. As President Joseph F. Smith taught, "the greatest things in this world are the greatest truths, and there are no truths of greater worth than the truths of salvation. To know and live those truths which bring us again into the presence of God is the crowning achievement of man."[2] Joseph Fielding Smith, President Smith's son and later president of The Church of Jesus Christ of Latter-day Saints, taught in a similar vein that the "truths of salvation [are] easily understood" and that "salvation should be a subject uppermost in the minds of all men. It is, without question, the most important subject that could possibly be considered, . . . as it may be applied in their lives."[3]

The truths about salvation help us understand our eternal nature and our special relationship with our Heavenly Father and his Son, Jesus Christ. These eternal doctrines of the gospel help prepare us to enter a covenant commitment with God, and knowing and believing them help us more faithfully keep his commandments. Living true to these beliefs will allow us to "be saved in the kingdom of God, which is the greatest of all the gifts of God; for there is no gift greater than the gift of salvation." (D&C 6:13.)

We have a long path to travel before we stand before God to see if we are ready and worthy to receive his gift of salvation. Until then, the gospel truths of salvation can bring peace and purpose into our lives. As President Ezra Taft Benson stated: "Thank God for the eternal truths of the gospel of peace and salvation. Thank God for the anchor, the feeling of security, the inner calm that the everlasting truths of the gospel bring to every faithful child of God."[4] By carefully studying and then diligently applying the gospel principles, we place ourselves upon the path of eternal life, which will bring us back into our Heavenly Father's presence.

In this book, our study of basic LDS beliefs will be in five segments.

First, we will review the nature of truth and seek an understanding about the members of the Godhead and the ways they communicate to us through prayer, revelation, the prophets, and the scriptures. Second, we will learn about the plan of salvation with emphasis upon the purpose of this earth life and the reality of our eternal existence, glorified through the atoning sacrifice of the Savior. Third, we will study the basic gospel principles and ordinances of the gospel, learning how we can mature spiritually as children of God. Fourth, we will review the commandments of God and LDS religious practices, many of which are found in traditional Christianity, while others are similar to the religious behavior observed in non-Christian religions. Finally, we will study the priesthood roles and offices and the purposes and programs of The Church of Jesus Christ of Latter-day Saints, including its role in preparing God's children for Christ's second coming.

PART 1

THE MEMBERS OF THE GODHEAD AND OUR RELATIONSHIP TO THEM

CHAPTER 1

WHY SEARCH FOR TRUTH?

At times, we all contemplate the ultimate meaning of our existence. Our reflections often arise when we are in the presence of something mysterious or awe-inspiring, such as the innocence of a newborn child, the sublime thought of a philosopher, the inspiration of the scriptures, the unsurpassed beauty of nature's panorama, or the grief at a loved one's death. At such moments, we join humanity in a pursuit of truth.

Our search for truth might be compared to a wandering young man who came upon an ancient sage. He asked the old man to teach him all the wisdom he had accumulated. Wondering about the young man's commitment to such an education, the sage replied by asking the lad to accompany him to a nearby lake. Standing chest deep in the water, the wise man then said, "If I am to teach you, you must first learn to trust me by putting yourself completely into my hands." The youth agreed and soon found his hands tied firmly behind his back. Then the old man grabbed the lad's head and held it underwater. Before long, the lad started to struggle, twist, and kick, but he could not pull his head out of the water. The old man kept the young man's face under the water until he was just a moment from unconsciousness. When the old man finally released the youth's head, the lad burst out of the water and gasped for air. "Young man," the mentor said, "when you desire learning and truth with the same zeal you just had for air and life, then come and I will teach you."

How do people measure their desire to master truth? Is learning experienced like normal breathing—a thing done casually, without thought or appreciation? Or is learning manifested like the breath of life—something individuals intensely desire with a probing, constant effort and great sacrifice? And what keeps people searching for understanding until they feel they have mastered the topic at hand? Various circumstances seem to motivate humans with a longing to understand the ultimate verities of existence. For example, the wonders of nature might prompt such a period of meditation as one studies the still splendor of a moonlit night, observes the verdant beauty of a misty forest, gazes at a flaming sunset over a desert valley, or watches a new day dawn over a mountain peak. The quest for truth may be roused within the walls of a classroom, a library, a laboratory, or a private study. One person may feel the need to be completely alone as he or she ponders some new knowledge. Another may need the company of others to stimulate thoughtful probing by raising questions or suggesting answers about important truths.

The inquiring minds of scientists, philosophers, and other curious people have invested countless hours, energy, and wealth in the pursuit of truth. Most have searched for truth with their eyes: observing nature and human behavior, looking at microscopes and gauges, and studying manuscripts and computer printouts. Some have sought truth through their other physical senses: listening to sounds and tones, noting tastes and smells, and detecting chemical and physical conditions. Others have tried to find truth through the mind: pondering problems and perspectives, discussing ideas and arguments, and developing theorems and conclusions. Still others have pursued truth with their inner soul or spirit: sensing unseen dimensions and powers, responding to conscience and promptings, and seeking inspiration and revelation from higher sources of divine intelligence. And although many truths have been learned through these approaches, we know that many, many more truths await discovery.

Some people, young children especially, have a natural desire to discover new truths. This desire does not necessarily leave us as we finish school or become older, but it often becomes secondary to other priorities. However, regardless of age, inclination, or education, we sense that most knowledge remains beyond our understanding. Daily we face questions and situations beyond our comprehension. How often we think: "What's going on here?" or "I wish I knew!" Many people shrug off these moments of ignorance, learn little from them, and continue their daily routine. Others accumulate some bits of knowledge through these circumstances as they journey through life. Still others, really wanting to understand, use these opportunities to pursue new knowledge, searching for understanding.

Not only do we vary in the settings where we search for insight, but most of us usually discriminate and select the certain areas of knowledge we want to pursue. We are selective because we sense there are greater, more important and eternal truths compared to lesser, more mundane and temporal truths. For example, the truth about exactly when the sun will set tomorrow is not as important as knowing the rules of good health, which will enable us to enjoy many more years of sunsets. President Benson taught that "all truths are not of the same value. The saving truths of salvation are of greatest worth."[1] We somehow feel that if we, personally, could possess the more valuable truths, they would grant us wisdom, honor, and even wealth. While a mastery of pure truth entices us like an elusive pot of gold at the end of the rainbow, we accept with some frustration the reality that we mortals are very limited in our capacity to learn and apply the great truths of the universe. So we are caught in a constant dilemma—we want to know more truths, especially those of an eternal nature, yet we do not usually know where or how to find them.

In short, there are a variety of types or levels of truth. The Prophet Joseph Smith revealed this principle in modern scripture, saying that "all truth is independent in that sphere in which God has placed it." (D&C 93:30.)[2] Among other things, this means that distinct realms of truth exist, each with its own method or approach to understanding. A simple model encompassing the different types and dimensions of learning truth will be helpful. To begin, we need to examine three spheres of truth: physical, moral, and spiritual.

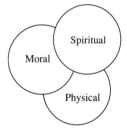

THE SPHERE OF PHYSICAL TRUTHS

We experience our first and primary contact with reality through our physical senses. We say we "know" what we can see, hear, taste, smell, touch, and feel through our senses. In such an empirical approach, we practice the scientific method, collecting data and drawing conclusions that can be verified by further observations. With experience and maturity, we appreciate that the physical body is a marvelous instrument through which we learn much about the universe.

We observe early on, however, that our bodies are imperfect and our physical senses are often deficient. Though human beings are intellectually superior to animals, many animals have more highly developed senses. As examples, people cannot see as well as cats, hear as well as dogs, or move as easily in the dark as bats.

Furthermore, the senses we do possess are vulnerable and easily deceived. A preschooler realizes that the world seems to spin when viewed from a merry-go-round and that a stick will appear bent in water when it really isn't. Older children wonder why lukewarm water seems hot to snow-chilled fingers and why a lemon tastes especially sour when eaten after a sweet dessert. Youth have amused themselves by blindfolding a friend and offering him an apple to eat, while holding an onion under his nose, and then laughing as the confused friend naturally refuses to take a bite. There are many ways our physical senses fail us.

A third limitation of physical senses is that the knowledge we gather through them is often incomplete. Most of our understanding is limited to how much reality we experience and understand. We are often blind to the whole dimension of truth—like the six blind men who had no previous knowledge of elephants and based their interpretation of elephants on the single animal part they first touched. The first, holding the trunk, thought the elephant was a giant snake; the second, touching a tusk, considered it a curved spear; the third, grabbing an ear, believed this animal was a huge leaf or fan; the fourth, touching the stomach, knew it was a leather tent canopy; the fifth, rubbing a leg, assumed it was a large tree trunk; and the sixth, holding the tail, thought an elephant was a whip. They each were correct but incomplete in their understanding.

A fourth challenge we face in our physical perception of truth is that our understanding is always conditional upon our point of view. Numerous examples illustrate this dilemma of natural, human bias. One compares the perspectives of a group of people who had each raised and studied many roses from their own gardens. In listening to them discuss the rose bush, one would think they each were talking about a different plant. A botanist highlights the colors and texture of the flower. A perfumer, with eyes closed, describes the roses' fragrance. A cook tells how to make rose tea from the dried petals. A tailor compares the thorn's sharp points and their hardness with that of needles. A farmer explains how rose vines strung along the fence rows protect his watermelon patch from careless teenagers. A weaver talks of roots that can be woven into a strong cord. Each of these people has a true but completely different perspective that affects their orientation and discussion of a common plant.

In summary, our physical senses are valuable avenues for learning, but they are also weak, vulnerable, limited, and biased. We need to continually increase our understanding of physical truths by expanding our perception of the world around us and by multiplying the means through which we seek these truths.

THE SPHERE OF MORAL TRUTHS

Our perceptions in the second dimension of truth, within the moral sphere, also begin as innate learning skills. Every person is born with a conscience, an inner knowledge of basic right and wrong. Though different ages and cultures have exhibited slight variations in this "moral law," most peoples have possessed common values of justice, mercy, honesty, loyalty, sexual restraint, respect for life, and so on. (See Alma 29:8; 2 Ne. 2:27; 29:7–13.)[3] In the human race as a whole, the idea of decent behavior is accepted as the moral standard.[4]

Moral truths, as they affect behavioral motives, go beyond the physical realm into our souls. Physical truths might describe *how* we act, but moral truths reflect *why* we act. Moral truths define conformity to established sanctioned codes and accepted notions of right and wrong. They also evaluate ethical questions of fairness, integrity, and virtue. The moral dimension incorporates our spirit or conscience in the search for truth.[5]

Unfortunately, our understanding of moral truths can also be weakened or twisted out of balance. Abusive upbringing, peer pressures, corrupt life-styles, and negative influences can dilute and distort our moral perspectives. Just as some people become blind, deaf, or otherwise physically handicapped, a few individuals may become seriously impaired in moral understanding, especially if they are raised in a corrupt environment or if they abuse moral values with destructive, egotistical, and selfish behavior. As will be discussed later, a regular pattern of upright behavior and personal integrity strengthens moral character and leads to a far greater understanding and appreciation of moral truths.[6]

THE SPHERE OF SPIRITUAL TRUTHS

Unlike physical learning and moral perception, spiritual sensitivity, which is the highest realm of truth, is not easily accessible or inherent to our existence. Indeed, the quest for truths within the spiritual sphere often goes against the grain of human nature and contemporary society. Spiritual truths cannot be attained by the usual empirical method through the normal physical senses; they must be learned through the Spirit. Jesus taught that the Holy Ghost, also known as the Spirit of God, is the means to receive truth. Indeed, Christ promised that the Spirit would guide us "into all truth" since he reveals only what the Father gives him. (John 16:7–15, especially v. 13.)

The Apostle Paul taught the Corinthians that the natural person cannot receive spiritual truths except through the Spirit of God. He said that God has prepared insights for us that can be neither physically seen by the eye nor heard by the ear, "but God hath revealed them unto us by his Spirit." He also taught that although we know our own thoughts, "the things of God knoweth no man, except he has the Spirit of God." The words of the apostle Paul make it clear that spiritual knowledge is available only by revelation from God through his Spirit. (1 Cor. 2:6–16, especially vv. 10–11, JST.)

The prophet Joseph Smith learned from the Lord that those seeking spiritual insight should learn both by study (using the physical and mental senses) and by faith (using the spiritual senses). (See D&C 88:118.) He also taught that whatever intelligence and understanding we acquire in this life will remain with our spirits after our death. (See D&C 130:18.) Additionally, we should learn spiritual truths because the glory of God is intelligence, and we cannot be saved in his presence in ignorance. (See D&C 93:36; 131:6.)

Studying spiritual truths is eternally important because our perception of them teaches us eternal values about the purpose of existence and includes an understanding of the glory, nature, and purpose of God. These truths are revealed through visions and revelations recorded by ancient prophets in the Holy Scriptures, are taught through the teachings of modern-day prophets, and, finally, are received through personal enlightenment by the Holy Ghost. Sometimes, enlightenment into spiritual truths comes to us directly and profoundly. Usually, however, we receive spiritual insights indirectly and subtly through gentle spiritual whisperings. Whether learned or sensed, the most valuable and enduring truths cannot be learned in a laboratory; they can be perceived only through the Spirit. Such personal revelation requires a great deal of effort on our part because we must exercise faith in things not perceived by our senses, open our souls to spiritual promptings through meditation and prayer, and keep God's commandments. (See D&C 93:27–30.) In summary, a genuine personal commitment, along with keen spiritual sensitivity, is necessary to learn truths of the spiritual realm.[7]

PHYSICAL, MORAL, AND SPIRITUAL TYPES OF PEOPLE

As we look about us in the world, we can see these levels of truth — physical, moral, and spiritual — reflected in the lives of different types of people. Those who think almost entirely within the physical realm are those for whom everything must be apparent and measurable to be "proven." Searching for data and raw knowledge, they feel comfortable with scientific discoveries and the theories of evolution and natural selection, which seem to explain the physical world around us. Unfortunately, a knowledge of physical truths and powers carries no guarantee that they will be applied for society's best good. For example, a knowledge of the physical laws of atomic power can lead to destructive bombs. Also, dependence upon physical strength alone can lead a society to justify gross behavior upon weaker members — such as demonstrated by Nazi manipulation during the Holocaust. It is no wonder, then, that a common theme of our modern age has been the "survival of the fittest"; for, especially in the natural world, it seems that "might makes right" and the "law of the jungle" prevail. In the physical world, fear and selfishness motivate people while force and oppression often seem to rule.

The search for truth should move beyond these attitudes and platitudes because a complete dependence upon natural, physically observable truths weakens our potential to perceive transcendental moral and spiritual truths. Following personal intuition and centuries of reasoning based upon the observation of society, most people innately believe in the higher, moral laws mentioned earlier. As enlightened by their conscience and motivated by their desire to improve society, people following moral laws bring us out of an animal-like existence into a friendly, productive social order. Modern scripture describes those people as the "honorable men of the earth." (D&C 76:75.) These are people governed by the "strength of justice," rather than the brute force of the "survival of the fittest." Higher moral values provide their ruling principles. Moral people do not seek to manipulate or dominate others, but they try to use personal, social, and legal means to promote the general good. In the moral world, logic directs human behavior as the power of reason governs.

Finally, those sensitive to the promptings of the Holy Spirit are the people who are enlightened and motivated by spiritual truths. Responding to personal revelations, they live by faith in the word of God. While not neglecting the good and the enjoyment that can be experienced on earth, they hope for a future that lies beyond what is humanly possible. Spiritual people desire to share their insights and hopes with others. Looking beyond the "survival of the fittest" or even the "strength of justice," they strive for what can be called the "glory of the righteous," which is eternal life and service in the presence of God. In the spiritual world, love permeates society as the power of righteousness prevails.

Our understanding of most truth is relative to our individual perceptions and is conditional upon our evaluation of perceived reality in the various physical, moral, and spiritual levels. Indeed, insights from the three different levels motivate our relationships with other people. Next, we need to appreciate how insight and knowledge within these three spheres of truth have dramatically expanded in the past century.

FROM ABSOLUTE IGNORANCE
TO COMPLETE LIGHT

To add another dimension to our model of truth, let us now imagine a horizontal plane bisecting any one of our spheres of physical, moral, and spiritual truths. As the spheres lie open before us, in their center lies darkness, or complete ignorance; on the outside edges is light, or an absolute knowledge of all truth within that sphere.

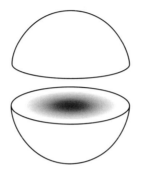

Considering just the physical world, movement toward the light has made remarkable progress as mankind's knowledge of the material world has expanded more in the last century than in all preceding ages combined. Physical truths about the universe have always surrounded us, but we have not always understood them. The principles governing electricity, nuclear energy, satellite communication, microchip technology, and many other modern marvels may have always existed, but they were independent of man's knowledge until recently. We have now progressed to the point where we have learned enough about some of these laws so we can put them to use. As an unknown thinker said: "Truth is never changing, but our perception of it is ever changing."

We are now living in the midst of a "knowledge explosion," in which scientific information is growing at an ever-increasing rate. To illustrate the dramatic nature of this phenomenon, consider a youth graduating from high school today. Since the child entered first grade just twelve years ago, man's knowledge has expanded tenfold. Ninety percent of current scientific knowledge has been discovered during his school years. With finer new instruments to take more exact measurements, newer computers and programs to sort and organize data, and continuous study in all scientific fields, much more is added daily to the store of information. New discoveries correct earlier ideas, challenge old theories, and open up completely different avenues for understanding. Since so much seems to remain unknown, we probably have not progressed very far along the spectrum from complete darkness and ignorance towards absolute light and knowledge. Indeed, some wonder if we can even know how much knowledge is available or how we can ever reach the end.

In a moral and spiritual sense, every person is born in ignorance and darkness, the same condition in which Adam and Eve lived before they ate of the forbidden fruit and acquired the knowledge of good and evil. Unlike the physical realm, where knowledge is expanding faster than any single person can begin to keep up, in the moral realm each individual has to learn the moral verities and values for himself or herself. As we mature, our innate moral sense develops, aided by the teachings of others and our own experiences and challenges. Eventually, we can develop the same foundation and appreciation for lasting moral values as any other person.

While building a secure, consistent moral foundation, we often search beyond ethical principles and seek spiritual truths to support our moral values and to give eternal purpose to our lives. We receive spiritual enlightenment from family, friends, teachers, religious leaders, and the prophets. As in the physical realm, where one's education in math begins with simple calculations and progresses to complex equations and theories, our development in the spiritual realm follows the same pattern of going from the simple to the sophisticated. At the top of the pyramid of learning and intelligence stands God. Latter-day Saints believe that God has a mastery of all truth—he is omniscient, all knowing. (See Ps. 147:5; 2 Ne. 9:20.)

We also understand that God gradually reveals his eternal truths to us as we are able and willing to accept them: "Whom shall he teach knowledge? and whom shall he make to understand doctrine? them that are weaned from the milk, and drawn from the breasts. For precept must be upon precept, precept upon precept; line upon line, line upon line; here a little, and there a little." (Isa. 28:9–10.)

Even with progress, however, Isaiah points out that our earthly understanding of eternal principles will always be severely limited when compared with God's infinite understanding: "For as the heavens are higher than the earth, so are my ways higher than your ways, and my thoughts than your thoughts." (Isa. 55:9.)

God has revealed much truth in the physical, moral, and spiritual spheres to many, but he has so much more knowledge that he could reveal to us collectively and individually. As we hearken unto divine counsels and learn wisdom, God promises us new truths and understanding. (See 2 Ne. 28:30.) Eventually, the Lord will reveal all things about this earth to its inhabitants, and then we will have access to a complete knowledge of physics, chemistry, geology, botany, and so on. (See Alma 12:10; D&C 101:32–34.) Thus, God's influence in our search for truth takes us to the frontiers of knowledge and new dimensions of intelligence and understanding.

TRUTH: PAST, PRESENT AND FUTURE

Adding a third dimension to our model of truth will help further illustrate our difficulty in coming to absolute light and knowledge. This dimension of learning takes us through the time periods of the past, present, and future. We need to add this dimension because modern scripture defines truth as a "knowledge of things as they are, and as they were, and as they are to come." (D&C 93:24.) Revelation also tells us that God knows all things — past, present, and future — because "all things are present" before his eyes. (D&C 38:2.) Although God has known all things from the time before the beginning of this earth, we study truth within the context of our own time and then expand our understanding into the past and the future.

For the most part, we live exclusively in the present, with some understanding of the recent past. Certain fields of human endeavor are making inroads into understanding the past (such as archaeology and ancient textual studies) and even the future (such as scientific projections based on environmental factors). We remain, however, basically ignorant of either the past or the future of our own earth, and we are even less aware of our earth's relation to the rest of time and space.

Returning to our model of the sphere that had been cut open, we need to draw a line on the horizonal plane of the flat interior surface. This line represents knowledge about one particular topic in the time periods of the past, present, and future. The line is hard to draw because the beginning of knowledge on any topic is hidden in our past and because we are uncertain how knowledge will continue into the unknown future after it passes through our present stage. This line weaves around on the plane through the sphere, showing that sometimes knowledge is lost or distorted and must be regained. What we now know may be more or less about that topic than was known in the past or than will be known in the future.

Truth

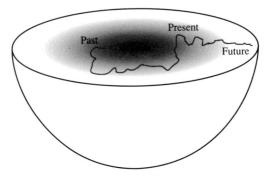

In summary, our model of truth shows that most of man's knowledge lies in the present physical realm, knowledge that is also recently acquired and, at the most, only tenuous. Basic moral understanding has remained more constant throughout history, but it too is limited, unable to elevate man much above human nature. Of absolute, spiritual truths, we know the very least, yet it is significant that what we do know is unchanging and most valuable.

Much of the value of eternal spiritual truth also lies in the way it can illuminate our understanding of the other realms of truth. For example, an understanding of God's past role as Creator of heaven and earth enables us to establish present moral values and to anticipate future order and progression in the universe. The theory of human evolution, on the other hand, necessarily attributes the origin of mankind and humanity's progress to random chance, rendering our existence both physically and morally insecure.

When human beings are reduced to mere animal status, we search for truth like moles searching for food beneath fruit trees at night. The fruit the moles find is that lying on the ground, bruised and half rotten, like many partial truths among the "commandments of men." (JS–H 1:19.)[8] Through the light of divine truth, however, we can look up, find, and enjoy the rich, ripe fruit hanging from God's trees of knowledge and life. (See 1 Ne. 8:10–12.) We can then learn to master and apply various truths for our own edification and the betterment of others.

Knowledge — Learning — Wisdom: Stages of Applied Truth

The process of understanding and applying truth requires at least three stages. First, we broaden the available information by gaining *knowledge* (the body of facts in a field of study) as we seek truth. This process can be compared to compiling data into a company's computer. Then, we evaluate and organize our material through a process of *learning* (the mastery of knowledge or a skill) as we come to an understanding of truth. This step is like organizing the data to recognize patterns or trends and printing them out. And finally, as we share and apply truth with others, we use *wisdom* (the discerning application of knowledge and learning) to achieve the desired results. This last stage is similar to presenting the insights to an executive meeting of the company to assist in making major policy decisions.

First, we need to gain *knowledge* by acquiring facts, data, and details within the physical, moral, or spiritual realm we wish to study. Within the physical realm, reading, asking questions, and observing are keys to acquiring the knowledge discovered by scientists, researchers, and others as they have been enlightened by the spirit of truth. We learn the moral truths by being sensitive to the feelings of our conscience and responding to the ethical teachings of noble people. We acquire the spiritual ideas by studying the inspiration revealed through prophets, apostles, psalmists, and other inspired men and women. All these bits and pieces of knowledge are like the separate pieces of a puzzle that must be gathered together before the puzzle can be constructed.

Second, we need to study and evaluate the things we know by sorting and organizing the information through a *learning* process. We learn to recognize linkages between facts and to compare the form, texture, and essence of different elements. We learn to appreciate the values of different physical items, moral ideas, and spiritual beliefs. Persistent study, analysis, and meditation help bring our facts, concepts, and creeds into sharper focus. This learning process is like joining the pieces of the outer edge of the puzzle together and connecting some puzzle clusters as the puzzle picture begins to develop.

Finally we need *wisdom* to apply what we have learned while joining all the pieces together in a meaningful way. A clear mental vision, combined with physical persistence, helps bring the learning project to fruition. In the physical realm, we experiment and observe as we follow the laws of nature and science. In the moral realm, we practice integrity and discipline as we live goodly lives. In the spiritual realm, we develop sensitivity and exercise righteousness as we follow the promptings of the Spirit. In all areas of our lives, we develop wisdom through applied learning, especially as we observe the results of our actions. Indeed, we hope the time will come when the puzzle is fully assembled and displayed with its organized picture clear to all.

THE VALUE OF TRUTH

Truth can be a powerful tool that blesses or intimidates mankind. God uses truth to bless others. As Ammon in the Book of Mormon declared: God has a comprehensive knowledge of all truth; he understands all fields of learning, and he applies truth with complete wisdom. The key to God's use of truth is that his absolute power is motivated by love as he brings salvation to the righteous. (See Alma 26:35.)

The key to the value of truth for humans also depends upon the person's intent. If a person acquires *knowledge* with a sincere desire to strengthen himself, then evaluates his *learning* with a positive attitude to help others, and finally applies his *wisdom* with a noble motive to serve God, the truths in his power will bless others and himself. As President Ezra Taft Benson taught, "Wisdom is the proper application of true knowledge." He also indicated that "the truths upon which our eternal salvation rests are the most crucial truths that we must learn."[9]

Truth should always be viewed first as a means to an end—and not the end itself. More specifically, truth needs to be seen as a means to a noble and righteous end that will benefit all. The members of the Godhead have a full understanding and mastery of truth, which they share for the understanding, glory, and blessing of the righteous. (See D&C 93:27.) We can summarize the value of applied truth by reviewing a question that members of one international service club ask of their words and deeds. After determining if something is true, Rotarians ask, "Is it fair, friendly, and favorable to all concerned?"[10] If all the truths that we know were only spoken or applied in situations that were "fair, friendly, and favorable to all concerned," then truth would surely benefit all.

Our knowledge of divine truth is the key to attaining, understanding, and righteously applying all knowledge that is available to us in this life. Divine truth comes to us first and foremost through the Holy Scriptures, which testify of Jesus Christ. (See John 5:39.) Jesus is our mediator with the Father, not only for remission of sins, but also for our reception of divine truth. Indeed, truth is embodied in him, as he said, "I am the way, the truth, and the life: no man cometh unto the Father, but by me." (John 14:6.) In the Doctrine and Covenants, the resurrected Lord further confirms our promise that we may eventually possess all divine truth: "He that receiveth me receiveth my Father; and he that receiveth my Father receiveth my Father's kingdom; therefore all that my Father hath shall be given unto him." (D&C 84:37–38.)

THE TRUTH WILL MAKE US FREE

When Jesus Christ was brought before Pontius Pilate, Pilate asked the age-old question, "What is truth?" (John 18:38.) Like many, he asked without really searching for an answer, although he, ironically, was in the presence of the very embodiment of truth. His attitude led Jesus to say, "Every one that is of the truth heareth my voice," meaning that one who lives by the Spirit of God is receptive to his message. Indeed, Jesus testified that he came into the world to bring truth. (See John 18:37.)

Christ promises us enlightenment if we will seek, search, and plead for the truth. (See Matt. 6:33; 7:7–8; D&C 11:7, 21; 2 Tim. 3:16.) Jesus particularly promises his obedient followers that they shall know the truth; so in addition to actively seeking and praying for truth, we need to live worthy of God's inspiration. (See John 8:31.)

The capstone of Jesus's promises concerning truth is that the truth will make us free. (See John 8:32.) Truth in every sphere brings us freedom. Researchers and scientists have discovered and applied many physical truths that make life safer and more enjoyable. In the fields of health and medicine, for instance, we are being freed more and more from disease and other infirmities of the flesh. The sages and philosophers have enlightened us with moral truths that make existence more compatible and stable, freeing us from fear and social chaos. And most of all, God has revealed spiritual truths that make the path to eternal life clearer, freeing us from ignorance and sin.

To receive these highest spiritual truths requires the greatest effort, but they yield the most valuable rewards. We must seek for and value them above all physical wants and desires, all worldly honors and successes. We must "hunger and thirst" after spiritual understanding, just as one gasps for the breath of life after his head has been held under water. As we do so, we will be "filled with the Holy Ghost," the revelator of all truth, and the mysteries of God will be unfolded to us. (See D&C 76:7; 3 Ne. 12:6.) As we know truth, it will free us from darkness, ignorance, superstitions, and lies. (See John 8:32.) As we learn the great, eternal truths, we will come to know God, our Savior, ourselves, and our bonds of love with each other. (See John 17:3.)[11]

To conclude our discussion, we can say that *TRUTH is an accurate understanding of physical, moral, and spiritual reality that God imparts through the ages to bless his children, bringing them freedom.* Although most truth is relative to our perceptions and is conditional upon our understanding of reality, absolute truth is a complete knowledge of all things (past, present, and future), which can be perceived on various physical, moral, and spiritual levels. To assist and bless mankind, God imparts many truths to his children, endowing them with opportunities for freedom. Truth does not just free us *from* damning bondages of ignorance, fear, and sin, but it also frees us *toward* favorable liberties of health, opportunity, and service. Truth frees us to make decisions with a full understanding of options and consequences. With the truth, and God's help, we are free to achieve the full measure of our creation. A fullness of truth brings freedom into our lives and gives them meaning and purpose. We need to constantly thank God for the blessings of truth.

For further study, refer to the following entries:

TG	BD	*EM*
Education	Knowledge	Knowledge
Knowledge		Philosophy
Light		Reason and
Truth		Revelation
		Revelation
		Truth

CHAPTER 2

ONE SUPREME BEING

David, the Hebrew psalmist, pondered about the greatness of God's creations compared to the insignificance of mankind, so he asked God: "What is man that you should spare a thought for him?" David recognized that man was God's crowning achievement, so he responded: "You have made him little less than a god." (Ps. 8:4–5, Jerusalem Bible.) Wondering people today ask a similar question: "Who is God that we should think of him?" Many answer: "He is a living entity far more glorious than man." Some respond: "He is probably just a higher force than man has yet discovered or developed." Others might comment: "Why worry about God? He doesn't seem to be present on this earth." A few may even say: "Some misguided men have made up the idea of a supreme being; he is no more than a figment of their imaginations."

Most people believe in some type of God, power, or force who rules the universe. Is their belief in God merely a response to intense feelings, or can this concept be substantiated by any sort of proof? In other words, is God a fantasy or is he a reality? And if God does exist, can we *know* it for ourselves, or must we rely upon our naïve faith or the belief of others? These are a few questions about God sincere seekers of spiritual truth often ask. The answers are found in the restored gospel. The first Article of Faith claims a belief in God the Eternal Father. He is viewed as the Heavenly Father of all human spirits, and all people may receive a personal witness of his reality.

WHO IS GOD THAT WE SHOULD THINK OF HIM?

Most people begin to think seriously about the possible reality and power of God after an intense emotional experience, either positive or

23

negative. Positive experiences might occur when we feel a oneness with nature and the universe. A quiet stroll on a starlit night, a peaceful walk through a vibrant forest, an intense observation of a gathering storm, or a careful study of plant and animal life—any of these might lead us to contemplate the order and majesty of the universe as the work of a supreme creator. Negative experiences might occur during periods of severe emotional distress, mortal danger, or personal tragedy. In these times, people who do not consider themselves "religious" often tend to appeal, almost instinctively, to some higher power for aid. Their prayer may be just a desperate effort, based only on faint hope, but it is also an indirect acknowledgement of the universal idea of God.

What constitutes the universal idea of God? To begin our investigation, let us first recognize that the idea of a supreme being or force in the universe forms the foundation of most traditional cultures—Christian and pagan, civilized and barbaric. But while the general idea of God is universal, a definition of his specific nature and purposes is not universally agreed upon, for many rival conceptions of God exist throughout the world.

The differences existing among religious systems today can be attributed to a diversity of teachings about God that have evolved through time as distinct world cultures developed. The primary ideological divergence exists between the Western and Far-Eastern religions. Judaism, Islam, and Christianity are the Western world's three great monotheistic religions (sharing belief in a single Supreme Being). They also share verified historical ties to Moses and Abraham, the prophetic heirs of the Adamic tradition. They proclaim a God who is separate and superior to nature, who in fact created and controls the universe.

As a contrast, the oriental religions of the Far East—Hinduism, Buddhism, Confucianism, and Taoism—all set forth "God" as a pervasive force within nature. Also, the Eastern religions emphasize the relationships of people with each other and with nature rather than the relationships between people and God. With religion and philosophy considered as a way of life, not as a mere social or intellectual activity, the aim of the Eastern religions involves a liberation from worldly cares and suffering. The orientals seek harmony with noble moral values and nature, including the higher ideals and powers of the divine within nature.

People today who do believe in a higher force of goodness and in other attributes credited to God have the weight of history and tradition in their support. Adherents of the Western religions also practice a monotheistic tradition supported through written scriptures. Through the Bible in particular, the world possesses a written canon that dates to the beginning of recorded time, containing the witnesses of prophets and others who claim to have seen and spoken with God.

There are important differences among the major Western religions as they attempt to describe God and the monotheistic nature of their own beliefs. Judaism and Islam are the most strictly monotheistic, with the Jews worshipping Yahweh and the Moslems following Allah. Among Christians, however, Catholics and many Protestants worship the Holy Trinity, which is one God, but composed of three parts—Father, Son, and Holy Ghost. Some Protestants reject a literal three-in-one God and are actually more "tritheistic," believing that the Father, Son, and Holy Ghost form a unified godhead, but are separate from one another. Some others, however, believe that God is simply a spirit or a force of nondescript form. Latter-Day Saints adhere to the tritheistic concept, proclaiming that the Father and Son are separate beings with perfected bodies of flesh and bones. Mankind is thus literally made in their image. The Holy Ghost is also a separate divine person with a spirit body in the image of God. Like most Christians, however, we maintain the belief that the members of the godhead are figuratively "one" in love, doctrine, testimony, purpose, and power. (See 3 Ne. 11.)

THE SKEPTICS OF GOD

Unfortunately, some individuals scattered throughout the world claim they do not believe in God at all. Others do not consider it possible or valuable to learn about God, even if one should exist. These skeptics fall into three general camps: atheistic, agnostic, and apathetic. The atheist denies that God exists; he believes in no divine power whatsoever. The agnostic is not quite so audacious; he just denies the possibility of knowing whether a divine being exists. The apathetic is not much concerned one way or the other; he considers the issue irrelevant. In any case, these groups leave God with few choices to manifest himself to any of them. Since the attitudes and ideas of the skeptics often confront God-believers and those seeking to know the reality and true nature of God, discussing the major arguments and fallacies of these three types of nonbelievers will be helpful.

ATHEISM

Atheists argue that if there were a God with supreme knowledge, power, and goodness, he would not permit the overwhelming injustice and innocent suffering that has often characterized human history. They point to the many examples of violence, wars, genocides, and holocausts that a divine, powerful being should be able to prevent if he really existed and had concern for people on this planet. Christians (and the followers of many oriental religions) respond that mankind is responsible for most of the evils of the world. God gave Adam and Eve agency—the power to choose—and let them have dominion over all the earth, to rule and take care of it. (See Gen. 1:26.) So we humans—not God—are the ones who both cause and tolerate most of the suffering of our own race as we yield either to our own selfishness or to the temptations of Satan.

The atheist would then question why a God would give mankind the agency to bring suffering upon each other, or why a God would not give people a more powerful conscience so they would avoid the injustices that otherwise prevail in the world. Granted, one might ask where the atheist develops his ideas of justice/injustice, or guilt/innocence in the first place. These ideas are an inherent part of universal moral truths that frame Western religions' concept of God. In other words, the atheist's criticism of God is based on inherent principles of conscience (a gift given by God) and on ideals derived from God's own divine character and laws (as recorded in the scriptures from God). Christianity claims that people have a conscience and agency to act as they will so that they can grow and develop within the moral and spiritual realms of truth.[1] A major purpose of mortality provides people the opportunity to develop spirituality in a corrupt environment.[2] In his own time and way, God will bring all people to a correct understanding of right and justice. (See Rom. 14:11–13; Isa. 45:23; 55:8–9.) The prophets declare and the scriptures witness that divine laws of eternal justice, as administered by God, will eventually rectify and compensate all the suffering that mankind brings upon itself.

The atheists then argue, if God exists, why does he not at least prevent the afflictions resulting from natural catastrophes? God may give people their agency, but nature should be under his dominion. Why, they ask, does he allow droughts, famines, earthquakes, diseases, and other natural sources of physical suffering? God himself answers this question through the scriptures, which record that the rains, the storms, and other natural phenomena are shared by all, the good and the evil, the rich and the poor. (See Matt. 5:45; 7:25; D&C 90:5.) However, according to the level of obedience to various physical, moral, and spiritual laws, the people who are prepared, righteous, and faithful will weather the storms and other natural catastrophes with less suffering and trauma. God chooses to not shelter us completely from the world of pain, but he desires to prepare us for life and the suffering that can be a part of it. He does give us inspiration and help to adjust to the temporary circumstances of the natural world, and he instructs us to help each other in times of disaster. He also commands us to assist the hungry, the thirsty, and others in need. If we did not complicate the situations of physical catastrophes with our injustices or selfishness, we could quickly alleviate most of the suffering resulting from the natural world.[3]

AGNOSTICISM

The agnostics are willing to concede that a God may exist, but to them he is unknown and unknowable. They think it is impossible to know whether there is a God or a future life, or anything beyond material phenomena. They would ask, even if God should exist, how does one obtain and maintain faith in a being who often has left man in such dire circumstances, like those described earlier as part of the atheist arguments? Another characteristic of agnostics, which atheists also share, is to reject the credibility of others who claim to have received revelation from God, saying that these people are deluded souls at best or outright liars at worst. Agnostics abstain from either affirming or repudiating the existence of God. They do not deny God's existence, but they deny the possibility of knowing him because such knowledge is beyond human comprehension. As agnostics refuse to make judgments concerning the realities of spiritual truths, they avoid both the power that religion could bring into their lives and the responsibility that religious conviction might impose upon them. Thus they forfeit opportunities for spiritual development.

APATHY

The apathetics do not want heated discussions—they are willing to let each believe and act as he will, as long as belief and action do not infringe on another's life-style. What these indifferent people really demand is that God reveal himself personally to them, or they will not believe or care whether he exists. But in refusing to search for an unseen and distant being, they reject the principles of faith, obedience, fasting, prayer, and so on—the very methods God has established for us to come to know him. If their hearts remain hardened against God, they will exclude themselves from ever knowing him. (See 1 Ne. 15:11.) Jesus warned against an apathetic attitude when he told those who were lukewarm that he would spew them out of his mouth like vomit. (See Rev. 3:16 and fn. 16b.) Insensitive individuals who procrastinate their spiritual development and reject the Lord because of worldly cares risk a forfeiture of the blessings and ordinances of the gospel. (See D&C 39:5–10; Alma 34:33.)

In the end, the atheist's arguments do not disprove the reality of God, they just cast doubt on his purposes and designs. The concerns of the agnostic, on the other hand, are not so much whether God exists, but whether it is possible for mankind to find the truth about God. Finally, the apathetic person feels that all the questions, concerns, and arguments about God have no direct bearing on his life, as long as he is free to pursue his own priorities.

THE SEARCH FOR TRUTH ABOUT GOD

In comparison, those who walk the path in search of truth about God must necessarily ask at least three key questions about God as they seek to establish his reality and purpose: "Is there a God?" "Does God ever reveal himself or his power on this world?" and "Would God ever make himself known to me?" Coincidentally, the answers to each of these questions also address the basic issues raised by the atheist, agnostic, and apathetic. The first key question we and the atheists must resolve is "Does God even exist at all?"

DOES GOD EXIST?

First, either there is a God or there is not a God. If God has ever existed in the past, he must by nature and definition still exist today because one of the divine attributes of God is that he must be immortal and unchanging in his essence. So, supposing the atheist could empirically search the universe for God, he would first need to know what he was looking for. The earliest concepts about God were recorded in the ancient scriptures, but they have since been dispersed and corrupted into many varied traditions and beliefs about God. If, however, the believer and nonbeliever could come to terms on what they were seeking, the only way to independently disprove the existence of God would be to explore instantaneously the entire universe with some sort of miraculous, superhuman vision. One would have to establish the fact that at any given instant, there was not on any planet, in any cloud, within any cave, behind any sun, indeed anywhere in creation any power, force, or being that could be identified as God. Only then could one be sure that God was nowhere to be found.

Ironically, to prove the truth or falsity of God's existence, one would himself have to be a god. Instantaneous observation of the whole universe and comprehension of all available data would itself require a godlike power. In the end, atheism is an unprovable proposition. (See Alma's response to Korihor's atheistic statements in Alma 30.) This brings us back to where we started: all that we know or can know of God is what he reveals to those he chooses. Thus, on the basis of no evidence (but with our own ideas about what God should be doing on earth), we can choose to ignore God. Or, on the basis of some evidence (and with personal hopes and feelings about what God might expect of us), we can choose to seek him. (See Mosiah 4:9.)

DOES GOD MAKE HIS PRESENCE KNOWN?

Assuming that God does exist, we and the agnostics then come to our second key question: "Does God ever reveal himself to people on earth?" If he should choose to remain hidden from us, we could never find him and come to know him. He must make his presence known to man, or his existence would mean nothing to us—our lives would be as frustrated and meaningless as if he were not there at all.

We have comfort, though, because God has revealed himself to many prophets throughout history: Adam, Enoch, Abraham, Moses, Jacob, Isaiah, and John the Baptist in the Old World; Lehi, Nephi, Jacob, Alma, Mormon, Moroni, and Joseph Smith in the New World; to name just a few. The scriptures provide a great written witness of the Lord's dealings with humanity over the course of thousands of years. Furthermore, Latter-day Saints believe that God continues revealing himself in the present day through appointed living prophets, "For do we not read that God is the same yesterday, today, and forever, and in him there is no variableness neither shadow of changing?" (Morm. 9:9.)

In addition to the prophets' voices, we also have the feelings and experiences of others who testify that they have received a personal witness of God's reality. These people, who have been prompted by the Holy Ghost to come to an understanding of God, let us know that God continues to communicate with some of us. Although their involvement is not as profound and expansive as the prophetic experience, they help us appreciate that God maintains contact with people on this earth. From the cumulative experiences of others, we can come to know more about the identity and attributes of God, especially that he exists and that he reveals his mind and will.[4]

DOES GOD MAKE HIMSELF KNOWN TO ME?

Though God may continue to reveal himself, does he communicate only with a select few, who in turn minister to the rest of us? Or is he personally accessible to everyone — common people like ourselves? This is the third key question that we ask as we search for God: "Does God communicate with me?" And with those who are apathetic, we would also ask: "Is it *important* that God communicates with me?" The answer of the restored gospel is an emphatic "yes!" The invitation to personally know God is extended to all. While God's criteria must be met before he chooses to reveal himself to us, we are the ones who must decide whether we seek to gain his communication. For his part, God pleads with us to keep searching: "Ask, and it shall be given you; seek, and ye shall find; knock, and it shall be opened unto you: For every one that asketh receiveth; and he that seeketh findeth; and to him that knocketh it shall be opened." (Matt. 7:7–8.) Again, every person can apply this formula: "For there is no respect of persons with God." (Rom. 2:11.)

On a few occasions — as with Paul in the New Testament or Alma the Younger in the Book of Mormon — God seems to have revealed himself to some people who did not seem interested in him, or who were actually rebelling against him. These cases, however, form a minority of the spiritual conversions recorded in the scriptures. For the most part, a divine response is rarely given unless an honest question is ardently asked with a sincere desire. For example, God's revelations to the Prophet Joseph Smith generally follow this pattern. From the First Vision, when the Father and the Son initially appeared to him, through the revelations recorded in the Doctrine and Covenants, most of the divine communications came in response to the prophet's prayers. Also, by the time Joseph asked a question, he was usually prepared in heart and mind to receive the answer and to live by it.

The Prophet Joseph Smith taught in his *Lectures on Faith* that the first man, Adam, had the correct perception of God because of his direct association with Heavenly Father in the Garden of Eden. "Adam, thus being made acquainted with God, communicated the knowledge which he had unto his posterity; and it was through this means that the thought was first suggested to their minds that there was a God, which laid the foundation for the exercise of their faith, through which they could obtain a knowledge of his character and also of his glory."[5]

Who Is God?

In order for each of us to receive our own personal witness of God, we must seek after him. We should first study the messages and witnesses of the prophets. Then we should ask God to send us our own individual witness through the promptings of the Holy Spirit.[6] As we study the word of God and respond to spiritual promptings, we begin to understand his character and attributes. With this perspective, we might define the nature of God as follows: *God our holy Father is an immortal, perfect being whose infinite wisdom, supreme power, and active love offer us immortality and the possibility of eternal life with him.*

First, God is *holy*. Holiness is an attribute of those who are dedicated and consecrated to sacred, eternal values of goodness and truth. God is full of goodness, light, and truth. His righteousness, glory, and sacredness are beyond description, and his ultimate desire is to help us become more like him. He has consecrated himself to eternally serve others, and he is dedicated to fostering holiness in his children and in all creation. We should join Moses and the ancient Israelites in singing, "Who is like unto thee, O Lord, among the gods? who is like thee, glorious in holiness?" (Ex. 15:11; see also Lev. 11:44–45; 2 Ne. 9:20.)

Second, God is the *father* of our spirits, since he provided our primal intelligence with an organized spirit body. That spirit body would later give life to the mortal body we call flesh. Thanks to God, we have the capacity to enjoy existence in our present state. God is also the father of the eternal plan of salvation, which his Son implements in our behalf. In the beginning, God also was the father or creator of this earth and of the physical bodies of our primal ancestors, Adam and Eve. In prayer and song, one of the most sacred names we invoke for God is expressed when we call him our Heavenly Father. (See Matt. 6:9; Acts 17:28–29; Mosiah 2:34.)

Third, God is *immortal.* His essence, or intelligence, is eternal, without beginning or end. In body and soul, he lives forever, and he has shown us the path towards immortality. The reality and power of his being cannot be destroyed or diminished. His will and purposes are unchanging—he is the same yesterday, today, and forever. (See D&C 20:12, 17–19; 1 Ne. 10:18; James 1:17.)

Fourth, God is a *perfect* being with a glorified, resurrected body. He is absolutely complete and pure in his physical, emotional, social, intellectual, moral, and spiritual nature. His perfection is so all-encompassing that multitudes of titles can barely begin to describe his glory. He enjoys the ultimate, highest form of existence and excellence. (See Matt. 5:48; Alma 42:15; D&C 130:22.)

Fifth, God is *all-knowing.* Past, present, and future are before him, and he sees the beginning from the ending. Not only is he master of all physical and spiritual laws in the universe, but he also knows each of us intimately and completely. We, too, were in the beginning with him, and from our eternal intelligences he created our spiritual bodies. God has knowingly and justly placed us each on earth in circumstances conducive to our individual development. He allows disease and hardship, wickedness and war to exist so mankind can experience a full range of feelings and can foster attributes of humility, sensitivity, and service. Ultimately, his knowledge and justice will rectify all temporal imbalances, and he will reward each as deserved. (See 1 Sam. 2:3; 1 Ne. 9:6; D&C 38:2; 88:6, 41.)

Sixth, God is *all-powerful.* He manifests his power through his works, his servants, and his priesthood. He controls the elements, performs miracles, and blesses the lives of his children both physically and spiritually. Though he allows mankind its agency to choose evil and thereby permits Satan temporary power on earth, the Almighty God will eventually cleanse the earth from all corruption and wickedness. He will then prevail forever because righteousness is the source of his power, which he uses only for the benefit of humanity. (See Rom. 13:1; Alma 26:35; 57:26; D&C 61:1.)

Seventh, God is *active.* He continues to create and sustain worlds, speak to prophets, answer prayers, and heal the physically and spiritually sick. He administers through his appointed servants on earth and by the Holy Spirit to direct and inspire us, his spirit children. His works also continue beyond death on this earth, extending to the spirit world, where the gospel is preached to all those who have died, and where individual spiritual progression continues toward resurrection and eternal life. God did not, as some modern philosophers contend, simply set the world in motion and leave us to our own devices. Modern revelation confirms that he is very much involved with us — indeed, as much as we allow him. (See Job 37:14; 3 Ne. 21:9; JS-H 1:17.)

Finally, God is *loving.* With no further perfection to gain for himself, his expanding glory and the sole purpose for his existence is our salvation, and his sole motive is love. This he succinctly revealed to Moses: "Behold, this is my work and my glory — to bring to pass the immortality and eternal life of man." (Moses 1:39.) To accomplish this end, God sent his Only Begotten Son, Jesus Christ, to show us the way of salvation and to atone for our sins so that we may follow the gospel path back to God's presence. (See John 3:16; 1 Jn. 4:8; 2 Ne. 1:15.)

These eight definitions highlight only a few key attributes of God. Many of them are summarized in a profound declaration of the Prophet Joseph Smith. As recorded in Doctrine and Covenants 20, he revealed some essential reasons why "we know that there is a God in heaven, who is infinite and eternal, from everlasting to everlasting the same unchangeable God, the framer of heaven and earth, and all things which are in them." (V. 17.) Almighty God's creation of humankind in his own likeness, his holy laws, the redemption of his Only Begotten Son, and the witness of the Holy Ghost are the primary means by which we know there is a God in heaven. (See vv. 18–28.) These manifestations of God will be discussed later as valid and personal demonstrations of the continuous love that Heavenly Father has for us, his children.[7] Our best response to these witnesses of God's existence is to follow the Prophet Joseph's admonition, declaring "that all men must repent and believe on the name of Jesus Christ, *and worship the Father in his name,* and endure in faith on his name to the end, or they cannot be saved in the kingdom of God." (V. 29; italics added.) As we study the scriptures and learn more about God our Father, we strengthen our resolve to worship him with sincerity of heart and conviction of spirit.

An understanding of God and his divine nature gives us confidence in his laws and teaches us about the purposes of our existence. The knowledge that God ultimately controls the universe is essential to comprehending our world's history and its present conditions. As discussed in chapter one, a proper knowledge of spiritual truths illuminates other spheres of truth and places our limited human understanding in its proper perspective. Remembering the divine attributes of Heavenly Father helps us counter the philosophies of men that would deny or distort God's power.

Some Philosophies of Man That Negate God

Through the ages, various theories, philosophies, and false religions have drastically distorted or even negated the teachings about the nature of God. As one example in our day, some concepts of the theory of evolution, or natural selection, challenge God's supreme position as creator and controller of the universe.

The Theory of Evolution

Evolution in its purest and simplest theory holds that all life forms as we know them on this earth evolved from a single life form — a simple cell — billions of years ago. This original cell, too, came into being quite by chance in one of this earth's primeval seas. Obviously, this theory takes God out of the picture, and man's achievements and native supremacy over other life forms becomes an amazing series of accidents.

Granted, the Latter-day Saint ideas of successive periods of creation (evolving ages), progression of life forms from spirit to physical to immortal bodies (a type of evolution), and the ultimate triumph of good over evil (the survival of the fittest) could be viewed as refined, spiritual interpretations of natural evolutionist theories. However, there are two critical areas where these theories of man and the scriptural accounts of God differ.

First, according to the theory of evolution, all forms of life on this earth had to originate and evolve from a state of primal lifelessness. Some aspects of this theory may be true in the universal development of life, but they may not apply specifically to this earth. For the evolutionists, no form of life could have entered this earth's biosystem from without, and no outside life forms could have influenced the natural course of earth life, for life evolves uniformly in a closed system. But the scriptures and the prophets declare that God (a powerful, living entity from outside this earth's natural biosystem) organized and created this earth. He prepared the earth to bring forth plant life and to sustain animal life. (See Abr. 4:11–12, 20–22, 24–25.) He ordered plants and animals to be placed on the earth, and he commanded them to multiply, each in their own kind. (See Moses 2:11–25.) Whether God received these plant and animal life forms from seed stock originating on this earth or from other biological sources is not revealed to us. This involvement of God runs counter to the basic tenets of the theory of natural selection.

Second, the theories of evolution emphasize the physical forms of existence, formed only here on earth. The scriptures record, however, that humans, animals, plants, and all forms of life had a spirit creation prior to their physical existence on this earth. (See Moses 3:5.) Thus the existence and form of living organisms were not determined solely by physical antecedents on earth, but also upon their spirit form and divine purpose, established before any physical material became a new organism — plant, animal, or human. This spirit entity gives both life and direction to the physical organism. Thus, external, physical life forms can be influenced by the spirit within.

The scientific problems and religious arguments surrounding the theory of evolution have filled thousands of volumes and cannot be adequately approached in this chapter. It is also important to remember that all the facts have not yet been revealed by God or discovered by man, and so differences and gaps remain between the theories of men and the limited records of God's revelations. But we should state that, at least in its most radical form, natural selection is ultimately incompatible with the teachings of the scriptures and the revealed gospel, especially as the theory of evolution takes God out of the picture and does not recognize his influence upon the life of this earth.

In summary, God's involvement in the creation and the influence of spirits within all life forms both affect our existence in ways that cannot be explained or understood by theories of natural selection and evolution. Every thinking person must therefore choose (on faith, if you will, in either some teachings of men or the declarations of the scriptures) his basic assumption—that the world was either formed completely by random chance or created purposefully by divine design—and proceed cautiously from there.[8]

IS THERE LIFE ON OTHER WORLDS?

Another increasingly popular theory also takes God out of our picture of earth life. While science strives to explain the world by wholly natural phenomena, a growing number of people in the "space age" explain some supernatural occurrences not as "miracles" from God, but as extraterrestrial intervention from even higher "life forms" than ourselves. The most widely known theory of this kind is outlined in various books of the supernatural and science fiction that hold that ancient Americans must have received help from extraterrestrial beings to develop extremely accurate calendars and to construct what, from high altitude photography, appears to be remarkable "airfields," or landing sites and other wonders.

Similar apologists for the Bible would say, for example, that the prophet Elijah was not taken into heaven by one of God's fiery chariots (as recorded in scripture), but rather in a spaceship belonging to superhuman beings. The fiery chariot was not a miracle; Elijah was just a member of an advanced society far ahead of the Israelites of his time. This would also explain his control over the weather, his raising people "from the dead," and other miracles. These advocates of extraterrestrial contacts with earth explain that by the same token, if some of us could travel years back in time on this earth or to some other place where we could visit more primitive people, we too could amaze and subdue these undeveloped people with the magic of a videocamera and a giant projection screen, an x-ray or sonar-graph machine, or any number of other modern electronic "miracles." We could also heal many of their number with our medications and bring prosperity through our application of agricultural knowledge until, within a short time, these people would worship us as gods or at least as angels of some supernatural divine being. As outlandish as extraterrestrial theories may seem, they illustrate the lengths to which some modern people will go to circumvent God and his truly miraculous and mysterious ways.

FAITH IN GOD

A simple belief and faith in God and his plan, however, does not completely explain all the mysteries and wonders of this earth. Neither the scriptures nor man's understanding have yet supplied ready answers to apparent contradictions within some fields of science and between some theories and theology. Many truths remain to be discovered, and until then God has seen fit to reveal what he considers to be most important for our spiritual development and salvation. His truths are sometimes called the "mysteries of God," and they are only slowly revealed to this children. But like a good mystery novel, where our major interest is to discover "Who did it?" and "Why did they do it?" God has revealed the answers to "who" and "why" in the scriptures. He tells us that *he* himself created, or organized, this earth and that he did it to help us progress toward immortality and eternal life. (See Moses 1:39.)

In addition, God reveals enough about himself and his plan that we can develop faith in him. His loving efforts are also manifest enough upon this earth so we can know that he remains active in our lives. A true knowledge of God anchors us in life so that we are not easily seduced by every new idea, "carried about with every wind of doctrine, by the sleight of men." (Eph. 4:14.) More important, a correct perception of God gives us a secure foundation on which to build a further understanding of unchanging, eternal, spiritual truths, such as the identity of God's Son, Jesus Christ, which will be treated in the next chapter.[9]

In conclusion, *GOD OUR HOLY FATHER is an immortal, perfect being whose infinite wisdom, supreme power, and active love offer us immortality and the possibility of eternal life with him.* A true knowledge of God profoundly enriches our lives. As we acknowledge his creative powers in our behalf, strive to keep his commandments, develop faith in his Son, and listen to the promptings of the Holy Spirit, we will come to know and love our Heavenly Father. As we study, ponder, and pray about his works and teachings as taught in the scriptures, we will appreciate his true nature. As we associate with others who have strong testimonies of God, we strengthen our own convictions concerning our holy Father and his expectations of us. And as we serve and love others, we serve and love him who gave us life.

For further study, refer to the following entries:

TG	BD	*EM*
Apathy	God	Elohim
God, Access to		God
God, Body of		God the Father
God, Creator		Holiness
God, Eternal Nature		Love
of		Name of God
God, Foreknowledge		Omnipotent God;
of		Omnipresence of
God, Intelligence of		God; Omniscience
God, Justice of		of God
God, Love of		
God, Manifestations		
of		
God, Mercy of		
God, Omniscience of		
God, Perfection of		
God, Power of		
God, Presence of		
God, Wisdom of		
God, Works of		
God the Father		
Holiness		
Holy, Holier, Holiest		

CHAPTER 3

OUR HOLY BROTHER

As people in the workplace observe many managers and supervisors, they soon recognize different qualities and styles of leadership. True leadership requires more than a position of authority, it includes proper training, a farsighted vision, a loving attitude, and diligent effort. Ideally, solid guidance and noble motives would permeate all levels of management in business, government, education, or wherever positions of influence are found. Typically, however, the one person who establishes the administration pattern for any organization is the head. The founder or leader determines the governing philosophy and directs the efforts of the whole group. People seeking employment would obviously prefer working in an association presided over by a wise, loving, and conscientious leader.

Similar expectations carry over into other social organizations, such as churches or religions. Without a doubt, one reason Christianity has become the largest religion in the world is because of the sterling qualities of its founder, Jesus, the humble carpenter's son and teacher of righteousness from Nazareth. Even the adherents of other religions usually recognize the example of his life and appreciate the values of his teachings. He is a model of holiness for the world.

Jesus is revered by one-third of humanity as the supreme Lord of this earth. Eventually all peoples and nations of the earth will recognize Jesus the Messiah as the Lord and King of this earth; then the prophecies of Isaiah and John the Revelator will be fulfilled. (See Isa. 45:23; Rev. 17:14; 19:16.) Until then, Christians have the responsibility to practice the Savior's teachings as they share his gospel with others. An in-depth understanding of the divine nature of Jesus will inspire his followers and educate non-Christians as they converse with each other.

39

To help understand who this person, Jesus, is, we will focus on three of his names that define his relationship to God the Father and ourselves. These are familiar names that we use in our earthly families: Son, Brother, and Father.

JESUS: THE SON OF GOD

Through the writings of the New Testament, Jesus Christ is familiar to Christendom as the "Son of God." Even so, many Christians consider the title to be the figurative expression of a mysterious and transcendental state of being. They accept the carpenter's son as a spiritual embodiment of divine holiness but do not believe that Jesus is the literal, physical Son of the living God. Through the revelation of the Prophet Joseph Smith, however, Latter-day Saints boldly declare that Jesus is literally the Son of God—his spirit child, his only begotten in the flesh, and his fully obedient offspring. The son of Mary was also the Son of Heavenly Father, spiritually, physically, and ideally.

THE FIRSTBORN SON OF GOD AS A SPIRIT CHILD

Spiritually speaking, Jesus was the first spirit being whom God the Father formed from the eternal intelligences that dwelt with him. The early apostles understood this important dimension of Jesus. Thus Paul taught that God knew Jesus beforehand and designated him to be formed in his image as his Son, that Jesus "might be the firstborn among many." (Rom. 8:29.)

Also, the gospel of John begins with an important reference to Christ's premortal existence. Though brief and somewhat cryptic, John's introduction reveals a great deal about the divinity and role of the Savior before he ever walked upon the earth: "In the beginning was the Word, and the Word was with God, and the Word was God. The same was in the beginning with God." (John 1:1–2.) To understand the meaning of these sentences, we must first consider the Greek term *logos,* which is generally translated into English as "word." *Logos* is akin to logic, the faculty of thinking, reasoning, or intelligence that man particularly possesses among all creation and that is evidenced above all through his use of language. Thus, in the beginning, there was an *intelligent being* who was both with God and became himself God.

The Lord Jesus clarifies his premortal status in modern revelation: "I was in the beginning with the Father, and am the Firstborn." (D&C 93:21.) Of all the eternal, primal intelligences in the presence of God, Jesus was the first that Heavenly Father formed into a spirit being—he was thus the "firstborn" in the spirit and was present with the Father from the beginning of the spirit creation of the earth's inhabitants.

The Lord further explained to Abraham that when "there are two spirits, one being more intelligent than the other; there shall be another more intelligent than they; I am the Lord thy God, I am more intelligent than they all." (Abr. 3:19.) The late apostle Bruce R. McConkie interpreted this passage to mean that through "obedience and devotion to the truth he [Christ] attained that pinnacle of intelligence which ranked him as a God, as the Lord Omnipotent, while yet in his pre-existent state."[1] To rephrase and interpret the beginning words of John: "From eternity there existed an intelligence, and this intelligent being was with God as his firstborn spirit child and became also himself a God." The spirit of Jesus in the premortal existence was the most advanced of all spirit beings. Through diligence and obedience, he was foreordained by God, and he acted as a member of the Godhead, with God's power, before taking upon himself a body of flesh and bones.

THE ONLY BEGOTTEN SON OF GOD IN THE FLESH

When Jesus was born on earth, his physical body was the offspring of a mortal mother and a divine Father. He was the firstborn child of his mortal mother, Mary, and more important, the Only Begotten Son of God in the flesh. (See John 1:14; 3:16; Moses 6:52.) Being the son of both a mortal and a divine being was "not in violation of natural law but in accordance with a higher manifestation thereof."[2] As the son of a mortal woman, Jesus "learned . . . obedience by the things which he suffered." (Heb. 5:8.) That is, he had to personally experience all the physical and spiritual hardships common to the human family. Thus, he became the great teacher or "rabbi" among the Jews of his time. On the other hand, Jesus was able to overcome all mortal difficulties, including the agony of sin and the bond of death, because he was the literal, physical son of God the Father. "He received not of the fulness at first, but continued from grace to grace, until he received a fulness. . . . And he received all power, both in heaven and on earth, and the glory of the Father was with him, for he dwelt in him." (D&C 93:13, 17.)

Jesus did not receive a physical body merely to experience life as we know it on this earth. He also needed a special body, empowered by the divine nature inherited from his Father, in order to become the Savior of mankind. The suffering of his atoning sacrifice in Gethsemane, the freewill offering of his life at Golgotha, and the liberating power of his resurrection from the garden tomb would have been impossible without the godly faculties inherent within his physical body.[3] As the Only Begotten Son of God in the flesh, Jesus was able to provide the gifts of immortality and eternal life to us, his spirit brothers and sisters.[4] In this, he became the exemplary son of our Heavenly Father.

THE OBEDIENT SON OF GOD IN ALL THINGS

Christ gradually obtained the full power of the Father because he was a fully obedient son. When any son honors his father through obedience and virtuous living, he is his father's son in the truest, most complete sense of the word. In contrast, an earthly father may "disown" his natural son if the son chooses a way of life contrary to the father's highest values. Furthermore, we naturally assume that children will "follow in their parents' footsteps," and we are shocked and surprised if they reject the values they have been taught from parents who are exemplary members of society and who have properly taught their children.

According to the scriptures and the teachings of the Prophet Joseph Smith, Christ patterned his life exactly after the Father. When criticized by the Pharisees for making himself equal with God, "then answered Jesus and said unto them, Verily, verily, I say unto you, The Son can do nothing of himself, but what he seeth the Father do: for what things soever he doeth, these also doeth the Son likewise." (John 5:19.) Joseph Smith expounded upon this scripture, teaching that the Father had earlier developed the faculties and feelings that Jesus would later experience, for "the Son doeth what He hath seen the Father do: then the Father hath some day laid down His life and taken it again."[5] Because the life of the Savior duplicated that of the Father in so many ways, Jesus could say, "He that hath seen me hath seen the Father." (John 14:9.) Not fully understanding the intimate relationship between Christ and the Father, many Christian sects have taken this and similar passages to mean that the Father and Son are simply manifestations of the same holistic person or abstract entity.

To summarize the roles of Jesus as a son—he was both a Son of Man and a Son of God. As the Son of Man, Jesus was the son in the flesh of an outstanding woman, Mary, and he remembered and cared for her until his dying day. (See John 19:26–27.) As the Son of God, he was the firstborn spirit son, the only begotten physical son, and the only perfect exemplary son of God. In fact, he became such a complete son of Heavenly Father that he appeared and administered like God, his father.

JESUS, OUR HOLY, ELDER BROTHER

Within his earthly family, Jesus was known as the brother of James and other family members. (See Gal. 1:19; Matt. 13:55.) Though he is not referred to as such in the scriptures, Jesus Christ has also been commonly called our "elder brother" by modern prophets. He has been given this title because we were all with him from the beginning as intelligent entities and later as spirit personages. (See D&C 93:21–23.) No doubt our common spiritual parentage is the source of Christ's great love for us, as it should be the wellspring of love among men. When we obtain Christ's love, we should develop further love for others: "In this the children of God are manifest, and the children of the devil: whosoever doeth not righteousness is not of God, *neither he that loveth not his brother.* For this is the message that ye heard from the beginning, that we should love one another." (1 Jn. 3:10–11; italics added.) The scriptures contain many sad examples of people, such as the murderer Cain, who turned away from natural affection and instead embraced envy and hatred for their brothers in the flesh. Christ, on the other hand, loves all his family of followers and "esteemeth all flesh in one," for he has redeemed all flesh. (1 Ne. 17:35.)

As God in the premortal, spirit world, Jesus was known as Jehovah (or *Yahweh*). As the firstborn and most righteous spirit son of God, Jesus set a noble example and became the primary supporter of God the Father. He became the chief advocate of God's plan of salvation, which would provide us with free agency and personal development. Due to the imperfection and weakness of human nature, this plan of redemption required the atoning sacrifice of a redeemer, and Jesus volunteered to be its foreordained savior. "The Lord said: Whom shall I send? And one answered like unto the Son of Man: Here am I, send me." (Abr. 3:27.) The role of the high priest in ancient Israel was to offer ritual animal sacrifices to God. Jesus Christ, the Great High Priest, would come to offer the ultimate sacrifice – himself. Thus he became the "author of eternal salvation" after the Father selected him as the administrator of his plan of redemption. (Heb. 5:9.)

Our elder brother, Jesus, not only advocates our Father's plan to us, but he also advocates our needs with the Father, pleading our case as any good older brother would in support of his siblings. And just as younger children look to their older brothers as examples of how to live, so Jesus is our teacher and role model: "Whither I go ye know, and the way ye know. . . . I am the way." (John 14:4, 6.) Like a stronger older brother who saves the younger from drowning or from other physical harm, Christ has the power to rescue us from sin: "Cry unto him for mercy; for he is mighty to save." (Alma 34:18.)

As our older brother, the premortal Jesus fulfilled a variety of important roles to prepare the world and its inhabitants for the salvation offered by Heavenly Father's plan. As the younger spirit brothers and sisters of Jesus would come to this earth, they would have opportunities for spiritual understanding and growth. Jesus provided spiritual help in his role as the Lord of the ancient patriarchs and prophets, who, in turn, instructed the children of God concerning the laws and commandments. Jesus was also the God of justice and mercy who extended the promises of divine retribution and redemption to peoples on earth. In all these callings, the premortal Jesus represented Heavenly Father as the legal administrator of God's plan.

THE GOD OF THE OLD TESTAMENT

Though, as we have shown, Jesus was a God before he came to earth and even before the earth existed, his complete identity has been unknown, obscured and misunderstood throughout the centuries. As Jesus told his followers, "The light shineth in darkness; and the darkness comprehended it not." (John 1:5.) Indeed, until Christ revealed himself as Jehovah to Joseph Smith and Oliver Cowdery (see D&C 110:3–4), his premortal role as God of the Old Testament had become virtually unrecognized in the Christian world. The Lord was also forgotten periodically in ancient times, such as among the children of Israel who grew up in Egyptian bondage. When Jehovah commanded Moses from the burning bush to deliver Israel, the prophet was not sure how to identify his God. "Moses said unto God, Behold, when I come unto the children of Israel, and shall say unto them, The God of your fathers hath sent me unto you; and they shall say to me, What is his name? what shall I say unto them?" (Ex. 3:13.) Jehovah replied with a name that embodies the preeminence of his being and power: "I AM THAT I AM: and he said, Thus shalt thou say unto the children of Israel, I AM hath sent me to you." (Ex. 3:14.)

In the original Hebrew, "I AM THAT I AM" is translated from three words, the first and last sharing the same root—*eh'yeh.* This is the verb signifying *being* or *presence.* The center word *'asher* is an all-purpose conjunction whose translation can vary among *that, so that, as, for, because,* and so on. Translations can vary slightly, then, but the common sense is that the being, or existence, of the Lord precedes and supersedes everything else. As expounded in modern scripture, "he comprehendeth all things, and all things are before him, and all things are round about him; and he is above all things, and in all things, and is through all things, and is round about all things; and all things are by him, and of him, even God, forever and ever." (D&C 88:41.)

Simply said, Jesus "is He who He is"—the Lord of this earth. The same Hebrew verb of being or presence that forms the root of "I AM" also provides the root for his premortal name "Jehovah." The original Hebrew was written without vowels, and thus there are varying transliterations of his name, with the standard King James Version being Jehovah. Transliterations closer to the original Hebrew phonetics would be *Yahweh,* or *Jahveh.* Two translations of the Hebrew *Yahweh* (or Jehovah) are currently advocated: one interprets Israel's God as "The One who is," while the other defines the Lord's name as "The One who causes to be" whatever comes to pass at his command.[6] *Yahweh* is who he is—our God. And he causes whatever he will—especially the glorification of this earth and its inhabitants.

From the words of John, then, we learn that Jesus was with God the Father from the beginning and that he became a God. Jesus directed the creation and became the light of the world. He was the God of the

Old Testament, even though most living on the earth, even many among the chosen people of Abraham, did not always recognize and follow him.

THE GOD OF JUSTICE

What the children of Israel needed to learn in the days of Moses was that the God of Abraham, Isaac, and Jacob still lived and governed as the supreme Lord of the whole earth. In antiquity, the captive Israelites, like other ancient peoples, seemed to believe that different lands were dominated by certain deities who required homage from the people in their territories. These local gods were capricious characters who often were angered with humans and could only be placated by many gifts and animal sacrifices.

Jehovah too required ritual sacrifices, but they were not given to feed or appease him. They served a symbolic purpose in pointing the people toward repentance, obedience, and the real redemption of man through the future sacrifice of the Messiah. In themselves, the sacrifices meant nothing to Jehovah: "The sacrifice of the wicked is an abomination to the Lord: but the prayer of the upright is his delight." (Prov. 15:8.) In contrast to pagan deities, Jehovah was a God who demanded righteousness and obedience to his laws.

Modern scripture helps us understand Jesus as the God of justice by revealing that spiritual laws, like God himself, were present "in the beginning" and are unchanging and eternal: "There is a law, irrevocably decreed in heaven before the foundations of this world, upon which all blessings are predicated—and when we obtain any blessing from God, it is by obedience to that law upon which it is predicated." (D&C 130:20–21.) Indeed, the Lord himself is subject to eternal law and operates within it: "I, the Lord, am bound when ye do what I say; but when ye do not what I say, ye have no promise." (D&C 82:10.)

After ancient Israel left Egypt, Jehovah gave them the Law of Moses, a group of "carnal" commandments that the Apostle Paul called a "schoolmaster to bring us unto Christ." (Gal. 3:24.) The children of Israel truly were like children during this time, in need of strict commandments with immediate rewards for obedience and punishments for wickedness. Israel often failed to acknowledge Jehovah's authority or to recognize the immediate link between actions and their consequences. From the record of forty years in the wilderness, we find that many disobeyed and immediately received the Lord's punishments, usually including death. Thus, Jehovah gained the reputation of being an overly harsh God, and this opinion remains today among people with only a superficial knowledge of the scriptures.

New sets of prophetic instructions were given, however, once Israel came into maturity and was established in the land of Canaan. Instead of instant, negative reinforcement for disobedience, God delayed the punishments, sometimes for generations. Jehovah sent prophets to warn the people of calamities to come from their wickedness, giving them opportunity to measure the spiritual effects of their acts and to exercise agency and repentance. Israel could then begin to act on faith and spiritual sensitivity, rather than to react in fear of instant physical punishment.

THE GOD OF MERCY

Nonetheless, the children of Israel in Canaan did not seem to reach the level of spiritual maturity later exemplified by the Nephites in the New World, who from the outset preached Jesus Christ while keeping the Law of Moses, so that their "children [might] know to what source they [might] look for a remission of their sins." (2 Ne. 25:26.) Because of their faith in Christ hundreds of years before his earthly ministry, the Nephites sought forgiveness from sin through the Atonement that was to come. (See Mosiah 26:20–22.) God rewarded their righteous efforts, and he extended a promise of forgiveness and redemption from sin if they would repent and look to Christ as their savior. (See Mosiah 4:6; 13:28.) The actual gift of redemption would not be given until the time of Christ's atonement, but the premortal Messiah could suspend their suffering for sin.

What is left for us to decide is the relationship we will establish with God's son. Whether we view the justice of God with fear and trembling or with hope and rejoicing depends upon where we personally stand in relation to eternal laws. If we are afraid of God's judgments, as Israel was in the wilderness, we reveal our own sinfulness and a need for the strict discipline of carnal laws. On the other hand, if we are glad that God is just as well as merciful, it is because we have hope of receiving rewards for our righteous acts. Finally, if we add good works to our faith in Christ, we can lay hold upon his mercy, which blesses the righteous and will "satisfy the demands of justice, and encircles them in the arms of safety, while he that exercises no faith unto repentance is exposed to the whole law of the demands of justice." (Alma 34:16.)

Those who live under carnal laws, then, receive a harsher judgment; those who have struggled to live spiritual laws earn the benefits of mercy. Slothfulness and wickedness become more difficult for all of us in the long run as their effects catch up with us. In contrast, spiritual industry and righteousness become easier for those of us who follow Christ as he shares his rewards with us. We choose, then, the manner of our own judgment before the eternal Christ, our holy, elder brother.

JESUS AS THE BROTHER WHO REPRESENTS THE FATHER THROUGH DIVINE INVESTITURE

Our elder brother could pronounce judgments and deliver punishments or grant forgiveness and promise redemption through the power he received from God the Father before this world was organized. When Jesus said "I am in the Father, and the Father in me" (John 14:10), he was speaking of what we call "divine investiture." As a God of justice and mercy, Jehovah represents the Father through the law of divine investiture. That is, God empowered the premortal Jesus to represent him in all the affairs of this earth. All that the Lord Jehovah proclaimed, bound, sealed, and promised was guaranteed effective by God Elohim.

The law of divine investiture is similar to, but far more encompassing than the so-called "power of attorney" that mortals can give one to another, in which one person gives another the power to act in his name in all legal affairs. To give someone power of attorney, we must have full confidence that the person will always act in good judgment and in our best interest. By Christ's diligence in antemortality (the premortal existence), he gained not only the Father's trust, but also his power, and through divine investiture of that power, Christ created the earth and its inhabitants. By later proving himself obedient in the flesh as well, Jesus received power to atone for the sins of mankind, bring all men to judgment, and exalt the faithful with himself. Thus in a glorious vision of the Savior, Joseph Smith and Sidney Rigdon beheld "that by him, and through him, and of him, the worlds are and were created, and the inhabitants thereof are begotten sons and daughters unto God." (D&C 76:24.) God the Father has decreed that Jesus is his representative to this earth, and anything of eternal value and divine power must be done in the name of Christ. (See Matt. 28:19; John 17:1–10; D&C 50:27.)

The Father has not only invested in the Son power to act in his name, but he has also declared that all things must be done through Jesus Christ to be binding on earth and in heaven. The Book of Mormon prophets clearly understood and emphasized this fact over and over again in their teachings: "This is the way; and there is none other way nor name given under heaven whereby man can be saved in the kingdom of God. And now, behold, this is the doctrine of Christ, and the only and true doctrine of the Father." (2 Ne. 31:21; see also 2 Ne. 25:20; Mosiah 3:17; 5:8.) Most religions of the world worship some form of Supreme Being akin to God the Father, though he is called by many different names. But unless men, when taught the truth, accept that God the Son has come in the flesh and call upon his name for redemption, they cannot be saved. Whoever Christ accepts, the Father will accept also, and whoever Christ rejects will not enter into the kingdom of heaven: "The keeper of the gate is the Holy One of Israel; and he employeth no servant there; and there is none other way save it be by the gate." (2 Ne. 9:41.)

JESUS, THE FATHER FIGURE ON EARTH

Understanding the principle of divine investiture, we can appreciate that Jesus' statement, "I am in the father and the father in me," is an expression of oneness in power, not identity. (John 14:10.) Revealing a fuller account of the apostle John's witness, the Lord expounded to Joseph Smith upon this point: "I am in the Father, and the Father in me, and the Father and I are one—the Father because he gave me of his fulness, and the Son because I was in the world and made flesh my tabernacle." (D&C 93:3–4.) Christ first became the Son of God in the flesh, and then later became like the Father when he received the fullness of God's glory and power.

In a more limited sense, this is the same way all human beings progress from children to adults. Each man is born a son to another. After having fully matured, the son himself becomes a father and brings life to yet another son. The same process, of course, applies to daughters and mothers. It follows, then, that as Christ has become as the Father, he begins to function more and more in the role of a father. There are many ways that Jesus serves us in a fatherly role, especially as the father of this earth and of our salvation.

THE "FATHER" OR CREATOR OF THIS EARTH

Holding the administrative authority and power of God, Jehovah was able to create the world: "All things were made by him; and without him was not any thing made that was made." (John 1:3.) God the Father directed and supervised the operation, but he delegated the actual process of creation to his firstborn, Jehovah, who was assisted in turn by the archangel, Michael, who later became the first man, Adam.[7]

Jehovah supervised the six creative periods including the creation of the Garden of Eden on this earth. He assisted the Father in placing Adam and Eve in the garden, and after their fall from grace, he directed them out of the garden and taught them about his redemptive powers and the gospel truths that would bring them salvation. For this reason, the Apostle John wrote, "In him was life; and the life was the light of men." (John 1:4.)

THE "FATHER" OR HEAD OF HIS KINGDOM

Jesus was foreordained to serve many important roles throughout time. As God's representative, he fathered or initiated some physical and many more spiritual things that continue to bless us. In the physical realm, Jesus was the creator or organizer of this earth. (See Heb. 1:2.) In the spiritual dimension, he is the father or head of his gospel and his church, which is called the Church of Jesus Christ. (See Col. 1:18.) As evidences of his love and power, he is the father of our salvation through the saving ordinances of his gospel, the redeeming powers of his priesthood, and the sanctifying grace of his atonement. (See Heb. 5:4–9; Rom. 5:11.) He is the acting head or father of his kingdom, both in heaven and on earth.

The fatherly role of Jesus is seen most vividly in the blessings he provides his disciples. Followers of Jesus are called "Christians" after they have accepted his gospel truths and entered into a covenant relationship within his church. As his gospel and priesthood blessings transform their lives, they are "born again," becoming spiritual children of Christ. King Benjamin in the Book of Mormon taught this concept, telling his listeners, "Because of the covenant which ye have made ye shall be called the children of Christ, his sons, and his daughters; for behold, this day he hath spiritually begotten you; for ye say that your hearts are changed through faith on his name; therefore, ye are born of him and have become his sons and his daughters." (Mosiah 5:7.)

Joseph Smith and Sidney Rigdon also bore witness of this fact: "For we saw him [Christ], even on the right hand of God; and we heard the voice bearing record that he is the Only Begotten of the Father—that by him, and through him, and of him, the worlds are and were created, and the inhabitants thereof are begotten sons and daughters unto God." (D&C 76:23–24.) Because we are spiritually reborn through Christ, Jesus is called the Father of our salvation.

Christ was the only person born on earth of a mortal woman and an immortal Father, allowing him the opportunity of opening the gates of resurrection and immortality. We all will be physically born into immortality through the Savior's gift of resurrection. However, if we are to become spiritually exalted as his true sons and daughters as well, we must follow the path he marked on earth as he "continued from grace to grace, until he received a fulness." (D&C 93:13.) Thus, the Savior's promise to us: "For if you keep my commandments you shall receive of his [the Father's] fulness, and be glorified in me as I am in the Father; therefore, I say unto you, you shall receive grace for grace. And now, verily I say unto you, I was in the beginning with the Father, and am the Firstborn; and all those who are begotten through me are partakers of the glory of the same, and are the church of the Firstborn." (D&C 93:20–22.)

Just as Jesus was an obedient son to his Father, we have the opportunity to follow Christ while he serves us as the father of his church and gospel. Just as Jesus' mortal life emulated that of the Father, we become Christ's sons and daughters in the truest sense as we follow, obey, and honor him. Finally, as Jesus took upon himself the name of Father in relation to us, so we, in baptism, take upon ourselves the name of Christ, "for by this name shall [we] be called at the last day." (3 Ne. 27:5.) In this light, the words of the Savior recorded by John become clearer: "At that day ye shall know that I am in my Father, and ye in me, and I in you." (John 14:20.) Christ is speaking of that heavenly, celestial state in which exalted beings are of one heart and one mind.

Though Jesus Christ is known by many different names and titles—

over one hundred in the Book of Mormon alone—his three most intimate are those we have elaborated in this chapter: Son, Brother, and Father. To summarize, *JESUS is the firstborn, literal, and perfect son of Heavenly Father, and he is also our holy, elder brother who became the chief advocate and administrator of God's plan, serving as the father of his gospel and our salvation. Indeed, he is the Lord of this earth!*

As a fitting capstone to this chapter, the language of the scriptures provides the best summation of the man whom we call Jesus. This rendition is based on an edition of the LDS *Church News* in 1980, where many titles describing Jesus were published in a special Easter article. This collection of major titles reads like a prose poem. The various names used in the scriptures define and describe the multitudinous roles and characteristics of the Son of God. They invoke many images while portraying the grand scope of this unique individual, Jesus, our Holy Brother:[8]

JESUS CHRIST, THE CORNERSTONE OF MORMON BELIEFS

We know that Jesus is the divine Son of God and the Father of our salvation, and we bear testimony of him.

THE SON

He is the Firstborn Son of God in the spirit, and thus is the Elder Brother of us all. He is the Only Begotten Son of God in the flesh— actually, literally, physically, and biologically—and from his immortal Father he received power to conquer physical death. He is the Beloved Son in whom the Father is well pleased because he speaks and does the will of the Father, submitting his desire to that of his Divine Parent. He is separate from God the Father in both spirit body and physical body, but is one with the Father in witness, testimony, truth, ideals, and goals; the work and glory of the Father is also the work and glory of the Son, "to bring to pass the immortality and eternal life of man." (Moses 1:39.)

THE FATHER

Jesus Christ also can be referred to rightfully as the Father. He is the only legal heir of the Father upon the earth, and the Father has bestowed his powers upon him by divine investiture of authority. Because the gospel was made efficacious upon the earth through his atonement, Jesus Christ is also the Father of those who accept his gospel and become his sons and daughters spiritually. Because the immortality of all mankind was assured through the gift of his life, Jesus Christ is the Father of all our resurrected bodies. Because the earth and its heavens were created and organized under his direction, Jesus Christ is the Father of the earth; all of the elements quickly and gladly obey the will of this God of nature and of miracles.

Jesus has many other honored titles, and he fulfills many other worthy callings.

THE ETERNAL ONE

He is Alpha and Omega, the first and the last, the beginning and the end. He is the GREAT I AM, the pre-earthly Existent One. As the pre-earthly Jehovah, he served as the God of the Old Testament, the God of Abraham, Isaac, and Jacob and thus of all Israel, the God who spoke with Moses on Mount Sinai and with all the ancient prophets. As the gloified Lord, he is God of the whole earth, forever and ever.

THE ANOINTED ONE

He is the Anointed One of Jewish hope and expectation, called the Messiah in the Old Testament. In anticipation of his coming, the ancients offered up sacrifice because he was the Lamb of God without spot or blemish who was foreordained from before the foundations of the world to be slain as a sacrifice in the meridian of time. He is the Anointed One of Christian belief and practice, called the Christ in the New Testament. His full name and title, Jesus the Christ, is the only name under Heaven whereby salvation and exaltation come.

THE SAVIOR

He is the Holy Child of Bethlehem, born of the virgin Mary. He is the boy of Nazareth and of the temple where he wanted to be about his Father's business. He is the Immanuel, or "God with us" of the Galilee and of Jerusalem. He is our Mediator with the Father. He is the promised Savior and Redeemer of us all, past, present, and future, having atoned for the transgression of Adam unconditionally and for our sins upon the condition of our repentance, and having provided for the resurrection of all mankind.

We should remember him and his atonement each time we partake of the sacramental emblems: the bread in remembrance of his resurrected flesh when he atoned for physical death, and the liquid in remembrance of the blood he shed in Gethsemane when he atoned for spiritual death.

THE LORD OF THIS EARTH

He is the Stone of Israel, the Rock of salvation; those who build upon him as their foundation shall be safe and secure from the winds and storms of the adversary. He is the Lord of the vineyard, and through partaking of the fruits of his gospel, we can enjoy the fruits of eternal life. He is the Good Shepherd and knows his sheep and is known of them. He desires to gather his sheep together that they might hear his voice and become one fold with him as their Shepherd.

He is the Founder and the Prince of Peace, and only through following his example and living his gospel can we find the peace that surpasses all understanding. He is the Eternal and Everlasting Judge; the Keeper of the Gate; a God of justice, law, and order; a God of mercy, kindness, and love. Only through him can we return unto our Heavenly Father.

THE MILLENNIAL RULER

He is the King of kings, who will return to the earth in the last days, cleansing it from all iniquity and establishing the conditions of peace and righteousness that shall last for a thousand years. From Zion—the New Jerusalem on the American continent—his law to govern all the earth shall go forth.

He is the Lord of lords, the High Priest over his Church, whose second coming in power and glory will fulfill the prayer, "Thy Kingdom come. Thy will be done in earth, as it is in heaven." (Matt. 6:10.) From the Old Jerusalem, which shall become a holy city at his presence, shall go forth his word to the faithful saints. May we be among that blessed number!

Of these things we bear witness concerning Jesus Christ, the divine Son of God.

For further study, refer to the following entries:

TG	BD	*EM*
Jesus Christ, Advocate	Advocate	The Father and Son: A Doctrinal
Jesus Christ, Antemortal Existence of	Christ	Exposition by the First Presidency and
	Firstborn	the Twelve
	Jehovah	Jehovah, Jesus Christ
Jesus Christ, Authority of	Jesus	Jesus Christ
Jesus Christ, Creator	Messiah	Jesus Christ,
Jesus Christ, Divine Sonship	Son of God	Fatherhood and Sonship of
Jesus Christ, Firstborn		Jesus Christ, Names and Titles of
Jesus Christ, Foreordained		
Jesus Christ, Head of the Church		
Jesus Christ — Jehovah		
Jesus Christ, Mediator		
Jesus Christ, Messiah		
Jesus Christ, Relationships with the Father		

CHAPTER 4

A MESSENGER OF TRUTH

Boy Scouts of America have long followed the motto "Do a good turn daily." As part of the spirit of this service, they are not to seek recognition or reward for their good deeds. In a similar service emphasis, groups of young women in local Mormon congregations often have a program of "secret sisters," where each girl is given the name of another young woman in the group. For a number of weeks they are to do special good deeds for their secret sister. Although the name of the Boy Scout or the identity of the young woman may not be known, evidence of their good deeds can be recognized as widows find their lawns mowed by unknown helpers and families find plates of cookies on their porches. One does not have to know or see the person rendering the service to receive and appreciate the good that has been done in their behalf. Similar acts of goodness by many anonymous people can bring many blessings into a neighborhood or among a group of friends.

In a similar pattern of service, the three members of the Godhead often help and assist us in many ways where we may not recognize their hand in the blessings we are receiving. This is particularly true for the abundant spiritual benefits that we receive through the promptings of the Holy Spirit. This third member of the Godhead, also called the Holy Ghost, is the least named in the scriptures, yet should be the most familiar to people because of their personal spiritual experiences. The scriptures are full of information regarding the character of both God the Father and his Son, Jesus Christ, revealed primarily through their personal interactions with the prophets and apostles. Except for these special witnesses, however, very few people have ever had direct contact with either the Father or the Son. On the other hand, relatively little has been revealed as to the personal origin, role, titles, and destiny of the Holy

Ghost. Yet all spiritual knowledge and guidance comes to people through the power of the Holy Spirit, and it is through him that most of us have come to know God the Father and his Son, Jesus Christ. All righteous people who search for spiritual guidance have access to the presence and influence of this obscure, yet personal, Godhead member — the Holy Ghost.

PERSONAL ATTRIBUTES OF THE HOLY GHOST

What we do know about the Holy Ghost's individual attributes we learn primarily through modern revelation: "The Father has a body of flesh and bones as tangible as man's; the Son also; but the Holy Ghost has not a body of flesh and bones, but is a personage of Spirit. Were it not so, the Holy Ghost could not dwell in us." (D&C 130:22.) Previous to his mortal birth through Mary, Jesus Christ also lacked a body of flesh and bones, but he was still a spirit son of Heavenly Father and the God of the Creation and the Old Testament, revealing himself and his power to men from the beginning of time. The Holy Ghost likewise is a spirit son of the Father and a God with eternal power, though his role is different from that of either the Father or the Son.[1]

Unlike the Father and Son, the Holy Ghost can "dwell in us." That is, his Spirit can enter into our bodies and commune directly with our own spirit. Mortal man cannot endure the glorified presence of the Father and Son unless his flesh be transfigured, so the Holy Ghost is sent to prepare men and lead them gradually back into God's presence. (See D&C 76:11–12.) It should not seem too strange that the Holy Ghost, as a spirit person, can actually enter into the body of a human being, since the scriptures record examples of spirits, both good and evil, who have entered into people. For example, the New Testament records one account where a legion of demons possessed a person's body to overwhelm and bind his whole soul. (See Mark 5:1–15; cf. Matt. 8:28–32.) Then, too, the power and influence of wickedness — like that of the Holy Ghost — can be spread throughout the world and among many people at once as Satan's legions undermine the spiritual influences of the members of the Godhead.

Because the Holy Ghost is a distinct entity, he does not and cannot transform himself into any other form, nor can he personally be in more than one place at one time. Thus, "a man may receive the Holy Ghost, and it may descend upon him, and not tarry with him." (D&C 130:23.)[2] However, the power of the Holy Ghost is infinite — for he is a God — and thus his influence can be manifested everywhere at any time. In this way, his power is like the effect of God's love or the Light of Christ, which at once permeates all creation and accompanies everyone in the world. (See D&C 121:46; 84:46.)

WHAT IS MEANT BY THE "SPIRIT OF GOD"?

The identity of the Holy Ghost is sometimes confused with the character of either the Father or the Son. As discussed in earlier chapters on both God and Jesus, these two members of the Godhead both have a spirit as an integral element of their divine being. Thus the term *Spirit of God* could refer to any of the three Godhead members. However, the usual context of this term in the scriptures is applied to the Holy Ghost, who is also called the Holy Spirit, Spirit of God, Spirit of the Lord, and the Comforter.[3] A brief discussion and example will clarify some distinctive spiritual roles of each member in the Godhead.

God the Father's own spirit exercises a subtle, loving influence through the nature of his divine being. He is the great planner and director of his plan of salvation for all his spirit children. Since he has delegated most of the responsibility for this earth and its inhabitants to his Son, his spiritual influence and pervasiveness appear refined and indirect.

More direct is the spiritual force emanating from Christ's own spirit, called the "light of Christ," which is the constant, goodly influence radiating into the souls of all, prompting them toward moral integrity and righteousness. (See Moro. 7:18; John 8:12.) This divine inducement interacts with us and is known as our conscience, telling us right from wrong. (See Moro. 7:12–19.) It is also the light that proceeds through Christ into the world, enlightening everyone coming to the earth and quickening human understanding. (See D&C 88:6–13, 41.) Since the light of Christ is an influence emanating from Jehovah, it should not be confused with the actual personage of either Christ or the Holy Ghost. Its purpose is to strive with the children of men until it brings them to the possession of the greater light and testimony of the Holy Spirit. Its effect seems both preliminary and preparatory to one's receiving the power and gift of the Holy Ghost.[4]

The Holy Ghost, also commonly referred to as the Spirit of God, manifests the most direct spiritual power in our lives; he is the *Spirit* sent by God the Father to this earth to minister to the spiritual needs of his children. The ancient prophet Nephi testified that the Holy Ghost is a "gift of God unto all those who diligently seek him. . . . For he that diligently seeketh shall find; and the mysteries of God shall be unfolded unto them, by the power of the Holy Ghost, as well as in these times as in times of old, and as well in times of old as in times to come." (1 Ne. 10:17–19.) The Holy Ghost is the great teacher and testifier of gospel insights.

The Prophet Joseph Smith has explained that the three members of the Godhead made an "everlasting covenant" before the organization of this earth. There they planned for the progress and salvation of mankind. Because of special assignments, they would be known to us as "God the first, the Creator; God the second, the Redeemer; and God the third, the witness or Testator."[5] He also taught that while the temporary influence of the Holy Ghost, the divine power of witnessing gospel truths, can be received before baptism, the lasting gift or constant companionship of the Holy Ghost can be received only after baptism and the laying on of hands.[6] Thus, the Holy Ghost is manifested to people on earth in two distinct ways: the *power* of the Holy Ghost and the *gift* of the Holy Ghost. Through his power, a person learns and receives a witness of gospel truths, even before he or she is baptized. Through his gift, a person receives the right for the constant companionship of the Holy Spirit after one's baptism.[7] Most of our discussion about the Holy Ghost in this chapter deals with the *power* of the Holy Ghost.[8]

Because we experience stages of spiritual darkness in mortality that cause us difficulty in distinguishing the spiritual manifestations of the three Godhead members, comparing these three spiritual influences with three forms of light will be helpful. Imagine being in a well-lit room at late dusk as a full moon is rising in the heavens outside. The electrical light is the most apparent illumination source in the room, and it can be compared to the power of the Holy Ghost, which is of greatest immediate aid in the coming night. The bright, silver light of the full moon outside is like the light of Christ, casting enough shadows so we can distinguish objects (or right and wrong) and providing enough light to assist us through the night. But as we look toward the west, we see the refracted light from the afterglow of the setting sun, which can be compared to the distant, subtle influence and love of God the Father softly illuminating the horizon, promising new light after the darkness.

Although the most powerful light of all—that of the fiery sun—is the furthest removed and the least visible to us, its power and glory surpass all else, sustaining life on this planet just as assuredly as the glory of Heavenly Father maintains spiritual life. However, just as mortals should not stand in the direct sunlight and look unprotected straight at the sun, we, as imperfect beings, cannot abide the direct light and glory of our Father in Heaven.

The light of the full moon is closer, reflecting the sun's light into our night of moral and mortal darkness. This light of Christ is sufficient to direct our paths if it is not blocked out by clouds of wickedness or the insensitivity of our souls.

The closest light, which assists us most directly through the night, comes into most homes through electrical energy, although many abodes are still lit with oil lamps and cooking fires. In any case, the light in the room derives almost entirely from the mineral and natural resources provided by God's prior efforts, but man's use of these sources is often affected by his understanding and action. Likewise, God has provided our lives with a source of valuable, spiritual light through the Holy Ghost. Just as we see much better in the forms of light available to us in our homes, we usually live better under the enlightening influences of the Holy Ghost. Prophets occasionally bask in the direct light of God as they receive profound revelations, but we would be blinded in such circumstances. Instead, we should strive to improve ourselves to be ready and worthy to receive daily, constant inspiration through the Holy Ghost. First, we must learn about the powers of the Holy Ghost and then understand how to gain access to them.[9]

THE THREEFOLD POWER
OF THE HOLY GHOST

To fulfill his role of bringing us to Christ and the Father, the Holy Ghost has a threefold manifestation of his power. He is a *revelator* of knowledge concerning the other members of the Godhead and of the gospel; he is a *testator* of the truthfulness of what he reveals; and he is a *comforter* to us in our earthly sojourn away from the presence of God.

REVELATOR OF TRUTH

In the first chapter on the nature of truth, we emphasized that just as human knowledge can be acquired only through human faculties, so also spiritual knowledge can be acquired only through revelation by the Holy Ghost. This is why, even when Christ was in the flesh among his disciples, the power of the Holy Ghost still had to reveal the Lord's divine identity to them: "When Jesus came into the coasts of Caesarea Philippi, he asked his disciples, saying, Whom do men say that I the Son of man am? And they said, Some say that thou art John the Baptist; some, Elias; and others, Jeremias, or one of the prophets. He saith unto them, But whom say ye that I am? And Simon Peter answered and said, Thou art the Christ, the Son of the living God. And Jesus answered and said unto him, Blessed art thou, Simon Bar-jona: for flesh and blood hath not revealed it unto thee, but my Father which is in heaven." (Matt. 16:13–17.)

Christ had already identified himself as the Savior to his disciples, and again in these verses he calls himself the Son of Man, referring to his unique relationship with the only exalted man at that time, God the Father.[10] Nonetheless, Peter could testify of Christ only because God the Father had revealed the Savior's divinity to him through the power of the Holy Ghost. In the verses that follow, Christ continues his lesson on the importance of divine knowledge through the Spirit because such knowledge serves as the foundation of his church: "Upon this rock [Christ's revelation] will I build my church; and the gates of hell shall not prevail against it." (Matt. 16:18.)[11]

As a member of the Godhead, the Holy Ghost knows the truth of all things. (See D&C 35:19.) He can reveal a knowledge of things past, present, and even future. (See 1 Pet. 1:2.) Those seeking eternal truth and salvation must be taught by the Holy Ghost because spiritual things can only be understood when taught and learned by the Holy Spirit. (See D&C 50:11–24.) Latter-day Saints are admonished to seek and teach by the power of the Holy Ghost as they go forth representing Christ. The Savior told them "to teach the children of men the things which I have put into your hands by the power of my Spirit." (D&C 43:15.) The Holy Ghost is such a valuable source of gospel knowledge that to have his constant influence is called the greatest gift a person can receive in mortality. (See D&C 121:46.)

The marvelous power of the Holy Ghost in his role as a revelator is demonstrated in the complex sophistication of his communicative abilities. As he interacts with our own spirits, even if just for an instant, he transmits simultaneous, instant, and personal messages. In simultaneous action, he speaks to many people at the same time through the miraculous nature of his spirit. His messages are also instant and spontaneous to the immediate situation; they are not prerecorded transmissions. Finally, his revelations are personal and tailored to the individual on the receiving end.

WITNESS OF GOD'S WORK

At the same time the Holy Ghost reveals knowledge to man, he also testifies that what he reveals is true. Whatever people speak under the influence of the Holy Spirit is scripture — sacred, inspired, and true. (See D&C 68:3–4.) When a person speaks by the power of the Holy Ghost, a spiritual conviction of the message's truthfulness is transmitted into the soul of the receiver. (See 2 Ne. 33:1.) This is why spiritual knowledge, though coming from the unseen world, is more sure than any temporal knowledge. No scientific or logical assertion can be its own proof — additional support from other sources is needed to establish validity. For example, mass confusion has resulted from both radio and television programs that were misinterpreted. A classic example is the Orson Wells radio drama *The War of the Worlds*. Many people thought it was a live news broadcast, and large numbers believed the earth was being attacked by alien invaders. A more recent example may be what appears to be a television news program where the footage or the newscaster's comments may not accurately portray what really is happening in that part of the world. We assume the reporting is truthful, but we do not really know until we can verify it with additional sources.

One might then ask, "How does a person *know* if he or she has received a true witness through the Holy Ghost?" To answer this question to a person who has never experienced the power of the Holy Spirit in their own soul is as difficult as describing the taste of salt to a person who has never tasted salt or the color green to a person blind from birth. The closest descriptions of the witnessing power of the Holy Ghost conveys a sensation of unusual warmth, often encompassing the whole being. Some people describe it as a special feeling of calmness and serenity, or even an "out of the physical body" experience of spiritual supernaturalness. The scriptures mention feelings of spiritual fullness, peace, joy, and power that accompany the Holy Ghost. (See Acts 13:52; Rom. 14:17; Moro. 6:9.) The best answer, as inconclusive as it may appear, is to encourage the questioner to plead and petition the Almighty for his or her own personal witness through the Spirit, for only the Holy Ghost can let a person *know* for a surety of the validity of any revealed truth.

To highlight, the Holy Spirit as a testator is both the medium of revelation and its confirmation. The Holy Ghost not only communicates information, but he simultaneously verifies the truthfulness of the data. Thus, the seemingly paradoxical words of Paul about faith make more sense: faith is not just a belief and hope in revealed truth, but also the "*substance* of things hoped for, the *evidence* of things not seen." (Heb. 11:1; italics added.)

COMFORTER FOR THE HUMAN SOUL

Furthermore, in the absence of direct communication and association with God and Christ, the Holy Ghost is a comforter to our souls. Though the power of the Holy Ghost revealed a testimony of Christ to Peter even while he enjoyed the Lord's presence, Jesus told the apostles: "It is expedient for you that I go away: for if I go not away, the Comforter will not come unto you; but if I depart, I will send him unto you." (John 16:7.) Even though Jesus dwelt personally among the apostles, he could not — as the Holy Ghost later could — dwell within them.

When the Spirit is within us, we receive comfort in the sense of the original Latin roots of the word: *com* = together + *fortis* = strong. As the Holy Spirit literally comes together with our own spirit, we receive great strength as well as peace, for the Spirit adds his power to our soul. An example of how the Spirit's comfort can strengthen a person is demonstrated in the Apostle Peter. The Peter who walked with Christ became weak in an hour of personal danger and denied the Savior three times. However, the Peter who later received the Comforter resolutely followed in the footsteps of Christ, even in the manner of his death. We, likewise, with the Spirit can have the inner peace and strength to overcome whatever heartache or hardship life may bring us.[12]

COMMUNICATION THROUGH THE SPIRIT

Within the past fifty years, the means of human communication have expanded and diversified in a way not previously imagined. Anciently, the spoken word could carry only as far as the strength of one's voice would allow; even the written word had to be hand copied and delivered. The rise of industrialization and technology has brought us improvements through the printing press, the telegraph and telephone, radio and television, and finally the computer and the facsimile machine. Through these inventions, many people can receive the same information, often at the same time. For example, many simultaneously watch satellite broadcasts from space as men circle the globe or walk on the moon's surface. Or, they observe the world Olympics from distant places. Through the medium of television, we see as though we are there, actually witnessing people and events very clearly although they occur thousands of miles away.

To appreciate how recent these technological advances are in human history, imagine the innocent ignorance of our great-grandparents when they were our age. How could we have described some of these things to them: what a television was, how people would see Americans walking around in space or on the surface of the moon, how clearly they could witness dozens of foreign Olympic events — some so clearly that they could see drops of sweat on the faces of athletes more vividly from thousands of miles away than people who were sitting in the grandstands personally witnessing the events could see them. Our great-grandparents would have been dumbfounded at our explanations and descriptions, and they might have even thought that we were crazy.

Communication technology has advanced greatly in the past few decades. Electronic and computer technology can now start to compensate for human defects in communication. For example, scientists are now developing a type of videocamera connected directly to the vision center of the brain to enable the blind to "see" images without their eyes. Also under research is a tiny microchip receiver of radio and television transmissions that could be implanted in the skull. Natural electrical impulses in the brain would conduct the signals directly to sound and sight centers of the nervous system, eliminating the need for external radio and TV receivers. With such advances, our great-grandchildren will consider the radios, televisions, compact disc players, and other devices of our age as historic relics of primitive communication.

Miraculous as these innovations are, they are still by no means as sophisticated as the means that God has developed through his supreme knowledge and power over the ages. His primary means of communication with us is to transmit information, truth, and comfort through the Holy Ghost. We mentioned earlier that only the Spirit can verify truthfulness while communicating. Also unique to the Holy Ghost is his ability to transmit personalized information to an infinite number of individuals at the same time. Each individual has a personal communication link with God through the Holy Ghost, and no matter how many people are seeking access at any moment, the circuits are never overcrowded.

A statement from the First Presidency of the Church in 1855 expresses some of the feelings that the Holy Ghost can bring into our souls: "Incomparable delight and happiness fill the soul of the faithful Saint, who has the testimony of Jesus and the Spirit of the living God to enlighten his understanding. Happiness supreme and love divine fill his bosom. . . . Thus our holy religion absorbs every feeling, desire, ambition, motive, and action of our natures. . . . It forms the vitality of our very existence. . . . This is true of every person who . . . has received the Holy Ghost, and continues to walk in the light, and be led by its gentle influence."[13]

In summary, we can say that *the HOLY GHOST is a spirit personage who serves as a revelator of truth, a witness of God's work, and a comforter for the human soul.* In other words, he *teaches, testifies,* and *transforms* us while he lovingly serves us as the third member of the Godhead.[14]

The intensity of revelation received through the Holy Ghost also surpasses any other mode of communication — Spirit speaking directly to spirit — and it has the power to motivate us to action as no word or image can. The Holy Ghost can bear a special, strong witness as he comes into our being, or he can inspire us through more subtle influences. His actual presence might last only a microsecond, but the residual afterglow could and should last for a much longer period. His effect upon our spirit can be like the catalytic agent in a chemical reaction — once the Holy Spirit starts the process, the reaction should continue long afterward until we weaken it with insensitivity or unworthiness. Finally, though the Holy Ghost can and does enlighten us in all types of learning, the spiritual knowledge alone that he conveys has the power to lead us to salvation.[15]

For further study, refer to the following entries:

TG	BD	*EM*
Holy Ghost	Comforter	Holy Ghost
Holy Ghost, Comforter	Holy Ghost	Holy Spirit
Holy Ghost, Mission of	Light of Christ	Light of Christ
Holy Ghost, Source of Testimony	Spirit, the Holy	

CHAPTER 5

THE GIFT OF PRAYER

Modern technology has provided society with marvelous means of communication. Particularly through the telephone, people can talk with each other around the globe. The same technology can sometimes be abused if it is not used properly, or it can be frustrating if it does not meet our needs. For example, telephone communication can be disrupted through atmospheric conditions or downed telephone lines. It can be abused by obscene or frivolous calls. Taped commercial messages or answering machines can frustrate our attempts to make effective use of our phone.

Prayer is much like our telephone communication — it is a great blessing if it is used frequently, wisely, and appropriately. But if neglected or abused, effective communication with our Heavenly Father can be severely weakened. We can also misuse prayer by asking for trivial things or things we should not ask for. Our Heavenly Father wants us to keep the lines of prayer open to him.

The divine command found most often in the scriptures is "to repent," perhaps because so many of God's children are inclined to turn away from him. The second most repeated injunction is "to pray," or to seek and ask God, a behavior that draws God's children nearer to him. (See D&C 4:7.) Prayer provides direction and comfort in our journey through life as we draw nearer to God. "Pray always," we are told, that we may "come off conqueror" — choosing good and conquering evil. (D&C 10:5.) Lacking the strength to prevail alone, we need to humble ourselves and seek help from God. In addition, prayer develops our understanding and testimony of gospel truths when the Holy Ghost bears pure witness. For these reasons, God has ordained that we should pray and has promised us that he will answer our prayers. The values, examples, and steps of prayer, along with its language and blessings, will be discussed in this chapter.

SPIRITUAL COMMUNION WITH GOD

Among all creations, only man has the ability to communicate through language with his maker. Because we possess this divine gift, we share a unique opportunity to establish contact with the supreme source of wisdom and compassion in our universe. When we realize and appreciate our relationship with God as his spirit children, we naturally and instinctively turn to him in prayer. When we ignore or disrupt this relationship, we find it difficult to pray. (See 2 Ne. 32:8–9.)[1]

Our prayers should be both simple and sincere. A *simple prayer* is the means by which the minds of the Father and the child are brought into connection with each other. A *sincere prayer* takes the contact one step further and brings the wills into harmony with each other. We do not pray to change God's will but to become sensitive to his desires so that we might request and receive the comfort, direction, and other blessings that he gives to those ready, worthy, and desirous to receive them. Some blessings from God, especially those of a spiritual nature, are conditional upon our asking for them, and if we ask, we will be answered. (See Matt. 7:7; James 1:5–6.) This requesting function of prayer reflects the ancient origin of the term *prayer,* which derives from the Latin *precarius,* meaning something "obtained by begging," coming from the Latin root *precari,* meaning "to entreat."[2] As we bring our will into contact and harmony with God, we entreat him for those things that he desires for us. As we understand his will, we find peace in our souls, knowing we are in the loving care of a divine being.

PRAYER IN THE TEACHINGS OF THE ANCIENT PROPHETS

The ancient prophets of the Bible and Book of Mormon indicate that prayers have been offered to God since the days of Adam and the patriarchs. (See Gen. 4:26; 12:8; 32:9–11.) Adam and Eve began praying to Heavenly Father after they were cast from the Garden of Eden. Although they were separated from God, they were able to communicate with him. (See Moses 5:4, 8.) The great patriarch Abraham often sought God in prayer as he requested blessings and protection from above. (See Gen. 12:8; Abr. 1:2–4; 2:6, 17.) The mighty prophet Moses often went to God in prayer seeking for strength and direction as the Lord's prophet.

(See Moses 1:20; Ex. 5:22; Num. 21:7.) Daniel knelt in prayer three times daily to give thanks to God. (See Dan. 6:10.) Enos and Alma in early Book of Mormon times also cried to God in mighty prayer. (See Enos 1:4; Alma 5:46; 8:10.) The ancient servants of God were often in contact with him through prayer.

Besides the prayers of the patriarchs and the prophets, the ancient scriptures record examples of various people praying: men and women, kings and common folk, individuals and multitudes. Prayers also took place in a variety of locations: at the temple and in the home, in public synagogues or street corners and in private closets and gardens, on mountain tops and in deserts.[3] Prayers were also given at different occasions: in times of war and peace, as expressions of sorrow and gladness, in periods of famine and prosperity, and at moments of private devotion and communal worship.[4] We learn much about prayer from the examples and teachings of the ancient prophets.

JESUS TEACHES US HOW TO PRAY

Jesus also provided valuable examples and instructions about prayer. He has constantly admonished us to "pray always." One way to have a constant prayer in our hearts is to remember that "to pray" means "to entreat or petition" God. If we wanted to effectively petition someone (such as our boss for a raise in pay or a neighbor for a special favor), we would surely spend time and mental effort in carefully pondering and preparing how we would communicate our desires with the person. In a similar manner, we should expend many moments of sincere thought prior to beginning a prayer with our Heavenly Father. In essence, we should be carrying a prayer in our heart at all times. (See Luke 21:36; 3 Ne. 18:18–21; D&C 81:3.)

Prayers are also meant to be personal and sincere. Prior to giving his exemplary prayer recorded in the Sermon on the Mount in Matthew 6, the Lord first warned his followers not to pray like the hypocrites, "to be seen of men." (V. 5.) This does not mean that public prayers are necessarily inappropriate but rather that prayers of a personal nature should be kept private. (See v. 6.) Similarly, Christ instructs his disciples to avoid "vain repetitions" (v. 7) characteristic of heathens petitioning their false, impersonal gods (who are perhaps hard of hearing as well as impotent). The living God, in contrast, knows our needs before we ask him, and before we even know them ourselves. (See v. 8.) With this introduction, Jesus then offers a prayer that is the model of humility, brevity, and sincerity:

> 9. After this manner therefore pray ye: Our Father which art in heaven, Hallowed be thy name.
> 10. Thy kingdom come. Thy will be done in earth, as it is in heaven.
> 11. Give us this day our daily bread.
> 12. And forgive us our debts, as we forgive our debtors.
> 13. And lead us not into temptation, but deliver us from evil: for thine is the kingdom, and the power, and the glory, for ever. Amen.
> (See also 3 Ne. 13:9–13.)

As discussed in chapter 3, the familiar and loving title of "Father" is preferred by God himself, and when we apply this title to deity, it is uniquely holy. After addressing God the Father, Jesus adds a phrase of acknowledgment and praise, which alternately translated from the Greek could read, "Let thy name be sanctified." (V. 9.) The Lord also voices a commitment to put God's will before his own. (See v. 10.) Christ repeats and fulfills this devotion later during his ministry in Gethsemane: "Father, if thou be willing, remove this cup from me: nevertheless not my will, but thine, be done." (Luke 22:42.) To bring our petitions into harmony with the will of God is a mark of mature prayer and the beginning of true spiritual confidence and power.

Verse 11 of Matthew 6 includes an element in prayer familiar to most of us—asking for help within the context of our physical lives. The infirmities of the flesh are so constant that we continuously need God's help to maintain our health and well-being. In establishing his covenant with Israel through Moses, God repeatedly promises the chosen people that if they would do his will, they would never want for the necessities of life. The first request of Jesus' prayer, in verse 11, recalls how God miraculously fulfilled that promise during Israel's forty years in the wilderness. It is also a humble admission of our daily dependence on God for life itself.

The Lord's next request highlights a most profound part of this model prayer—freedom from sin and spiritual faults. First, we should be willing to forgive others of their offenses as we would have God forgive our debts to him. (See v. 12.) The original Greek word translated as "debts" in this verse also means offenses, faults, or sins. We need relief from our spiritual debts and failures, and we should also be willing to help others relieve their burdens. In verses 12 and 13, the emphasis of the prayer shifts from ourselves and our personal needs toward the needs of others and our relationship with our Savior. We move from the physical into the moral and spiritual dimensions of our existence as we look at our hidden infirmities. Jesus teaches us here to ask for godly protection from sin and deliverance from spiritual weaknesses. The constant need to confess our weaknesses and to seek for divine forgiveness and aid is apparent in these important verses.

The Lord's Prayer concludes as it began, with a recognition of God's power and glory. It ends with the word "Amen," meaning "so be it," or "it is firm and true," an affirmation of our sincere entreaty with God.

In reviewing the Lord's Prayer, note that Jesus twice praises God, twice concerns himself with spiritual well-being, and only once asks for a material blessing (and then only for "daily bread," not the riches of this world). Most people, even Latter-day Saints, are often too preoccupied with material rather than spiritual needs and desires, and they need to remember the other elements of praise, thanksgiving, and devotion in their prayers.

THE SEVEN STEPS OF PRAYER

Children raised in the church are taught at a young age four basic steps of prayer: we *address God* as our Father in Heaven; we *thank him* for our blessings; we *ask him* for the things we need; and we *close our prayer* in the name of Jesus Christ. The Lord's Prayer adds two more important elements often found within prayer: *praising God* for his goodness, power, and glory; and *confessing our weaknesses* and sins before God. As Jesus taught his followers in the Book of Mormon, he built upon another element alluded to in the Lord's Prayer, *expressing commitment,* love, and devotion to God. (See 3 Ne. 19:20–23.) Except for the natural location of the introductory and closing parts of a prayer, there is no set order for the elements of a prayer. The following is a suggested order of these steps that might be reflected in many of our prayers:

Opening — addressing our Heavenly Father
Praise — recognizing God's glory and goodness
Thanksgiving — voicing appreciation for blessings received
Confession — admitting our sins and weaknesses
Petition — asking for personal and other people's needs
Commitment — expressing our love and sincere devotion
Closing — concluding in the name of Jesus Christ

Each of these steps warrants further explanation.

ADDRESSING HEAVENLY FATHER

Since the purpose of prayer is to commune with God, the creator of our spirits, we must first direct our mental and spiritual concentration toward that communication by specifically addressing Heavenly Father with any of the many appropriate titles by which we know him; such as, Heavenly Father, our Father who art in heaven, God our Father, God, Elohim, and so on. As we develop a trusting relationship with our Heavenly Father, we will feel comfortable addressing him in all types of circumstances — pleasant or painful, calm or chaotic, personal or public.

PRAISING GOD

Much of the beautiful language of the ancient psalms and the modern hymns is in the form of praises to God. As we understand his infinite knowledge, power, goodness, and glory, we have a natural desire to express our feelings through song and prayer. Praising God is not required by him so that he might condescend to listen to our prayers, rather it is a valuable element to bring us into a reverential feeling and to bolster our trust in him. Such feelings take us out of the natural world and bring us into a more holy sphere. Praising God at the beginning of prayer is like Moses taking off his sandals as he approached the Lord on Mt. Sinai — we come in awe and respect before God in prayer as we recognize and express appreciation for what God is.

THANKING GOD FOR BLESSINGS

One problem with prayers is that they tend to center more on what we want rather than what we have already received from God. No matter what our circumstances, we are commanded to "in everything give thanks: for this is the will of God in Christ Jesus concerning you." (1 Thes. 5:18.) Christian missionary Corrie ten-Boom included a moving account of this scripture about gratitude in her autobiographical book, *The Hiding Place*. During World War II, Miss ten-Boom was sentenced with her sister, Betsie, to a German concentration camp for hiding Jews and helping them escape from occupied Holland. Having been placed in a crowded, dirty, flea-infested barracks, Corrie complained:

"Betsie, how can we live in such a place!"

[Betsie muttered,] "Show us. Show us how." It was said so matter of factly it took me a second to realize she was praying. More and more the distinction between prayer and the rest of life seemed to be vanishing for Betsie.

"Corrie!" she said excitedly. "He's given us the answer! Before we asked, as He always does! In the Bible this morning. Where was it? Read that part again!"

"It was in First Thessalonians," I said. . . .

" 'Rejoice always, pray constantly, give thanks in all circumstances; for this is the will of God in Christ Jesus.' That's it, Corrie! That's His answer. 'Give thanks in all circumstances!' That's what we can do. We can start right now to thank God for every single thing about this new barracks!"[5]

In turn, then, Betsie gave thanks: that their Bible had not been discovered because there was no initial inspection; that crowded quarters meant more women could hear the word of God; and that they had the company of fleas. At this point, Corrie protested:

The fleas! This was too much. "Betsie, there's no way even God can make me grateful for a flea."

" 'Give thanks in all circumstances,' " she quoted. "It doesn't say, 'in pleasant circumstances.' Fleas are part of this place where God has put us."

And so we stood between piers of bunks and gave thanks for fleas. But this time I was sure Betsie was wrong.[6]

Betsie was not wrong, however, for the sisters later realized that the reason they were able to hold evening Bible meetings miraculously undetected was because the guards would not enter the flea-infested barracks. Corrie concluded: "My mind rushed back to our first hour in this place. I remembered Betsie's bowed head, remembered her thanks to God for creatures I could see no use for."[7]

As difficult as circumstances might be for any of us, surely we are not in such dire straits that we cannot give thanks as the ten-Boom sisters did. We all have many things for which we can be thankful, and we should express appreciation for these blessings in our prayers.

CONFESSING PERSONAL SINS AND WEAKNESSES

We often are able to quickly identify transgressions and imperfections in the lives of others, but we find it harder to recognize and admit these failures in our own character. John warns us that "if we say that we have no sin, we deceive ourselves, and the truth is not in us." (1 Jn. 1:8.) Before we can seek divine help in our weak areas, we must be aware of what they are. Through prayer and contemplation before God, our weaknesses can be revealed to us. Except for Christ, all have sinned, and we should concentrate on our own transgressions rather than finding fault in others.

As we recognize and admit the errors of our ways, we are ready to correct our faults. Confessing our sins becomes a healthy catharsis as we attempt to purge ourselves of our moral and spiritual blemishes. Latter-day Saint practice does not require public confession of all sins to a priesthood leader, but all are expected to confess their sins to the Lord, who alone can provide forgiveness.[8] Such confessions are best done in an attitude of prayer. When we come to the Lord with a contrite spirit and a willingness to admit areas of weakness, then we can establish an open, honest dialogue with our Heavenly Father. We have no secrets to camouflage, and with a sincere and humble confession, we are then in the spiritual framework to be taught and assisted by God's Spirit as we pray for his help to overcome our weaknesses. (See D&C 38:14; Ether 12:24–27.)

PETITIONING FOR HELP

After praising God, giving thanks for his blessings, and confessing our weaknesses, we are usually more discreet in what we then ask for from God. Nephi wrote from his experience, "My God will give me, *if I ask not amiss.*" (2 Ne. 4:35; italics added.) The Savior likewise counseled the Nephites, "Whatsoever ye shall ask the Father in my name, *which is right,* believing that ye shall receive, behold it shall be given unto you." (3 Ne. 18:20; italics added.) Even if we ask in faith and are worthy to receive God's blessings, if we ask for the wrong things, God reserves the right to withhold answers and favors from us if they would not be for our benefit.

The Prophet Joseph Smith learned this lesson in a bitter way when he persistently asked the Lord to allow him to lend the first 114 pages of the Book of Mormon manuscript to Martin Harris—even after the Lord twice told him "no." Finally, the Lord consented, presumably to teach Joseph a lesson, and gave him specific instructions for handling the manuscript. After Martin disregarded these instructions, the manuscript was lost, and the gift of translation was temporarily taken from the Prophet as punishment, which taught Joseph to be sensitive to God's will.[9]

Our ultimate goal, likewise, should be to refine our desires and conform them to the will of God. We accomplish this by learning to pray through the promptings of the Holy Ghost, for the Spirit "teacheth a man to pray." (2 Ne. 32:8.) When the things we ask for, as well as the answers we receive, are inspired by the Holy Ghost, we will not "ask amiss," and we will discover what we and our loved ones truly need to progress toward holiness.

EXPRESSING LOVE AND DEVOTION

Sometime during a full, sincere prayer, while we are recognizing God's glory, gifts, and forgiveness, or even while we are petitioning him for additional assistance, we should sense that he does so much more for us than we could ever do for him or others. Beyond a new expression of love and appreciation, such feelings motivate us with a desire to give rather than just to receive. We would like to do unto others as our Heavenly Father has done for us. With what few gifts and abilities we have, we want to share them with others to help and assist them. This dimension in prayer brings us into harmony with the most important commandments of God.

The first and greatest commandment is to love the Lord with all our heart, might, mind, and strength. (See Matt. 22:37; Deut. 6:5.) The second great commandment is like the first, as we learn to love and serve others. Prayer provides a beautiful opportunity to express our feelings toward God and our commitment to serve him and others. In these tender moments of divine communion, we find the love and empathy lacking in most of society. As we voice our love to God, we draw within the shadow of his protective care. As we proclaim our devotion to him and his teachings, we draw upon his strength and receive courage to meet the challenges ahead. And as we resolve and promise him that we will help others as he has helped us, we draw into a compact with God, vowing to do something for him. Prayer gives us the occasion to renew our commitments to our Father in Heaven, thereby maintaining a strong link with our Supreme Benefactor.

CONCLUDING IN CHRIST'S NAME

Jesus taught us that we should pray always and that our prayers should be directed to the Father in the name of Jesus Christ. (See John 14:13–14; 3 Ne. 18:19.) We truly pray in Christ's name when our mind and will are united with his. Our wishes will then be the same as his, and our requests will be possible for God to grant. (See John 15:7.) As we discussed earlier in the chapter on Jesus, he represents the Father in all aspects here on this earth, and any blessing we receive must come through his permission. As we conclude our prayers in Christ's name, we want to feel confident that our supplications are in harmony with God's mind and will so that God, through Christ, can accept our words and grant the righteous desires of our hearts.

The usual last word of a prayer expresses the sincerity of our communication. The word *amen* means "truly," and it witnesses a final oath of genuine expression. An *amen* is a seal and a pledge: with it, we both conclude our prayers to God and solemnly promise to remain faithful to the words of our communication. (See Deut. 27:14–26; 1 Chr. 16:36; D&C 20:77–79.) A proper *amen* focuses our whole soul upon the expressions of our prayer. (See Neh. 8:6.)

As a short review, the following simple prayer contains all seven steps:

> Father in heaven,
> Thou art good and kind.
> Thou hast blessed me abundantly.
> Forgive me, please, of my transgressions.
> Please help me with my material and spiritual needs.
> I commit myself into thy service,
> In the name of Jesus Christ, Amen.

Frequent inclusion of each of these seven steps within our prayers will greatly enrich our spiritual communion with God. Our prayers will be less narrow and selfish and will expand our perspective of life and appreciation for Heavenly Father.

UNANSWERED PRAYERS

Sometimes we feel that the Lord does not answer our prayers. On other occasions, we sense that perhaps he is communicating to us, but we do not recognize his methods. Joseph Smith received some specific counsel on how to recognize God's answers early in his prophetic experience. The Lord sent some instructions through Joseph to be given to Oliver Cowdery, and the advice remains fresh and pertinent for us today: "Behold, I say unto you, that you must study it out in your mind; then you must ask me if it be right, and if it is right I will cause that your bosom shall burn within you; therefore, you shall feel that it is right. But if it be not right you shall have no such feelings, but you shall have a stupor of thought that shall cause you to forget the thing which is wrong." (D&C 9:8–9.)

Many of our prayers, which we think were unanswered, may have been answered through the types of spiritual promptings and feelings just mentioned, but we may have been insensitive to them. On other occasions, it seems that God does not answer our prayers because he wants us to search and ponder some more before he responds, or he is waiting for us to first come to a decision before he can confirm that decision through the Spirit. In some situations, he respects our agency and spiritual maturity and lets us decide and act for ourselves. In other situations, he hesitates to respond because we are not spiritually mature or sincere enough to accept or even recognize his responses. Some prayers remain unanswered because they do not represent Christ's mind at all, but they spring out of the ignorance of a person's mind or the selfishness of his or her heart.[10] Rather than lose faith in God because he does not seem to answer our prayers, we need to evaluate the motives and attitudes of our prayers and work to improve our spiritual sensitivity. As with other important matters of eternity, we must be patient, for we might not receive an answer or witness until after a test of our faith and perseverance. (See 1 Pet. 1:7; Ether 12:6; D&C 105:19.)

THE LANGUAGE AND ATTITUDE OF PRAYER

The kind of language we use in general conversation indicates more than our knowledge and vocabulary—it also reflects our feelings and attitude. Prayer language is likewise very important since it is often influenced by our daily speech patterns yet needs to reflect our spiritual mood. Our divine petitions will not be readily answered if we are in the habit of careless, vulgar, or angry speech as in some normal conversations: "The tongue can no man tame; it is an unruly evil, full of deadly poison. Therewith bless we God, even the Father; and therewith curse we men, *which are made after the similitude of God.* Out of the same mouth proceedeth blessing and cursing. My brethren, these things ought not so to be. Doth a fountain send forth at the same place sweet water and bitter?" (James 3:8–11; italics added.)

Made after the similitude of God, we should strive to make our everyday language with our fellowman pure as a "sweet fountain" so that we may also confidently and effectively communicate with God in prayer, the highest use of the gift of language.

In our communication with God, we are commanded to "pray vocally as well as in . . . [our] heart." (D&C 19:28.) There are a couple of reasons why oral prayer can be more effective than silent prayer. Vocal prayers, spoken out loud, help us focus on ideas the same way our speech focuses our thought. Without external visual or verbal stimulus, the average span of attention on any idea is about twenty to thirty seconds for most adults, and even shorter for children. Also, thought and speech are so closely linked that an idea is usually not fully formed until it is expressed. If we say we understand something but cannot explain it, we probably don't fully understand it at all. In addition, we all know that talking over our feelings and problems with someone else helps us understand them more clearly and relieves our burden. In the same way, vocal prayer first makes our thoughts and feelings clear and precise and second brings us insight and comfort.

To help us elevate our verbal prayers to a higher plane, we are also encouraged to address the Lord using formal pronouns and adjectives like *thou, thee, thy,* and *thine,* rather than the familiar *you* and *yours.* Ironically, the now-formal English of *thee* and *thine* was originally used among people familiar with each other, such as family members and peers, and our present informal form of *you* and *yours* was used with strangers or superiors in class. Later political and social democratization weakened class distinctions in English-speaking countries. Public communication gradually eliminated the *thee* and *thine* form from common usage and changed the formal form to the universal *you* and *yours*.

The King James Bible and the works of Shakespeare are the major writings that have remained with us in the original, sixteenth-century idiom. Orally, the only type of speech that has retained the older patterns is prayer. In this way, the language of the scriptures and prayer has gradually assumed an unfamiliar and formal air. Despite the illogical historical reversal (taking what once was common, familiar speech and using it now in formal prayer language), the language of our prayers reminds us that prayer is no ordinary conversation with just anybody, but indeed it is sacred communication with God. As President Kimball has commented, "In all our prayers, it is well to use the pronouns *thee, thou, thy,* and *thine* instead of *you, your,* and *yours* inasmuch as they have come to indicate respect."[11]

Our priorities in prayer should be first to pray with genuine feelings and then to check if we are accurately expressing the correct terminology. Our greatest priority is to pray with full heart as we express our genuine, immediate feelings. We can foster this genuineness as we think and ponder while we pray and as we avoid vain repetitions and idle clichés. Our second priority is to search out the precise words and prayer style that best communicate our feelings. In any prayer, the use of proper language can help us remember the supreme, divine being with whom we are communicating. The formality of address or a special style of prayer need not be, nor is it meant to be, a barrier to communication. Children raised with the formal language in prayers find them completely natural, and even uninitiated adults who are unfamiliar with this style of speech can gradually adapt themselves comfortably to the elevated language of prayer. As an expansion of the simple prayer given earlier, a short prayer using the more traditional prayer style and including all the seven steps might sound like this:

> Father in Heaven,
> Thou art holy and righteous.
> Through thy love, thou hast given me life and many blessings
> that bring me comfort and peace.

Please forgive me of my sins against thee and of my transgressions against others.

Bless me, please, with the physical and spiritual necessities that my family and I need.

I pledge myself to be of service to thee and others.

I ask these things in the name of thy son, Jesus the Christ. Amen.

Besides using special language to show respect for the Lord, we should also seek a quiet, tranquil place and kneel to say our prayers—particularly our private prayers—whenever possible. On our knees with our heads bowed, we are in a position expressive of complete humility and trust. In ancient times, when one knelt before a king or conqueror, he placed himself not only at the ruler's disposal, but also at his mercy, for in a kneeling position the petitioner was physically vulnerable and unable to defend himself. When we kneel before God, then, we acknowledge both his greatness and our own helplessness and dependency on him for all we are and all we possess.

Prayers do not need to be long and complicated. A short, simple, and sincere prayer will be far more edifying than a lengthy, elaborate, and hypocritical one. Genuine prayers bond us with our Heavenly Father and increase our desire to communicate more often with him. As we listen to the whisperings of his Spirit and meditate upon the spiritual impressions we receive, we gain confidence in our capacity to commune with the Divine. Occasions will then arise in which we will want to have longer, more detailed prayers with our Father in Heaven. These longer prayers will need much earnest, spiritual intensity. Like any effective dialogue, a proper prayer requires effort and concentration on our part. The rewards for this spiritual endeavor will provide much spiritual nourishment for our souls.

We conclude this chapter with this summary: *PRAYER is the communication gift between God and mortals through which we praise Deity, give thanks, confess weaknesses, petition needs, and express devotion to our Heavenly Father in the name of Jesus Christ.* As we seek for strength and help from God, we need to remember that most blessings require some work and effort on our part. Often the physical and mental effort that we expend in the proper language and attitude of prayer results in more intense, sincere prayers, which in turn bring us closer to receiving the desired blessings. True prayer is a form of spiritual work, and it is God's appointed means for obtaining the highest of all his blessings.[12] Regular, sincere prayer is the single, most powerful spiritual quality that puts us onto the path of spirituality and keeps us in the way of righteousness.

For further study, refer to the following entries:

TG	BD	EM
God, Access to	Prayer	Amen
Petition		Family Prayer
Praise		Lord's Prayer
Prayer, Pray		Prayer
Supplication		Thankfulness
Thank		
Thanksgiving		

CHAPTER 6

GOD REVEALS HIS WILL

At times, all people have had the sensation of knowing certain facts but being unable to recall that information at a given time. For example, many humans have experienced the embarrassment of not being able to recall the name of an acquaintance when they see the person unexpectedly. They know they recognize the person, and they can even remember many experiences that they shared, but they cannot remember the person's name. This temporary forgetfulness is especially true when trying to recollect particular names and facts about people and events from one's youth.

As we search for a clearer remembrance of our past, a variety of aids can help refresh our memory. Sometimes as we read an old newspaper or periodical, leaf through a scrapbook, scan our high school yearbook, or review our comments in a teenage journal, certain images assist our recollection, bringing the past into immediate focus. We not only recall names and events, but we also bring to remembrance many concepts and opinions that we had believed as a youth and then forgotten and discarded during the later pursuits of life. As we refresh our mental memories, we occasionally recognize that some of the innocent ideas and images of our younger years were really very wise and valuable, and maybe we appreciate them even more now.

God's process of revelation fulfills a similar function in the spiritual dimension of our lives, his divine promptings bringing eternal truths into immediate focus. Indeed, the word "reveal" means "to unveil what was hidden." Some things that could be hidden from us might be a remembrance of our past or an understanding of our present and future. God's revelation unveils our recollections and the knowledge of him that we had in our premortal existence. Divine revelation also unveils the gospel truths that we had known or believed earlier, but that we have forgotten during the course of mortal life. In addition, spiritual revelation can unveil new insights and perspectives about our present and future life. Especially when coupled with the learning experiences our physical bodies provide, spiritual revelation helps us comprehend the purpose of life and our eternal priorities.

In the first chapter in this book, different levels of truth and their methods were outlined, with the conclusion that the highest form of truth — eternal and spiritual — can be known only as it is revealed by the Eternal One through his Spirit. We cannot understand the things of God through our own physical or mental faculties. As the Book of Mormon prophet Jacob so beautifully expressed: "Great and marvelous are the works of the Lord. How unsearchable are the depths of the mysteries of him; and it is impossible that man should find out all his ways. *And no man knoweth of his ways save it be revealed unto him.*" (Jacob 4:8; italics added.)

God has seen fit to reveal many truths about himself and his expectations for his children through the ancient prophets and apostles. Unfortunately, this religious knowledge and these spiritual truths were soon distorted and forgotten by later generations. Thus God has to continuously unveil what has become lost and hidden. In every dispensation, the knowledge of God, his plan of salvation, and the keys of the priesthood have been revealed anew to the prophets.

The remedy to avoid the loss of revealed truth is found in the New Testament. Jesus was the fountain of truth for his disciples, but toward the close of his ministry, he warned his followers that he would shortly be taken from them. To prepare his apostles for their leadership role, Jesus affirmed to Peter that revelation would be the "rock [upon which] I will build my church; and the gates of hell shall not prevail against it." (Matt. 16:18.)[1] When the apostles died and revelation ceased, Christ's true church lost its spiritual direction and the priesthood keys were taken from the earth.[2] Only through revelation could the gospel truths be restored. The restoration of Christ's church in the latter days naturally commenced with a divine revelation (the First Vision) to Joseph Smith. Joseph later affirmed the value of such revelations through his statement, "Salvation cannot come without revelation."[3]

The Prophet's declaration applies as much to individual members of the Church as it does to the inspired leaders of gospel dispensations. The same Spirit that has inspired the prophets can and must also enlighten us. Only through divine inspiration can we come to know the mysteries of God and God himself. This is the promise of the scriptures: "Verily thus saith the Lord: It shall come to pass that every soul who forsaketh his sins and cometh unto me, and calleth on my name, and obeyeth my voice, and keepeth my commandments, shall see my face and know that I am." (D&C 93:1.) This promise can only be ours as we follow the promptings of the Holy Ghost, who will lead us to God. We cannot receive personal salvation without this enlightenment and guidance of the Holy Ghost: "For the natural man is an enemy to God . . . unless he yields to the enticings of the Holy Spirit . . . and becometh a saint through the atonement of Christ." (Mosiah 3:19.) The Spirit communicates to us through various forms of revelation.

TYPES OF REVELATION

Ranging from majestic, personal visitations from members of the Godhead to simple insights gained while studying the scriptures, the ways in which God reveals truth to us are almost innumerable. Divine revelations may be direct and profound experiences, encompassing our whole physical and spiritual senses, or they may be manifest as subtle spiritual promptings. In fact, the Prophet Brigham Young taught that any time truth is communicated to us, either directly through the Holy Ghost or indirectly through others, we have received revelation: "No person [has] received knowledge, only upon the principle of revelation, that is, by having something revealed to them. . . . Who reveals? Everybody around us; we learn of each other."[4]

Since God the Father does not regularly communicate face-to-face with us, he has prepared many ways and means by which he may reveal truths to us. A few messages are delivered personally by him, and many more by his representatives. Other communications are given by heavenly and inner voices, through visions or dreams, or by the gentle instruction of the Spirit. God also uses physical objects, miracles, scriptures, the prophetic word, worship services, and a host of other means to reveal his will to his children. Initially, God can communicate to us directly or indirectly, and either on a one-to-one basis or as a member of a larger group. There are at least three general categories of revelation through which we usually receive divine communication: person-to-person visitations, supra-spiritual channels, and subsidiary means of revelation.

PERSON-TO-PERSON VISITATIONS

When we think of communication, we usually associate two or more people in conversation or contact with each other. Communication between individuals is an important source of revelation. God can either reveal himself and his message directly to an individual, or he can do it indirectly through angels or mortals, such as prophets and apostles.

Direct Personal Manifestation of God. The rarest and most profound of personal revelations is to have God the Father or Jesus Christ appear directly to an individual. Moses records that the ancient patriarchs, such as Enoch and Jacob, saw God and walked together with him. (See Gen. 5:24; 32:30.) Moses could easily identify with this special direct, divine manifestation because he and seventy elders of Israel shared a similar experience. (See Ex. 24:9–11.) Later prophets and apostles also bore a similar witness. Although Jesus promised that the pure in heart will see God, few mortals have had the purity or calling to see God while in the flesh. This form of personal revelation is primarily reserved for the prophets. It is significant that the founder of Christ's church in our day, the prophet Joseph Smith, had such a profound experience when he saw both the Father and the Son. (See JS–H 1:17.)

In the few recorded occasions when God the Father has clearly unveiled himself to mortals, he has usually introduced and testified concerning his Son, such as at the baptism of Jesus, at the transfiguration, or in his witness to the Book of Mormon peoples just prior to the resurrected Christ appearing to them. (See Matt. 3:17; 17:5; 3 Ne. 11:7.) Thereafter and in most cases where the prophets record a visitation from God, it is usually the Son who communicates directly with the mortals on earth.

Angelic Appearances. From the experiences recorded in the scriptures, a personal visitation from God the Father and/or the Lord Jesus Christ is generally reserved for prophets who are called to open a gospel dispensation or perform a significant work. Premortal spirits, resurrected beings, and other heavenly messengers are more frequently employed by

God to make personal visits. According to the root meaning of "angel," any messenger sent by God to people on earth is an angel.

Adam, Lot, Jacob, Daniel and other people had angels appear to them during the Old Testament period. (See Moses 5:6; Gen. 19:1; 32:1; Dan. 8:15.) Angels appeared to Nephi, Jacob, and Samuel in Book of Mormon times. (See 1 Ne. 11:14; 2 Ne. 6:9; Hel. 14:9.) Angels also appeared to Mary, Joseph, Philip, John, and others during the New Testament period. (See Luke 1:30; Matt. 1:20; Acts 8:26; Rev. 10:9; 17:7.) Angels were also used as messengers during the restoration of the gospel, as when Moroni delivered the gold plates to Joseph Smith, when the Prophet received the Aaronic and Melchizedek priesthoods from John the Baptist and Peter, James, and John, respectively, and when other angelic beings appeared to Joseph. (See JS–H 1:30–33, 68; D&C 27:5–12.) John the Revelator prophesies that the fullness of the gospel is to be restored through the ministry of angels in the last days. (See Rev. 14:6.) Mormon also records that God has used angels through the ages to reveal gospel truths. (See Moro. 7:22–32.)[5]

Inspired Prophets and Church Leaders. Just as God can send angelic messengers from heaven to minister to his children, he can direct people on earth to pass on important truths and revealed guidance. Prophets and apostles of the Lord can transmit divine counsel to all Church members, while local Church leaders can act as God's intermediaries to us. Heads of families, priesthood leaders, teachers, and home and visiting teachers have the spiritual right to receive revelation and inspiration concerning those in their stewardship.

Accepting counsel from inspired leaders is a type of indirect revelation where others receive the communication, and we must have the spiritual sensitivity and courage to act upon their words. Action on their inspired wisdom can eliminate the sorrow of sin and spiritually enrich our lives. Such counsel includes general conference addresses and other talks given by Church leaders, as well as private counsel from our local leaders. For example, receiving inspired direction from a bishop provides an immediate, personal form of revelation. Unless we recognize these leaders as inspired and respect the stewardship they have over us, receiving such counsel may be difficult. However, if we accompany their counsel with prayer, we can receive confirmation that it is a type of revelation directed to us. We can then act with a spiritual confidence knowing that we are responding to Heavenly Father's will.

SUPRA-SPIRITUAL CHANNELS

Normally, our spirits are incapable of "tuning in" to God's divine will because of the limitations and distortions caused by the physical body and our wicked, worldly environment. We have to go beyond the usual, natural capacities of our spirits and refine their ability to recognize God's will. Sometimes Heavenly Father will dramatically enrich our spiritual understanding through special, profound types of revelation. However, he usually encourages us to develop the spiritual gifts that he gives us so we can become sensitive to our spiritual feelings and recognize what he desires to communicate to us. In any of these examples, we become "supra-spiritual" beings, at least for a while. The prefix "supra" means "beyond." In other words, a supra-spiritual revelation is something *beyond* the normal spiritual experience that a person would have. Supra-spiritual channels of revelation can include hearing a voice from heaven, seeing a vision or special dream, and feeling definite spiritual promptings.

A Voice from Heaven. The voice of God or other angelic beings may be audible and heard through our physical ears. (See Matt. 3:16–17; 2 Pet. 1:17–18; Hel. 5:33; D&C 130:13.) As examples, the children of Israel heard the voice of God on three important occasions. The Lord God spoke to assembled Israel at Mount Sinai as he gave them the Ten Commandments and other instructions. (See Ex. 20:1, 19, 22.) Some heard God's voice from heaven near the Jordan River when Jesus was baptized by John. (See Matt. 3:17.) The voice of God was heard by the people gathered at Bountiful before the resurrected Christ appeared to them. (See 3 Ne. 11:7.) These few examples demonstrate that God can literally speak from heaven as he gives revelation.

In another direct manner, God can communicate clearly to our minds as he implants a message straight into our consciousness. As an example, the prophet Enos recorded this experience after he had gone into the forest one day, "My soul hungered; and I kneeled down before my Maker, and I cried unto him in mighty prayer and supplication for mine own soul; and all the day long did I cry unto him. . . . And there came a voice unto me, saying: Enos, thy sins are forgiven thee, and thou shalt be blessed." (Enos 1:4–5.) Because of Enos's great humility and diligence in seeking the Lord, and also because the Lord called him to the ministry and gave him specific promises concerning the Nephites and Lamanites, Enos received a revelation through the actual voice of God himself. Enos describes it as "the voice of the Lord" coming into his mind. (Enos 1:9–10.) Whether one hears God's voice through human ears or directly in the mind, the listener receives the clear communication along with a sure witness through the Holy Ghost, testifying that the voice and message are from God.

Visions. In our age of tele*vision,* we can surely relate to the reality of people communicating directly to individuals over vast distances. Although the physical eyes of the viewer do not actually see the other person (they see instead the image on the screen), they are able to bridge the gap of space. Just as we can transmit movies, photos, and other images through television and facsimile machines, God reveals much to his children on earth through visions. Instead of having personal appearances, hearing words spoken, or receiving subtle promptings, this visual mode of communication presents distinct images into the mind. (As examples, see Ezek. 40:2; Acts 10:9–17; Ether 3:19–26; D&C 67:10–14; 76:12–14; 93:1.)

Visions are a powerful means of divine communication that takes the recipient beyond the realm of his or her normal physical senses. For example, upon receiving the first ordinances of the temple endowment, Joseph Smith recorded: "The heavens were opened upon us, and I beheld the celestial kingdom of God, and the glory thereof, *whether in the body or out I cannot tell.*" (D&C 137:1; italics added.) One LDS scholar has stated that visions "anchor all the rest of God's communion by a visual link with an ordinarily unseen world that directs the destiny of humankind. They provide a vivid sense of the nature of God and his design for the world that gives coherence to all other scripture and inspiration."[6]

Dreams. Some great men among the Gentiles, such as the pharaohs of Egypt and the kings of Babylon, have received revelations through dreams and then sought for their interpretations from the prophets of the God of Israel. For example, Joseph interpreted a pharaoh's dreams, and Daniel clarified a number of King Nebuchadnezzar's dreams. (See Gen. 41; Dan. 1–5.) Of course, the prophets and apostles themselves have also had great dreams and visions, usually concerning events to come or the mysteries of heaven.

A distinction is sometimes made between dreams and visions—the former received during sleep and the other experienced while awake. In either case, important insights are disclosed as images are viewed in the consciousness of the mind. They are real experiences that mortal man normally cannot perceive with the physical senses. Like X-rays or atomic particles that we cannot see or feel, these divine manifestations are real, but they can only be perceived and understood when the person is quickened by the Spirit of God. Although dreams may take place outside normal consciousness, they do provide indelible impressions that the person remembers after awakening. As clarified and confirmed by the Holy Spirit, visionary dreams can be an insightful means of heavenly communication.

Definite and Subtle Promptings of the Spirit. Responding to firm promptings from the Spirit gives us opportunity to apply the truths revealed to us. We may feel compelled to speak to a friend about faith or a special gospel teaching. We may receive a prompting to call someone, cancel a vacation, turn down a job that otherwise looks acceptable, or write a family member a letter. If we listen to the "still, small voice" of the Holy Ghost, we can receive day-to-day direction on how to live our lives. (See 1 Kgs. 19:12–13.)

Often the promptings of the Spirit will be so soft and subtle that we may not appreciate how much they influence us. Often it is only when we lose the gift of the gentle, constant companionship of the Holy Spirit that we realize how much it has been a part of our lives. Spiritually sensitive people recognize immediately when they have lost this spiritual companionship, and they usually strive to regain it.

We should not become disappointed if we do not receive a vision or supra-spiritual experience every time we seek religious insight or divine guidance. Revelation does not have to be an overwhelming experience; sometimes the subtle spiritual promptings affect us even more, especially as they are a more constant part of our daily lives. Among the many ways that revelation may come to us, Heavenly Father prefers the gentle promptings of the Spirit. The guidance of God is most often a feeling within us put there by his Spirit. This guidance is as important and meaningful as any of the other types of revelation.

God respects our agency, and thus he desires to treat us like mature, spiritual beings. Like a parent, especially with older children, he would prefer to counsel a child with mild words of wisdom and gentle prompting rather than with shouts, threats, overwhelming evidence, or signs of power. God does not want to be a harsh taskmaster or a supreme power-broker. Instead, he prefers to be a loving shepherd who gently drives the sheep while personally attending the needs of the weak. (See Isa. 40:11.) With spiritual gentleness, he leads us by the subtle promptings of the Spirit through the darkness of this worldly wilderness.

SUBSIDIARY MEANS OF OBTAINING REVELATION

In addition to the more personal, direct, and individualized types of revelation discussed above, Heavenly Father also uses a variety of secondary, subtle, and general means of communication with his children. His will can be revealed through physical means (miracles, signs, a Urim and Thummin, etc.), through the message of his word (as it is passed on either orally or in written form, such as in the scriptures), and through association with other inspired people. A brief discussion of some of God's supplemental means of revelation helps us appreciate just a few of the many ways he is trying to communicate with us.

Signs and Miracles. Because of their dramatic and sacred nature, revelations such as the voice of God or the appearance of heavenly messengers remain quite rare in the records of the scriptures. A more common manifestation of the divine will comes through signs and miracles, especially when they are accompanied by a witness of the Spirit. Miraculous signs can sometimes be a highly effective way of demonstrating God's power and of calling even the most wicked to repentance.

Both the Apostle Paul and Alma the Younger were shocked and frightened to repentance by such manifestations. (See Acts 9:1–22; Mosiah 27:8–32.) Laman and Lemuel, unfortunately, were not so moved, and their revelations became condemnations because of their increased accountability before God. (See 2 Ne. 5:19–25.) Many of the wicked Nephites at Zarahemla were more receptive to a great sign, and they came to believe in Christ when a day, a night, and a day passed without darkness at the time of his birth. (See 3 Ne. 1:15–22.)

Usually, however, visitations, signs, and miracles are withheld from the unrighteous because they would not heed them anyway. So the Lord speaks to the wicked of their physical and spiritual destruction by means of earthquake, fire, war, and pestilence: "O, ye nations of the earth, how often would I have gathered you together as a hen gathereth her chickens under her wings, but ye would not! How oft have I called upon you . . . by the voice of earthquakes, and great hailstorms, and by the voice of famines and pestilences of every kind . . . but ye would not!" (D&C 43:24–25.) Miraculous signs will strengthen the faith and understanding of the righteous while confounding and condemning the wicked.

Physical Instruments. One physical method of revelation is worth mentioning, though it is only rarely discussed in the scriptures. From time to time, or perhaps more than we know, the prophets have possessed certain instruments to aid them in receiving revelations. For examples, the Liahona guided Lehi's family to the promised land, the Urim and Thummim helped prophets obtain revelation and translate languages, and seer stones helped some prophets see into the future.

Though these types of instruments may seem strange to us on earth, they are apparently common fixtures in heaven: "The place where God resides is a great Urim and Thummim. This earth, in its sanctified and immortal state, will be made like unto crystal and will be a Urim and Thummim to the inhabitants who dwell thereon." (D&C 130:8–9.) Individuals living on the earth as celestial beings at that time will also have their own physical means of learning the truths of the universe with an individualized seerstone. John the Revelator indicates that those in Christ's church who are true and faithful will receive a special seerstone with a new name, a special key word, written in it. It will apparently help the recipient to receive "hidden manna," or special spiritual strength and understanding from God. (See Rev. 2:17.) Joseph Smith reveals that "the white stone mentioned in Revelation 2:17, will become a Urim and Thummim to each individual who receives one, whereby things pertaining to a higher order of kingdoms will be made known." (D&C 130:10.)

Scriptures. A primary source of spiritual truth is, of course, the written words of God as found in the Holy Scriptures. Studying the scriptures provides an opportunity to "feast upon the words of Christ; for behold, the words of Christ will tell you all things what ye should do." (2 Ne. 32:3.) More than just running our eyes over the words of the page, "feasting" includes searching, pondering, praying, and living the gospel principles outlined in the passages. As we search for God's truths in the scriptures, the Spirit will accompany our reading and testify of their validity. The Spirit will also bring passages of scripture to mind when we are in need of counsel and inspiration.

Although most scriptures were recorded many centuries ago, the application of their messages find value in our contemporary lives. God's will and directions to his children in ancient times should be a source of personal inspiration to us. Through the stories and teachings in the scriptures, we come to know Heavenly Father and his Son and their dealings with the children of men. As the Spirit prompts us during our scripture studies, we also come to know ourselves and our relationship to the gospel. We should read the scriptures as if they were written to us, and then open our spirit for the Spirit of God to instruct us accordingly. Thus the scriptures will be a constant source of inspiration, regardless of what we are reading at the time.[7]

Inspired Family Records. Along with the scriptures, the written experiences of others, especially our own ancestors and family members, can strengthen our testimonies. The canonized scriptures are themselves largely records of certain key families throughout the gospel dispensations. Just as we can benefit from the spiritual insights and religious experiences of other people, we can spiritually help and strengthen others through our writings. If we write our own records under the influence of the Holy Ghost, as did the prophets of old, our posterity can receive the spirit of revelation through them. Likewise, we can look to the inspired writings of our progenitors, when they are available, for guidance, testimony, and insight.

Priesthood Blessings. Blessings through the power of the priesthood of God are available to Latter-day Saints today, just as they were to the ancient Israelites and early Christian Saints. We see numerous examples of such blessings in the scriptures, some with promises carrying over into many generations, such as Jacob's and Lehi's blessings on their children. (See Gen. 48–49; 2 Ne. 1–4.) Father's blessings are still a form of revelation by which righteous priesthood bearers can direct their children. Church patriarchs also draw upon the powers of revelation to give patriarchal blessings to those Saints who are worthy to receive counsel from the Lord. (See D&C 107:39–53.) Priesthood leaders give blessings of inspiration and revealed counsel as they perform priesthood ordinances, set members apart to Church callings, anoint the sick, and perform other priesthood blessings. These blessings can offer personal, specific direction and revelation to their recipients.

As many bishops can testify, one of the most physically demanding, emotionally exhausting, and spiritually challenging experiences of their calling is giving appropriate blessings when performing ordinances or directing and comforting individuals in times of need. Bishops also have many opportunities to give blessings to young people coming from part-member, nonmember, or inactive families, who have never before received a father's blessing. Giving blessings is an exhilarating opportunity for priesthood leaders as they struggle to become in tune with the Spirit and to give the counsel that the Lord himself would give if he were speaking. In a similar fashion, patriarchs say that it is physically strenuous for them to give more than five or six blessings at a time because such intense spiritual experiences are physically exhausting. Latter-day Saints should appreciate the spiritual direction that this avenue of revelation can provide.[8]

Oral Messages and Testimonies. Church members also have a tradition of sharing their spiritual experiences with one another formally in fast and testimony meetings, as well as informally among family and friends. And, when righteous Church members speak, "whatsoever they shall speak when moved upon by the Holy Ghost shall be scripture." (D&C 68:4.) Thus bearing and receiving testimonies, when accompanied by the Spirit, can be a form of revelation for both parties. This is one effective means of edifying each other that fulfills a commandment: "When ye are assembled together ye shall instruct and edify each other, that ye may know how to act . . . upon the points of my law and commandments which I have given." (D&C 43:8.) As righteous saints testify to each other, either in formal meetings or informally as visiting and home teachers, family members, and friends the Spirit can reveal new spiritual strengths and insights to all those sensitive to its promptings.

Temple Worship. Participation in temple ordinances also provides a great source of revealed knowledge for all worthy saints. Indeed, temples are built for the dual purpose of administering ordinances of salvation and obtaining revelations. (See D&C 94:3; 124:40–41.) As we worship in the temples, we receive guidance on how to walk in godly paths. Not only can we receive general instructions meant for all temple-going Saints, we can also receive personal revelation and spiritual confirmations as a part of our temple visits. After completion of the Kirtland Temple, the Lord appeared there, declaring, "I have accepted this house . . . and I will manifest myself to my people in mercy in this house." (D&C 110:7.) Every temple has been built to serve as a "house of learning" for the righteous who seek to know God's will concerning them. (D&C 88:119.)[9]

Prayers. The revelatory potential through prayer is one of the most readily available and effective means for receiving divine communication. The Lord promises, "Surely shall you receive a knowledge of whatsoever things you shall ask in faith, with an honest heart, believing that you shall receive. . . . Behold, I will tell you in your mind and in your heart, by the Holy Ghost. . . . *This is the spirit of revelation.*" (D&C 8:1–3; italics added.) The scriptures are full of examples of individuals who received guidance from the Lord only after sincere and fervent prayer. (As examples, see Dan. 9; Luke 9:28–31; 1 Ne. 1:5–6; D&C 121; Moses 1:24–26.)

Although we may not receive revelation every time we pray, we do place ourselves in a state of mind to receive counsel and guidance from our Heavenly Father. In company with sincere asking, listening for these answers is a vital element of prayer. With continued effort and honest desire, an answer will be given through our prayers. (See Moro. 7:9.) If we follow the guidelines of prayer as explained in the scriptures and outlined in the previous chapter, we can receive revelation in response to our heart's desires.

Pondering Gospel Topics. Pondering is not only an important element of both prayer and scripture study, it is also an opportunity to receive revelation in and of itself. Pondering involves a careful consideration of a concept, thinking deeply about it, especially in terms of its validity, significance, or outcome. Christ recognized how searching for such insights can instruct through the Spirit. When he saw that his listeners were having difficulty understanding all he taught, he asked them to go "home and ponder." (3 Ne. 17:3.)

In order for pondering to be a means of revelation, we must search in faith for the truthfulness and importance of the things we ponder. For example, we may ponder, "Is Joseph Smith a true prophet?" As our mind wanders through different mental channels in an effort to understand this and related principles, various spiritual promptings in harmony with gospel truths will attend the ponderings. As we ponder further, we can also receive revelation on how to act upon these truths. The Lord's counsel for pondering is, "You must study it out in your mind; . . . and if it is right . . . your bosom shall burn within you; therefore, you shall feel that it is right." (D&C 9:8.) Pondering is an important subsidiary step leading to revelation.

The Light of Christ within our Conscience. As we faithfully seek truth and come unto Christ, we shall feel his presence with us. As we desire to do good continually, his spirit will become our guiding light. The scriptures promise us that we can receive the light of Christ: "The Spirit giveth light to every man that cometh into the world; and the Spirit enlighteneth every man through the world, that hearkeneth to the voice of the Spirit." (D&C 84:46.) The light of Christ enhances our ability to distinguish right from wrong and to know which doctrines come from Christ. (See Moro. 7:15–19; John 8:12.) This subtle inspiration can prompt our own conscience to tell us whether a decision we are pondering is good or bad. In order to make correct, inspired judgments, we need to live righteously and allow his light to lead us.

WHY SO MANY VARIATIONS OF REVELATION?

God chooses to reveal his will at different times, through a variety of means, to meet various needs. Since every person is different, God can reveal his truths to each according to the timely needs of the individual. We do not need to see God or an angel in order to have our questions answered or to receive divine direction. If we remain ever worthy to receive his guidance, we may need only a gentle prompting to understand his will. It seems that Heavenly Father prefers to reveal quietly the knowledge that a person is seeking.

If stronger or more powerful means of communication are needed, he can use them in special circumstances. Especially when a revelation pertains to an entire body of people, such as the House of Israel or the membership of the Church, God often uses more direct means of communication and spiritual verification. Our responsibility is to seek counsel from God and allow him to lead us as he will. As we grow in the principles of revelation, our manifestations may become even more specific and distinct, according to both our worthiness and our need.

THE SPIRIT OF PERSONAL REVELATION

Since experiences of direct, personal revelation are so important to our ability to endure to the end, outlining some of the ways in which the

Holy Ghost may manifest himself to each of us should be helpful. Through diligent prayer and spiritual experience, we may come to recognize which of these ways the Holy Ghost usually chooses to speak to us—for they vary from one person to another, according to their nature and receptivity. Some people feel a burning sensation in the body when the Spirit is present. (See D&C 9:8.) Some feel a sense of peace or joy, making them feel like praising or even singing God's glory and blessings. Others experience a tingling sensation or a quickening of the mind. Many people experience a variety of these feelings at different times when receiving special spiritual communication from God.

One common manifestation of the spirit of revelation is when a sudden idea or insight comes into our minds after we have been pondering over a question or problem. It is so common and universal that we see it illustrated even in comic strips as the light bulb suddenly clicking on to illuminate a difficult situation. The Prophet Joseph Smith described it in this way: "A person may profit by noticing the first intimation of the spirit of revelation; for instance, when you feel pure intelligence flowing into you, it may give you sudden strokes of ideas, . . . and thus by learning the Spirit of God and understanding it, you may grow into the principle of revelation, until you become perfect in Christ Jesus."[10] Ideas presented to our minds are not only the primary form of revelation, they are also a foundation that we build upon to seek, accept, and understand further revelation.

The ideas and insights we receive from the Spirit are also confirmed by feelings of peace. When Oliver Cowdery desired a second witness that the translation of the Book of Mormon was divine, the Lord replied, "Did I not speak peace to your mind concerning the matter? What greater witness can you have than from God?" (D&C 6:23.) Shortly thereafter, God reminded him again how to recognize the manifestation of his Spirit: "I will tell you in your mind and in your heart, by the Holy Ghost, which shall come upon you and which shall dwell in your heart." (D&C 8:2.)

On the other hand, we can recognize that the spirit of truth is not with us when we feel confused, as if we are in a stupor of thought. (See D&C 9:9.) We might also feel a darkness of evil influence or a sense of despair, which "cometh because of iniquity." (Moro. 10:22.) Thus, any course of action we may decide upon that leaves us agitated or uncertain has not been confirmed by the Holy Ghost. It may even indicate that we need to strengthen ourselves spiritually before we will be ready and worthy to receive personal revelation.

The more a person lives the commandments, spends time with edifying people, and prayerfully searches for spiritual direction, the more he or she will come to recognize and depend upon God's revelatory powers. The gift of spiritual light is given to every mortal, which enables us to receive spiritual confirmation of true and significant gospel principles. (See D&C 84:45–47.) When the Holy Ghost comes to dwell in our hearts, the mental and spiritual peace we feel may be accompanied by a literal, physical sensation of warmth, or spiritual "fire" within our bodies. Again, the Lord's instructions to Oliver Cowdery apply to us as well: "I say unto you, that you must study it out in your mind; then you must ask me if it be right, and if it is right I will cause that your bosom shall burn within you; therefore, you shall feel that it is right." (D&C 9:8.)

A TESTIMONY OF TRUTH THROUGH THE SPIRIT

The most important blessing we can seek through prayer is a testimony, a spiritual conviction concerning gospel truths. Although study and reasoning can assist truth seekers in laying a foundation of correct teachings and principles, only the spirit of truth, as manifested through the Holy Ghost, can confirm a person's testimony. The Apostle John taught that a testimony consists of knowledge that comes through revelation, "for the testimony of Jesus is the spirit of prophecy." (Rev. 19:10.) The late Elder Bruce R. McConkie instructed us in three key elements of a true testimony: "Three great truths must be included in every valid testimony: 1. That Jesus Christ is the Son of God and the Savior of the World (D&C 46:13); 2. That Joseph Smith is the Prophet of God through whom the gospel was restored in this dispensation; and 3. That The Church of Jesus Christ of Latter-day Saints is 'the only true and living church upon the face of the whole earth.' (D&C 1:30.)"[11]

As we receive a spiritual witness concerning these three truths, we also by inference gain divine knowledge concerning other important concepts. As we receive a testimony of Jesus, we come to understand the gospel of Jesus Christ (which will be discussed in later sections of this book) and his relationship with the Godhead (the subject of the first section of this book). As we strengthen our testimony of Joseph Smith, we better understand God's work with prophets and apostles, both ancient and modern, and we better appreciate the scriptures that they have brought forth. As we receive a spiritual witness of the restored church of Jesus Christ, we will learn more about God's priesthood and saving ordinances, especially those performed in his holy temples.

The Book of Mormon provides a valuable pattern for seeking truth and testimony. At the end of the Book of Mormon, the prophet Moroni suggests at least five important steps: A person must have a *desire* to know the truth. He or she must *search* and *study* the scriptures to see what has been recorded concerning God's doings and counsel. (See John 5:39.) The person must *remember* what God has done and *ponder* the Lord's intentions and efforts with his children. And finally, he or she must *ask God,* in the name of Christ, with "a sincere heart, with real intent, having faith in Christ," and then God will manifest the truth to this individual by the power of the Holy Ghost. And through the power of the Holy Ghost, a person can then come to know the truth of all things. (Moro. 10:3–5.)

One receives such a testimony, or witness of truth, with a feeling of calm assurance and unwavering certainty. People know they have received a special witness through the Holy Spirit when they can say, as Alma did: "I testify unto you that I do know that these things whereof I have spoken are true. And how do ye suppose that I know of their surety? Behold, I say unto you they are made known unto me by the Holy Spirit of God. Behold, I have fasted and prayed many days that I might know these things of myself, and now I do know of myself that they are true; for the Lord God hath made them manifest unto me by his Holy Spirit." (Alma 5:45–46.)

A testimony is the beginning of significant spiritual growth in the life of any person. As will be seen in later chapters, a testimony is not, however, the end of an individual's spiritual development. For starters, one's simple testimony of the Godhead can and should be strengthened with additional testimony of the prophets, the Church, the scriptures, and other gospel truths. In addition, great spiritual values exist beyond simply gaining, maintaining, and building a testimony. Some "born again" Christians and other pentecostal followers in some religions may believe that a fervent declaration of faith is all they need to gain entrance into God's kingdom, but closer study reveals that further study, effort, commitment, and righteous service is required to enjoy eternal peace with God.

THE POWER OF PERSONAL REVELATION

With all the sources of truth around us, there is still no substitute for personal, direct revelation through the Spirit. Joseph Smith taught, "Could we read and comprehend all that has been written from the days of Adam, on the relation of man to God, ... we should know very little about it. Reading the experience of others, or the revelations given to them, can never give us a comprehensive view of our condition and true relation to God. ... Could you gaze into heaven five minutes, you would know more than you would by reading all that ever was written on the subject."[12] Personal revelation, besides being the most comprehensive channel of divine knowledge, is also essential to developing the faith and testimony needed to endure the tribulations of the last days. President Heber C. Kimball warned, "To meet the difficulties that are coming, it will be necessary for you to have a knowledge of the truth of this work for yourselves. ... The time will come when no man nor woman will be able to endure on borrowed light. Each will have to be guided by the light within himself."[13]

The only ways that a testimony or spiritual knowledge can be weakened is through neglect and transgression. If we fail to study the gospel and to seek new spiritual insights, we begin to lose our spiritual focus in life. If we disobey the commandments, we forfeit the spiritual inspiration that otherwise would lead and direct us. The knowledge of God and his sublime truths cannot remain in us when we are in a sinful state. Through disobedience, God's great truths have repeatedly been lost to mankind — within religious communities and not just within individuals. The Book of Mormon describes this process: the sinful dissenters "became more hardened and impenitent, ... entirely forgetting the Lord their God." (Alma 47:36.)

Unfortunately, we probably recognize this pattern in others more easily than in ourselves. How painful it is to watch people close to us go against God's laws and the truths to which they once held closely. As they break the commandments, we can observe a forgetting that takes place as the spirit of revelation leaves them and they are left to their incomplete knowledge. This tragedy of spiritual forgetfulness is far more serious than forgetting the name of an old acquaintance. We can avoid this spiritual calamity by seeking further revealed light and truth, working to preserve God's truths through faith, repentance, obedience, and service.

We conclude this chapter with this summary: *REVELATION encompasses a variety of means chosen by God to communicate divine truth and his will to his prophets and his children—without it, the true gospel and church could not exist on earth. TESTIMONY is our spiritual witness of divine truths.* As the Spirit testifies to us, we can learn to recognize revelation in its many forms. We should be constantly seeking revelation in our lives by all the means at our disposal in order to learn divine truths, to benefit our testimonies, and to receive personal guidance from God. Sincere prayer along with studying and pondering will lead to personal inspiration, which will reveal and strengthen our testimony of Heavenly Father and his work. This spiritual insight and witness give us the guidelines and conviction to continue our spiritual journey toward God and his glorious presence.

For further study, refer to the following entries:

TG	BD	*EM*
Angels	Angels	Inspiration
Dream	Dreams	Light of Christ
God, Privilege of	Light of Christ	Revelation
Seeing	Revelation	Testimony
Holy Ghost, Source	Scripture	Vision
of Testimony	Urim and Thummim	Urim and Thummim
Light of Christ		Visions
Revelation		
Testimony		
Vision		
Visitation		
Voice		
Witness, Witnesses		

CHAPTER 7

GOD'S SPOKESMEN

Though the names and settings may change, the story is often told of a young hard-working American rising to the top of his field. He wanted to work for a major business but did not have any professional experience. He started out at the bottom of the corporate structure as a messenger boy, but he worked hard and productively, receiving more and more responsibility until some years later he became one of the chief executives in the firm. He effectively represented the company president as the corporation developed a new product and opened up a productive market in a new area of the world. His climb up the corporate ladder was not out of personal ambition or with a desire to become wealthy; he just wanted to do well and to enjoy a sense of success. He was then able to share his knowledge with others, both within and without the company. Eventually his expertise qualified him to be an international spokesperson for one of the world's most successful businesses. Imagine his feelings when he saw how his service not only benefited his company, but also helped make the world a better place. This man's feelings only begin to approximate those felt by a prophet as he is called to be the Lord's messenger on earth and God's spokesman to all mankind.

A PROPHET IS GOD'S MOUTHPIECE

Instead of personally administering to the children of men, the Lord has ordained prophets to act in his name. A prophet acts as God's messenger by declaring his divine will. While some forms of revelation are open to all who diligently seek heavenly communication, God has reserved certain manifestations for his special representatives. Throughout the ages these men testify of and for God as they teach divine truths by proclaiming the gospel to the ignorant and wise, the faithful and unbelieving. These special, divinely appointed witnesses are called "prophets," a title derived from the Greek word *prophetes*, which means "inspired teacher." The Greek root is *prophanai*, meaning literally, *pro* "for" + *phanai* "to speak." A prophet is simply one *who speaks for God*, one who is his inspired mouthpiece.[1]

The challenging task of serving God as his prophet-spokesman has caused some prophets to hesitate when called to their office. For example, Enoch said, "Why is it that I have found favor in thy sight, and am but a lad, and all the people hate me; for I am slow of speech; wherefore am I thy servant?" (Moses 6:31.) Moses resisted his prophetic calling for a while and repeated some of the same uncertainties when he was chosen to prophesy to Israel: "O my Lord, I am not eloquent . . . but I am slow of speech, and of a slow tongue." (Ex. 4:10.) Despite, or perhaps because of their limitations, God chose both Enoch and Moses so that he could show forth his own great power and eloquence through them. To Enoch, he replied, "Open thy mouth, and it shall be filled, and I will give thee utterance," and to Moses, "I will be with thy mouth, and teach thee what thou shalt say." (Moses 6:32; Ex. 4:12.)

SPEAKING FOR GOD

As God's spokesman or mouthpiece to the world, the prophet reveals the mind and mysteries of God to an ignorant or searching people. Foreordained prophets have stood at the head of God's religious communities throughout the ages, from the day of Adam to the present.[2] The Lord has declared that prophets are his primary means of communicating his will to the people. (See Amos 3:7.) Indeed, essential truths will be taught and testified to the world by two or more prophetic witnesses. (See 2 Cor. 13:1.) These multiple prophets often live during different times, even on different continents, suggesting the importance of the words they give us, as recorded in the scriptures.

Though prophets speak the word of the Lord as personally revealed to them, the message has always carried the same basic themes: repent and draw near unto the Lord, keep the commandments, and serve one another. The prophets' primary function, then, is not necessarily to reveal new truths, but to remind the people of what they should already have learned from the scriptures and earlier teachings. Thus the prophets speak more as *forth*tellers than as *fore*tellers — men delivering God's will for his children more than declaring his plans for the future. As a prophet receives special revelations from above, he may also include the predictive element of prophecy in his teachings. He then serves as a seer and revelator. In the main, however, the prophet's most common and authentic role as God's spokesman is to interpret earlier laws and traditions and apply them as guides to unify and establish norms amid new problems and circumstances.

Each prophet naturally builds upon the foundation of truth laid by the prophets before him: the laws of God revealed to Moses in the first five books of the Old Testament (also know as the Torah or Pentateuch) became the reference point for later Old Testament prophets; Isaiah's teachings established an important theological foundation for later Bible and Book of Mormon prophets and apostles; the Brass Plates of Laban formed the basis of Nephi's teachings; and the Book of Mormon and the Bible revealed the gospel to Joseph Smith. Our modern prophets continue this pattern as they teach us from the ancient scriptures as well as from the translations and contemporary revelations of the Prophet Joseph recorded in the Book of Mormon and the Doctrine and Covenants.

THE TEST OF A TRUE PROPHET

Our living prophets speak forth with spiritual power and conviction when they deliver God's word. They add their witness to the many who have preceded them, and they speak with the same prophetic authority as the ancient prophets. Indeed, when a living prophet closes his remarks "in the name of Jesus Christ," he bids us to obey the divine word just as the ancient prophets did when saying, "thus saith the Lord." Hence we receive the word of God through modern-day prophets as they build upon ancient prophetic traditions and authority.

Unfortunately, other individuals have come forth proclaiming to be prophets when they do not represent God. "Beware of false prophets," warned the Master. (Matt. 7:15.) Joseph Smith taught, "When a man goes about prophesying, and commands men to obey his teachings, he must either be a true or false prophet. False prophets always arise to oppose the true prophets."[3] Jesus particularly warned of false prophets who would deceive many in the last days before his second coming. (See

Matt. 24:11, 24.) Note that nowhere in his teachings did Jesus say there would be no prophets at all after him. However, he did admonish us to be aware of false, deceiving prophets — implying that there would also be true, edifying prophets in the last days.

Fortunately, Jesus also provided guidelines to measure the truthfulness and authority of a prophet. He first forewarned that false prophets come in deceit as "in sheep's clothing," while they are actually "ravening wolves." (Matt. 7:15.) His primary criteria was that "ye shall know them by their fruits." (V. 16.) He then gave two "fruits" by which to measure them: first, by the fruits they gather, and second, by the fruits they produce. (See vv. 17–20.) The Lord, through Moses, had earlier mentioned another way to recognize a false prophet — if they prophesy or promise something in the name of the Lord but "the thing follow not, nor come to pass," then it was not the word of the Lord. (Deut. 18:22.) The fruits that a false prophet (or preacher and minister) gathers include money, fame, political influence, and other worldly attractions and false promises inconsistent with a truly spiritual mission. The fruits that a false religious leader produces include corruption, dishonesty, loss of trust, infidelity, sorrow, confusion, and any form of wickedness or heresy, including false prophecies.

In comparison, a true prophet gathers fruits of righteousness, seeking for the glory of God (rather than his own self-aggrandizement), the edification of the saints (rather than control over his followers), the building of God's kingdom (rather than his own religious empire), and the verification of truth (rather than his vain rhetoric and verbose deceptions). The fruits that a true prophet produces include righteousness among his followers, virtue and honesty as standards of moral behavior, increased testimony and conviction, spiritual gifts and manifestations, clear gospel teachings and admonitions, and other manifestations of uplifting and spiritual leadership. Likewise, if a prophet prophesies something that comes to pass, it is a sign "that the Lord hath truly sent him." (Jer. 28:9.)[4]

THE SPIRIT OF PROPHECY

The critical fruit that a true prophet both seeks and produces is the spirit of prophecy. The spirit of prophecy is a testimony of Jesus the

Messiah that a person receives by revelation through the Holy Ghost. (See Rev. 19:10.)[5] The words of the prophets always bear record of the Lord and his commandments. Accordingly, every prophet testifies of Christ — "to him give all the prophets witness" (Acts 10:43; see also Jacob 4:4) — although they may call him by any of a number of titles.[6] All true servants of God enjoy the spirit of prophecy, a gift that allows them to benefit others through words of "edification, and exhortation, and comfort." (1 Cor. 14:3.) On the other hand, anyone who "denies the spirit of prophecy, is a liar, and the truth is not in him; and by this key false teachers and impostors may be detected."[7]

But how can one measure the sincerity of a person who claims to have the spirit of prophecy?

> A person claiming to be a true spiritual leader might present such a good imitation of a true prophet as to deceive those who do not themselves have the guidance and inspiration of the Spirit. But in addition to giving lip service to the assertion that Jesus is the Christ, a true prophet must conform his life to the divine pattern; he must conform to the laws and ordinances that the Lord has revealed. 'He that speaketh,' the Lord says, 'whose spirit is contrite, whose language is meek and edifieth, the same is of God if he obey mine ordinances.' [D&C 52:16.][8]

Thus, the authenticity of the spirit of prophecy is demonstrated in the pattern of righteous obedience that these people exemplify. They not only speak what sounds to be right, but they also do what is known to be right. Such prophetic people not only teach and witness of the truth, they also serve as examples of godlike devotion — blessing themselves and those who will follow them. (See John 18:37; Eph. 4:13.)[9] Studying the lives of the ancient prophets, we recognize courageous men who lived what they preached as they spoke out against the wickedness of the people and testified concerning Christ and his commandments.

THE GIFT OF PROPHECY IS AVAILABLE FOR ALL PEOPLE

During a meeting of ancient Israel's elders at the tabernacle in the wilderness, a young man ran to Moses in alarm, saying that two other men were prophesying outside the camp. "Joshua the son of Nun, the servant of Moses, . . . answered and said, My lord Moses, forbid them. And Moses said unto him, Enviest thou for my sake? *Would God that all the Lord's people were prophets,* and that the Lord would put his spirit upon them!" (Num. 11:28–29; italics added.) Moses did not want to reserve all the spiritual powers, especially the gift of prophecy, for himself, but he desired that all of Israel should be as prophets.

The Apostle Paul likewise told the early Christian church, "Ye may all prophesy one by one, that all may learn, and all may be comforted." (1 Cor. 14:31.) In a similar manner, any contemporary member of the Church of Jesus Christ who has received a testimony of Jesus Christ through the power of the Holy Ghost is authorized, indeed commanded, to bear witness of the same. (See Luke 22:32; Acts 22:15; D&C 14:8; 88:81.) As we testify of the truth, we are prophets, "for the testimony of Jesus is the spirit of prophecy." (Rev. 19:10). Like the prophets of old, we can know for ourselves the truths contained in the scriptures and add our testimony to theirs.

Furthermore, in our own stewardships and callings as parents, priesthood leaders, and fellow saints, we are entitled to revelations for ourselves and those for whom we are responsible. Thus, we can also become seers and revelators within our own sphere of jurisdiction and influence. We have prophets to guide us in our spiritual development and accountability. We can receive personal revelation to know the truthfulness and personal application of what the prophets have taught us. Then we can receive additional revelation for our stewardship responsibilities. All that the Father has is not promised to his prophets alone; all who seek him and do his will may receive the spirit of prophecy. (See D&C 20:26.) As we have strong prophets, seers, revelators, and apostles in close contact with the Lord, and as we fulfill our charge to receive and develop the gift of prophecy for ourselves and those in our charge, then all of us in Christ's kingdom are strengthened and blessed.

A SEER OF NEW TRUTHS

In the minds of most people, a prophet has had such significant personal experiences with God that he has developed an extraordinarily high level of the spirit of prophecy. The Lord has shared important truths with the prophet, who now has the responsibility to share his newly found insights with the people. Sometimes, these insights include visions into the future. Indeed, the term "prophet" is often associated with the capacity to prophesy into the future. True prophets in all ages have shared their prophetic insights about important future events. Before a prophet can share his insights into the future though, he must first gain a divine perspective through careful study of previous prophetic writings and through his own personal revelation. As he thus gains new insights and visionary perspectives, he becomes more than a prophet—he is also a seer, one who sees into new dimensions of truth.

As one LDS scholar noted, "A seer is a person endowed by God with a special gift for seeing spiritually."[10] The membership of The Church of Jesus Christ of Latter-day Saints accept the president of the Church as more than a living prophet; they sustain him as a "prophet, seer, and revelator." In functioning as a *seer*—literally "one who sees"— the prophet possesses the gift of perceiving new truths, gaining new perspectives on known truths, or seeing again old truths that were known among previous prophets but that were later lost during periods of apostasy.

The office of a seer extends the prophetic calling "to a capacity for envisioning future and past."[11] Marveling that King Mosiah could translate the twenty-four gold plates of Zeniff, King Limhi of Zarahemla declared that "a seer is greater than a prophet." Ammon replied that "a seer is a revelator and a prophet also; and a gift which is greater can no man have, except he should possess the power of God." (Mosiah 8:15–16.)

As an aid to some seers, like Mosiah, the Lord provided a visionary medium, a physical instrument, called a Urim and Thummim, consisting of two special stones called seerstones or interpreters. A Urim and Thummim is used both in receiving direct revelations and in translating ancient records from unknown languages. The earliest scriptural reference to a Urim and Thummim is found in the revelations of the brother of Jared. (See Ether 3:21–28.) Abraham possessed another set (see Abr. 3:1–4), as did Aaron and succeeding high priests in Israel (see Ex. 28:30; Lev. 8:8; Num. 27:21; Deut. 33:8; 1 Sam. 28:6; Ezra 2:63; Neh. 7:65). King Mosiah used his Urim and Thummim to translate the Jaredite record (Book of Ether) and handed it down to his prophetic successors until

Moroni buried it with the gold plates. (See Omni 1:20; Mosiah 8:13–19; 21:26–28; 28:11–20; Alma 63:12; Ether 4:1–7; Moro. 10:2.)

Joseph Smith recovered Moroni's Urim and Thummim with the gold plates, used it to translate the Book of Mormon, and then returned it with the plates. (See JS-H 1:51–52.)[12] Joseph also possessed another seerstone, with which he may have worked on his translation or inspired version of the Bible.[13] In any case, for the Inspired Version of the Scriptures (now called the Joseph Smith Translation), the Prophet received an expanded revelation of Moses' Genesis accounts of the Creation and the Fall and more of the teachings of Enoch and Noah. Apparently, these portions and versions of the text were known anciently but were omitted by the time our Bible was compiled: "Now of this thing Moses bore record; but because of wickedness it is not had among the children of men." (Moses 1:23.) As a seer, Joseph was able to see and restore these ancient visions, along with important insights into the life and teachings of Abraham. (See the books of Moses and Abraham, which contain these revelations.)

A seer may sometimes see things in visions or dreams with symbolic imagery that he does not understand unless he is given the keys to the symbols. As a hypothetical example, a person might have a symbolic dream in which a bear and an eagle chase a groundhog carrying a valuable gold disk in and out of several holes. The person may recall the dream and know that he has seen something significant, but he must understand the symbolic imagery in order to recognize that he has seen the Russian and United States basketball teams in the pursuit of an Olympic gold medal.

The Book of Mormon presents an example of this principle early in its pages. Lehi has a dream of the tree of life and sees many things, but the immediate message he derives from it is that two of his sons will reject some spiritual blessings offered by God. Lehi's son, Nephi, after asking to know more, sees the same vision and receives specific keys to the meaning of many symbols and images in the dream. Both Lehi and Nephi were seers, but Nephi saw and understood more. (See 1 Ne. 8, 11.)

Joseph Smith describes the process of seership as a gift of special spiritual awareness. As he and Sidney Rigdon saw the great vision concerning the many kingdoms of God's creation, the prophet states that through "the power of the Spirit our eyes were opened and our under-standings were enlightened, so as to see and understand the things of God." (D&C 76:11–12.) With or without a physical instrument, a seer's eyes are enhanced through the Spirit so he can see things and understand truths that are obscure or hidden to others. As he shares his insights with us, we are likewise blessed with greater understanding.

On the other hand, some manifestations to the ancient and modern seers were seen by them but never spoken of or written down, since the Lord forbid it. (See JS-H 1:20.) Truth being "knowledge of things as they are, and as they were, and as they are to come," seers have often had visions encompassing truths from the whole of human history, but have kept back part, particularly concerning the latter-days. After Nephi wrote about his vision of events up until the time of John the Revelator, he concluded: "I, Nephi, am forbidden that I should write the remainder of the things which I saw and heard . . . and I have written but a small part of the things which I saw." (1 Ne. 14:28.) We can be thankful that much of what the seers have seen they have revealed to us, because their revelations help us understand God's dealings with people on this earth, especially in the last days.

A Revelator of Relevant Truths

When a seer does make known the new truth he has received, he acts as a *revelator*. As first and second elders of the early restored church, Joseph Smith and Sidney Rigdon were assigned duties as revelator and spokesman, respectively. To Elder Rigdon, the Lord explained, "I will give unto thee power to . . . be a spokesman unto him [Joseph], and he shall be a revelator unto thee, that thou mayest know the certainty of all things pertaining to the things of my kingdom on the earth." (D&C 100:11.) In other words, the Prophet (acting as revelator) was to teach doctrine to Rigdon, and Rigdon (acting as the Prophet's spokesman) was to expound it to the Church, using the scriptures.

In many instances, a revelator is restricted in what he reveals. Initially, he may be limited in what he receives, because his knowledge is usually limited to those words of God meant for this earth's inhabitants at a particular time. (See Moses 1:35–36.) Secondarily, he is often restricted in what he is allowed to pass on to others. (See 3 Ne. 26:11.)

This second limitation is usually based upon the worthiness and readiness of the people to receive what the prophet would reveal unto them. (See Moses 1:42.) In addition, some sublime truths and feelings are not revealed because mortals are sometimes incapable of expressing or writing what they have seen and felt. (See 3 Ne. 19:32.) Or, there might not be enough time to speak or enough space to write all that is known by a prophet. (See 3 Ne. 26:6.) The prophets have revealed much to us, and we know that if we will accept and obey what they have told us, greater truths will be given to us. (See 3 Ne. 26:9; D&C 76:7.) Those who continue in righteousness are promised that eventually the very mysteries of heaven will be revealed unto them. (See Alma 12:9; D&C 76:7.)

In summary, the duties and gifts of a prophet, seer, and revelator are somewhat distinct, yet obviously related. The prophet testifies of known truths; the seer sees new or hidden truths; the revelator declares some new truths or old ones previously hidden. Today, the title of "prophet, seer, and revelator" is applied to some members in the presiding councils of The Church of Jesus Christ of Latter-day Saints, particularly the members of the First Presidency and the Quorum of the Twelve Apostles. They continue the ancient prophetic tradition into our contemporary times.

APOSTLES: SPECIAL WITNESSES OF CHRIST

In ancient times, prophets held the priesthood of God, just as they do today. Before the coming of Christ, several prophets often lived and ministered as contemporaries, though one was generally recognized as the preeminent prophet. This was the case, for example, with Isaiah and Jeremiah, who both left comprehensive accounts of their ministries and served also as the prophetic spokesmen in their day to Israel's kings and foreign heads of state. When the ancient prophets' promise of a Messiah became a reality, the priesthood prophetic structure changed somewhat. Christ established himself as the preeminent spokesman of his gospel and church, but also appointed apostles (forming an official Quorum of Twelve) to testify of him after his death and resurrection. After the Lord's ascension, the senior apostle, Peter, took Christ's place as leader and became spokesman for him to the Church members.

In one sense, an apostle is simply a New Testament version of an

Old Testament prophet. For four thousand years, the ancient prophets testified of the coming of Christ, trying to prepare Israel to receive her own, but she would not. (See John 1:11.) As promised and prophesied, Jesus became the universal Savior and Messiah, having drunk the bitter cup, atoned for the sins of all mankind, and given and taken up his life again, thus fulfilling all righteousness. His primary work finished, he then needed special witnesses to proclaim his divine role and to administer the spreading of his gospel to all the world, not just Israel. (See Matt. 24:14; 28:19; Acts 1:8.) Thus, the apostles assumed one important role different from the prophets before them, testifying not that the Messiah would come, but that he had already come and redeemed mankind.

The apostles of the restored church today are called and sent forth to testify in the same way as were those personally called by the mortal Christ. Any worthy Melchizedek priesthood holder may be called to the office of apostle—a special witness for Christ. He usually becomes part of the Council or Quorum of the Twelve Apostles, all of whom (along with the members of the First Presidency) are also set apart as "prophets, seers, and revelators" to the Church. However, only the presiding apostle—our modern-day senior prophet and president of the Church—fully functions and directs all the keys in those offices, for he is Christ's mouthpiece. Members of the Quorum of the Twelve within their sphere of responsibility may very well testify of truth as prophets, receive visions and revelations as seers, and teach some of what they know as revelators, but they may not do so in a way that is binding on the Church as a whole. This duty pertains only to the presiding apostle—the prophet and president—of Christ's kingdom on earth. (See D&C 107:91–92.)[14]

THE PREPARATION OF A PROPHET

Like the young business executive who had worked up the corporate ladder until he found himself in a position of importance and influence, servants of the Lord usually spend years in service and spiritual maturation before they are called as prophets of God. Although there is no formal "school of the prophets," opportunities for religious learning and leadership training are provided as men work and serve in the religious community. A few prophets who were called in their youth, such as Samuel, Daniel, John the Baptist, Nephi, and Joseph Smith, gain this experience as they serve in their calling. Ancient and modern prophets have come from a variety of vocational and social backgrounds, including farmers, fishermen, shepherds, craftsmen, educators, business men, attorneys, and governmental officials. Some, such as Isaiah, have willingly accepted an opportunity to serve, while others, such as Jeremiah, have reluctantly taken on the responsibility. Regardless of their ages, backgrounds, and initial attitudes, they all seem to share a courageous faith, a sensitivity to the Spirit, and a sincere devotion to the Lord. They all have demonstrated years of faithful commitment in building the kingdom of God on earth.

One does not seek to become a prophet, as one might choose to become a farmer, accountant, or doctor. No true prophet ever calls himself; instead, one is called by God to this position. Indeed, "we believe that a man must be called of God, by prophecy." (A of F 5.) Often the prophetic call is accompanied with divine manifestations and supra-spiritual experiences, such as hearing the literal voice of God, seeing visions, receiving angels, and witnessing physical signs of the Lord's power. When these manifestations are sealed by the spirit of prophecy, they personally validate the calling for the prophet, who then goes forth to serve.

Men and women who heed the counsel of the prophets are sometimes called the "children of the prophets." Many faithful ancient Israelites, early Christians, and modern Latter-day Saints, as they follow the Lord's servants, share in edifying spiritual experiences similar to those of the prophets themselves. All workers in a successful business or enterprise cannot and should not sit on the executive board of that group. Likewise, the workers in building God's kingdom do not all belong in the leading councils of the Church. As the general membership of the Church works together under the leadership of the prophets, they help bring a mighty work along.[15]

In conclusion, we can say that *PROPHETS are called through divine authority and revelation to represent the Godhead, and they are often endowed as seers, revelators, and apostles as they speak for God and build Christ's kingdom on earth.* As we follow the prophets, building upon their counsel and developing our own spiritual gifts, we are better able to assist them in strengthening Christ's kingdom and to help each other along our path back to Heavenly Father's presence.

For further study, refer to the following entries:

TG	BD	*EM*
Apostles	Apostle	Apostle
Prophecy	Prophet	Prophecy
Prophets, Mission of	Seer	Prophet
Revelation		Prophet, Seer, and
Seer		Revelator
		Seer

CHAPTER 8

THE POWER OF GOD'S WRITTEN WORD

Automobile owners receive handbooks to instruct them about their vehicles, computer owners receive manuals, and even the recipients of small appliances receive some written material instructing them how to best use and care for their machine. However, these instructions become obsolete as the mechanical and electrical appliances age and eventually wear out. Automobile and computer owners all own another possession far more valuable than any physical machine — each human has a priceless physical body and spirit. Yet many people do not have a copy of the owner's manual for the soul, and others who have a copy do not read and follow the instructions. A wise Heavenly Father has provided a guidebook for the life and welfare of our souls. This aid is a helpful resource for parents on how to raise his spirit children. Friends, leaders, counselors, and teachers can also use such inspired instructional material to assist and direct those in their circle of influence. We all need direction in conducting our lives and building our spirituality, but where is such written help to be found?

The Holy Scriptures provide the direction and guidance detailing God's instructions for us. They tell us how to best use and care for our souls, how to become more godlike, and how to truly help others. Just as a sophisticated machine or computer is practically useless without careful attention to directions in the manuals, life can be vain and empty without study and the application of God's inspiration found in the scriptures.

SCRIPTURES ARE LIKE PRECIOUS PEARLS

Any word of God, recorded as holy scripture, can be compared to a "pearl of great price," something so precious that a person is willing to sell personal possessions in order to acquire it. (Matt. 13:45–46.) Like pearls that are not to be scattered before swine, the prophetic writings contain sacred truths that are not to be carelessly cast to those who do not appreciate their eternal value. (See Matt. 7:6.) Why are the scriptures so valuable and sacred? Why has God provided and preserved them through the ages, and what personal insights and power can they bring into our lives today, even this very day?

To answer these questions, we should first appreciate that the written word of God found in the Holy Scriptures is our most accessible source of information about our relationship to the Godhead and the plan of salvation. The scriptures bear witness of God and define our covenant relationship to him. They also give an account of the life of Jesus Christ, his works and teachings. Through prayer accompanied by serious study and meditation of God's written word, our soul is opened to the promptings of the Holy Spirit, and we learn truths of eternal value.

In addition, the inspired writings provide an important resource through which we learn how God relates to and works with his children. We see how he teaches his children through inspired prophets and other leaders. We read about his feelings as he observes his children make right and wrong choices in their thoughts, words, and actions. We sense his love as he patiently seeks to strengthen and improve his children.

God's written word also links together vital doctrines within a system of correlated teachings and witnesses that he has provided for our spiritual growth and accountability. In the scriptures, the Lord has stated that by "the mouth of two or three witnesses shall every word be established." (2 Cor. 13:1.) He has, however, given us many more than just two or three witnesses of his eternal truths, with holy writ constituting the primary resource and foundation of them all.

A TESTIMONY OF OUR COVENANT RELATIONSHIP

The title page of the Book of Mormon contains an inspired statement about the twofold purpose of scriptures—to teach and to testify. Moroni writes that the records of Mormon were written "to show unto the remnant of the House of Israel what great things the Lord hath done for their fathers; that they may know the covenants of the Lord, that they are not cast off forever." Besides teaching Israel the history, covenants, and prophecies of the Lord, Moroni declares that this scripture was also written "to the convincing of the Jew and Gentile that Jesus is the Christ, the Eternal God, manifesting himself unto all nations." More than a record of the relationship between God and humans, the Book of Mormon and all sacred writings are a testimony of the Lord. These statements of Moroni are inspired keys to understanding scripture.

THE DOINGS OF THE LORD

Scriptures are basically a family history of God the Father's dealings with his children on earth. The prophets and other inspired writers record the hand of God in their history, showing how he has worked through the ages to bring about their redemption. Moroni also writes that as the spiritual heirs of Israel read the scriptures, they should "remember how merciful the Lord hath been unto the children of men, from the creation of Adam even down until the time that [they] shall receive these things." (Moro. 10:3.) The scriptures are not meant to be a complete historical document of the chronological sequence of mankind. Instead, it is a selective record of how God fulfills his word. As many students of the Bible have recognized, holy writ is not as much *history* as it is *His story*.

THE COVENANTS OF THE LORD

The historical framework of the scriptures provides the context for the important covenant relationship between God and his children. The written word of God contains the stipulations and promises of the covenants that Heavenly Father has established with his chosen people through the ages. The greatest fulfillment of the covenant promises will come in the last days when the Messiah reigns over his people. (See Ether 13:8–11.) Moroni testifies that his words are true and that latter-day Israel should "no more be confounded, that the covenants of the Eternal Father which he hath made unto thee, O house of Israel, may be fulfilled." (Moro. 10:31.) The sacred writings are the great depository of the covenant teachings and promises of the Lord.[1]

THE PROMISES OF THE LORD

The scriptures not only teach God's expectations of us in our covenant relationship, they also promise his rewards according to our faithfulness in the covenant. When Moroni talks about the covenant prophecies being fulfilled for the House of Israel in the last days, he includes a promise that can bless us individually. As we come unto Christ, deny all ungodliness, and love God with all our being, "then is . . . [God's] grace sufficient for you, that by his grace ye may be perfect in Christ." (Moro. 10:32.) Having personally experienced God's promised grace and his other gifts, we are able to bear witness of God's divine love and power. Our testimony will then join together with the prophets' and the scriptures' affirmations that God lives and that his work is manifest through his Son, Jesus Christ.

JESUS IS THE CHRIST

The Bible is the first great witness about the Lord of this earth, beginning with a record of his premortal work (as found in the Old Testament) and continuing through his ministry as a resurrected being (as recorded in the New Testament). The Book of Mormon is another testament or witness of Jesus, who is also to be revered as the Christ or Messiah (the "Anointed One"). Nephi's eyewitness account of Christ's resurrection ministry in the Americas (as abridged by Mormon) includes three important sermons and profound acts of prayer and blessing.[2] These records verify Jesus as the promised Anointed One. Moroni adds his exhortation to "come unto Christ" and be perfected in him through the sanctification of his atonement. (Moro. 10:30–33.) Thus, the scriptures provide ample testimony that Jesus is the Christ.

JESUS IS AN ETERNAL GOD

The written words of God as revealed through the prophets also witness the eternal nature of Jesus as a God. In the last passage of the Book of Mormon, Moroni uses a name and a title to indicate the eternal nature of Jesus. He identifies him first as "the great Jehovah," a variation of *Yahweh,* a name by which he was known among the ancient patriarchs and prophets. (See Ex. 6:2–3, JST.) The meaning of the name is probably "the One who is," indicating the absolute, unchangeable, and eternal nature of this God. The second term used by Moroni, "the Eternal Judge," is a clear reference to his unending nature. As the scriptures testify, Jesus is an eternal being, a God full of love and power.

JESUS MANIFESTS HIMSELF TO ALL PEOPLES

The sacred writings also witness that Jesus has manifested himself to many peoples and that he will yet reveal himself to all the nations. His mortal ministry, which began in Bethlehem, did not see him travel more than three hundred miles from the place of his birth. But as a resurrected being, he visited remnants of the House of Israel on at least two different continents. When he comes in power and glory, he will circle the whole world and all peoples will know that he reigns over this earth. In the periods of time between the personal visitations of the Savior, Moroni indicated that Jesus manifests himself to humanity indirectly through a variety of spiritual gifts, "and all these gifts come by the Spirit of Christ; and they come unto every man severally, according as he will." (Moro. 10:17.) In one way or another, people who live on the earth receive the opportunity to have Jesus reveal himself and his power to them. The scriptures testify of the many ways, means, and times that Jesus has manifest himself to mankind.

Readers of the scriptures should remember these two keys to understanding the written word of God—scriptures *teach* of the Lord's doings, covenants, and promises; scriptures *testify* of Jesus as the Christ, the Eternal God, and the One who manifests himself unto all nations. Any student of holy writ should then look for these teachings and testimonies as he or she reads and ponders the mighty word of God.

A GUIDELINE FOR DAILY LIVING AND ETERNAL LIFE

Without question, the scriptures contain some of the most inspirational literature that has ever been written. In many schools, courses evaluate the Bible as a classic literary work of lasting value. Scholars will accept portions of the sacred writings as models of inspirational literature even though they may not accept them as holy writ.

In the writings of the Old Testament, the wisdom of the proverbs, the beauty of the psalms, the doctrines and poetry as presented by Isaiah, and the covenant teachings of Moses continue to motivate many people toward righteousness centuries after they were first written. From the New Testament, the teachings of the Master, the counsel of Paul, and the intriguing revelations of John provide important insights into Christ's kingdom on earth. In the Book of Mormon, the prophecies of Nephi, the discourses of Alma, and the inspired commentaries of Mormon and Moroni are inspiring more and more people as this work of scripture is translated and disseminated throughout the world. In the Doctrine and Covenants, Joseph Smith's vision into the three degrees of glory, his "olive leaf discourse," and his wise counsels for leadership are examples of beautiful literature and profound doctrine. (See D&C 76, 88, 121.) Although these sacred writings have come to us over the course of many centuries and through the hands of many writers, they all demonstrate the wisdom of God, the guiding mind of the Lord, and the inspiration of the Spirit. In reality, the scriptures are not the writings of man — they are the mind and word of God.

After recognizing God's teachings, testimony, and inspiration in the sacred writings, the reader is better able to identify how the written word can find place in one's own heart. The wise student of the scriptures will want to take it one step further and convert the power of the written word into personal action. The word of God then comes alive for that person as he or she receives inspiration and feels a new surge of spiritual strength.

Unfortunately, there are many written works and other media forms that erode a person's spirituality. The scriptures counterbalance these evil influences. One poignant lesson that holy writ teaches us is that opposition exists in all things. (See 2 Ne. 2:10–13.) Assuredly, our world has always contained positive and negative influences: the light of Christ versus the natural, carnal desires of humans; the promptings of the Holy Ghost contrasting with the temptations of Satan; true prophets competing with false ones; the righteous struggling against the wicked; and scriptures and moral writings opposing erotic and pornographic literature. Scriptures and other inspired works of literature have always embodied the highest values of their respective cultures and served as a standard for measuring the righteousness of society. They provide unity, purpose, and vision to a people. Recognizing their prime importance, good men in all cultures have struggled to preserve holy writ over time.

In contrast, satanic or evil literature has been created anew by wicked men each time cultures have fallen into decadence. The false ideas in these works teach people to disbelieve God and the scriptures. In addition, the writings of men often contain worldly philosophies that distort truth and may encourage people to doubt the sacred writings. Writings such as these generally appear in a society that has become corrupt and has ceased to cling to scriptural ideals. In time, these corrupt writings have almost always been lost or destroyed as wiser people in later generations have recognized their negative influence and discarded their heresies. Although some portions of the scriptures have been lost during times of severe war and persecution, many of their sacred writings have remained until today, making them the oldest literature of the world still in active circulation.

The degree to which a people cling to their scriptures has often been *the* deciding factor in their spiritual progress or decline. For example, the Book of Mormon provides a telling comparison between two offshoots of Old World culture who transplanted themselves in the New World during the same period. The people of Lehi and the people of Mulek both left Jerusalem during the reign of Zedekiah to escape the imminent Babylonian conquest (587 B.C.). The people of Zarahemla (the Mulekites) took no records with them; consequently, their language and religious teachings became completely corrupted within two hundred years. (See Omni 1:15–17.) In contrast, the descendants of Lehi (the Nephites)—who preserved the ancient records and kept current ones—flourished for one thousand years, until the entire people willfully rejected traditional religious teachings.

Scriptures preserve religious teachings and traditions that can strengthen people anytime and anywhere who read and apply the word of God in their lives. Regular scripture reading is necessary to counter many of the world's evil influences that otherwise would weaken a person's spirituality. In addition, the scriptures are an important link in a system of witnesses that connect all of God's teachings and works together into one, unified, whole gospel.

A BOND IN GOD'S SYSTEM OF WITNESSES

God's system of witnesses originates with the Godhead. The three members of the Godhead themselves form a model for the nature of divine scriptural witnessing, as they all testify of each other. The resurrected Christ explained this pattern to the Nephites: "I bear record of the Father, and the Father beareth record of me, and the Holy Ghost beareth record of the Father and me." (3 Ne. 11:32.)

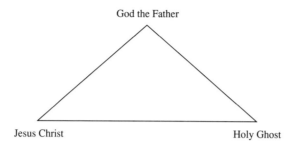

One major purpose of the scriptures is to bring us to Jesus Christ, whose atoning sacrifice provides us the gift of the Holy Ghost and sustains his role as our mediator with the Father. In addition to the testimony of the scriptures concerning the Savior, we also have the witness of modern prophets and the validation of the restored gospel that direct us to Christ.

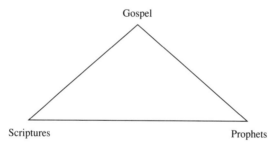

Within the various volumes of scripture, we find an interrelated system of witnesses. Each book testifies of the other while bearing witness of Christ. In the Bible, the Old and New Testaments complement each other as they present the Lord's work. The Book of Mormon, as its subtitle "Another Testament of Jesus Christ" indicates, builds upon many Old Testament writings, affirming the validity of its prophecies. The Book of Mormon also validates the contents of the New Testament concerning Christ's teachings and the establishment of his apostolic church. The latter-day scriptures—the Doctrine and Covenants and part of the Pearl of Great Price—give us a modern witness of Jesus Christ and the teachings of both the Bible and the Book of Mormon. The still-hidden records of the lost Ten Tribes of Israel, mentioned in the Book of Mormon, will someday provide yet a fourth scriptural testimony of Christ's resurrection and ministry. (See 2 Ne. 29:12–13.)

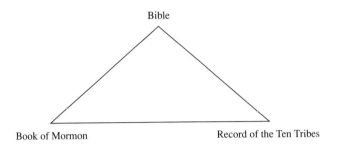

Appreciating the contributions of all types of personal and scriptural testimonies, our interlocking system of divine witnesses forms a series of pyramids, with God the Father at the apex. Below him, we have the other members of the Godhead, and then the prophets, the gospel, and finally the scriptures, which help anchor the base. Each book of the scriptures supports and complements the others, forming the foundation of our spiritual understanding of divine truths.

How Have the Scriptures Come to Us through the Ages?

Certain steps were necessary in the historical formation of the scriptures to make them available to us today. An understanding of these steps increases our personal readiness to receive, comprehend, and apply the written word of God. Each of the following eight steps in the development of God's word are conveniently labeled with words formed with the Latin prefix *trans* (meaning movement *through, across,* or *beyond*) and with the suffix *ion* (signifying a *state of being* or something that exists). Combined, these terms describe "something that has passed through time." This derivation reminds us that the scriptures are not dead, static words on a page, but living, dynamic revelations as vibrant and pertinent today as when they were received and recorded.

Transcension

The initial three steps outline how the scriptures first came into existence as spiritual experiences, historical documents, and written records. The first step in the origin of the scriptures was a special spiritual experience or a transcension. Each prophet who recorded a divine revelation and each poet or psalmist who wrote an inspired verse needed spiritual edification. To accomplish such inspired literature, each had to transcend, or be lifted above, a normal human level of understanding. Many times the prophets and seers were also simultaneously carried up to a high mountain, the physical counterpart of their elevated mental and spiritual state. As we, in turn, read these sacred accounts, asking the Holy Ghost for enlightenment, we can also be lifted above our normal capacity for understanding divine truth. Otherwise, the strange language and images accompanying many revelations and visions would be quite difficult to envision and interpret.

TRANSACTION

Besides being a record of heightened spiritual experiences, the scriptures also provide an account of many day-to-day transactions in ancient times. The interactions between God and his prophets, as well as the relations between the prophets and God's children, prophets and kings, kings and citizens, tribes and neighbors, Israelites and Gentiles, are recorded. Much of the time, the account is not very flattering to God's children. It contains a bit of everything—the good and the noble, the bad and the base. Some of their social experiences and ritual practices may seem strange, boring, or even silly to us, separated from them as we are by time and culture. However, recorded transactions help to place spiritual happenings in a historical context, so that the more we study and become acquainted with these ancient cultures, the more we understand God's workings with his children in ancient times. We can then better relate to our own experiences with him. We thereby see more clearly the pertinence of revelation and his help in our own age and individual lives.

TRANSCRIPTION

Each revelation and transaction found in scripture is a transcription, something written down at some point by someone. At least once, in the case of the Ten Commandments, the Lord wrote his own words on stone tablets. Often the prophets wrote their own manuscripts or had a scribe who recorded for them. Sometimes, though, events were recorded years after the fact by people who were not actual witnesses. Some writers indicated how hard it was for them to accurately and fully portray what they felt and observed. Nevertheless, a written record was made. The permanency of the written record indicates the original importance and continued value that the scriptures have. Likewise, important events and feelings in our lives, which we record in our journals and pass on to our posterity, can find value in their lives, however hurried and incomplete our personal record may be.

The next three steps highlight how the scriptures passed from ancient societies to modern readers, explaining some of the difficulties we now have in understanding them. They also seem to be the pivotal steps implied in Joseph Smith's statement when he said, "We believe the Bible to be the word of God *as far as it is translated correctly.*" (A of F 8; italics added.)

TRANSMISSION

For us to receive scriptural accounts, there was a transmission of the records from ancient times to the present. Parchment scrolls, papyrus manuscripts, and other records were copied and recopied by hand innumerable times and passed on for centuries in this manner. The possibility of error in making copies was naturally very great. In fact, wherever different ancient copies do exist of the same text, there are almost always minor errors and some major contextual differences.[3] Although we may sometimes feel burdened with the responsibility to read, understand, and apply all the material recorded in the scriptures, we should appreciate that so much of God's "manual of spiritual instruction" has been transmitted to us in such good condition.

Unfortunately, as far as we know, there are no surviving original documents for any of the ancient biblical sacred writings. Not even the tiniest fragment of the Torah or of one of Jeremiah's scrolls or any of Paul's epistles remain. Nor do we have an original compilation of what later became the Old or New Testament. In this light, it seems strange that the Book of Mormon should be criticized, as it often is, simply because the gold plates are not presently available for study or display. At least the Book of Mormon can claim to be a direct translation from an original document, which the Bible cannot.

TRANSLATION

Even if the original documents of the Torah or Jeremiah's prophesies or Paul's epistles were available, only a few scholars could read them in their original language. Following transmission of the scriptures, a translation from the earliest copies of these ancient writings must be made into modern languages so that everyone can read the word of God in his or her own tongue. This includes translation of older versions of a language into its modern counterpart, as has happened over several thousand years with Hebrew. As difficult as it is to translate between modern languages, the problems are compounded when dealing with ancient languages and texts. A literal, word-for-word translation is inevitably awkward and actually distorts, rather than enhances meaning. So there is need, as well as justification, for various interpretations. For this reason, all important religious and secular works have been translated several times by different scholars having a variety of opinions on their texts.

The beauty and remarkable accuracy of the King James version of the Bible derives from the unsparing efforts of many dedicated and faithful commissioned scholars during a renaissance of language and learning. The Church of Jesus Christ of Latter-day Saints accepts this version, as the Prophet Joseph Smith stated, "as far as it is translated correctly." Why did the Prophet qualify his acceptance of the King James Bible? Again, a correct translation does not merely require finding a good modern equivalent for each original word or phrase in the old language. Ideally, the translator should have a mastery of the ancient language and also a thorough knowledge of the prevailing ideas and culture of the ancient age. The King James Bible translators were certainly among the most qualified of their time in these respects. Even so, sacred texts demand more than linguistic clarity. Isaiah, Nephi, and other ancient prophets stated that even the most learned might read a message, but still not understand it unless they are edified by the Spirit. (See Isa. 6:9; 29:9–12; Matt. 13:14–15; 2 Ne. 27:6–23.)

How, then, is a correct translation of holy writ possible? A doctrinally correct translation can come only by revelation, the way in which prophecies were originally received. The words of the prophets, Nephi explains, can be completely understood only by one who himself possesses the spirit of prophecy. (See 2 Ne. 25:4.) Therefore, Joseph Smith carefully studied the King James Bible and its original languages, then prayed for revelation on problematic passages to help him write the Inspired Version of the Holy Scriptures. Parts of this new translation, the Book of Moses (cf. Gen. 1–6), and Joseph Smith-Matthew (cf. Matt. 24) in the Pearl of Great Price, are invaluable additions to the Latter-day Saint canon. When we likewise read and ponder the best modern-language translations of the scriptures, we gain valuable insights and inspiration for our own lives.

TRANSMUTATION

Aside from inherent problems in translation, the absence of original documents, and errors in existing copies, many purposeful transmutations occurred in the scriptural texts from time to time. In making some changes, well-meaning scribes no doubt felt they were clarifying or improving the original lines, which may have been incomplete or hard to read. Other changes were malevolent, however. If a ruler thought the writings of a contemporary prophet were unfavorable toward his policies or threatened his authority, he might order the script altered or destroyed altogether.

In ancient times, it was common practice for a conquering nation to absolutely destroy the libraries, archives, and temple records of the vanquished people, in order that their past might be forgotten.[4] In a similar vein, wicked King Manasseh of Judah plunged his nation into gross idolatry during his fifty-five year reign (c. 696–642 BC). (See 2 Kgs. 21:1–18; 2 Chr. 33:1–20.) He wanted no witnesses or records of the Israelite Mosaic religion to remain. According to Jewish tradition, he had Isaiah put to death and ordered the destruction of all sacred writings and the death of their owners. Only limited religious records were later retrieved and partially restored during the religious reformations of King Josiah and the prophet Jeremiah. Some of these documents were then lost during the Babylonian captivity, which soon followed in 586 BC. Shortly thereafter, Nephi prophesied in the Book of Mormon that some early religious leaders after the time of Christ would deliberately alter the Bible to conform to their own ideas and ends. The result was that "many plain and precious things" were taken away. (1 Ne. 13:29.)

For these reasons of accidental and deliberate distortion, as well as the natural destruction of materials over time, we can only guess how many valuable insights and writings were lost before our present Bible was finally compiled. Both the Bible and Book of Mormon mention missing writings of several prophets, and Paul wrote other epistles that are not included in the canon of the New Testament.[5]

The formulation of the Hebrew Old Testament as we know it was not finalized by the rabbis in Palestine until sometime in the first century AD. The Greek New Testament took its final form during the third century AD. The early Christian church had already fallen into apostasy after the death of the apostles, and so the church leaders were left to choose some books (from different versions) and omit others from the canon without direct revelation to guide them. Though obviously incomplete and imperfect, the Bible we now possess is still a miracle, in that it has been so well preserved through so much time and difficulty. However, if we neglect or distort the scriptures in our own time, their preservation for us is in vain.

TRANSPOSITION

The last two steps in the development of the scriptures pertain directly to us as readers. Number seven is transposition, which literally means "to change position." When two people are having a disagreement, a third party often recommends that each disputant view the situation from the other's point of view. "Try to put yourself in his shoes," the arbitrator says. This is transposition. Understanding the scriptures is also a two-way street: on the one hand, we strive to comprehend the ancients' cultural and historical context, even as they looked prophetically to our age; on the other, we glean eternal truths from past events and apply them to our current situation. In this way, Nephi says, we can "liken all scriptures unto us, that it might be for our profit and learning." (1 Ne. 19:23.)

TRANSFORMATION

When we come to feel the real value and urgency of scriptural messages in our personal lives, they can truly help us make a spiritual transformation. Without this final step, the scriptures are of no ultimate value to us, except to satisfy our curiosity or even to lead to our condemnation. "Search the scriptures," the Savior said to the Pharisees, who though steeped in intellectual scriptural knowledge and tradition, lacked full spiritual sensitivity and insight, "for in them ye think ye have eternal life: and they are they which testify of me. And ye will not come to me, that ye might have life." (John 5:39–40.) If our knowledge does not lead us to Christ and his saving power, all else is vain. (See 2 Ne. 9:29.) But as we internalize the scriptures through study, prayer, and obedience, they lead us to him and transform us to a higher level of spiritual development. We will not be satisfied with where we are now, but will seek to become perfect as Christ is. We will become altogether new men and women. In the scriptures we will have found eternal life, and the transcendent experiences of the prophets will have become our own.

What Can the Scriptures Do for Us Today?

To summarize the social and personal value of holy writ, we can identify five specific functions of scriptures: they record, teach, inspire, verify, and testify. As discussed earlier, the scriptures first *records* God's plans, words, works, glory, and even personal joys and sorrows. In the pages of holy writ, we see how a loving Heavenly Father has worked so carefully and lovingly to provide an earth with abundant resources and to nurture the physical and spiritual welfare of his children. In the scriptures, we learn his plans to give origin to our immortality and eternal life, and we also recognize his works to bring about these special gifts.

Second, sacred writings *teach* and instruct us about our relationship with God. They are our source for God's commandments and covenants. They teach us the plan of salvation and the laws and covenants by which we can return to Heavenly Father's presence. Through the scriptures we learn that God's commandments are not restrictive barriers or stumbling stones to the full enjoyment of our life on earth; instead they are helpful guideposts and building blocks for peace and fulfillment, both for now and into eternity.

Third, the scriptures *inspire* and edify. As we read and ponder them we can be mentally enlightened and spiritually refined. They are beautiful works of literature and the source of general moral truths and eternal gospel principles. As we study God's written messages, they help us to establish eternal priorities, chart a productive course for our lives, live peacefully with our fellow brothers and sisters, and know and seek the "abundant life." (John 10:10.) In short, the scriptures help lift us to a higher plane of existence.

Fourth, sacred writings *verify* that God the Father has not forgotten us. In the record of holy writ, we find his prophecies about us, who are his children with divine potential, and about this earth, which is a place of his ultimate celestial glory. One important point about the scriptures is that their promises give us great hope in the world to come. Through righteousness, we can obtain hope of deliverance from the disappointments of this life and from physical and spiritual death. Just as rain falls upon "the just and the unjust," the Saints are not immune to the difficulties of this life. A knowledge of the scriptures gives our challenges and suffering a meaningful and ennobling quality. (See Matt. 5:44–45.) In the scriptures, God promises that he will ultimately triumph over evil and introduce a millennial, or paradisiacal, order of life on earth. Eventually, he will grant the great gifts of resurrection and immortality to all people. If we also triumph over evil, we are further promised eternal life and a place with him in his heavenly mansions, including this celestial earth.

Fifth, the scriptures *testify* concerning God the Father and his Son, Jesus Christ. They specifically emphasize the nature and mission of the Savior, Jesus Christ, and bear witness of his atonement and how we can partake of it. The witness of the scriptures will also testify of us to our Father. We will be judged "out of those things which were written in the books" of God. (Rev. 20:12.) They measure how our behavior lives up to divine expectations. They serve as a canon, a measuring rule or standard, by which the world will be judged. (See Dan. 7:10; Rev. 20:12; D&C 128:8.) They are an integral element in God's divine system of witnesses and teachings that present his gospel to the world. Nations and individuals that possess the scriptures will be judged according to the heed and diligence they have given to the sacred writings. Initially, we will be held accountable as to whether we have read them, and then, if we have understood and lived by them.

WHAT SPECIFIC STEPS CAN I TAKE TO INTERNALIZE THE SCRIPTURES?

Two key scriptures help us recognize the value of the scriptures and the way we can gain a personal, spiritual witness of their truthfulness. The teaching of Jesus in John 5:39 can be viewed in a positive context: "Search the scriptures; for in them ye think ye have eternal life." As we search the scriptures we can better envision eternal life with our Heavenly

Father, and as we think about life with him, we should be motivated to live worthy of such a sublime existence. Thus our thoughts lead to actions lifting us closer to God.

A second valuable scripture is found at the end of the Book of Mormon. In Moroni 10:3–5 we learn some key steps to studying and gaining a testimony of the scriptures. Starting in verse three, Moroni says to *read* the messages that God has provided through his prophets, and he admonishes us to *remember* how merciful the Lord has been through the ages in his dealings with the children of men. He then stresses the important step to *ponder* what the Lord has done as recorded in the scriptures before we are to *pray* with sincere intent and faith in the name of Christ.

"INTO THE DARK WOODS": A PARABLE OF SCRIPTURE READING

Our experience of reading and pondering as we go through the scriptures might be compared to walking through thick, dark woods in the middle of the night. Our first reading of the scriptures is like the first trip we make through a foreign forest. With barely enough light from the heavens to guide us, we often stumble and feel lost, wondering if we will ever get through. Eventually we find our way out to the other side. The next time or two through the scriptures, we find the journey a little easier and more enjoyable. We bring tools to light our way — cross-references, maps, definitions, and background notes for the scriptures, which act as our candles and flashlights. We quickly find familiar paths and are able to weave through the more difficult passages with greater ease.

However, it is usually not until the third or the fourth time through the scriptures that we notice that we are not traveling through just any forest, but rather an orchard loaded with rich fruit. The first couple of times through, we want to plod through or work our way around the forest of our ignorance. With later, more enlightened perspectives, we are ready to stop and harvest gems of spiritual fruit from the scriptural passages. Hereafter it is with anticipation, not dread, that we approach the scriptures and the rich storehouse they provide. With careful, prayerful study, our reading of the scriptures will bear rich spiritual fruit.

The scriptures strengthen our spirituality as they provide a written witness of God's work, a record of his commandments, a source of his inspiration, a blueprint of his eternal purposes, and a standard by which all things are judged — all of which help us find eternal life. In summary, we can say that *SCRIPTURES are pearls of divine wisdom and gems of sacred writing that record God the Father's plans and works, teach his commandments and covenants, inspire expressions of his truths through great literature and profound doctrine, verify his prophecies and promises, and testify of him and his Son.* As we study and follow his guidebook of spiritual instruction, we will take better advantage of earthlife and draw closer to his heavenly existence.[6]

For further study, refer to the following entries:

TG	BD	*EM*
Bible	Bible	Book of Mormon
Book of Mormon	Bible, English	Bible
Scripture	Canon	Doctrine and
Scriptures, Study of	Ephraim, Stick of	Covenants
Scriptures, Value of	Gospels	Pearl of Great Price
Scriptures, Writing of	Joseph Smith	Scripture
	Translation	Standard Works
	Judah, Stick of	
	Pentateuch	
	Scripture	

NOTES TO INTRODUCTION AND PART 1

INTRODUCTION

1. *TETB*, 336–37.
2. *GD*, vii.
3. *DS*, 2:1.
4. *TETB*, 468.

CHAPTER 1

1. *TETB*, 504.

2. D&C refers to the Doctrine and Covenants, a collection of modern-day revelations received by Joseph Smith and others, which the Latter-day Saints accept as scripture.

3. These references (and most of those not in the Bible) are to books in the Book of Mormon, a volume of scripture compiled, abridged, and written by an ancient-day American prophet named Mormon and his son Moroni. See chapter 8 for a discussion of the scriptures and their purposes.

4. See C. S. Lewis, *Mere Christianity* (New York: Macmillan/Collier, 1960), 18. The role of our conscience and its growth through the Spirit is presented in more detail in chapter 12.

5. Chapter 19 on the gifts of the Holy Spirit highlights this process in greater detail.

6. For more insights, see chapter 24 on obedience to God's laws.

7. Chapters 16 and 20 will provide more specific guidelines into developing our understanding of spiritual truths.

8. The Joseph Smith–History (JS–H) is found in the Pearl of Great Price, a collection of a few, major inspired writings of Joseph Smith.

9. *TETB*, 295.

10. Condensed from Rotary's "Four Way Test."

11. See chapter 2 on God the Father.

CHAPTER 2

1. Ideas on moral and spiritual development are developed further in the previous chapter (truth), in chapter 12 (the sinful nature of mankind), in chapter 17 (repentance), and in chapter 20 (spiritual growth).

2. Chapter 11 contains more details on the purposes of life on this earth.

3. A lengthy discussion on human agency and God's role in it is presented in chapter 10. The purposes of this earth life, including suffering and pain, are presented in chapters 11–13.

4. Further information about the many means by which God reveals himself and his will is found in chapters 6 and 7. The written record and witness of God's earlier involvement with people on this earth is in the scriptures, the subject of chapter 8.

5. *LF,* 2:31.

6. The importance of faith and prayer in this search for understanding God is discussed in further detail in chapters 5 and 16.

7. The creation, nature, and purposes of life on earth are presented in chapters 9–14. The edifying values of God's commandments are discussed in chapters 24–30. Jesus Christ and his atoning roles are highlighted in chapters 3, 13, and 16–18. The testifying gifts of the Holy Ghost are reviewed in chapters 4 and 19–20.

8. For differing views by LDS authors on resolving the evolution/religion controversy, see A. Lester Allen, "Science and Theology: A Search for the Uncommon Denominator," in *BYU Studies* 29, no. 3 (Summer 1989): 71–78; and Reid E. Bankhead, *The Fall of Adam, the Atonement of Christ, and Organic Evolution* (Levan, Utah: RAM Books, 1978). Both authors quote authoritative Church leaders to support their positions, which can at least serve to direct the reader to original Church statements and sources on the subject.

9. God's plan of salvation for us and this earth will be discussed in chapters 6–10. We can draw nearer to God both as we learn more about his messenger of truth, the Holy Ghost (addressed in chapter 4), and also as we understand the power of prayer (written about in chapter 5).

CHAPTER 3

1. *MD,* 129.

2. James E. Talmage, *Jesus the Christ,* Classics in Mormon Literature edition (Salt Lake City: Deseret Book Company, 1982), 77.

3. Further insights into the atonement, crucifixion, and resurrection of Jesus the Messiah are found in chapters 13 and 15.

4. The key principles and ordinances necessary for us to receive these gifts are outlined in chapters 16–20.

5. *TPJS,* 312.

6. *The Interpreter's Dictionary of the Bible* (New York: Abingdon Press, 1962), 2:410.

7. See *MD,* 169–70.

8. "Jesus Christ Is Basis of LDS Beliefs," *CN,* March 29, 1980, pp. 8–10, 13.

CHAPTER 4

1. See *EM,* 2:649.

2. See also *TPJS,* 190; *GD,* 61–63.

3. See *EM,* 2:649; BD, 776–77.

4. See BD, 725.

5. *TPJS,* 190.

6. See *TPJS,* 199.

7. See BD, 704.

8. More insights into the *gift* of the Holy Ghost are presented in chapter 19.

9. Some keys to understanding how this spiritual influence is generated through our prayers and how it develops into a strong testimony are presented in the next chapter.

10. See *MD,* 742–43 for further explanation of this title of deity.

11. Joseph Smith interprets the rock as "revelation." (See *TPJS,* 274.)

12. An important, eternal role of the Holy Ghost is discussed in chapter 19, which describes his power as he sanctifies our souls in a "baptism of fire" and reveals many great spiritual gifts.

13. *Latter-Day Saints' Millennial Star,* 17:503.

14. We assume that the Holy Ghost will have an opportunity some time and place to receive his own body of flesh and bone in order to achieve his own ultimate, personal perfection. Without further revealed insights, we can only speculate under what circumstances this would take place.

15. The next chapter discusses in more detail the process of prayer, through which we communicate with God and receive our own testimony of his truths. Additional insights into how the Holy Ghost and the spiritual gifts from God can transform us into spiritual children of our Heavenly Father are discussed in chapter 19 on the gift of the Holy Ghost.

CHAPTER 5

1. See also BD, 752–53 for further insights. Additional details about our spirit-child relationship with God are discussed in chapter 9.

2. See *WNTCD,* 1414.

3. See BD, 752.

4. See index, Book of Mormon.

5. *The Hiding Place* (New York: Bantam Books, 1971), 197–98.

6. Ibid., 198–99.

7. Ibid., 209.

8. See *EM,* 1:309.

9. See *HC,* 1:21–23; D&C 3, 10.

10. See BD, 753. Further perspectives into recognizing answers to prayers and understanding the different types of revelations are discussed in the next chapter.

11. *EM,* 3:1119.

12. See BD, 753.

CHAPTER 6

1. See also *TPJS,* 274.

2. More details about earlier gospel dispensations and this period of apostasy from early Christianity are found in chapter 31.

3. *TPJS,* 160.

4. *DBY,* 39.

5. See *EM,* 1:40–41.

6. See *EM,* 4:1511.

7. Chapter 8 contains more insights about the role and values of the scriptures.

8. Chapter 22 contains further insights about the variety and power of priesthood blessings and ordinances.

9. Further insights about the temple and its ordinances and values are found in chapter 23.

10. *HC,* 3:381.

11. *MD,* 786.

12. *TPJS,* 324.

13. *Life of Heber C. Kimball* (Salt Lake City: Bookcraft, 1945), 450.

CHAPTER 7

1. The Hebrew root for *prophet* is *nabi',* meaning "one who speaks by inspiration" or "one who speaks, announces, proclaims, or testifies" for God. The root can also imply "one who is called by God" before he can qualify as "one who calls out for God" as his spokesman.

2. See *EM,* 3:1165.

3. *TPJS,* 365.

4. In these latter days, the Lord has said that his church will be like a judge by which false prophets will be known. (See D&C 64:37–39.)

5. See *TPJS,* 119, 312.

6. See pages 52–54 in this book.

7. *TPJS,* 269.

8. *MD,* 608.

9. *TPJS,* 12–13.

10. *EM,* 3:1292.

11. Ibid.

12. See also *HC,* 1:2, fn.

13. See *DS,* 3:225–26.

14. More details on Church organization and leadership are found in chapter 33.

15. Chapter 33 reviews the role of prophets and others in the leading Church councils. Chapters 34 and 35 discuss the mission of the Church and the success that Latter-day Saints are helping to bring about under prophetic leadership.

CHAPTER 8

1. The purpose and process of entering into covenants with the Lord is discussed in greater detail in chapters 18 and 23.

2. The three sermons are the Sermon at the Temple (3 Ne. 12–14) — basically the Sermon on the Mount as recorded by Matthew in the New

Testament, with important additions; the Law and Covenant Discourse (3 Ne. 15:1–17:3); and the Covenant People Discourse (3 Ne. 20:10–23:5).

3. For example, we find differences in almost forty percent of the verses of the early Greek Septuagint and Hebrew masoretic texts of the book of Jeremiah.

4. We have vivid examples of this in our own century under Josef Stalin's Communist regime, in which Russia's history was entirely rewritten along revolutionary lines, and under Adolph Hitler's Nazi Germany, in which massive book burnings took place.

5. See TG, Scriptures, Lost.

6. Chapter 20 contains helpful suggestions for establishing a regular scripture reading program.

PART 2

GOD'S PLAN OF SALVATION

CHAPTER 9

OUR INTELLIGENT SPIRIT PERSONALITY

Professors and researchers in the physical sciences often probe into the nature of matter and energy. They ask questions like "What are the mass, atomic structure, and chemical properties of this substance?" They may also want to study various physical forces, such as electricity, temperature, gravity, and so on, which affect the subject matter under investigation. In the end, they hope to understand the real world around us.

Professors and scholars in the social sciences usually probe into the nature and properties of humans. While it seems obvious that our physical bodies are real, along with all things that we can see, feel, hear, taste, and smell with our physical senses, social scientists want to evaluate the validity of our observations and the significance of our thought processes. They ask a different set of questions, for example, "What is reality and can we identify it?" and "How does one think and rationalize?" "Is there something else within us, like a spirit, psyche, intellect, or vital essence, and can we identify it?" and "How do humans establish moral values?" — questions often asked by philosophers and theologians. The answers to these questions are not as obvious as those dealing with the physical body. Thus there are many theories and explanations for the unseen rational and moral qualities that seem to distinguish humans from all other forms of life on earth.

After all truth is gathered into one great body of information, the questions of the physical and social scientists will be answered. Modern prophets, such as Joseph Smith and Joseph F. Smith, have declared that eventually all truth will be circumscribed into one great whole, with the laws of the universe and the gospel unified together.[1] As one small but important example of this, in the twentieth century, Albert Einstein concluded scientifically what the Prophet Joseph Smith had taught doctrinally in the nineteenth century: matter can be neither created nor destroyed, but merely changed from one form to another. Einstein's discovery of relativity between matter and energy in the physical world revolutionized modern science, just as the Prophet's revelations on the eternal nature of elements in the human spirit transformed traditional Christian ideas about man's creation and progression. In this chapter, the restored doctrine of eternal identity and its implications for our immortal potential will be explored.

CREATED OR ORGANIZED MAN?

Since the time of the great apostasy, orthodox Christianity has alleged that the earth and man were created by God *ex nihilo,* or "out of nothing." Through the teachings of Joseph Smith and with careful study in the scriptures, we see that this Christian creed, which developed during the early Middle Ages, is inconsistent with other traditional beliefs like man's soul having some eternal elements and man's spirit living before the creation of this earth. To begin, the Prophet Joseph taught that the physical elements in the universe have always existed: "The elements are eternal. That which has a beginning will surely have an end; take a ring, it is without beginning or end—cut it for a beginning place and at the same time you have an ending. . . . If the soul of man had a beginning it will surely have an end. In the translation [concerning creation] . . . the word 'created' should be 'formed,' or 'organized.' "[2]

God did not create the world out of nothing; it was organized out of existing materials and elements. The scriptures do not tell us what the nature and history of these elements were before they were organized as a part of this earth, but we do know that God was the power who formed the earth as it now is. Joseph Smith taught that although the elements are eternal, they can be reorganized: "The pure principles of element are principles [or component parts] which can never be destroyed; they may be organized and reorganized, but not destroyed. They had no beginning, and can have no end."[3]

A simple study of the skin cells of our own body will illustrate the eternal nature but changing form of physical elements. The normal human body creates millions of new skin cells daily to replace those lost through abrasion, cleaning, and the normal functions of the body. The material to build these skin cells comes from the food we eat. In other words, a few hours before this material became a part of our body, it was in some form of food. The food could have been fresh vegetables from the garden or processed products that had been prepared weeks earlier, but it has now become a new, vital part of our body.

Even then, weeks and months before the food was available for our human consumption, its materials were parts of plants and animals living and growing somewhere on this planet. Sometime prior to that, this same material was part of the soil of the earth. Much of the soil consists of decomposed matter from earlier living organisms, particularly plants. In other words, the physical material that forms the fiber and body of plants, animals, and humans is constantly recycled and reorganized by various living entities developing, growing, and dying. Thus the physical elements that now comprise our skin cells have always existed, but only very recently in their long history did they exist as a part of our body. Matter is eternal, but its form and function may change through time — it might be a simple piece of soil or an essential part of the human brain.

Some material in the universe is so refined that we cannot see or observe it with our physical eyes. Most of the electromagnetic spectrum, such as cosmic radiation, X rays, microwaves, and electric current, falls into this category, although we now have equipment to measure much of it. Other forms of matter are not yet observable by human eyes or machinery. One such refined essence is the spirit found within each living person, "For man is spirit. The elements are eternal, and spirit and element, inseparably connected, receive a fulness of joy." (D&C 93:33.) The human spirit is composed of real, refined matter. As the Prophet Joseph taught, "all spirit is matter, but it is more fine or pure, and can only be discerned by purer eyes; we cannot see it; but when our bodies are purified we shall see that it is all matter." (D&C 131:7–8.)

Another unseen part of humans is their mind, that special capacity to think and decide. Joseph Smith taught that the "mind or the intelligence which man possesses is co-equal [co-eternal] with God. . . . The intelligence of spirits had no beginning, neither will it have an end. That is good logic."[4] He also said, "Intelligence is eternal and exists upon a self-existent principle . . . from age to age, and there is no creation about it."[5] As we will see later in this chapter, the element of eternal intelligence within our being is the essential ingredient that determines our personality. It is the guiding force behind our decision-making capacities and thus determines whether we are wise in our pursuit of truth and righteousness.

In summary, the Prophet Joseph Smith teaches that the principle ingredients of physical and spirit elements have existed and will continue to exist in some form of organization forever. The doctrine of the restored gospel, then, is that the elements of the body and spirit of each human have always existed. At some point in the distant past, God brought eternal intelligence and other spirit elements together in the form of a spirit body. Later, he placed that living spirit within an embryo or fetus made of the physical elements of this earth. As a new life was born, the infant body grew until it became the mature body we now possess. Although some may argue that God *created* the whole man (intelligence, spirit, and body) from nothing, God's own revealed word declares that God *organized* man from already existing material, both physical and spiritual.

THE NATURE OF INTELLIGENCE

Of all the component parts of the human body, *intelligence* is the most valuable and enduring. Indeed, man's fundamental essence is referred to in modern scripture as intelligence. (See D&C 93:29–39.)[6] The word *intelligence* can have a variety of meanings. In temporal or secular terms, intelligence is defined as "the rational ability to assimilate and apply knowledge." In eternal or spiritual terms, intelligence encompasses more than just thinking capacity; it is a rational faculty with moral priorities that understands and applies knowledge *to righteous action.*[7] Both the secular and religious meanings draw from the Latin root *intelligere,* meaning "to perceive" or "to understand between choices." Switching the Latin components into an English sequence, *legere* + *inter* mean "to gather or select" + "between." Mentally, one who *gathers* and understands many facts is one of high intelligence. In a spiritual context, a person with great intelligence is one who *selects* truth for goodly purposes. The Lord revealed this nature of intelligence to the Prophet Joseph Smith: "The glory of God is intelligence, or, in other words, light and truth. Light and truth forsake that evil one." (D&C 93:36–37.)

In what particular form or capacity our original intelligence existed, we cannot begin to say. For example, could unorganized intelligence move itself or communicate with any other form of intelligence or life? Was it something that could act for itself, or was it only acted upon by other powers and entities? We lack both scientific knowledge and divine revelation to answer these questions and fully understand precisely what eternal intelligence is. However, lacking a complete comprehension of the entity need not prohibit us from observing its influence and experiencing its effect in our own lives. This dilemma is similar to mankind's incomplete knowledge yet beneficial application of electrical power. Scientists do not always agree as to the exact nature of electricity or of the light that it generates, and engineers do not fully understand how these energy forces actually work, but they know enough to develop and harness electrical power to greatly bless mankind. Our best measurement of intelligence is not in studying its nature but in evaluating its influence.

As quoted earlier, the scriptures define intelligence as "light and truth." Light makes seeing and distinguishing things possible. Physical light aids us in seeing material objects, while spiritual light reveals more the inner workings of our lives and this world. Truth, as defined in chapter one, is a correct perception of physical, moral, and spiritual things. So to have light and truth means one both sees and understands things ranging from the physical to the spiritual realms. This refined intelligence encompasses and greatly expands our mental capacity. Indeed, the development of this intelligence is a sign that we are in the image of the great Creator.

Intelligence is both a necessary ingredient for a full human life and also a faculty that can strengthen and enrich the quality of eternal life. In this aspect, it might be compared to a more easily understood part of the body—muscles. Every viable human has to have some functioning muscles, particularly in the heart and lungs. However, people can also develop many muscles throughout the body, increasing their strength and capacity to do more things with their body.

Likewise, rational and accountable humans need some basic level of initial intelligence. One can usually recognize intelligence early in the life of an infant, although, as we will later see in this chapter, the capacity of one's intelligence to demonstrate itself might be severely handicapped by mental or physical impairments. People also have the capability to develop further intelligence as they receive light and truth from "grace to grace" until they come to a fullness of understanding. (See D&C 93:11–13, 27–30.) Intelligence increases as people choose to follow the Lord and keep his commandments. (See D&C 93:1–2, 28, 37.) Also, whatever principles of intelligence they gain in this life will continue with them into the postmortal existence. (See D&C 130:18–19.) On the other hand, intelligence is lost through disobedience, insensitive hearts, and adherence to false traditions. (See D&C 93:39; Mark 8:17–21.) As people with intelligence seek more light and truth, as they conduct themselves like true children of God, they rise above the animals and those of animal-like behavior.

Man's ability to communicate through the ages and to reason and make moral choices distinguishes him from the animals on earth. The righteous application and expansion of his intelligence will draw him and others nearer to God. Indeed, his unique and superior intelligence is what has defined him from eternity: "Man was also in the beginning with God. Intelligence, or the light of truth, was not created or made, neither indeed can be. All truth is independent in that sphere in which God has placed it, to act for itself, as all intelligence also; otherwise there is no existence." (D&C 93:29–30.) In brief, an intelligence is an independent entity capable of acting for itself. Every intelligence has an eternal existence and is free to act within the realms established by God. Greater intelligence can be acquired through added light and truth as a person chooses good and lives righteously.

THE INDIVIDUALITY OF ETERNAL INTELLIGENCE

Some teachings of the Prophet Joseph Smith build upon the passages quoted above and maintain that in the primal state of intelligence, people were separate entities: "Intelligence is eternal and *exists upon a self-existent principle.* It is a spirit [individual entity] from age to age, and there is no creation about it."[8] The prophet Lorenzo Snow also taught about the importance of our individuality: "We are immortal beings. That which dwells in this body of ours is immortal, and will always exist. Our individuality will always continue. . . . Our identity is insured. We will be ourselves, and nobody else. Whatever changes may arise, whatever worlds may be made or pass away, our identity will always remain the same; and we will continue on improving, advancing and increasing in wisdom, intelligence, power and dominion, worlds without end."[9] There is something about our personality and individual identity that has always existed and that is forever ours alone.

An understanding of the eternal dimensions of our individual existence is hard to comprehend. The finite mind can hardly grasp the concept of eternity—a time without a beginning or an end. But neither can mortals understand the opposite—an end or a beginning to time. They would ask themselves, "What happened before time began?" or "What will happen the day after time ends?" The concept of "no time" is as incomprehensible as one of "all time," or eternity.

Nevertheless, the passage of time through eternity is marked off in periods of beginnings and ends as various events, epochs, dispensations, and cycles are recorded in the scriptures. For example, "in the beginning" of this earth's history as it is now organized, God took seven periods of creation to develop this world with all the forms of plant and animal life now found on it. (See Gen. 1.) After the fall of Adam and Eve, the earth entered a new stage of temporal, telestial existence, which will continue through seven cycles of dispensations, using one unit of measurement, or through seven periods of time, each a thousand years long, using another means of measurement. (See D&C 110:12–16; 77:6–7; 121:31.)

OUR FIRST ESTATE

In a similar fashion, our own passage through eternity is marked with periods of beginnings and ends as we experience birthdays and death dates—times of new starts and final conclusions. The scriptures identify such a major time period as an "estate," meaning a "dominion," a "stage of life," or a particular condition and state of existence.[10] (See Jude 1:6; Abr. 3:26.) Our first estate was our eternal premortal existence, which continued until we were born on this earth; we are currently in our second estate, which continues after death into the postmortal spirit world; the third estate will begin with our resurrection and continue through eternity.

Our existence as unorganized intelligence comprised the major portion of our first estate. At some point, however, God the Father took what is called primal or unorganized intelligence, combined it with other spirit elements, and organized them into intelligent spirit personages— each unique, independent, and endowed with the power to think and act for itself as his spirit child. The process by which this spirit came into being is called a spirit birth, for "the Spirit itself beareth witness with our spirit, that we are the children of God" and joint heirs with our elder brother, Jesus Christ. (Rom. 8:16–18.) As with our natural birth, two parents were involved—our Father in Heaven and a lesser-known but vital Mother in Heaven.[11] As one Mormon writer noted, "Latter-day Saints believe that all the people of the earth . . . are actual spiritual offspring of God the Eternal Father (Num. 16:22; Heb. 12:9). In this perspective, parenthood requires both father and mother, whether for the creation of spirits in the premortal life or of physical tabernacles on earth. A Heavenly Mother shares parenthood with the Heavenly Father. This concept leads Latter-day Saints to believe that she is like him in glory, perfection, compassion, wisdom, and holiness."[12]

This understanding helps explain a puzzling passage in Genesis that describes God as creating mankind "male and female" in the image of the Divine. One modern translation of the key verse reads: "God created human beings in his own image; in the image of God he created them; male and female he created them." (Gen. 1:27, Revised English Bible.) A statement of the First Presidency of the Church clarifies that each spirit personage "was begotten and born of heavenly parents" as "off-spring of celestial parentage." It also teaches that "all men and women are in the similitude of the universal Father and Mother, and are literally the sons and daughters of Deity."[13] Thus, we are all the spirit children of God.

These spirit personages are also called *organized intelligences.* (See Abr. 3:22.) The late Elder Bruce R. McConkie wrote that "this name designates both the primal element from which the spirit offspring were created and also their inherited capacity to grow in grace, knowledge, power, and intelligence itself, until such intelligences, gaining the fullness of all things, become like their Father, the Supreme Intelligence."[14] So it seems that, though independent and individual, unorganized intelligences in their earliest stage of existence could not act much for themselves until formed into spirit personages entering their next stage of existence. This creation of our spirit body was our first, or spiritual "birthday," the highlight of our first estate in the premortal world.

Our existence as an organized spirit being initiated a new stage of our pre-earthly life. This part of our first estate was a heavenly, celestial type of existence where we lived in the presence of our Heavenly Father. There he instructed us preparatory to our coming to earth. (See D&C 138:56.) Our spirit personages were as unique and different from one another as each of our bodies are in mortality. The scriptures even go so far as to suggest that we even looked different as spirits: "That which is temporal in the likeness of that which is spiritual; the spirit of man in the likeness of his person, as also . . . every other creature which God has created." (D&C 77:2.)

God's infinite number of spiritual offspring also developed varying levels of intelligence, or light and truth: "If there be two spirits, and one shall be more intelligent than the other, yet these two spirits . . . have no beginning; they existed before, they shall have no end." (Abr. 3:18.) The pre-earthly or antemortal spirit being of Jesus was the most intelligent of all spirit children of God, and the rest varied in their degree of intelligence and spirit improvement. (See Abr. 3:19.)

Some intelligences did worse than develop very slowly—they openly rebelled against God and were cast out of his presence. (See Jude 1:6; D&C 29:36.) In contrast, some had already greatly excelled in their intelligence: "Now the Lord had shown unto me, Abraham, the intelligences that were organized before the world was; and among all these there were many of the noble and great ones; and God saw these souls that they were good, and he stood in the midst of them, and he said: These I will make my rulers; for he stood among those that were spirits, and he saw that they were good; and he said unto me: Abraham, thou art one of them; thou wast chosen before thou wast born." (Abr. 3:22–23.) Though some, like Abraham, came to earth with more spiritual intelligence than most, all of us born on earth had gained enough light and truth to accept God's plan of salvation for us and to agree to its conditions. In the language of the scriptures, we "kept our first estate."

THE GRAND COUNCIL IN HEAVEN

In addition to the growth and development that our intelligences experienced in the spirit world, we also had the opportunity to witness the planning of this earth and the circumstances that would later surround us here. At a council in heaven convened by God the Father, he presented his plan for the creation of this earth and the development of his children. (See Abr. 3:24–26.) We rejoiced with him when he presented his plan. (See Job 38:4–7.)

Crucial to our situation on the earth would be the freedom, also called agency, that God had already given us to act for ourselves. Earth life would be a time when we would be tried and tested. (See D&C 29:39.) We would have opportunities to learn good and evil and to choose our own path of righteousness or wickedness. (See D&C 101:78; Moses 5:11.) This agency carried with it a large risk, because as God's children should choose to sin and become impure, they could not return to the holy, pure state of celestial existence with God. Not knowing how we would conduct ourselves in an environment so foreign to our heavenly home, we undoubtedly wondered if we had the spiritual qualities to successfully pass through this time of probation. Heavenly Father counseled us that his plan would include the means by which we could overcome our imperfections and impurities and become qualified to return to his presence. (See Moses 7:32–40.)

Jesus became the primary advocate of Father's plan, and he and others like him encouraged us to support it. Other spirit children were not as ready to accept the whole plan. Lucifer, for example, wanted to modify our agency so that there would be no opportunity at all to sin, thus enabling all God's children to return to their celestial existence.[15] Many wondered, however, how such restrictions on our freedom might adversely affect our moral growth and personal development. We were also hesitant in that Lucifer wanted the full control, glory, and credit for the implementation of God's plan. (See Isa. 14:13; D&C 29:36.)

After much discussion and debate, God moved his plan one step closer to implementation as he asked for a volunteer, a special person who would serve as the Redeemer and Savior of his plan. Jesus responded first and said: "Here am I, send me." (Abr. 3:27–28; see also 1 Pet. 1:19–20.) Lucifer answered second and said: "Here am I, send me." After God chose Jesus, Lucifer rebelled against the Father; as a result he and his followers were cast out of heaven while God and his angels wept at their departure. (See Moses 4:1–4; D&C 76:25–29.) The impact of this rebellion and the resulting expulsion of one-third of the hosts of heaven was so powerful that it, more than any other single event of the premortal existence, is highlighted in many scriptures. (See Luke 10:18; 2 Pet. 2:4; Rev. 12:7; 2 Ne. 2:17; D&C 29:36–38.)

We who chose not to rebel have since become the beneficiaries of God's plan. He has blessed us with the opportunity to come to earth, to receive a physical body, and to learn and grow in the physical, emotional, social, mental, moral, and spiritual dimensions of our lives. This earth life is our greatest reward for keeping our first estate.[16]

Premortal Decisions Affecting Our Situation on Earth

We need to appreciate the fact that right now we are in the pivotal period of our own individual existence. We have already passed through the two important stages that constituted the first estate: primal or un-organized intelligence and premortal spirit world. There are also two important stages that follow this earth life in the flesh: the postmortal spirit world and the resurrected state thereafter. Although hard to con-ceive, just as the first stage of unorganized intelligence had no beginning, the last stage of resurrected glory will have no end—we are living the focal point of our eternal destiny.

Given the fact that our life here is so pivotal, one might ask, "Why are we all born into such diverse situations in the world?" Many in the English-speaking countries live in relatively comfortable, civilized sur-roundings, although some struggle in impoverished, crime-ridden neigh-borhoods. Most reading this book might ask, "Why are we not members of other families fighting tsetse flies or experiencing famines in Africa, or barely surviving in Afghanistan? Or why are we not among the hundreds of millions in China for whom Christianity is merely a vague concept? Why are we in the circumstances we are in today?"

There are at least three possible connections between who we are here on earth and who we were in our earlier antemortal existence. One possible explanation is that our pre-earthly behavior may have earned something, bad or good, that determined the circumstances of this life, to test or to stretch us where needed. A second plausible explanation is that we are here by need or by assignment. The need could be our own, or our families', or one of our associates' here on the planet. Maybe

Heavenly Father placed us here because somebody else requires special help, and we can meet those needs. We may have received a service opportunity by special assignment from a loving Father. A third possibility is that we may have requested a certain time and circumstance on earth, and our request was honored. But, of course, we could receive the request only if it corresponded with the mind and will of our Heavenly Father.

We usually do not know why we were born into our individual circumstances. We may not particularly have deserved to be where we are, or we may not sense any particular needs that we are meeting, and we may not have really asked for our station in life. As we learn more about our real nature, enhance our sensitivity to others, and take advantage of service opportunities, we usually sense that this earth life is a natural continuation of our earlier life from the first estate.

Individuals who may be privileged to enjoy the more favorable circumstances of life should appreciate their blessings and take advantage of their opportunities. For example, some individuals in the scriptures, by virtue of their birth into the house of Israel, received an inheritance from the Lord. The Old Testament prophets, as they talked to these ancient Israelites, warned the descendants of Abraham that they were chosen to be a role model for the world and that if they failed this opportunity, they would have fared better not to have been born at all, because they would be cast out and become as orphans. (See Lam. 5:3.)

With citizenship in the house of Israel anciently, or with membership in Christ's church today, comes responsibility. Assuming that we knew what situation we could be born into, some of us in the premortal life may have thought, "That Israelite (or Christian) community has got to be the 'in group' and the choicest family on the earth. I want to be a part of their inheritance." If we appreciated the seriousness of that commitment, of being an Israelite or a Christian, and if we did not take advantage of the responsibility or opportunity in this life — instead of being a blessing, it would become a condemnation.

In another vein of thought, some people wonder why a loving Heavenly Father places spirit children in disjointed, even abusive, families. This does not seem fair to the young, tender children. One should not prejudge and assume the child is being cursed because of spiritual weaknesses in the premortal life. It could just as easily be an opportunity for an especially noble, choice spirit to help reform a wayward family and end the chain of abusiveness that might otherwise continue through future generations.[17]

To highlight, it could be that some of us, in essence, were deliberately placed in our stations in life. Maybe we were among the more faithful, valiant ones in the premortal life, and God wants to use us as the spiritual catalysts and the stalwarts of the faith to build his kingdom here on the earth. He is going to take the best spirits and put them in the situations where they can serve the best and have the greatest influence for the greatest good. (See D&C 138:53.) He could put them in an organization that is to be the light of the world as well as provide a social order that will become the standard of existence for all the world during the Millennium. The Lord needs his choicest, most dependable followers in this organization. Although we may not know the particular reasons why we have an opportunity to become his servants, we probably sense that a primary reason for it lies in our actions and choices long before we were born.

Most of us, if not all of us, probably had much the same attitude in the premortal life that Jesus exhibited in the Garden of Gethsemane, where he prayed to the Father, "Not my will, but thine be done." (Luke 22:42.) We were willing to go wherever and whenever God would send us. Many of us exhibit this attitude now in earth life, and we likely had that attitude in our first estate since our personalities here reflect the personalities we developed there. One thing is certain—the decision was made with the Father's will because his wisdom is so much greater than ours.

NURTURING ONE'S INTELLIGENCE

To what do we owe the difference, or inequality, in the faculty of intelligence among spirits? Speaking temporally of rational ability alone, some people are simply born smarter than others, some are reared in a more intellectually stimulating environment, and others receive a better education. Some of these varied circumstances could result from natural differences in heredity and the environment that we experience on earth. Other differences could come from the weaknesses that God sometimes places upon us. (See Ether 12:27.) Spiritual intelligence, however, was not doled out in random, unequal, or unfair amounts. Its expansion was based upon obedience to divine truth, and all spirit beings could progress in intelligence according to their diligence. (See Abr. 3:24–26.) Spiritual intelligence, then, may not be at the same level as one's mental or physical intelligence.

As in our premortal existence, although family and friends can influence our attitude toward spiritual light and truth, the potential of our spiritual progress during our earth life is determined wholly by individual choice, not predetermined by heredity or other external factors. This fact helps explain why we observe greatly varying degrees of spirituality among members of the same family or with people living in similar social and economic situations.

Despite the differences in the development of our intelligences in the first estate and our different spiritual and physical circumstances in this second estate, we are all still capable of infinite progress. The Prophet Joseph Smith confirmed that though some people are born more spiritually advanced than others, "all the minds and spirits that God ever sent into the world are susceptible of enlargement."[18] We have made marvelous progress since our primal existence as unorganized intelligences. We continued to mature in the spirit world phase of our first estate, and we know that those who continue to progress in mortality and "keep their second estate shall have glory added upon their heads for ever and ever." (Abr. 3:26).[19] Since we have already progressed so far, we need to view the magnificent possibilities ahead of us and continue our spiritual way of life until we reach our ultimate destiny.

The Lord teaches us that as we mature spiritually, we learn and grow "precept upon precept" and "here a little and there a little." As long as we are willing to receive from the Lord and hearken to his counsel, he will give us more wisdom so our spiritual growth can continue. (See 2 Ne. 28:30.) This process of spiritual growth is like the nurturing of our physical body. Nurturing our body takes effort on our part—we obtain and eat food, ingesting the nutrients that in turn provide health and energy. However, most of the work is done internally by our body organs without our active thought and direction.

In a similar manner, as we take in God's light and truth, our intelligence and spirituality are strengthened. We do this through such things as daily prayer, gospel study, and service to others.[20] Nevertheless, the increased spirituality within us does not come about by our conscious control. God's Spirit works mysteriously and wonderfully with our own spirit to bring about this blessing. He is the giver of the great spiritual gifts that enlighten our understanding and increase our intelligence.

The following definitions and descriptions highlight the attributes of our intelligence:

> Intelligence is the eternal essence of our being; therefore, it is the nucleus of our identity and individual personality.

> Intelligence is our will, our capacity or power to make decisions; it is the part of our being with which we think; and it is our ability to reason and to form sound judgments.

> Intelligence is the light of truth expanding our understanding, and it is our sensitivity to the reality and power of all truth.

> Intelligence is an inclination to do right and to serve others; it motivates us to become more like God our Father, and it is our most valuable application of personal agency.

> Human intelligence distinguishes us from all other life forms, and its essential influence in our lives characterizes us as true children of God.

Intelligence is an eternal gift of the universe, the essence of our reality. God has magnified our intelligence through his own light and truth and with the blessing of spirit bodies; otherwise, we would still be unorganized, weak, and primal intelligence. Now, in this life, we have constant opportunities to magnify our intelligences even more.

To summarize: *In our first estate, we existed as primal INTELLI-GENCES until our Heavenly Father provided us with spirit bodies, thus allowing us new dimensions of organization, experience, and progression.* What we saw and experienced in our premortal existence with our Heavenly Father was a necessary and valuable foundation that prepared us for earth life. Heavenly Father has provided us this earth and the opportunity to receive a physical body so we can continue to expand and develop our intelligence and so we can help others to do the same. Christ has guaranteed us the promise to achieve our full potential destiny through the powers of the gospel, the priesthood, and the Atonement. If we are truly intelligent, we will thank God for these blessings and use our intelligence to bless ourselves and others.

For further study, refer to the following entries:

TG	BD	*EM*
Council in Heaven	Spirit	Council in Heaven
Foreordination	War in Heaven	First Estate
Intelligence		Foreordination
Man, Antemortal		Intelligences
Existence of		Plan of Salvation,
Spirit Body		Plan of Redemption
Spirit Creation		Premortal Life
		Spirit Body
		War in Heaven

IT'S YOUR CHOICE — THE NATURE OF AGENCY

When people think of "freedom," their first thoughts usually center either on their political rights as citizens or on the appetites and liberties their physical bodies might have. These political and physical freedoms are, at best, only temporary, since we do not know how long we will have them. Social freedoms can be taken from us as others gain control of government or as physical abilities are lost through accidents or ill health. A third type of freedom is much more enduring and important — it relates to our moral and spiritual decisions. The situation (and opportunity) that allows us to make moral choices — to decide the type of person we want to become and then to develop a corresponding character — is called agency. Although influenced by our social and physical environment, this freedom of deciding our own attitudes, beliefs, and commitments remains within us and cannot be taken from us. Freedom in a gospel context provides us the possibility of choosing who we want to be and where and how we want to live in the eternities.

Agency to make moral and spiritual decisions can be present within any political system, although maintaining this freedom can be difficult. Historically, in spite of oppressive societies and malicious persecution, the followers of righteousness have been able to maintain their faith in God, sometimes at great sacrifice. In the extreme examples of the twentieth century, the human capacity to retain religious beliefs and a loving attitude toward others has been demonstrated by many survivors of the Nazi and Communist concentration camps. Ironically, the people who freely gave in to their emotions and appetites were not the ones who found lasting inner freedom; rather those with the greatest self-control and inward discipline retained the greatest freedom over their own personality and spirituality. To be free, one needs to learn how to act with self-control instead of simply responding to the forces acting upon him or her.

"To Act" or "To Be Acted Upon"

The most succinct and beautiful scriptural treatment of agency is found in the Book of Mormon, in the Prophet Lehi's deathbed sermon and blessing to his son Joseph. In his admonition, Lehi emphasizes that "opposition in all things" is necessary to existence, and that God has placed all creation into two major categories: "things to act and things to be acted upon." (2 Ne. 2:11, 14.)

Among all forms of animal life that God has created, humans have the fullest opportunity to act for themselves. (See Hel. 14:30–31.) Inanimate objects, such as rocks, dirt, and bodies of water, are devoid of agency and are always acted upon by external forces. Plants and most forms of lower animal life basically act under the governance and influence of the laws of nature—they have little freedom for independent action. Even higher intelligent animals are mostly governed, or acted upon, by natural instinct, and their ability to choose or act is limited. Though man shares many instincts with animals, he possesses a higher, rational capacity for moral choice to govern his life (if he chooses). This capacity, which in the gospel we call "agency," is the first and most fundamental gift given by God to man. (See Moses 7:32.) The meaning of agency, the choice of where and when to act, the consequences of our actions on others, and the reasons for agency are the subjects of this chapter.

The Essential Elements of Agency

Let's begin with a metaphor familiar to everyone—driving an automobile. First, a driver (the agent) is needed who knows how to maintain and drive a vehicle. Correspondingly, a car (the object acted upon) is needed, or the driver cannot fulfill his desires. Since automobiles are designed to operate according to laws of combustion, friction, motion, and so on, the driver must first learn how the car functions and then comply with those laws, supplying the necessary fluids and maintaining the machinery. He must also possess basic skills for maneuvering the car in traffic, skills that improve with experience. Now he is ready to drive. However, if he fails to comply with the preparatory steps or the rules of proper driving, the car will fail him or his driving privileges will be revoked. His freedom to drive will be suspended until the car is fixed or his license is restored.

Like the model of the driver and his car, certain elements are necessary in life before we make choices and engage in various activities. To act as an agent, a person must have an *identity* apart from the object of action. He then must acquire *knowledge* and the *freedom* and *power to act.* The things he acts upon — the choices he makes — are governed by *law,* and as his knowledge and experience increase, his *efficacy* or ability to achieve also expands. Finally, the *preservation* of his rights depends on his wisdom in prior choices and the privileges granted him by governing powers.

Let us discuss each of the seven essential elements of agency: identity, knowledge, freedom, action, law, efficacy, and preservation.

INDIVIDUAL IDENTITY

Identity or intelligence is the unique characteristic of human personality — it is the core element that makes each person original, individual, and distinct. A person's capacity to think and decide is his *will,* which becomes the director of his soul. With "free will," a person can think, decide, and act. (See D&C 58:26–29.)

In modern scripture, the Lord revealed to Joseph Smith an indispensable truth about the identity (or personality, intelligence, and will) of man hitherto unknown in the religious world: "Man was also in the beginning with God. Intelligence, or the light of truth, was not created or made, neither indeed can be." (D&C 93:29.) If, as in traditional theology, God created man's spirit "ex nihilo" (out of nothing), man could not be a free agent since either his personality would have been programmed (like a computer) by God, or his choice of acts would be ultimately controlled (like a robot) by God.[1] But since our prespirit essence — our intelligence — has always existed independently, we are each unique, autonomous, and free to choose the course of our own personality and destiny.[2]

KNOWLEDGE

Although our primal intelligence (or will) has always existed, our capacity to experience life's different dimensions and to choose from a full range of options was not fully formed in the beginning. We, as spirit beings, came to earth to receive physical bodies, to develop our ability to choose good over evil, and to grow in knowledge. Like Adam and Eve, we all begin our lives in innocence and ignorance, making choices – often poor ones – without a full understanding of the consequences. Our knowledge expands rapidly as we satisfy curiosity, grow in experience, and learn from our errors. This expanded learning provides insight into our potential. Just as Adam and Eve first received knowledge of good and evil and then acquired greater freedom to experience a fuller range of growth, we too learn to act in light after we gain a vision of our opportunities. A knowledge of the truth makes us free to choose from more options. (See John 8:32.)

Knowledge not only multiplies our options, but it also affects our accountability before God. Because small children lack understanding, they are guiltless before God when they make wrong choices. Indeed, any person's justification or condemnation before the Lord is relative to his understanding of the eternal laws and commandments governing his choices: "Therefore to him that knoweth to do good, and doeth it not, to him it is sin." (James 4:17.) Besides children and the mentally incapacitated, people who have not been taught the commandments are not held fully accountable for disobeying them. (See 2 Ne. 9:25–26; Moro. 8:22.)

FREEDOM OF CHOICE

In case anyone should think that ignorance of the commandments is bliss, we should quickly add that the greater our knowledge, the greater our range of choice. Not many people would really wish to return to the restrictions of childlike understanding and learn everything over again "the hard way." Freedom of action – freedom from the recurrent disappointment of harsh and unforeseen consequences – is a privilege well worth its price of understanding and obeying eternal laws. Agency involves the freedom to move to the left or right, forward or back, toward good or evil, or whatever the case may be. Opposition is a natural part of life as different forces work for and against each other and as various and sometimes opposing choices are placed before us. (See 2 Ne. 2, 9; esp. 2:11.)

Freedom of choice is a critical dimension in our religious lives. As one LDS scholar noted: "The gospel of Jesus Christ does not represent freedom merely as a philosophic concept or abstract possibility, but establishes it at the foundations of the creation of the world and *as the fundamental condition of God's dealings with his children*."[3] Freedom of a greater range of choices places humanity at the top of all forms of life on this earth. As people are free to control their own paths of life and to influence others, they can live the law of the jungle and seek dominion, or they can live the golden rule and give service, or they can choose any number of options in-between. Those who choose to live the golden rule rise above the animal kingdom and live more like God.

A responsibility of Latter-day Saints is to help others to have full religious freedom so that all can enjoy the same privilege of worshipping "how, where, or what they may." (A of F 11.) Satan's followers seek to manipulate or even eliminate opportunities for full freedom of worship. The followers of God must be constantly vigilant in order to retain their rights as strong agents for good on the earth.[4]

EXERCISING OUR AGENCY THROUGH ACTION

In discussing "free agency," a phrase commonly used by Latter-day Saints, they sometimes emphasize the term *free* but neglect the word *agency.* Note that the two words in the phrase "free agency" do not appear side-by-side anywhere in scripture. Both ancient and modern prophets have often stressed the importance of the gift of agency. Agency is the active force or power by which something is done. It is the means by which hopes and expectations are made into reality. A knowledgeable agent with freedom of choice must initiate action and actually start to do something — otherwise, the freedom to exercise available options remains an unfulfilled opportunity. Indeed, the scriptures and the prophets stress active involvement in the concept of agency as much as they include the idea of freedom and choice when talking about the moral and spiritual dimensions of agency.[5]

Agency refers to both the actions and the accountability for those actions. People with greater intelligence, knowledge, and freedom to act are more accountable in exercising their golden opportunities. Ideally, they should use their agency toward good, but in no case can they remain neutral or "lukewarm" (Rev. 3:16) because those who are not for the Lord are against him (see Matt. 12:30). When knowledgeable people do not work in God's behalf, they are not using their agency for good, thus they are condemned. Even if people do something wrong, if they are wise, they will learn from the errors of their ways, repent, and do better in the future. But no action whatsoever means no potential for learning or service. If we think that the object of our existence is to do nothing, we could just as well have remained as unorganized intelligence. At least then our undeveloped potential would not have required the wasted work and efforts of others, especially our Heavenly Father, in our behalf. Where much has been given to us, much is now expected.

LAWS AND THEIR REWARDS

When we exercise our freedom to act, the results of our actions are based upon the eternal laws governing our existence. With the consequences of all actions based on unalterable and unbending law, we can confidently move forward with less fear of failure toward our chosen goals. Without fixed, unchanging laws rewarding our actions, we could not be agents; we would be subject to a random, disorderly universe and its whimsical god. Through the law, we know what the consequences of our actions will be and can make better choices. By law, the results of our actions are determined, and we can systematically work toward full achievement. (See D&C 29:34; 88:36–39, 42; 132:5.)

Subjecting ourselves to laws brings freedom not bondage. As one LDS philosopher noted: "Thus, in the LDS concept of agency, obedience and agency are not antithetical. On the one hand, Church leaders consistently stand against all coercion of conscience. . . . On the other hand, obedience — willing and energetic submission to the will of God even at personal sacrifice — is a central gospel tenet. Far from contradicting freedom, obedience is its highest expression."[6] Indeed, the extent to which we keep the laws of God and master the laws of the universe will influence the degree to which we can find freedom.[7] Brigham Young stated that obedience is the only way to truly become free. Such obedience does not contradict one's agency, because the person "who yields strict obedience to the requirements of Heaven, acts upon the volition of his own will and exercises his freedom."[8] The freedom to be free depends upon our freewill obedience to eternal law.

IMPROVING OUR EFFICACY

Since no one besides God is completely powerful and free, each of us must learn to do the best with our available opportunities. Efficacy is the power to produce intended results. Greater efficacy or effectiveness results in greater accomplishment. Developing patterns of personal growth will help us to become more perfect and effective in our use of agency. As we learn to strengthen and improve ourselves in one area of our lives, we learn a discipline that can be applied in other areas. For example, a person who develops self-discipline in controlling his thoughts and speech can apply the same principles to his physical and moral behavior. On the other hand, a person who has not maintained self-control in at least one area of his life will find it difficult to establish self-control in any area.

In a similar manner, as we improve our capacities in some areas of our lives, we find it easier to continue this growth pattern in other areas. As we evaluate the range of our freedoms and agency, we recognize many limitations, especially when compared to God. Rather than become discouraged, we should pause and appreciate the development we have already achieved. We have progressed from the spirit world to a physical one; we have mastered many simple tasks and can now learn more difficult skills; and we have accumulated wisdom, experience, gifts, and talents that we carry with us into the future. Although short of our ultimate goal, we have made great progress.

Since we are all born with limitations, the only way to overcome them is to recognize our weaknesses and to follow God's plan for redemption until we are born again of the Spirit and become new, more Christlike persons. Then, our agency can become more effective. Without the "mighty change in our hearts" (Alma 5:14), we "cannot see the kingdom of God," nor will we become like God (John 3:3). Unless we improve our efficacy to its full potential, we will be forever limited in how much of our agency we can apply. As we improve our range of choices by making good, correct decisions, we expand our agency and increase our effectiveness to pursue our course of personal destiny, to become perfect before God. (See Matt. 5:48.)

We are all aware, however, of certain circumstances in which a person's efficacy or effectiveness may be diminished or enhanced. But in these cases, according to eternal laws of justice and mercy, the judgment of God is likewise modified. For example, as briefly mentioned earlier, a mentally handicapped person who cannot develop a mature understanding of right and wrong will be judged for what he or she is—a little child. Also, modern psychology has greatly illuminated the lasting effect that each child's upbringing has on the ability to mature and act as an agent for him- or herself. In cases where normal people have been so maltreated or poorly taught as children that they can never accept full responsibility for their actions, God does not hold them fully accountable.

On the other hand, intelligent, capable people who possess a wide range of freedoms, powers, and even divine gifts are placed on a higher level of accountability before God. (See Ezek. 18:20–30.) Indeed, many factors, including mental and physical capacity, upbringing, education, economic status, culture, and nationality contribute to an individual's efficacy. On a larger scale, of all the people in the world, those in a few Western nations have a wide range of social, political, and religious choices. God has placed people in a myriad of different and difficult circumstances that affect their agency, so all individual and collective variables are weighed fairly by him. (See Mosiah 4:7–9; D&C 76:2–3.)

Why does God first grant us agency and then allow obstacles or even create challenges that seem to limit our effective freedom? The answer is found in the Book of Mormon: "I give unto men weakness that they may be humble; and my grace is sufficient for all men that humble themselves before me; for if they humble themselves before me, and have faith in me, then will I make weak things become strong unto them." (Ether 12:27.) In other words, God gives us weaknesses in the hope that, realizing our limitations without him, we will choose the path of repentance and self-improvement that he has given us.

GUARANTEED PRESERVATION

The last necessary element in agency is its preservation, a guarantee that the conditions and promises of agency will be maintained throughout the eternities. God himself acts as preserver, promising that the consequences of our actions will be fair, consistent, and eternal. He guarantees that the laws of the universe and the gospel, which are a part of our lives, will be preserved so that our hopes and plans for the future might be realized. (See D&C 88:34.)

As we exercise our agency, we must act in faith that the Eternal God recognizes and rewards all that we think, say, and do. His desire is that we should be completely free to choose good and live righteously so that we and others can enjoy many of his blessings while in mortality. He

wants us to have the physical strength, emotional health, political freedom, and intellectual understanding to make good and proper moral and
spiritual decisions. The more we gain power and freedom in each of
these areas of our lives, the more we preserve and strengthen our agency
in the other areas. The primary way that we begin to lose the capacities
of agency is when we (or others) choose to disobey the laws of God and
the universe. The negative results of such disobedience usually restrict
someone's agency – at least temporarily. As we follow God's directions,
particularly as recorded in the scriptures, we can regain lost freedoms
and enhance others so that we can live as true, free children of God.[9]

DEVELOPING THE GIFT OF AGENCY

Each of the elements of agency we have discussed – identity, knowledge, freedom, action, law, efficacy, and preservation – are indispensable
to our exercise of this heavenly gift. To help illustrate this, let us turn
to something familiar to most of us – a simple game of basketball.

A basketball team, though it performs as a whole, is composed of
five individuals with distinct *identities* and functions. To perform their
roles, they must have a *knowledge* of the game in general and of their
individual roles in particular. Then, of course, the players must have the
freedom to play the game and must *act* to take advantage of their knowledge and opportunity. They are also bound by certain *laws* or rules of
the game, which carry consequences when obeyed or disregarded. In
addition, certain immutable physical laws – like the law of gravity – also
govern the results of their actions. Granted, not all basketball players
are created equal. Some are inherently better, or more *effective,* at the
sport than others. For this reason, some allowance is made in the rules
depending on whether the players are children or adults, men or women,
amateurs or professionals. Without all these conditions, the game would
either not be possible, or we would say it was unfair. Finally, officials
and administrators supervise the game and *preserve* its integrity. The final
outcome of the game depends on the applied agency of one team's players
as opposed to the players on the other team.

Let us try to imagine another set of rules for agency. The scriptures
tell us that when God presented to the hosts of heaven his plan of
salvation, he met with opposition from Satan, who wanted to modify this

plan. Satan wanted to eliminate our freedom to choose between right and wrong—we would have to follow him in his choice of what he thinks is right. (See Moses 4:3; D&C 29:36.) True, Satan proposed only one change, but (returning to the metaphor of driving) what use is a beautiful, powerful car without a steering mechanism? Without individual choice, we lose our *identity;* we become programmed robots without personal development and continuing *efficacy* in our actions. We are deprived of personal *action* in choosing between good and evil, which would otherwise increase our *knowledge* of opposing forces in the universe. Also, if we have no choice in our moral actions, eternal *laws* and their consequences serve no purpose, for they are made to *preserve* human agency and growth. The value of all existence would become meaningless, as Lehi stated, "having no life neither death, nor corruption nor incorruption, happiness nor misery, neither sense nor insensibility. . . . Wherefore, all things must have vanished away." (2 Ne. 2:11–13.)

Without full agency, Satan's alternate plan would have returned us to our Heavenly Father in almost the same condition as when we left: innocent, unrefined children like Adam and Eve in the Garden of Eden. We, with our new physical bodies, would be with God, but we would not be like him. Adam and Eve themselves understood this after they learned, through the Holy Ghost, the plan of salvation: "In that day Adam blessed God . . . saying: Blessed be the name of God, for because of my transgression my eyes are opened. . . . And Eve, his wife . . . was glad, saying: Were it not for our transgression we never should . . . have known good and evil, and the joy of our redemption, and the eternal life which God giveth unto all the obedient." (Moses 5:10–11.) Eternal life is life as God knows it, with unlimited knowledge and power to act with him in edifying his children as part of his eternal purposes.

Under his plan, God allows us opportunity to share his limitless power and glory if we can prove that we will use them for noble purposes. Under Satan's plan, we would have had no power, and the devil would have retained all glory, as he said: "Behold, here am I, send me, I will be thy son, and I will redeem all mankind, that one soul shall not be lost, and surely I will do it; *wherefore give me thine honor.*" (Moses 4:1, italics added.)

For now, Satan wields considerable influence on earth among the wicked, but his reign here is limited. The irony of Satan's fate is that, instead of obtaining absolute rule over all inhabitants of the earth, the results of his choices will place him beneath the least of the children of men. Satan's works are "works of darkness" (Hel. 6:28; see 1 Ne. 8:23–24), and darkness equates with evil, disorganization, cold, and chaos— situations existing before this earth was organized. It also refers to outer darkness, perdition, or emptiness—the final abode of Satan and his followers. Although the devil desires to rule over all people and over everything, his final kingdom will literally be dark, cold, and disorganized nothingness. (See Alma 40:13–14.)

SHARING FREEDOM WITH GOD

God's own plan also has its irony. By giving us our agency, God gives himself more freedom. After we have proven ourselves through tribulation, we become trustworthy, faithful, valuable servants in God's kingdom on earth and in heaven. In this life we help him by spreading the gospel to his children; in the life to come we assist his work by creating new worlds with new generations of spirit children. We, as his fellow servants and as his kings and queens, his priests and priestesses, literally share the burden of his work and free him to pursue his goal more rapidly, which is "to bring to pass the immortality and eternal life of man." (Moses 1:39.)

Indeed, the kingdom of heaven expands as God shares all that he has with other righteous beings. We come to earth to exercise our agency, to be tested and refined until we become spiritually mature and independent. In particular, as members of God's church applying our agency, we are entrusted with important tasks: strengthening our families and fellow members, preaching the gospel throughout the world, and performing saving ordinances for the dead.[10] We stand at the crossroad with the choice of following either Satan or God. Satan, by seeking to control us, not only loses his own rights and freedoms, but also brings us into his bondage; God, by giving us agency and responsibility, both gains exalted children, and also blesses us as we share his expanded power, glory, and freedom.

That God has no other purpose for his existence but to improve our potential for eternal life shows not only how much he loves us, but also how much trust and faith he has in that potential. Satan would reduce us to little more than mechanical animals, but God shows great faith in our abilities. First, he created our spirits from unorganized intelligences, then organized the world for our habitation. More important, he gave us dominion over the earth and granted us agency during our earth life — our training ground for celestial responsibilities. While many of us may not reach our full potential in the eternal scope of personal destiny, the exaltation of those who do achieve perfection is reward enough for God. Furthermore, most of God's children will live, learn, and grow during mortality, and they will eventually enjoy an eternal, resurrected state far superior to their earlier existence.[11]

In conclusion, God is the prototype for all loving, wise parents. Loving parents do not overprotect their offspring or keep the children completely dependent on them. Wise parents let the children make choices — right and wrong — within their ability so that their capacities can grow. Otherwise, the child remains a child. Our Heavenly Father gives us our agency to foster this growth in us, his children. *The divine gift of AGENCY is an eternal principle that permeates our relationship with the Almighty, and it requires identity, knowledge, freedom of choices, action, law, efficacy, and preservation to be in full operation.*

Heavenly Father has guaranteed us our agency so that we can meet and overcome the challenges of this life, enabling us to grow to our full potential as celestial beings like himself. If we do not choose eternal life, we may be with God our Father, but we could never be like him. (See 2 Ne. 2:10, 13, 27–29.) Under his plan, God allows us opportunity to become independent, trustworthy children. He will then share his limitless power and glory with us since we have proven that we will use his gifts for noble purposes. Under such celestial conditions, we will enjoy freedom far beyond anything to be experienced in mortality. The wise choice of our limited freedoms now will determine the ultimate agency we will experience in the eternities.

For further study, refer to the following entries:

TG	BD	*EM*
Accountability		Accountability
Agency		Agency
Free		Freedom
Freedom		Opposition

CHAPTER 11

EARTH LIFE — OUR PIVOTAL STAGE OF EXISTENCE

On almost any given morning, we might lie in bed and ask ourselves, "Why do I have to get up today?" This feeling is especially strong on days when we face unwelcome tasks. On the other hand, on mornings when we anticipate pleasant activities, we can hardly wait to get out of bed so we can start with our pursuits. Our approach to life in general reflects this same pattern: when we dread what lies ahead, we hesitate to do anything; when we foresee valuable opportunities, we accelerate our efforts. Heavenly Father recognizes these human tendencies, and he constantly reminds us of the valuable purposes and joyous experiences that should be the essence of our earth life. With these eternal values in mind, we can then approach life with determination and hope.

To find purpose in our life, we often ask ourselves, "Why are we here?" Prior to answering this question, we need to appreciate our present situation by first answering the questions, "Where did we come from?" and "Where are we going?" In chapter nine, we examined the two phases of our first estate in the premortal world: first, we existed without beginning as unorganized intelligence, and God then organized our intelligence at some point into a spirit body. In this antemortal existence, our spirit progressed in knowledge, understanding, faithfulness, and obedience until it was prepared to take on a physical body.

After entering our second estate through mortal birth, we now experience mortality in the flesh and continue to prepare ourselves for the future through learning, trials, and experiences. The future promises two further major stages of development, which will be explored in the next two chapters. First, we will experience death and enter postmortality as a spirit being in another spirit world. Eventually, we will exit the postmortal spirit world and be reunited with our physical bodies, judged, and assigned to our third and final estate.

The answer to our initial question is, in short, "We are here to build upon our past and to prepare for our future." Our past first estate had no beginning since our intelligences have always existed; and our future third estate will have no end because we will live forever as resurrected beings. However, our present stage of earth life, though temporary, sets the pattern for and determines the quality of our future destiny. It is critical, then, to understand the nature of our pivotal second estate, what it requires of us, and what it promises us concerning our future existence.

MORTALITY UNITES SPIRIT WITH FLESH

We do not know exactly how long all the inhabitants of this earth existed as organized, intelligent spirit beings before entering their second estate. For those souls now living on the earth, they are at least six thousand years old, since all spirit children of God participated in the premortal council prior to his sending Adam and Eve to begin the human family. In any case, our spirits had more time to grow and develop in premortality than any of us have in mortality. What is it then—in this short, critical time of earth life—that our spirit, united with our flesh, needs to accomplish?

The answer lies in realizing that for the first time in our existence, we live—albeit temporarily and imperfectly—as a complete person, with intelligence, spirit, and body. These three elements will also comprise our future immortal beings as we exist forever after the resurrection. This life, then, is the best facsimile of eternity and provides the only total, intensive training ground in which we can harmonize all the elements of our being in preparation for our final estate: "Therefore this life became a probationary state; a time to prepare to meet God; a time to prepare for that endless state . . . which is after the resurrection of the dead." (Alma 12:24.)

Before we meet God and are judged by him, we must concentrate our efforts during mortality on training our mature spirits to develop, control, and utilize our relatively new and immature physical bodies. To complete this preparation and probationary period, we need to enrich ourselves in three dimensions, experiencing a new life through our physical bodies, building new families and social relations with our spirit brothers and sisters, and developing a renewed bond with our Heavenly Father, his Son, and the Holy Spirit.

PHYSICAL LIFE WITH A NEW BODY

With a new physical body, we experience new sensations of the flesh—exciting appetites and feelings. Through our physical senses, we have new avenues for learning about the natural world and some laws of the universe. We also soon learn that our body and spirit can compete with each other for control of our being, but they can also work in harmony for the edification of the whole soul. In essence, we need a physical body and earth life as a time to discover ourselves, learn sensitivity, make choices, live a full life, develop self-control, and expand talents.

A TIME TO DISCOVER OURSELVES

Our first opportunity of earth life is to learn who we are—to come to an understanding of our basic self and our role in the eternities. To achieve this self identity, we had to leave our existence with God, where we lived as his spirit children. We were provided a new dimension in an entirely different framework of physical existence without an active remembrance of our earlier life. This situation provided us with an opportunity to foster new faith in our Heavenly Father.

Separated from our heavenly parents, we first became dependent upon physical parents, and later we also separated from them to become even more independent. As we grow, we usually choose some individuals as role models, and if we are fortunate, we can develop positive bonds with good people with whom we can have supportive, trusting, and loving relationships. As we carefully observe other people, we come to know ourselves better. With experience and insight we develop into mature adults and learn more concerning our true identities.

A TIME TO LEARN SENSITIVITY

One of our constant priorities in life is to seek, learn, and apply truths in the physical, moral, and spiritual realms of existence. As we study the universe from a new perspective, earth life becomes a marvelous opportunity to develop both sensitivity and a special sense of awareness in these realms of truth.

Physical Sensitivity. Some things can be learned only through the experiences of the physical senses, which is one important reason why we are separated from our Heavenly Father. He, no doubt, told us many things about what we would experience here on earth, and we agreed to the conditions of our existence. However, we needed to move from a theoretical conception to practical experience; therefore, we came to earth to explore the physical world through learning and experience.

One way we learn is by study—reading books and journals, taking classes, attending lectures, and pursuing other areas of academic education. Intellectual study is helpful, but it becomes more interesting as we expand upon what we have learned by conducting experiments, making field trips, and personally getting involved in various aspects of the learning process. As we become active participants, we not only enjoy our studies more, but we also remember more. The more senses we use in the educational process, the more vivid the learning experience is.

We enrich our observation skills as we view sunrises and rainbows, as we study the colors in nature, and as we behold the beauty of flowers and human faces. Our noses smell flower fragrances, pine forests, freshly baked bread, and other aromas. Our ears hear the music of birds and instruments, the patter of rain and children's feet, and the tones of the wind and tender voices. We feel the morning dew on our bare feet, the fabric textures through our fingertips, and the sensations of temperature and pressure through our skin. We taste the freshness of sweet fruit, the savor of finely cooked foods, and the flavor of healthy herbs and vegetables.

We also develop our internal physical senses as we respond to feelings of hunger, thirst, fatigue, stress, and pain. By far the best way to enhance any of these senses is to use them regularly, with intensity and concentration. Imagine the challenge of describing the color green to a person who has been blind from birth. Or try, for example, to explain the difference in taste between salt and sugar without referring to your own experience with foods containing these two substances. Colors become clear only to those who see; bitter and sweet tastes must be experienced to be known. Without personal experience, developing these senses is extremely difficult.

Moral Sensitivity. Likewise, so it is with the moral sensitivities in life — they must be experienced and compared to be understood. Among its many attributes, moral sensitivity encompasses the abilities to make good decisions, judge others righteously, and discern right from wrong. Justice and injustice, evil and good, and their consequences can be recognized from experience and put in perspective through wisdom. As we become sensitive to the suffering and needs of others, we learn more about our attitudes toward others and the nature of God and ourselves.

We soon learn that we cannot easily explain why one sometimes suffers for no apparent reason. To understand why a person receives affliction and tribulations, we should automatically look not into their past but into their future. Instead of being punished for previous deeds, perhaps they are being refined for later excellence. If they become better people after their trials and sufferings, their adverse experiences have proven to be valuable developments in their earth life. The guidelines of not judging unfairly or without a full understanding also apply to many of our own unexplainable negative experiences. As we review our particular circumstances, we might identify opportunities that increase our learning and faith. As we expand our horizons in studying history, observing human behavior, and responding to the promptings of our conscience, we develop the moral sensitivity that will enrich our lives and will bless the lives of others.

Spiritual Sensitivity. Our highest priority should be to develop our spiritual sensitivity. To do so, we must first regain in the flesh the spiritual association we possessed as spirit children in God's presence. Our mortal bodies and their imperfect perceptions can act as barriers in communication between our spirit and the Holy Ghost. When divine Spirit communicates directly with our spirit, that communication is plain and pure. Through earnest prayer, we can gradually learn to distinguish between our own prejudices and desires and the pure revelation of the Spirit. Without spiritual sensitivity, God's desires for us will be constantly filtered and distorted by the predisposition of our physical nature.

A TIME TO MAKE CHOICES

Earth life is a unique time of testing. We are tested in mortality to determine the nature of our character. Our character is seen in the attitudes we develop, the thoughts we have, the priorities we establish, the words we utter, the habits we form, and the actions we perform. (See Alma 12:13–14; Rev. 3:21.) Life is a probationary period; we show whether we obey God and overcome evil, or we follow Satan and oppose righteousness. (See D&C 98:14–15.) The intent of our hearts is examined to see why we speak and act as we do. All of us are continually being so tested.

Different people experience their "tests of life" in vastly different circumstances: adversity challenges some, while others find it complicated to handle prosperity; some are tried in times of health, while others find their challenges in illness. Contrary to the attitudes of many, the circumstances of life that we face are not our major tests in mortality—our greatest test is in how we handle these situations. As examples, parenthood is a wonderful demonstration of selfless service for some, but a dreaded responsibility or an opportunity for selfish manipulation for others. On the other hand, being single or without children can be a great opportunity for personal improvement, community involvement, and church service for some, but an excuse for self-depredation, isolationism, and antagonism for others. Even two people of the same family can face the same set of circumstances, such as divorce or the death of a parent, and react quite differently. We must learn to endure and grow through our many trials rather than use them as excuses for ill-advised behavior.

Sometimes we learn that we can react very differently in the same situation, depending upon our mood or understanding at the moment. One simple story illustrates this point. Imagine being in the back of a crowded elevator when a large man steps heavily on your foot. You cry out, "Watch where you're stepping, you blind fool." The man turns around and you recognize that he *is* blind—what feelings do you have? Or compare the feelings you would have had if you had known from the beginning that he was blind. He may have still accidentally stepped on your foot, and the pressure and pain would have been the same, but you probably would have reacted much differently. Thus we see that the actual situation (such as a large man stepping on our foot) is not what determines our character but rather how we respond to the circumstances (with anger or patience).

Daily we face a variety of situations. How we handle each one contributes to the development of our personality. Our decisions carry us further on the paths of righteousness or wickedness, and our acts strengthen our patterns of selfishness or selflessness. Through the choices we make, we are forging our future in the postmortal life and our selves during this earth life.

A TIME TO LIVE LIFE'S TRAGEDIES

The trials of life are often experienced in the toughest of times, during tribulation, calamity, adversity, or frustration. (See 2 Tim. 3:12.) In a spiritual context, the righteous are promised that they will not be tempted or tried beyond their ability to endure. (See 1 Cor. 10:13; Alma 13:28–29.) In the physical and social context of life, we may experience obstacles that we are not able to overcome, such as ill health, old age, divorce, or wayward children. We have to learn how to adjust to these less favorable situations while maintaining our moral integrity and spiritual strength. We will grow spiritually and receive eternal rewards if we remain faithful during such times of adversity. We are also told that by experiencing the bitter, we are then better able to taste and appreciate the sweet experiences of life. (See 2 Ne. 2:1–11; D&C 29:39.)

In spite of tribulations, or (in the case of some people) because of tribulations, earth life becomes our opportunity to live by faith in God. (See Gal. 2:20.) As we reviewed in the earlier chapter on God, he allows calamities to exist on earth, and we must decide whether we will still believe in him. These trials also give us experience, try our souls, measure if and how we endure, and provide us opportunities not only to make the best of the situation, but also to improve the lot of others. (See D&C 90:24; Rom. 8:28.) In short, the true quality of our faith, hope, and charity is usually refined, improved, and measured through adverse situations.

If such tribulations enhance and strengthen these great spiritual gifts, then the positive, eternal rewards of these trials become far more valuable than the negative, temporary experiences of anguish and sorrow. (See 1 Cor. 13.) Peter, in fact, saw such tribulation as a time to rejoice because of the fruit it could yield: "Wherein ye greatly rejoice, though now for a season, if need be, ye are in heaviness through manifold temptations: that the trial of your faith, being much more precious than of gold that perisheth, though it be tried with fire, might be found unto praise and honour and glory at the appearing of Jesus Christ." (1 Pet. 1:6–7; see also 1 Pet. 2:19–23; 3:14–18; 4:12–19; D&C 122:7; Moses 5:10–11.) If we learn goodness in periods of adversity, times of earthly toil become step-ping stones of personal and spiritual growth.

A TIME TO ENJOY LIFE'S TRIUMPHS

There exists another, more pleasant way to develop divine personal attributes—through righteous behavior. God rewards those who dili-gently seek him. The wise person learns to seek God at all times, not just when intense challenges must be faced. By learning to love and serve others in times of peace, prosperity, and health, we improve our character in a positive environment. Tasting the fruits of righteousness strengthens our character and encourages our resolve to continue on the gospel path. Constant searching and receiving positive reinforcement are much more valuable and lasting incentives toward learning and growth.

In addition, God desires that we would experience joy during our life here on earth because "men are, that they might have joy." (2 Ne. 2:25.) Like other emotions and spiritual gifts, joy usually comes to those who look for it. In an attitude of faith and hope, we should look for and enjoy the simple pleasures found during the journey through life. Al-though few of us achieve success to the degree that we may desire, we still have many accomplishments that we can feel good about. Rather than regret the times we are stuck in traffic or occupied with mundane tasks, we should look for something beautiful or seek a learning oppor-tunity. Instead of being upset because we are separated from old friends, we should foster and enjoy new friendships. Although we do not expe-rience constant happiness on earth, eventual, lasting happiness is God's object and design for our existence. In times of either accomplishment or adversity, we always have the comfort of God's promises, knowing that eternal joy and divine gifts will be our eventual reward as we inherit his kingdom. (See Matt. 25:21.)

A TIME TO DEVELOP SELF-CONTROL

We must also learn to do good in the flesh according to our knowledge of what is right and good. This is often a difficult thing because our bodies are inherently weak and hard to tame. Thus, Paul wrote, "For what I would [do], that I do not; but what I hate, that do I." (Rom. 7:15.) Likewise, the disciples were overcome by fatigue when they should have been watching and praying with the Savior in Gethsemane. The Lord sadly, though understandingly, commented, "The spirit indeed is willing, but the flesh is weak." (Matt. 26:41.) Moroni wrote that we are given weaknesses in the flesh so that we may learn the discipline and humility of overcoming them with help from the Lord: "For if they humble themselves before me, and have faith in me, then will I make weak things become strong unto them." (Ether 12:27.)

Ideally, a person will be responsive to the counsel of others and the promptings of conscience in order to learn control over the whole self—mind, spirit, and body. We refine ourselves by working on the little tasks of self-control, many of which are reciprocal. For instance, we need to control our thoughts, which leads to better control over our words and actions. We need to learn how to love our friends, which enables us to better love our enemies. We need to say and mean "yes" when we have an opportunity to make a righteous commitment so we will have the courage to say and mean "no" when we are in a situation of temptation. We need to learn to accept victory and defeat with the same graciousness and humility. In essence, we need to keep the directions and commandments of our loving Father in Heaven, whose prophets, scriptures, and Spirit provide the necessary resources to learn true self-mastery.

All of us spend considerable effort in the first years of life simply learning to control bodily functions and coordinate basic motor skills. As we grow older, both social and religious constraints require that we also learn to defer physical gratification of our appetites and passions. In the restored church, the covenants we make bind us not only to control, but also to purify our physical bodies through obedience so that they can endure the glorious presence of God: "Who may abide the day of his coming? and who shall stand when he appeareth? for he is like a refiner's fire, and like fullers' soap." (Mal. 3:2.) Now, above all other times in our stages of existence, is the ideal time to learn self-control so that our whole being can be strengthened and purified.

A TIME TO EXPAND TALENTS

Earth life is an opportunity for us not only to receive a body, but also to enhance and improve it. According to the parable of the talents, if we develop the talents God has given us, they will be multiplied even more. (See Matt. 25:14–23.) Each of us has special gifts and talents that can not only bring us a sense of joy and fulfillment, but also provide enrichment and pleasure for others. Gifts of music, communication, compassion, service, and concern for community are just a few examples of gifts that bless both the person who possesses them and those who witness and experience them.

Even our weaknesses can be overcome and turned into strengths through expanding our talents. (See Ether 12:27, 35.) As we gain control over some weaknesses, we develop patterns of personal growth that allow us to strengthen other areas of imperfection. The ultimate goal of our personal development should be to become perfect as our Father in Heaven is perfect. (See Matt. 5:48.) With God's help and through the grace of the Atonement, we can achieve the full measure of our creation — godliness. (See Eph. 4:12–13.)[1]

Life on earth with a physical body is meant to be a time of individual development whereby we experience physical growth, emotional pleasure, social enrichment, intellectual learning, moral refinement, and spiritual improvement. As we experience and recognize these opportunities, we feel good about ourselves, we relish life, and we thank God for the marvelous blessings of earth life.

SOCIAL LIFE WITH NEW OPPORTUNITIES OF SERVICE

Earth life is more than a time to receive — it is also a time to give. Just as we receive life from heavenly and earthly parents, we can give physical life to other spirit children through parenthood, and we can strengthen the spiritual lives of others through righteous service. We, who have received an earth with great natural resources and beauty, can exercise wise stewardship and show concern for our natural environment to make it a more productive and pleasant place. Organized as families and joined in social contacts with many other people, we receive much emotional and social reinforcement. This interaction brings stability into our lives, so in turn we should help provide similar stability for others.

Almost everything we receive on earth, we can share with others. Physically, we can help provide better health and nutrition. Emotionally, we should support and uplift each other with genuine care and love. Socially, we strengthen one another through families, in Church settings, and within the community. Intellectually, we have a responsibility to improve and pass on the heritage of knowledge and understanding that we have received. Morally, we should go beyond setting a good example and politely but firmly encourage others to do the same. Spiritually, we teach gospel principles, bear fervent testimony, and exercise spiritual gifts to bless the lives of others. Any who have received blessings of earth life have a moral responsibility to share them with others.

As other chapters in this book outline the opportunities and blessings we receive through the grace of God, the work of Christ, and the companionship of the Holy Ghost, suggestions will also be given on how we can encourage others to seek for and attain the marvelous blessings God has provided his children. We need to remember, however, that not all people will have the desire or capacity to receive all the blessings that earth life can offer. Infants who die young, children raised in extremely adverse circumstances, and people with severe handicaps do not enjoy a full range of opportunities while in the flesh. Some people will experience severe adversities or calamities that afflict their physical and emotional health throughout mortality. In the hereafter, these negative circumstances will be counterbalanced, and the wounds that they inflicted will be remedied. A wise, loving Heavenly Father will measure how each person deals with such trials.

The Supreme Judge will also measure how each of us has added to or taken away from the suffering that his children experience. Sometimes people suffer because of their own mistakes; on other occasions their suffering comes through no fault of their own. We should not judge or condemn any who are sick, afflicted, or suffering. More than a trial of their capacity to endure, adversity might be a test of our willingness to help. Part of our responsibility on earth is to lessen the burdens of others. As God's children unitedly exercise such an attitude, the quality of life improves for all.

SPIRITUAL LIFE WITH NEW GIFTS AND POWERS

In the premortal existence, we needed a new setting without God's continuous physical presence in order to have the opportunity to foster new faith in our Heavenly Father. Now, as we faithfully seek God during mortality, his presence returns, and we enjoy a greater guidance and peace in our lives. As we enter into and keep sacred covenants with our Father in Heaven, the blessings and promises of the priesthood ordinances are granted us through the power of Christ's atonement. As we listen to the promptings of the Holy Spirit, we receive special spiritual gifts that prepare us for eternal service in God's celestial kingdom. Spiritual refinement and improvement is an important dimension of mortality.

A TIME TO SECURE BLESSINGS

One major purpose of earth life is to draw closer to God by participating in certain covenants and ordinances. Jesus himself set the proper example by being baptized, and he stated that no one can enjoy the blessed presence of God without being purified through the covenant ordinance of baptism by water and the Spirit. (See John 3:3–7.)

Besides covenanting to maintain a relationship with God, our covenants also take us one step further, making us at least partially responsible for the progression of our brothers and sisters here on earth. The first covenant we make, that of baptism, is also our initiation into the society of the church of Jesus Christ, and part of our commitment is to sustain and serve one another in the faith. (See Mosiah 18:8–10.) When receiving our temple endowment, we expand upon the baptismal covenant. It is significant that two of the four temple covenants specifically address the greatest temptations of the flesh: unlawful sex (which is controlled through obeying the law of chastity), and covetousness for material possessions (which is harnessed through obeying the law of consecration). These are the two primary earthly attractions we must overcome to subdue our physical bodies as we are tested and proven worthy for God's future blessings.[2]

Finally, when we have children, we assume full responsibility to raise them in the covenants of the Church: "Inasmuch as parents have children in Zion . . . that teach them not to understand the doctrine of repentance, faith in Christ the Son of the living God, and of baptism and the gift of the Holy Ghost by the laying on of the hands, when eight years old, the sin be upon the heads of the parents." (D&C 68:25.) Bearing and rearing children in the light of the gospel is one of the most important and serious experiences of mortality because Heavenly Father desires that all his children should be reared in a strong gospel environment. Our service to family and ward members again benefits us in the future stages of existence because we will be doing similar work with later generations of spiritual offspring while we live as resurrected beings in the celestial realm.

EARTH LIFE IS A PREPARATORY SCHOOL — NOT A PLAYGROUND

As discussed previously, earth life is a marvelous opportunity to learn knowledge, grow with our physical body, and give and share as we serve others. As such, mortality serves as a school preparing us for the style and status of life that follows. However, too many of God's children either do not know or have forgotten why they are here, and they treat mortality as a time for personal gratification rather than as an opportunity for learning and training. They want to be in the playgrounds of the world enjoying the excitement and pleasures of the body with little thought for the long-range effects of their attitudes and behavior.

Mortal life is more than a learning period of our existence, it also serves as a probationary period — a time for us to prepare to meet God and to live thereafter in his presence. (See Alma 12:24; 34:32; 42:4, 10.) Thus, as in any preparatory school, if the student does not take advantage of the schooling, future opportunities are restricted. We are tested in mortality to show our obedience to God's directions and commandments in order to demonstrate whether we are ready for further light, truth, and service in his celestial realms. (See Rev. 3:21; D&C 98:14–15; 124:55; 136:31; Abr. 3:25–26.) The tests of earth life come to us through varied challenges and opportunities, trying us in the financial, physical, emotional, social, mental, moral, and spiritual dimensions of our existence. (See 2 Tim. 3:12; 1 Pet. 1:7; Rom. 5:3–5; D&C 101:2–4; 121:1.)

Note that God will give us spiritual direction and help us beyond our natural ability to bear the challenges and endure the sufferings so that we can learn and grow from life's experiences. (See 1 Cor. 10:13; Alma 13:28–30; 38:5.) Although we are separated from God's direct presence, we still have access to him through the promptings of the Spirit. Mortality becomes our opportunity to develop faith and to act in love. (See Gal. 2:20; 3:11; John 13:35; 14:15.) As we maintain faith in God through the temptations and trials of life, and as we seek for God's glory, our eternal character is strengthened. (See Rom. 8:28; D&C 58:2–4; 90:24; 121:7–8; 122:5–9.) God the Father and his Son, Jesus Christ, love us and realize that such challenges and trials provide a strengthening and purging effect in our lives. (See Titus 2:12; Ps. 65:3; Prov. 25:4–5.) As we taste the bitter experiences of life here on earth, with the help of God we can learn to relish the sweet blessings of our existence now and in the future. (See 2 Ne. 2:1–11; Moses 6:55; D&C 29:39.)

To summarize, earth life is a necessary step in the progression of God's children. One major purpose is to receive a physical body and to be tested in how we use this body. The whole person or soul of man is complete only when the intelligent spirit and the physical body are brought together in one being. (See D&C 88:15; Gen. 2:7.) A physical body enhances our learning capacity and is essential to our obtaining a fullness of joy. (See D&C 93:33.) Life with a physical body becomes a trial period in our existence, during which we should learn to properly use the natural bodily appetites and powers. We prove ourselves as we determine whether the spiritual and moral aspects of our nature will maintain control over the physical and selfish desires of the flesh. As we master ourselves and become more godlike, we can take better advantage of the full range of physical, social, and spiritual opportunities that earth life provides.

The experiences of earth life should expand beyond the personal learning experiences in the flesh. We should look beyond the small communities we live in to broader horizontal and vertical dimensions. Horizontally, we require involvement with other people on earth as we both gain and give: we gain a body, knowledge, assistance, talents, and much more from others; we give our lives, our time, and our talents as a blessing for others. Vertically, as we strengthen our relationship with Heavenly Father, we both receive and share blessings from God: children, gospel truths, covenants, revelation, saving ordinances, and joy. In all dimensions, we experience highs and lows as we journey through life's trials and triumphs, and through it all, we become more fully developed children of God.

In short, *EARTH LIFE is a probationary state that separates us from God's presence and provides us with a physical body. Mortality provides an opportunity to discover the physical world, to serve others in new dimensions of unselfishness, and to increase our spiritual stature.* Earth life gives us opportunities to learn truth and discipline, to experience life's tragedies and triumphs, to choose between good and evil, to develop faith and love, to receive heavenly gifts and ordinances, and to give time and service as we develop godlike attributes. Each new day should be anticipated as another opportunity to learn, serve, and become more refined. As our bodies become healthy tabernacles for our spirits, we perceive and experience life more fully, and we end up serving both ourselves and others. Through these processes, we become more like God as we draw ourselves and others closer to him. The ultimate measure of our creation and the fulfillment of our destiny are to achieve godliness through the grace of God, the power of Christ, and the sanctification of the Holy Ghost. (See Eph. 4:12–13.)

For further study, refer to the following entries:

TG	BD	EM
Body		Adam
Flesh and Blood		Birth
Man, Physical		Creation, Creation
Creation of		Accounts
Mortality		Earth
		Eve
		Mankind
		Mortality
		Natural Man
		Origin of Man
		Physical Body
		Purpose of Earth
		Life
		Second Estate
		Suffering in the
		World
		Trials

CHAPTER 12

SIN — LIFE'S SPIRITUAL DETOURS

Most travelers have been on trips when they want to get quickly to their destination. Looking at a map or at their surroundings, they see a shortcut that might save time. But soon after deviating off the main road, the traveling becomes more difficult and slow. The wise traveler soon recognizes the problem and immediately returns to the main road. Although he has lost some time, returning to the highway and continuing on it still provides the quickest way to his destination. However, some people do not appreciate the detour's difficulty or they stubbornly persist on the "shortcut," thinking the difficulty will soon end, even though the route seriously delays their travel. In fact, some shortcuts become so difficult and hazardous that a mechanical breakdown can stop the trip, or an accident in an isolated location can endanger the lives of the travelers.

Taking such a detour is very similar to experiences in life. Usually there are time-proven, well-traveled highways toward our goals in life. Instead, we look for shortcuts to health, wealth, social recognition, and success. We take diet pills instead of following a moderate diet and exercise program; we gamble or make risky investments instead of maintaining solid financial management; we buy the latest fashions or join an elite social club to enhance our community standing instead of consistently giving community service; and we try to run up the ladder of corporate success instead of continuing our education or providing steady, productive work. Almost always these shortcuts delay our progress, and many times they take us to places we really didn't want to go to. If we are wise, we will ignore such shortcuts and follow the trustworthy highways of life.

Likewise, one's spiritual life on this earth should be a journey—a return to Heavenly Father's realm. He wants his children to enjoy peace,

love, and joy in his glorious presence. However, earth life offers enticements and apparent shortcuts disguised as excitement, power, or pleasure. These alternatives almost always lead toward sin as the traveler
turns away from God's directions and commandments. Unfortunately,
people usually do not recognize the sinful entanglements of this path
until they have traveled some distance along it. How is it that anyone
would even put him- or herself on such a detour of sin?

THE FALL OF ADAM

Traditional Judaism and Christianity claim that our sinful behavior
is simply the nature of humanity resulting from the fall of Adam. In
contrast, the restored gospel provides an optimistic view of the Fall and,
thereby, human nature. The ancient prophet Lehi best summarized this
perspective: "Adam fell that men might be; and men are, that they might
have joy." (2 Ne. 2:25.) Several important doctrines are implied in this
brief passage and clarified in other scriptures. First, Adam's fall was not
a result of chance or bad luck — it had a foreordained purpose: to populate
the earth and spiritually develop humankind. Second, because of (and
not in spite of) the Fall, people are able to experience joy both in this
life and more fully in the life to come.

The New Testament confirms that the Fall was not an unfortunate
accident by declaring that Jesus Christ was foreordained as our Redeemer: "Ye know that ye were not redeemed with corruptible things,
as silver and gold . . . but with the precious blood of Christ, as of a lamb
without blemish and without spot: who verily was foreordained before
the foundation of the world." (1 Pet. 1:18–20.) Jesus would not have
been set apart as Savior "before the foundation of the world" if the Fall
had not also been an integral part of the plan of salvation from the
beginning.

OPPOSITION IN ALL THINGS

The Fall was a prerequisite to mortal life because the opportunity
for growth through choosing between a variety of opposites is the very
foundation of our second estate. Lehi explained this principle beautifully:
"For it must needs be, that there is an opposition in all things. If not
so, . . . righteousness could not be brought to pass, neither wickedness,

neither holiness nor misery, neither good nor bad." He went on to say that "all things must needs be a compound in one," or in other words, our existence "must needs remain as dead, having no life." (2 Ne. 2:11.)

Though Lehi was concerned primarily with moral and spiritual opposition, we find upon inspection that the physical world is based on opposites as well. For example, in physics, the atom is composed of a positively charged nucleus counterbalanced by negatively charged electrons. Among plants and animals, male and female elements must come together to propagate the species while competing with other life forms in an ecological niche. Opposition is also a natural part of the human world. The engineer designs a bridge based on balance and counterweight. The poet gives language its most potent form through the tension of conformity versus contradiction in meter, sound, and symbol.

Returning to spiritual things, the scriptures teach that to understand the purpose of life, we must experience the principle of opposition ourselves. Born into an already fallen world, we find that many opposing experiences await us: pleasure and pain, health and sickness, good and evil, happiness and misery. We experience the effects of opposing conflicts both as a result of others' actions (dating back to the Fall) and also through our own decisions. From our experiences, though, we gain the knowledge to make informed, responsible choices. In the Garden of Eden, there existed no consequences of prior actions. Thus, Adam and Eve were in a state of untutored innocence, unable to knowingly choose either good or evil. God himself walked and talked with our first parents, but they could not fully appreciate his goodness or understand why they should trust his word, since they knew nothing else. Therefore, God allowed Satan into the garden in opposition to his own glory.

God had warned Adam and Eve that if they ate of the tree of the knowledge of good and evil, they would die (first spiritually, being cast out of his presence, and later physically, returning to the dust from which they were created. [See Moses 4:25, 29.]) But having never been lied to before, Eve in her gullibility (for she was "beguiled") just as readily accepted Satan's side of the story: "Ye shall not surely die; for . . . your eyes shall be opened, and ye shall be as gods, knowing good and evil." (Moses 4:10–11.)

Since Adam and Eve were morally immature and a full explanation was beyond their comprehension, the Lord had warned them of the ill

consequences of eating the forbidden fruit but not tried to explain everything. All parents of young children do the same thing. Children must
grow up, though, and some things are best learned only through experience. Thus God added to his warning: "Nevertheless, thou mayest
choose for thyself, for it is given unto thee." (Moses 3:17.) Learning
through personal experience always means making some mistakes, but
Satan tried to simplify the issue by lying about the pitfalls (spiritual and
physical alienation) and emphasizing only the benefits (awareness and
knowledge like the gods).

Because Eve partook of the fruit without fully understanding the
commandment and its consequences, we say that she *transgressed* the
law, not that she willfully *sinned:* "To him that *knoweth* to do good, and
doeth it not, to him it is sin." (James 4:17; italics added.) Unlike Satan
(who with full understanding openly rebelled in the presence of God),
Eve lacked knowledge of good and evil and was not fully accountable.
Even though Satan encouraged Adam and Eve to do what had to be
done anyway to bring God's plan into place on earth, Satan's intent was
selfish and evil. (See Moses 4:6.) Thus he was punished more severely
than Adam and Eve.

To unknowingly break one of God's laws is a transgression, while to
disobey knowledgeably and willfully is a sin. Unfortunately, just as innocent contact with fire still burns our flesh whether we know it will or
not, our first parents had to face the consequences of their transgression.
Thus, Adam and Eve were temporarily cut off from the presence of the
Lord and had to experience the trials and tribulations of life, including
physical death.

THE HARD LESSONS OF MORTALITY

Although some negative consequences and risks entered the world
with the Fall, more positive benefits and values began at the same time.
President Joseph Fielding Smith taught that prior to the Fall, the immortal bodies of Adam and Eve were sustained by the Spirit, for they
were in the presence of God. Once banished from his presence, blood
became the life of their flesh, and they "were thus subject to the ills of
the flesh which resulted in their gradual decline to old age and finally
the separation of the spirit from the body."[1] The introduction of death,
however, was also the introduction of mortal life; Adam and Eve, now

physically as well as spiritually prepared, could have children. Without the Fall, we could not be here. We would have remained innocent and inexperienced spirits in the presence of God, like our first parents in Eden. We would have been with him, but not like him, knowing and choosing "good from evil."

As the posterity of Adam and Eve, we follow a similar pattern of learning and accountability. As young children or "innocent" adults, we may make mistakes and even transgress some laws of God without knowing it. Like Adam and Eve after partaking of the fruit of the tree of knowledge of good and evil, we can become mature, knowledgeable, accountable children of God. In spite of our knowledge, however, we may still choose evil over good and commit sins even when we know they are wrong. Hopefully we will quickly learn the error of our ways and follow the path of our first parents.

Having gained knowledge by experience in the flesh through transgression and repentance, Adam and Eve were prepared again to receive the Spirit of the Lord and eventually return to his presence. Thus, when the Holy Ghost taught them about the redemption through Jesus Christ, Adam praised the Lord: "Blessed be the name of God, for because of my transgression my eyes are opened, and in this life I shall have joy, and again in the flesh I shall see God. And Eve, his wife, heard all these things and was glad, saying: Were it not for our transgression we never should have . . . known good and evil, and the joy of our redemption, and the eternal life which God giveth unto all the obedient." (Moses 5:10–11.) From this scripture, we see the blessings of the Fall given to Adam and Eve and ourselves: our "eyes are opened" to understanding good and evil; we have joy in this life in the hope of our redemption; we can dwell eternally with God again as resurrected beings; and we can have children in the flesh who can enjoy these same blessings. The potential of all these benefits far outweighs the risk—though very real—of failing to learn by our own experience and of remaining outside the presence of God. To help us avoid this possible failure, we need to recognize the difference between God's time-proven way of life and Satan's alluring shortcut of sin.

To stay on God's path, we should follow the Savior's pattern for spiritual success, seek after righteousness, establish testimonies of the truth, keep the commandments, and actively support and build Christ's kingdom. Though not perfect, we need to be aware of our personal spiritual deficiencies and try to overcome them, strengthening our spirituality while serving others and helping them to do the same. As long as we follow the Lord's example and continuously strive for spiritual growth and service, we will remain on the path of righteousness. If not, our spiritual commitment may weaken, and we may stray from the way leading to eternal life and wander onto the path of sin.

THE PATTERN OF PERSONAL APOSTASY

The pattern of sin among individuals often follows a common trail marked by a few clear warning signals. By identifying these signs, we can avoid traveling the wrong path. Or, we can recognize when we have strayed onto a spiritual detour and quickly turn around before digressing any further. What, then, are these downward steps on the path of sin?

1. COMPLACENCY—A SYMPTOM OF LAZINESS OR A SIGN OF PRIDE

Sometimes people do not do anything really wrong; they just get spiritually lazy. They may commit small acts of omission by failing to do their home or visiting teaching or not diligently fulfilling their Church calling. Or, they may be going through the motions of Church activity, but their faith and testimony are not being strengthened. They are active in the Church, but not in the gospel. They are in danger of gradually slipping away as their faith and testimony weaken.

Nephi warns us of this first step toward apostasy: "Wo be unto him that is at ease in Zion! Wo be unto him that crieth: All is well!" (2 Ne. 28:24–25.) As soon as a righteous individual feels that "all is well," or "it is enough," he no longer feels the need to repent and progress, and he is in danger of falling into error. Being righteous does not imply freedom from sin, since "all have sinned, and come short of the glory of God." (Rom. 3:23.) Rather, being righteous suggests a willingness to repent and constantly correct or improve one's spiritual health, an attitude not found among the wicked.

This willingness to repent and conform to the truths we possess is also a necessary prerequisite to receiving more truth. Thus Nephi continues: "Wo be unto him that shall say: We have received the word of God, and we need no more of the word of God, for we have enough!"

(2 Ne. 28:29.) Spirituality is a lot like physical health — it is something we need to consistently work on to improve and maintain. Just as we do not yet know the ultimate potential of the human body in such areas as running speed, lifting strength, or endurance, we also do not know the ultimate spiritual strength within us.

In spiritual terms, there is never such a thing as "having arrived." We are either progressing or regressing, adding or subtracting from the divine knowledge and power we possess. We can know the word of God only by doing it — by either growing in knowledge through obedience or weakening due to a lack of repentance or improvement. Nephi concludes the Lord's admonitions for eternal progression with both a promise and a warning: "Thus saith the Lord God: I will give unto the children of men line upon line, precept upon precept, here a little and there a little; and blessed are those who hearken unto my precepts . . . ; for unto him that receiveth I will give more; and from them that shall say, We have enough, from them shall be taken away even that which they have." (2 Ne. 28:30.)

Thus, the first step to personal apostasy begins with our attitude. If we are spiritually insensitive or think we are spiritually strong and we do not have to persist in righteousness anymore, then we are setting ourselves up to lose the spiritual health which we now enjoy.[2] Complacency, the lack of zeal for spiritual things, is the warning signal that the first step has been taken. Theologians may argue whether this attitude of complacency is just a simple symptom of religious laziness or a subtle sign of spiritual pride, but the results remain the same — a person's spiritual growth stops.

2. MAKING PERSONAL EXCEPTIONS — SETTING ONESELF UP FOR A FALL

With personal apostasy, we begin to weaken in our spiritual commitment. This may begin very subtly, as our religious duties and observances lose priority in our lives. It might begin with acts of omission as we consistently or deliberately neglect our Church calling, personal prayer, or gospel study. For example, schooling, work, or even family may be used as an excuse for not attending church on Sunday. Or, acts of commission may result in disobeying some of the commandments. A teenager might become too intimate during a date. A worker could "borrow" something from the job site. In an important social setting, an individual might go against Church and personal standards and drink an alcoholic beverage. The list of possibilities continues, but somewhere the person takes a spiritual detour by making an exception for him- or herself in one area of spiritual behavior. In short, this exception declares that the person has enough religion and needs no more, although the individual would never directly state such a blasphemy.

Granted, a variety of situations might lead to this "first sin." The person may have become neglectful or distracted by other priorities. The individual may have acted in ignorance or with spontaneous foolishness. He or she may have been falsely persuaded or unduly influenced by someone else. On the other hand, the individual may have thought over, discussed, and deliberately entered this course of action. In any case, one has deviated from the path of righteousness to the shortcut of sin. The clear warning signal of this detour is the loss of the companionship of the Holy Ghost. In essence, the person has stepped from light toward darkness, and his or her spiritual strength begins to weaken. To counteract this step, the person must remain spiritually sensitive and constantly strive to stay on the path of righteousness. Otherwise, persistent sin may develop.

3. THE EXCEPTIONS BECOME THE NORM— ONE'S SLIPPERY SLIDE SWIFTENS

Soon the exceptions made under unusual circumstances become the rule, and behavior that was once sporadic becomes periodic and then habitual. Not only does one lose the Holy Spirit as a constant companion, but the person rejects the promptings of a conscience calling one to repentance. Along with the warning sign of habitual disregard for one commandment, another danger signal often accompanies this third step—other commandments are broken as a pattern of disobedience is gradually established.

This step is sometimes difficult to recognize, either by the person or others. It takes a while to realize that the few, earlier, "justifiable" exceptions have now become the norm of one's behavior. Even family members, home teachers, or ecclesiastical leaders might not perceive that someone in their sphere of influence has slipped into a pattern of disobedience. This is when daily prayer, weekly sacrament covenant renewal, monthly fasting, and periodic interviews with priesthood leaders should help Church members evaluate their faithfulness and stop any problems before they become difficult habits to break.

Satan, on the other hand, tries to influence us toward entrenched wickedness. He will try to weaken us through our pride, selfishness, sensualness, and fear. Our pride might allow us to feel neglected or to take offense at others in the Church who make mistakes affecting us or our family members. Our selfishness may cause us to feel we are not benefiting enough from our Church association, especially in return for all the sacrifices we are asked to make. Our sensualness can entrap us in habits of drug abuse, inappropriate sexuality, or other weaknesses of the flesh. Our fear could lessen our tolerance against peer pressure or the mocking persecution of the world and even result in scorn for those striving to live righteous, pure lives. We need to recognize our vulnerability in these areas and quickly strengthen our spirituality before we slide into the next step of apostasy.

4. SEEKING JUSTIFICATION — FINDING EXCUSES EVERYWHERE

Having changed the patterns of our behavior for the worse, the fourth step is to free ourselves from guilt by justifying our behavior. The easiest way to do this is to blame someone else: thus, we might blame our parents for not rearing us properly, or we find offense with another Church member or complain of a "personality conflict" with the ward bishop or other Church leaders. This step is particularly dangerous because not only is the person moving further off the path of righteousness, but it also seems he or she does not want to return to it.

Former active members who have traveled some distance on the detour of sin almost always blame another person for their own dissatisfaction with the Church. Failure to pay tithing, or to come to church, or to keep some other commandment is usually linked to some event or altercation with a Church member. Furthermore, when this excuse is waved like a banner for all to see, we can be sure this person is proceeding further down the road to apostasy. This step of justification is often accompanied with a weakening knowledge of what is right and wrong. Some irrational behavior may also be exhibited. Either the person may encourage others in his family or circle of influence to disregard the commandments, or he or she may become very critical and judgmental of any who deviate even slightly from expected religious behavior. In any case, the responsibility for one's own behavior is cast upon or shared with other people.

Ironically, these same "other people" are often the ones who still have the greatest opportunity to help the sinful person turn his or her life around. They must remain patient and loving, without taking personal offense themselves, as they try to bridge the gaps growing between the sinful individual and themselves and also between the sinner and God. Tragically, at this critical stage, some people will turn against those who can help the most.

5. HYPERCRITICISM—
DISSATISFACTION WITH GOD'S SERVANTS

Once people blame their own transgressions on someone else, the next logical step is to belittle others as they transfer their dissatisfaction of the Church and the gospel as a whole. This fifth step reflects universal human nature: we try to bring others down to our own level when we do not live up to expected standards. Not bold enough to blame God for personal spiritual weaknesses, and not daring to chastise God, sinful people who have apostatized naturally turn against his representatives on the earth. So, they criticize Church leaders, considering their real or imagined weaknesses as legitimate reasons to deny their priesthood authority. They also dispute the revealed doctrines because they no longer live them. If such individuals look into the scriptures, they find fault with the teachings because of supposed awkwardness or ambiguity in the style of writing, irrelevancy, or some other historical or literary quirk. We are signaled that people have taken this step when their faith in God and his restored gospel is severely weakened and when they become hypercritical.

The obvious solution at this step is to humbly recognize God's power and to turn to his servants and the scriptures for counsel; otherwise, as Nephi warned: "Wo be unto him that hearkeneth unto the precepts of men, and denieth the power of God!" (2 Ne. 28:26.) When people reach this step, they are under the influence of those outside God's realm. Indeed, they are beginning to turn against God, his teachings, and his representatives.

6. WITHDRAWAL FROM GOD—
LOSING FELLOWSHIP IN HIS CHURCH

After denying the fundamental authority of Church leaders and the power of God in the Church, the sixth step to apostasy is complete withdrawal from the Church and inactivity. Personal behavior and attitude make the individual feel awkward associating with other Latter-day Saints. Some apostates simply disassociate themselves from any kind of religion, while others seek out religions that may promise as much or more than the restored gospel but make fewer demands on their behavior.

Whether Church disciplinary action is sought or given, the inactive person feels alienated from the Church. At this stage, family and ward members also recognize the obvious signs that the person is outside the circle of Church association. Concerted efforts of fellowship and counseling are necessary to help the individual turn his or her life around. Fellowshipping must be undertaken with pure motives. A wave of disproportionate friendliness by the masses upon recognition of a person's inactivity will never substitute for the consistent encouragement of close friends. Such a turnabout, though very difficult, is not impossible.

By this stage, the critical attitude is sometimes accompanied with bitterness and frustration. Like the intense bitterness that sometimes develops between family members and former friends, backbiting, name-calling, slander, and open argumentation sometimes develop. Most often, the root of the bitterness is buried by this external anger. Long periods of hatred can fester unless the original source of antagonism is identified and resolved. With apostasy, the true root (usually sin) is often covered by murmuring against authorities, insinuations, and doctrinal denials; failure to get to this root can lead to years of misery.

7. DESPONDENCY AND ANTAGONISM—
THE FINAL FRUITS OF APOSTASY

The final stage of personal apostasy is reached when the person gives up and becomes despondent about ever finding peace and fellowship in the Church. This bitter despondency may turn to cynical attacks against the Church or its members, including relatives and former close friends. It is plain to see how accurately Nephi describes Satan's influence on the primrose pathway to apostasy: "Others will he pacify, and lull them away into carnal security, . . . and [he] leadeth them away carefully down to hell. And behold, others he flattereth away, and telleth them there is no hell; and he saith unto them: I am no devil, for there is none—and thus he whispereth in their ears, until he grasps them with his awful chains." (2 Ne. 28:21–22.) Not only will some people give themselves over to Satan's influence, but they may also go one step further and actively persecute and fight against the Church. In other words, they may leave the Church, but they cannot leave it alone.

How easy it is for even faithful followers of Christ to slip from making an occasional exception to the rule to habitual sinful behavior, from activity to inactivity within the Church, from affirming to rejecting authority, from obeying to disobeying the commandments, from maintaining a testimony to denying the faith, and from righteousness to wickedness. The final sad result is that one ends up at the opposite dimension from spirituality. The person has completely traversed the spiritual spectrum from light to darkness, from joy to misery.

TURNING BACK

To reclaim someone from apostasy is difficult, for he or she must go beyond blaming someone else for personal disaffection and instead admit individual errors and sins. If an active member can establish a relationship of trust, then love and a good example—rather than judgments and accusations—can help the inactive or less-active member admit his or her mistakes and regain the desire to have the gospel blessings. Somewhere and somehow, though, a person must recognize one's own spiritual condition and then develop the desire to turn back toward God and his people. Simply stated, one needs to repent—to return to the path from which one has detoured.[3]

The climb back is often a reversal of the seven steps of apostasy: (7) finding a glimmer of hope for changing attitude and behavior; (6) seeking fellowship with the Saints; (5) criticizing one's own actions instead of others' misdeeds; (4) finding reasons for obedience; (3) keeping all the commandments; and (2) striving to overcome weaknesses while (1) increasing spirituality and service. Once back on the path of righteousness, the person continues on it, led by the promptings of the Spirit and one's conscience.

Before leaving the topic of sin and apostasy, it will be helpful to

discuss both the role of our conscience as the enticements of sin are
presented to us and also the possible dangers and values in our struggle
against wickedness.

OUR CONSCIENCE HELPS US RECOGNIZE SIN

Every child of God is born into the world freely endowed with the
light of Christ as a gift. (See D&C 84:45–48.) By virtue of this endowment,
people intuitively know right from wrong and are encouraged to do what
is right. (See Moro. 7:16.) This gift, which enlightens the mind and
prompts righteousness, is called conscience. "Conscience" literally means
"knowing together," a process where our awareness corresponds with
what God wants us to know. It is an inborn sense of right and wrong
even in the absence of all the facts, an instinctive feeling to do right and
to be good. It is a help toward appropriate thoughts, words, and actions.

Every person's conscience is pure and clean at birth. (See D&C
93:38.) However, after an individual arrives at an age of accountability
(when he becomes mature and knowledgeable enough to bear responsibility for his choices), his conscience can be clouded by sin or strengthened by righteousness. Willful disobedience scars and weakens the conscience. (See 1 Tim. 4:2; 1 Cor. 8:7; Titus 1:15.) Spiritual integrity leads
to the companionship of the Holy Ghost. (See Rom. 9:1.)

Wickedness invariably leads to a suppression of conscience, until a
person could lose all influence of the Lord's Spirit. (See 2 Ne. 26:11;
Ether 2:15.) However, a full awareness of sin will smite a person when
in the presence of the Lord or his power. (See Alma 12:1; 29:5; 42:18.)
Ideally, sinful people will recognize their spiritual shortages and repent
so they can regain the Spirit that they enjoyed in their innocence. (See
D&C 1:32–34.) Thus, even though a person has been evil, a change of
attitude and behavior accompanied by a remission of sins can lead to a
restoration of peace and conscience. (See Heb. 9:14; Mosiah 4:3.)

THE DANGERS OF CONFRONTATIONS WITH SIN

Throughout mortality, all of us succumb, at least temporarily, to some
sin or another. We cannot assume that we or anyone else will repent,
although turning back is possible at any of the stages of personal apostasy
discussed earlier. Therefore, we should not step intentionally onto the
path of sin while planning to repent later. There are many dangers

surrounding the path into sin, any one of which may restrict us from turning back to God and thus result in a spiritual death for us. These dangers include destructive friends, behaviors, and attitudes.

As individuals separate themselves from religious, believing people, they tend to choose new friends whose life-styles and behavior reinforce a pattern of disobedience to God's commandments. A teenager who breaks the Word of Wisdom will often "hang out" with other kids with the same habits. A sexually promiscuous man may feel uncomfortable with other Church members and will seek friends with lower standards. The new associates make returning to a religious way of life more difficult.

Once we step onto the path of sin, becoming entrenched is easy because one type of improper or destructive behavior often leads to another. For example, we might not just do something bad, but we may also stop doing good. As we do acts of commission, such as being dishonest or immoral, we might also commit sins of omission, such as not praying or not going to church. President Spencer W. Kimball taught that "the effect of both types of sin can be serious, not only intrinsically but because each type leads naturally to and reinforces the other." He gave an example of an act of commission (fishing on Sunday) that involves an act of omission (neglecting sacrament meeting attendance). Or conversely, "simple non-attendance can, over a period, condition a person to spend Sunday in non-Sabbath pursuits like fishing. Either way Satan wins."[4] As we get entangled in more and more types of spiritually destructive behavior, we are less likely to establish good religious habits.

Whenever we observe problems and catastrophes, it becomes easier to falsely condemn ourselves or to wrongly judge others. Like the friends of Job, we may assume that all disasters and illnesses are the result of wickedness. When the natural tragedies of life hit us or others, we may say, "It serves us (or them) right, and this must be a punishment from God." Such an attitude may bring fear into our lives, but it is not the best attitude to effectively motivate the healthy repentance process. Indeed, we may feel we are hopelessly lost because we fear God's judgments without any hope of redemption.

Other subtle and long-term dangers of sinful behavior exist, all leading to the same result—we give up on ourselves and remain enmeshed in wickedness. We are witnessing the destructive results of sin when our attitudes or actions draw us toward bad and away from good, and it becomes increasingly difficult to leave this path. As we persist in sin, these dangers increase and become more powerful.

SOME VALUES OF CONFRONTATIONS WITH SIN

At times we can learn more from sin than the error of our ways. We learn that the more serious consequences of our improper choices are internal and spiritual rather than outward and physical. God may choose to send tragedies upon us as punishment, but usually the most serious punishment results from the loss of his guidance. But what else can we learn from the sinful behavior of others and ourselves?

As we travel the paths of wickedness, we learn the importance of outside influences, especially friends. Although we have independent spirits, associates and family members definitely affect our attitudes and behavior. Sometimes disturbing experiences with some people teach us about the negative direction our association is taking us. Developing a sense of discernment, we then learn to identify our true and valuable friends—those who uplift and edify us and whose companionship we will cherish throughout eternity. If a few negative experiences encourage us to develop this gift of discernment, then our future, long-term social relationships will be much stronger and more worthwhile.

As we observe our patterns of behavior and areas of weakness, we gain valuable tools that can help us overcome our faults. All of us have weaknesses in one area or another. Indeed, God gives us some weaknesses to humble us and to teach us how to overcome weak things. (See Ether 12:27, 35–41; D&C 50:16.) The scriptures teach us that with faith and endurance, we can turn our weaknesses into strengths. (See 2 Cor. 12:9–10.) With the Lord's help, we can change potential stumbling stones of trials and temptations into stepping stones of spiritual growth. As we learn to overcome, we prepare ourselves to receive God's glory and his eternal blessings. (See Abr. 3:25; D&C 136:31.)

Ironically, it is sometimes in darkness that we finally see ourselves as we really are. Through conflict, we sometimes get to know ourselves and our true nature. As we improve our behavior and come out of darkness, we recognize our capacity to change and appreciate the kind of person we want to become. We learn that we are children of God, drawing nearer to him and increasing our capacity to help others do the same. As we fight and conquer sin, we feel the strength and help we can receive from others, especially God. We witness his love and spiritual powers, along with the value of good, persistent friends. We sense the unity that should prevail in Christ's church on earth and that will permeate God's celestial realm. Sometimes a taste of the bitterness of Satan's hell not only helps us appreciate the sweetness of God's kingdom, but also gives us incentive to help bring it about on earth.

A wise traveler does not have to take the shortcut to realize the advantages of driving on the highway. Likewise, the wise, sensitive person does not have to taste sin to know its bitterness. Observation of others and empathy for their spiritual trials can help us avoid the pitfalls of wickedness. Whatever the taste or experience we may have had with sin and its results, if we have learned to turn back from them and avoid them, then we have gained from our exposure to the world of wickedness. Even better, if we have gained spiritual strength and commitment to build God's kingdom, then others may also benefit from our learning.

In conclusion, *SIN develops when we pervert truth and goodness by disobeying God's commandments, rationalizing our wickedness, criticizing God's works and servants, then becoming despondent, even antagonistic.* The sooner we learn the error of a sinful detour and turn back toward God, the sooner we gain spiritual strength through overcoming temptation, and we can then quickly progress on God's way of righteousness.

For further study, refer to the following entries:

TG	BD	*EM*
Apostasy of	Devil	Apostasy
Individuals	Fall of Adam	Apostate
Darkness, Spiritual	Lucifer	Buffetings of Satan
Disobedience,		Devils
Disobey		Evil
Evil		Fall of Adam
Rebellion, Rebel		Opposition
Sin		Sin
Transgress,		Spiritual Death
Transgression		Temptation
Wickedness, Wicked		

CHAPTER 13

LIFE'S PERFECT WAY THROUGH CHRIST'S ATONEMENT

When embarking on a new and difficult task, we benefit greatly from having a guide or mentor. For example, in learning how to rock-climb, an experienced guide is a must. The guide teaches the principles of climbing before we begin the ascent; he leads the way while scaling the cliff, identifying the best handholds and footholds; additionally, he is capable of rescuing us in case of an accident. In short, a strong, qualified guide makes it possible to safely traverse treacherous terrain, resulting in an exciting and safe experience.

In a similar fashion, to whom do we turn when we need special help, such as after suffering an accident, when struggling with debt, while working through intense family problems? Ideally, we want to consult a wise, loving parent or a caring, capable older sibling or relative. Similarly, Jesus of Nazareth serves as our experienced guide and help through mortality. He has taught us the truths of salvation and lived perfectly, showing us the safest path through life. Finally, through his atonement, he has the power to rescue us. Thus, Jesus Christ is our teacher, role model, and redeemer.

Unfortunately, we do not always heed the Redeemer's gospel teachings or follow his perfect example. Since we all have sinned, we must turn to him, who can not only show us the way out of bondage, but also deliver us unto freedom. We must rely on our divine guide, Jesus Christ.

As discussed in chapters three and nine, Jesus (also known as Jehovah or *Yahweh*) attained spiritual perfection and power in premortality, thus qualifying and enabling him to act in his Father's name to create this world and to administer Elohim's plan of salvation. To carry out that plan, Jehovah himself came to earth to show all mankind the way back to our Heavenly Father's presence. He was born of a mortal woman so that he could experience life as a man and achieve his own salvation in the flesh. But the Messiah was also the only person on this earth to be physically born of the Immortal Father, empowering him both to lead a perfect life and also to ransom himself for the salvation of imperfect human beings.

By looking at some of Christ's own statements in the New Testament, we can grasp the essential reasons why Jesus is our Savior. He particularly made a variety of bold declarations about himself as recorded in the gospel account of John. Reflecting various dimensions of his life and mission, these pronouncements are all prefaced with "I AM." This emphatic form of speech is unusual in Greek, since the personal subject of the verb or the pronoun *I* is not normally expressed. However, this pattern is used in the Greek translation of the Old Testament, particularly when rendering words spoken by God. The phrase "I AM" echoes back to earlier Israelite history when Moses asked the name of the God who had sent him as a prophet to Israel; the Lord told him to say that "I AM hath sent me unto you." (Ex. 3:14.) This compares with modern prophetic references recorded in the Doctrine and Covenants to the "Great I AM," even Jesus Christ. (See D&C 29:1; 38:1; 39:1.)

Nine "I AM" declarations recorded by John provide a helpful outline and comprehensive foundation for our discussion about Jesus and why he is our Savior. The first four use temporal objects and physical terms (*bread, light, door, shepherd*) to symbolize various divine roles. As Elder McConkie stated: "Where ideas and attributes are concerned Deity is the embodiment and incarnation of them. Where inanimate objects are chosen as his names, they are chosen to teach that as they perform a certain temporal function, so the Lord of heaven performs a similar spiritual function which is symbolized by the temporal."[1]

I AM THE BREAD OF LIFE:
JESUS AS THE COMMON MAN

Jesus says he is the "bread of life," using an object of food to demonstrate that just as bread is a necessary staple of life for mortal beings, his life provides essential spiritual sustenance. (See John 6:35, 41, 48, 51.) As indicated in the sacrament prayers, the bread represents his body (see D&C 20:77), which went through physical life in humble circumstances. Like the bread of the earth, the body is a natural, physical object of the soil. Christ's body experienced the common encounters faced by humans, but unlike all other people of this earth who sin in the flesh, Jesus mastered all things material and spiritual in his physical tabernacle.

Simply to gain a mortal body, Jesus might have been born in any number of different physical, social, and economic circumstances. However, he came not just to receive a body, but to experience life in the flesh just like the ordinary masses. Thus, the extreme lowly circumstances of his life and death are no mere coincidence. Without even considering the suffering of the Atonement, the mortal life of Jesus was undoubtedly more difficult than any of ours and yet similar to each of them.

Examples of his common circumstances are found throughout his life. Jesus was not born in a hospital or even at home. His homeless birth was among livestock in a stable. His first few years were spent in humble conditions, first in Bethlehem and then with his refugee family in Egypt. He was not raised in upper-class high society but spent his youth as the stepson of a small-town carpenter in an unprogressive area of a minor Roman province. He received no formal education from any of the renowned Roman, Greek, or Jewish academies of the time, but gained a simple education from the local synagogue and learned the carpentry trade from his stepfather, Joseph. As for his physical appearance, Jesus was not exceptionally striking or handsome. (See Isa. 53:2.) At age thirty, he left his simple trade to become a homeless, itinerant preacher. Jesus endured many types of deprivation during his lifetime: hunger, thirst, fatigue, social ostracism, and public ridicule. He finally was executed as a common criminal and buried in a borrowed tomb. It is actually quite an understatement, then, to say that Jesus received no special privileges on earth, even as the Son of God.

Like the simple bread of the earth, which provides physical life, Jesus lived a humble earth life for a noble spiritual purpose, as recorded by Alma: "He shall go forth, suffering pains and afflictions and temptations of every kind; and this that the word might be fulfilled which saith he will take upon him the pains and the sicknesses of his people. And he will take upon him death . . . and he will take upon him their infirmities, that his bowels may be filled with mercy, according to the flesh, that he may know according to the flesh how to succor his people according to their infirmities." (Alma 7:11–12.) Jesus lived his life and died his death so that when we come to him with our mortal sufferings, he truly knows how we feel.

I AM THE LIGHT OF THE WORLD: JESUS OVERCOMES EVIL

The mission of Jesus was not, of course, just to empathize with our mortal miseries. Many people who have lived and died in poor circumstances could do the same. Christ can enlighten us on how we can overcome not merely the physical hardships, but also the moral and spiritual infirmities of the flesh. We need to know how to come out of the darkness of sin into the light of righteous living. Jesus called himself the "light of the world" and promised that his followers could walk a lighted path through life. (See John 8:12; 9:5.)

The youthful and early adult years of Jesus, the son of Mary, served as basic training for what he was to endure and overcome as the Son of God. His superhuman trials began with forty days in the wilderness prior to the formal beginning of his ministry. Preparing himself with a self-imposed, divinely inspired fast, Jesus squarely faced and conquered the three primary temptations of Satan: abuse of physical appetites, misuse of power, and lust for worldly wealth and glory.

The devil first tempted the physically weakened Christ to make a show of his divine power by turning stones into bread. Then, Satan asked for proof that angelic hosts would support the Son of God in times of danger. Finally, the tempter offered the Lord dominion over the kingdoms and riches of the world. (See Matt. 4:1–11.) The Joseph Smith translation of Matthew's account makes it plain that these were not just token challenges, but very real temptations for the Savior: "When he had fasted forty days and forty nights, *and had communed with God,* he was afterwards an hungered, *and was left to be tempted of the devil.*" (Matt. 4:2, JST; italics added.) Though first strengthened by the Father, Christ was then left to resist the evils of the mortal world of which he was a part. When it was all over, Jesus needed more than bread and water to revive himself physically — "angels came and ministered unto him" as well. (Matt. 4:11.)

Shortly thereafter, Jesus began his public ministry and brought the light of his gospel teachings to the public. As the "light of the world," the example of his triumph over temptation encourages us to overcome the influences of the evil one. Jesus made it clear that he was the example that all should follow in life. When teaching the Nephites upon the American continent, he declared: "I have set an example for you. . . . I am the light which ye shall hold up — that which ye have seen me do." (3 Ne. 18:16, 24.) Later, Christ asked them: "Therefore, what manner of men ought ye to be? Verily I say unto you, even as I am." (3 Ne. 27:27.)

I AM THE DOOR OF THE SHEEPFOLD: JESUS JUDGES OBEDIENCE

In a short allegory, Jesus compared himself to the door of the sheep-fold. (See John 10:7–9.) In Judea, the sheepfold was a cave, sheltered overhang, or four-sided structure with only one entranceway. At eventide, the shepherd would stand in the gateway of the sheep pen and check each sheep for bruises or cuts as it entered. Only by walking past the shepherd could the sheep enter. Thus, the shepherd literally became the door; there was no other way for the sheep to enter the fold. The shepherd was the evaluator; the door was the way. Through Christ alone are healing salvation and heavenly refuge obtained. Just as baptism is the gateway to eternal life, no one comes to the Father except they pass the judgments of the keeper of the gate, the Son of God. Jesus will allow past him only those who know his voice — his disciples.

The word *disciple* has the same root as *discipline,* meaning one who has learned or an obedient pupil. The source of Jesus' learning was Heavenly Father, and he had disciplined himself to obey all that the Father asked him to do and to become all that Elohim wanted him to be. As Christ's disciples, he expects us to do and become the same.

Jesus also set an example by being obedient to the covenants of the gospel. He was without sin, yet at the beginning of his ministry he went unto John the Baptist to be baptized. Matthew records that Jesus said he was baptized to fulfill all righteousness. (See Matt. 3:15.) The Book of Mormon adds that Christ "humbleth himself before the Father, and witnesseth unto the Father that he would be obedient unto him in keeping his commandments. . . . Again, it showeth unto the children of men the straitness of the path, and the narrowness of the gate, by which they should enter, he having set the example before them." (2 Ne. 31:7, 9.) As the door of the sheepfold, Jesus sets the standard by which his disciples will be measured. Christ's life clearly illustrated the significance and importance of obedience and exemplary living.

I AM THE GOOD SHEPHERD:
THE ADMINISTRATOR OF GOD'S COVENANTS

In Old Testament and ancient Near Eastern tradition, the shepherd symbolized a royal caretaker of God's children on earth. The Lord himself is the "Shepherd of Israel." (Ps. 23:1; 80:1; Isa. 40:10–11; Ezek. 34:11–16, 23.) The shepherds had great responsibility and accountability. Thus, even worse than thieves were the false shepherds who led the flocks astray or did not protect them. (See Isa. 56:9–12.) God promised to send Israel the true shepherd. (See Ezek. 34:23.)

Heavenly Father appointed Jesus as the Good Shepherd because he knew that Jesus would faithfully tend God's precious sheep. Indeed, the shepherd would be willing to lay down his life for the sheep. (See John 10:11–18.) Also, as Jesus told the Nephites, his responsibility as a shepherd extended beyond his death and resurrection to teaching and ministering to the scattered remnants of Israel. (See 3 Ne. 15:11 – 16:3.) As the Good Shepherd, Christ works diligently, teaching his sheep to recognize his voice. Those belonging to Christ's flock should hear his voice and respond to his call. (See 3 Ne. 16:5, 11–12; 20:10–14.) His purpose is to fulfill the covenant promises made to the ancient patriarchs.

Unfortunately, even sheep of the best shepherd's flock wander off occasionally. However, Jesus has assured us that even if only one sheep is lost, he will go in search of it. When he finds that lost sheep, he rejoices greatly. (See Matt. 18:1–13.) As members of his flock, we can be assured that the Good Shepherd loves and serves us on an individual basis. When we stray in life, he will search for us, calling our name and reaching out a loving arm to bring us back into the fold.

Being the Good Shepherd and the appointed caretaker of God's children on earth, Christ is the administrator of God's covenants. He also tends the flock as he gathers the sheep from the four quarters of the earth, brings them the fullness of his gospel, and stewards them during the Millennium. (See 3 Ne. 16:5, 10; D&C 133:25.) Being a true and good shepherd requires more than just knowing the sheep of the fold; it also involves nourishing and caring for them. Jesus is the exemplary shepherd.

I AM THE RESURRECTION:
JESUS GUARANTEES OUR IMMORTALITY

Moving from temporal symbols to eternal dimensions, John records Christ's declaration, "I AM the resurrection." (John 11:25; emphasis added.) Resurrection is a capstone of Christ's gospel because it contains the promise of living forever with an immortal body. Because of Jesus and his sacrifice, we all are assured of immortality, and if we live in a way conducive to his will, we can live eternally with him and the Father.

According to Webster, the word *resurrect* can be defined as, "to bring to view, attention, or use again." Because of Christ, we receive hope that immortality seems obtainable, and our attention is directed toward having the best eternal use of our renewed bodies. Shortly before bringing Lazarus back from death, and only a few weeks before his own death, Jesus promised that he was the source of regeneration and life. (See John 11:25.) This is an unconditional, universal promise that guarantees all people a release from physical death because eventually everyone's body and spirit will be reunited through the resurrection.[2] While most mortals fear death, Jesus' promise of universal resurrection supplants fear with peace and hope.

As the firstfruits of the resurrection, Jesus proved the reality of this miracle by appearing to many groups of people throughout the world during the forty days after that first Easter Sunday. When he appeared to his disciples in Judea and Galilee, he ate with them and allowed them to touch him. Thus they finally understood the reality of the resurrection. During these same weeks, Jesus appeared on the American continent where he was seen and touched by great multitudes. The reality of the gift of resurrection was further reinforced as many others also arose from the grave with regenerated bodies. (See Matt. 27:52; 3 Ne. 23:9–10.) Christ's own resurrection had begun the fulfillment of his promise of universal resurrection.[3]

Later, ancient witnesses such as Paul, Mormon, and Moroni also saw the resurrected Christ. In modern times, Joseph Smith and Oliver Cowdery have seen the resurrected Lord. Other resurrected beings have also appeared in this dispensation, including John the Baptist, Peter, and Moroni. Among his visions of the resurrection, the Prophet Joseph Smith records that when the spirits of people are joined with immortal physical bodies, "the same glorious spirit gives them the likeness of glory and bloom. . . . No man can describe it to you — no man can write it."[4] Because of the appearance of Christ and other resurrected beings in ancient and modern times, we know that our Redeemer lives and that we can also obtain a renewed body. This knowledge of Jesus' gift to all brings new hope and understanding into our journey through life.

I AM THE TRUTH:
JESUS TEACHES THE PERFECT DOCTRINE

In John 14, Jesus teaches his apostles on the night before his death about his imminent departure. He explains that he is leaving them but that they should not be troubled, for he is preparing a place for them. In verse four, he states, "Whither I go ye know, and the way ye know." Thomas, perhaps trying to understand this statement in a literal way, asks, "Lord, we know not whither thou goest; and how can we know the way?" (V. 5.) Jesus responds by saying, "I am the way, the truth, and the life: no man cometh unto the Father, but by me." (V. 6.)

What does Jesus' response mean? The key is found in the central element: "I am the truth." Jesus did not teach any falsehoods. He testified concerning the truth of God's existence and love. He taught truth concerning how we may come back into God's presence. His doctrine was pure. Matthew records that "the people were astonished at his doctrine: for he taught as one having authority, and not as the scribes." (Matt. 7:28–29.) Luke adds that "his word was with power." (Luke 4:32.) The people sensed that Jesus was not teaching his own ideas or interpretations — they could tell through his manner and the spiritual power with which he taught that he spoke the truths of God. Jesus himself declared, "My doctrine is not mine, but his that sent me." (John 7:16.) Jesus is thus the truth — his doctrine is the pure doctrine of the Father, untainted by the philosophies of men. We must *know* the truth as he taught and lived it.

Once we accept the truth, the Lord promises us that the truth shall make us free. (See John 8:32.) In view of the Savior's statement, "I am the truth," the meaning becomes clear. Freedom from the bonds of sin can come only through the doctrine of repentance and the power of Christ's atonement. Bruce R. McConkie also explains that the truth shall make us "free from the damning power of false doctrine; free from the bondage of appetite and lust; free from the shackles of sin; free from every evil and corrupt influence and from every restraining and curtailing power; free to go on to the unlimited freedom enjoyed in its fulness only by exalted beings."[5] If we accept Christ and his gospel as truth, we will enjoy the priceless gift of freedom.

I AM THE WAY:
JESUS SHOWS THE PERFECT EXAMPLE

In addition to correct belief, Jesus teaches us correct practice. In religious studies, the technical term for "correct belief" is *orthodoxy,* and the term for "correct practice" is *orthopraxy.* Some religions, such as some modern Protestant movements, emphasize correct belief (ortho-doxy) at the expense of practice. Other religions, such as Islam, stress correct practice (orthopraxy) without major emphasis upon beliefs. When Jesus said he was the *way* and the *truth,* he was teaching that both orthopraxy and orthodoxy are necessary to enter into God's kingdom.

After Jesus triumphed over Satan's three major temptations in their initial encounter, the Lord embarked upon his ministry to teach us how to do the same. For centuries prior to Christ, the wisest of the pagan philosophers instructed men how to judiciously use power and wealth to reward friends and punish enemies—the same tactics Satan uses. Jesus corrected such worldly wisdom with simple, revolutionary doctrines that comprise the core of his message on how to live.

First, Jesus taught that we should be the masters of our whole bodies and that we should control not only the appetites of the flesh, but also the thoughts of the heart. (See Matt. 5:27–30.) In addition, he instructed that emotions and feelings can be controlled and directed to positive, edifying means of expression. (See Matt. 5:21–26, 38–42.) He also taught both the power and importance of fasting and the weaknesses of gluttony and excess. (See Mark 9:29; Matt. 11:19; 23:25.) If we trust in the Lord and truly seek his kingdom, he will provide the food and clothing we need to sustain us and our families. (See Matt. 6:31–33.)

Second, Jesus was not distracted—as many honorable Gentiles were—with how one can quickly earn and spend money. Instead, he told his disciples not to place their priority upon worldly treasure, "for your heavenly Father knoweth that ye have need of all these things. But seek ye first the kingdom of God, and his righteousness; and all these things shall be added unto you." (Matt. 6:32–33.) To not even try to gain wealth is poor financial advice according to many world's economists, and to purge all desire for wealth would be heresy according to the gospel of Satan. Ironically, those who promise that anything in this world can be bought with money do not acknowledge the creative source and ultimate distributor of all material things—God.

Third, when his own disciples were arguing among themselves as to which of them would have supremacy in the kingdom of heaven, Jesus gently rebuked them for seeking power like the Gentiles, saying, "Whosoever will be chief among you, let him be your servant: even as the Son of man came not to be ministered unto, but to minister, and to give his life a ransom for many." (Matt. 20:27–28.) Loving service, not manipulative control, is the trademark of the Master and his disciples.

In summary, Jesus contrasts his ways to the ways of the Gentiles, and he supplants the basic worldly formula for personal benefit: "Ye have heard that it hath been said, Thou shalt love thy neighbor, and hate thine enemy. But I say unto you, Love your enemies, bless them that curse you, do good to them that hate you, and pray for them which despitefully use you, and persecute you; that ye may be the children of your Father which is in heaven." (Matt. 5:43–45.) Christ overcame the world by overcoming evil through love.

These doctrines, with an emphasis on love, prepare us to counter Satan's three major temptations. The Lord's sublime teachings become the truth and the way to ultimately live in the kingdom of heaven, and they also enable us to live peacefully and joyfully in the present world. The truths Jesus taught truly do make us free—free from dominating appetites, worldly materialism, selfish jealousy, and the corrupting lust for power and revenge.

Jesus' doctrines are simple to understand but sometimes difficult to live. How can we overcome the desire to gain power and glory? How can we be in the world but not be overly concerned with wealth, materialism, comfort, and security? And how can we sincerely seek good for those who attempt our destruction? The answer is that we cannot without the Savior's assistance. We must rely upon the godly power of Christ, remembering that his doctrine did not stop at "I will *teach* you the way," or even "I will *show* you the way." Rather, he says, "I *am* the way . . . : no man cometh unto the Father, but by me." (John 14:6; italics added.) Thus, proper conduct—patterned after Jesus—is the "way" to exaltation.

This is reflected in what Jesus taught elsewhere. Jesus also says, "For I have given you an example, that ye should do as I have done to you." (John 13:15.) To his disciples, Jesus states, "Whosoever will come after me, let him deny himself, and take up his cross, and follow me." (Mark 8:34.) In the good-shepherd discourse, he adds, "My sheep hear my voice, and I know them, and they follow me." (John 10:27.) In his resurrected ministry in the Book of Mormon, he explains in a more direct manner, "Therefore, what manner of men ought ye to be? Verily I say unto you, even as I am." (3 Ne. 27:27.) Thus, when Jesus proclaims that he is the way, he means that if one desires salvation, one must follow the model of conduct he gave. Jesus is our role model. We must not only *know* his truth and *do* his will, but we need to *be*come as he is.

Compared with great exemplary people who have lived on this earth, our Lord and Savior Jesus Christ is greater than all. In his life we can find every quality that will help us progress toward perfection. (See 3 Ne. 12:48.) President Ezra Taft Benson commented, "While many men have admirable qualities, there is only one man who ever walked the earth who was without sin, whose father of his physical body was God the Father, and who had the power to resurrect his own body. This Jesus is our exemplar and has commanded us to follow in his steps."[6]

I AM THE LIFE: JESUS' ENDURING GIFT

The third attribute of Christ listed in John 14:6 is that Jesus is the *life*. The meaning of this phrase is more apparent than the first two elements of *truth* and *way* because Christ is our Resurrector and Savior. Only through his atoning sacrifice may we return to live with the Father.

Latter-day Saints understand that the Atonement had a twofold purpose. First, Christ redeemed humanity from physical death: *all* shall be resurrected. (See 1 Cor. 15:20–22.) Second, Christ atoned for our sins so we could return to the presence of the Father if we would repent. (See 1 Pet. 2:24.) These two concepts were taught by the Book of Mormon prophet Jacob: "He [Christ] cometh into the world that he may save all men if they will hearken unto his voice; for behold, he suffereth . . . this that the resurrection might pass upon all men, that all might stand before him at the great and judgment day. And he commandeth all men that they must repent, and be baptized in his name, having perfect faith in the Holy One of Israel, or they cannot be saved in the kingdom of God." (2 Ne. 9:21–23.)

When Jesus says that he is the life, the doctrine goes beyond the promise of physical resurrection — he is speaking about the second sense of his atonement. This distinction appears in John 11:25, where Jesus seems to separate the promise of a general resurrection of all people and his atonement for the sins of the repentant: "I am the resurrection, and the life: he that believeth in me, though he were dead, yet shall he live." In other words, when Jesus teaches that he is the life, he means that only through him may we return to live with the Father. This is exactly what he says in John 14:6: "I am . . . the life: no man cometh unto the Father, but by me." We must *accept Christ* as our Savior and repent if we want eternal life with him and the Father.

Thus, we understand Jesus' teaching, "No man cometh unto the Father, but by me," as meaning, "In order to enter the Father's kingdom, you must do as I have done, you must know the truths of the gospel as I know them, and you must accept me as your Savior so that your sins may be cleansed from you." In this manner Jesus is the way, the truth, and the life.

I AM THE TRUE VINE:
OUR SOURCE OF SPIRITUALITY

The vine culture is well known in the Mediterranean area. The vine draws nutrients and moisture from the soil and air and then passes them on to the branches, which produce the fruit. Without the vine, the branches are dead kindling. Pruning is necessary to increase productivity. When a gardener prunes his vineyard, he cuts off the dead, withered sections and the less-productive branches. He also prunes the productive branches so they can produce bigger fruits. A good husbandman carefully tends the fruitful branches to insure a steady, good crop.

Christ likens us to the branches on a vine. He teaches, "I am the true vine, and my Father is the husbandman. . . . I am the vine, ye are the branches: he that abideth in me, and I in him, the same bringeth forth much fruit: for without me ye can do nothing." (John 15:1, 5.) This profound analogy contains many lessons. God the Father is the supreme supervisor, and Jesus is the direct source of strength by which we bring forth the fruits of the gospel. Our good fruits should be a godlike life (see Matt. 3:8; 7:16–20) and a noble character (see Gal. 5:22–23; Eph. 5:9; Philip. 1:11). However, just as the branch cannot bear fruit by itself, we cannot produce anything of value without or apart from Jesus.

Applying the abstract precepts and teachings of Christ in our daily lives prepares us to receive true salvation, just as the mere human experiences of Jesus prepared him to fulfill his duties as the transcendent Son of God. The mysterious, miraculous, but literal transformation of human beings into sons and daughters of God (the fruit) is made possible through the atonement of Christ (the vine). His atoning sacrifice is the real and only way we, who are imperfect, can follow the Perfect One in the perfect way.

JESUS THE JUST AND THE MERCIFUL

Before we can fully appreciate Christ's atoning sacrifice, we must understand the relationship of the law of justice and the law of mercy. These two laws are best understood when we know about the necessity of "opposition in all things" and the choices placed before Christ before he took upon himself the sins of the world.

The clearest discussion about the necessity of opposition and choice is given by Lehi in 2 Nephi 2:11–27. He explains the interplay between law, punishment, blessings, and agency:

   1. Every law has both a punishment and a blessing attached to it.
   2. Disobedience to law requires a punishment that results in misery.
   3. Obedience to law provides a blessing that results in joy.

4. Without law there can be neither punishment nor blessing, neither sorrow nor happiness — only innocence.

5. Thus joy can exist only where the possibility of misery also exists.

6. In order to exercise agency, we must have freedom of choice; in a world without law, no choices between right and wrong could exist, and thus our freedom to choose and to exercise our agency would be nonfunctional. (See also Alma 12:31–32; 42:17–25.)

Lehi does not say that choosing evil is necessary to recognize good and evil, but he does make it clear that a choice between opposites is necessary for spiritual growth. Indeed, Christ's perfect life demonstrates that the most simple and sure way to attain eternal joy and celestial perfection is to never choose evil but to always follow the Father. (See D&C 130:20–21; 132:5.)

The divine law of justice is a natural manifestation of the principles both of opposition and of agency. It relates to the other divine laws, or commandments, and provides the means by which people receive their just reward. In essence, the law of justice might be summarized by these three points:

1. Every law has both a punishment and a blessing attached to it.

2. Whenever the law is transgressed, a punishment must be inflicted.

3. Whenever a law is obeyed, a reward must be given.

The choice between good and evil presupposes agency; the exercise of our agency activates the law of justice and its resulting blessings and punishments. On the other hand, without choices, we cannot exercise agency and thus experience the full range of blessings and punishments.[7] Many passages in the Doctrine and Covenants indicate that blessings and punishments are predicated upon the laws and judgments of God. God is absolutely just in rewarding each individual according to his or her works, based upon individual levels of knowledge, accountability, motivation, and so on. (See, for example, D&C 82:10; 121:36–37; 130:20–21; see also Rom. 2:5–6; 2 Ne. 9:25; Mosiah 3:11; Alma 41:2–6; 3 Ne. 27:14.) The relationship of agency, laws, choices between good and evil, and the other elements of the law of justice may be diagrammed as a flow chart like this:

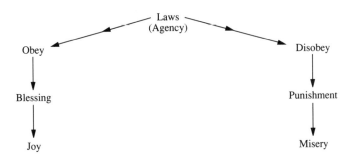

If we are free to choose between good and evil after the laws of God have been given to us, then we are free to receive either the blessings and joy for our obedience or the punishment and misery for our disobedience. Freedom of choice does not mean freedom from consequences.

Christ's atonement satisfies the law of justice. However, as Isaiah explains in 53:4–6, Jesus did not have to suffer for any of his own sins, because he lived a perfect life. God satisfied the demands of justice by allowing Christ to accept our punishment. At first thought, Christ's suffering for our sins does not seem just, since the law of justice requires that God be impartial. Indeed, as the Lord has said: "I, the Lord, am bound when ye do what I say; but when ye do not what I say, ye have no promise" (D&C 82:10); and, "When we obtain any blessing from God, it is by obedience to that law upon which it is predicated" (D&C 130:20–21). Rather, the reason Christ accepted our punishment has to do with mercy.

WHY IS JESUS SO MERCIFUL AND KIND?

The law of justice can make no allowances, and by it, everyone stands condemned because "all have sinned, and come short of the glory of God." (Rom. 3:23.) Our just yet loving Heavenly Father has thus allowed his Son to suffer for our sins, so justice is thereby satisfied and we are spared. This provision is called the law of mercy. In effect, this law becomes part of the law of justice for it introduces the possibility of vicarious payment for broken laws.

The law of mercy might be paraphrased as follows: whenever a person transgresses a law, a payment must be made; however, the person who transgressed the law does not need to make the payment *if* he or she will repent of this disobedience and *if* he or she can find someone else who is both *able* and *willing* to make the payment. The law of mercy expects that the demands of the law of justice will be fully met. Alma explained the relationship this way: "Justice exerciseth all his demands, and also mercy claimeth all which is her own; and thus, none but the truly penitent are saved. What, do ye suppose that mercy can rob justice? I say unto you, Nay; not one whit. If so, God would cease to be God." (Alma 42:24–25.)

Christ's atonement provides an essential element in both the law of justice and the law of mercy. The law of justice made the atonement of Jesus Christ *necessary.* When Adam fell, he transgressed a law that carried physical and spiritual death as its punishment. Thus, the law of justice demanded payment (or reparation, which is one meaning of atonement) for the broken law. The law of mercy made the atonement of Jesus Christ *possible.*

In order for Jesus Christ to pay fully for the law that Adam transgressed, the Savior had to be both *able* and *willing* to make reparation. He was *willing* to make payment because of his great love for mankind, and he was *able* to make payment because he lived a sinless life and, as the Son of God, he had the power and calling to atone for the spiritual and physical death introduced by the Fall. Because of his atoning sacrifice, he is rightfully referred to as the Savior and Redeemer of all mankind.[8]

Interestingly, the word *forgive* does not appear in Isaiah 53, where Isaiah has written about the vicarious suffering of the Messiah, although the Hebrew root *nasa,* from which the word *forgive* is usually translated, does appear twice, as "borne" in verse four and "bare" in verse twelve. (See also Isa. 2:9; 33:24.) Christ "bore" or carried our sins so that we do not have to carry their burden. (See John 1:29; 1 Pet. 1:18–20.) Or, as we say, "He has *forgiven* us," meaning he "gave" the price "before." Indeed, almost two thousand years before our time, he gave the necessary payment in the Garden of Gethsemane. As we realize the benefits of his suffering and are cleansed, we can find the joy that God wants all of us to experience becoming worthy to live in his presence. (See 2 Ne. 2:25; 9:21.)

The relationship between the law of justice, the law of mercy, and Christ's atonement may be illustrated like this:

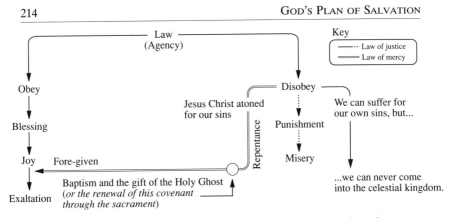

Before the law of mercy can apply in our lives, we must take advantage of Christ's atonement by repenting of our sins.[9] The prophets have constantly reminded God's children of the necessity to repent and seek for the blessings of the Lord.

Some of the blessings promised Israel and other peoples are not conditional upon the people's repentance and righteousness. For example, every person benefits *unconditionally* from one major aspect of the Atonement—the resurrection and Christ's payment for the original transgression of Adam and Eve. The Atonement also unconditionally satisfies the demands of justice for sins committed by ignorant and unaccountable individuals. (See Mosiah 3:11; Moses 6:54.) However, there are also *conditional* aspects of the Atonement, and in order to benefit from these, we must repent of our sins. Otherwise, "mercy could have claim . . . no more" (Mosiah 3:26) upon the person because "none but the truly penitent are saved" (Alma 42:24).[10]

HOW IMPERFECT BEINGS ARE PURIFIED THROUGH THE ATONEMENT

In the Sermon on the Mount, Christ gives the injunction, "Be ye therefore perfect." (Matt. 5:48.) The thought of being perfect in any dimension of our lives is overwhelming. Many think that being perfect in every aspect of life and character is impossible. But if Jesus was the only person on earth capable of achieving perfection, is his commandment legitimate? We know that with God, nothing is impossible. (See Luke 1:37.) What does he mean when he wants us to be perfect?

The answer becomes clear as we consider the definition of "perfection." Perfection can be defined as "setting out for a definite point or goal and achieving it." The Hebrew and Greek roots of the Bible terms translated as *perfect* or *perfection* refer to wholeness or completeness. In other words, "Be ye therefore whole (or complete) even as your Father in Heaven is whole (or complete)."[11] This gives us some hope that we can obtain perfection in a step-by-step, gradual, and sure process.

Our Heavenly Father knew that all of us would sin during mortality; thus Jesus was foreordained to be our Savior. Since we cannot save our imperfect selves, we need Christ's help. Perfection is a process: when we sin, we need to follow through with all the steps of repentance and thereby take advantage of Christ's atonement. The Lord's admonition to Abraham gives us a pattern to follow: "Walk before me, and be thou perfect. And I will make my covenant between me and thee, and will multiply thee exceedingly." (Gen. 17:1–2.) There are a few keys in these verses that direct us in our perfection process.

First, the Lord says, "Walk before me." When we walk in the Lord's presence by the way we live, surely then we are on the path toward perfection. We walk before the Lord in our actions and thoughts, and we become one with him because our desires are united with his. Second, the Lord says, the covenant is "between me and thee." He wants us to succeed, and he promises to help us. Working toward perfection is not only a commandment, but a covenant into which we enter with the Lord. If we truly desire and strive to fulfill this commandment, the Lord will help us to obtain it. Third, the Lord promises, "I will multiply thee exceedingly." He can bless us with gifts, helps, and capacities untold — both in this life and especially in the life to come.

As we keep the commandments and repent of those we have transgressed, we gradually become righteous and perfect in more and more areas of our life. The state of being perfect is not necessarily a measure of all we have ever done; rather, it is a measure of our attitude and our pattern of spiritual growth and development. A person who continually strives to correct misdeeds through repentance and the Atonement can be cleansed of the past and be placed on the proper path toward perfection. President Spencer W. Kimball said, "Perfection really comes through overcoming."[12] Patient, persistent people striving for perfection are described in the scriptures as "they who are just men made perfect through Jesus the mediator of the new covenant, who wrought out this perfect atonement through the shedding of his own blood." (D&C 76:69.) With Heavenly Father's spiritual treasures, gifts, and blessings, and through Christ's atonement, perfection can still be gained.

We must remember, however, that although individual repentance is a prerequisite for receiving God's greatest blessings, nothing we can or ever could do by ourselves is sufficient payment to satisfy all the demands of justice. Ultimately, redemption and salvation are Heavenly Father's gifts to us, "for we know that it is by grace that we are saved, after all we can do." (2 Ne. 25:23.) We do not earn God's mercy; he shares it with us as a freewill offering out of his infinite love.

In conclusion, we see that Jesus has not only shown us the way to live through his gospel teachings and perfect life, but he has also helped us by providing the means to overcome death and hell. In summary, *JESUS of Nazareth lived a sinless life, taught eternal values, and became the PERFECT WAY—showing all people the path toward happiness, holiness, and exaltation; his ATONEMENT satisfied both the demands of justice and the expectations of mercy, bringing salvation to God's children.* We should constantly thank our Heavenly Father for the life and mission of his Son, our Savior. As we follow Jesus in our thoughts and attitudes and in our words and deeds, we will be on the path of eternal life leading us back to God's presence. And as our being becomes more like his, filled with love and goodness, we will be united and perfected with him and our Heavenly Father.

For further study, refer to the following entries:

TG	BD	EM
Atonement	Atonement	Atonement of Jesus
Jesus Christ,	Blood	Christ
Atonement through		Jesus Christ
Jesus Christ,		Justice and Mercy
Redeemer		Justification
Jesus Christ, Savior		Perfection
Justice		Sanctification
Mercy, Merciful		
Perfection, Perfect,		
Perfectly		
Salvation		

CHAPTER 14

DEATH'S NEW BEGINNINGS

Life frequently presents favorable times for new beginnings. Children move from school to school as they advance through the educational system, adults change jobs, and families move to different homes or apartments. New starts may produce some anxiety and stress as people are forced to leave loved ones and adapt to new settings. New beginnings also provide opportunities for new friends and service while adjustments to new environments and sets of activities are made. Before long, the new locations become "home." However, there is one final move that all people dread because of the many unknowns surrounding it. This transition is more than a change of location; it is a change of existence, an exit from the land of the living through the gateway of death.

From our limited perspective as mortals on earth, death appears to be the end of our existence. However, from the perspective of the scriptures, the prophets, and many people who have closely faced death, it is just a new beginning. Death is not the end of life but a transition to a different sphere of existence, a passageway into a new dimension—the postmortal spirit world. The promise of life after death and the eventual resurrection of the physical body is a cornerstone of Christian faith.

WHAT IS DEATH?

Death is a benchmark in the continuation of our lives as spirit beings, marking the date when our physical shells are laid to rest. At death, body and spirit separate for a time. (See James 2:26; Eccl. 12:7.) Though we may be upset that the fall of Adam and Eve eventually brings death to every one of us, we should also remember that the results of death are temporary because Christ's atonement and resurrection will rescue us all from death. (See 1 Cor. 15:21–22.)[1]

The scriptural promises of a spirit life after physical death are complemented with the accounts of people who have had "near-death" or brief "after-death" experiences; they often no longer fear death because they see life in a new context. In the best-selling book *Life after Life,* and in its sequel *Reflections on Life after Life,* Raymond A. Moody, Jr., M.D., compiled and analyzed "out-of-the-body" experiences of people who were revived from clinical death. Dr. Moody and others talked about individuals who have had "after-death" experiences and who have gone through a different dimension of space until they realized they were in a different existence in the presence of a glorious being.

This being radiated extreme dignity, power, light, and love. They knew, by looking at this person, that this being knew all there was to know about them. They sensed that there was a partial judgment about to take place. They were given the option of having their spirit return into the physical body and living for another number of years. Almost all of these individuals no longer fear death but rather live under a more noble, eternal set of priorities in which service to others and love are more important than honors and material possessions. Death was an actual experience they had "lived through," and they no longer dreaded it. More importantly, they developed a new set of more eternal priorities.

From these combined sources, we learn that we need not fear death. (See D&C 101:36.) As we grow in faith and knowledge, our fears about the natural experience of death will be calmed.

Nevertheless, we are often curious about the conditions of life we will experience after our physical body dies and our soul still lives. When we die, we leave behind the physical body and its sensations of hunger, thirst, pain, and weariness. Although all material and earthly things are left behind, we carry many possessions of greater worth with us into the future spirit world, such as our accumulated knowledge, the memories of our experiences, our social and family relationships, our eternal intelligence, and other spiritual gifts. Our spirit is free to move and communicate and remains full of life and vigor. Brigham Young stated that when we have moved through the veil of death, we "have passed from a state of sorrow, grief, mourning, woe, misery, pain, anguish and disappointment into a state of existence, where [we] can enjoy life to the fullest extent as far as that can be done without a body."[2]

A SPIRIT WORLD WITH NATURAL CONTRASTS

Although we shed our physical body at death, the memories of the flesh remain with us. The influences of a physical body also remain with us to the extent that we have allowed them power over our spirit. If we have successfully conquered the attractions and appetites of the flesh, our disciplined spirits are freed from the temptations and pains of earth life and enter into a spirit bliss, a tranquil heaven. On the other hand, if our bodies have sinfully ruled our souls in mortality, our spirits remain in bondage to the cravings of the flesh, which cannot be satisfied in a spirit world—thus, we are consigned to a spirit torment, a terrible hell. Recognizing how this life affects the next, an ancient prophet, Alma, wisely warned us: "If we do not improve our time while in this life, then cometh the night of darkness wherein there can be no labor performed. . . . For that same spirit which doth possess your bodies at the time that ye go out of this life, that same spirit will have power to possess . . . [you] in that eternal world." (Alma 34:33–34.) Spirit beings are influenced by the yearnings of the physical world even though they are no longer a part of it. No longer able to manipulate or control a physical body, their relative tranquility or torment depends upon how independent their spirit was of the flesh before death separated the body and spirit.

The teachings of the ancient prophets coincide with some modern findings in the medical profession. The studies of Dr. Moody describe various aspects of the realm of spirits, including a portrayal of those still bound to the desires of the flesh:

> Several people have reported to me that at some point they glimpsed other beings who seemed to be "trapped" in an apparently most unfortunate state of existence. Those who described seeing these confused beings are in agreement on several points. First, they state that these beings seemed to be, in effect, unable to surrender their attachments to the physical world. One man recounted that the spirits he saw apparently "couldn't progress on the other side because their God is still living here." That is, they seemed bound to some particular object, person, or habit. Secondly, all have remarked that these beings appeared "dulled," that their consciousness seemed somehow limited in contrast with that of others. Thirdly, they say it appeared that these "dulled spirits" were to be

there only until they solved whatever problem or difficulty was keeping them in that perplexed state."[3]

Note how this description concurs with that of Alma. First, they
cannot change the desires or attitude of their spirit "because their god
[or physical habit] is still living here [as a part of the earth]." Second,
their "dulled" or restricted spirits are in a "night of darkness wherein
there can be no labor performed."

When an angel visited and taught him, Alma received later insights
about the period directly after death. He recorded: "The spirits of those
who are righteous are received into a state of happiness, which is called
paradise, a state of rest, a state of peace, where they shall rest from all
their troubles and from all care, and sorrow. . . . The spirits of the
wicked . . . shall be cast into outer darkness; there shall be weeping, and
wailing, and gnashing of teeth, and this . . . [is] a state of awful, fearful
looking for the fiery indignation of the wrath of God upon them; thus
they remain in this state, as well as the righteous in paradise, until the
time of their resurrection." (Alma 40:12–14.)

Thus a partial judgment occurs after death as people enter the world
of spirits — the righteous to a state of rest and peace; the wicked to a
state of darkness and fear. These two states are called *paradise* and *prison,*
and we remain in this spirit world in either state until our resurrection.
(See Luke 23:43; 1 Pet. 3:19; D&C 138:16.) Eventually, each of us will
enter one of these two postmortal existences. Since the state we find
ourselves in is dependent upon the way we live, a preview of both states
may help us decide how to conduct our lives.

SPIRIT PARADISE

The spirits of those who are righteous are received into a state of
happiness called paradise, where they enjoy respite from earthly cares,
expand in wisdom, increase their gospel understanding, serve the Lord,
and prepare for a resurrected state of eternal glory. In short, they continue their progression as eternal intelligences.

And who will enter the state of paradise? It will be peopled by the
spirits of just, good, and pure people: innocent children who die before
the age of eight, followers of God who are faithful in their testimony,
people who are humble and selfless, and individuals who sacrifice for

the Lord and suffer for righteousness' sake. (See Alma 40:12, 14; D&C 138:12–13.) What is life like in paradise? For innocent children and the severely handicapped, who die before reaching an age or stage of accountability and who thus have not sinned before God, paradise is a place of enlightened learning and social companionship. For those righteous older mortals who have struggled with and prevailed against the enemies of God, paradise is a peaceful spiritual haven. But more than a place separated from the trauma and temptations of earthlife, paradise is a state of tranquility, rest, and peace; a time of joyful reunion with family and friends; an experience of joy, gladness, and happiness; and an opportunity to learn, grow, and progress.

Spirit paradise is more than a resting stage removed from physical and moral obstacles, it is an enhanced preparation period for the eternities. Not only do we build upon the learning and understanding we gained in the flesh, but we also gain spiritual growth and learning much faster in this spirit realm for a variety of reasons.

First, since the physical demands of our bodies will have vanished, the necessity of working for daily bread and of sleeping to rejuvenate our bodies will disappear, and other limitations of the flesh will be left behind. As spirit beings with new dimensions of time and energy, we can concentrate on acquiring spiritual knowledge faster and more fully than now. Second, physical restraints on our spiritual understanding will have disappeared, making our learning time much more effective. As Brigham Young taught, all things will be easily understood because we will understand natural things, and our ability to learn will be greatly facilitated.[4] Third, the dimensions of the world will open as the barriers of time and space fall away: "If we want to behold Jerusalem as it was in the days of the Savior; or if we want to see the Garden of Eden as it was when created, there we are, and we see it as it existed spiritually, for it was created first spiritually and then temporally, and spiritually it still remains."[5] In addition, we will gain a remembrance of our premortal spirit existence and will be able to observe and understand things from a more eternal perspective.

So, though frustrated in some ways without the normal, pleasurable sensations of the physical body, God's spirit children in paradise are freed from earthly demands and are liberated in other ways to pursue knowledge and do the work of the Lord while awaiting resurrection.

SPIRIT PRISON

The spirits of those who are evil and wicked are cast into a state of misery called prison, where they experience darkness and uncertainty while suffering for sins and transgressions. For the duration of their time there, they suffer the punishing presence of Satan and dread the future judgment of God.

Who will be cast into this spirit prison, which is also commonly called hell? It will be occupied by the spirits of the wicked and ungodly, individuals who reject the promptings of moral conscience or spiritual testimony, people who are unrepentant and selfish, those who give themselves over to Satan's power, and those who cause others to suffer. (See Alma 40:13–14; D&C 76:103–6; 138:20, 29.) What is life like in prison? It is a state of turmoil, chaos, and confusion; a place of darkness, weeping, and wailing; an experience of guilt, anguish, and sorrow; and a period to suffer the wrath of Almighty God by being turned over to the buffetings of Satan, as the devil torments, taunts, and harasses those under his subjection. This spiritual state is a hellish environment because of the contentions of Satan, fears for the future, and the inhabitants' awareness that they are suffering this anguish because of their transgressions on earth. They will see where they are in contrast to what they might have obtained through righteous living.

Spirit prison is more than just a punishment for the past; it is also a purging for the future. Recognizing the evil designs, hatred, and torment of Satan in spirit prison will convince telestial people that, in contrast, God is indeed good, loving, and fair. The manifestation of opposites helps them appreciate the true nature of God and the devil. Their hatred of Satan also encourages a hatred of evil. Thus their suffering in hell not only punishes for their past but turns them away from wickedness. Through such a bitter experience, they learn to never sin again. Some, however, though they have left behind evil and wickedness, may still not want to serve God and others with full, genuine love. This may be like a reformed drug or substance abuser who leaves the negative, destructive past behind but does not choose to be a strong, supportive member of the family or community.

A variety of attitudes will be manifest in spirit prison. Some people will persist in their wickedness, a few will simply turn aside from bad behavior, and others will not only give up the bad but also strive to do good. Most spirits in prison will eventually pay the full price for their wickedness, and at the end of this earth's temporal history, they will be called up in the resurrection of the unjust, ready for their less glorious eternal state. For a very few of the most evil spirits, however, spirit prison is just the beginning taste of a hell they will experience forever.[6] (This spirit prison is but a temporary station until they are cast out with Satan and his other followers into the final and eternal hell of outer darkness.) On the other hand, many spirits will learn of their past ignorance and mistakes and will seek more righteous attitudes. For these, the experience in prison will convince them to change their behavior.

Dr. Moody observed this aspect of the spirit world when his patients said that it appeared that those "dulled spirits" in bondage were to be there only until they solved whatever problem or difficulty was keeping them in that perplexed state.[7] This concept agrees with New Testament teachings and LDS doctrine, for when the spirits in prison repent, they can leave their hell and join the righteous in spirit paradise as they await their resurrection. It is important to outline, however, what is required for this release from spirit prison.

RELEASE FROM PRISON

Before the time of Christ, the spirits held in prison were unable to gain paradise, because the Savior had not yet atoned for mankind's sins in the flesh. Thus, as Nephi saw in vision, there was "an awful gulf, which separated the wicked from the tree of life, and also from the saints of God." (1 Ne. 15:28; see also Luke 16:19–26.) This gulf was bridged, however, after the Atonement was completed. Writing an account of his vision of the spirit world, Joseph F. Smith states that between the crucifixion and resurrection, the Savior visited spirit paradise, "declaring liberty to the captives [of death and the spirit world] who had been faithful," for even the righteous "had looked upon the long absence of their spirits from their bodies as a bondage." (D&C 138:18, 50.) Jesus instructed and commissioned the righteous spirits, then sent them from paradise to preach the gospel to the spirits in prison, both "those who had died in their sins, without a knowledge of the truth," and those "in transgression, having rejected the prophets." (D&C 138:32.)

Why didn't the Lord himself go to declare liberty among the unjust? First, aside from the fact that he was in the spirit world for only a brief time, Christ withheld his presence and direct influence from the wicked so they might legitimately receive a chance at salvation under conditions similar to those on earth. Spirit beings in prison needed to learn the principles of faith and testimony. They had to prove that they would accept the prophets' words, which they either had not known or had disregarded in mortality. This gives them the chance to respond to the Lord's messengers when gospel truths are clearly presented to them.

Second, because of their unrighteous acts in the flesh, they had to suffer for their own sins (to the degree of their accountability) in the spirit before they could be released. (See D&C 19:15–20.) While in the flesh, all men have potential superiority over Satan and his hosts, who have only bodies of spirit. But if the flesh and spirit together are not redeemed through the Atonement and the ordinances of salvation, Satan can and does have dominion over the wicked after death. Having had bodies, however, spirits in prison can repent for deeds done in the flesh and seek for Christ's deliverance and for the companionship of the righteous in spirit paradise.

Third, spirit beings must receive earthly ordinances performed vicariously for them in holy temples by the living. Many of the dead have waited literally for centuries for this work to be done, but only in the last hundred years have the Saints performed vicarious ordinances on a large scale. Unfortunately, too, for spirits in the spirit world, "the last shall be first and the first shall be last," since more recent genealogy must necessarily be completed first and then traced backward.[8]

To liberate themselves, then, the unrighteous must accept the gospel preached to them by the Lord's spirit missionaries. Then, they must repent and accept responsibility for their sins and take advantage of Christ's atoning sacrifice. And finally, since they no longer possess physical bodies, they must wait for others to perform vicarious ordinances for them on earth. Thus, President Smith concluded the record of his vision with these terms: "The dead *who repent* will be redeemed, *through obedience to the ordinances of the house of God,* and *after they have paid the penalty of their transgressions,* and are washed clean, shall receive a reward according to their works, for they are heirs of salvation." (D&C 138:58–59; italics added.)

Apparently there are at least four primary paths by which humans pass through the postmortal spirit world: (1) They are righteous during mortality and thus qualify to enter paradise in preparation for a celestial resurrection. (2) They commit transgressions but live without the gospel light during mortality, and thus they are sent to spirit prison where they accept the gospel and later join the company of the righteous in paradise. (3) They are wicked in this life and reject the gospel when it is presented and witnessed to them, and thus they go to spirit prison, where they suffer until their sins are paid for. Then, depending upon the nature of their attitudes and past behavior, they are eventually resurrected on a terrestrial or telestial level. (4) They are grossly wicked in this life, sinning against light and truth, and they refuse to accept that God's judgments are just, continuously rebelling against him. Thus they are sent to hell where their suffering begins and continues beyond the time when they are finally resurrected and sent into outer darkness.

Though all who have possessed physical bodies may overcome the temptations of Satan and become heirs of salvation, those who remain unrepentant and unwilling to follow God, even after gospel truths are witnessed to them, will not achieve glory in the celestial kingdom with those who are faithful in accepting the Lord and Savior. Those who could have lived righteously on earth but chose not to may still in spirit prison learn from their past mistakes. They may yet turn aside from wickedness and qualify for the lesser glories of the terrestrial or telestial kingdoms. Ideally, all of God's children would quickly learn to love and follow him in righteousness. For those who learn this later, even in the postmortal spirit world, there are still marvelous blessings awaiting them.[9]

A CONTINUATION OF OUR SECOND ESTATE

The postmortal spirit world is a natural continuation of earth life. It comprises the other vital portion of our second estate. The second estate began with our birth as our spirit and physical body were joined together, and it continues until they are reunited again in a resurrected state. Since the world currently exists on an incomplete, telestial type of existence, the postmortal spirit phase is necessary to complete the full range of development that the second estate should provide.

This spirit world after death is quite different from the spirit world we experienced before birth. For one, the postmortal spirit world of paradise and prison remains here on earth, separated from Heavenly Father's celestial presence.[10] That is, the postmortal spirit world is here but in a different dimension of existence than our own mortal existence. We generally coexist without being aware of each other and without knowing what is happening in the other realm. Quite possibly, the inhabitants of the spirit world may be much more aware of us and our doings than we are of them. We understand that the veil between us will be removed during the Millennium when open and cooperative association between mortals and spirit beings will be possible.[11]

We also know that the experiences of mortality greatly enrich the learning dimensions of the later spirit world as we build upon what we learned in the flesh. Furthermore, the premortal spirit world was the major beginning of our personal growth and spiritual development, while the postmortal spirit world will conclude our preparation opportunities for improving and perfecting ourselves.

Opportunities missed here on earth, as well as injustices not balanced out, will be taken care of in the postmortal world before we as individuals can reach our final eternal destiny. Both phases of the second estate are probationary periods where we learn, develop, and test our spiritual commitments. Our priorities must be developed and refined before we can exit from the postmortal spirit world.

As we compare the opportunities of earth life with those of the postmortal existence, we note the main difference is that in the former we gain a body and in the latter we lose it. However, the possibilities of gaining experiences, developing talents and abilities, and increasing knowledge and understanding remain with us. Although one may not gain the ability when separated from the physical body to throw a javelin or run a personal best time in a mile race, new experiences will be available for many people. For example, people born blind in mortality will enjoy vision as spirit beings. Their memories will not bring back visual images from earth life, but they will have keen remembrances of sounds, tastes, and other sensations that will come to mind and enrich their studies and development in the spirit world.

We mentioned earlier that after Christ's visit in the spirit world, the gulf between spirit paradise and spirit prison was finally bridged. Individuals from paradise visit people in prison and may convert some of them and prepare them to go to paradise. The option of developing faith and making a religious commitment is available, but people still retain their agency. The bridge was open for movement back and forth, much as in this earth life where individuals can share gospel truths and people can change their behavior and come into a new religious community. Life in the postmortal spirit world will reflect many of the same patterns of religious movement as seen here on earth.

Satan seems to rule in many parts of earth as well as in spirit prison. In reality, however, Heavenly Father governs over all. Part of the purpose of this second stage of existence is to allow Satan to influence us. Those who follow him and refuse to repent, especially after they have known the gospel light and truth, are turned over to the buffetings of Satan. Sinful people carry their attitudes with them from mortality into spirit prison until they finally learn to reject Satan's temptations and go to paradise. Both phases of the second estate encourage, on the one hand, our recognition of God and his loving justice and, on the other, our recognition of Satan and his evil designs. Eventually all will recognize both God and Satan for who they are. (See Isa. 45:23; D&C 88:104.)

To conclude, *AFTER DEATH, we continue learning truth, deciding moral and spiritual issues, and serving others in a postmortal spirit world, where we either enjoy peace with the righteous in restful paradise or suffer torment with the wicked in the hell of spirit prison.* This spirit world becomes the final stage in our spiritual development for the eternities.

For further study, refer to the following entries:

TG	BD	*EM*
Death	Death	Afterlife
Heaven	Heaven	Buffetings of Satan
Hell	Hell	Death and Dying
Paradise, Paradisiacal	Paradise	Heaven
Prison		Hell
Spirits, Disembodied		Paradise
Spirits in Prison		Spirit Prison
		Spirit World

CHAPTER 15

LIFE EVERLASTING

A wise teacher desired to identify the most penetrating issues that his students wanted to discuss. He presented the following hypothetical situation to the students in his university philosophy class: "Suppose instead of being granted three wishes by a genie, you would be given three keys of knowledge through the following opportunity: *You are granted a complete and truthful answer to any three questions you have in your heart!* What would your three questions be?" Based upon the common, probing topics presented by many philosophy and religion students, a set of three burning questions lies in the hearts of many people. First, they ask, "Is there life outside or after our life on this earth?" If the response is positive, they often ask, "What type and quality of existence will this afterlife be?" And the next, natural question is "What, if anything, can I do to affect the nature of this afterlife?"

Mankind's study of religion over the ages has often resulted from a preoccupation with these questions concerning life after death. Regardless of their station or situation in life, most people want to know if and how life exists beyond death. The previous chapter of this book taught that our spirit lives after our physical body dies. This spirit existence has been briefly seen by many who have experienced "near-death" or "after-death" episodes. Life after death is not to be feared; this idea is supported by many prophetic teachings as found in the scriptures and witnessed by the Spirit. The belief in a postmortal life forms a doctrinal basis for many religions. However, the sequential stages or the physical nature of our bodies within this afterlife are less well known. The scriptures present a limited look into this future life—they witness the reality of a physical resurrection, and they highlight some available options and the varied dimensions of life for these people. Some of what is known about the

228

physical resurrection and the quality of postmortal life will be the topic
of this chapter.

RESURRECTION

The testimonies of apostles and the promises of scriptures reveal
that the grave is not the end of existence, for all people will receive their
bodies again in a resurrected state. Paul, a special witness of the resurrected Jesus, so promised: "Now is Christ risen from the dead, and
become the firstfruits of them that slept. . . . For as in Adam all die, even
so in Christ shall all be made alive." (1 Cor. 15:20, 22.) God has promised,
as a basic element of his eternal plan, a resurrection for every one of his
children who has lived on this earth. (See Alma 11:41; D&C 29:26.)

Just as death is the separation of the spirit from the physical body,
resurrection is the reuniting of the spirit with the physical body. (See
D&C 88:14–17.) As discussed in the previous chapter, the spirit lives an
active life during the period between death and resurrection. However,
the person lacks a fullness of joy without the physical body and yearns
to be reunited with it. (See D&C 93:33–34.) The gift of resurrection
comes from God and is made effective through Christ's atonement. (See
1 Cor. 6:14; 15:20; 2 Ne. 2:8; 9:12.) The act of resurrection, or new life
with our physical bodies, is just as miraculous and natural as the earlier
gift of life that we received when our bodies first came into physical,
material existence.

Both the physical body that we now have and our future resurrected
body are comprised of physical elements. These elements constitute the
individual cells of the body and are made of finite material that is eternal.
The minute particles in this physical material, however, have gone
through different stages of existence or organization. Each of our physical
bodies started with just two cells—one from each of our parents. These
primal cells divided and multiplied, and our bodies grew with the additional nutrients provided by our mother before our birth and by our
own eating and ingestion during our lifetime. The actual building blocks
or elements of our new cells came from the food—plants and animals—
that we ate. Earlier, in turn, the physical material of the plant and animal
life existed as part of the minerals, moisture, and soil of the earth.

At death, our body cells disintegrate and revert to the basic elements of the earth, such as they were before they became part of the plants or animals we consumed. Thus the physical matter of our body is not eliminated; it is merely disorganized. The power of the resurrection is to gather disorganized elements and material back into an organized body structure, complete with all parts so that not even one hair of the head will be lost. (See Luke 21:18; Alma 40:23; 41:2.) Apparently, the resurrection is similar to the constant regeneration provided by the genetic pattern of our DNA. Just as the physical elements in our bodies are constantly changing as old cells die and new ones are made, the genetic structure remains the same and gives instructions for the type and function of the new cells.

Although we do not yet understand the precise method of physical restoration, we know that the source for the power of the resurrection comes from God through Jesus Christ.[1] The instrumentation of the resurrection is provided by the human spirit, which, endowed with power and knowledge, will be able to gather dormant, disorganized physical elements back together into an organized, living body of resurrected glory. (See 2 Ne. 9:12; D&C 88:12–17, 27–32.) The prophet Joseph F. Smith taught about the important role of the spirit in giving the body life. Without spirit, the physical material is just lifeless clay. Eventually, it is the spirit now within us that "will redeem these tabernacles and bring them forth out of the graves."[2]

The teachings of the prophets and the scriptures provide further insights into various dimensions of the resurrection. One prophet's vision of the redemption of the dead records that those in the spirit world eagerly awaited the coming of the Son of God after his crucifixion so he could redeem them from the bands of death. President Joseph F. Smith knew much about life after death because he had received his own great visions into the afterworld, one of which culminated several divine communications and is now recorded as the last section of the Doctrine and Covenants. He saw Christ's ministry in paradise among the righteous dead and the way they were preparing for their day of resurrection: "Their sleeping dust was to be restored unto its perfect frame, bone to bone, and the sinews and the flesh upon them, . . . that they might receive a fullness of joy." (D&C 138:17.)

In a sermon to the wicked Zeezrom, Alma the younger suggested that in the resurrection we will appear physically just as we are when we die: "This restoration shall come to all, both old and young . . . ; and even there shall not so much as a hair of their heads be lost; but everything shall be restored to its perfect frame, *as it is now, or in the body.*" (Alma 11:44; italics added.) The Prophet Joseph Smith concurred with this idea, saying: "They must rise just as they died; we can there hail our lovely infants with the same glory. . . . They differ in stature, in size, the same glorious spirit gives them the likeness of glory and bloom; the old man with his silvery hairs will glory in bloom and beauty."[3] The Prophet also taught that after resurrection, the bodies of children will grow to the full maturity and stature of the adult spirits that possess them.[4]

At the moment of resurrection, people will have the same stature and appearance as when they died. Infants and children will resurrect at the stage of development they were in when they died. Adults and the aged will also resurrect, appearing as they did at their death, for, as the Prophet Joseph Smith taught, "all men will come from the grave as they lie down, whether old or young."[5] Joseph F. Smith also taught: "The body will come forth as it is laid to rest, for there is no growth or development in the grave. As it is laid down, so will it arise, and changes to perfection will come by the law of restitution."[6] In the natural course of time as resurrected beings, children will grow to maturity since "the body, after the resurrection will develop to the full stature of man."[7]

Adults and the aged will quickly achieve the full measure of their creation as their bodies "will be restored to their proper, perfect frame immediately."[8] President Smith taught about the state of resurrected beings who go through this transformation: "We will meet the same identical being that we associated with here in the flesh — not some other soul, some other being, or the same being in some other form, but the same identity and the same form and likeness, the same person we knew and were associated with in our mortal existence. . . . Deformity will be removed; defects will be eliminated, and men and women shall attain to the perfection of their spirits, to the perfection that God designed in the beginning."[9] The exact timing required for this transformation is not recorded, but it is assumed that the power of the priesthood and the spirit will be able to quickly bring it about. The time for an infant to be raised by its mother or some other loving person to full maturity will probably take longer, but possibly not more than the almost twenty years as now required in mortal existence.

President Smith's teachings about the complete effects of this transformation were expressed beautifully in the remarks he delivered at the
funeral services of Rachel Grant, the mother of the later prophet Heber
J. Grant. In this sermon, he gave poignant examples of two people to
illustrate how the resurrection will affect individuals:

> Therefore, I look for the time when our dear Brother William
> C. Staines . . . will not remain the crippled and deformed William
> C. Staines that we knew, but he will be restored to his perfect
> frame — every limb, every joint, every part of his physical being will
> be restored to its perfect frame. . . . Aunt Rachel . . . will not always
> remain just as she will appear when she is restored again to life,
> but she will go on to perfection. Under that law of restoration that
> God has provided, she will regain her perfection, the perfection of
> her youth, the perfection of her glory and of her being, until her
> resurrected body shall assume the exact stature of the spirit that
> possessed it here in its perfection, and thus we shall see the glorified,
> redeemed, exalted, perfected Aunt Rachel.[10]

Literally, the word *resurrection* means "to rise again." Our ultimate
goal in resurrection is to rise again to a glory that can withstand God's
presence, so that we may enjoy eternal life with him. As we rise again,
we add a refined physical body to our mature spirit so that we may go
on to achieve the full measure of our creation. The precise timing and
the absolute quality of resurrected life for any individual will be determined by the Lord as a part of his final judgment.

JUDGMENT

As we pass from one stage or estate of our eternal existence to the
next, we also experience a judgment of our performance in the former
estate, which largely determines the condition of our next stage. As
reviewed in chapters nine and eleven, the spirits who kept their first
estate were rewarded with physical bodies and mortal life on earth. The
judgment passed upon us as we enter this life, however, is far from
complete. All children of God on earth have the opportunity to seek
varied degrees of glorious everlasting life, even to gain eternal life with
God in the highest degree of glory, the celestial kingdom.

As we pass from mortality, however, our future options are limited
by our previous actions. For example, if people have developed attributes

of love, service, and spiritual commitment on earth, these qualities will continue after death with further enrichment and reward. On the other hand, people entrenched in attitudes of selfishness and abuse will have a difficult time changing their behavior, which will bring them further conflict and anguish in the postmortal spirit life. In the words of Nephi, "they who are righteous shall be righteous still, and they who are filthy shall be filthy still." (2 Ne. 9:16.)

As an example, if people had ample opportunity to embrace the gospel in the flesh but failed to do so, they will not suddenly become righteous as they enter the postmortal realm and thereafter seek the highest degree of heavenly glory. People with a lack of interest or effort in the pursuit of truth and righteousness in mortality will probably continue that pattern. Additionally, individuals will not have the opportunity in the afterlife to qualify for all the Father has if they have rejected the Spirit of the Lord in mortality. (See Alma 40:13–14.) In the postmortal spirit world, though, others who were not exposed to gospel truths and were thus less accountable in the flesh may yet qualify for all the Father possesses. Opportunities for growth and change continue until we reach our ultimate resurrected state. Finally, at the close of our second estate, as we are resurrected into the last stage of our existence, the time to repent is past, and all men receive their final judgment and assignment to a kingdom of glory.

FINAL JUDGMENT MADE BY CHRIST ALONE

The pathway between each of our three estates has been blazed by the Savior himself. Through the eternal principle of what we have called "divine investiture" (see chapter 3), God the Father gave his Son, Jesus Christ, the power to undertake the creation and salvation of this earth and its inhabitants. In our first estate, Christ was the advocate of the Father's plan through his appointment as Redeemer. Without Christ's prior agreement to take upon himself the sins of the world in the flesh, the plan of salvation could not have become effective, and we, as spirits, would all have remained in our premortal state, limited in our progression as spirit entities.

Fortunately, Christ did agree to fulfill the terms of the plan of salvation and so prepared the way for us to enter our second estate. Having helped create men in the flesh, the Savior then inspired the ancient prophets to direct God's children toward higher moral and spiritual plateaus. Later, he took upon himself a mortal body, so that he could lead the way to salvation. He showed us how to live and how to give even our lives, if necessary, to building God's kingdom. Without his direction and leadership, our spiritual growth would have been meager at best.

But mortals who had died and entered either spirit paradise or spirit prison before Christ's life and atonement were stopped, or "damned" and delayed in their progression—they were restricted in their development as postmortal spirit beings. Again, the Author of Salvation took the lead. When he died and passed into the spirit world, he miraculously unlocked the gates of hell and set the captive spirits free. (See D&C 138:18, 29–31.) Thus, Christ's own resurrection broke "the bands of death that the grave should have no victory," causing that all men might be resurrected and attain their third estate. (Mosiah 16:7.) As he promised, "in my Father's house are many mansions: . . . I go to prepare a place for you." (John 14:2.)

Having personally marked the way in every phase of mankind's existence, Christ fully earned the authority he possesses to determine our final station in eternity. Thus, while we may be instructed and judged by surrogate priesthood leaders in mortality and even in the spirit world, we must all eventually face the Lord for final judgment: "O then, my beloved brethren, come unto the Lord, the Holy One. Remember that his paths are righteous. Behold, the way for man is narrow, but it lieth in a straight course before him, and the keeper of the gate is the Holy One of Israel; and he employeth no servant there; and there is none other way save it be by the gate; for he cannot be deceived, for the Lord God is his name." (2 Ne. 9:41.) The Lord cannot be deceived or swayed in his judgment, for he intimately knows the pains and pitfalls of eternal progression. At the last day, "when all men shall stand to be judged of him," even the wicked will "confess, who live without God in the world, that the judgment of an everlasting punishment is just upon them." (Mosiah 27:31.)

WITNESSES AT OUR JUDGMENT SCENE

To guarantee that a just judgment is given and to assure the person being judged that he or she has been fairly and accurately evaluated, various witnesses, records, and other forms of evidence can be brought forth. We do not know whether the witnesses can include family members, friends, and associates who can testify concerning a person's circumstances and behavior. The scriptures do indicate that certain ecclesiastical leaders, particularly apostles (who have callings as "judges in Israel"), can bear witness concerning members of Christ's church and kingdom. The Lord's apostles have a notable role as they help judge the covenant members of the house of Israel: the New Testament apostles will particularly judge from all the tribes of Israel, while the twelve Nephite disciples will assist in judging the Nephite-Lamanite descendants of Joseph's tribe. (See Matt. 19:28; D&C 29:12; 1 Ne. 12:9–10; 3 Ne. 27:27.) In a similar fashion, the Lord's living apostles can participate in our future judgment, testifying concerning the gospel teachings and spiritual directives they have given us through general conference talks, writings, and their special testimonies. In addition to "judges in Israel" and people who have lived with us on earth, heavenly witnesses or angelic beings can add their corroborating evidence.

Since each of us is to be judged according to our own level of knowledge, accountability, and opportunity, various records on earth and in heaven have been maintained from which we can be judged. (See Rev. 20:12; 2 Ne. 29:11; D&C 128:6–7.) As the Prophet Joseph instructed early priesthood leaders in the Church, "Our acts are recorded, and at a future day they will be laid before us, . . . they may there, perhaps, condemn us; there they are of great consequence."[11] The Church has consistently pursued accurate record keeping and historical departments. Also, Latter-day Saints have been admonished to keep complete, accurate personal and family records, particularly of gospel ordinances and priesthood offices.[12] All of these records will be part of our judgment, although their greatest value appears to be mostly for us. God already knows us and the level of our righteousness and goodness. These records and witnesses will help us better understand the opportunities we have had and how we have taken advantage of them.

Perhaps the most important witness or record that will be brought forth at our judgment will be the record of our soul. All the desires, thoughts, words, and deeds of our previous existence will come into clear remembrance, and by them we will be judged. (See Alma 12:14; 41:3; D&C 33:1; 137:9.) As God's Spirit touches our memory core, we will remember all the acts and ordinances in which we have participated.[13] Standing in the presence of supreme truth, we will know ourselves and the true nature of our being. Unable to resort to evasion or hypocrisy, we will be able to evaluate our attitudes and actions, and we will know how they have been in or out of accordance with God's will. (See Matt. 7:21–23; D&C 4:3; 82:2–3.) As the Savior then pronounces final judgment, we will know that his reward is both just and loving. (See 2 Ne. 9:46; Mosiah 16:1; 27:31; 29:12–13.) Until then, one key question remains unanswered—what are we doing now to prepare ourselves for that day when Jesus will call us before his judgment bar?

RESURRECTION AND RESTORATION OF THE JUST AND UNJUST

Some of our earliest ancestors on this earth have already been resurrected and received their judgment from the Lord. As will be explained later in this chapter, resurrected beings will experience a variety of levels of resurrected life. Jesus promised to his disciples that he was preparing many mansions for them as a part of his Father's kingdom. (See John 14:2.) Paul also indicated that there would be at least three major, different degrees of resurrected glory, comparable to the differences of the sun, the moon, and the stars. (See 1 Cor. 15:40–44.) Joseph Smith used the terms *celestial, terrestrial,* and *telestial* to distinguish these three levels of resurrected life. (See D&C 76.) In addition, a certain order of resurrection will be followed where the righteous and just individuals will be resurrected prior to the wicked and selfish people on the earth.

When the Lord himself was resurrected on earth, he ushered in what is called the "morning" of the first resurrection as a part of the resurrection of the just: "The graves were opened; and many bodies of the saints which slept arose, and came out of the graves after his resurrection, and went into the holy city, and appeared unto many." (Matt. 27:52–53.) Note that only the righteous "saints" came forth at this time, and among them we assume were the ancient prophets, such as Abraham, for the Lord revealed to Joseph Smith in 1843 that Abraham "hath entered into his exaltation and sitteth upon his throne." (D&C 132:29.) Whether all the righteous dead arose at this time or even sometime afterward we do not know. We do know, however, that the morning of the first resurrection will continue to the beginning of the second coming of Christ. At the sound of the first trumpet, those then living or those who have previously died and lived in paradise under a heavenly or celestial[14] law will be "caught up to meet him in the midst of the pillar of heaven—they are Christ's, the first fruits." (D&C 88:97–98.)

At the sound of the second trump, the "afternoon" or "evening" of the first resurrection will ensue, bringing forth for the first time the dead who lived an honorable earthly or terrestrial[15] law. This resurrection also ushers in the millennial reign of Christ and will continue throughout the thousand years of peace on earth. In fact, the earth itself will be elevated from a lesser worldly or telestial[16] state to its original terrestrial, or paradisiacal order, which it enjoyed before the fall of Adam. This is why wicked, or telestial, beings alive on earth must be destroyed and the dead "sinners stay and sleep until I [the Lord] shall call again." (D&C 43:18.) Telestial beings simply cannot participate in or even physically endure the glory of a terrestrial world. (See D&C 88:23.)

All terrestrial beings still alive during the Millennium, however, may continue to progress toward a celestial existence, if they choose, for agency will still be in force. (See D&C 29:22.)[17] Any who live and die during the Millennium will experience an immediate resurrection as the time of separation between death and restoration will be in the "twinkling of an eye." (D&C 63:51.)

At the end of the Millennium, the Lord will finally call forth the wicked in the second and last resurrection, or "the resurrection of the unjust." It will include the spirits of all those beings still in spirit prison who did not repent, "and are found under condemnation. . . . There are found among those who are to remain until that great and last day, even the end, who shall remain filthy still." (D&C 88:100, 102.)

Every person, then, will be resurrected to that glory whose law he lived during mortality and, in some cases, attained during postmortality in the spirit world. The spirit of each individual will have lived God's law at different levels of righteousness, and thus each individual will be resurrected at his or her level of spiritual maturation. For these reasons, Alma the younger instructed his wayward son, Corianton: "If their works are evil they shall be restored unto them for evil. Therefore all things shall be restored to their proper order, everything to its natural frame. . . . The one raised to happiness according to his desires of happiness, or good according to his desires of good; and the other to evil according to his desires of evil. . . . Do not suppose, because it has been spoken concerning restoration, that ye shall be restored from sin to happiness." (Alma 41:4–5, 10.)

THE DIFFERING LEVELS OF RESURRECTED BODIES

Much more important than physical maturity or appearance in the resurrection will be the degree of righteousness our spirits have obtained by that day, for that will determine our final assignment to a kingdom of glory. All persons who kept their first estate (premortality) and received a body of flesh in their second estate (mortality) will inherit some degree of glory as their reward, "except those sons of perdition who deny the Son after the Father has revealed him." (D&C 76:43.)

THE MOST WICKED IN OUTER DARKNESS

Sons of perdition, instead of accepting Christ and his authority, continue their rebellion against God with bodies in a resurrected state of nonglory. They are consigned to outer darkness with Satan, who is also called Perdition, and his devilish angels who were cast out of heaven in the beginning. (See D&C 76:26.) Let us clarify, therefore, exactly what type of rebellion against the Father qualifies a person to become a son of perdition, one who denies the sure witness of divine truth.

The first basic requirement is for individuals who have experienced a sure manifestation of absolute truth through a great, personal manifestation of the Holy Ghost to then lie about and rebel against that knowledge. Since most people have felt at least some spiritual promptings and may have even rejected or acted contrary to them, some may wonder if they have sinned so seriously against the promptings of the Holy Spirit that they might be sent to outer darkness. It is safe to say that any person who has to ask whether he or she has received such a sure witness does not qualify for eternal damnation, for we are not talking about manifestations of the Holy Ghost alone, however dramatic they may be.[18]

To commit this level of spiritual rebellion, a person "must receive the Holy Ghost, have the heavens opened unto him, and know God, and then sin against Him."[19] For example, when the witness of the Holy Ghost is accompanied by the presence of the Father and/or the Son as well, then the individual knows he or she has received such a sure witness.

This is the type of manifestation that the Prophet Joseph Smith received in the Sacred Grove, which he "could not deny . . . , neither dared . . . do it." (JS–H 1:25.)

The Prophet wrote that to deny a sure witness of the Savior after a direct manifestation of his glory is to commit "the unpardonable sin": "What must a man do to commit the unpardonable sin? . . . He has got to say that the sun does not shine while he sees it; he has got to deny Jesus Christ when the heavens have been opened unto him, and to deny the plan of salvation with his eyes open to the truth of it; and from that time he begins to be an enemy."[20]

The Father and the Son can give few greater gifts to people than to reveal themselves to them and show them the glory they may someday share with the Godhead. So, if a person denies this great witness and rebels against God, there is no hope for his or her salvation. Having rebelled and turned away from the brightest light, sons of perdition inherit instead the darkest chaos and torment for their eternal reward: "They shall go away into everlasting punishment . . . to reign with the devil and his angels in eternity, where their worm dieth not, and the fire is not quenched, which is their torment — and the end thereof, neither the place thereof, nor their torment, no man knows." (D&C 76:44–45.) Sons of perdition join Satan and his devilish angels, who likewise rebelled against God and Christ even as they dwelt in their glorious presence.

If it seems difficult to understand how anyone could rebel against God after knowing him so intimately, consider that the scriptures specifically name very few individuals who, after having kept their first estate, became sons of perdition. Cain, the murderous son of Adam and Eve, is the classic example of a person who will be consigned to outer darkness. His eternal miserable fate comes not because he murdered his brother, Abel, but because, knowing both God and Satan, he "rejected the greater counsel which was had from God" and "loved Satan more than God." (Moses 5:18, 25.) Outer darkness is reserved for those who love themselves beyond all others and love Satan more than God.

TELESTIAL GLORY FOR THE WICKED

Aside from sons of perdition, even the most wicked people of this earth will eventually recognize the reality, power, and goodness of God. They will obtain a kingdom of glory, but only after they have suffered during a long sojourn in spirit prison for their sins of the flesh. The unrepentant among them who continue their perversions in the face of truth and goodness reject the redemption that Christ has already purchased through his own bitter suffering. Their anguish must also complete the demands of eternal justice, and they are thus warned: "Repent, lest I smite you . . . and your sufferings be sore — how sore you know not, how exquisite you know not, yea, how hard to bear you know not. For behold, I, God, have suffered these things for all, that they might not suffer if they would repent; but if they would not repent they must suffer even as I; which suffering caused myself, even God, the greatest of all, to tremble because of pain, and to bleed at every pore, and to suffer both body and spirit." (D&C 19:15–18.) Indeed, the scriptural descriptions of spirit prison, or hell, and outer darkness are strikingly similar, with the important exception that spirit prison is, however long, still only temporary.

Among those who, after their sufferings, will inherit the telestial kingdom are "they who are liars, and sorcerers, and adulterers, and whoremongers, and whosoever loves and make a lie." (D&C 76:103.) During mortality, these individuals have given themselves over to bodily appetites and physical passions; they seek for emotional dominion and monetary power as they yearn for personal glory and influence. In other words, telestial people are selfish, self-indulgent people who do not care for others and think only of themselves. They truly live the "law of the jungle" and believe in the "survival of the fittest." Nonetheless, after they are purged of their sins in the hell of spirit prison, they will be judged according to their works, and "these all shall bow the knee, and every tongue shall confess to him who sits upon the throne forever and ever." (D&C 76:110; see also vv. 81–85, 98–106.)

Living in the telestial kingdom, people of a telestial glory will be governed by the Holy Ghost, with rulers and administrators gathered from the terrestrial worlds. (See D&C 76:86, 88.) Although living in the least of the resurrected states of glory, they will enjoy an existence of far greater comfort and enjoyment than is now experienced by any mortal on this earth. In fact, the glory of a telestial existence surpasses all understanding for us mortals. (See D&C 76:89.) Telestial beings need not fear death, disease, or infirmity ever again. They are also freed from the social banes of taxes, wars, bills, and menial labor. They apparently will be free to socialize, travel, learn, observe, and enjoy life with a great variety of options on a variety of worlds, differing from one another as the stars in the heavens. (See 1 Cor. 15:40–42; D&C 76:98.) In their own way, they will be "servants of the Most High; but where God and Christ dwell they cannot come." (D&C 76:112.) The range of their experiences, however, while much better than anything on earth, will pale in comparison to the quality of life enjoyed by beings of a terrestrial order. (See D&C 76:91.)

TERRESTRIAL GLORY FOR THE HONORABLE PEOPLE

In contrast to people living a telestial law, terrestrial beings are "they who are the honorable men of the earth." (D&C 76:75.) They are just, good people who live a moral law above that of the jungle, caring for the needs of others and trying to improve the condition of this world. But because these "honorable" people are "blinded by the craftiness [or philosophies] of men" they remain—however just, good, and ethical they may be—uncommitted to becoming Christ's disciples and progressing toward saintliness or godhood. (D&C 76:75.)

In order to qualify for the celestial kingdom, one must accept and live the gospel when it is first presented to him or her, especially while in mortality. The person needs an opportunity to hear enough of the gospel to make a sound judgment, along with a possibility to live the gospel principles. Terrestrial beings, on the other hand, reject their initial opportunity to learn and live God's law, for they "received not the testimony of Jesus in the flesh, but afterwards received it" after death. Others, having died without the gospel law, did not accept it even when taught in the postmortal spirit world. (See D&C 76:72–74.) They also include those who, having accepted the gospel, were "not valiant in the testimony of Jesus." (D&C 76:79; see also v. 74.) So whether good, decent people refuse to enter into the gospel ordinances, or whether they fail to keep the covenants they have made, their neglect causes them to "obtain not the crown over the kingdom of our God." (D&C 76:79.)

Living in the terrestrial mansions and worlds prepared for them, terrestrial people are governed by Christ with assistance from the Holy Ghost and other celestial beings. (See D&C 76:77, 87.) In every dimension of glory, power, might, and dominion, they enjoy a life far more glorious than the telestial one. (See D&C 76:91.) In addition to the range of social and learning experiences available to telestial people, terrestrial beings enjoy the association with more pleasant, honorable, decent people. So they will be of service in administering God's kingdoms, they can also assist in governing telestial worlds. (See D&C 76:88.) But the glory of their existence and the intensity of their service appear dim and weak in comparison to what is enjoyed by celestial beings residing in God's presence.

CELESTIAL GLORY FOR GOD'S TRUE CHILDREN

While heirs to the terrestrial kingdom may be "nice people," heirs to celestial glory are "just men made perfect through Jesus the mediator of the new covenant." (D&C 76:69.) Having completely reconciled themselves with God by accepting Christ and the saving ordinances, they are true in their faith and endure in righteousness to the end. (See D&C 76:51–53.) Because of their faithfulness, celestial people "are they into whose hands the Father has given all things." (D&C 76:55.) They inherit "thrones, kingdoms, principalities, and powers" (D&C 132:19) from Heavenly Father in part because they assisted in bringing to pass the immortality and eternal life of other individuals (see D&C 76:54–70; 132:19–20; Moses 1:39). They are literally transformed into "new creatures" and angels on high, some becoming as their heavenly parent, fulfilling their ultimate destiny as gods and goddesses. (See 2 Cor. 5:17; D&C 76:58.)

Celestial beings enjoy association directly with Heavenly Father. (See D&C 76:92.) They are governed by God himself and assisted by Jesus Christ and the Holy Ghost, as they bask in the Father's celestial glory, within his heavenly mansions. (See John 14:2.) While free to serve God as kings and queens, priests and priestesses, and ministering angels of the Most High in his kingdom, celestial people also assist Jesus in his administration of the terrestrial worlds. (See D&C 76:56–60, 87.) They alone will be able to abide with the Father and the Son on this earth after it becomes a celestial sphere. (See D&C 88:19–20; 130:9.) This celestial glory is the promised, prepared destiny for those who are truly the children of God.

After having reviewed much that has been revealed about the promised resurrection and our eventual entrance into one of the three kingdoms of glory, we can summarize with the following statement: *RESUR-*

RECTION and the FINAL JUDGMENT are gateways into eternity whereby God's children enter into one of his many kingdoms, the joy and glory of which depend upon how they have lived and proven faithful. To evaluate how our own personality best matches a particular eternal state, we need to measure where we are and, more important, in which direction we are moving. To assist in this evaluation, we should study the essential gospel principles and then determine whether we are participating in the eternal ordinances that God expects of us. The next section of chapters provides these perspectives.

For further study, refer to the following entries:

TG	BD	*EM*
Celestial Glory	Degrees of Glory	Celestial Kingdom
Eternal Life	Heaven	Degrees of Glory
Judgment, the Last	Hell	Eternal Life
Outer Darkness	Resurrection	Exaltation
Resurrection		Immortality
Telestial Glory		Immortality and
Terrestrial Glory		Eternal Life
		Judgment
		Judgment Day, Final
		Resurrection
		Sons of Perdition
		Telestial Kingdom
		Terrestrial Kingdom

NOTES TO PART 2

CHAPTER 9

1. See *TPJS*, 163; *GD*, 86.

2. *TPJS*, 181; cf. 354.

3. *TPJS*, 351–52.

4. *TPJS*, 353; see fn.

5. *TPJS*, 354.

6. Joseph Smith, in his masterful "King Follett Discourse," used a number of terms synonymously to refer to this eternal element of people: soul, mind of man, immortal spirit, mind, intelligence, immortality of the spirit of man, intelligence of spirits, spirit of man, mind of man, spirit, and mind and spirit. (See *TPJS*, 352–54.)

7. See *GD*, 58.

8. *TPJS*, 354; italics added. The late Elder B. H. Roberts felt that the Prophet said "a spirit" to specifically denote individuality. (See *TPJS*, 354, n. 9.) This agrees with the list of terms given in the reference of note 6 above.

9. CR, April 1901, 2.

10. *WNTCD*, 625.

11. See *EM*, "God the Father" (2:548ff); "Mother in Heaven" (2:961).

12. *EM*, 2:961.

13. Ibid.

14. *MD*, 387.

15. The necessary elements, values, and risks of agency are discussed in the next chapter.

16. One valuable dimension of our earlier existence that carried over into our mortal life here is the essential element of agency, which is discussed in the next chapter. Other elements of our earth life and the promises of the future are discussed in chapters 11–15.

17. Chapter 12 contains more insights into the nature of sin and the dangers of judging others.

18. *TPJS*, 354.

19. The blessings, opportunities, and probationary nature of mortality are discussed in more detail in chapter 11.

20. Chapter 20 provides more details on how to develop strong, regular spiritual growth.

CHAPTER 10

1. From the *ex nihilo* misconception arise the equally misguided doctrines of predestination and salvation strictly by grace.

2. Chapter 9 presents more insights on the nature of our eternal intelligence.

3. *EM,* 2:525; italics added.

4. Chapter 36 highlights further responsibilities that the Latter-day Saints have as citizens of the world.

5. See TG, Agency.

6. *EM,* 1:27.

7. Chapter 24 provides more important insights into the liberating and eternal values of God's laws.

8. *JD,* 18:246.

9. Material in later chapters will examine how lost agency can be regained through the gifts of the gospel. See particularly chapters 13 (gifts of the Atonement), 18 (repentance), 20 (sources of spiritual strength), and 21 (personal growth).

10. These responsibilities are reviewed in greater detail in chapter 34.

11. This will be discussed in the next chapter and in chapter 15

CHAPTER 11

1. Many specific suggestions about how we can develop our gifts and talents are found in chapter 35.

2. For a more detailed discussion on temple covenants, see chapter 23.

CHAPTER 12

1. *DS,* 1:111.

2. Further insights and suggestions on developing spiritual health are in chapter 20.

3. Further details on this process of repentance will be presented in chapter 17.

4. *MF,* 91.

CHAPTER 13

1. *MD,* 571.

2. See TG, Resurrection. Further details about the resurrection and our final judgment will be presented in chapter 15.

3. See *EM,* "Resurrection," 3:1222–23.

4. *TPJS,* 368.

5. Bruce R. McConkie, *Doctrinal New Testament Commentary,* 3 vols. (Salt Lake City: Bookcraft, 1973), 1:456–57.

6. *God, Family, and Country,* 155–56.

7. Further insights into the conditions of agency were presented in chapter 10.

8. For further information, see *MD,* 60–66; *DS,* 1:126.

9. The key steps of repentance will be discussed in chapter 17.

10. See Boyd K. Packer, "The Mediator," *Ensign,* May 1977, pp. 54–56; also published as *The Mediator* (Salt Lake City: Deseret Book Company, 1978).

11. Note, for example, LDS footnote "b" in Matthew 5:48.

12. *MF,* 209; cf. Revelation 2:7, 11, 17, 26–28; 3:5, 12, 21.

CHAPTER 14

1. More details about the fall of Adam and Eve are provided in chapters 11 and 12. The effects of the Atonement are discussed in chapter 13.

2. *JD,* 17:142.

3. *Reflections on Life after Life* (New York: Bantam/Mockingbird Press, June 1977), 18.

4. See *JD,* 8:10.

5. *DBY,* 380.

6. The state of nonglorious resurrection in outer darkness is briefly discussed in chapter 15.

7. See *Reflections,* 18.

8. Further teachings and details about ordinance work for the spirits in the postmortal spirit world are presented in chapter 23.

9. In the following chapter, we will discuss the varying degrees of salvation and exaltation awaiting God's children after their resurrection.

10. See *TPJS,* 310.

11. See *JD,* 378.

CHAPTER 15

1. Chapter 13 provides further details about why and how Jesus became the firstfruits of the resurrection.

2. *JD,* 25:250.

3. *TPJS,* 368.

4. See *GD,* 455–56.

5. *TPJS,* 199–200, 368.

6. *TPJS,* 200 fn.

7. *IE,* 7:624; see also *EM,* 3:1223.

8. *DS,* 2:292.

9. *GD,* 23.

10. *GD,* 23–24.

11. *TPJS,* 69.

12. See *DS,* 2:204–15.

13. See Daniel H. Ludlow, *Latter-day Prophets Speak* (Salt Lake City: Bookcraft, 1948), 56–58.

14. The term *celestial* has a Latin root *caelestis* (or *caelum*), meaning "sky" or "heaven." (*AHD,* 216.)

15. The term *terrestrial* derives from a Latin root *ters-a* (or *terra*), meaning "of the earth (or the dry land)." (*AHD,* 1546.)

16. The exact meaning of *telestial* is uncertain, though it appears to come

from a Greek/Latin root *tel* (or *tele*) meaning to lift, support, and weigh, as in the making of a payment. (*AHD*, 1545.)

17. Some details on the millennial era and the final celestial status of the earth and its inhabitants are included in chapter 38.

18. For details on types of revelation through the Spirit, see chapter 6.

19. *TPJS*, 358.

20. Ibid.

PART 3

BASIC PRINCIPLES, ORDINANCES, AND BLESSINGS OF THE GOSPEL

CHAPTER 16

CULTIVATING FAITH

Have you heard of someone described as a "con man"? The term derives from "confidence man," meaning one who swindles through misplaced trust. It is often used in irony because instead of having confidence in someone, the term means we have lost all confidence in that person. Unfortunately, most of us have been betrayed or deceived by someone. After experiencing sour business deals, disreputable service repairs, or false promises, we naturally begin to question our faith in other humans. Because of uncertainty within the human character, many people have more trust in animals or machines than in people.

However, we can learn to be more discerning as we deal with different people. After experience, we generally realize that we should not judge someone too quickly on outward appearances or after a limited relationship. Likewise, we should not believe everything everyone says. Through time and interaction, we come to know the nature and truthfulness of most people. If we could gain these insights upon first meetings, however, we could choose better friends and trustworthy associates.

As we learn to carefully select the people we trust, we are refining a process that can also enhance our spiritual perspective of God and his nature. To most people, the concept of having "faith in God" simply means to believe that God actually exists. But beyond knowing that God exists, we need to understand his character and essence. As we pursue this quest, we go beyond naïve belief and dutiful obedience; our faith and understanding of God increase and we come to feel his great love for us. Jesus promises eternal life to those who come to know the only true God. (John 17:3.) Eventually we learn that to "know God" requires more than simple study or scripture reading. It goes beyond believing in his existence; it develops only as we become more and more like him.

As we obey his commandments and serve others with love, we understand the nature of deity because it is reflected in our souls. The spiritual ingredient that encourages us to understand God and become more like him is *faith*.

WHAT IS FAITH?

The most widely known definition of faith in Christendom was given by the apostle Paul to the early Hebrew saints: "Now faith is the substance of things hoped for, the evidence of things not seen." (Heb. 11:1.) "From this," the Prophet Joseph Smith said, "we learn that faith is the assurance which men have of the existence of things which they have not seen, and the principle of action in all intelligent beings."[1] That is, faith is not just an airy hope in something we would like to believe. It is the *substance* (Greek = *assurance*) and *evidence* on which we pattern our lives, thus motivating us to action.

In general terms, faith is the force behind action in temporal as well as spiritual pursuits. The farmer plants his seeds in faith that he will reap a harvest; the university student studies in faith that he will obtain a degree; the physician performs an operation in faith that his patient will be healed. The list could go on and on—all human action is done in the faith that it will yield certain desired results. In spiritual terms too, true faith is always followed by righteous action: "He that *believeth* and *is baptized* shall be saved." (Mark 16:16; italics added.) Naturally, "faith without works is dead," having not borne the attending fruit of obedience. (See James 2:20.)

Finally, beyond both belief and the motivation to do good, the Prophet Joseph taught, "Faith is not only the principle of action, but of power also, in all intelligent beings, whether in heaven or on earth."[2] Thus, as Paul wrote, "Through faith we understand that the worlds were framed by the word of God." (Heb. 11:3.) In its totality, then, faith is an attribute of godly character—like justice, mercy, or love—from which springs God's omnipotent power over all temporal and spiritual things. "Faith, then," Joseph concludes, "is the first great governing principle which has power, dominion, and authority over all things; by it they exist, by it they are upheld, by it they are changed, or by it they remain, agreeable to the will of God."[3] Thus, we see that faith can have great power and influence in our lives.

There are three key dimensions of our faith: principles of truth, relationships with others (especially God), and effect upon our own behavior. Faith is first of all *an assurance of unseen truths* that we have developed since our first experiences in childhood. We may not understand all the laws of mathematics, energy, nuclear physics, and the universe, but we are comfortable in our belief about some of the principles and truths in these fields. We have an assurance that the sun will rise tomorrow, bringing life-giving light to this earth, even if we do not know all the laws and powers that effectuate this daily phenomenon. Believing in things we cannot see, we use electricity even if we do not know the absolute structure and influence of an electron. Thus, we have faith in certain truths. In a gospel context, as we develop faith in the saving principles of truth contained in the words of God and his Son, we look forward to receiving the blessings promised by God. As we kindle this hope of divine promises, we gain a better understanding of not only who we are, but also what our destiny might be.

Second, we develop faith in living entities, primarily in God but also in others. LDS scholars describe faith as having "confidence in something or someone."[4] As we develop a *feeling of confidence in God,* we want to learn not only who he is, but also how we can please him. Thus faith influences our attitudes and provides us a motivation toward righteous living.

Third, beyond influencing our beliefs and attitudes, faith also generates activities that affect our behavior. True and noble faith stimulates us to live good, godlike, and Christian lives. As *a principle of action centered in Christ,* its greatest power is demonstrated as we seek to obey his words.[5] Faith thus becomes a powerful catalyst that generates spiritual life when we attempt to do all that God has asked of us. Ultimately, we begin to fulfill the Savior's most difficult commandment: "Be ye therefore perfect, even as your Father which is in heaven is perfect." (Matt. 5:48.)

HOW DO WE DEVELOP FAITH?

So we see that there are several levels of faith: our initial belief and hope develop into the motivating force behind righteousness and culminate as a divine attribute of godly character and eternal power. Naturally, we do not experience all these levels at once. We seem to progress through six major steps as our faith matures.

Since all God's creations ultimately owe their existence to the power of faith, it follows that we, as eternal, intelligent spirits, have always possessed some degree of faith. In speaking of the premortal existence as compared to mortality, Latter-day Saints often say that we previously walked by sight, but now by faith. (See 2 Cor. 5:7.) True, as spirits living in the presence of God, we did not have to exercise faith in his existence. However, in order to accept the plan of salvation, we did have to exercise faith in God's ability and willingness to save our souls and bring us back into his presence. In contrast, Satan and his hosts were also in the presence of God and they knew him, but they chose not to exercise faith in God's wisdom and goodness or in man's eternal potential, thus rejecting the plan of salvation.

To continue exercising faith in God's power and mercy while on earth, we must first regain at least some of our premortal knowledge of his existence and character. Thus, the Prophet Joseph Smith taught: "The real design which the God of heaven had in view in making the human family acquainted with his attributes, was, that they . . . might be enabled to exercise faith in him."[6] But where do we gain this knowledge of God?

1. WITNESSING THE FAITH OF SOMEONE ELSE

If you do not know what or where something is, you will have difficulty finding it. Human beings have naturally searched for answers to the great questions of life, and they tend to look first toward those who seem to have found the answers. Accepting and building upon others' beliefs then takes a certain amount of faith.

The Prophet Joseph repeatedly taught that "faith comes by hearing the word of God."[7] Thus, the first step for engendering faith in any person is to preach to him the true and living God; false teachings about the nature of God cannot produce true faith, only misplaced belief. Engendering faith is what Alma had in mind when he taught the Zoramites, who held a perverted concept of God. He said, "Faith is not to have a perfect knowledge of things; therefore if ye have faith ye hope for things which are not seen, *which are true*." (Alma 32:21; italics added.) As people hear new truth, witness a person's devout act of faith, or feel the power of a true believer's testimony, they sense the genuineness of the experience, and they may recognize that new spiritual dimensions are available for them. (See D&C 46:13–14; 50:17–24.) They should then seek out that new spirituality for themselves.

2. DEVELOPING A PERSONAL DESIRE TO BELIEVE

When we perceive someone with tremendous faith, we may temporarily lean on that person's testimony. But eventually, like children growing up, there comes a time when one must learn these things for oneself. A modern scientist and apostle, John A. Widtsoe, said, "A conviction of the truth of the gospel, a testimony, must be sought if it is to be found. It does not come as the dew from heaven. It is the result of man's eagerness to know truth. Often it requires battle with traditions, former opinions and appetites, and a long testing of the gospel by every available fact and standard."[8] In his continued preaching to the Zoramites, Alma explained, "If ye will awake and arouse your faculties, even to an experiment upon my words, and exercise a particle of faith, yea, even if ye can no more than *desire to believe,* let this desire work in you, even until ye believe in a manner that ye can give place for a portion of my words." (Alma 32:27; italics added.)

At various points in our lives, we are exposed to new ideas and opportunities. At those moments, we may have a burning desire to find the truth in them and to incorporate them in our lives. Whether this is ever accomplished depends upon our level of desire. (See Alma 29:4.) We must sincerely desire to have faith if we are to obtain it. Regardless of our current level of faith, we need to maintain a desire to increase it. Another modern apostle, Bruce R. McConkie, stated, "All faithful people have the desire, born of the Spirit, to grow in faith and be more like [Jesus]. All the saints desire to increase in faith and godliness."[9] An ancient prophet expressed a similar admonition when he said, "Thus saith the Lord God: I will give unto the children of men line upon line, precept upon precept, here a little and there a little; and blessed are those who hearken unto my precepts, and lend an ear unto my counsel, for they shall learn wisdom; *for unto him that receiveth I will give more.*" (2 Ne. 28:30; italics added.)

To receive faith in God and the gospel truths, we must turn to him who knows and gives all. We must seek to obey all the Master has asked of us, and we must tune in our spirits to the gentle promptings of the Holy Spirit. Elder McConkie also stated, "Working by faith [is not] merely a mental desire, however strong, that some eventuality should occur. There may be those whose mental powers and thought processes are greater than any of the saints, but only persons who are in tune with the Infinite can exercise the spiritual forces and powers that come from him."[10] Moroni also expressed the fact that this desire to develop in faith is more than a mental wish and must include sincere, sensitive petitions to God: "I would exhort you that ye would ask God, the Eternal Father, in the name of Christ, if these things are not true; and if ye shall ask with a sincere heart, with real intent, having faith in Christ, he will manifest the truth of it unto you, by the power of the Holy Ghost . . . [by which] ye may know the truth of all things." (Moro. 10:4–5.)

The second step then is to awaken a desire within us to receive our own witness of faith. If we lack faith, we must go to our Heavenly Father for inspiration and strength. We must search for this gift from God, who can reveal all truths to us. To recognize his spiritual promptings, we must set our lives in spiritual harmony with the promptings of his Holy Spirit and then petition him through prayer with a sincere heart and real intent.

God not only allows us to make this petition to him, he desires this of us. Indeed, the most repeated constructive injunction in the scriptures is to "ask"—to seek, to knock, to inquire, to petition, to search, and to pray.[11] (See, for examples, Matt. 7:7–8; D&C 88:63.) After we have heard a new truth or witnessed a sincere testimony, the first responsibility of gaining faith rests with us, and we must resolve to ask God for our own spiritual witness.

3. RECEIVING THE GIFT OF FAITH THROUGH GOD'S GRACE

After a person desires to gain a true knowledge of God's nature, faith usually develops along a pattern identified by the prophet Alma: "Now, we will compare the word unto a seed. Now, if ye give place, that a seed may be planted in your heart, behold, if it be a true seed, or a good seed, if ye do not cast it out by your unbelief, that ye will resist the Spirit of the Lord, behold, it will begin to swell within your breasts; and . . . ye will begin to say within yourselves—It must needs be that this is a good seed, or that the word is good, for it beginneth to enlarge my soul; yea, it beginneth to enlighten my understanding." (Alma 32:28.) Thus, knowing just a portion of the word, we can develop faith that, in turn, leads us to further knowledge by "enlightening our understanding."

Notice that the planter of the seed needs to act and hope as he plants the seed. Also, he should not discard the truth from the beginning through unbelief or resistance to the Spirit of the Lord. The only way to gain faith and understanding of any gospel principle is to plant the seed. Desire is not enough since action must build upon the thought.

Please note that the germination of the seed (the first real sign of spiritual awakening in a person's soul) is beyond our control. The actual germination of truth and the budding forth of faith requires a special witness of the Spirit. Just as a physical miracle causes the dead seed to burst forth with new life, a divine gift quickens our weak, numb spirit to radiate with new life. The Apostle Paul told the Ephesians, "By grace are ye saved through faith; and that not of yourselves: it is the gift of God." (Eph. 2:8.)

This gift comes at a time and place determined by God. We may plead for a spiritual witness or a confirming answer to our prayers for days and weeks before we recognize God's spiritual response to our petitions. The Apostle James tells us that if we patiently petition God, he will give us an answer. (See James 1:3-5.) Alma indicates that eventually, if it is a "good seed" or if the word is good, we will recognize a feeling of peace and comfort within us — the first signs of faith. (See Alma 32:29-31.) Alma also tells us that we can know the reality of the spiritual experience we are having. It will be discernible, and we will recognize it for the light and goodness it brings into our souls — further signs of faith. We can no longer deny the reality of our spiritual witness; therefore, we "know that it is good." (Alma 32:35.) This sweet spiritual feeling not only removes our doubts about the validity of the seed, but it also impels us to cultivate and nourish the seedling.

4. PREPARING OUR SOULS TO RECEIVE GOD'S WORD

In Christ's parable of the sower, he indicates that the eventual fruitfulness of seeds is often dependent upon the type of earth in which they sprout. Seeds cast upon hard or rocky soil could not produce mature plants at all. Seeds growing in different fields produced according to the soil's fertility — some thirtyfold, some sixty, some a hundred. (See Matt.

13:3–8.) Just as a gardener should prepare the soil and enrich its nutrient base before planting seeds, we must prepare our souls to receive divine truths. The personal nutrients we need are humility, a sensitive spirit, diligence, and a willingness to sacrifice.

Humility. We must be teachable if we wish to be taught the things of God. An attitude of humility softens our soul for the planting of God's word. Humility, either compelled by external circumstances or developed through internal attitudes, is a vital prerequisite to faith. Alma indicates that those who are humble before they are introduced to the gospel will be blessed as they come to know and believe in the word of God. (See Alma 32:13–16.) Christ admonishes us to humble ourselves as little children, and he provides a perfect example. (See Matt. 18:2; 20:27; John 13:3–10.) The Prophet Joseph also revealed that humility is an important condition for Latter-day Saints receiving the blessings of God's kingdom. (See D&C 61:37.)

One cannot receive and develop faith without humility; thus, these two qualities are often linked together in the scriptures. (See Mosiah 4:11; Alma 37:33; Ether 12:27; D&C 5:24; 104:79.[12]) Indeed, as Mormon indicated, the development of humility corresponds with a growing faith. (See Hel. 3:35.) Humility should be carefully cultivated into the fertile ground in which our seeds of truth may be planted and nurtured.

As we strive to develop humility, we might ask, "What attitudes help a person become humble and teachable?" One dual answer would probably suffice: "Sincerity and gratitude." The ancient prophets stressed the importance of sincerity in our prayers to God. (See Hel. 3:27; Moro. 10:4.) Gratitude for the things we have already received from God can also help develop our humility. (See Alma 34:38; 3 Ne. 10:10.) With a sincere, grateful attitude, our hearts are softened and ready to receive spiritual guidance. On the other hand, when we are vain and arrogant, the Spirit cannot reach us. Pride and faith are mutually exclusive: the proud feel no need to seek God's help, whereas the humble receive it and are strengthened. (See Hel. 6:35; 2 Ne. 9:28.) As sincerity and gratitude enrich our humility, we are prepared to receive God's spiritual knowledge. (See 1 Pet. 5:5–11; 2 Ne. 9:42; D&C 1:28.)

Sensitivity. The story is often told of a man in a loud, bustling city who heard the chirping of a bird over the city noises. As he looked around him, he noted that no one else heard the beautiful sounds of nature in the urban environment. As a test of the citizens' hearing ability, he dropped a large coin on the pavement. Immediately many people looked in his direction. The sound of money, not the bird, caught their attention. In a like manner, the whisperings of the Spirit may be echoing around us, but our attention may be centered on the mundane, material things of life. Sensitivity to the Spirit should be like a warm, moist climate within our souls that will allow our seeds of truth to germinate into new, vibrant seedlings.

In order to feel the Spirit, one must listen. As Jesus said, "Who hath ears to hear, let him hear." (Matt. 13:9.) We must tune our spiritual ears to personal revelation from God. Pondering and feeling are the attributes that cultivate this spiritual sensitivity. We need to separate ourselves from the distractions around us and ponder our own relationship with Heavenly Father. (See Moro. 10:3.) We also need to arouse the faculties of our souls and recognize with our inner spirits the feelings of truth, love, warmth, and goodness that the Spirit of God might manifest within us. (See Jacob 3:11; Alma 32:27–28; Moro. 7:16; D&C 9:8.)

Diligence. The ancient Hebrews were told of the diligence necessary to gain the full assurance or faith they needed to keep their hope strong and to gain their promised blessings. (See Heb. 6:10–15.) Latter-day Saints have also been admonished to seek diligently to increase their learning and faith. (See D&C 88:118.) A farmer's diligent work plows and tills the ground so the roots can grow in the loose, oxygenated soil. Our study and work cultivate the soil of our faith so our seedlings of faith can take root and grow.

Two key attributes will strengthen our diligence — patience and persistence. We need patience because the Lord's timetable for our spiritual development may not coincide with our own. Like spiritual teenagers, we may think we are mature and ready for new, profound revelations when actually we first need to master the basic necessities of simple faith. (See D&C 19:22.) Persistence is required because spiritual growth, like our physical health and fitness, is gained in gradual steps over long periods of time. (See 2 Ne. 28:30.) With patient, persistent diligence, our faith will grow stronger and stronger. (See Alma 32:42.)

Sacrifice. The Prophet Joseph taught "that a religion that does not require the sacrifice of all things never has power sufficient to produce the faith necessary unto life and salvation." He continued by saying that through the ages, "the faith necessary unto the enjoyment of life and salvation never could be obtained without the sacrifice of all earthly things."[13] Like the farmer who forfeits his easy chair and spends much time in his fields to increase their productivity, true sacrifice means a willingness to place religious concerns over material pursuits. Some of the easier pleasantries of life must be set aside to concentrate on more important spiritual questions. (See Matt. 6:19–24; D&C 97:8.)

We fulfill the expectations of sacrifice as we give of our time and means to build God's kingdom. We do this in two basic ways: first, we build and strengthen ourselves through righteous devotion, and second, we help others through missionary work and Christian service. Sacrifice and faith are intertwined to lead a person toward eternal life. We must sacrifice to gain faith, and we must have faith to gain eternal life. If we are willing to sacrifice all, as our Savior did, our faith in him and his plan of salvation will help reunite us with him and our Heavenly Father for the eternities. Such is the ultimate fruit of faith.

5. CULTIVATING FAITH THROUGH STUDY, PRAYER, AND OBEDIENCE

After the soil is prepared, the seedling must be nourished and cultivated. Alma's teachings and the Savior's parables in the New Testament warn us how easily the seedling's growth can be hindered. Alma taught that the young plant needs to be nourished "with much care" so it can take root, grow, and bear fruit. But he warned that even a good plant can die if the ground of our personal spiritual environment is barren, for "if [we] neglect the tree, and take no thought for its nourishment," it will not take root and the sun's heat will cause it to wither and die. He applied this process to our spiritual growth when he said, "If ye will not nourish the word, looking forward with an eye of faith to the fruit thereof, ye can never pluck of the fruit of the tree of life." (Alma 32:40.)

In the parable of the sower, the Savior warned us about the influences of Satan and the natural difficulties of nurturing a seed until it bears fruit. (See Matt. 13:3–9, 18–23.) In fact, we might not even receive great spiritual witnesses until after our faith has been tried and tested. (See Ether 12:6.) But he that nurtures the seed in the good ground hears and understands the word until it bears fruit, even a hundredfold. (See Matt. 13:23.)

The parable of the talents also shows us how easily the spiritual gifts can be hindered if we do not develop them. The servant with one talent did not invest it but rather hid it for safekeeping. When he presented his master with the same talent, the master took the talent away and chastised him, saying, "For unto every one that hath shall be given, and he shall have abundance: but from him that hath not shall be taken away even that which he hath." (Matt. 25:29; see vv. 14–30.) We will have our spiritual talents or seeds taken away from us if we do not plant and cultivate them. As we learn obedience, we will know the truths of God's doctrines. (See John 7:17.) Desire is not enough; we must nurture the seed of truth if we want the fruits of faith and righteousness.

Just as the successful cultivation of a plant requires light, water, and food, three areas of spiritual nurturing will bring about a stronger, more fruitful faith: study, prayer, and obedience.

Study. Anyone seeking faith in a gospel principle must first study and learn about that teaching. Our primary resource for gospel learning should be the scriptures. Jesus admonished his followers to "search the scriptures" for help in understanding eternal life and his special calling. (John 5:39.)[14] As we feast upon the scriptures (see 2 Ne. 32:3), study the words of the modern prophets, and ponder the inspired messages we hear at church meetings and classes, gospel ideals and eternal truths will enrich our understanding and stimulate our quest for further insights. Just as garden plants need light for survival, we need the light of the gospel to strengthen our testimonies.[15] When our gospel study reveals new precious seeds of truth, we must foster a desire to understand their underlying principles and to develop faith in their worth.

Prayer. Prayer is a primary means by which eternal truths are communicated from God.[16] In order to cultivate our faith, we must communicate daily with our Heavenly Father. In contrast, anyone neglecting regular spiritual contact with the Almighty will inevitably find their faith and commitment wavering. Prayer, like water for a plant, is a constant need. If neglected, signs of distress (thirst) will appear; if maintained, a healthy relationship (growth) is encouraged.

As we regularly study the gospel and daily petition God for direction, the Holy Spirit maintains our faith and strengthens our spirituality. The prophets and apostles have promised that through the Holy Ghost we can eventually "know the truth of all things." (Moro. 10:3–5; see also 2

Cor. 2:5–12.) New truths are revealed to us while we are cultivating our faith.

Obedience. Though knowledge of God is the foundation of faith, we can see from Satan's example that knowledge alone will not produce faith. As one of the most intelligent spirits in premortality, Satan was also the most proud. He thought his plan was better than Heavenly Father's. When his plan was rejected by God and the great majority of the premortal spirits, he rebelled. For his disobedience, he was cast out and left to his own devices, not knowing the things of God. (See Moses 4:3–6.) Obviously, knowledge alone did not cultivate his faith.

Obedience to the laws of God is a necessary catalyst that stimulates an increase of godly knowledge and a growth of spiritual faith. Elder Bruce R. McConkie wrote, "Faith is a gift of God bestowed as a reward for personal righteousness. It is always given when righteousness is present, and the greater the measure of obedience to God's laws the greater will be the endowment of faith."[17] As mentioned earlier, God and Jesus Christ should be the first objects of our faith. Therefore, if we wish to receive the full fruits of our budding faith, we must nurture it by patterning our lives after Christ, who embodies the divine principle of faith in our Heavenly Father. Our faith and obedience should be like his. Thus he counsels us, "Therefore, what manner of men ought ye to be? . . . Even as I am." (3 Ne. 27:27.)

To know what God knows, to possess the faith he possesses,[18] we must become as he is. Our seeds of knowledge and faith, when compared to the eventual full fruits of these attributes, are like the genetic material contained in a human embryo compared to a full-grown human being. All human potential is contained in the embryo, but it must be properly nourished to fully mature. Any seed or form of life requires food for growth. In spiritual terms, righteousness through obedience is the nutrient necessary for transforming our attributes from the natural into the divine.

The apostle John wrote: "Beloved, now are we the *sons* of God, and it *doth not yet* appear what we shall be: but we know that, when he shall appear, *we shall be like him; for we shall see him as he is.* And every man that hath this hope in him purifieth himself, even as he [God] is pure." (1 Jn. 3:2–3; italics added.) Those who will again enjoy God's presence will have become righteous and loving like him. In summary, like the necessary sun, water, and nutrients in a plant's growth, these catalysts — study, prayer, and obedience — produce a spiritual reaction that develops our faith. We must incorporate these three ingredients in order for our seeds of truth to produce sweet fruit.

6. TASTING THE FRUITS OF FAITHFUL LIVING

A cyclical process — truth begetting faith begetting good works begetting truth begetting faith, etc. — continues in a spiral pattern as the seed of knowledge takes root in us, the tender plant of faith grows within us, and eventually the tree of righteousness bears the fruit of spirituality: "Ye shall feast upon this fruit even until ye are filled, that ye hunger not, neither shall ye thirst." (Alma 32:42; cf. Heb. 12:9–11; D&C 52:34.) If we nurture the seedling until it bears fruit, we will no longer lack for truth, faith, or spiritual gifts because we will possess them as attributes of our character, as does God himself. (See Gal. 5:22–25; Eph. 5:9.)

On the other hand, though Satan was one of the most innately intelligent of God's spirit children, "a son of the morning," his chance to develop eternally was cut off through disobedience and a lack of faith. He rejected the pattern of spirituality and brought spiritual death and damnation into his own life. He now desires to bring the same catastrophes into the lives of others. Ironically, while trying to subvert the plan of salvation after his expulsion from heaven, "he sought also to beguile Eve, for he knew not the mind of God, wherefore he sought to destroy the world." (Moses 4:6.) But instead of destroying the world by deceiving Eve and Adam, Satan thereby brought the plan of redemption into force. We are now able to come to the earth and develop our spirituality.

As a true saint of Christ takes advantage of the plan of redemption and tastes the fruits of increased faith, a spiral pattern of expanding spirituality is developed. If we can maintain this pattern despite worldly and personal challenges, then we are following a path that leads to life eternal with the Father and the Son. (See John 17:20–23.)

In premortality, we were not called upon to exercise our faith in God until we agreed both to leave behind our intimate knowledge of his existence and also to develop faith in his power to bring us back to him. The bulk of our development of faith must then take place here on earth, away from him. If we regain his presence, our knowledge will be perfect, supplanting faith; the eternal cycle will be complete for us as our faith is transformed into divine power. Therefore, faith remains throughout our progression as "the first great governing principle which has power, dominion, and authority over all things."[19] Once we transform our faith into power, we can assist in beginning a new cycle by organizing intelligences into spirits and creating worlds on which they can develop their faith.

THE COMPANIONS OF FAITH

Before we leave this chapter on faith, we need to make comparisons between faith and some principles closely associated with it: faith and belief, faith and knowledge, and faith and works.

FAITH AND BELIEF

For many people today, faith seems to mean little more than belief. Belief is a mental conviction that a person has of something, whether it is real or imagined. Faith adds a spiritual context or confirmation to the mental conviction, which usually leads to some action. For example, belief is defined as a "mental act . . . of placing trust or confidence in a person or thing" or as the "mental acceptance or conviction in the truth or existence of something."[20] Faith is defined as "a confident belief in the truth, value, or trustworthiness of a person, idea, or thing," as a "belief that does not rest on logical proof or material evidence," and as a "belief and trust in God and in the doctrines expressed in the Scriptures."[21] Notice that belief is mostly a mental act while faith seems to be a step beyond that. The LDS Bible Dictionary supports this relationship and indicates that faith is more than belief "since true faith always moves its possessor to some kind of physical and mental action."[22]

However, the ancient prophets and apostles did not distinguish between the terms *faith* and *belief.* In the writings of the scriptures, especially the Bible, the two concepts were synonymous. Indeed, the basic terms *believe* and *faith* come from the same Hebrew and Greek roots. The Old Testament Hebrew root is *'aman,* meaning "to build up or support," "to render (or be) firm or faithful," or "to trust or believe."[23] The New Testament Greek root is *pistis,* meaning "credence, conviction, assurance, belief, faith, or fidelity."[24] Thus, while some people may feel that faith is a step above belief, the scriptural sources will not have that same distinction.[25]

FAITH AND KNOWLEDGE

Some skeptics consider faith and knowledge to be mutually exclusive, that faith simply explains some voids that knowledge has not yet filled. The prophets indicate, however, that they mutually complement each other. Moses and Joseph Smith taught that a knowledge of God's existence has been on the earth since the days of Adam, and this knowledge has helped Adam's posterity in the development of their faith.[26] Faith in God and gospel principles cannot exist without a knowledge of some basic facts. We must know something about a concept or person before we can develop faith or understanding about it.[27] Or as Paul asked, "How shall they believe in him of whom they have not heard?" (Rom. 10:14.) Thus a certain amount of knowledge must precede faith.

The prophets also taught that our knowledge continues to grow as our faith develops. Alma taught that "faith is not to have a perfect knowledge of things" (Alma 32:21), but we can at least know when the object of our faith is good and true. (See Alma 32:28, 33–36.) The amount of knowledge, especially in spiritual matters, that we receive seems to be dependent upon our faith, spiritual maturity, and God's desires. (See 2 Ne. 28:30; Alma 18:35.) A greater knowledge and understanding of God cannot be obtained without an adequate amount of faith and spiritual help. (See D&C 121:26–28.) Eventually, when we see Christ and know all truth, our faith will be replaced with a "perfect knowledge." (Alma 32:26; see also Ether 3:19–20; D&C 93:1, 26–28.) Therefore, the two are intertwined with each other like spiritual cords within a rope — we must have knowledge upon which to build our faith, which in turn increases our knowledge — until both are fulfilled.

FAITH AND WORKS

One last term often associated with *faith* is *works*. The ancient Apostle James taught that faith and works go together: faith without works is dead, and by works faith is made perfect. (See James 2:14–26.) We must not only express to God our faith in him, but we also need to live as he would have us live — obedient to all the commandments and full of love. (See 1 Jn. 2.) Jesus also taught that we can recognize the nature of someone by his or her fruits — a good tree will bring forth good fruits. (See Matt. 7:15–20.)

As discussed earlier, a growing faith will naturally motivate us to bring forth good works of Christian service. Our faith and love should be evidenced in our works. Alma states clearly that real faith will bring forth abundant good works. (See Alma 7:24.) Beyond the natural Christian service that we might give, we may also benefit from special spiritual works resulting from true faith, such as "miracles, visions, dreams, healings, and all the gifts of God that he gives to his saints."[28] Thus, the greater our faith — the greater our works.

As a final comparison, knowledge, faith, and works are like three cords woven together in a strong spiritual rope. Each cord is necessary; without one of them, the rope weakens and eventually breaks. As they reinforce each other and are strengthened and enlarged through the Spirit of God, they become a mighty cable of spirituality in our lives.

In conclusion, we can say that *FAITH is an assurance of unseen truths, a feeling of confidence in God, and a principle of action centered in Christ, which provides us a hope of divine promises, a motivation toward righteous living, and a catalyst that generates spiritual life.* We must cultivate this gift of God and share its transforming power with others as we grow toward more complete spirituality. As we develop faith in Heavenly Father, we come to know someone we can trust, a divine being who loves us. As he nurtures our faith in his truths, his Son, and ourselves, we receive a more perfect knowledge and perform more righteous works. As we encourage others to develop faith on their way of spiritual life, we also come to recognize that faith is indeed the first eternal principle of Christ's gospel.

For further study, refer to the following entries:

TG	BD	EM
Assurance	Faith	Faith in Jesus Christ
Believe		First Principles of the
Faith		Gospel
Trust in God		Lectures on Faith

CHAPTER 17

TURNING BACK: THE PROCESS
OF REPENTANCE

Have you ever been in a dirty, cluttered home or messy apartment and felt it reflected the personality of its occupant? Think of the task of cleaning and organizing everything in that dwelling. Even more challenging, imagine assuming the responsibility of helping the occupant to develop a whole new life-style of cleanliness and tidiness. When a dwelling is filthy and messy, it is less attractive and habitable. Besides being more difficult to maintain tidiness and a healthy environment, it may even foster antisocial behavior. Although housecleaning may be a major project, it is necessary to break out of unhealthy patterns and maintain a neat and functional residence.

Even greater difficulties arise when one tries to cleanse filthiness from a person's soul that the wickedness of the world has corrupted. When our spirit is sinful, we offend others and disturb ourselves, which leads to frustration and straying from God's path. Repenting is like cleaning a dirty house and establishing new habits—we may not look forward to cleansing and changing our life, but we must do it if we are to achieve spiritual purity and harmony.

WHAT IS REPENTANCE?

The New Testament terms translated into *repent* and *repentance* come from a Greek root, *metamorphoō,* meaning "to transform, change, or transfigure." This same root has evolved into the term *metamorphosis.* In biology, metamorphosis is the natural change in the structure and habits of an animal during normal growth—such as when a caterpillar transforms into a butterfly or a tadpole transfigures into a frog. In our spiritual life, when we reverse our negative behavior and enhance our spirituality, we initiate a process of transformation called repentance.

The word *repent* shows up relatively few times in the Old Testament. When it does, it is usually derived from the Hebrew word *nacham,* meaning "to sigh heavily" or "to be sorry." However, the Hebrew term used much more often to describe the repentance process in the Old Testament is *shuv,* usually translated as "to return" or "to turn back." The idea is to simply turn away (from sin) and to return (to goodness). To turn back or return to a state of goodness implies that though once good and righteous in the sight of God, we have detoured off that path of righteousness in our journey through earth life. The sorrow (or "heavy sighing") results from our feelings of disappointment.

As discussed in chapter twelve, we all have experienced physical and spiritual detours during our lives. We neither wanted nor planned them, but they have occurred anyway. Our spiritual detours resulted from associating with the wrong people, exploring foolish ambitions, or behaving improperly. Repentance is simply to return as soon as possible to where we should be—to get back on the right path. The emphasis may at first weigh on the negative, turning away from sin, but it should quickly shift to the positive, turning back to God as we begin new, more faithful lives.

Unfortunately, our image of repentance often carries heavy, dark, negative undertones dating back to early Catholic Christianity. The English term *repent* inherited a major flaw from its Latin origins, *repoenitere,* meaning "to experience pain, grief, or distress." Apostate medieval Christianity emphasized grief rather than the original dominant concept of a change of direction. Exhortations of ancient prophets, the Savior, and the apostles demonstrate that "change," especially a change of mind, was the primary focus behind the original terms, while grief, behavior modification, and other characteristics were secondary elements of the repentance process.[1]

How does repentance relate to the earlier example of a filthy room? Every newlywed couple probably plan to have a neat, clean dwelling. But despite expectations, they may find that their residence has instead become dirty and disorganized. They have detoured from their expectations, and they see a need to *change,* or repent, to get their house back in order. Obviously, they first must recognize that present conditions are unsuitable. They then need to feel some sense of embarrassment over the sorry state of things and decide to change their behavior, giving up previous habits and committing to new patterns. They probably could use the help and support of others during this important time of readjustment. Eventually, they will be able to harmonize their expectations with their behavior, and cleanliness and peace will dwell in their home.

Similarly, remedying the spiritual imperfections of our lives goes through a process. For ease in classifying and remembering the process, it has been broken down into six steps, each of which has been "tagged" with the beginning letter *R*: recognition, remorse, renunciation, resolution, restitution, and reconciliation. As one goes through the repentance process, these steps often overlap, but they are all necessary before the process can be completed.

RECOGNITION

Words like *sin, wickedness,* and *repentance* are almost never heard in public discourse nowadays — in an age when personal accountability has been undermined by popular psychology, they are considered at best old-fashioned and at worst offensive. Fittingly, LDS scholar Hugh Nibley writes: "The fatal symptom of our day is not that men do wrong — they always have — and commit crimes, and even recognize their wrongdoing as foolish and unfortunate, but that they have *no intention of repenting,* while God has told us that the first rule that he has given the human race is that all men everywhere must repent."[2] Although a tendency to blame personal faults on someone else or something beyond our control is prevalent in today's society, a willingness to accept responsibility for one's actions is the first requisite for repentance.

Before we can undertake the steps of repentance, we must feel that our present life is unsatisfactory, probably as a result of our own actions. In short, we must desire to change. If we value our spiritual well-being, we will want to rid ourselves of sin. This inner feeling motivates us to seek something better in life. A modern apostle, David B. Haight, has said, "If we could feel or were sensitive even in the slightest to the matchless love of our Savior and his willingness to suffer for our individual sins, we would cease procrastination and 'clean the slate,' and repent of all our transgressions."[3]

As discussed in chapter ten on agency, we are all influenced in some degree by circumstances outside our control. But within all people lies their conscience, the light of Christ, which prompts them to recognize the right and repent of their wrongs. Furthermore, the light of Christ leads people to the Holy Ghost, through whose power they may overcome faults and inhibitions.[4] Thus, the Lord promises, "My grace is sufficient for all men that humble themselves before me; for if they humble themselves before me, and have faith in me, then will I make weak things become strong unto them." (Ether 12:27.)

This desire to change must be fed by a hope that lasting results will occur. Here, a friend or family member who is strong in the faith can be of inestimable value—for the nonmember seeking a new Christian lifestyle, the less-active member wanting to return to the fold, and the member struggling to overcome weaknesses. A trusted confidant can gently encourage and help the repentant one to recognize the promptings of the Holy Ghost, which brings both hope and power to change. Trust in a friend and a realization of the power of the Holy Ghost leads the repentant to faith in God—faith that God can be approached and that he will forgive.

Now the purification process of repentance can begin. In fact, the first step has already been accomplished. This step—as all children raised in the Church learn at an early age—is to *recognize* our errors and sins. Despite how we may have been originally deceived or coerced into sin, the recognition of sin through the light of Christ and the Holy Ghost places the burden of repentance squarely on our shoulders. If we argue that our guilt is unfair, we are not yet ready to repent. Thus Alma the younger counseled his son Corianton, who had committed fornication while serving a mission to the Zoramites, "Do not endeavor to excuse yourself in the least point because of your sins, by denying the justice of God; but do let the justice of God, and his mercy, and his long-suffering have full sway in your heart; and let it bring you down to the dust in humility." (Alma 42:30.)

Remorse

When we cease to rationalize our behavior and are willing to humble ourselves before God, we are then prepared for the second step of repentance. This is genuine *remorse,* which Paul referred to as "godly sorrow" for sin when he addressed the repentant Corinthians: "Now I rejoice, not that ye were made sorry, but that ye sorrowed to repentance:

for ye were made sorry after a godly manner, . . . for *godly sorrow worketh repentance* to salvation . . . but the sorrow of the world worketh death." (2 Cor. 7:9–10; italics added.)

The step of remorse is closely associated with the original Latin meaning of *repent,* meaning "in response to sorrow." However, there are different types of sorrow. Godly sorrow is abhorrence of sin because it is inherently wrong and harmful. Worldly sorrow, on the other hand, is like the sorrow felt by a thief who doesn't regret that he stole, only that he was caught and is going to jail. Godly sorrow implies action and a determination to turn one's life around with God's help. Worldly sorrow is to feel self-pity and a sense of helplessness. Bruce R. McConkie expressed it well by saying, "Godly sorrow is born of the Spirit; it is a gift of God that comes to those who have a broken heart and a contrite spirit. It includes an honest, heartfelt contrition, a frank recognition of sins committed, and a firm determination to go and sin no more."[5] Thus, remorse for the past must be sincere and come from within for it to truly affect future attitudes and behavior.

One may ask, "How can we help someone else through this step of remorse?" It is *not* the responsibility of other people, even Church or family members, to "make the person feel guilty." If they are aware of the sinful behavior of a person, their most helpful service is to encourage the person to pray to God and to go to proper Church leaders so the repentance process can begin in the errant person's life. With an attitude of trying to help the person rather than one of not trying to punish him or her, they can inform the person of the immediate harmful effects and the possible future consequences of sinful acts. They can also remind the person of the blessings and peace that can come as a change for the better is made.

Unsought, self-righteous counsel and condemnation, however, must be strictly avoided; rather than helping someone along, these actions usually promote bitterness and resentment. If the sinful person has already recognized the error, and he or she is experiencing remorse, then family members and friends should strengthen, encourage, and hold out hope for the individual to continue through the other steps of repentance. Their primary goal should be to help individuals to help themselves, not to alienate or belittle them.

RENUNCIATION (INCLUDING CONFESSION)

Recognizing and feeling sorry for sins is not enough. Third, the sinner must *renounce and confess* the transgression to the Lord and, in many cases, to others as well. In this step the one seeking change actually turns away from improper behavior. This is a pivotal step, where the person actually begins to leave the sin behind. As he forsakes negative behavior, he needs to admit his errors to those affected by his acts.

Only through confession are private feelings of remorse transformed into a tangible commitment to change: "For with the heart man believeth unto righteousness; and with the mouth confession is made unto salvation." (Rom. 10:10.) The confession is more than just an admission that a mistake was made — it should also indicate a total separation from that negative behavior. As Orson Pratt stated, "A confession of sins, unaccompanied with the resolution to forsake, is a solemn mockery before Him, and will add to our guilt, and increase the displeasure of heaven against us."[6]

With any sin, we offend God and often others. In most cases, a confession of sin need take place only to God and to those persons directly wronged by it. With a few more serious sins, we may have so misrepresented the behavior expected of Christ's disciples that our fellowship in his church may be affected. "Major" sins (defined by the late President Spencer W. Kimball as sexual sins and "other sins of comparable seriousness," such as felony crimes, family and drug abuse, and so on) must also be confessed to proper Church authorities. "This procedure," President Kimball continues, "assures proper controls and protection for the Church and its people and sets the feet of the transgressor on the path of true repentance."[7]

Going to proper Church authorities is not easy, but it is occasionally necessary. Latter-day Saints should remember that bishops, stake and mission presidents, and General Authorities are set apart as special judges in Israel. As such, they have the right and responsibility to receive special inspiration in counseling the repentant Saint. They can also help the person recognize the true seriousness of his or her transgressions and the ways one's fellowship in the Church is affected. As the Lord told an ancient prophet and judge, "Go; and whosoever transgresseth against me, him shall ye judge according to the sins which he has committed;

and if he confess his sins before thee and me, and repenteth in the sincerity of his heart, him shall ye forgive, and I will forgive him also." (Mosiah 26:29.)

The Church leader has four basic courses of action that he can follow: First, he may feel the member has genuinely repented and should be so informed, as well as comforted and strengthened in the resolve to continue on the path of righteousness. Second, he may feel the repentance process is under way but not yet complete, and so the member is placed in a state of probation with certain restrictions and expectations as defined by the leader. Third, the sin may be serious enough to require the disfellowshipment of the member, with certain prescribed restrictions (such as no Church callings or public talks and prayers) placed upon the person. Finally, the sins may be so serious that the person is beyond the behavior even closely resembling that of a true Christian and thus the person is excommunicated from the Church.

The last two courses of action are very serious and require a formal procedure of Church discipline (formerly called a "Church court") with the sustaining support of both counselors (for a bishop's action) as well as of the local high council (for a stake president's action). Ironically, such serious disciplinary actions often help wayward members recognize the seriousness of their behavior, serving as a spiritual catalyst and motivating many to reform their lives. Probationary and disfellowshipped members may be brought back into full, active fellowship within a short period of time, as determined by the Church leader. Excommunicated members generally need to wait at least a year, during which they must demonstrate the fruits of repentance and righteous devotion. Then they can reapply for Church membership and the restoration of former priesthood and temple blessings. (Note that any case of Church discipline may be appealed through Church channels. That is, a bishop's action may be appealed to the stake president, or a stake president's action may be appealed to Church headquarters. Thus the member is insured a fair hearing with both his interests and those of the Church being justly evaluated.)

This step of renunciation is more than just privately or publicly recognizing the wrong; it also involves making a clean break and leaving that wrong behind while beginning to change for the better. For this step to take effect, especially with serious sins, the help of loved ones, family members, and Church leaders is vitally important. They can encourage the repentant one in removing the burden of sin from the soul so the person can move forward on a path of righteousness.

RESOLUTION

President Kimball has said, "It is imperative that when one has once put his feet on the path to recovery and mastery there must be no turning back."[8] Once a sin has been cast off, the repentant transgressor must make a firm *resolve* or commitment to forsake that weakness and to live righteously. "By this ye may know if a man repenteth of his sins—behold, he will confess them and forsake them." (D&C 58:43.) At this fourth step or stage, the person has turned the corner of repentance. Elder Neal A. Maxwell said, "Real repentance consists of turning away from that which is wrong and also turning to God. A full revolution! This is the most lasting and beneficial of all revolutions!"[9] This pivot point is where we turn to God with a promise to obey him.

Without a firm commitment to both forsake our sin and live righteously, recognition, remorse, and renunciation of earlier misdeeds will bring only empty bitterness to the soul. (Remember the Latin root of *repentance,* with its emphasis upon sorrow.) Instead of looking back and regretting the problems we have caused, we must resolve to look forward to the blessings our Father in Heaven can now give us. (Remember the Hebrew root of *repentance,* meaning to turn back or return to the Lord.)

We cannot look in two directions at once with clear vision, especially backward and forward. Indeed, we are told to "look forward with steadfastness unto Christ." (2 Ne. 25:24.) Elder Bruce R. McConkie elaborated on this point, saying that ceasing from sin is the commencement of repentance; "To turn to righteousness and keep the commandments is a greater and more ennobling course, as when the immoral sinner not only forsakes his unchaste ways, but keeps the commandments in general, thus assuring himself of forgiveness."[10] We must have faith that the Lord and the Holy Spirit will give us strength as we begin the uphill course of repentance. Again, this commitment should be made with God, Church authorities (if necessary), and even those who have been wronged by the sin.

Bishops are often intensely involved with these steps of repentance, especially concerning repentance of sexual sins among young people. Once the transgressors and the bishop have assessed, through confession, how much deviation from the strait and narrow path has occurred, a discussion of the repentance process and a renewal of personal goals help the members to unify themselves again with the Church and God. Oftentimes, a bishop who has won the confidence of the repentant person can be a great strength in sharing the burdens and challenges of the repentance process. The transgressor who genuinely wants to overcome sin will work hard to do what is right, not only to avoid disappointing himself and the Lord, but also to keep the confidence of his ally, the bishop, as well.

Usually, the repentant set their goals and timetable around partaking of the sacrament[11] on Sunday. As a bishop clears repentant individuals to partake of the sacrament, they know that they have reached an important milestone in renewing their baptismal commitment to the Lord. For both "minor" transgressions between individuals and the Lord and "major" ones where the bishop has been involved, the sacrament is provided weekly for forgiveness and spiritual renewal. The fact that it is available weekly should remind us of our continuous need for repentance and recommitment. It is significant, too, that we do not partake of the sacrament privately but together, as a public admission that we "all have sinned, and come short of the glory of God." (Rom. 3:23.)

The serious sins of others do not permit us to pass judgment or feel superior to them. Rather, let us act as saviors on Mount Zion by empathizing, listening, and encouraging. This positive environment will help the sinner return to a state of happiness.

RESTITUTION

Whenever possible, the repentant transgressor must try to make *restitution* for his sins. With this fifth step, the person leaves the last burdens behind and continues up the path of spiritual progression. Currently, this portion of the sinner's reformation is often neglected in the secular courts. However, just restitution remains critical in religious matters. In fact, because repairing or returning exactly what was lost, especially moral and spiritual damage, is difficult, the person should do as much as possible to balance the scales of justice.

Anciently, the law of Moses required not just equal restoration of defrauded property but additional punitive damages as well. For example, "if a man shall steal an ox, or a sheep, and kill it, or sell it; he shall restore five oxen for an ox, and four sheep for a sheep." (Ex. 22:1.) In other words, sin holds so many unforeseen consequences that a higher quality product should replace what has been lost. It is like a debt whose interest rapidly accrues. One should try to give back more than what was taken so that justice will be more than satisfied.

For example, if a person borrows a neighbor's lawn mower and severely damages it, he should at least have it repaired in even better condition than when he borrowed it. If the damage cannot be repaired, he would probably need to purchase a new machine, or at least a good used one. If the neighbor gets a better machine back, he may be upset that his lawn mower was damaged, but he should feel good about the other person who went the second mile in restoring his equipment. Thus no hard feelings should develop between the two people, and a relationship of respect and trust can be built.

This step heals the sinner as well as the victim. Rather than forgetting about the other people involved, it helps prepare for forgiveness and reconciliation, especially with the Lord. By restoring more than what was taken, the offender not only clears his or her debt, but also, to a certain degree, brings the other person into a forgiving, loving mood. This step is even more difficult when one is trying to provide restitution for spiritual, moral, and emotional offenses. One must demonstrate to Heavenly Father and others that he or she is diligently striving to bring much more good into the world than the evil the individual has caused. As powerful examples in the scriptures, note how Paul in the New Testament and the sons of Mosiah and Alma the Younger in the Book of Mormon spent the rest of their lives trying to provide restitution for the serious sins and acts of their earlier lives. (See Acts 9:4–19; 22:7; 26:14; Gal. 1:15–16; Mosiah 27:32–28:8; Alma 5:3–61; 36:3–21.)

RECONCILIATION THROUGH FORGIVENESS

The sixth and last step of repentance is *reconciliation* between the sinner and the offended parties. Now that the transgressor has broken from the past by renouncing and compensating for his past errors, he is ready to ask God and others for forgiveness. Reconcilement with those we have wronged will hasten the cleansing process within our souls and bring a feeling of peace and harmony with family and friends. This rapprochement will only occur when the past is forgotten and all parties are willing to forgive and forget.

Harmony with God is the most important reconciliation. He and his Spirit cannot abide with us unless we are free of sin. Reconciliation occurs when we conform ourselves to God's will, remembering that salvation comes through his grace. (See 2 Ne. 10:24.[12]) The prophets and apostles have taught that we receive this harmony through the atonement of Jesus Christ. (See 2 Cor. 5:17–20.) It is necessary before we can be in full fellowship with Christ's saints. (See D&C 46:4.)

The act of forgiveness is the crucial element in this step. Forgiveness has three stages: (1) we ask others to forgive us, (2) we express willingness to forgive others, and (3) we receive forgiveness from others. The model petition for forgiveness is in the Lord's prayer where he instructs us to ask Heavenly Father to "forgive us our debts,[13] as we forgive our debtors." (Matt. 6:12; see also Mosiah 26:31; D&C 42:88.) This is a classic example that illustrates that one cannot simply ask for a gift but must first give before receiving.

Separating the prefix from the root of "fore-give," we can see that the literal meaning of the word is "given in advance." The Old English term (*forgiefan*) is a translation of the Medieval Latin word for *pardon* (*perdonare*), meaning "to give wholeheartedly." The Greek root means "to send forth." The Hebrew root means "to carry away" or "to pardon or spare." So when we forgive someone, we carry away, send forth, or spare their burden of transgression. This is a gift we should give wholeheartedly, not begrudgingly. Similarly, when we receive the gift of forgiveness, we should accept it with sincere appreciation. True forgiveness heals the wounds of both the transgressor and the person who was wronged.

Unfortunately the act of forgiveness is sometimes one directional. That is, only one party is willing to forgive. Either the repentant person requests but does not receive forgiveness from the offended one, or the offended person offers a pardon but the transgressor does not feel that he or she is worthy to receive forgiveness. Also, there are cases where both parties have offended, but only one is willing to extend forgiveness. The one not receiving forgiveness should not hold it over the other, demanding or expecting forgiveness. Sadly, people unable to forgive are usually hurting themselves more than others, although all suffer to a certain extent until reconcilement is achieved. Instead, turning to the Lord, who forgives all freely, will bring the peace and blessings that come from harmonizing our love with his. (See Mosiah 26:22–24.)

REMISSION OF SINS

After completing these six steps of repentance, culminating with reconciliation and forgiveness, we are ready to receive a full remission of or release from our sins. This occurs when we enter the waters of baptism or renew the baptismal covenant through the sacrament. Like a glorious Sabbath day of rest after a week of soul-searching labor, one could call this the seventh and most wonderful capstone step of repentance. Remission gives us a new, free beginning to the rest of our lives. Guilt flees as we know that God not only has forgiven us, but also has chosen to forget our transgressions—thus the burden of the past is gone. (See Jer. 31:34; Heb. 8:12; 10:17.) The sweet companionship of his Holy Spirit comes into our lives and confirms the cleansing process.[14] The peace that comes into our lives results from the greatest blessing of repentance—a release of our sins through Christ's atonement.

The peace that accompanies a remission of our sins will come only if we have faith. Faith unto repentance leads us through the steps of repentance because we trust in the power of Christ's atonement, leaving our sins with him, letting go of our guilt, and seeking for a new purity. One clear example of faith unto repentance is in the book of Enos. After "wrestling" before God for a remission of his sins, Enos recorded, "There came a voice unto me, saying: Enos, thy sins are forgiven thee, . . . thy faith hath made thee whole." (Enos 1:5–8.)

In a simple comparison, repentance is like updating a computer file. Once it replaces the old file, only the new one needs to remain in the memory bank. The cleansing, sanctifying power of the Atonement allows us the opportunity to remove the imperfections from our soul and to come forth clean and pure. Thereafter, our record of recollection will be the final, polished edition. Until that day of final cleansing, we will retain some recollection of earlier transgressions. This remembrance keeps us humble and helps us avoid repeating similar mistakes. In addition, we can better empathize with others and their weaknesses. We can also wisely counsel others on the pitfalls of sin and the struggles of repentance. And if we have truly repented and been forgiven, this recollection should not renew the bitter anguish of guilt.

IF WE DON'T REPENT, THEN WHAT?

Of course, we have the agency to choose whether or not to repent. Although we may escape the consequences and punishment for our wicked deeds temporarily, eventually we will have to fully pay for them ourselves. (See Matt 5:26.[15]) Suffering for sin is so severe that Jesus admonishes us to avoid it by partaking of his atoning sacrifice. If not, we must suffer as he did in the Garden of Gethsemane, "which suffering caused [him]self, even God, the greatest of all, to tremble because of pain, and to bleed at every pore, and to suffer both body and spirit." (D&C 19:18.)

The prophets use graphic language in trying to describe this suffering, comparing it to a lake of fire and brimstone, a place of endless torment, and a burning in the lowest depths of hell. (See Rev. 20:14; Mosiah 3:25; Luke 16:28; Deut. 32:22.) No one will know how bitter it is until they suffer it themselves. Jesus warned us, saying, "Repent, lest I smite you . . . by my wrath, and by my anger, and your sufferings be sore – how sore you know not, how exquisite you know not, yea, how hard to bear you know not." (D&C 19:15.)

Although all of us make mistakes during our probationary state on earth, surely we are not so foolish as to turn aside the promises of repentance so that we will have to suffer ourselves for all of our sins. We should choose now, today, to begin our repentance process instead of procrastinating the day of our repentance until it is too late. (See Alma 12:37; 34:33.) Death may, at any time, cut off our chances for repentance in the flesh. Or we may not have enough time to work through the process of repentance and forgiveness. Or we may simply lose our desire to repent. Any of these will leave us in the awful state the prophets have often described.

In conclusion, *REPENTANCE means both feeling genuine sorrow for our sins and turning our hearts toward God. It is a process involving recognition of our transgressions, sincere remorse, renunciation of wickedness, a firm resolve to become more godlike, restitution to those we have wronged, and reconciliation through forgiveness (and a willingness to for-*

give) — qualifying us for a release from our burdens through Christ's atonement. The act by which we formally receive a remission of our sins is initially through baptism[16] and thereafter through renewal of our baptismal covenant by partaking of the Lord's sacrament. Once we are free from sin, we are then worthy to have God's Spirit with us. The light of his love will then shine upon us as we learn and live the truths of salvation.

For further study, refer to the following entries:

TG	BD	*EM*
Confession	Confession	Confession of Sin
Forgive, Forgiveness	Repentance	Disciplinary
Punish, Punishment	Restitution;	Procedures
Reconciliation,	Restoration	Remission of Sins
Reconcile		Repentance
Remission of Sins		
Repent, Repentance		

CHAPTER 18

THE CLEANSING COVENANT
OF BAPTISM

Few people today take the foolish risk of major financial commitment based only on good feelings and a verbal agreement. Instead, to protect themselves and their property, most people draw up written contracts in precise legal form. In contrast to this strict legalistic approach to temporal affairs, however, modern people are generally quite lax concerning the formalities of religious observances. This is most evident in the ordinance of baptism—once the foundation of all Christian religions—which is no longer even performed in some denominations professing Jesus Christ. In these cases, philosophic sentiment has supplanted symbolic ritual.

Just as in legal matters in which people are judged by their actions as manifestations of their intents and feelings, religious beliefs must manifest themselves in acts, including symbolic ones, to have saving power. Legally, a contract is a necessary indication of a person's intention; likewise, religious commitment is demonstrated by symbolic ordinances. The gospel of Jesus Christ requires baptism as its first and primary symbolic ordinance. Baptism not only marks one's entrance into Christianity, it also opens the way for spiritual regeneration.

THE FOURFOLD PURPOSE OF BAPTISM

Before discussing how a symbolic ritual creates actual, literal changes in our being, we should first study the purpose of baptism. As revealed through ancient and modern scripture, baptism has four main functions. First, baptism in water is a *symbol* of cleansing and rebirth preparatory to the baptism of fire by the Holy Ghost. Second, it is an *ordinance* that culminates the last step of repentance for those seeking a remission of sins. Third, baptism is a *covenant* in which one takes the name of Christ

281

upon oneself and vows to keep his commandments. Finally, baptism is a *gateway* admitting the person first to membership in Christ's church on earth and later into the celestial kingdom. Thus, baptism starts the disciple on the strait and narrow path leading to eternal life.

BAPTISM AS A SYMBOL OF NEW LIFE

Symbolic rituals among foreign, primitive cultures are quickly identified but rarely understood by visiting strangers. Although some study these rituals out of curiosity and others try to imitate them, most people from "civilized" nations consider any such rituals to be out of place in modern society. But as materialistic, straightforward, and modern as our culture may appear, all types of symbols and representations permeate it.

Even simple, common acts can be loaded with symbolic importance, even though we often do not think of the meanings behind the acts. A simple handshake, for example, has symbolic meanings of friendship and trust. In medieval times, a handshake in which armed men extended bare hands was a token of trust that meant they were *not* bringing forth their weapons. "Let's shake on it" can still mean the honored end of a negotiated contract between people. These symbolic meanings rarely come to mind when two people grasp hands as a quick gesture of greeting or parting.

Other symbols in our society obviously represent something, though people disagree as to their meanings. For example, in contemporary society, men and women argue over the implied messages of a man opening the door for a woman, or a woman asking a man out to lunch. Objects can also represent status in society, such as cars, houses, clothing, and so on, though status symbols do not mean the same thing to different people. Symbolic acts and objects are thus a natural part of modern life, though their meanings are not always understood or remembered.

To understand the ramifications of a symbolic ordinance such as baptism, we must first understand what a symbol is. Our English word is transliterated from the Greek word *symbolon,* which means "something brought together." The original symbolons were coins or potsherds (small pieces of pottery) broken into two pieces to identify the parties in a legal agreement. Each fragment became a symbol representing the agreement, and the two were brought together again when the conditions of the bargain were fulfilled. In simplest terms, then, a symbol is a concrete representation of something abstract and greater than itself, which leads us to comprehend or obtain something of value. Likewise, baptism is a physical act that symbolizes the union of spirit and flesh, cleansing, and rebirth.

A Symbolic Ritual Uniting Spirit and Flesh. In baptism, the concrete symbol is a physical act of bodily immersion in water, representing a subjection of our will to God, which, in turn, can transform a person's soul. By virtue of the ritual act, we achieve for a brief moment in mortality what can only be sustained in eternity: complete unity between the flesh and the spirit (like two Greek symbolons brought together). "For man is spirit. The elements are eternal, and spirit and element, inseparably connected, receive a fulness of joy; and when separated, man cannot receive a fulness of joy." (D&C 93:33–34.)

Most of the time on earth, the spirit and elements (flesh) are at variance with one another, harboring conflicting desires. Thus, our joy is not full. Symbolic ritual brings body and spirit into harmony by elevating the flesh to the level of the spirit in order to transform the soul, for "the spirit and the body are the soul of man." (D&C 88:15.) Perhaps this explains why many adult converts to the Church, who have previously not felt this binding of body and spirit, report such a joyous experience as they come out of the waters of baptism. The human spirit must learn to subdue its flesh so that the entire soul may become divine. Baptism is a symbol of such submission and unity.

A Symbolic Cleansing of Body and Spirit. The specific form of baptism, by immersion, also has symbolic richness. It illustrates better than any other ordinance the symbolic power of ritual. Since a major purpose of baptism is the remission of sins, this washing away of guilt is represented by water. But why water? Hugh Nibley explains that "water is not only a symbol of cleansing, cooling, refreshing, and reviving: it actually does all those things, at one and the same time."[1] Thus the associations between the concrete actions of water and the abstract quality of purity it represents correspond exactly. Equally important is the total immersion in water to achieve a complete cleansing from impure to pure. (Note that something not completely pure is impure. There is no such thing as partially pure.)

Having cleansed the flesh from sin by water, the soul is ready for a second baptism—the sanctification of the flesh and spirit together by fire, the Holy Ghost. Fire is an apt symbol for the Holy Ghost, since it consumes earthly matter and dissipates it invisibly heavenward. Temporal elements are literally changed in their chemical makeup by flames, just as the carnal flesh is elevated to a spiritual level through the Holy Ghost. With body and spirit thus united and transformed, the symbolic rebirth of the soul is complete. Without it, there is no salvation. Thus, Jesus explained, "Except a man be born of water and of the Spirit, he cannot enter into the kingdom of God. That which is born of the flesh is flesh; and that which is born [transformed] of the Spirit is spirit." (John 3:5–6.)

A Symbolic Rebirth Foreshadowing the Resurrection. The baptismal ritual further expands the age-old symbolic association between birth and death by adding atonement and resurrection. In ancient pagan cultures, birth and death were passages in the life cycle, first from a premortal (spiritual) to mortal (physical) life, and then from the mortal to post-mortal (again, spiritual) existence. This cycle of spiritual-{birth}-physical-{death}-spiritual would continue throughout eternity. It remains a basis for some contemporary religions, such as those teaching reincarnation. Through the resurrection and glorification of the flesh through Christ, on the other hand, the phases of life build upon one another in linear rather than in cyclical form. Thus, the soul, spirit and body, may progress eternally.

Associating the image of death with baptism, the apostle Paul wrote that "we are buried with him [Christ] by baptism into death." (Rom. 6:4.) The important difference, of course, is that pagans believed only the spirit is eternal, while Paul affirmed that the flesh is also: "For if we have been planted together in the likeness of his death, we shall be also in the likeness of his resurrection." (Rom. 6:5.)

Water is a dominant symbol in pagan death myths, just as it is in Christian baptisms. In Egyptian and Grecian lore, for example, the spirits of the dead were ferried across rivers of water to the underworld. Though various traditions share water as a symbol of passage unto death, the uniquely Christian symbol for redemption from death unto resurrection is blood. In a revelation to Moses, the Lord explained how the symbols of water, spirit, and blood relate to birth, baptism, and resurrection: "By reason of transgression cometh the fall, which fall bringeth death, and inasmuch as ye were *born into the world by water, and blood, and the spirit,* which I have made, and so became of dust a living soul, even so ye must be *born again into the kingdom of heaven, of water, and of the Spirit, and be cleansed by blood, even the blood of mine Only Begotten;* that ye might be sanctified from all sin, and enjoy . . . eternal life in the world to come, even immortal glory." (Moses 6:59; italics added.)

Every unborn spirit is sustained in its mother's womb and aided in its passage into mortality by her water and blood surrounding it. Likewise, Christ was baptized in the waters of Jordan to fulfill all righteousness as confirmed by the Holy Spirit in the form of a dove, and he shed his blood both in Gethsemane and on the cross to bring us a new eternal life with him. Appreciation of these symbolic elements of baptism helps us better understand its nature as an essential Christian ordinance.

BAPTISM AS AN ORDINANCE OF SALVATION

Imagine walking down a city street and observing two people in a heated discussion in front of a store. Suddenly the conversation ceases, they bend over, and each of them takes off one shoe and gives it to the other person. "What a strange act!" you say to yourself. But if you later found out that the shoe exchange was deliberately done in public as the symbol of a special contract between these two people, it might make a little more sense, especially if this were a frequent act within the community. (See Ruth 4:7–8.)

Baptism is an unusual act or ceremony. It is not often that people will, fully clothed, immerse themselves completely into a body of water, especially in front of others. However, baptism is readily recognized worldwide as a Christian ordinance. Although various forms of the ritual might take place, its nature as a religious ceremony is easily identifiable. Thus it becomes a visible, public declaration of allegiance to the Christian faith. Christians also view the ordinance as the culmination of a repentance process, as discussed in the previous chapter. Whether viewed as the last step of repentance or as the first step, or threshold, of Christian commitment, it is an extraordinary act of fellowship.

Joseph Smith identified baptism as the foundation ordinance of the Church, an act done "by immersion for the remission of sins." (A of F 4.) Because of their sacred nature, LDS baptisms are conducted in meetinghouse baptismal fonts where private religious services can be held. When such fonts are unavailable, secluded open bodies of water are used. Family members and friends customarily attend, and the presence of two priesthood holders is required for the act to be considered binding. The unusualness of the act provides additional impact to the ordinance; the person being baptized must have genuine intentions before participating in such a unique act. This is one reason why children under the age of accountability, eight years old, are not baptized. (See D&C 68:25–27.) Since the act is at least semipublic, it indicates the humility of the older child or adult being baptized. But baptism is meant to be more than an unusual public act of humility; it is also a sacred ordinance.

An ordinance can be either a law (teaching, directive, or commandment) or an act (ritual, rite, or ceremony). Ordinance acts are just one important subcategory within the ordinance laws of the gospel.[2] In general LDS practice, however, the term *ordinance* usually refers to the act, such as baptism, laying on of hands, sealing, and so on.

Baptism, as an ordinance, is both a law and an act. As a law of the gospel, baptism is a commandment to all who wish to return to Heavenly Father's celestial presence. (See John 3:5.) As an act of the gospel, baptism is essential to our salvation in God's kingdom. Few divine laws have such specific rituals to symbolize their fulfillment. For example, there is no specific religious ceremony accompanying the commandments to love the Lord our God or to honor parents, although social customs may indicate accepted ways that obedience to these commandments is recognized.

Ordinance-acts of the gospel are divided into two categories: ordinances of salvation and ordinances of blessing. The ordinances of salvation include baptism, confirmation (the gift of the Holy Ghost), and temple ordinances, especially the endowment and marriage sealings.[3] These ordinances are necessary for exaltation in the highest realms of God's celestial kingdom.

The blessing ordinances give us comfort, strength, and direction while in our probationary estate. Although not necessary, they include, among others, blessing children, healing the sick, receiving patriarchal blessings, dedicating graves of the deceased, and so on.[4] The blessing ordinance that comes closest to being a salvation ordinance is the sacrament. Though not mandatory, the sacrament ordinance is expected of faithful

Latter-day Saints as they constantly strive to bring their lives into spiritual harmony with Christ and his commandments.[5]

Because the soul is spirit and body united, ordinances of salvation must be performed by people in the flesh to achieve their purpose. But just as Christ suffered and atoned vicariously for our sins in the flesh, his ordinances may be performed by one person on behalf of another, provided that the ordinances are performed by people in the flesh and that the recipient of the proxy ordinances has him- or herself experienced mortal life. The third of the hosts of heaven who refused the opportunity to come to earth and gain a mortal body are excluded from salvation — at least in part — because their complete souls were never formed.

Through the baptismal ordinance, the participant incorporates theoretic and symbolic meanings of the commandments and demonstrates obedience to divine law through an actual, prescribed ritual. By being baptized and uniting our body and spirit with God's will, we actually experience with our own flesh the symbolic values of the ritual. When the ordinance of baptism is properly performed, body and spirit are both cleansed and then transformed in a manner similar to the resurrection. Thus, the symbolic becomes a reality.

BAPTISM AS A COVENANT OF COMMITMENT

By participating in the burial and resurrection of Christ through our own baptism, we are prepared to receive the gift of the Holy Ghost, which empowers us to follow him in our daily lives, gradually conforming to the symbolic perfection achieved in ritual. A strong personal commitment must be associated with the ceremony, or it will remain nothing more than an empty, hypocritical gesture. We demonstrate our sincerity through entering and keeping covenant promises with the Lord. Since covenants include solemn promises to God, we need to understand the nature and purpose of covenants in order to appreciate the covenant promises of baptism.

The Nature of Covenants. The first two definitions of the word *covenant* in Webster's dictionary are both appropriate to the covenant context of baptism. First, Webster defines the word as "a binding or solemn agreement by two or more persons, parties, etc." The second dictionary definition amplifies the meaning of baptism, explaining covenants to be "the promises of God to man, usually carrying with them conditions to be fulfilled by man, as recorded in the Bible."[6] From these definitions, we learn that covenants are binding agreements with conditional promises.

The language roots of the Old Testament provide helpful ancient meanings of *covenant* and *covenant making.* As a noun, *covenant* derives from the Hebrew word *b'rith,* which has roots in the Semitic languages of the ancient Near East. According to which language etymology one follows, the term *b'rith* has three possible meanings, each applicable to Latter-day Saint covenant tradition:

First, one meaning comes from the Hebrew root *bara,* meaning "to select" or "to choose." This root conveys the analogy of a woodcutter going into the forest to select or mark certain trees to harvest with his ax. God does not arbitrarily enter into a covenant relationship with each and all of his children. He selects those with faith and commitment and enters into a covenant relationship with them after they have chosen to come unto and obey him, as witnessed in the waters of baptism. Thus, a covenant is a selective choice, carefully entered into by both parties.

This definition of *covenant* also matches a common verb used to describe the process of "entering into a covenant." The technical phrase for "making a covenant" most frequently used in the Old Testament is *karat b'rith,* meaning literally to "cut a covenant," similar to the phrase heard today, "to cut a deal." The origin of this expression may lie in the ancient covenant ceremony of sacrificing animals by *cutting* their throats, which symbolized a point of finalization and personal commitment in the contractual process. In other words, when the two parties came to an agreement, they would indicate it through an unusual act — such as cutting the throat of an animal to be used as a sacrificial offering or as the main dish for their feast of celebration. Today, we participate in the unusual act of bodily immersion as a symbol of our covenant contract.

Second, *covenant* means a "bond" or "joining together." Many scholars believe *b'rith* in this context is derived from the Akkadian root *biritu,* which means "fetter" or "chain." We may feel uncomfortable with such strong language of being fettered or chained; for us, covenants are voluntary, not obligatory. However, once a mutual commitment has been made, the two parties are linked or "chained together." *Biritu* can thus represent an absolute, binding compact between God and his children, as symbolized in the baptismal covenant. This binding dimension of covenants is also evident when Latter-day Saints talk about sealings as a part of the "new and everlasting covenant" in LDS temple ordinances.

Indeed, when one looks at covenant making and the meaning of "cutting" a *b'rith* in this second context, the symbolism of the cutting motion represents a penalty if one breaks a solemn oath. Ancient Near Eastern contracts often went so far as to list the penalties for breaking the agreements. So to "cut a bond" can mean to commit yourself to dire consequences if you break your promise. However, when we think of "cutting a bond," there is also a positive dimension and the implication of a liberation if one maintains the vow. In a gospel context, as we cut ourselves from the chains of sin by entering into a baptismal covenant relationship with Christ, we free ourselves to achieve our ultimate, eternal destiny.[7]

Third, the root of *covenant* also has a more unusual meaning. According to some scholars, the Hebrew root *bara* really means "to eat bread" with someone. This concept is probably best understood in the Semitic tradition of hospitality and guest protection. According to the Arabian and Bedouin customs, even if someone is your fierce enemy or a complete stranger, when you invite that person into your home or tent and share bread with him, you are duty-bound to defend and protect this guest—even at peril of your own life. This external, physical act of breaking bread together symbolizes an internal, moral commitment that obligates the host to protect his guest.

Although many might find this act of eating bread a bit unusual as a covenant process, Latter-day Saints see it as a natural part of making covenants because they renew covenants on a weekly basis by partaking of the bread of the sacrament. The cutting or breaking and eating of bread may be much closer to covenant making in the ritual sense than we generally think. Among the direct parallels between the performances of sacrifice in the Old Testament and sacrament in the New Testament, we remember that, as a part of their covenant-making and covenant-renewal process, the levitical priesthood holders and the Israelites together ritually cut or divided and then ate the important and common peace offering. Today, we follow an ancient procedure as our priests separate or break the bread, representing Christ's sacrifice, and we all eat it together in a renewal of our baptismal covenant.

In review, a covenant is a binding, solemn agreement between God and man, conditional upon certain scriptural stipulations. Entering into a covenant requires a voluntary binding between the covenant parties, often symbolized by some special act, such as baptism or eating bread together.[8]

The Purpose of Covenants. Knowing what covenants are, it is helpful to appreciate why God uses covenants to bind our relationship with him. God's work and glory is to "bring to pass the immortality and eternal life of man." (Moses 1:39.) For us to achieve this divine purpose, we need help and direction. Our covenants with God provide the directives and motivate us past important measuring posts in our path back to Heavenly Father's presence, helping us establish a pattern of faithful obedience. Let us review four ways that covenants help us by providing important teachings, incentives, gateways, and patterns.

Covenants help us first as gospel *teachings* by informing us of God's expectations for achieving eternal life. A major part of the temple endowment, for example, instructs us about ourselves and God's plan and eternal purposes. The laws and commandments attached to the covenants teach us how to draw nearer to God and how to become more like him.

Second, covenant oaths and blessings provide helpful *incentives* to stay on the path toward the celestial kingdom. For example, the seriousness of any oath with God prompts us more toward obedience in moments of temptation or weakness than a simple knowledge of right and wrong. Also, the enticement of promised blessings encourages us to obey when we feel discouraged or lost. Covenants promise us divine help and assistance in reaching our eternal goals. The Lord says he is obligated to bless us as we obey his laws, and this gives us courage and incentive to remain faithful to our covenants.

Third and most important, covenants serve as necessary *gateways* through which we must pass if we are to return to God's presence. After passing through the gates of water and spirit baptism, we then prepare to enter into higher temple covenants that draw us closer to God's highest glory. The major covenant teachings of the temple provide the measurements by which we determine where we are in our path toward perfection and which gateways we still have to go through. When we are found ready and worthy to enter into higher covenants, we sense we are getting closer to our highest potential—the gateway to eternal life with our families.

Finally, when we maintain covenant oaths, we establish *patterns* of obedience that become a part of our eternal nature. We gradually become the type of person who remains faithful to God and dedicated to goodness, love, and righteousness. We are then ready to help the next generation establish a pattern of celestial life.

Thus we see that God's covenant ordinances — along with their accompanying laws, commandments, and promises — give us help and hope in reaching toward eternal life. The scriptures not only provide details about the specific covenants, but they also give the eternal context of our covenant relationship with God. As stated on the title page of the Book of Mormon, scriptures provide both the past historical context for these covenants and also the future prophetic promises for their blessings. Baptism in particular has many commandments and promises attached. To receive the full benefit of baptism, we must understand the promises made during the ordinance.

The Covenant Promises of Baptism. The baptismal covenant is an external act indicating our internal commitment to God. When we are "desirous to come into the fold of God," we make certain promises with him, best summarized by Alma in his discourse at the waters of Mormon. Our initial covenant of baptism includes a willingness (1) "to be called his people," that is, to take upon us the name of Christ; (2) "to bear one another's burdens, that they may be light"; (3) "to mourn with those that mourn; yea, and comfort those that stand in need of comfort"; (4) "to stand as witnesses of God at all times and in all things, and in all places . . . even until death"; and (5) to "serve him and keep his commandments." (Mosiah 18:8–10.)

In return, the Lord promises those who honor their baptismal covenant that he will (1) "pour out his Spirit more abundantly upon" them; (2) they will be "redeemed of God, and be numbered with those of the first resurrection"; and (3) they will "have eternal life." (Mosiah 18:9–10.) These three blessings, when combined with the valuable one mentioned earlier of receiving a remission of sins, promise us not only deliverance from sin, but also the companionship of the Holy Ghost throughout our life. This baptismal covenant is renewed weekly through the sacrament of the Lord's supper, wherein we promise (1) to remember Christ, (2) to take his name upon us, and (3) to keep his commandments.

In turn, the Lord promises us one great blessing—that we "may always have his Spirit" to be with us. (D&C 20:77.)

Finally, baptism prepares us for our eventual resurrection with the righteous. Along with the baptism of fire, it continues a sanctifying process that continues until the symbolic resurrection with Christ through the waters of baptism becomes literal. The symbolic again becomes actual.

BAPTISM AS A GATEWAY TO RIGHTEOUS LIVING

To further help us in our journey toward perfection, baptism grants us membership into Christ's church, his kingdom on earth. Baptism is the one required gateway through which all must pass. It also grants symbolic citizenship into the celestial kingdom, which gradually becomes reality as one continues on the strait and narrow path leading to that kingdom of glory. One must be in a state of absolute purity to actually enter into Heavenly Father's realm, for "there cannot any unclean thing enter into the kingdom of God." (1 Ne. 15:34.) Since we have become impure through sin, we must be cleansed in order to meet God's heavenly environmental expectations. (See Mark 16:16; 3 Ne. 11:33; D&C 112:29.)

The Lord himself showed us the gate by which we enter the kingdom of God. Nephi, referring to the Lord's example, wrote: "Do the things which I have told you I have seen that your Lord and your Redeemer should do; for, for this cause have they been shown unto me, that ye might know the gate by which ye should enter. For the gate by which ye should enter is repentance and baptism by water." (2 Ne. 31:17.) Later emphasis in this book will show how much remains to be done once one has gone through this critical portal. Initially, though, we must prepare ourselves to go through this gateway if we want to return to Heavenly Father's presence. Once through the entrance, God will help us, primarily through the Holy Ghost, to continue on the path toward eternal life. Eventually, all these baptismal symbols will become actualized in our very lives, as we follow the example of our Savior.

UNITING THE SYMBOLIC AND ACTUAL IN THE SAVIOR'S LIFE

Though Jesus himself was sinless and did not need baptism for remission of sins, he prepared himself for this ordinance as he matured and "increased in wisdom and stature, and in favour with God and man" (Luke 2:52) and "learned obedience by the things which he suffered" (Heb. 5:8). The experiences of his youth gradually refined and prepared him for his own baptism. His compliance with this initial eternal ordinance "fulfilled all righteousness" (Matt. 3:15), enabling him to receive the baptism of fire by the Holy Ghost, which John the Baptist described, saying, "I saw the Spirit descending from heaven like a dove, and it abode upon him. And . . . he that sent me to baptize with water, the same said unto me, Upon whom thou shalt see the Spirit descending, *and remaining on him, the same is he which baptizeth with the Holy Ghost.* And I saw, and bare record that this is the Son of God." (John 1:32–34; italics added.)

This passage written by John the Beloved indicates a second difference in the baptism of Christ as compared to the rest of us. Because he was sinless, because his flesh and spirit were not at odds with one another, the Spirit that descended upon him remained with him thereafter, and he became the one "which baptizeth with the Holy Ghost." (See also John 14:16–18.) Baptism was not an empty formality, then, even for the Savior. The reception of the Holy Ghost both prepared him for and prompted him to seek out his forty-day trial in the wilderness, which immediately followed his baptism. (See Matt. 4:1–11.) The ritual also foreshadowed and forearmed the Savior for his actual atoning sacrifice when the symbolic meaning of baptism became literal in Gethsemane and on the cross.

REQUISITES FOR BAPTISM

When John the Baptist began his ministry, preaching repentance and baptizing in the wilderness, people sought him out from all Judea "and were baptized of him in Jordan, confessing their sins." (Matt. 3:6.) Thus, the first requirement for baptism was and still is confession and promise of commitment in an interview with an authorized priesthood holder.

Christ also sought baptism by water from John because the Baptist was a bearer of the Aaronic Priesthood. Likewise, today, a priest in the Aaronic Priesthood may perform baptism by immersion, though only Melchizedek Priesthood holders may confer the gift of the Holy Ghost. (See D&C 20:41; 55:3.) In the case of the Lord's own baptism, the Father himself was the one who conferred his Spirit, saying "This is my beloved Son, in whom I am well pleased." (Matt. 3:17.)

God the Father was a witness to his Son's baptism, along with John the Baptist, just as two priesthood witnesses are required today to ensure that the baptized person is fully immersed and the baptismal prayer is properly recited. (See D&C 20:72–74.) Furthermore, the presence of witnesses binds the agreement and makes it impossible for the recipient of baptism to deny the covenant's validity and return with impunity to his or her former way of life. Thus, the spirituality of the person seeking baptism, the authority of the one who performs it, and the proper formality of the ordinance must all be observed before the legality of the ritual can be effectual and binding.

PERSONAL PREPARATION (SPIRITUALITY)

Before a race, the runner prepares for the event. Before an exam, the student prepares for the test. Before a job interview, the prospective employee prepares for the vocation. Before many stages of life, we make important personal preparations. With the responsibility associated with the sacred covenant of baptism, one naturally would want to prepare properly and fully.

The Lord gave the Prophet Joseph some guidelines on preparations for baptism. After humbling ourselves before God and desiring to be baptized, we should "come forth with broken hearts and contrite spirits," witnessing before the church that we "have truly repented of all . . . [our] sins." We must also be willing to take upon us the name of Jesus Christ, "having a determination to serve him to the end." Our works should already demonstrate that we "have received of the Spirit of Christ" unto the remission of our sins. When these steps are completed, we "shall be received by baptism into his church." (D&C 20:37.) Each of these important preparations helps the person about to be baptized turn from worldly influences toward the kingdom of God. (See 3 Ne. 12:19; Moro. 6:2.)

President Ezra Taft Benson has given additional insight on preparing for baptism. He said, "Before investigators are baptized they should commit themselves to each of the principles of the gospel. An investigator who will not commit to praying, going to Church, or living the Word of Wisdom is certainly not prepared for the serious baptismal covenant."[9]

These steps of personal preparation, spirituality, and commitment are essential before a person is baptized.

OFFICIAL ADMINISTRATOR (AUTHORITY)

After humility, faith, and a repentant attitude have brought the individual to the waters of baptism, that person needs to be baptized by one having authority. In any major social order, corporation, or government, unless the legal head of the body has either personally signed certain documents or authorized others by legal power of attorney to do so, any contract or agreement with that entity is not valid. So it is with the covenant contract of baptism.

To be received of God, baptism must be performed by one with the proper power and authority. If priesthood authority was not important, why did Jesus go to John to be baptized? John held the Aaronic Priesthood, which contains the authority from God to properly baptize a person. (See D&C 13:1.) Joseph Smith received this priesthood from John the Baptist, and he and his successors have transmitted to the priesthood holders of the Church the power, keys, and directions to perform this saving ordinance.[10] Proper priesthood authority is necessary so that a true, divinely accepted baptism can be performed.

CORRECT PROCEDURES (FORMALITY)

Paul taught the Ephesian Saints the importance of unity in Christ's church. He indicated that just as there is one Lord (Jesus) and one God and Father of all, there is also "one faith, one baptism." (Eph. 4:3–6.) There is only one type of proper baptism—by immersion. The word "baptism" itself has a Greek root meaning "dipping" or "immersing" in the water. In Greek, to say "baptism by immersion" is redundant; like saying "immersing by immersion." This proper form of baptism was practiced in the New Testament, as witnessed in the account of Jesus being baptized when he came "straightway out of the water." (Matt. 3:16.) Also John baptized in areas where there was "much water" (John 3:23), as did Philip when he and the Ethiopian "went down both into the water." (Acts 8:36–38.) As discussed earlier, only through immersion does the full, rich symbolism of the ritual become actualized.

RITUAL CORRECTNESS (LEGALITY)

In different countries, depending on the time of year, location, and cultural traditions of an area, the physical setting of LDS baptisms may vary. However, the basic act will be the same because certain steps are required. The absolute essential elements of a baptism are (1) recommendation by an authorized priesthood leader who carefully interviews the baptismal candidate (age eight or older) according to the guidelines of Doctrine and Covenants 20:37, (2) a body of water large enough for the immersion, (3) a priesthood holder to perform the baptism—either a priest of the Aaronic Priesthood or a Melchizedek Priesthood holder, (4) modest, clean, white clothing, (5) two Melchizedek Priesthood holders to serve as witnesses, (6) the proper prayer according to Doctrine and Covenants 20:73, and (7) full immersion of the whole body in the water. In addition, three necessary steps are completed immediately or soon after the baptism: (1) ordinance of confirmation, which includes bestowal of the gift of the Holy Ghost, (2) baptismal data entered into the records of the Church, and (3) sustaining of the person in a sacrament meeting as a Church member.[11]

Besides the required elements of a proper baptism, other features can also enhance a baptismal service. Additional complementary aspects of a baptism can include a quiet, worshipful environment and physical setting, including privacy, dressing rooms, warm water, and so forth. A preliminary program with prayers, hymns, talks, or videos about baptism and the Holy Ghost, and testimonies can enhance the reverence of the meeting and the understanding of the ordinance. The presence of family, friends, and ward or branch members shows support and encouragement; these people are especially helpful whether the prospective Church member is a child or an older convert. A personal historical record of the event, including pictures, journal entries, simple program, and notes will help the convert remember this pivotal day in his or her life.

Any other form or method of baptism is a counterfeit act. Satan constantly tries to substitute different types of baptism or membership rites for the genuine ordinance. As Elder Bruce R. McConkie commented, "Apostate substitutes . . . are found both among pagans and supposed Christians. Perverted forms of baptism were common among the mystery religions of the old world." He also indicated that "some . . . churches of modern Christendom deny the necessity of baptism and talk in terms of salvation coming by the mere act of confessing Christ with one's lips. Others . . . enlarge the doctrine to include children who have not arrived at the years of accountability [eight]."[12]

The Lord has designated one baptism, however, that is correct and approved in his sight—baptism by immersion with the proper form and authority. (See D&C 20:73–74.) God is "the same yesterday, to-day, and forever" (1 Ne. 10:18), and he will not change his doctrines to fit the desires of men (see Isa 55:8). Starting with Adam, the children of God have been baptized by immersion, and the practice continues in this dispensation. (See Moses 6:64.) Thus, the way one is baptized enriches the symbolic meaning of the ordinance as well as fulfills the purposes and ways of God.

To summarize, we can say that *BAPTISM is a symbolic ordinance of cleansing and new life, and it is also the covenant gateway into Christ's church and God's celestial kingdom.* A baptism that is properly performed by an authorized priesthood holder will bring the genuine disciple a remission of sins and prepare him or her for the reception of the Holy Ghost. Baptism is an essential ordinance of salvation and a blessing of peace for God's children on their pathway back toward his presence.

For further study, refer to the following entries:

TG	BD	*EM*
Baptism	Baptism	Baptism
Baptism, Essential		Baptismal Covenant
Baptism, Immersion		Baptismal Prayer
Baptism,		Joining the Church
Qualifications for		
Covenants		

CHAPTER 19

THE GIFT AND COMPANIONSHIP
OF THE HOLY GHOST

The story is told of the Viking chieftain who wanted to reward his warriors after a particularly successful trading voyage. He announced that each man could take whatever he wanted from the chieftain's storehouse — as long as he could carry it home by himself. The storehouse was filled with furs, clothes, tools, furniture, and many other precious objects. Like children in a toy store, all the men but one quickly selected large loads of goods to carry home. The exception — one of the biggest, strongest warriors — selected the smallest, least costly item: the one and only key to the treasure vault. Through this, he accumulated abundant wealth, which he used to build his community. Not surprisingly, the elders elected this man a few years later to be their next chieftain. Sometimes a seemingly small, simple gift can be the key to many blessings.

In a similar manner, if the Lord were to grant every new convert into his church the spiritual gift of their choice, people would likely choose impressive spiritual powers, like the ability to heal, speak in tongues, see into the future, and so on. However, the most precious gift is so simple that it might be overlooked; yet it could, in turn, bring forth any and all of the other spiritual gifts. This key gift is the constant companionship of the Holy Ghost.

In the previous chapter on baptism, we touched on how the gift of the Holy Ghost helps us fulfill our baptismal covenants, gradually elevating our behavior to match the symbolic purity achieved in the baptismal ritual. Our baptism of water is a one-time occurrence, instantly washing away all our previous sins. Although the actual confirmation of the Holy Ghost is also a singular ordinance, internal purging by the fire of the Holy Ghost is a sustained effort that influences future actions and leads to greater spiritual manifestations. Our spiritual refinement must continue over time through repentance and spiritual persistence.

In order to regularly sharpen our spiritual focus, the corollary ordinance of the weekly sacrament was instituted. The emblems of bread and water direct our minds to the physical elements of Christ's atonement—his flesh and blood. In partaking of the emblems, we remember the Atonement and renew our baptismal covenants so that we may continuously have the Holy Ghost to be with us. (See Moro. 4:3; 5:2.)

The relationship between our continuous spiritual refinement and the ordinances of baptism and confirmation can also be compared to mortal birth and subsequent physical development. The newborn infant has received a body containing all the genetic material it needs to become a full-grown man or woman. The physical potential of the infant's body is like the spiritual potential embodied in the ordinance of confirmation. The process of the infant becoming an adult, however, requires time for the cells to develop and multiply. Even after reaching maturity, new cells in the body continue to replace old, worn-out ones. In a sense, then, the infant's physical rebirth continues with new growth throughout his or her lifetime, just as our spiritual rebirth continues beyond the confirmation ordinance until we reach perfection.

A MIGHTY CHANGE OF HEART

Our spiritual rebirth begins in our hearts. Before his death, King Benjamin delivered a rousing sermon to his people, exhorting them to fulfill their covenant relationship with the Lord. His words moved the people to seek forgiveness; as a result, they received a witness through the Spirit that their sins had been remitted. (See Mosiah 4:1–3.) After further instruction, they felt the influence of the Spirit upon them, "and they all cried with one voice, saying: Yea, we believe all the words which thou hast spoken unto us; and also, we know of their surety and truth, because of the Spirit of the Lord Omnipotent, *which has wrought a mighty change in us, or in our hearts, that we have no more disposition to do evil, but to do good continually.* " (Mosiah 5:2; italics added.)

The change of heart that accompanies spiritual rebirth does not mean that we will never sin again but that we are now inclined to do good. To paraphrase an earlier portion of King Benjamin's sermon, we have put off "the natural man" and yielded to the enticing of the Holy Spirit. (Mosiah 3:19.) Though we may still have human weaknesses, our fundamental natural preference is changed from carnal to spiritual.

This change in our hearts through the fire of the Holy Ghost is as literal as the chemical change in physical elements exposed to natural flame. Just as chemical change can be verified through scientific analysis, a spiritual transformation is evidenced by our belief in the words of Christ, our desires for righteousness, our good works, and even our very appearance. Thus, Alma the younger asked Church members who had become lax in keeping the commandments: "Have ye spiritually been born of God? Have ye received his image in your countenances? Have ye experienced this mighty change in your hearts?" (Alma 5:14.) Though Alma's people had been baptized and had received the confirmation and gift of the Holy Ghost, the spiritual transformation of the ordinance had not remained in effect because of their unrighteousness.

In contrast, Alma the younger relates how his own father, who had been among the wicked priests of King Noah, was spiritually born again: "Did not my father Alma believe in the words which were delivered by the mouth of Abinadi? . . . And according to his faith there was a mighty change wrought in his heart." (Alma 5:11–12.) With a change of heart, the Holy Ghost assists us in becoming new men and women in Christ.

Latter-day Saints who have been brought up in the Church, led righteous lives, and enjoyed the gift of the Holy Ghost from their childhood may relate to the Spirit's subtle influence as they do to the sun's constant light and warmth—something that has always worked in them to gradually transform them into "new creatures" in Christ. (2 Cor. 5:17.) They may even take for granted the Spirit's presence and only appreciate the Spirit were they to experience its prolonged absence, after which they would need a mighty change of heart, like a convert. For many converts coming from the spiritual darkness of the world, however, the sudden presence of the Holy Ghost may seem more like a brilliant, raging fire.

VARIOUS MANIFESTATIONS OF THE SPIRIT

Generally, manifestations of the Holy Ghost follow a gradual, progressive pattern as we reject worldly influences and seek spiritual enlightenment. Our relationship with the Holy Spirit seems to go through at least four stages. We first experience the *influence or power of the Holy Ghost;* this prompts us to accept the truth and be baptized. We then receive the *gift and companionship of the Holy Ghost,* helping us to remain faithful. As we continue in righteousness, our spirituality brings forth various *gifts of the Spirit.* Finally, perhaps in this world but probably in the postmortal paradise, our soul and righteous works are sealed by the *Holy Spirit of Promise.*

Most of these steps are recognizable in the New Testament account of Cornelius, the Roman centurion. This humble, pious man feared God, did much good, and was influenced by the Spirit. As Peter the Apostle taught him and his household, the gift of the Holy Ghost poured upon them and they spoke in tongues, partially as a witness to the early Jewish-Christian Saints that the Gentiles were worthy for these greater spiritual manifestations. (See Acts 10:30–31, 44–48.) Like Cornelius, we may experience these four stages in our lives: spiritual influence, spiritual companionship, spiritual gifts, and spiritual sealings.

SPIRITUAL INFLUENCE

When any person—Church member or nonmember, Christian or otherwise—receives spiritual knowledge or guidance, he receives it through the power of the Holy Ghost. The Spirit may manifest himself to that person in any of his capacities as messenger, revelator, testifier, or comforter.[1] Thus, an investigator of the Church receives a spiritual witness that the Book of Mormon is true "by the power of the Holy Ghost." (Moro. 10:4.) But unless the investigator acts upon this revelation through repentance, baptism, and confirmation, the testimony of the Spirit will not remain with him.

Expounding upon the New Testament account of the conversion of Cornelius, the Prophet Joseph Smith clarified the difference between the influence of the Holy Ghost and the gift of the Holy Ghost: "Cornelius received the Holy Ghost before he was baptized, which was the convincing power of God unto him of the truth of the Gospel, but he could not receive the gift of the Holy Ghost until after he was baptized. Had he not taken this sign or ordinance upon him, the Holy Ghost which convinced him of the truth of God, would have left him."[2] As a member of the Godhead, he can expand our intelligence, witness to gospel truths, and provide comfort to our souls. However, these influences will be irregular and fleeting without a confirmation of the gift of the Holy Ghost. We should all desire the companionship of this member of the Godhead so we can have his constant help in developing our godly qualities.

SPIRITUAL COMPANIONSHIP

When the gift of the Holy Ghost is "confirmed" (Latin *com,* together, or *con* [intensive!] + *firmare,* to make firm) or "firmly bonded together" with us, we have the right to his strength and companionship whenever we desire and need it. Like the constant light of the sun, the Spirit will light the paths of our lives if we are worthy members of the Church. The key to making the ordinance of confirmation effectual in daily living is our personal righteousness. Thus, Elder Bruce R. McConkie wrote, "The gift of the Holy Ghost is the *right* to have the constant companionship of the Spirit; the actual *enjoyment* of the gift . . . is based on personal righteousness. . . . The Spirit will not dwell in an unclean tabernacle."[3]

Even righteous people, however, are sometimes left without the companionship of the Spirit (as was the Lord himself during the crucifixion) so they can develop their ability to discern light from darkness. Thus, President Joseph F. Smith taught, "It does not follow that a man who has received the presentation or gift of the Holy Ghost shall always receive the recognition and witness and presence of the Holy Ghost himself, or he may receive all these, and yet the Holy Ghost [might] not tarry with him, but visit him from time to time."[4] (See D&C 130:23.)

The importance of striving for the spiritual companionship of the Holy Ghost was stressed early in Church history in a fascinating episode between the first two presidents of the Church, Joseph Smith and Brigham Young. Some time after the Prophet Joseph's death, he appeared to President Young in a dream and gave him the following instructions: "Tell the people to be humble and faithful, and be sure to keep the spirit of the Lord and it will lead them right. Be careful and not turn away the small still voice; it will teach them what to do and where to go; it will yield the fruits of the kingdom." Brigham was also told to admonish the Church leaders "to keep their hearts open, . . . so that when the Holy Ghost comes to them their hearts will be ready to receive it." After further, similar admonitions, Joseph repeated again, "Tell the people to be sure to keep the spirit of the Lord and follow it, and it will lead them just right."⁵ Brigham Young obeyed this counsel and emphasized these spiritual priorities for the early Saints.

Following the Holy Ghost's direction continues to be of utmost importance to Latter-day Saints, especially in the trying times of contemporary society. As a modern apostle, James E. Faust, has counseled us, "The comforting Spirit of the Holy Ghost can abide with us twenty-four hours a day: when we work, when we play, when we rest. . . . That sustaining influence can be with us in joy and sorrow, when we rejoice as well as when we grieve. . . . The Holy Ghost will also help us solve crises of faith. The Spirit of the Holy Ghost can be a confirming witness, testifying of heavenly things. Through that Spirit, a strong knowledge distills in one's mind, and one feels all doubt or questions disappear."⁶

SPIRITUAL GIFTS

Having received the gift of the Holy Ghost, members of the Church are also entitled to seek and receive particular spiritual gifts to further help themselves and others progress on the strait and narrow path to the celestial kingdom. In Section 46 of the Doctrine and Covenants, the Lord counsels the Saints on the purpose and use of spiritual gifts: "Beware lest ye are deceived; and that ye may not be deceived seek ye earnestly the best gifts, always remembering for what they are given; for verily I say unto you, they are given for the benefit of those who love me and keep all my commandments." (Vv. 46:8–9.) The Lord adds that "all have not every gift given unto them. . . . To some is given one, and to some is given another, that all may be profited thereby." (Vv. 11–12.) This revelation echoes 1 Corinthians 12, in which Paul describes how each member of the body of Christ (the Church) is necessary to the functioning of the whole. Thus, the purpose of spiritual gifts is to unite the Saints in faith and give them greater powers to strengthen one another.

The scriptures exhort us to "covet," "seek," "lay hold upon," and "exercise" these gifts. (See, as examples, 1 Cor. 12:31; D&C 46:8; Moro. 7:19; D&C 6:11.) Like the gifts of faith, testimony, and other spiritual blessings, we are to earnestly seek after these things. And as in the parable of the talents, if these gifts are used, they will be added upon; if they are neglected, they will be lost. As different gifts are received and developed by the saints, the full range of gifts will be found in the Church so "that all may be profited thereby."

A great variety of gifts are mentioned throughout the scriptures. In Doctrine and Covenants 46, 1 Corinthians 12, and Moroni 10, we find three valuable lists of the primary gifts of the Holy Spirit. These gifts seem to be either gifts of spiritual learning and knowledge or gifts of spiritual powers and manifestations, sometimes called "miracles." The first tend to be more internal and personal while the second are external and public. Among the gifts of "spiritual learning," we find the following:

- knowing that Jesus is the Christ
- knowing that God lives
- having faith in Christ through the witness of others
- receiving the word of knowledge
- receiving the word (gift) of wisdom
- teaching others knowledge and wisdom
- discerning various spirits and influences.

Among the gifts of "spiritual powers," we find these:

- prophesying
- speaking in tongues
- interpreting tongues
- working miracles
- healing
- receiving the faith to be healed.

Since the gifts of "spiritual learning" are obviously influenced by the Holy Ghost, we will discuss them in more detail.

Knowing That Jesus Is the Christ. One of the first gifts we should seek is knowledge that Jesus is the Christ. In section 46 of the Doctrine and Covenants is stated, "To some it is given by the Holy Ghost to know that Jesus Christ is the Son of God, and that he was crucified for the sins of the world." (V. 13.) A person does not need to see the resurrected Christ to have a testimony of his life and mission. This we can know through the manifestations of the Spirit.

Several different ways in which we may know of the sacred Sonship of Christ include some that are direct and profound and others that are indirect and subtle. Direct knowledge could come from a personal appearance or manifestation of the Savior himself or through the special testimony of God the Father (such as, "This is my beloved Son . . . "), but such examples of direct witnesses are extremely rare. More common sources of knowledge include receiving personal revelation through the Holy Ghost and sensing the validity of a testimony borne by individuals who have already gained a personal witness of his divinity. To have the knowledge that Jesus is the Christ is truly a great gift.

Knowing That God Lives. Similar to knowing that Christ lives, this gift relates to the testimony we receive concerning the reality and nature of our Heavenly Father. This knowledge is especially valuable when we first develop our faith. Some rudiments of this gift seem to be present among most peoples and religions of the world, for they have an innate belief about the reality of a supreme being. Although God rarely appears to mortals, evidence of his existence and works is found in nature, the scriptures, and the words and acts of godly people. As people search for God and respond to the whisperings of the Spirit, they accept the reality of a powerful, loving divine being whom they have not seen.[7]

Having Faith in Christ through the Witness of Others. Those who do not yet know that Jesus is the Christ, the Son of God, can temporarily rely on someone who does have that knowledge. Missionaries recognize this fact in their teaching of nonmembers. Bruce R. McConkie elaborates on this gift by saying, "Individuals who have not yet advanced in spiritual things to the point of gaining for themselves personal and direct revelation from the Holy Ghost may yet have power to believe what others, speaking by the power of the Spirit, both teach and testify. They have power to recognize the truth of the words of others who do speak by the power of the Spirit, even though they cannot attune themselves to the Infinite so as to receive the divine word direct from heaven."[8]

Modern-day revelation explains this spiritual gift by stating, "To others it is given to believe on their words [that Jesus Christ is the Son of God], that they also might have eternal life if they continue faithful." (D&C 46:14.) This gift is dependent upon the strong testimonies of others, but it still has the power to encourage one onward in the path towards eternal life.

Receiving the Word of Knowledge. Knowledge is something we seek throughout our lives. It gives us understanding and helps us reason things out. Many times, as we start to piece things together, we desire to gain more knowledge and additional understanding. Godly knowledge includes understanding the Father and the ways we can be like him. The

Doctrine and Covenants tells us the importance of knowledge: "If thou shalt ask, thou shalt receive revelation upon revelation, knowledge upon knowledge, that thou mayest know the mysteries and peaceable things — that which bringeth joy, that which bringeth life eternal." (D&C 42:61.) Joseph Smith tells us that "it is impossible for a man to be saved in ignorance" (D&C 131:6), indicating the eternal importance of learning. Knowledge is a broad gift, so we should first seek for important truths: we can gain knowledge of God and his plans for mankind, knowledge of good and evil, and eventually a knowledge of all truth.[9]

Receiving the Word (Gift) of Wisdom. To some is given the gift to understand wisdom, something different and perhaps greater than knowledge since it denotes practical or applied knowledge. One can have knowledge and be able to expound the gospel doctrines, but the one who truly understands the ways that knowledge fits into daily life and who wisely uses it will be greatly blessed. Paul illustrates the role of the Holy Ghost in receiving wisdom, saying, "We have received, not the spirit of the world, but the spirit which is of God; that we might know the things that are freely given to us of God. Which things also we speak, not in the words which man's wisdom teacheth, but which the Holy Ghost teacheth." (1 Cor. 2:12–13.)

The process of learning wisdom should be started early, as Alma noted while giving some fatherly advice to Helaman, "Remember, my son, and learn wisdom in thy youth; yea, learn in thy youth to keep the commandments of God." (Alma 37:35.) He indicates that by keeping the commandments and acting upon knowledge, one can distinguish between knowledge and wisdom. Thus, wisdom is active, not passive. The Lord revealed to Joseph Smith some rewards of gaining wisdom, "Thou shalt observe all these things, and great shall be thy reward; for unto you it is given to know the mysteries of the kingdom, but unto the world it is not given to know them." (D&C 42:65.) Through the gift of wisdom, we receive insight into the mysteries of the kingdom, which, in turn, helps our progression on the path to eternal life.

Teaching Others Knowledge and Wisdom. As we attain knowledge, we have the responsibility of teaching and helping others gain understanding. As we instruct others by word and example, both the teacher and the learner are blessed since they both move to higher levels of knowledge strengthen and enrich their understanding. The ability to teach words of knowledge and wisdom is another of the gifts of the Spirit. (See Moro. 10:9–10.) For example, as missionaries teach investigators new truths, the investigators build upon their previous understanding, and the missionaries learn new applications of their previous learning.

In teaching and receiving knowledge, those who are humble and want to learn more will receive knowledge and understanding "precept upon precept; line upon line." (Isa. 28:10.) Their learning will come through other people, the scriptures, conference talks, church meetings, and innumerable other sources. As we pursue truth, teaching others is one of the best ways to increase our spiritual gifts and understanding.

Discerning Various Spirits and Influences. We can be influenced by many spirits sharing this earth with us. Some, like ours, are in bodies of flesh and bone; others can be spirits without a body. Bruce R. McConkie tells us, "To all men in some degree and to the faithful saints in particular is given the spirit, gift, and power of discernment." He also states, "If a man has power to part the veil and converse with angels and with the ministering spirits who dwell in the realms of light, surely this is a gift of the Spirit."[10] We can discern good from evil spirits with the help of the Holy Ghost and we receive this gift and the right to heavenly ministering angels if we live worthily.

The Apostle John gives us advice on how to develop this gift of discernment: "Believe not every spirit, but try the spirits whether they are of God: because many false prophets are gone out into the world. Hereby know ye the Spirit of God: Every Spirit that confesseth that Jesus Christ is come in the flesh is of God: and every spirit that confesseth not that Jesus Christ is come in the flesh is not of God: and this is that spirit of antichrist, whereof ye have heard that it should come; and even now already is it in the world." (1 Jn. 4:1–3.) As John tells us, a testimony of Christ quickly distinguishes between the spirits of truth and error. The gift of discernment insures that we will recognize the proper sources of truth and goodness. This gift includes knowing how spiritual gifts are administered and recognizing the various operations of the Spirit. With it, we can fully develop all the spiritual gifts of learning.

Spiritual Gifts of Power. Occasionally God will empower his servants with special spiritual gifts that both assist his work and demonstrate his power. We usually call these spiritual manifestations miracles because we do not yet understand the laws and powers by which they are actualized. Among them are the gifts of prophesying, healing, speaking and interpreting in tongues, and so forth. The gift of prophecy begins with a testimony of Christ and can culminate in marvelous visions for one who is endowed as a prophet, seer, and revelator.[11] The gift of healing is the most common miracle recorded in the scriptures and during Christ's ministry.[12]

The gift of tongues and their interpretation includes spiritual assistance both in learning foreign languages and in speaking and understanding unknown languages without premeditation. Although the first type is more common, the second is more dramatic. Primarily given to assist in preaching the gospel, the gift of tongues usually magnifies one's efforts in studying and communicating in a foreign tongue, and Paul emphasizes its value over the more dramatic manifestation. (See 1 Cor. 14:19.) However, as special circumstances may require, the Holy Spirit may miraculously assist with special communication abilities. (See Acts 2:1–12.) Since this gift can be easily imitated by Satan's followers, the gift of discernment and proper interpreters are required factors.[13]

Other gifts of power include such mighty miracles as the parting of seas and rivers, producing water from desert rocks, walking on the water, bringing people back from death, moving mountains and rivers, and changing the weather. These are extremely rare and are manifest by the Son of God and his prophetic servants. Normal mortals are not given these spiritual powers over the earth and its elements. (See Matt. 17:20; Ether 12:30; Jacob 4:6; Hel. 10:9.) Although we are commanded to seek after spiritual gifts, we are warned against seeking after miraculous signs. (See D&C 63:9–12.)

Most Latter-day Saints will develop the gifts of learning long before, if ever, they will demonstrate the gifts of power. Different people, even in the same family, have their own unique gifts. Notice, for example, that the ability to speak in tongues and to interpret tongues are separate gifts and might not be possessed by the same person. This reminds us that members of the body of Christ are all dependent upon each other and that these gifts are given not to be "consumed upon their lusts" but "in order that every member may be profited thereby." (D&C 46:9, 29.)

Furthermore, a careful look at the list of spiritual gifts reveals that these endowments are attributes of God himself, which he uses solely for the benefit of his children. He desires that we receive and develop these gifts. As we perfect our unselfish use of whatever spiritual gifts God sees fit to give us here on earth, we will receive further gifts in preparation to obtain all divine attributes of godliness in our eventual exalted state.[14]

SPIRITUAL SEALINGS

As a final manifestation of the Holy Ghost in our lives, all ordinances performed in the flesh — such as baptism, temple endowment, or celestial marriage — must be approved by the Holy Ghost to be effectual when the body and the spirit are reunited in the resurrection. Acting in this capacity, the Holy Ghost is known as the Holy Spirit of Promise. As the Lord revealed to the Prophet Joseph, "All covenants, contracts, bonds, obligations, oaths, vows, performances, connections, associations, or expectations, that are not made and entered into and sealed by the Holy Spirit of promise . . . are of no efficacy, virtue, or force in and after the resurrection of the dead; for all contracts that are not made unto this end have an end when men are dead." (D&C 132:7.)

The Holy Spirit of Promise verifies that "ordinances and other righteous acts performed on this earth . . . are ratified, validated, and sealed in heaven as well as on earth."[15] The Holy Spirit seals our covenants upon us by testifying before the Lord that we have entered into them in righteousness and that we have been "just and true" in fulfilling them. (D&C 76:53.) The Spirit also promises, or confirms, to us that the Lord has accepted our acts. We may thus pursue our eternal course with confidence, knowing that Heavenly Father has accepted our righteous acts.

If we enter into a covenant unrighteously, or if we are not faithful in keeping that covenant, the act will not be spiritually ratified. However, if we repent and make ourselves worthy, we can still receive the promise. Similarly, an ordinance originally sealed by the Spirit can be later rendered ineffectual if we break our covenant.[16] As with all other manifestations and workings of the Holy Ghost, the seal of promise is contingent upon our righteousness.

THE SANCTIFYING POWER
OF THE HOLY GHOST

The greatest blessing of the Holy Ghost in our lives is the spiritual refinement of our souls. The baptism of water may cleanse us, but his baptism of fire purges us until no sign of the former blemishes exists. The scriptures sometimes refer to the Lord's cleansing as a "refiner's fire." (Mal. 3:2; 3 Ne. 24:2; D&C 128:24.) A refinery uses extreme heat to purify metal. By burning away the dross and impure particles, a piece of metal is strengthened. Each one of God's children needs to pass through a spiritual refiner's fire in order to enter his presence. This refiner's fire is defined as a purification or sanctification process.

Sanctification means that a person becomes pure and spotless through the process of time. Paul states, "If any man be in Christ, he is a new creature: old things are passed away; behold, all things are become new." (2 Cor. 5:17.) The scriptures teach us that the Holy Ghost assists in this transformation process. Bruce R. McConkie adds, "Sanctification is a state of saintliness, a state attained only by conformity to the laws and ordinances of the gospel."[17] We need to understand the purpose of sanctification before we can see how we can become sanctified.

Sanctification means "to consecrate" or "to make holy." It is a prerequisite to return to Heavenly Father's presence. The Lord taught that no unclean thing can enter the kingdom of heaven. (See 1 Ne. 15:34; Eph. 5:5.) Since all but Jesus Christ have sinned and have become unclean and unworthy before God (see Rom. 3:23), no one qualifies for the kingdom. However, the atoning blood of Jesus Christ, upon the conditions of repentance, is what prepares the way for our purification so we can be led back to our Father's presence.

One LDS scholar, Robert L. Millet, clarifies this by saying, "Jesus Christ is the means by which men and women are sanctified, made holy and clean, and his is the only name through which fallen creatures may be renewed and renovated and lifted spiritually to that plane which characterizes him who is the embodiment of holiness."[18] After Christ has opened the gates of redemption for us, we must go through them to receive the potential blessings. These thoughts are echoed in the well-known words of the "Battle Hymn of the Republic," "As he died to make men holy, let us live to make men free."

The Holy Ghost is the means by which sanctification is accomplished within us individually. The process of purifying the soul comes after the cleansing of baptism, and it requires a baptism of fire through the Holy Ghost to be completed. As Elder McConkie stated, "It is the Holy Spirit . . . that erases carnality and brings us into a state of righteousness.

We become clean when we actually receive the . . . companionship of the Holy Ghost. It is then that sin and dross and evil are burned out of our souls as though by fire. The baptism of the Holy Ghost is the baptism of fire."[19] Heavenly Father controls the power and conditions for sanctification; the atonement of his Son provides the means by which a holy consecration can occur, and the purging of the Holy Ghost completes the sanctifying process within our souls.

Sanctification is a process that occurs in gradual steps. It comes to those who yield their hearts to God, who are personally righteous, and who endure faithfully and valiantly in the gospel of Jesus Christ. (See Hel. 3:35.) Bruce R. McConkie highlights the importance of enduring to the end by emphasizing, "Nobody is sanctified in an instant, suddenly. But if we keep the commandments and press forward with steadfastness after baptism, then degree by degree and step by step we sanctify our souls until that glorious day when we're qualified to go where God and angels are."[20] Sanctification is the personal perfection process.

When we are sanctified by the Holy Ghost, we become a new person. Our habits, personality, desires, and passions are changed. We view ourselves and others around us differently. This change is accomplished because of the refining powers of the Holy Ghost. We become like the people during King Benjamin's time when we witness "a mighty change in us, or in our hearts, that we have no more disposition to do evil, but to do good continually." (Mosiah 5:2.) As we are purged from the effects of sin, all the desires and temptations of sin are rooted out of our hearts, and we become more like Christ.

Indeed, we are not actual members of Christ's true church without the gift of the Holy Ghost. When Joseph Smith was asked what primary factor separated The Church of Jesus Christ of Latter-day Saints from the other religions of the day, he responded that it was in "the gift of the Holy Ghost by the laying-on of hands, . . . [and] that all other considerations were contained in the gift of the Holy Ghost."[21] Thus, Christ commissioned the Nephites, "Now this is the commandment: Repent, all ye ends of the earth, and come unto me and be baptized in my name, that ye may be sanctified by the reception of the Holy Ghost, that ye may stand spotless before me at the last day." (3 Ne. 27:20.) Since the gift of the Holy Ghost is the great distinctive factor separating the true church of Jesus Christ from all other churches and religions, experiencing the constant companionship and sanctifying power of this member of the Godhead should be our primary goal in life.

In conclusion, *the GIFT OF THE HOLY GHOST is shared among God's children as the Holy Ghost confirms our membership in Christ's church, as his power and gifts transform us spiritually, and, as a God, he sanctifies our souls preparatory to receiving celestial glory.* The reception of the Holy Ghost, like the little iron key to the Viking chieftain's treasure vault, can open the door to further gifts. These blessings of the Spirit are designed to help us achieve our divine potential. As we spiritually progress from receiving the subtle promptings of the Holy Spirit to experiencing more of his constant companionship and gifts, his power will seal the ordinances of God that we have received. We may not have every gift yet, but by sharing those we do have, we can experience joy and obtain eternal life.

Ultimately, not only is the Holy Ghost a witness to us of God the Father and Jesus Christ, but, through the Holy Spirit of Promise, he can also testify to them of our worthiness to be in their presence. The Lord revealed the value of this celestial goal when he spoke through the Prophet Joseph Smith to the Latter-day Saints, "If you keep my commandments and endure to the end you shall have eternal life, which gift is the greatest of all the gifts of God." (D&C 14:7.) To prepare us for eternal life, the gift and influence of the Holy Ghost is the greatest gift God has given us in mortality. (See D&C 121:46.) The companionship of the Holy Ghost is God's valuable gift to enlighten us so that we are able to return to his celestial presence and receive his greatest endowment — the gift of eternal life.

For further study, refer to the following entries:

TG	BD	*EM*
Confirm	Confirmation	Baptism of Fire and
Holy Ghost, Baptism of	Holy Ghost	of the Holy Ghost
Holy Ghost, Gift of		Confirmation
Sanctification, Sanctify		Gift of the Holy Ghost
		Gifts of the Spirit

CHAPTER 20

SPIRITUAL HEALTH

The daily need for food to sustain physical life is so pressing that few people purposely neglect or inadvertently forget it. Consider the hypothetical example of a superathlete who, after winning a major championship, claims he will keep his high state of physical fitness intact. But afterward, he refuses to eat, drink, or rest. Severe health problems, even death, would result within days if such a foolish course were taken. After only a few hours without food, the body reminds us of its need for nourishment through numerous physical symptoms — hunger pain, stomachache, headache, fatigue, and so on.

The daily need for spiritual nourishment to the human soul is equally important, yet individuals are more inclined to ignore its symptoms, which are subtle but real. They include unhappiness, irritability, insensitivity, abuse, selfishness, hard-heartedness, and even some types of depression. People easily neglect these symptoms and thus mistreat their spiritual selves far more than their physical bodies. In addition, they may also seek diversion from spiritual weaknesses through materialistic pursuits, frivolous distractions, physical gratification, and drug abuse. Needless to say, such diversions as these only intensify the dearth of their spiritual condition.

Proper physical nutrition includes daily intake from the four basic food groups: grains and cereals, fruits and vegetables, proteins and dairy products (including beans, meats, and eggs), and fats and oils. Similarly, four minimum daily requirements for sound spiritual health are necessary: prayer (along with pondering and occasional fasting), scripture and gospel study, service to family and others, and personal development and well-being. If we nourish ourselves daily in each of these areas, we enrich our eternal spiritual welfare while tending to our temporary physical needs.

PRAYER (ALONG WITH PONDERING AND FASTING)

Before entering mortality through birth, we all dwelt in the presence of God. Communicating with him required little effort: we spoke to him, heard his voice, and received direct counsel and instruction. Like little children under the tutelage of earthly parents, we were closely directed in our spiritual growth by our Heavenly Father. Now, like young adults away from home and parents, we no longer enjoy the immediate presence of God. To continue receiving his direction for our spiritual progress, we must pray.

For this reason, Adam and Eve, upon being driven from the Garden of Eden, "called upon the name of the Lord, and they heard the voice of the Lord from the way toward the Garden of Eden, speaking unto them, and they saw him not; for they were shut out from his presence." (Moses 5:4.) By the Lord's voice within the garden, Adam and Eve received commandments, the first of which was to pray, calling upon God in the name of the Son for forgiveness of sins. Having done this, Adam and Eve then received the Holy Ghost, which brought them knowledge of their mortal condition and joy in their eventual redemption. (See Moses 5:5, 8–11.)

We, likewise, should pray for forgiveness of our sins and for the companionship of the Holy Ghost to help us overcome the power of Satan, whose presence seems all too strong in this world. (See Moses 5:13.) As children of God, we are free to approach our Heavenly Father on any subject and for any of our spiritual or temporal needs. Following the Savior's example, we should also remember others and pray for their needs. The Book of Mormon disciple Amulek made a representative list of the things for which we should pray, including not only divine mercy, eternal salvation, and other spiritual concerns, but also material possessions such as our fields and flocks, our houses and households. Further, we should also pray for others, both our enemies and neighbors. (See Alma 34:17–27.) In short, our prayers should involve all our activities, responsibilities, and aspirations.

Amulek also counsels concerning when we should pray: "Cry unto him . . . morning, mid-day, and evening . . . and when you do not cry unto the Lord, let your hearts be full, drawn out in prayer unto him continually." (Alma 34:21, 27.) It is significant that we should pray at least as often as we eat. If we feed our spirits as often as our bodies, we will live fuller lives on earth and obtain eternal life in the world to come.[1]

We receive subtle spiritual help through daily moments of quiet pondering and introspection. As we meditate on personal concerns we have opportunity to search for meaning and purpose in our existence. Gentle whisperings of the Spirit assist us in the many decisions and acts we must do daily. As we listen and respond to these promptings, we learn that a loving Heavenly Father is guiding us in paths leading to spiritual growth.

Strengthening Our Prayers and Spirituality through Fasting

Occasional fasting strengthens the effectiveness of our prayers and enriches our sensitivity to God's spiritual promptings. Both prayer and fasting are admonished in the scriptures. Interestingly, prayer is often mentioned in the scriptures without any link to fasting, but fasting is rarely mentioned without a reference to prayer in the adjoining verses. A major purpose of fasting is to make our prayers more effective; but fasting without prayer is merely depriving oneself of food and will not lead to spiritual strength. Prayer is a necessary element throughout fasting, and more rewarding prayers are a noticeable result of diligent fasting.

The spiritual nourishment we can receive through fasting cannot be overestimated. In fact, many of the greatest miracles and revelations recorded in the scriptures were brought about through fasting and prayer. Alma the younger and the sons of Mosiah found success in converting the formerly unrepentant Lamanites because of their knowledge of the scriptures and because they "had given themselves to much prayer, and fasting; therefore they had the spirit of prophecy, and the spirit of revelation, and when they taught, they taught with power and authority of God." (Alma 17:3.)

Significantly, three spiritual giants of the Bible — Moses, Elijah, and the Lord Jesus Christ — all retreated to the wilderness in fasting and prayer for forty days and nights to prepare themselves to serve their people. Through willingness to subdue the flesh, they received marvelous revelations and were physically and spiritually sustained through communion with heaven. (See Ex. 34:28–29; 1 Kgs. 19:8–18; Matt. 4:2, 11.)

These three servants also exemplify three notable purposes for fasting: to strengthen ourselves, to serve others, and to draw nearer to God. Through Moses, the Lord instituted the first required fast among the children of Israel on the annual Day of Atonement. On this fall day all the congregation fasted, while the high priest, dressed in white linen, made sin offerings and burnt offerings for himself, his household, and the people: "For on that day shall the priest make an atonement for you, to cleanse you, that ye may be clean from all your sins before the Lord." (Lev. 16:30.)

The ritual Day of Atonement was also a symbolic representation of the actual atonement of Christ, who offered his own sinless flesh as a sacrifice so that we might be purified and thereby enter with him into the presence of God. (See Heb. 9:24.) Thus, one major purpose of our fasting is to strengthen ourselves spiritually as we purge ourselves of weaknesses and shortcomings. Furthermore, as the priest assisted others in the time of fasting, we can aid others through intensive fasting commitments. Elijah learned this value of fasting late in his ministry.

Elijah was in extreme despair when he began his forty-day fast. He felt he had failed in his calling to bring the Israelites closer to God, even after his miraculous confrontation with the priests of Baal. Frustrated and disappointed, he wanted to die. But after his fasting, he felt spiritually rejuvenated and ready for further callings from God. He was a better, more enlightened person after this fasting experience, and he spent many more years among the people as their servant. Elijah also came to recognize the gentle spiritual whisperings that allow us more complete communion with God, and thus grew closer to him. (See 1 Kgs. 19.) After a sincere fast, we likewise are spiritually strengthened, we receive new understanding and commitment toward serving others, and we find we have drawn nearer to our Heavenly Father.

Jesus' atoning sacrifice symbolizes the potential value of a fulfilling fast. His fast was a valuable preparation for his mortal ministry, culminating in his atoning sacrifice. When we fast, we symbolically reenact the sacrifice of Christ in our own flesh: we deny ourselves the things that sustain our physical being so as to bring our spirits into communion with God, and this makes us better Saints. We also pay a fast offering for the poor when we fast, not only for the good it does them, but also to remind ourselves that Christ sacrificed himself for others. In fasting we reconcile ourselves spiritually to God and sacrifice our physical means for our fellowman in a truly Christlike manner.

TEN STEPS TO A FULFILLING FAST

In modern scripture, the Lord equates genuine fasting and prayer with a time of rejoicing. (See D&C 59:14.) How many Church members, however, anticipate fast Sunday with dread rather than joy? The following outline, if used as a guideline for fasting, can help transform what might normally be a day of mere physical deprivation into a spiritual feast.

1. *Plan ahead.* A few days before you fast, review these ten steps and start thinking about a purpose for your fast. Since most of our fasting involves a major portion of a Sunday, prepare your schedule so that you can start the fast properly on Saturday, thus making yourself spiritually ready for the fasting experience throughout the Sabbath.

2. *Have a particular purpose or goal* in mind as you begin the fast. Perhaps you desire personal enlightenment or strength, such as an answer to a doctrinal question, help in solving a problem, or inspiration in strengthening your testimony. Or, you may desire help and direction in counseling sensitively with a troubled family member, aiding a neighbor, sharing the gospel with a nonmember, or in performing some other form of service. Fasting can also be a time of thanksgiving or appreciation. Select a primary goal and perhaps one corollary goal on which to concentrate during your fast.

3. *Start the fast with a private prayer* — preferably vocal — while you are alone and on your knees. Remember, fasting without prayer is simple starvation. The Lord has never commanded us to abstain from eating except for spiritual purposes. Although voluntary abstinence may strengthen self-discipline, it will not have spiritual value without prayer. Include thanks to the Almighty for your blessings, especially for the bounty of food you may have enjoyed, and express your desires concerning your fasting purposes.

4. *Direct your thoughts, words, and actions toward keeping the Spirit with you.* Set a spiritual tone for the whole fasting period by rising above the normal physical plane. Keep Saturday evening activities uplifting, especially those of a social nature, in order to set the proper mood for the fast and the Sabbath.

5. *Abstain from two meals.* Since most Mormons conclude their fast

sometime Sunday in the late afternoon or during the evening, ideally you should start your fast following your evening meal on Saturday. Thus, you would be fasting for twenty to twenty-four hours, refraining from all food and drink, if possible. In case of health problems, fast and restrict your intake according to your limitations. Sick individuals, pregnant women, and nursing mothers are advised not to fast. As you discipline yourself physically, you prepare yourself spiritually to fulfill your fasting purpose.

6. *Study possible means toward your purpose or goals* while you fast. For example, look up possible answers to your gospel question or problem by reading the scriptures, draft some possible solutions to personal or family problems, talk with someone in whom you have confidence to get ideas before counseling a troubled friend, write in your journal to solidify feelings and valuable learning experiences, and so on. (Depending upon your Sunday meeting schedule, this step and the next one may be reversed.)

7. *Attend all your church meetings on Sunday.* By this time you should be fifteen to twenty hours into your fast—a period, studies have demonstrated, when most people can think more clearly, concentrate more deeply, and (in a religious setting) listen to the Spirit more intensely. Listen to the speakers, teachers, and the Spirit for ideas concerning your fasting purpose.

8. *Pay a full fast offering* as determined by the cost of the two meals you have missed and your ability to give. Church leaders have counseled us to be generous in our fast offerings, multiplying them as we desire in order to assist the poor and needy (which is the only purpose for which these funds are used).[2]

9. *Ponder and meditate.* Before concluding your fast, set aside some time, preferably twenty to thirty minutes, to meditate, pondering the possible solutions to the problem or answers to the question you have been considering. Read Moroni 10, especially verses one through five, for helpful counsel.

10. *End the fast with a private prayer,* taking time to listen to spiritual promptings and to receive an answer from our Heavenly Father. Finally, break the fast by eating a simple meal "prepared with singleness of heart that thy fasting may be perfect, or, in other words, that thy joy may be full." (D&C 59:13.)

Aside from the spiritual benefits of fasting, physiological studies in recent years have confirmed that periodic fasting helps purify the body. Furthermore, during a fast, blood circulation normally devoted to digesting food is available to the brain, enabling fasting individuals to react faster and think more clearly. Twelve to twenty hours into the fast, heightened physical and mental capacity help put us in a proper spiritual state to receive the direction and revelation we desire. Having disciplined ourselves, focused on a purpose, assisted the needy, and enriched our spirituality, a proper fast will be a time of rejoicing!

SCRIPTURE AND GOSPEL STUDY

Just as Amulek counseled us to pray as often as we eat—morning, noon, and night—so the prophet Nephi admonished us to "feast upon the words of Christ; for behold, the words of Christ will tell [us] all things what [we] should do." (2 Ne. 32:3.) The words of Christ, which are revealed by the Holy Ghost, are available to us primarily through the scriptures and our personal study and pondering.

The scriptures do not answer every individual question or problem; they alone cannot tell us everything we should do—for this, pondering and praying are necessary. What the scriptures do give, however, are the eternal truths and commandments on which to base deliberations, judgments, and decisions. They also give examples, or "case studies," of how other men and women have dealt with similar difficulties of life throughout the ages. They furthermore demonstrate God's constant love for his children—a comfort and promise for today.

Daily prayer and scripture study should, therefore, go hand in hand. The scriptures help prepare our minds and hearts for meditation and prayer as they raise questions to consider that we might not have thought of and as they expand our understanding of God's work. In return, our prayers help us better understand the written word of God as we "liken all scriptures unto us, that it might be for our profit and learning."[3] (1 Ne. 19:23.)

A helpful way to read the scriptures is to organize a systematic, regular reading program. Some people set aside a regular period each day for scripture reading, such as fifteen to thirty minutes. Other individuals set a goal to read a certain number of pages or chapters daily or weekly until their objective is met. Orienting the goal toward chapters is usually more practical, since they present more logical breaks. Sometimes, a person will decide to read a work of scripture during a short vacation or other selected period. Usually, the reading is spread out in smaller portions throughout the year. For the reader's information, the following chart indicates the number of chapters in each of the Standard Works:

Old Testament	929
New Testament	260
Bible (total)	1189
Book of Mormon	239
Doctrine and Covenants	140[4]
Pearl of Great Price	16
Total	1584 chapters
	(2480 pages)

Adult Latter-day Saints usually orient their scripture-reading program around the subject matter of the Gospel Doctrine classes in the Sunday School, which are currently on a four-year rotating schedule in this order: Old Testament (and the Moses and Abraham portions of the Pearl of Great Price), New Testament, Book of Mormon, and Doctrine and Covenants (with the rest of the Pearl of Great Price). Additionally, many Latter-day Saints have a yearly goal of reading the Book of Mormon.

Scripture reading can be a fun, positive experience for individuals and families, especially if appropriate incentives or rewards are a part of the program. For example, a special ice-cream treat may reward the completion of a book (such as Matthew or First Nephi) or the end of a reading period (such as a month or a set number of weeks of daily reading). Recognition of intermediate goals reinforces our resolve to complete our annual goals. In addition, while reading the scriptures, family members should learn the importance of discussing important passages and of using various scripture aids, such as footnotes, the Topical Guide and Bible Dictionary entries, maps, and so on. Scripture-reading programs, even if they are not daily successes, will help establish spiritual priorities for the family. They also instill good reading and gospel study habits for all involved, especially children.

SERVICE TO FAMILY AND OTHERS

LDS scholar Hugh Nibley once said, "If you pray for an angel to visit you, you know what he'll do when he comes. He'll just quote the scriptures to you — so you know you're wasting your time waiting for what we already have."[5] In a similar vein, President Spencer W. Kimball wrote, "God does notice us, and he watches over us. But it is usually through another person that he meets our needs."[6] In other words, if we look for miraculous intervention in our lives, we usually anticipate too much. Most of the needed knowledge and understanding can be found in the scriptures, and most of the desired blessings and assistance can be received through service from and to others. Our primary duty as Saints of God, then, is to love and serve others, following the Savior's example. We then can become his messengers in performing miracles of service to others.

The Pharisees, who seemed more concerned with law than love, asked the Savior which was the greatest commandment in the law. Christ responded with two: "Thou shalt love the Lord thy God with all thy heart, and with all thy soul, and with all thy mind. This is the first and great commandment. *And the second is like unto it,* Thou shalt love thy neighbour as thyself. On these *two* commandments hang all the law and the prophets." (Matt. 22:37–40; italics added.) The two great commandments are inseparable, and the second is "like unto" the first because through the second we fulfill the first commandment. We demonstrate our love for others by caring for their temporal and spiritual needs. Jesus set such an example when he provided the five thousand with a meal along with a spiritual feast. (See John 6.) He also admonished us to care for the needy as a witness of our service and love for him. (See Matt. 25:31–46.) In other words, God is not present with us here on earth; we can serve him only by serving others. (See Mosiah 2:17.)

If, on the other hand, we spend all our energies serving ourselves, we ultimately become servants of Satan. He encourages men to pile up goods for their own material security, without regard for the needs of their neighbors. Because of this practice, the Lord says, "the world lieth in sin." (D&C 49:20.) Christ also warns, "No man can serve two masters: for either he will hate the one, and love the other; or else he will hold to the one, and despise the other. Ye cannot serve God and mammon."

(Matt. 6:24.) *Mammon* is transliterated from a Greek word (derived from Aramaic) meaning personal riches. The true Saint realizes that there is no such thing as *personal* riches: the fullness of the earth and all its riches belong to God and should be used to provide equally for all.

Instead of allowing material wealth to be our means of public recognition, perhaps we should follow the Semitic example where internal virtues rather than exterior possessions are the basis of public honor. For example, the story is told of a distinguished traveler coming to an Arab village and being invited to a special feast. Only the most honored members of the community were invited to the dinner, and they came in their finest robes. But the traveler was surprised when the person seated next to him was dressed in beggar's rags. He asked the host if this was not the same poor man he had seen begging at the village entrance just a few hours earlier. The host replied that he was, and sensing the traveler's next question, he explained:

"This man is the poorest person in our village, yet he is our most honored and esteemed citizen. His knowledge and wisdom are legendary, and his literary and musical talents are without equal. And until a few months ago, he was the wealthiest man in the valley, noted for his generosity to the poor. But after a devastating scourge destroyed most of the townspeople's flocks, he used all his wealth to buy food for the people and distributed all of his livestock, except for one camel, among them. He was journeying with his camel to a far land, where he had earlier traded and gained much wealth, when a starving family crossed his path. Without hesitation, he slaughtered his last camel and provided abundant food for the famished strangers who were guests in his tent. Poor and penniless, but rich in honor and dignity, he now lives with us in our village. He is the most distinguished citizen we could seat next to you." If more societies recognized such generosity, the destitute would truly find all of their basic needs fulfilled.

Besides harboring a selfish attitude towards material goods — "After all, I earned it myself" — many people today are also caught up in popular movements promoting "personal priorities" and "self-fulfillment." But instead of enlarging and refining character, constant focus on self produces gross egoism, which clouds the mind and hinders spiritual growth. The paradoxical truth about abstract ideals such as fulfillment and happiness is that they can be obtained only when we do not consciously seek them: "He that findeth his life shall lose it: and he that loseth his life for my sake shall find it." (Matt. 10:39.) President Kimball expounded on this paradox when he said concerning service, "The more we serve our fellowmen in appropriate ways, the more substance there is to our souls. . . . Indeed, it is easier to 'find' ourselves because there is so much more of us to find!"[7]

PERSONAL DEVELOPMENT AND WELL-BEING

In order to better serve others, we usually need both temporal resources and spiritual strength. Indeed, it is difficult to assist others when we are weak and destitute ourselves. President Marion G. Romney of the First Presidency encouraged us to develop our means and our talents so that we can be more profitable servants: "Without self-reliance one cannot exercise these innate desires to serve. How can we give if there is nothing there? Food for the hungry cannot come from empty shelves. Money to assist the needy cannot come from an empty purse. Support and understanding cannot come from the emotionally starved. Teaching cannot come from the unlearned. And most important of all, spiritual guidance cannot come from the spiritually weak."[8]

CARING FOR OUR BASIC NEEDS

To enable ourselves to serve others well, we should be mindful of all temporal and spiritual areas of personal welfare. A helpful checklist might include the financial and vocational, physical, emotional, social, intellectual, moral, and spiritual aspects of our lives.

Most people have daily work to provide for the financial needs of themselves and their families. Within many families, however, *financial and vocational* instability is a major cause of marital stress and is often listed as a major cause for divorce. As President Heber J. Grant counseled, "If there is . . . one thing that will bring peace and contentment into the human heart, and into the family, it is to live within our means, and if there is any one thing that is grinding, and discouraging and disheartening it is to have debts and obligations that one cannot meet."[9] Latter-day Saints are therefore counseled by one of the Lord's prophets to stay out of debt and to "plan and work in a way that will permit you to be happy even as you do without certain things that in times of affluence may have been available to you. Live within your means and not beyond them. . . . Strive to save a portion of that which you earn. . . . Teach your children these basic principles in your family councils."[10]

Solid educational and vocational training along with modest monetary expectations, spending discipline, and careful budgeting will lead to financial independence and material security. On the other hand, if we constantly live beyond our means and always worry over our daily maintenance, we feel in bondage to financial necessities. In addition, our minds and hearts are not free to seek higher things or to think of others' needs. Furthermore, we feel we have no surplus material goods to share with others in their times of need.[11]

The second item on our personal-welfare checklist involves our *physical* body. As discussed earlier, when we fast, we subdue physical needs to gain spiritual blessings. When we are not fasting, however, we should remember that the physical body is a temple that houses the spirit, and we should care for it accordingly. (See 1 Cor. 3:16.) Some Church members may not recognize the correlation between spiritual and physical health. Our physical well-being cannot be neglected without suffering ill consequences spiritually, for "the spirit and the body are the soul of man" (D&C 88:15) and "when separated, man cannot receive a fulness of joy" (D&C 93:34). Regular exercise and a wise diet, as advised by the Word of Wisdom, will bring us not only physical strength and endurance, but also spiritual revelation: "Wisdom and great treasures of knowledge, even hidden treasures."[12] (D&C 89:19.)

The third area we need to work on is our *emotions.* The prophet Lehi provides valuable insight into the strongest emotional feeling we should experience in mortality: "Men are, that they might have joy." (2 Ne. 2:25.) Note that Lehi did not say something like, "Men are that they will have joy," indicating that joy is reserved only for future celestial life. On the other hand, he did not guarantee complete, constant joy by saying "Men are that they have joy." Instead, men are that they *might have* joy—hopefully a good share of it now and a complete measure of it in the eternities.

In other words, we do not have to wait for our final destination to experience joy—it can be part of our earth life now. If our attitude is one of faith in Christ, of hope in our future with God, and of charity for others as prompted by the Holy Spirit, then we will daily look for the best in life, in others, and in ourselves. Ultimate joy comes through exaltation, and exaltation results from full personal growth. Such joy and emotional contentment will come only as we fulfill Heavenly Father's planned destiny for us. Thus, as we grow and progress, we will generally retain a positive, peaceful spirit about us that brings us joy.[13]

The fourth item on our personal development checklist involves our *social* habits. In modern scripture, the Lord chastened early leaders of the Church, including Joseph Smith, and commanded them to "set in order" their homes and families. (See D&C 90:18; 93:43, 50.) Without love and harmony as the social patterns in our own families, we are ill-equipped to share the gospel and set a Christlike example for others. For both parents and children, sound family relationships foster a secure environment that enables family members to succeed in social relationships outside the home. Our role as unique individuals in the family largely determine how we will function in society. It influences whether we will love only ourselves or learn to love our neighbors as ourselves. We need to learn how to build upon our family foundation so we can expand into other social relationships.[14]

A fifth area for development is our *mind.* Besides needing to set his family in order, Joseph Smith was commanded to "set in order the churches, and study and learn, and become acquainted with all good books, and with languages, tongues, and people." (D&C 90:15.) The Latter-day Saints are committed to intellectual progress throughout life and even beyond the grave, since the glory of God is intelligence (see D&C 93:36) and since the degree of intelligence and knowledge we acquire in this life will accompany us into the spirit world (see D&C 130:18–19). President Brigham Young counseled that, while the fundamental truths of salvation are contained in the holy scriptures, these should not be the end of our study, or we will overlook much beneficial knowledge and many inspired truths: " 'Shall I sit down and read the Bible, the Book of Mormon, and the Book of Covenants all the time?' says one. Yes, if you please, and when you have done, you may be nothing but a sectarian after all. It is your duty to study to know everything upon the face of the earth in addition to reading those books. . . . The truth that is in all the arts and sciences forms a part of our religion."[15]

In addition to enriching our minds, we need to constantly strengthen ourselves in a sixth area: our *moral* integrity. As we maintain and strengthen our moral values, we demonstrate social responsibility and an attitude of fairness and justice. And when we speak of morality, we mean more than the moral-sexual relationship between men and women—for morality also refers to honesty, ethical values, and all interpersonal relationships.[16]

Finally, as we evaluate our checklist for personal well-being, we must appreciate that *spirituality* is the most important ingredient. Spiritual progress—like happiness and fulfillment—cannot be sought after directly. Rather, it is a by-product of daily prayer, fasting, scripture reading, study, service, and personal development and refinement in many areas. A spiritual person is one who cares not for the wealth and honor of this world, but who loves truth and patterns his life upon noble, eternal principles. As President David O. McKay so succinctly expressed: "Spirituality, our true aim, is the consciousness of victory over self and of communion with the Infinite."[17]

Our personal well-being requires constant attention in all the seven areas we just discussed. As we strengthen ourselves, we are better able to help others. In addition, as we feel good about ourselves, we should want to assist others in feeling good about themselves. We can accomplish this through genuine service. Some of the best means and values of service are illuminated in the scriptures. Regular scripture reading and gospel study keep our personal and service priorities in line. To insure that our priorities correspond with Heavenly Father's will, we need to pray to him many times each day. An occasional fast accentuates our communication with God as we augment our religious commitment. All of these actions enhance our spiritual health.

Although the signs of spiritual weakness are not as obvious as symptoms of illness, they are just as sure if we do not tend to our spiritual health. Champion athletes at their peak would be foolish to claim no need for proper nourishment, exercise, and rest. They would quickly lose their health and could even endanger their lives. Similarly, people cannot become complacent and claim they no longer need to pray, keep the commandments, or strengthen themselves spiritually.

We need to regularly strengthen our SPIRITUAL HEALTH through daily activities like prayer (along with occasional fasting), scripture and gospel study, service to others, and personal development in one or more of the financial and vocational, physical, emotional, social, intellectual, moral, and spiritual areas of our lives. As we maintain our spiritual health, we will find peace and purpose in life while preparing ourselves for the joy and contentment of eternity.

For further study, refer to the following entries:

TG	BD	*EM*
Fast, Fasting	Fasts	Church Educational
Prayer, Pray	Prayer	System
Scriptures, Study of		Education
Service		Fasting
		Institutes of Religion
		Physical Fitness and
		Recreation
		Prayer
		Scripture Study
		Seminaries

PERSONAL GROWTH—OBEYING THE COMMANDMENT TO BE PERFECT

There are times when each of us wishes for something more than what we have—be it health, wealth, beauty, skills, or possessions. We wonder how we can improve our life-styles and the lives of others. As a barometer of these desires, think of how often we have said or heard sentences beginning with these phrases: "I wish I had ...," "I wish I could ...," or "I wish you would ... "? Most often we look outside ourselves for the fulfillment of these dreams.

We wish we could be like the servants in the parable of the talents who received money from their master, doubled it, and then received a generous reward from their lord. In the parable, Jesus said simply that the wealthy man "called his own servants, and delivered unto them his goods. And unto one he gave five talents, to another two, and to another one; to every man according to his several ability." (Matt. 25:14–15.) He then related that two of the servants benefited from the wise increase of their talents. Because they had been "faithful over a few things," the master would make them a "ruler over many things." However, Jesus did not share with us *how* the servants were wise and faithful in multiplying their talents, other than to say they were traders. (See Matt. 25:16; Luke 19:15.) What did they trade, and why were some more successful than others? We are not told the details of their success. We wish we knew some special secret, not only to multiply our wealth, but also to increase our gifts, talents, skills, and successes.

Most people, regardless of their social status, financial condition, or spiritual strength, would like to improve their station of life. For example, a variety of interesting surveys have found that most people feel they need just a little more income than what they now have. They believe if they had just 10 percent more, they could easily get by. This was true across the whole economic spectrum, whether the people already had very limited or seemingly large sources of income. Most people believe that just a little bit more will make them happy. Likewise in a spiritual dimension, many people sense that their spiritual level is below their expectation and potential. They feel they need just a little more spirituality, sensitivity toward others, understanding of the scriptures, and other spiritual attributes. And although they naturally look elsewhere for the satisfaction of these desires, most often their achievement comes from within.

THE QUEST FOR PERFECTION

Mormons often share these same material and spiritual expectations. Sometimes, they confuse the relationship between the two types of success. They are often a pragmatic people who believe that solid effort produces results. Some assume that material increase and social growth reflect greater spirituality, believing that the Lord materially blesses those who are righteous and that his tangible blessings are easy to see. Wiser Latter-day Saints recognize, however, that God's blessings are usually spiritual and less obvious. Wanting to receive these spiritual blessings, many might place especially rigorous demands upon themselves. Their ultimate goal is to fulfill the Savior's admonition, "Be ye therefore perfect, even as your Father which is in Heaven is perfect." (Matt 5:48.) Thus many strive for personal excellence or perfection in the various areas of their lives.

To outsiders, Mormons may be grouped together with Jews, Orientals, and others who have a reputation for high academic performance and business aggressiveness. Within the LDS community, some members sense that very high expectations can place some people under a great amount of stress—so much so that it can be damaging. Latter-day Saints are challenged to maintain a wise balance between academic and professional expectations and other priorities in life. On the one hand, they are promised that if they are obedient, they can "run and not be weary." (D&C 89:20; see also Isa. 40:31.) On the other hand, the Lord admonishes them through the Prophet Joseph Smith to not run faster than they have strength. (See D&C 10:4; Mosiah 4:27.) Thus, Latter-day Saints need to thoughtfully develop individualized approaches to personal perfection as they seek to follow Christ's example and receive divine help through his atoning sacrifice.[1]

DEVELOPING GIFTS AND TALENTS

People first face the challenge of discovering how self-improvement or success is achieved. Some feel that just plain hard work is required to succeed in life, yet history is full of people who worked busily but accomplished little of consequence. Too often, people are so involved in busywork that they do not accomplish things of greater, lasting value. Their efforts can be like the energy within lightning or the wind that is wasted because it is not directed or controlled.

Some other people believe that luck or circumstance leads to wealth or success. They wish that they were related to some rich ancestor or that the next lottery would bring them riches. They wait for good fortune to drop into their laps. Their circumstances vary little from those who simply wait for whatever life brings them, without trying to take control of their destiny. For these people, the elements of chance rather than the principles of control govern their lives.

Ultimately, mature people recognize that although just plain work or chance may lead to some success, the most dependable means toward personal fulfillment comes when we try to direct our own progress. In the previous chapter, we talked about areas in which we should all be striving to gain control in our lives. We learned that both physical and spiritual fitness come through inspired, diligent effort. Daily, we physically need to eat, exercise, and rest. Likewise, we should spiritually improve ourselves through prayer, gospel study, service, and personal development. This chapter will share guidelines on how we can improve ourselves and our life-styles through principles of proper preparation and effective achievement.

Amid the pressures of modern living, it is difficult — in fact, impossible — to give equal attention to all areas of personal development every day of our lives. The range of our financial, physical, emotional, social, intellectual, moral, and spiritual problems and potentials boggles the mind. To try to rigidly adhere to a fixed routine of personal development is to set oneself up for frustration and failure, for life will stubbornly refuse to conform itself to our desires. On the other hand, if a person sets no goals or priorities, his or her life will become completely governed by outside pressures and circumstances.

Seven Steps
for Personal Development

To realistically improve our lives, we must not try to do it all at once. Instead, we must identify our objectives and available resources, establish priorities, commit ourselves to reach attainable goals, and use our efforts wisely to attain those goals. We need to ask ourselves three key questions: (1) "What are we supposed to do?" (2) "How do we accomplish our objectives?" and (3) "How do we maintain our growth pattern?" As we answer these three questions, seven key steps become apparent.

What Are We Supposed to Do?

To begin, we need to decide where we are going and how we plan to get there. We prepare various guidelines as we go through the first three steps:

1. *Strive for true, noble, and eternal purposes.* However much we value industriousness, we need to look at the purpose behind our work. Sometimes we can get so caught up in busywork that we lose the vision of our grand, divine purpose on earth, which is ultimately the same purpose of God in heaven: "This is my work and my glory—to bring to pass the immortality and eternal life of man." (Moses 1:39.) All that we do should be done with an eye focused on the eternal life of ourselves and others. If what we desire has a negative bearing or no bearing at all on our eternal progression, how can it possibly be worth our time?

A declaration of purpose, a personal mission statement, or an organizational theme focuses attention upon the central objectives of the person or group. Such objectives encompass many areas of influence and should contain long-range perspective. A mission statement declares both what we want *to do* and what we want *to become,* and it will also probably suggest *why* we want to do it. Such a creed states the principles or values that motivate and give purpose to our activities. We do not need to be a company or a group to prepare a declaration of purpose or a personal mission statement for ourselves.

To assist us in this search for purpose and value in our efforts, we need to seek and follow the Holy Spirit. The prophet Jacob counseled that the revealed word of Jesus Christ through the Holy Ghost will "tell [us] all things what [we] should do." (2 Ne. 32:3.) We cannot help the Lord promote the immortality and eternal life of man without the aid of his Spirit. If we fix our minds on priorities and goals without the Spirit, we tend to cut ourselves off from his subtle whisperings, and we will most likely pursue the wrong things: "For my thoughts are not your thoughts, neither are your ways my ways, saith the Lord." (Isa. 55:8.) Like the Liahona given to Lehi, the Spirit should be our compass in life, not only pointing us in the right direction, but also giving us specific instructions along the way. Without the Spirit, we are truly lost. After identifying our mission in life, we can study how we can move toward our objectives.

2. *Identify individual roles and available resources.* On any given day, each of us may function in a variety of interpersonal roles: one person may be a husband, father, employee, Scoutmaster, neighbor, handyman, sportsman, and so on, while his marriage partner assumes her own roles as a wife, mother, employee, Primary teacher, volunteer worker, house-keeper, aerobic instructor, to name some possibilities. As we seek to bring the vision of our personal mission statement into realization, we should take into account the various, specific roles we play in life. We identify our varied roles and functions and compare them with the talents, assets, and other resources available to us (time, money, transportation, interests, and abilities, for example). Since we have only so much time and energy, we need to keep a sense of balance and proportion in our existence. As we recognize the personal, family, professional, and social dimensions of our lives and carefully use our resources, we will find it easier to organize our productive efforts toward the fulfillment of our personal missions.

An analogy will help us understand this process. Imagine remodeling a house for a family in need of larger living quarters. First, we need a set of blueprints (a mission statement) so we can know what the end product is supposed to be. We then need to identify our work skills so we can see which tasks we can accomplish (identifying our roles). We must also be sure we have the proper tools (resources) to get the job done.

To assist us in building our own lives, we need our own tools — the aids and helps that will allow us to get the job done. Two types of resources can be used: (1) those *personal abilities within* ourselves or those working with us, such as individual capacities, attitudes, skills, perspectives, experiences, and strengths; and (2) those *physical assets outside* ourselves, such as material possessions, tools, written works, financial means, Church programs, community services, and so forth. As we appreciate the resources available to us, we gain a better understanding of our potential achievement.

As we pursue the noble, eternal purposes of life, we should also remember that God will help us. President Abraham Lincoln believed that "God is the silent partner in all great enterprises."[2] As in the parable of the talents, God will reward those who work faithfully in his service, blessing them with additional gifts, strengths, and abilities to achieve their righteous desires, for those "which hath shall be given" more. (Luke 19:26; cf. JST.)

3. *Establish a plan of action with meaningful, challenging goals.* After reviewing our mission-based roles and resources, we are ready to map a course of action where we select our most important goals. We must schedule our priorities toward productive activities so we can improve the quality of both our performance and our life-style. Our plan should include balanced, systematic, and timely goals in the appropriate areas of our life.

Mottos and programs abound that encourage us to set goals. We are told that hopes and desires without plans to achieve them will always remain unfulfilled wishes, and those who fail to plan should plan to fail. In office-supply stores and bookstores, we find various time-management systems that provide guidelines, forms, and planner notebooks so we can organize our time more effectively. They give motivation and a structured framework for planning and accomplishing what matters most in our lives. As one LDS leader counseled, "successfully balancing life's demands requires careful long- and short-term planning and prioritizing, as well as constant review of one's values."[3]

As we plan, we should not be afraid to set difficult goals if they are what we truly desire and what the Lord would have us do. The ultimate goal of all believing Latter-day Saints is to become like God himself, which is humanly impossible, but attainable through the aid of the Atonement and the Holy Ghost.[4] We will reach only what we aim for, so we must aim high. Or as the British poet Robert Browning so elegantly stated, "Ah, but a man's reach should exceed his grasp, or what's a heaven for."[5]

HOW DO WE ACCOMPLISH OUR OBJECTIVES?

We are now ready to translate our values, resources, and plans into action. We do it through personal involvement with three further steps:

4. *Getting started—do it now!* At some time, we have to move from theory into practice. We need to commit ourselves and to start working hard to achieve our best. Our personal commitment to our projects or goals is vitally important because success or failure depends more upon attitude than upon aptitude. Making a commitment to others as well as ourselves is extremely helpful in reinforcing our desires to improve. We should confide our goals to a trusted parent, spouse, or friend. Through their acceptance of us as we are, they can best encourage and help us to improve amid obstacles and setbacks. A private commitment can easily be ignored or hedged upon, but when we include others in our goals, we can combine their strength with ours to help us succeed. This is one reason why all saving ordinances in the Church must be publicly witnessed and recorded. It is also why part of every Church member's baptismal covenant is to be "willing to bear one another's burdens, that they may be light." (Mosiah 18:8.)

Change almost always becomes harder and rarely becomes easier when it is postponed. If the saying, Nothing of lasting value is achieved without hard work, is true, then it is better to err in initiative and effort than in inactivity. We need to begin now. This concept is embodied in President Spencer W. Kimball's oft-repeated admonition, "Do it!" But given our human nature, we tend to procrastinate and delay. Although many motivating forces may get us going, five of them seem to be common: desperation, dissatisfaction, obligation, idealism, and faith.

Desperation catches up with us as deadlines arrive, crises arise, and pressing matters demand our attention. Things just finally have to get done, and so we go out and do them. Stress and frustration almost always accompany this compelling motivation, but at least we get the burdens off our back so we can go on with more pleasant activities.

Dissatisfaction is a more subtle but powerful motivating force. As we are dissatisfied with imperfections, incompleteness, and mundane efforts, we desire to improve things. Failure itself is not the problem; rather, our view of failure can make it a problem. Babies fail countless times before they learn to walk — in this, is a simple principle: success does not come with the first try. If we are satisfied or content with our failure, then our failure becomes permanent. The inventor Thomas Edison, who failed hundreds of times before perfecting the electric light bulb, said, "Discontent is the first necessity of progress."[6]

In striving to perfect ourselves, we will fall short of our own expectations many times. Whether we give up or keep trying, though, is the measure of our inward resolve strengthened by the Spirit. Sins and imperfections can be fully overcome only as man "yields to the enticings of the Holy Spirit, and putteth off the natural man and becometh a saint through the atonement of Christ." (Mosiah 3:19.) Unless through the Spirit we catch a glimpse of what we can become, we will likely be content with what we are. The Lord is not content with us the way we are, either, and for this reason he says, "Whom I love I also chasten that their sins may be forgiven, for with the chastisement I prepare a way for their deliverance in all things out of temptation." (D&C 95:1.)[7]

Obligation motivates us when we feel a sense of responsibility to get a job done. A work assignment, Church calling, or community commitment may provide this feeling. We are not always doing the task because we have to or because we want to. Sometimes, we just feel that someone ought to do it, and so we acquiesce. This incentive is usually not as frustrating as the motives discussed above, but it does not always provide the sense of fulfillment we would desire.

Idealism generates out of a positive desire to help others. It is the other side of the coin from the element of dissatisfaction discussed earlier. A negative incentive, such as discontent, will not always motivate us long enough to really solve the problem unless we also have some positive, lasting reasons that propel us forward. The gospel of Jesus Christ, the plan of salvation, and the threefold mission of the Church[8] provide a valuable positive framework for our actions. Likewise, some political philosophies and social programs give us positive incentive to extend our reach and help ourselves and others.

Faith is the sublime spiritual motivator in our lives. With this working as a spiritual catalyst, we want to actively participate in righteously living and helping others. Instead of negative, frustrating motives prompting us to action, and even nobler than dutiful or idealist motivations, this incentive brings love and spirituality into our behavior. We truly want to help ourselves and others for the best good of all; all this we do for God's work and glory. Faith, coupled with love and righteousness, guarantees that our motives are pure and our results will be optimal.

Whatever our incentive for getting started, we need to remember that no formula for success will work if we do nothing. With maturity and understanding, our motives will become more noble and will reflect more and more the long-range, charitable desires of our hearts. As our incentives for action generate out of higher motives, we will find that our efforts in these activities will be more rewarding and fulfilling.

5. *We increase our effectiveness through beneficial teamwork.* When people work well together, they often enjoy the benefits of synergy. Synergy is a process where the whole end product is greater than the sum of the individual parts. Edifying cooperation becomes a catalytic, empowering, and unifying force leading to far greater success than any individual could produce by him- or herself. Teamwork improves effectiveness and productivity as people synergize their efforts.

Working with others provides valuable experience in observing and learning their strengths and skills. As we emulate the positive attributes of others, we become better people more rapidly than if we tried to develop the same characteristics independently through trial and error. A progressive family or organization encourages the sharing of ideas and the mutual development of abilities. A weak group, on the other hand, often settles to low standards of performance, with members tolerating and reflecting each others' weaknesses. It can also foster unhealthy competition as members seek to bring down each other. As we emulate the good rather than emphasize the bad in each other, our relationships will edify ourselves and others.

Obvious examples of synergetic effort are found in the sports world and in business. Effective teamwork often allows a group of less-talented players to excel over a collection of gifted but selfish athletes. A company united from top to bottom toward quality production and genuine service will outperform far larger corporations. Likewise, LDS families, wards, stakes, and missions working together in love and harmony will find strength, success, and fulfillment in great abundance.

In our search to enlist the cooperation of others, or in our insistence to do things ourselves, we often overlook the assistance that the members of the Godhead can provide. As declared in the scriptures, "with God all things are possible." (Matt. 19:26; Mark 10:27.) Heavenly Father's help, along with Christ's direction and the Holy Ghost's inspiration, will give us great power to succeed in all our noble endeavors. In fact, all divine goals are impossible without their help.

6. *We overcome obstacles and achieve success in gradual steps.* Certainly godhood would exceed every person's grasp if it had to be attained all at once. Yet it is not impossible to find, or even be, a person who is perfect in one or more ways—absolutely honest, completely dependable, fully chaste, and so on. The key is to perfect those areas of our lives where we are nearly perfect already, while applying the discipline and spiritual strength we have acquired to more difficult areas. Thus, we will reach our ultimate goal—and any long-range goal we set for ourselves—one step at a time. "For precept must be upon precept, precept upon precept; line upon line, line upon line; here a little, and there a little." (Isa. 28:10.)

When the Lord came to young Solomon in a dream, saying, "Ask what I shall give thee," the new king did not desire the luxuries of courtly life but rather the wisdom to solve the problems of his kingdom: "Give therefore thy servant an understanding heart to judge thy people, that I may discern between good and bad." (1 Kgs. 3:5, 9.) Discernment between good and bad and, even more challenging, between good and better is an essential gift in making our many daily decisions.

These many little decisions and the resultant acts combine over the years to formulate our character. We need spiritual guidance and courage to conquer the many little obstacles in life. We should pray not for a life of ease, but for the capacity and strength to face and overcome life's challenges. As any wise mariner would agree, "A ship in harbor is safe, but that is not what ships are built for." Just as ships are built for sailing out on the seas, human beings are created to experience the challenges of life and to learn to "subdue all things" like our example, Jesus Christ. (Philip. 3:21.)

To ensure personal growth, we need to measure our performance. As President Thomas S. Monson has often said, "Performance measured and reported will consistently improve."[9] By doing little things well and measuring our increased capacities, we become more capable of doing big things better until we find success in all the important areas of our lives. As Jesus said, those who are faithful in little things will be given power over many things. (See Matt. 25:21; Luke 19:17.)

HOW DO WE MAINTAIN OUR GROWTH PATTERN?

Once we witness personal development and improvement, we want to expand and maintain it. We need to establish a lasting pattern of personal development through one important step:

7. *We should continue our progress by reviewing and renewing the previous six steps.* By establishing a regular habit of evaluation and reevaluation, we establish a cycle of growth that spirals upward. No matter how we may fail at times, the review and renewal sends us upward again. As we learn from our mistakes and successes and continue on in our efforts, we develop patterns of perfection that carry over into other areas of our lives. We gradually become the type of people we truly desire to be.

To keep ourselves on track, we should periodically review our goals in light of our eternal goal of immortality and exaltation. Then, with the help of the Spirit, we should reevaluate our priorities and adjust our goals accordingly. Through prayer, self-discipline, and the help of others, we will find ourselves progressing step by step. Eventually, we will know all that we need to know, we will do all that should be done, and we will fulfill our divine potential.

OBSTACLES TO PERSONAL DEVELOPMENT

Challenges, obstacles, and stress are a natural part of life and personal development. But just as muscles need physical resistance to develop, meeting challenges straight on can actually become a positive character-building opportunity. As the scriptures record, we learn and grow line upon line and here a little and there a little—just as in muscle and body building—but when we say we have enough, we begin to lose the strength and testimony that we had. (See 2 Ne. 28:30.) When challenges present themselves in our lives, we can either avoid them as we separate ourselves from them, or we can meet them head-on and try to overcome them.

Two key obstacles represent the different challenges we face—handling stress and solving problems. Stress can be an emotionally disruptive influence in our lives; it is usually an internal battle we face, although others can influence it. Problems become difficult situations that impede our progress, conflicts that may involve others, or problems within ourselves. If we can master these hindrances, we will develop the technique and strength to overcome life's obstacles.

HANDLING STRESS

Stress or tension usually affects the emotional dimension of our life, but it can also influence our physical and social well-being. Some tension is a natural part of earth life. Almost everything around us causes some pressure — the air we breathe, the food we eat, every motion we undertake. All of it generates some form of strain. Stress is not only natural but valuable. For example, without tension in a rubber band, muscle, watch spring, violin or guitar string, the instrument would not function. However, too much tension can be destructive, as witnessed by a guitar string that snaps, or a muscle that suffers a sprain. Our challenge is to maintain a healthy balance of moderate stress.

The amount of stress we experience is usually divided into three levels: low, medium, and high. Low (or no) stress frequently results in immediate low productivity, while high stress usually results in long-term low productivity. Medium stress consistently results in a high productivity level. Therefore, we should strive to maintain a constant, moderate level of stress.

A look at the major physical, emotional, and social stresses in our lives will help us appreciate their values and dangers. Physical stress causes a person's energy and strength to temporarily increase, often resulting in keener physical sensitivity through the body senses. Recognized by the presence of adrenalin and other hormones, physical stress assists the body to access all available energy resources. It can also help the body increase its defenses against disease. Prolonged, heavy stress leads to fatigue, high blood pressure, and weakness in fighting disease. Signs of too much physical stress include ulcers, headaches, and eating disorders.

Emotional stress sharpens a person's attitude and helps him or her become more sensitive. Moderate stress develops an attentive, positive, steady disposition as witnessed by a calm, steady demeanor and a patient but persistent behavior. Increased stress naturally results as we experience change — such as when we move, take on a new job, alter our family structure, suffer illness, face dangers, and the like.

The three usual sources of emotional stress are fear, guilt, and pressure. Fear includes phobias and dangers, both real and imagined. Guilt is sometimes called "fear inside out," and it comes from knowing we are not living up to God's expectations and being afraid of what the possible consequences might be. Pressure is the most common source of emotional stress. Pressure comes from both within and without ourselves, and it usually results from a gap between expectations and performance. Healthy pressure motivates us to do better, while severe pressure can burden us as others sometimes expect too much of us, or we may place unrealistic demands upon ourselves. Prolonged, heavy stress causes a person to become nervous, agitated, anxious, worried, fearful, or lethargic. Signs of too much emotional stress include depression, moodiness, frustration, and tenseness.

Social stress occurs as we strive for success and work harder to enhance our relations with others. A person under moderate social stress wants to be an involved, committed citizen, and he or she earnestly attempts to become more outgoing, concerned, and friendly. Prolonged, heavy stress leads to high anxiety levels and aggressive, selfish, or "driven" behavior, which often disrupts one's relations with others. Signs of too much social stress include either withdrawal and escapism on the one hand, or conflict and power struggles on the other hand.

To maximize our time under healthy, moderate stress, we need to work in all three areas. Physically, we should exercise regularly, maintain healthy diets and sleep habits, and learn to relax and enjoy life. Sometimes just a few deep breaths or a short walk can release physical stress. A balanced, healthy life-style is the best guarantee for handling physical stress. Emotionally, we should focus on feelings and problems we can influence, learn not to be so categorical or emphatic, and develop positive images and attitudes. For short-term effects, a quick question to oneself, such as, "Why am I acting this way?" helps us get our emotional perspective into balance. A sense of humor and an appreciation of our eternal self-worth provide long-term help in handling emotional stress. Socially, we should be active with others, take advantage of service opportunities, and develop love and patience. A simple kind word or deed can quickly bring friendliness into a relationship. Personal integrity and a genuine concern for others will usually foster harmony and help us handle the social stress in our lives.

Stress is like the wind of life that moves us over the seas of existence. Whether it moves us toward or away from our objectives depends upon the set of our sails (our physical conditions), the direction of our rudders (our hopes and attitude), and the stability of our keels (our strength or "weight" received from others, especially God). Since our Heavenly Father knows us and our circumstances so well, his Spirit is the best guideline for monitoring our stress level. He knows when we need a little more tension and push in our lives and when we are weakening through too much strain. He will help us handle a healthy level of stress. With appropriate, moderate stress in our lives, we can accomplish much in God's service, both for ourselves and for others.

Solving Problems

Problem solving is a natural part of life, starting as toddlers who must learn how to stand, walk, and run in spite of the forces of gravity and the awkwardness and weakness of developing bodies. The process of learning and growing continues in school as students learn to write and communicate and to analyze and solve many types of problems. This problem-solving pattern continues as we face and overcome a variety of life's challenges. Learning how to turn potential obstacles into personal strengths leads to a stable growth pattern that a person can apply in many areas of his or her life.

Most of us want to help God and serve others, but sometimes we make mistakes and cause problems for others. Or, we may be aware of problems facing us and others, but we feel weak and ineffective in overcoming them. Although we may not be "problem creators" (in that we willingly cause problems), many of us tend to be "problem observers" (people who resist getting involved) rather than "problem solvers" (people who courageously seek solutions). One characteristic of a successful life is becoming a problem solver. There are some basic steps to solving problems:

1. Identify and state the problem.

2. Study the problem, along with its sources, attributes, and challenges.

3. Propose a tentative solution.

4. Preview the possible effects of that solution, review how it fits within one's stated mission and goals, and see if any better alternative is available.

5. Decide what to do, referring to one's applicable goals and the relevant timetables and taking inventory of helpful resources.

6. Confirm the decision and proposed program through the Holy Spirit so that you can know that it is right and good — and then do it!

The reason many people fail to overcome their problems or obstacles is that they ignore at least some of the above steps. Often they will do the odd-numbered steps without taking the time and effort to do the work involved in the even-numbered steps. All of the steps are valuable in overcoming most problems.

If we are frustrated in our lack of success or spirituality, we might want to look at the above steps so that we can identify and remove any obstacles. Sometimes our initial efforts fail, and we need to start over again with steps one and two. Repeated attempts are usually necessary to overcome difficult or habitual problems, especially if we do not have a lot of outside help. As we transform obstacles from stumbling stones into building blocks, we develop patterns of growth that we can then carry over into all areas of our life.

In conclusion, we can say that *PERSONAL GROWTH through wise, consistent patterns of character development, preparation of value-oriented goals, and commitment to cooperative success will lead to self-fulfillment and individual perfection and help us progress toward our personal destiny.* Our value-oriented plan of action will develop more effectively through evaluating our purposes and needs, deciding our strengths and weaknesses, anticipating our obstacles and successes, and setting our priorities and goals.

We begin to accomplish our objectives as we commit ourselves to steady, cooperative work, and we begin to realize success as we use our time, talents, resources, and energy wisely. Often, we must review and repeat any necessary steps until we overcome our obstacles and achieve our goals. Ultimately, our efforts coupled with the Lord's assistance will help us achieve our personal destiny. No longer will we need to wish we had done or become something better—we will have reached our personal quest for perfection.

For further study, refer to the following entries:

TG	BD	*EM*
Perfection, Perfect, Perfectly	Education	Enduring to the End
Self-mastery		Eternal Progression
Skill		Perfection
Talents		Purpose of Earth Life

CHAPTER 22

CHURCH BLESSINGS AND
PRIESTHOOD ORDINANCES

Before joining a new social club, aerobics class, or fraternal organization, a person usually asks, "What's in it for me?" Prior to joining a service club or supporting a charitable organization, one should ask, "What does it provide for others?" As a prospective member of a new church or religious denomination, one might combine both of these questions and ask, "Will this church really provide me the salvation it promises, and will it help me assist my family and friends to fulfill their spiritual and personal needs?"

Similarly, longtime members of a group or church should periodically ask themselves if they are receiving acceptable benefits from their association and if the organization is fulfilling its purposes. If both personal and group expectations are being met, then justifying a move to another group would be difficult. If the response is weak or mixed, then they need to study the situation to determine whether the weakness lies in themselves or the organization. If people have not really applied themselves, they should be careful about criticizing the group, but if the organization is deficient, they should either seek to improve it or search out a more compatible association. This type of review should bring positive results — at the very least, a new appreciation of the group.

A study of The Church of Jesus Christ of Latter-day Saints highlights a variety of blessings and benefits available to its members. For example, peace and joy are often mentioned in the scriptures along with other blessings as rewards for righteous living. Many blessings and spiritual strengths are available to Church members through their faithfulness and by the power of the priesthood. Some blessings, such as faith, hope, and charity, are received through righteous living, through disciples gaining

344

gospel knowledge, receiving spiritual gifts, and serving. In addition, other blessings may be received through specific ordinances performed by the power and authority of the priesthood of God.

THE BLESSINGS OF FAITH, HOPE, AND CHARITY

The prophet Mormon and the apostle Paul both wrote about three important attributes of a true Christian—faith, hope, and charity. (See Moro. 7; 1 Cor. 13.) These three qualities are among the ultimate aspirations of a faithful follower of Christ.

Faith is a gift of God received after one has sincerely petitioned Heavenly Father for an understanding of him and his Son and our relationship to them.[1] Our faith in Jesus Christ grows as we pray regularly, study the scriptures, and strive to keep the commandments. As we strengthen ourselves spiritually, we become more sensitive to the promptings of the Holy Ghost and enjoy more often and for longer periods the companionship of this special member of the Godhead. Receiving comfort, guidance, and powerful, personal, and spiritual knowledge direct from these divine beings is a marvelous blessing. Faith is a pivotal blessing promised to righteous members of Christ's church.[2]

Jesus also promised his followers the blessing of peace, not in the worldly, political sense, but as an abiding, spiritual response within their souls. (See Matt. 11:28–30; John 14:27.) This special peace is likewise a gift from God, bearing its own fruits of joy and hope within us. Because we are doing what the Master desires, we have the assurance that we are on the path of righteousness. Having received the saving ordinances of Christ's gospel, we also anticipate with great hope the time when we can be reunited with him and our Heavenly Father. Hope is another blessing enjoyed by God's obedient children.

The third blessing, charity, is a gift from God and something we can also develop within ourselves. Charity is defined as the "highest, noblest, strongest kind of love" a person can have.[3] It is also called the "pure love of Christ." (Moro. 7:47.) But as we experience the pure love of Christ, we find that love flows both ways—we sense his love emanating from him, and we feel our love increasing toward him. As we receive his love, we find our own love developing and growing until we can no longer contain it within us, and we desire to share our love with him and others. Indeed, the best way to develop love is to be sensitive of the love others have for us and to reciprocate by giving of ourselves. By doing so, we will experience and receive more in our lives than we have ever given! Basking in the warmth of this pure love, our charity toward others naturally increases, and we find ourselves encircled with eternal friends. Charity is one of the greatest blessings of the restored gospel of Christ.

In addition to the three blessings of faith, hope, and charity, membership in Christ's church provides access to a variety of blessings through the priesthood. We receive these blessings through certain acts or prayers known as ordinances. Sometimes ordinances are also called rites or ceremonies, especially when they are performed in the temple. The root of the words *ordain* and *ordinance* is order. Hence, the purpose of priesthood ordinations and ordinances is to put in order the affairs of God's kingdom on earth: "Mine house is a house of order, saith the Lord God, and not a house of confusion." (D&C 132:8.) There are two general types of ordinances: those essential to our salvation in God's kingdom, and those that edify and strengthen us during mortality.

ORDINANCES OF SALVATION

Of all the priesthood ordinances, only four (five for men) are rightly called ordinances of salvation, meaning that they are required for passage into the celestial kingdom and for exaltation within that kingdom. These essential ordinances are baptism, confirmation (laying on of hands for the gift of the Holy Ghost), priesthood ordination for men, personal endowment in the temple, and celestial marriage in the temple.[4]

BAPTISM AND CONFIRMATION

The major ordinances in a member's life as a child, and the first ones for converts to the Church, are baptism and confirmation. These ordinances are the passageways of water and spirit required of all responsible persons who want to enter into God's kingdom. (See John 3:5.) The confirmation ordinance is also valuable because the priesthood holder conferring the gift of the Holy Ghost has the opportunity to give an inspired personal blessing to the individual being confirmed.

Full-time missionaries for the Church are naturally excited and anxious to baptize new converts, but the greater responsibility actually rests with the Melchizedek Priesthood holder who confirms the new member. The words of the prayer for the baptism (an Aaronic Priesthood function) are set and must be given word perfect, but the confirmation prayer allows for personal inspiration and spiritual communication. The newly baptized child has reached an age where he can understand and appreciate a personal blessing; the new convert yearns for spiritual guidance to help remove himself from the world and into the kingdom of God. The priesthood holder needs to be in tune with the Spirit in providing guidance that will assist the newly baptized person to honor the covenant commitment and to make the transition into full Church fellowship as quickly and completely as possible. Thus, baptism and confirmation are a double blessing, fulfilling the requirements for salvation into God's kingdom and providing inspired encouragement for new members.

PRIESTHOOD ORDINATIONS

A priesthood ordination is not a single act received only once in the life of most priesthood holders. Since there are different offices in the priesthood and different callings within any priesthood quorum, an active Latter-day Saint man will receive a number of priesthood ordinances. In particular, he will have either the Aaronic Priesthood or Melchizedek Priesthood conferred upon him and be ordained to an office within that priesthood (such as deacon, teacher, or priest in the Aaronic Priesthood; or elder or high priest in the Melchizedek Priesthood). Thereafter, he might be ordained to other offices in that particular priesthood. A young male member of at least twelve years of age, however, always has the Aaronic Priesthood conferred upon him.[5]

On occasion, he could also be set apart in a calling to lead or teach other priesthood holders within his quorum. Elder Bruce R. McConkie defined the three major types of priesthood ordinances and wrote that "modern usage of terms conforms to this pattern: Priesthood is *conferred* upon an individual; he is *ordained* to an office in the priesthood; and he is *set apart* to a position of presidency or administration."[6]

In this last kind of ordinance, priesthood leaders give the people being set apart the keys, or authority, to function in their "callings." This is done through special priesthood blessings. Stake presidents, who must be high priests, are called and set apart by General Authorities to preside over the Melchizedek Priesthood offices in their stake. The stake presidents supervise the ordinations of all high priests and elders in their stake, and they, with their counselors and the high council, provide jurisdiction over the high priests groups and elders quorum presidencies in the local wards. Given the voluntary, lay leadership characteristic of the priesthood and the customary rotation of callings, an active man in the Church typically receives many priesthood callings during his life.

An interesting pattern has developed in the past few generations concerning priesthood ordinances. Previously, ordinations and settings apart usually took place during priesthood meetings with only quorum members present. Now, family members are encouraged to be present, whether the act takes place during quorum meeting or in the stake president's or bishop's office. This shift emphasizes the importance of the priesthood calling to the entire family. It also fosters family unity, encourages spiritual experiences, and provides role models for children.

TEMPLE ENDOWMENT AND SEALING

The temple ordinances consist of a number of rites and ceremonies essential for exaltation in the celestial kingdom: baptism and confirmation, washing and anointing, ordination to the Melchizedek Priesthood, endowment, and sealing. You will note that three of them, baptism, confirmation, and priesthood ordination, can take place outside the temple. In fact, people must receive them on their own behalf prior to going to the temple. In the temple, these three ordinances are performed exclusively for those who are deceased. Washing and anointing, endowment, and sealing are ordinances first received once by the living. Thereafter, individuals may receive them vicariously for the deceased.[7]

The washing and anointing ceremony reminds temple patrons of the special, noble purposes of our physical bodies. This rite teaches members some of the ways they can consecrate themselves to God's service. As the name implies, the "endowment" is a special gift from God that helps his children attain the knowledge necessary to qualify for his special celestial blessings. Endowed members understand the purpose of life and commit to build God's kingdom. The sealing ceremony is of two types— sealing of spouses to each other in the covenant of eternal marriage, and the sealing of children to their parents in the family order of God's celestial society. These sealings eternally bind in heaven what would otherwise be valid only on earth in mortality. All the temple ordinances are sacred rites crucial to our exaltation, that is, becoming like and living with our Heavenly Father.

ORDINANCES FOR EDIFICATION

In addition to the ordinances necessary for salvation and exaltation, many other ordinances and blessings are given through the power of the priesthood to comfort, console, and encourage. Among these edifying ordinances, some provide reminders of our covenant relationship with God and our service relationship with others, especially family members. Others bless the body and strengthen the spirit of an individual, especially in times of illness, distress, or loss. The general requirements and procedures for these priesthood blessings vary from ordinance to ordinance, depending upon their function and setting.[8]

THE SACRAMENT

Of the edification-type ordinances, the sacrament service comes the closest to being a salvation-type ordinance, both because of its symbolic representation of Christ's atonement and also because it renews the covenant of the baptism and the temple vows. The bread and water represent the body and blood of Christ, who suffered for us. As we partake of the sacrament, we not only remember him, but we take his name upon ourselves and covenant to keep his commandments, as we did in the waters of baptism and at the temple altars.

Like the baptismal prayer, the sacramental prayers have fixed wording and are recited word for word. If part of the prayer is inadvertently omitted or a phrase slightly changed, the prayer must be recited again from the beginning. One responsibility of the presiding authority at sacrament meeting is to decide if the sacramental prayer is acceptable. Priests or Melchizedek Priesthood holders offer these prayers, and any worthy priesthood holder can pass the emblems of the sacrament to the members, who then pass them to those seated next to them.

All who participate in administering and passing the sacrament should do so solemnly and reverently. Those who partake of the sacrament should do so sincerely, with the intent to honor the vow they make with the Father. If we honor our part of the sacrament covenant, God promises us the constant companionship of the third member of the Godhead, the Holy Ghost. This divine association brings many spiritual gifts into our lives.[9] No wonder the brethren admonish the Saints to attend their sacrament meetings weekly so they can maintain their spiritual priorities and remain worthy for this valuable spiritual power.[10]

SETTING APART

An ordinance of "setting apart" is performed by one or more priesthood leaders laying hands on the head of a person, "setting them apart" for a Church calling, and pronouncing a blessing related to that calling. After a person has been called to a position of leadership, teaching, or service by the proper Church leader and has been sustained by the common consent of the local members, he or she is set apart to perform the duties and responsibilities of that new calling. Settings apart are required for missionaries and for people called to leadership positions over ecclesiastical units (wards and stakes), priesthood quorums, and auxiliary organizations. In the setting apart, the recipient receives the authority and the charge to act in that calling. Additional words of counsel, instruction, and blessing are usually included. For members called as teachers, advisors, musicians, librarians, and for other positions of service, a setting apart is usual though optional.

Settings apart benefit both the Church and the person. The ordinance gives authority to a person in a new calling and reinforces the obligations and blessings of the office so that more responsible service can be rendered. As the person pronouncing the setting apart is prompted by the Spirit, words of instruction can enlighten the person and words of blessing will edify him or her. Naturally, the blessings and rewards of the calling are conditional upon faithful service. An inspired setting apart immediately assists the person in serving more effectively—an advantage for all who are affected by the calling.

NAMING AND BLESSING OF INFANTS

The naming and blessing of an infant is generally the first ordinance performed for members of the Church. This blessing is given by a Melchizedek Priesthood holder, usually the infant's father, who may be accompanied by other bearers of the same priesthood.

Children are traditionally named and blessed during the monthly fast-and-testimony meeting in the ward, but this ordinance can also be performed on other Sundays, in the bishop's office, or at home if the family desires more privacy or needs to accommodate schedules of visiting relatives. In case of trauma at birth, the blessing can even take place in the hospital, but the family should remember that the blessing is not in any way essential for the child's salvation should the infant die without it. Wherever the ordinance is performed, a member of the ward bishopric should be present to make an official record for the Church.

The child first receives a name for the general records of the Church and then whatever personal blessing the father (or other officiator) desires. The privilege of giving personal blessings belongs only to the Melchizedek Priesthood and should be exercised by righteous holders of that priesthood. The father should rely on inspiration to discern the child's needs and offer counsel to guide the infant and the family. He should not merely repeat common phrases and niceties but should seek for personal inspiration to know the appropriate words of blessing and promise. Since the baby cannot understand the blessing, the family will often record some of the key elements in a journal for the infant; thus, the blessing can become a source of later inspiration and direction.

PATRIARCHAL BLESSINGS

Shortly before his death, the prophet Jacob (Israel) gave patriarchal blessings to his twelve sons, predicting what would befall them and their posterity. (See Gen. 49.)[11] As literal or "adopted" descendants of Jacob, all members of the Church are likewise entitled to a patriarchal blessing. Such blessings are given by ordained patriarchs, men holding the Melchizedek Priesthood office, who officiate in their stakes.

In a letter dated June 28, 1957, to all stake presidents, the First Presidency (David O. McKay, Stephen L Richards, J. Reuben Clark, Jr.) gave this definition and counsel on patriarchal blessings:

> Patriarchal blessings contemplate an inspired declaration of the lineage of the recipient, and also where so moved upon by the Spirit, an inspired and prophetic statement of the life mission of the recipient, together with such blessings, cautions, and admonitions . . . for the accomplishment of such life's mission, it being always made clear that the realization of all promised blessings is conditioned upon faithfulness to the gospel. . . . All such blessings

are recorded and generally only one such blessing should be adequate for each person's life. The sacred nature of the patriarchal blessing must of necessity urge all patriarchs to most earnest solicitation of divine guidance for their prophetic utterances and superior wisdom for cautions and admonitions.

Like the naming and blessing of a child, a patriarchal blessing is not a required ordinance for salvation, nor is there a set age at which the blessing is necessarily given. Generally persons in their late teens or older, on the assumption that they are mature enough to understand and appreciate the gift, receive patriarchal blessings. Such blessings contain sacred, personal counsel, which is a type of personalized scripture or "word of the Lord" for that individual (but which should not be regarded as canonized scripture for others). Comparing blessings randomly with others is also generally not a wise practice, for this may breed a sense of jealousy or competition if one feels his specific promises are not as glorious as those of someone else. The greatest blessing God can give to anyone — eternal life and exaltation with him in the celestial kingdom — is universally granted to every member of the house of Israel who faithfully keeps his covenants. Who could ask for more?

A patriarchal blessing is sometimes compared to a "road map of life" in that it indicates general directions, destinations, and obstacles. The details of the actual journey, however, are left to the individual. Thus it is imperative that the person remain spiritually in tune so he or she can know how to follow the course God has outlined. Also, the promises of a patriarchal blessing are almost all conditional upon continued righteousness. If one does not heed the counsel given by God through his ordained servants and is not worthy for the companionship of the Holy Spirit, one may detour from the journey that God would desire of him or her, the rewards and promises may be forfeited, and the person's divine destiny may not be met.

FATHER'S BLESSING

A father's authority and responsibility to bless his family members in times of need is a special privilege of the Melchizedek Priesthood. Unlike other blessings for set occasions, the father may take the initiative in discerning when one of his children is in special need of divine assistance. Children are also free to ask for such a blessing.

A father's blessing is appropriate when a child needs help in school, encounters serious social problems with peers, has difficulty keeping a particular commandment, or desires to develop a certain attribute of character. Transitional periods such as starting school, preparing for baptism, receiving the priesthood, beginning to date, or leaving home for an extended time also afford good opportunities for a father's blessing. Especially when a child is about to leave for a mission, enter military service, or be married, a father's blessing not only provides words of inspired counsel, but also builds bonds of love between father and child. Such blessings can be recorded and transcribed so that the child may look back upon them for additional strength and guidance, but they are not preserved by the Church as are patriarchal blessings.

BLESSINGS OF COMFORT AND COUNSEL

Melchizedek Priesthood bearers may also give special blessings of comfort and counsel to close personal acquaintances. An individual may request — or a priesthood holder may offer on his own initiative — personal blessings in times of spiritual, physical, emotional, social, or financial stress. Husbands particularly can give inspired blessings of comfort to their wives in times of personal or family turmoil, and such a blessing and concern enhance their relationship.

Even in the absence of the Melchizedek Priesthood, members may petition the Lord through fasting and prayer for needed blessings. In the New Testament, Book of Mormon, and Doctrine and Covenants, all disciples are admonished to seek spiritual gifts regardless of age, sex, length of membership, priesthood office, or any other consideration. The only requisite is faith. In fact, the unified prayer and fasting of a faithful group is likely the most effective means of communication with heaven (in the temple endowment, it is referred to as the highest form of prayer).

ADMINISTERING TO THE SICK

Normally, two Melchizedek Priesthood holders administer to the sick. If no other Melchizedek Priesthood holder is available, one can both anoint and seal the anointing. In a family where the father or an older brother holds the Melchizedek Priesthood, he along with another priesthood holder should administer to family members. This ordinance is performed upon request from either the sick person or a close relative or friend, for the healing itself is effected through the faith of those involved. (See D&C 24:13–14.) The ordinance is performed in two parts.

First, one of the Melchizedek Priesthood holders anoints the head of the sick person with a small amount of pure, consecrated olive oil (see discussion of consecrating oil in the following section), lays his hands upon the person's head, calls the person by name, and states that by the authority of the Melchizedek Priesthood the person is being anointed with oil consecrated for the healing of the sick, and then closes in the name of Jesus Christ. These elements must be included in the prayer, but exact words are not prescribed.

Second, the anointing is sealed by two or more Melchizedek Priesthood holders, with one being voice. They lay their hands on the head of the ill person, and the spokesman calls the sick individual by name, states the Melchizedek Priesthood authority by which the ordinance is performed, and seals the anointing. He then gives a personal blessing by adding such words of comfort and promise as the Spirit dictates. Perhaps at no other time is it so crucial for the one acting as "voice" to be sure that his words are in harmony with the promptings of the Spirit. One should not attempt to invoke the Lord's power through a priesthood blessing to do what is contrary to the Lord's will. If constrained not to promise the sick a return to health, the giver of the blessing should offer appropriate, inspired words of comfort, counsel, and strength.

One priesthood leader recalls the surprise he once had when called upon to give a sick woman a blessing in which he was prompted not to promise a return to health but to advise her that her time on earth was shortly to end and that she should prepare for her imminent death. He did promise her, however, comfort and understanding in this experience. Within forty-eight hours of the blessing, she died, and the blessing lightened her burden of anxiety and fear during those final moments.

Such a blessing is within the guidelines of the Church leaders. They advise that when severe illness strikes and when dying becomes inevitable, death should be looked upon as a blessing and a purposeful transition into the next phase of our eternal existence. Members should not feel obligated to extend mortal life by unreasonable medical means or through unwise prayers and petitions. Competent medical advice and spiritual promptings (after prayer and fasting) should be followed in such situations.[12] Although no one wants to be separated from a loved one, death should be accepted as an inevitable, natural part of our existence. If we are worthy, we will enjoy full fellowship with loved ones in the postmortal spirit world and the resurrected life to follow.

Consecrating Olive Oil for the Blessing of the Sick

As part of the ordinance of administering to the sick, the head of the sick person is anointed with a small amount of olive oil, consecrated for this purpose before it is used. To consecrate the oil, a good grade of olive oil is selected and placed in a small container, usually a little plastic bottle or metal vial. Holding the open container, the Melchizedek Priesthood holder consecrates the oil and sets it apart for its holy purposes — blessing and anointing the sick and afflicted. Since only a few drops of consecrated oil are used in each healing administration, a few years will probably pass before a new supply of oil will need to be consecrated. The use of the oil helps concentrate the attention, faith, and prayers of all involved on the important act of administering to the sick.

The source of this oil, the olive tree, is a major source of livelihood in the Holy Land. In the scriptures, the olive tree represents the house of Israel. (See Hosea 14:6; Rom. 11:17; Jacob 5; D&C 101:43–62.) The olive branch has long been considered a symbol of peace, and the oil has been used since ancient times in religious rites. The Old Testament records that olive oil has been used to anoint priests (see Ex. 29:7; Lev. 21:10–12), kings (see 1 Sam. 10:1; 16:3), and objects used in sacred worship (see Gen. 28:18–19; Lev. 8:10–12). It was also given as a tabernacle/temple offering. (See Ex. 25:1–6.) The New Testament records its use in anointing the sick (see Mark 6:13; James 5:14) and lighting lamps (see Matt. 25:3; cf D&C 33:17). Olive oil has a rich history of religious connotation, and the use of consecrated oil in anointing the sick and in anointing in the temple is very appropriate.

Dedicating Homes, Chapels, Temples, Lands, Countries, and Graves

The ordinance of dedication is an act of consecrating or setting apart something for a specific purpose. This priesthood ordinance deals not with people directly but with their places of abode and worship. Since homes and chapels are places where LDS families spend so much time and where they become strongly molded in their spiritual attitudes, it is important that a special spirit of peace and righteousness reign there.

A family's dwelling should be a haven from the world, where family members can find refuge and security. Melchizedek Priesthood holders may dedicate their apartment or home as a sacred abode or edifice in which the Holy Spirit can reside. Some Church members falsely assume that their home must be debt-free before it can be so dedicated, but this is not true.[13] A worthy member can dedicate his home "as a sanctuary for his family where family members can worship, find safety from the world, grow spiritually, and prepare for eternal family relationships."[14]

In addition, places of worship, such as meetinghouses and temples, and other Church buildings and properties are also dedicated. After appropriate open-house activities to which the general public is invited, an appropriate priesthood authority, usually a General Authority, conducts the dedication services, and local members are especially invited to attend. Unlike home dedications, Church buildings must first be completed and be debt-free. Also unlike the members' private dwellings, the chapels and temples are specifically dedicated and consecrated to the Lord to serve as holy places for worship and covenant making. Church schools, welfare facilities, office buildings, historical sites, and other properties are also dedicated to the Lord for their intended purposes.

Lands and countries are also dedicated so they can become places where God's work can progress. Under the direction of General Authorities and with the assistance of local members, many countries and areas within different nations have been dedicated for the preaching of the gospel. Any of these dedications of dwellings, Church buildings, or lands help God's children find truth and spirituality as they call upon the powers of heaven for enlightenment. They help the missionary work in such places and lands to go forward, often in miraculous ways.

A related ordinance performed by the Melchizedek Priesthood is dedicating a grave as the final resting place of one's body. The burial plot is consecrated for this purpose, and, if so prompted by the Spirit, the priesthood holder may petition God to hallow and protect that spot of earth until the time when the body will be resurrected and reunited with its spirit. Again, some inspired words of blessing may accompany the ordinance, addressing the needs of the deceased's family while providing counsel and comfort in their emotional distress and grief.

WHO COMPOSES THE WORDS
OF A BLESSING?

While the priesthood holder, officiator, or patriarch acts as "voice" for the Lord in any of these Melchizedek Priesthood blessings, the recipient should not presume that the Lord always dictates his message word for word through his mouthpiece. Priesthood bearers, particularly many patriarchs, state that they generally receive ideas and impressions concerning the person they are blessing. It is then up to them to deliver these thoughts in their own words. On occasions, though, some report that they do receive revelations in complete and exact phrases.

Indeed, exact phraseology may on occasion be necessary to insure that God's precise message is given. One bishop recorded a case where he was called upon to set apart a young man, a returned missionary, to be a Sunday School teacher. As he proceeded to add words of counsel and direction, he became aware that the words were coming not from him but were merely passing through his mouth as if he were, in fact, a mouthpiece or speaker for someone else's message. Some of this counsel was quite direct and rather harsh.

The two counselors participating with the bishop also remarked afterward that they had noted a change in his tone and manner of speech. The young man wanted to talk with the bishop later, for he was disturbed by this portion of the blessing. A couple of days later, he brought his patriarchal blessing to the bishop and asked him to read it. One paragraph was recorded word for word the same as the bishop's pronouncement in his blessing. The young man admitted that he had not read his patriarchal blessing for many months and that he was humbled by the censure he had thus twice received.

This experience, along with many others that numerous Melchizedek Priesthood bearers have witnessed, confirm the very real power and line of communication given by the Lord to those who act with authority in his name. When priesthood holders use their gift wisely and worthily, they receive important inspiration that can bless the lives of the members for whom they are performing a priesthood ordinance.

Remember that the efficacy of all these blessings and ordinances derives from the love and priesthood power that God has so graciously shared with his children on earth. These ordinances are performed through the power of God's priesthood with the keys he has invested through his Son, Jesus Christ, to the prophets. Thus, as part of most of the ordinances mentioned above, the priesthood holder or officiator will state the authority of the Melchizedek Priesthood by which the ordinance is performed, and in each of them he will conclude the act by closing in the name of Jesus Christ.

In summary, we recognize that *a variety of spiritual BLESSINGS (or GIFTS) edify the Saints through their righteousness; and various sacred priesthood ORDINANCES magnify the Saints through God's power.* We should be eternally thankful that God is willing to bless us so abundantly while we are separated from him. The ordinances and blessings of his holy priesthood provide direction and spiritual infusion in our lives. Because Heavenly Father amply rewards and strengthens us now as we journey through life, eventually we can enjoy the even greater blessings that await us when we are again in his celestial realms.

For further study, refer to the following entries:

TG	BD	*EM*
Blessing	Laying on of hands	Blessings
Ordinance		Dedications
		Fathers' Blessings
		Oil, Consecrated
		Ordinances
		Patriarchal Blessings
		Priesthood Blessings
		Sick, Blessing the

CHAPTER 23

TEMPLES OF HOLINESS

When families or individuals must relocate to some distant place, adjusting is often traumatic. Working in a new environment with new colleagues, attending new schools, and associating with new neighbors all place stress upon a person. Such a transition is especially challenging if the person or family has never made a major move before and if they receive little help from others.

The trauma of moving from one place to another is intensified if people are completely changing their social and vocational condition. For example, prisoners who have spent long times in confinement have a hard time adjusting to a normal civilian life. From the first day in incarceration, most prisoners look forward to their release date. Yet when the day finally arrives, many experience great stress in the adjustment. Inmates are the first to admit that prison life is genuine hell on earth, but many of them return to prison because they are not prepared for the freedom and responsibility of civilian life. Indeed, part of the problem for some inmates is that they have rarely had a prolonged, positive experience in their family background or in society; thus, they do not really know how to take a productive role in society. If they are not prepared, they revert back to their former, negative behavior and end up back in confinement.

Most inmates require assistance in making the transition into being normal, productive citizens. For those inmates who really have the desire and potential to succeed in society, a "halfway house" can be an important aid. In a halfway house, ex-convicts are still restricted in many ways, yet they receive close supervision, direction, training, and motivation as they work outside the prison in a normal work place. Increased family visits and social contacts are allowed as they establish new behavioral patterns and rebuild their lives. Eventually they may be ready for the free life as productive, valuable citizens.

As a more positive example, refugees from oppressed societies or devastated lands are constantly striving to obtain citizenship in productive, progressive, free countries. Special refugee camps, often under the sponsorship of international organizations, assist these homeless people as does a halfway house and help prepare them for a new life in a new land.

Although few of us have ever been confined in a prison or had to live in a refugee camp, all of us are living in a corrupt world. Rather than being a heaven on earth, mortality often provides unpleasant work assignments, burdensome taxes, restrictive laws, painful ill-health, and other negative aspects of earth life. We sense that when we are finally freed from the burdens of mortality, these problems and limitations will not exist in our life after death. We anticipate a future existence of greater freedom and opportunity.

In order to prepare for this future life, we could be assisted by a transitional place that would make us ready for a heavenly style of spiritual life. We need help in preparing for our potential heavenly existence, for although we all existed in God's presence in our premortal life, we have no guarantee of returning unless we learn to live like him. Like the sweet, fresh innocence of childhood, which many of us now yearn for but did not understand or appreciate when we were growing up, we now need a renewed perspective about what celestial life is like and how we can obtain it. We need a spiritual training school, a university for eternal life, where we can receive inspired guidance, long-range instruction, special preparation, and genuine inspiration for obtaining the celestial life that might be ours to enjoy. This place would be God's halfway station between heaven and earth. Actually such a place already exists. It is called a temple, a place where holiness is learned and experienced.

THE TEMPLE STRUCTURE AS A SYMBOL

We are invited into the Lord's house of learning to seek knowledge from him about the requirements of celestial life. In the Old Testament, the English references to *temple* come from two different roots: *hekal,* meaning a large place, such as a temple or palace; and *beth,* meaning a house, particularly a house of God. Combining the two Hebrew terms, the temple could be called "God's Great House." In many references, the sacred place of worship is called the *House of the Lord,* a place where God can come to earth and visit his prophets and followers in a pure, spiritual setting. (See Isa. 2:2–3.) It is also called a *house of prayer,* where our petitions ascend from the temple altars directly to God. (See Isa. 56:7; Matt. 21:13.) The temple is also identified as a *sanctuary,* a place of holiness set apart for sacred purposes. (See Ex. 25:8; Lev. 19:30; Ps. 150:1.) In summary, the Old Testament context of temple is that of a great, sacred place where people gather to learn, pray, and worship.

The term *temple* is also used frequently in the New Testament. It has two basic Greek roots: *hieron,* meaning a holy place; and *naos,* meaning a shrine or temple. According to Hugh Nibley, our English word *temple* comes from the Latin *templum,* which was first used by the Roman scholar Marcus Terentius Varro (116–27 B.C.) to describe a building used for interpreting heavenly signs and omens. Nibley also adds that the root *tem-* in both Greek and Latin means the cutting or intersection of two lines at right angles, or—referring specifically to the temple—the point where the four corners of the earth come together.[1] A close cognate of *templum* is our English *template,* which is any sort of guide, pattern, or mold for making something else. From this brief etymology, then, we can see that a true temple is a central, pivotal point on earth designed to show mankind the pattern of heavenly things.

The key word used to describe temples is *holy.* The phrase "Holiness to the Lord" was inscribed on the gold plate on the brim of the cap of the High Priest Aaron and his successors who officiated over the tabernacle and temple worship of the ancient Israelites. (See Ex. 28:36; 39:30.) The same inscription is over the eastern entrance of modern LDS temples. The temples are holy because they are dedicated to the Lord, who has manifest himself within them. They are also the place where God's children learn more about the Man of Holiness, Jesus Christ, and the purpose of his atoning sacrifice. Finally, it is in the temples where those with "clean hands, and a pure heart" (Ps. 24:3) receive special instruction about the process of being made holy (see vv. 3–6; cf. Isa. 33:14–16).[2]

For ancient Israel, the temple at Jerusalem was the center of the world, and the prophets foretold that in the last days Israel would be gathered there from the four corners of the earth to meet their God. (See Isa. 11:11–12.) Today, in temples on every settled continent in the world, worthy Latter-day Saints can gather to commune with God and receive instruction and blessings at his hand. Besides unifying all the faithful Saints on earth, modern temples unite the living with their deceased relatives, who now live in a postmortal spirit existence, and also the past with the present, all with a view toward a glorious eternal future.

The purpose of temples—uniting people and preparing them for eternity—is expressed in the location and design of the buildings themselves. Whenever possible, temples are built in a central location, representing the center of the earth, or on elevated ground, representing the meeting of earth with heaven. In ancient times, both types of places were points of contact with deity. For example, before the Israelites had established themselves in Canaan and centered their government and worship at the temple in Jerusalem, they built altars on mountains in the wilderness. Abraham climbing Mount Moriah to sacrifice Isaac, and Moses ascending Sinai to receive the Ten Commandments provide two notable examples of worthy men pressing forward in faith to do and receive God's word on his holy mountains. Nephi, in the Book of Mormon, also received instruction from the Lord on a mountain, which eventually led to his and his family's voyage to America. (See 1 Ne. 17:7–8.)

The external structure and foundation of most temples is rectangular, and the interior design and upper levels usually include a circular or a progressive pattern focused on the celestial room as one comes from the temple courtyard or grounds into the temple itself and then into the holy of holies or the celestial room. The rectangular shape establishes a firm footing and recalls the gathering from the four corners of the earth; the circular design gathers us together and reminds us that all the elect are joined into one eternal family, like a circle that has no beginning and no end.[3]

Many temples, ancient and modern, also have three distinct levels, representing our movement upward as we progress through the three degrees of glory: telestial, terrestrial, and celestial. Each building is usually mounted by one or more spires ascending into heaven, for the temple is where Saints receive revelation from God, and only through the ordinances of the temple do they gain passage to him in the celestial realm.[4]

The temple is more than a symbol of God's heavenly abode, it is a sacred place where one can feel his Spirit. Even nonmembers of the Church have recognized a special spirit at the temple, especially when they have entered a temple during a special public open house. Prior to the dedication of any new temple (or the rededication of an extensively remodeled older temple), the Church invites the public to visit and view its various facilities. This open-house period gives members and non-members alike the opportunity to see the beauty and craftsmanship in the temple construction and furnishings. They also learn about the purpose and sacred nature of the temple ordinances. Most importantly, it provides them an opportunity to feel the special spirit that resides in the temple.

For example, when the LDS Temple was dedicated in Freiberg, East Germany, many visitors waited for hours in the rain to view the temple and then immediately got back in line so they could have the experience one more time. When asked why they were willing to wait so long in unpleasant weather conditions for such a relatively short temple revisit, they responded that never in their lives had they felt such a spiritual sweetness and power as when they were in the temple, and they wanted to bask in that spiritual environment one more time. Many of them even returned a day or two later, often with friends and relatives, so they could enjoy the experience anew.

A COVENANT PEOPLE WITH TEMPLES

There are certain patterns of spiritual behavior not normally learned in our social environment that are essential to our readiness for celestial life. Reverence for the sacred, and especially its expression through symbolic ritual, is far removed from modern life and therefore strange and incomprehensible to many people who live only in what they call the real, or practical, world. For a covenant people who take ordinances literally and seriously, however, the temple, as a model of the eternal world to come, is one place on this temporal earth that is truly significant. By participating in temple instruction and ordinances, Latter-day Saints prepare themselves and their kindred dead to enter into that eternal world.

Hugh Nibley has written, "The temple is the primal central holy place dedicated to the worship of God and the perfecting of his covenant people."[5] God himself has revealed the instructions and ordinances that take place in this pure spiritual environment. The temple teachings have been restored through living prophets, and their sacred nature sets them apart from the profane teachings and practices of the world. Indeed, "so sacred and holy are the administrations performed that in every age when they have been revealed, the Lord has withheld them from the knowledge of the world and disclosed them only to the faithful saints in houses and places dedicated . . . for that purpose (D&C 95:8–9; 124:25–41; Luke 24:59)."[6]

The temple also represents the divine principles and truths of the universe. "It is the school where mortals learn about these things," Professor Nibley has written. "The temple is a model, a presentation in figurative terms, of the pattern and journey of life on earth."[7] Temple covenants provide God's children with essential spiritual instruction— the knowledge of the conditions and promises of eternal life in the celestial world to come.[8]

TEMPLE COVENANTS AND ORDINANCES

The temple is more than a halfway station between earth and heaven where we temporarily escape the distractions of earth life and experience a taste of celestial environment. Since the temple is a sacred place unique in all the world, those who wish to receive its blessings must be worthy and prepared to do so. Only members of the Church who have a testimony of the gospel and are striving to keep the commandments are ready to receive greater spiritual knowledge and take upon themselves the responsibility of added covenants. For this reason, temple applicants must be carefully interviewed by both their bishop and stake president before receiving a temple recommend. Whoever can honestly qualify for entrance into the temple and who desires, like Abraham of old, "to be a greater follower of righteousness, and to possess a greater knowledge" (Abr. 1:2) will find the temple endowment a rich and rewarding experience.

INITIATORY ORDINANCES

After baptism and prior to making further covenants and receiving an endowment of knowledge and blessings, each person receives initiatory ordinances called *washings and anointings*. The men and women go to separate areas in the temple where men administer these ordinances to men and women administer them to women. Somewhat like baptism, the washings are symbolic acts of purification, followed by anointings that give the recipient certain powers and blessings—some immediate, and some to be fulfilled later, even in the next life. As the ancient priests in Israel were purified and anointed prior to their standing as representatives of the Lord, we today are similarly prepared in the temple to become spiritually begotten sons and daughters of the Savior.

The ancient priests also put on special clothing symbolic of the Lord's covenants with Israel. Today, symbolic of our transformation into "new creatures in Christ," we also put on sacred clothing, a new *garment,* after the initiatory washing and anointing ordinances. We wear this special white underclothing afterward throughout our lives as a reminder of our covenants and as protection through our close association with the Holy Spirit.[9] Since the initiatory ordinances prepare us to become truly begotten sons and daughters of Christ, we begin to assume a new spiritual identity, symbolized with a *new name,* before proceeding to the endowment session itself.[10] (See Rev. 2:13–17.)

ENDOWMENT

Presented by means of a symbolic drama, the endowment is a gift of special spiritual knowledge. The New Testament phrase "to endow" comes from the Greek *enduein,* meaning both to clothe or put on garments, and to put on attributes or receive virtue.[11] As noted in the root meaning, "to be endowed" involves both external acts (putting on sacred clothing) and internal edification (committing to righteous behavior). The endowment involves the physical, aesthetic, intellectual, and spiritual human faculties through art, drama, symbols, and scriptural representations. In the newer and recently remodeled temples, the drama is presented on film, though a few older buildings still have sessions with live actors and a change of scenery by movement of the congregation through a series of rooms, some with extensive murals and paintings. The endowment session consists of three interwoven parts: instruction, covenants, and keys (crucial information).

Divine instruction through symbolic representation has always been a part of temple ritual. Despite variations and various degrees of corruption, many temple rites in ancient cultures included a drama of the creation and redemption of the world. For example, the ancient Israelites were commanded to assemble at least three times yearly at the tabernacle or temple, where they sang psalms and received instruction from the Torah, the sacred writings of Moses. The same is true of our modern temple narrative, which builds upon the revelations in the first and second chapters of Genesis and the books of Moses and Abraham in the Pearl of Great Price. These scriptures are excellent reading material as preparation for the temple experience. Our modern temple narrative also includes additional revealed information from dispensations prior to the restoration. The essential, cardinal teachings of the endowment place the entire gospel structure into a divinely inspired eternal framework.[12]

Elder James E. Talmage succinctly summarized the contents of the latter-day endowment thus:

> The Temple Endowment, as administered in modern temples, comprises instruction relating to the significance and sequence of past dispensations, and the importance of the present as the greatest and grandest era in human history. This course of instruction includes a recital of the most prominent events of the creative period, the condition of our first parents in the Garden of Eden, their disobedience and consequent expulsion from that blissful abode, their condition in the lone and dreary world when doomed to live by labor and sweat, the plan of redemption by which the great transgression may be atoned, the period of the great apostasy, the restoration of the Gospel with all its ancient powers and privileges, the absolute and indispensable condition of personal purity and devotion to the right in present life, and a strict compliance with Gospel requirements.[13]

Beyond providing instruction, the endowment gives opportunity for personal commitment. Just as the Prophet Joseph Smith never received a revelation without being bound to live by it, so the divine knowledge in the temple endowment is given only in conjunction with certain covenants, which commit us to principles of devotion, charity, righteousness, purity, and diligence.

After receiving instruction concerning the creation, the Fall of Adam, and the early laws given him by God, we can follow Adam's example and claim allegiance to God, promising to obey him and covenanting to be willing to sacrifice our time and talents to building his kingdom. As the narrative progresses to include teachings from Christ's original apostles, we covenant to keep the laws of the gospel and to work together in a spirit of unity. Two particular commandments represent our worthy intentions—the law of chastity and the law of consecration, signifying the degree of purity and commitment that God desires of his dedicated disciples.[14]

Having pledged our all to God and his kingdom on earth, we are then privileged to participate in prayer circles surrounding the temple altars and to receive certain keys in the form of specialized instruction necessary to return back to God's presence. Prayer circles are collective prayers petitioning God's blessings for mankind, his Church and its leaders and missionaries, and for those with special needs, particularly those whose names are on the temple prayer rolls (consisting of names submitted by those attending the temple).[15]

Keys are referred to often in the Doctrine and Covenants in the context of God's power to govern and the means "whereby something is revealed, discovered, or made manifest":[16] "This greater priesthood [the Melchizedek Priesthood] administereth the gospel and holdeth the key of the mysteries of the kingdom, even the key of the knowledge of God. Therefore, in the ordinances thereof, the power of godliness is manifest. And without the ordinances thereof, and the authority of the priesthood, the power of godliness is not manifest unto men in the flesh; for without this no man can see the face of God, even the Father, and live." (D&C 84:19–22.) In the temple, therefore, the keys symbolically take us into the presence of God, into the celestial room, which represents the place where God himself dwells. If we keep our covenants, these keys will someday admit us to God's celestial kingdom.

Thus, we gain a sense of the divine presence at the culmination of the endowment. As President Kimball stated, there is an "aura of deity" in the temples that the worthy members feel.[17] The endowment session concludes in the *celestial room,* a place of aesthetic splendor and quiet contemplation. The celestial room "represents the highest degree of heaven, a return to the presence of God, a place of exquisite beauty and serenity, where one may feel and meditate 'in the beauty of holiness' (Ps. 29:2)."[18] Here the endowed, committed Saint can meditate upon the mysteries of God and his holiness in a sacred place erected to his glory. (See D&C 88:119.)

SEALINGS

To receive exaltation in the highest degree of God's celestial kingdom, however, yet another temple ordinance is required—celestial marriage and the sealing of families into an eternal union. One meaning of *sealing* means the securing of a lasting bond of legitimacy. Temple sealings refer to the marriage of a husband and wife and the joining together of children and parents into eternal family units. As the culminating temple ordinance, a sealing ceremony is an inspiring and solemn rite performed in specially dedicated sealing rooms of the temple. The couple to be married or the family members to be joined together kneel at an altar. An officiator performs the sealing in the presence of two witnesses. Close friends and family members usually witness the ceremony as well. Sealings become a spiritual foundation for a marriage and family—they sustain the family in life and unite its members after death, establishing eternal continuity for the family.[19]

Eternal families are the nucleus of heaven. Family members born or sealed in the holy covenants of God are heirs for his highest blessings and become like him. Through God's sealing power, all such celestial beings will be linked in an unbroken family chain. Divine parenthood is the ultimate potential of these sealings because "the saintly life is not in renunciation but in glorification of the family." Thus, "the quest for happiness and completeness within the marital state is transformed from the banal and temporary toward the divine and eternal."[20]

Those who are endowed but not sealed in marriage and family lines to other endowed Saints will be "ministering servants" in the celestial kingdom, serving as God's administrators, such as his kings and queens and his priests and priestesses, "to minister for those who are worthy of a far more, and an exceeding, and an eternal weight of glory." (D&C 132:16.) Those worthy persons sealed in eternal families will enjoy not only the presence of God, but also his power, inheriting "thrones, kingdoms, principalities, and powers, dominions, all heights and depths." (D&C 132:19.)

Unlike civil marriages between two persons performed under authority of the state, temple marriages, conducted under the authority of

God, form a special covenant relationship between three individuals—husband, wife, and God. As with baptism, the covenant is sealed in the name of the Father, the Son, and the Holy Ghost. Therefore, the sealed man and woman have the right to call upon the Holy Ghost to bless and guide their union. Furthermore, by sealing themselves together, their children will be born under the covenant of an eternal family and will remain their rightful posterity throughout all eternity.[21]

Naturally, these promises are conditional upon the righteousness of the family members, and the hope of their fulfillment becomes the foundation of a loving, caring, and united family. The sealing of families through the "new and everlasting covenant of marriage" (D&C 131:2) is the culmination of all ordinances performed in the temple. Without this last ordinance, the "whole earth would be utterly wasted at his [Christ's] coming," for the family relationships we hold so dear would be dissolved at death.[22] (JS–H 1:39.)

PERSONAL PREPARATION FOR VISITING THE TEMPLE

In biblical times, the temple was such a sacred place that the special ordinances could be performed only by selected individuals who met certain required qualifications. Likewise today, only Church members who meet certain requirements are granted a temple recommend with which they can then visit any temple and participate in the sacred ordinances there.

In order to maintain the spiritual purity of the temple environment, ecclesiastical leaders ask certain qualifying questions of Church members so that both parties can feel good about the the members' spiritual preparation and worthiness to attend the temple. Among other things, they are asked about their belief in God the Father, Jesus Christ, and the Holy Ghost. They also affirm their testimony of the restored gospel and their sustaining of Church leaders. Their Christian behavior with family members and others is also reviewed, along with their diligence in keeping the major teachings and commandments of the gospel. They themselves decide and declare whether they feel they are worthy to visit the temple, enjoy the spirit there, and share the purpose of that sacred place. Complete honesty in this introspection process and sincere evaluation of one's spiritual direction are invaluable steps in preparing a person to attend the House of the Lord.[23]

Additional preparation can include selected reading from the scriptures and other written resources as advised by the bishop. In addition, most wards and branches have periodic temple preparation courses that provide specialized instruction to selected small groups of people. Anyone even thinking of preparing for the temple endowment should meet with the bishop or branch president and request such instruction. Ultimately, the best preparation for the temple is to live worthily and to seek earnestly for its blessings. A worthy, prepared member will feel peace and find valuable spiritual insights in the temple, God's house of spiritual training.

DOING TEMPLE WORK FOR OUR DECEASED RELATIVES

All temple ordinances, from baptisms to sealings, may be performed by proxy for people who died without the opportunity of receiving these rites for themselves. In order to perform vicarious ordinances for the living spirits of the deceased, Church members must first receive these ordinances for themselves. They can then act as agents or proxies for others, particularly their deceased ancestors, and do the ordinance work in their name, in their behalf.[24]

As outlined in the *Encyclopedia of Mormonism,* five fundamental principles underlie LDS beliefs concerning salvation for the dead:

1. Life is eternal, and each stage of existence provides new divine enlightenment and blessings.
2. Repentance and personal commitment are possible in the postmortal life as well as in this one, especially for those who did not have an opportunity to accept the gospel teachings in mortality.
3. Family bonds, as sealed in holy covenants and ordinances, extend beyond death in uniting the living with their deceased ancestors.
4. Salvation ordinances can be performed by proxies (living people in the flesh) for the dead (or, more specifically, for the living spirits of those whose physical bodies lie dead in the earth).
5. Temple ordinances are not mere signs; they are vital acts that are as real and binding as if the deceased person had done them

during mortality. These ordinances are not binding, however, if that person in the postmortal spirit world does not freely choose to accept them.[25]

Understanding these key teachings of salvation for the dead helps us appreciate why the Church builds temples and why Latter-day Saints spend so much time and effort in pursuing family history research and genealogy and in returning often to the temple to do the ordinance work vicariously for others.

An additional value of doing temple work for others is the review and reminder we receive of our own temple vows. It provides an opportunity for us to learn something new about the purpose of life and our responsibilities toward our families. These labors fulfill some of the promises of Malachi and Elijah in turning the hearts of fathers and children toward each other.[26] (See Mal. 4:6.) Temple work brings the blessings of the Savior's redemption into the lives of others, and thus we join with him as saviors on Mount Zion.[27] (See Obad. 1:21.) Indeed, without this vicarious work, the greatest blessings of God's plan and Christ's atonement would not be available for many of our spirit brothers and sisters. A major purpose of this earth life would be so frustrated that the Lord himself would come and "smite the whole earth with a curse" and consume all flesh before him. (D&C 98:16–17.) Temple work is a key element and a valuable blessing in this stage of our existence.

God has given us temples to enable us to prepare for his celestial kingdom. Providing a spiritual training school for the eternities, they help us sense the divine while living on earth. In temples, we learn about our Heavenly Father's plan of salvation, the nature of mortality, and our purposes for being here. There we can enter into sacred covenants wherein we promise to obey his commandments and whereby he endows us with promised gifts, especially eternal life with him. We also receive specific instructions or keys to enable us to enter into his highest realms. In addition, we are also privileged to act as proxies for others who have passed away, so they may benefit from these blessings. Through temple sealings, we can be united as eternal families in the service of our Heavenly Father. The temple stands as a symbolic yet real reminder of God's love for us, his expectations of us, and our potential as his children.

In summary, *Latter-day Saints, like the ancient Israelites, are a covenant people who worship in TEMPLES, where they learn about their relationship with God, make sacred commitments, receive key directions about returning to God's presence, and do ordinance work for their deceased relatives.* Latter-day temples are a gift from God where we receive sacred instruction and covenants. Different from all other buildings, the temple is a place of refuge from the world, a spiritual retreat where God's peace is felt, and a university of eternal life where sublime truths are learned and where all members of the Godhead work for our edification. It is the house of the Lord Jehovah on earth, where we can learn the mysteries of God the Father through his Holy Spirit. God invites us all to prepare and partake of the temple blessings. As we worthily prepare ourselves for the temple and then earnestly strive to keep our temple covenants, we come to know the glory and presence of God. (See D&C 97:15–16.)

For further study, refer to the following entries:

TG	BD	EM
Covenants	Temple	Baptism for the Dead
Endowment, Endow		Covenants
Genealogy and		Endowment
Temple Work		Garments
House		Marriage
Marriage, Celestial		Salvation of the
Temple		Dead
Temple, House of		Sealing
the Lord		Temple Ordinances
		Temple Recommend
		Temples
		Washings and
		Anointings

Notes to Part 3

Chapter 16

1. *LF,* 1:9.
2. *LF,* 1:13.
3. *LF,* 1:24.
4. BD, 669.
5. BD, 670.
6. *LF,* 4:2.
7. *HC,* 3:379; 5:355; *LF,* 3:1.
8. *Evidences and Reconciliations* (Salt Lake City: Bookcraft, 1987), 15.
9. *NWAF,* 186.
10. *NWAF,* 192.
11. The command to repent and to turn back or return to the Lord is the most common warning of the scriptures.
12. See TG, Humility, for other helpful scriptures.
13. *LF,* 6:7.
14. See also chapters 8 and 20 in this book for further insights about the values of scripture study.
15. The relationship between gospel study and spiritual growth is highlighted in chapter 20.
16. The importance of prayer was discussed earlier in chapter 5.
17. *MD,* 264.
18. Even though faith, in one sense, "is not to have a perfect knowledge of things" (Alma 32:21), God and Jesus Christ, who know all things, are nonetheless perfect in faith. In fact, two of the names of Christ are "Faithful and True" (Rev. 19:11; see also 1 Cor. 10:13; Heb. 2:17.) Since faith is also a principle of action and of power, God operates by faith. Thus, a person who has perfect knowledge will still need to be faithful in all things.
19. *LF,* 1:24.
20. *American Heritage Illustrated Encyclopedic Dictionary* (Boston: Houghton Mifflin, 1987), 166.
21. Ibid., 601.
22. BD, 670.
23. James Strong, *The Exhaustive Concordance of the Bible* (Nashville: Abingdon Press, 1890, 1980), "Hebrew and Chaldee Dictionary," 14.
24. Ibid., "Greek Dictionary of the New Testament," 58.

25. See Doctrine and Covenants 20:23–29; 42:43, 48–52 to note how Joseph Smith intertwined both terms in his revelations.

26. See *LF*, 2:30–33.

27. See *LF*, 2:18; 3:6.

28. BD, 670.

CHAPTER 17

1. See Theodore M. Burton, "The Meaning of Repentance," in *Repentance* (Salt Lake City: Deseret Book Company, 1990), 9–14.

2. "BP," 297.

3. "Our Lord and Savior," *Ensign*, May 1988, p. 23.

4. Sanctification through the Holy Ghost is discussed in chapter 19.

5. *NWAF*, 235.

6. *A Series of Pamphlets by Orson Pratt* (Liverpool: Franklin D. Richards, 1852), reprinted in *Orson Pratt Works*, vol. 2 of *Important Works in Mormon History* (Orem, Utah: Grandin Book Co., 1990), 32.

7. *MF*, 179. A detailed discussion of the law of chastity and the reasons why confession to ecclesiastical leaders is required for serious sexual sins is found in chapter 26.

8. *MF*, 86.

9. *Men and Women of Christ* (Salt Lake City: Bookcraft, 1991), 27.

10. *NWAF*, 237.

11. See chapter 25 for a discussion on the important role of the sacrament.

12. See also TG, Reconciliation.

13. The Greek word can mean debts, offenses, faults, or sins.

14. The sanctifying cleansing of the Holy Ghost is discussed in chapter 19.

15. See also TG, Punish, Punishment.

16. Baptism is discussed in the next chapter.

CHAPTER 18

1. *Message of the Joseph Smith Papyri: An Egyptian Endowment* (Salt Lake City: Deseret Book, 1975), 94. Baptism originally occurred in running water (i.e., a river or stream), symbolic for washing sins away (downstream). The Jewish ritual of washing or immersion in the Mikveh of the synagogue also stipulates running or flowing fresh water, whenever possible.

2. *MD*, 548–49.

3. The gift of the Holy Ghost is discussed in the next chapter; the temple ordinances are explained in chapter 23.

4. These ordinances are discussed in more detail in chapter 22.

5. Chapter 25 contains further details about the sacrament ordinance.

6. *WNTCD*, Baptism.

7. This promise of freedom was also given in the Book of Mormon as King Benjamin spoke to his covenant Israelites in Mosiah 5.

8. Chapter 23 contains further insights into the steps and requirements of making covenants.

9. *TETB*, 75.

10. See BD, Baptism. More details about the priesthood and the necessary keys for performing such ordinances are presented in chapters 22 and 32.

11. See *EM*, 1:92–95.

12. *MD*, 72.

CHAPTER 19

1. Further details on these basic roles and functions of the Holy Ghost are in chapter 4.

2. *TPJS*, 199.

3. *MD*, 313.

4. *GD*, 61.

5. S. Dilworth Young, "Gift of the Holy Ghost," *IE*, Nov. 1968, 75–76.

6. "The Gift of the Holy Ghost—A Sure Compass," *Ensign*, May 1989, 32–33.

7. The nature of God the Father was discussed in chapter 2.

8. *NWAF*, 372.

9. See TG, Knowledge. Chapter 1 discusses truth and man's search for truth.

10. *MD*, 197; see also *NWAF*, 374.

11. The roles and purposes of prophets and prophecy were discussed in chapters 6 and 7.

12. The ordinances of anointing the sick and blessing the sick are presented in greater detail in chapter 22.

13. *NWAF*, 374–75.

14. Further examples of priesthood and spiritual blessings are found in chapter 22.

15. *EM*, 2:651.

16. See *DS*, 1:55; 2:94–99.

17. *MD*, 675.

18. *By Grace Are We Saved* (Salt Lake City: Bookcraft, 1989), 52.

19. *NWAF*, 290; see also *TPJS*, 314.

20. *Doctrines of the Restoration: Sermons and Writings of Bruce R. McConkie* (Salt Lake City: Bookcraft, 1989), 53.

21. *HC*, 4:42.

CHAPTER 20

1. See chapter 5 for further discussion on prayer.

2. See chapter 28 for further information on the use of Church financial resources.

3. See chapter 13 for further insights about the scriptures.

4. This includes the two Official Declarations of the Church.

5. "Gifts," paper delivered March 13, 1979, Brigham Young University.

6. "Small Acts of Service," *Ensign,* Dec. 1974, p. 5.

7. Ibid., 2. Further suggestions for Christian service are found in chapters 34 and 35.

8. "The Celestial Nature of Self-reliance," *Ensign,* June 1984, p. 6.

9. "President Heber J. Grant," *Relief Society Magazine,* 1932, p. 302.

10. Spencer W. Kimball, "Follow the Fundamentals," *Ensign,* May 1981, p. 80.

11. The importance of work and vocational preparation is emphasized in chapter 29. The same chapter also talks about the proper care and use of material goods, such as food, clothing, housing, appliances, automobiles, and so on. Chapter 28 discusses means by which our financial resources can assist the Lord and help our families and others.

12. Further insights on the Lord's commandments concerning physical health are found in chapter 27.

13. Christ's role and his expectations for us in this personal perfection process were presented in chapter 13.

14. Further insights on the significant role of families in both earthly and heavenly society are discussed in chapter 30.

15. *DBY,* 256, 332. See also chapters 1 (truth), 8 (scriptures), and 16 (cultivating faith) for further insights about how knowledge and study can enrich our spirituality.

16. God's primary moral expectations for his children are found in the Ten Commandments, which are discussed in chapter 24. The sexual laws concerning moral purity are presented in chapter 26. Issues surrounding our work ethics are evaluated in chapter 29.

17. CR, Oct. 1969, 8.

CHAPTER 21

1. Chapter 13 contains further insights into how Christ can help us to come closer to being perfect.

2. *Treasures of Love and Inspiration* (New York City: Galahad Books, 1985), 317.

3. Hyrum W. Smith, "Life's Many Demands Create 'Time Traps,'" *CN,* Dec. 30, 1989, p. 13.

4. See note 1 above.

5. *The Treasure Chest* (New York: Harper and Row, 1965), 17.

6. *Quotable Quotations* (Wheaton, Illinois: Victor Books, 1985), 310.

7. Chapter 17 contains further insights about the power of change and repentance in our lives.

8. Chapter 34 discusses the Church's threefold mission: proclaim the gospel, perfect the Saints, and redeem the dead.

9. From personal notes and conversations with President Monson while the author was a mission president in Frankfurt, Germany.

CHAPTER 22

1. See chapter 16 for an examination of faith.

2. See BD, Faith.

3. BD, Charity.

4. These ordinances are discussed at length in chapters 18 (baptism), 19 (gift of the Holy Ghost), 23 (temple covenants), and 32 (priesthood).

5. See Chapter 32 for a more detailed discussion of the priesthood.

6. *MD*, 549.

7. The nature and purposes of the temple are discussed in the next chapter.

8. A guideline for performing the priesthood blessings and ordinances is usually printed in the back of each year's Melchizedek Priesthood manual.

9. See chapter 19 for a discussion of spiritual gifts.

10. Under the bishop's direction, the Aaronic Priesthood can take the sacrament to the sick and housebound. Chapter 25 has some further insights about the sacrament and its role in our Sabbath worship services.

11. See also *TPJS*, 151.

12. *GHI*, 1989, 11–6.

13. *GHI*, 1989, 11–2.

14. *MPLH*, 1984, 29; see also *GHI*, 1989, 11–2; *Melchizedek Priesthood Personal Study Guide 2*, 141.

CHAPTER 23

1. See *EM*, 4:1458.

2. See *EM*, 2:648–49, 4:1463.

3. Cf. *EM*, 4:1458–59.

4. Ibid.

5. *EM*, 4:1458.

6. *MD*, 227.

7. *EM*, 4:1458.

8. See chapter 24 for further insights on the nature and purpose of covenants.

9. Note, as a contrast, that the clergy and many of the committed members in almost all major faiths wear special symbolic clothing outside rather than under their normal attire. (See *EM*, 2:535.)

10. See *EM*, 2:534–35, 4:1444–45, 1461.

11. See *EM*, 2:454.

12. See *EM*, 2:455, 4:1460.

13. *The House of the Lord* (Salt Lake City: Deseret Book, 1976 rev. ed.), 83–84.

14. See *EM*, 2:455, 4:1444.

15. See *EM*, 1:37, 3:1120–21, 4:1449.

16. *MD*, 410; see also TG, Priesthood, Keys of; *EM*, 2:780–81.

17. *TSWK*, 535.

18. *EM*, 4:1445.

19. See *EM*, 3:1289.

20. *EM*, 4:1445.

21. See *EM* 1:218, 4:1445.

22. More insights about the eternal roles of the family are found in chapter 30.

23. See *EM,* 4:1446–47.

24. See *EM,* 1:95–96, 4:1445.

25. See *EM,* 3:1258–59.

26. See *EM,* 2:452, 3:1258–59.

27. See *EM,* 4:1449.

PART 4

THE LORD'S COMMANDMENTS
FOR OBEDIENCE AND BLESSING

CHAPTER 24

GOD'S LAWS TO BLESS

Most people would gladly work for an enlightened employer who puts their welfare above his desires for increased profits. A wise boss will run a business that not only clears a profit, but is also socially conscious and helps the workers feel worthwhile. If employment is more than just making money, also benefiting society by making valuable commodities or performing good service, then people are more willing to be productive workers. To ensure that workers' needs are addressed while various noble goals and financial ends are achieved, such an employer sets up rules and expectations so that each individual's personal efforts lead to the desired overall productivity. He also sets up some kind of a profit-sharing program so that all are rewarded when the company does well. Recognizing the company's rules and expectations as requirements for their best welfare, the workers should follow them willingly.

Although we may never work for an ideal employer in the professional world, we can all be in the service of the ultimate wise and loving supervisor, our Heavenly Father. God has placed us on this earth with a unique opportunity to learn, grow, and develop. To help us progress, he has provided rules and guidelines, which we call commandments. These divine laws are like road signs and fences in our lives. As road signs, the commandments direct us toward noble purposes and measure how close we are to Heavenly Father's expectations. And like fences, God's laws protect us from detouring into dangerous areas. His instructions derive from his great love for us and his desire to bring about our immortality and eternal life. (See Moses 1:39.) His divine wisdom and the natural laws of the universe serve as a foundation for his directives. He knows that only through obedience to them will we experience ultimate happiness.

Many traditional theologies conceive of God as some type of divine power, the "first cause" or "prime mover" of the universe, the self-creating, self-motivating source of all creation and progression. Many theologians claim that nothing existed before him, and that all things derive from him. Latter-day Saints, on the other hand, assert that God progressed to his present state of perfection and glory by strict adherence to eternal law. In Mormon theology, law is the first cause and prime mover of the universe, and by adherence to it, people may become like God.[1] Thus, in modern revelation we read: "There is a law, irrevocably decreed in heaven before the foundation of this world, upon which all blessings are predicated—and when we obtain any blessing from God, it is by obedience to that law upon which it is predicated." (D&C 130:20–21.) In this chapter, we will learn how eternal principles form the foundation for God's commandments and how adherence to his commandments determines our level of spiritual progress.

From Principles to Particulars

Isaiah and other prophets understood that relative to God's understanding, all people are spiritually as little children who must be instructed in concrete particulars and simple laws before they can understand abstract principles and complex commandments: "Whom shall he [the Lord] teach knowledge? and whom shall he make to understand doctrine? them that are weaned from the milk, and drawn from the breasts. For precept must be upon precept, precept upon precept; line upon line, line upon line; here a little, and there a little." (Isa. 28:9–10.) The prophet Nephi speaks for God and adds a promise to this pattern of learning by stating, "Blessed are those who hearken unto my [God's] precepts, and lend an ear unto my counsel, for they shall learn wisdom; for unto him that receiveth I will give more." (2 Ne. 28:30; see also D&C 98:12.) Thus, the Lord will instruct us in knowledge and doctrine by teaching us precepts, line upon line, a little bit at a time—as we receive his truths, he will give us more.

Along with the knowledge and doctrine that the Lord teaches us are the fundamental ideas or *precepts* upon which he operates. A precept is a "principle imposing a particular standard of action."[2] Among the principles motivating God's actions are his love for us and his desire to help good conquer evil. His divine actions harmonize with the eternal principles of light and truth as he pursues our eternal welfare. Meanwhile, as we come to understand the governing precepts and eternal purposes of existence, we come into harmony with God. The eternal principles of the universe are the basis for God's higher laws and the framework for his actions—as we understand them, we begin to appreciate *why* God acts as he does.

Within the framework of governing principles or higher laws, Heavenly Father ordains temporal laws, or particular commandments, to govern our behavior. The commandments are given "line upon line," an image reminiscent of the straight horizontal and vertical measuring lines and rods used to erect strong buildings from the ground up. Literally, the Hebrew phrase is equivalent to "rule upon rule" and can be considered as a proper course of conduct or policy. Similarly, in Lehi's dream, the iron *rod* represented "the word of God, which led to the fountain of living waters, or to the tree of life," meaning eternal life. (1 Ne. 11:25.) A certain straightness and firmness is necessary in any command for it to have power to move people to action, especially if they do not understand the purposes behind the instructions. God's commandments, given line upon line, contain his directions to us—telling us *what* he wants us to do.

The phrase "here a little, there a little" can be thought of as the private guidelines we set for ourselves to help us keep the commandments we receive. God expects us to learn his truths and to apply a few of his directions for our personal development a "little" at a time as we grow spiritually. He tells us to walk before we run and to not run faster than we are able. (Mosiah 4:27.) In the Isaiah passage quoted above, his truths are given to those weaned from infancy and ready for higher truths. The gradual means by which we learn and apply God's commandments are the personal resolutions and increased capacities we develop as we draw nearer to God. These personal laws structure our individual application of the commandments—they demonstrate *how* we live God's laws.

In other words, eternal precepts define *why* we should behave a certain way as eternal beings and spiritual offspring of our Heavenly Father. The commandments, or "lines" that direct and measure our behavior show us *what* to do—i.e., "thou shalt" and "thou shalt not."

Finally, the "here a little" and "there a little" guidelines frame *how* we come to comply with the law.

PROTECTIVE FENCES OR PROHIBITIVE BARRIERS

In Jewish tradition, personal application of law is called a "fence" around the law. These fences protect one from accidentally or inadvertently breaking any commandment. As one applies a commandment in his own life, he establishes how he will interpret the Lord's law and put it into practice. To fully obey the law, he may need to narrow its parameters, putting a fence around his behavior to protect himself. For example, within the eternal principle that declares "life is sacred," God has given the commandment that we "should not kill." A personalized law or little "fence" that would protect us from life-threatening situations might be "Don't get angry with someone" or "Don't even threaten another person." Another example, within the wise precept "keep spiritual priorities in mind" would be God's commandment to "remember the Sabbath day and keep it holy." A personal application might be to "not engage in any sports activities on Sunday" or to "carefully select the music to listen to on the Sabbath."

Unfortunately, in trying to live the commandments, we can easily mistake our own adaptations and interpretations of the law for the law itself. For example, some Mormons interpret the commandment to keep the Sabbath day holy to mean that they should not watch television on Sunday. If not watching TV helps a family to properly observe the Sabbath, by all means they should avoid TV viewing. This does not mean, however, that they should automatically condemn other people who do watch television as being Sabbath-breakers. Nor should they assume that avoiding television is the same as keeping the Sabbath day holy. This attitude was the mistake of the Pharisees, who, over the centuries, built their "fences" around the law of Moses to protect people from disobeying it. Eventually, as the letter of the law strangled the spirit of the law, the protective fences actually became barriers to living the Mosaic law. It had degenerated so far that Jesus—accused of violating the Sabbath by healing the lame—had to ask the obvious question: "Is it lawful to do good on the sabbath days, or to do evil? to save life, or to kill?" (Mark 3:4.)

If not misapplied or carried to the extreme, fences around the law are very helpful. What driver, for example, does not appreciate warning signs and barricades around a road construction project, especially at night or during a storm? Likewise, a disciple of Christ appreciates and respects guidelines given by priesthood authorities to aid in living the gospel. Fences around the law of chastity are a good case in point.[3] The prophets and apostles have specifically instructed Church members not to masturbate, neck, or pet, not only because they are sins, but also because such activities bring one to the brink of the pit of fornication and adultery, the most serious sin next to murder. Because sexual immorality is so prevalent in society at large and occurs far too often among Church members, a Latter-day Saint would be wise to construct his or her own fence, a fence that would keep the individual from getting into compromising situations where such sins could occur. Members should learn their own limits and weaknesses in the areas of obedience and should govern themselves accordingly.

OBEDIENCE PRECEDES
DIVINE UNDERSTANDING

Just as fences around the law can be highly individualized (like our example concerning the Sabbath) or nearly universal (like present-day advice concerning chastity), the commandments themselves may undergo modification according to circumstances. For example, both the ancient Israelites and modern Latter-day Saints have rather strict health codes, though they differ according to the health hazards of their respective times. The codes are related, however, because they are based on the same eternal principle—the physical body is a temple for the eternal spirit and the Holy Spirit as well.

The eternal principle reflected in each commandment is not always obvious, however. This may be because we are unable or unwilling to understand the "why," as in the instance with the early Israelites, who were not prepared to accept the higher laws of the gospel, and therefore were given the "carnal" commandments of the law of Moses. (See Heb. 9:9–12.) Or, to test our faithfulness and obedience, we may not be given knowledge of the principle that a law is based on. For example, upon expulsion from the Garden of Eden, Adam and Eve received a command to offer sacrifice to the Lord: "After many days an angel of the Lord appeared unto Adam, saying: Why dost thou offer sacrifices unto the Lord? And Adam said unto him: I know not, save the Lord commanded me. And then the angel spake, saying: This thing is a similitude of the sacrifice of the Only Begotten of the Father, which is full of grace and truth." (Moses 5:6–7.) Adam had to obey the law of God before the law's higher meaning was revealed to him.

A modern example of obedience preceding understanding is the 1833 revelation on the Word of Wisdom, which warns the Saints against using tobacco, hot drinks, and alcohol, while encouraging them to eat little meat and lots of grains, fresh fruits, and vegetables. More than a century later, scientific research began verifying the ill effects of nicotine, caffeine, and alcohol. Even more recently, nutritional studies have proven the Word of Wisdom to be a good, basic blueprint for a healthy diet. But even before the Word of Wisdom was verified scientifically, adherents to its principles knew it was sound counsel because they had received the promised blessings of "health in their navel and marrow to their bones; . . . wisdom and great treasures of knowledge."[4] (D&C 89:18–19.)

Thus it is with all the commandments. As we do the will of the Father, we come to know the doctrine. (See John 7:17.) Our faith thereby increases, and we become able to accept correct, higher principles and govern ourselves without having to be commanded in all things.[5] (See D&C 58:26–27.)

THE TEN COMMANDMENTS

Understanding the eternal governing principles and some modern applications will enrich our appreciation of the Ten Commandments. The Ten Commandments form the foundation of the Mosaic law, but their basic values are still fundamental to God's kingdom today. Given to Moses over three thousand years ago, later prophets of the Book of Mormon and in modern times have reemphasized their relevance. (See Mosiah 12:33–13:24; D&C 42:18–28; 59:5–13.) Living the letter of the Ten Commandments is only the beginning of their relevance—understanding the spirit or principle of the laws brings their values into focus.

Jesus made this differentiation as he taught in the New Testament and the Book of Mormon records. He emphasized that man must live according to the spirit of the law as well as to the letter. As we apply the commandments within the context of our modern lives, we find spiritual strength and blessings.

WORSHIPPING THE TRUE AND LIVING GOD

The first four commandments provide direction on how we should worship God.

1. *"Thou shalt have no other gods before me." (Ex. 20:3.)* Beyond acknowledging Heavenly Father as supreme, we need to love and worship him with all our heart, might, mind, and strength. He is the source of all good things, which come from him as he works to bring about our immortality and eternal life, and his laws and ordinances are designed to bring us supreme joy and absolute peace. An appreciation of his wisdom, power, and love brings our whole existence into proper perspective.[6]

2. *"Thou shalt not make unto thee any graven image." (Ex. 20:4.)* Originally, this commandment was a prohibition given to the children of Israel against making idols and worshipping them. Many think this law no longer applies in the modern world, but as long as we make things that we worship (the meaning of "graven images"), we have a problem obeying this commandment. When we pursue our own selfish interests, we set up idols of materialism, power, and honor that distract us from our noble relationship with God and his other children.[7] We end up chasing empty, temporary images — paper money, cars, houses, television, corporate positions, and so on — instead of seeking the full, eternal essentials provided by God.

3. *"Thou shalt not take the name of the Lord thy God in vain." (Ex. 20:7.)* To take the name of God or Jesus Christ in vain is more than cussing or using profanity, either in moments of anger or in casual conversation. Those who falsely claim to be empowered by God when they do not have his authority are also guilty of this sin. In addition, people who make vows or promises in the name of the Lord have committed to keep covenants; to not do so is to take the name of Deity in vain because they have not endured true to their vow. As we take the name of Christ upon us, we should not only avoid blaspheming his name, but we should

also live so that others could use Christ's name in a statement like "Now there is a true Christian!"

4. *"Remember the sabbath day, to keep it holy." (Ex. 20:8.)* A true Sabbath realigns our spiritual compass, like the Liahona used by father Lehi. (See 1 Ne. 16.) We thus keep our eternal priorities in line and recommit ourselves to follow God and serve others as we obey his commandments. Proper worship and scripture study on this day also recharge our spiritual batteries. We receive inspiration from sacrament meeting talks and class instructors and are better prepared for the following week.[8]

SHOWING RESPECT FOR OTHERS

The next four commandments emphasize our relationships with other people.

5. *"Honour thy father and thy mother." (Ex. 20:12.)* This commandment is the only one of the ten with a specific promise—that our days will be long upon the land that the Lord has given us. Beyond respect for our immediate parents, this commandment suggests appreciation for earlier ancestors and relatives who have provided so much for us—stretching back to Father Adam and Mother Eve and even earlier to our Heavenly Father and Mother. Our greatest gift to our first parents is to live as they would wish us to live within the spiritual environment of the gospel, the Church, and the temple. When extended family lines are bound together by the sealing powers of God, we not only enjoy a pleasant life with family members for however long we live in mortality, but we also will live with our families on this earth in its eternal celestial state. Thus our days will be forever on this land.[9]

6. *"Thou shalt not kill." (Ex. 20:13.)* The sanctity of life is so significant that God has declared that the deliberate breaking of this law is an unforgivable sin. (See D&C 42:18–19.) Jesus challenged us to live a higher law in avoiding the anger and hatred that can lead to taking another person's life. The Prophet Joseph Smith stated that beyond not killing, one should not even do anything like unto it. The commandment can extend beyond blatant murder and include participating in or encouraging acts destructive to life, such as abortion, gang violence, and drug abuse.[10] Abuse of the body, whether by beating others or defiling our own, indicates a disrespect for life and is a type of killing. Rather, we should foster life and help others to enjoy the necessities of a good and

healthy life. We must improve the mind and body as we perfect ourselves and others.[11]

7. *"Thou shalt not commit adultery." (Ex. 20:14.)* Again with an appreciation for the sanctity of life, God has given us the law of chastity. He desires that each of his spirit children be born into a loving family environment, with devoted, married parents and a good prospect for a healthy beginning in earth life. Transgressing the law of chastity tampers with this life-beginning process and brings complications into the lives of all involved, whether guilty or innocent of the initial transgression. Jesus desires a wholesome, clean environment around us and he asks us not only to maintain purity in the flesh but also to be chaste in our thoughts and words. The power of purity frees us to better fulfill our purposes of earth life.[12]

8. *"Thou shalt not steal." (Ex. 20:15.)* Anything that we take from another is stealing—be it material possessions, virtue, honor, dignity, or other personal qualities. We can even steal from God if we do not return to him what he has requested. (See Mal. 3:8.) Stealing sometimes results from desperation when individuals do not have life's necessities (often because others have not shared), but it is usually an act of selfishness. We need to move toward the opposite: honesty instead of stealing, and generosity instead of selfishness. When we take from others, we suffer as well. When we share with others, all are blessed together.[13]

DEVELOPING INTEGRITY WITHIN OURSELVES

The last two commandments encourage further self-control and an honest, personal evaluation of our words and ambitions.

9. *"Thou shalt not bear false witness." (Ex. 20:16.)* Empty as storm clouds that do not bring rain is the person who continuously promises but never fulfills his word. (See Prov. 25:14.) A false promise or statement, especially with the intent to deceive, is a grievous sin.[14] This is the most serious accusation hurled against Satan. He is a spirit being, without a body, thus he cannot commit some of the other serious sins available to us mortals. He fosters our greatest errors through the deception he brings into the human mind, for he was and is a master liar, even the father of all lies. (See 2 Ne. 2:18; 9:9.) How much better to be known as one who always tells the truth, even as God—for he never tells a lie. (See Heb. 6:18).[15]

10. *"Thou shalt not covet . . . any thing that is thy neighbour's."* *(Ex. 20:17.)* The danger of this sin is that it is the beginning of most other sins. First one desires something, and then instead of working for it, the person chooses a shortcut and decides to take it from someone else, even by deceit or murder. We should not covet material possessions or the gifts possessed by others.[16] The only things we should covet are spiritual gifts that God is willing to share with us. (See 1 Cor. 12:31.) Spiritual gifts, such as faith, hope, and charity, multiply and become stronger as we share them; when we seek to misuse or steal material possessions, they are lessened, damaged, and even destroyed. If our desires are for things spiritual and in heaven, then our hearts and actions will move us and others up in that direction. We can start by instilling noble values into the hearts of the children.

PERSONAL PATTERNS OF OBEDIENCE

One of the earliest challenges of parenthood is teaching children to obey. The word *obey* has an interesting Latin root meaning "to listen to." Young children have a hard time listening to parents or authority figures for long periods, especially when it involves modifying their behavior. Each child has his or her own spirit, which must be individually approached and taught concerning this important principle. Children learn obedience best from example. No matter what we teach, they are influenced more by our deeds than by our words. A harmonious example of our own faithful words and corresponding actions, accompanied with a positive, spiritual attitude, will be the greatest teaching lesson we can give.

In addition, we should appreciate that obedience or "listening to" parents (whether earthly or heavenly) requires at least three key elements: agency, attitude, and attention. As we respect our children's *agency,* we will teach them correct principles and then provide a nurturing environment in which they learn to govern themselves. Ultimately, each individual must learn to exercise his or her own agency toward obedience if that person wants to follow God's laws.[17]

Our *attitude* reflects our motivation toward obedience, whether it be fear, logic, or love, and it greatly affects both our incentive to obey and the rewards we receive from compliance. We need to help our children understand that not only what we do but also why we do it brings the blessings of obedience into our lives.

Attention means that we can never give up our allegiance to God but must stick to our commitments and endure to the end. The concept of enduring to the end is sometimes called the fifth principle of the gospel, a continuation of the set of the first four principles and ordinances of the gospel in the fourth Article of Faith.[18] Parents must have the courage to pay attention to their own behavior and that of their children. If together they are obeying the commandments of God with a proper spirit, they will strengthen one another as they progress together.

As we obey some commandments, we find it easier to keep others until we find we are keeping most, if not all, of God's laws. The value learned by doing small and easy things is that we gain strength to do greater and harder things. We need to start somewhere to establish a pattern of obedience that can carry over into all aspects of our spiritual lives. Unfortunately, the converse is also true. If we start to neglect some of the commandments we have been keeping, neglecting other laws of God becomes easier. We must strive to keep all the commandments so that our pattern will be one of spiritual growth and increased commitment.

WHY DO WE OBEY?

We experience different levels of motivation and incentive in obedience as we progress through life and develop varying attitudes toward individual commandments. In general, we tend to act out of three motivation levels: fear, logic, or love.

FEAR

The first reason we usually obey a law or command, be it from God or some other authority, is out of fear. Often a small child can be convinced to do something by telling him the negative consequences of a wrong action. Other children, with an independent attitude, will test the authority figure to see if the punishment will be given. Having been punished for wrongdoing, they likely will not transgress the command again for fear of the consequences. For example, some young children can be told that they should not touch a hot stove. When told of the hurt that can occur, many will not touch the stove out of fear. Some children might still touch the stove. For them, the resulting pain should teach them to fear the hot stove.

Many individuals lack the desire and motivation to live the commandments of God with a cheerful heart. Nevertheless they obey out of fear, the least virtuous motivation for submission. Their fear can be directed toward God or others. They may fear the punishment of God, or they may fear what others may think of them or do to them if they disobey. In any case, they are acting out of a negative response that is not always strong enough to influence a person. For example, older teenagers or young adults usually lose their fear of parental punishment as they grow and become more independent. Fear can also be misdirected. Youth often fear the loss of popularity among their peers more than they fear the displeasure of their parents or Heavenly Father. At best, fear should be a temporary, emergency motivator toward obedience.

REWARD (INCLUDING LOGIC, DUTY, INSTINCT, AND HABIT)

The next level of obedience comes when people experience the positive consequences and rewards of compliance. An individual who has obeyed a commandment and found that his or her life has been blessed as a result may then keep the commandment out of logic. Or a person may sense the responsibility of setting a good example and keep the commandment out of duty, particularly if a promise has been made to someone else to keep this law. Sometimes we act out of natural, healthy instinct to keep a commandment. Or, after living it for a longer period, it becomes a valuable habit. Abstaining from cigarettes is a good example for all of these motivators. An individual may enjoy the better health that nonsmoking brings, especially if he or she has witnessed the problems of smoking (logic). A parent may abstain for the good health of other family members (duty). Someone else may just have a natural aversion to cigarette smoke and irritation (instinct). Others may have abstained for so long that they no longer have a desire to start smoking again (habit). In any case, these motivating factors are more positive and lasting than the primary motivator of fear. Our family and friends are also better influenced by these motivators, while we recognize the benefits they bring into our lives.

LOVE

The highest and purest level of obedience, though, is displayed by the person who lives righteously out of noble love for his Heavenly Father, others, and self. This acquiescence usually develops from one of the aforementioned types of motivation, as a result of earlier obedience to God's laws. Personal concerns move into the background when one acts out of love. We do not have to have a logical reason to keep the commandment, we just sense that God loves us and only has our best interest at heart. We trust his word and strive to keep it.

Out of God's infinite love for us, he gives us commandments that help perfect us and bring us back into his presence. As we keep his laws, we develop love for God and are able to accept and live higher laws. The highest and all-encompassing law is love itself: "For God so loved the world, that he gave his only begotten Son, that whosoever believeth in him should not perish, but have everlasting life." (John 3:16.) Christ overcame sin and death because of love—love of the Father and of us. "Therefore," he said, "those things which were of old time, which were under the law, in me are all fulfilled." (3 Ne. 12:46.) We transcend temporal commandments to live divine principles in the same way. We love God through loving our neighbor: "Love worketh no ill to his neighbour: therefore love is the fulfilling of the law." (Rom. 13:10.)

The pure motivator of love is also easily transferred from one commandment to another. As we have a strong, positive, loving experience in keeping one law, we are more willing to trust in God when he asks us to keep others. As we progress in righteousness, we learn to rely on the Lord and to strive to keep all his commandments. In addition, others are more likely to follow our example when we act and obey out of love.

DO IT!

Finally, the only way to learn why we need to follow God's laws and commandments is by experience, whether negative or positive. The wise person does not need to "burn oneself" spiritually to learn the value of obedience. One need only observe the destructive results in others' lives to appreciate the wisdom of following God's advice. As we learn firsthand the blessings that the Lord sends, we relish their sweet taste and want to do more. Obedience then becomes a natural part of our being, as normal as eating and sleeping.

But somewhere, sometime, we must start. As President Kimball stated, we must *Do it* and *Do it now!* In fact, his advice to the Church members shortly after he became President of the Church led to the popular primary song "Keep the Commandments." For whatever reason, we should start to keep the commandments now. As we keep them, our level of obedience and the personal rewards we experience through that righteousness will rise to more fulfilling dimensions. We will taste and rejoice in the sweet fruits of obedient living.

THE VALUES OF OBEDIENCE

Obedience is a requirement of heaven and, therefore, a cardinal principle of the gospel. Part of God's purpose for his children on earth is to "prove them herewith, to see if they will do all things whatsoever the Lord their God shall command them." (Abr. 3:25; D&C 98:14.) To regain Heavenly Father's presence, we must first "listen to" (or *obey*) all that he has commanded. Thus, "obedience is the first law of heaven, the cornerstone upon which all righteousness and progression rest."[19] Our compliance to God's laws will ultimately prove our worthiness to return to live with our Father in Heaven and Jesus Christ again.

Obedience is not passive. It is an active commitment to a decision, including the courage and discipline to personally carry that decision to completion. In today's world, as always, one must fight to remain in harmony with all the commandments of God. But some will ask: "Why must we be obedient? Isn't required obedience oppressive? Doesn't obedience restrict our own free agency and choice?" These are legitimate and important questions that need to be answered.

Two key principles become the foundation for our answers. First, God knows, comprehends, and understands all things. We are all dependent upon our Father in Heaven for correct understanding, knowledge, and truth. Second, God gives us commandments to bless our lives. Every commandment is given with the purpose to lead men and women back to his presence.

WHY MUST WE BE OBEDIENT?
OBEDIENCE BRINGS BLESSINGS AND HAPPINESS

By obeying God, we are happier and eventually will become like him, dwelling in eternal joy. God commands us that we may benefit from his infinite wisdom. When we obey, we are happier and we grow closer to God in knowledge and truth. When we disobey, our lives are full of sorrow, regret, and pain as we move further away from him. Joseph Smith taught: "Happiness is the object and design of our existence; and will be the end thereof, if we pursue the path that leads to it; and this path is virtue, uprightness, faithfulness, holiness, and keeping all the commandments of God. But we cannot keep all the commandments without first knowing them, and we cannot expect to know all, or more than we now know unless we comply with or keep those we have already received."[20]

The kingdom of heaven is governed by law, and when we receive any blessing, it is by obedience to the law upon which that blessing is based. (See D&C 130:21; 132:5.) By keeping all the commandments of God, we prepare for eternal life and exaltation. Nephi taught us that the Lord will give no commandment without preparing a way for us to accomplish what he has commanded. This can help us when we think that a commandment is too hard to live. Like Nephi's brothers, we may say, "It is a hard thing which [you] have required of [us.]" (1 Ne. 3:5.) Yet, like Nephi, we can be sure that when God gives a commandment, he prepares a way for us to obey him.

Sometimes we do not know the reason for a particular commandment, or we may think that it is not very important. The scriptures tell of a man named Naaman who thought that way. (See 2 Kgs. 5:1–14.) Naaman had leprosy, and he traveled from Syria to Israel to ask the prophet Elisha to heal him. Elisha's instruction to Naaman, by way of a servant message, was to wash seven times in the river Jordan. Naaman replied, "Are not . . . [the] rivers of Damascus . . . better than all the waters of Israel? May I not wash in them, and be clean?" His servants commented, "If the prophet had bid thee do some great thing, wouldest thou not have done it? How much rather then, when he saith to thee, Wash, and be clean?" (2 Kgs. 5:12–13.) Naaman thought the commandment insignificant, yet he was wise enough to follow the Lord's instruction. Because he did, he was healed.

Joseph Smith commented on this matter of obedience in seemingly small matters: "The object with me is to obey and teach others to obey God in just what He tells us to do. It mattereth not whether the principle is popular or unpopular, I will also maintain a true principle, even if I stand alone in it."[21] We show our faith and trust in God when we obey him without knowing why, and he rewards us with blessings and happiness.

ISN'T OBEDIENCE OPPRESSIVE?
OBEDIENCE LEADS TO PERSONAL PERFECTION

Perhaps the most difficult test ever given, save Christ's, was Abraham's commandment to sacrifice his son Isaac, as recounted in Genesis 22. Abraham had waited many long years for the birth of Isaac—the son whom God had promised and through whom a prophesied lineage was to descend. How could Abraham now lose his son and the promise by killing him in sacrifice? The deed must have been most repugnant to Abraham, partially because he himself had barely escaped being a human sacrificial offering. (See Abr. 1:7, 12, 15–20.) Yet he disregarded his own feelings and chose to obey God. Not until the knife was raised did the Lord intervene. Abraham, by passing this most trying test, had portrayed his unquestioned obedience before the Lord.

Why the test? Hugh B. Brown commented, "Abraham had to learn something about Abraham."[22] Joseph Smith taught, "Whatever God requires is right, no matter what it is, although we may not see the reason thereof till long after the events transpire."[23] Our love of God, not the hope of reward, must be our highest motivation if we are to pass tests of life similar to Abraham's.

King Saul is a sad example of one who fell out of harmony with the Lord because of disobedience. The Lord had commanded Saul to utterly destroy the Amalekites, including their cattle. Saul, relying upon his own wisdom and fearing his people more than God, spared the best cattle and the Amalekite king, Agag. The Lord, through Samuel the prophet, told Saul, "Hath the Lord as great delight in burnt offerings and sacrifices, as in obeying the voice of the Lord? Behold, *to obey is better than sacrifice.*" (1 Sam. 15:22; italics added.) Because of his disobedience, Saul was rejected by the Lord as king of Israel.

Christ, himself, set the perfect example of obedience for all of us. At the start of his ministry, he was baptized to witness "unto the Father that he would be obedient unto him in keeping his commandments." (2 Ne. 31:7.) The scriptures teach us that he did not receive of the fullness at first but continued from grace to grace. (See D&C 93:13.) The apostle Paul wrote, "Though he were a Son, yet learned he obedience by the things which he suffered." (Heb. 5:8.) Christ said: "I came down from heaven, not to do mine own will, but the will of him that sent me." (John 6:38.) His whole life was devoted to obeying his Father; yet it was never easy for him. During the time of the great atoning sacrifice as he bled from every pore of his body, he cried: "O my Father, if it be possible, let this cup pass from me: nevertheless not as I will, but as thou wilt." (Matt. 26:39.) Jesus' obedience led to his perfection, "and being made perfect, he became the author of eternal salvation unto all those that obey him." (Heb. 5:9.) Our obedience allows us to follow him on the path toward our perfection.

DOESN'T OBEDIENCE RESTRICT AGENCY?
OBEDIENCE BRINGS MORE FREEDOM

At the beginning of this chapter, we looked at the example of the wise employer who placed the welfare of his employees above making more profit. As the workers trusted in his noble purposes, they willingly worked harder and longer. As the quality of their work improved, the company's reputation and profits increased, and all were amply rewarded through their profit-sharing program. How a person becomes free and happy by obeying someone else's laws and expectations is hard for many people to understand, just as workers at another firm might not appreciate how the employer mentioned above could really be genuine in his beneficent motives. The only way one knows is to become active within the system and to experience its rewards.

As God directs us on earth, he seeks for our eternal welfare, and so his laws include blessings of lasting value. Among the greatest rewards for obedience to his commandments is further freedom. As we are faithful in a few things, the Lord rewards us with greater powers and opportunities. (See Matt. 25:21.) To become a part of God's social system, one must learn to obey God's commandments. Yet this obedience should be given freely while respecting God's authority. The delicate balance between obedience, individual agency, and authority is beautifully expressed in a brief statement by the First Presidency in one edition of the LDS *General Handbook of Instructions*:

A distinguishing characteristic of the Church organization lies in its balance of authority and individual rights. Priesthood is a brotherhood, and in its operation the highest capacities of man—his capacity to act as a free agent and his capacity to be spiritual — must be respected and enlarged. Leaders invite, persuade, encourage, and recommend in a spirit of gentleness and meekness. Members respond freely as the Spirit guides. Only this kind of response has moral value. An act is moral only if it expresses the character and disposition of the person, that is, if it arises out of knowledge, faith, love, or religious intent. Fear and force have no place in the kingdom because they do not produce moral actions and are contrary to God's gift of free agency.[24]

Individual freedom must be the premise by which a person chooses to obey. We are all free to choose whether or not to obey God's commandments. Because our agency is so important to him, he will not take it from us or force us to obey him. As Elder Boyd K. Packer stated: "Obedience to God can be the very highest expression of independence. Just think of giving to him the one thing, the one gift, that he would never take. . . . Obedience — that which God will never take by force — he will accept when freely given."[25] We always have the freedom to obey.[26]

In addition, freedom becomes a natural gift resulting from obedience. By subjecting our will to God and following his Spirit, we are entrusted with greater blessings and responsibilities because Heavenly Father knows we will use our agency to further his purposes. As we obey more and more of God's laws, he blesses us with increased knowledge and power and thus enhances our capacity to do even more in the future. Continuing the words of Elder Packer: "He [God] will then return to you freedom that you can hardly dream of — the freedom to feel and to know, the freedom to do, and the freedom to be, at least a thousandfold more than we offer him. Strangely enough, the key to freedom is obedience."[27] Compliance to God's instructions brings us lasting freedom along with peace and many other blessings associated with keeping his commandments.

We know that obedience to the physical laws of health, diet, and exercise leads to greater physical capacity and well-being. We also learn that obedience to spiritual laws results in increased spirituality and spiritual gifts. As a contrast, neglect of physical laws may jeopardize our health, while disobedience to spiritual laws will lead to the bondage of sin. (See Rom. 7:14–23; Alma 41:11.)

Obedience to the laws of nature and God increases our freedom and joy. For example, as we place our devotion to God above material desires, we receive spiritual direction that can inspire a more effective use of our time and talents. Through greater productivity, we are free to pursue personal priorities that bring us a sense of peace and fulfillment. Thus, obedience to God's commands is no long-term sacrifice, but rather an inspired path to achieving our personal destiny and joy.

To conclude, we learn that *out of God's love for us, he gives us diverse COMMANDMENTS and makes OBEDIENCE to him the first law of the gospel; as we learn to obey him and to serve others because of love (more so than logic or fear), we receive multiple timely blessings.* As we wisely and truly "listen to" (obey) God's directives, we willingly keep his commandments and enjoy the blessings of obedience. With Heavenly Father as our overseer, we will find joy and purpose in our journey through life as we help ourselves and others on our way back toward God's presence.

For further study, refer to the following entries:

TG	BD	*EM*
Commandments of God	Commandments, The Ten	Accountability
Obedience, Obedient, Obey		Commandments
Vow		Obedience
		Ten Commandments

CHAPTER 25

A Holy Day of Restful Service

A radio, flashlight, or toy fails to perform when its batteries no longer carry an electrical charge. People often select rechargeable batteries for such products rather than buying new batteries at every need. Over time, rechargeable batteries cost less and have less adverse environmental impact because less energy is required to recharge them than to manufacture new ones; furthermore, they provide fewer disposal problems. With recharged batteries, the appliance or toy is again able to perform its functions.

Sometimes we feel run down and without energy, not necessarily physically tired but emotionally drained or spiritually weak. We sense that our emotional and spiritual powers need to be built up again. How would it be to have special spiritual batteries that we could just replace or plug in somewhere to be recharged? Actually, there is a spiritual battery recharger available—a weekly holy day called the Sabbath. Like batteries, it takes less effort to regularly recharge our spiritual powers than waiting to completely rebuild spiritually after losing all energy. If on a weekly basis we rejuvenate our spirits, our spirituality will remain stronger through the work days. The Sabbath has the potential of providing constant spiritual recharging.

The very first decree God made upon completing the creation of the world and its inhabitants was that the seventh day should be a *Sabbath,* a sanctified "day of rest" from weekly labor: "God blessed the seventh day, and sanctified it: because that in it he had rested from all his work which God created and made." (Gen. 2:3.) The primacy of a holy day, when one rests from the normal work routine, was thus established literally "in the beginning" and remains a fundamental observance among all true followers of God.

Sabbath observance is a practice that readily distinguishes the people of God from those of the world. The three great religions that have primarily influenced western civilization — Judaism, Christianity, and Islam — all celebrate a Sabbath.[1] In resting from our daily labors one day each week, we give ourselves formal occasion to acknowledge God as the creator of all blessings and to engage ourselves in his service rather than in our own ambitions. Through rest, worship, covenant renewal, and service to others, we acknowledge the Sabbath as the Lord's day, not our own.

HOW DID SABBATH WORSHIP COME INTO PRACTICE?

For ancient Israel, many Mosaic laws involved Sabbath requirements and restrictions. In addition to the weekly Sabbath, holy days of abstaining from work were established for special festivals. When the Lord led Israel out of bondage from Egypt, he established the first Sabbath feast — the Passover — to show "that the Lord doth put a difference between the Egyptians and Israel." (Ex. 11:7.) Following the flight from Egypt, the Feast of the Passover was instituted as an annual, week-long celebration and sanctification stretching from one Sabbath rest day to the next. Sabbath days in general became days not only of rest, but also of worship, thanksgiving, and sacrifice wherein the Lord was acknowledged as Creator and Redeemer, one who had to "buy back" Israel from her slavery or spiritual bondage.

The Lord taught Israel more about Sabbath observance during the forty years of the Exodus, as he fed them with manna from heaven six days a week, giving a double portion on the sixth day to supply the seventh. Israel could not have survived in the wilderness without their "daily bread"; thus they were constantly reminded that their sustenance came from the Lord, not their own labors, and that the Sabbath was a time for rest and remembrance.

Once established in a land of plenty, Israel formally celebrated the Lord's assistance in Canaan by letting their fields lay fallow every seventh year and living off the surplus God had previously provided. He had promised them that if they would keep the Law of Moses (emphasizing Sabbath observance), they should never want for anything: "I will give you the rain of your land in his due season, . . . that thou mayest gather in thy corn, and thy wine, and thine oil. And I will send grass in thy fields for thy cattle, that thou mayest eat and be full." (Deut. 11:14–15.)

To further acknowledge the Lord's gifts, Israel set aside every fiftieth year (after seven times seven) as the greatest Sabbath celebration of all, the Year of Jubilee. In this year all outstanding debts were forgiven, all mortgaged lands reverted to the original families, and all indentured Israelite servants were set free. Thus the Sabbath became a time for forgiving and doing good to others, as God does to us. Jubilee was a dramatic reminder that the richness of the earth does not belong to any one man over another, but that everything is the Lord's, and all blessings flow from him. Other feasts, celebrations, and customs were added to Israelite tradition over the years, each enriching the character of the Sabbath while maintaining the essential elements of rest, worship, and sacrifice.

Unfortunately many Israelites paid little attention to the spiritual dimensions of the Sabbath and often ignored the major Sabbaths of the land. The prophets witnessed repeatedly that the Sabbath was either improperly observed or altogether ignored. Amos chastised those who impatiently waited for the passing of the Sabbath so they could continue their dishonest pursuits. (See Amos 8:5.) Isaiah condemned his contemporaries for the iniquity of their Sabbaths and religious celebrations. (See Isa. 1:13.) He also rebuked their strifes and wickedness on the fast days. (See Isa. 58:4.) Jeremiah exhorted his listeners to refrain from their Sabbath labors, but they ignored his admonitions. (See Jer. 17:21–23.) Because the children of Israel continually disregarded the Sabbath and other Mosaic laws, the divided kingdoms of Israel and Judah were subjugated by other nations, culminating first in the Assyrian invasion and scattering of Israel in 721 B.C. and second in the Babylonian conquest and destruction of Judah and Jerusalem in 586 B.C.[2]

During the Babylonian captivity, the prophet Ezekiel repeatedly noted continuing Sabbath neglect. (See Ezek. 20:12–24; 22:8; 23:38.) After Babylon fell to the Persian Empire, the conquering emperor Cyrus allowed the Jews to return to Jerusalem, to rebuild their temple, and to reestablish their Sabbath practices. From that time onward, Judah remained predominantly subjugated under various foreign powers—the Persians, Greeks, and then the Romans. During this period, some Jews

developed particular and even fanatical practices in their Sabbath observance while others became more lax. For example, Nehemiah rebuked
the Jews of his day for profaning the Sabbath, and he ordered the city
gates closed to prevent travel and trade. (See Neh. 10:31; 13:15–22.)
Some of the more strictly observant rabbis believed that redemption from
foreign rule would come only if *all* Jews would just honor and obey one
complete Sabbath, and therefore they pushed even harder for their Sabbath practices.

HOW DID JESUS OBSERVE THE SABBATH?

Judah was laboring under Roman rule and suffering internal conflicts
between differing Jewish religious attitudes when the Great Redeemer
was born. Though many Jewish leaders strictly adhered to outward forms
and traditions of the Mosaic law, they would not acknowledge the supreme lawgiver himself when he appeared among them.

A frequent charge levied by the Jews against Jesus was that he broke
the Sabbath by failing to observe some customs, traditions, or protective
fences built around the law by the scribes and sages. In reality, Jesus
attended faithfully to the letter of the original Mosaic law, and more
important, he exemplified its spirit. For example, on one occasion, the
Pharisees accused Jesus and his disciples of violating the Sabbath because
they plucked and ate grain while walking through a field. (See Mark
2:22–28.) The Mosaic law stated, however, that in passing through a field
or vineyard in Israel, anyone who was hungry was free to eat as he went:
if the owner refused him, the owner broke the law; if the wanderer took
more than he needed, then he broke the law. (See Deut. 24:19–22.) Thus,
the fruits of the field, when collected and eaten casually, were not considered a type of labor, even on the day of rest.

Immediately after the incident in the grainfield, Jesus entered the
synagogue, saw a man with a withered hand, and promptly healed him.
Again the elders were outraged at what they felt was an act of labor on
the Sabbath, but Jesus silenced them by asking, "Is it lawful to do good
on the Sabbath days, or to do evil? to save life, or to kill?" (Mark 3:4.)
In conclusion, he said, "The Sabbath was made for man, and not man
for the Sabbath: therefore the Son of man is Lord also of the Sabbath."
(Mark 2:27–28.)

As the Lord of the Sabbath, Jesus not only lived the Mosaic law, but he also introduced symbolic observances that would make future Sabbaths more meaningful for his followers. The most dramatic symbols dealt with bread and blood. When Jesus broke a few pieces of bread and fed five thousand, the people wanted to make him their earthly king. Jesus, however, wanted the people to realize that, though he was the giver of earthly bread, he was more interested in their spiritual sustenance: "Your fathers did eat manna in the wilderness, and are dead. . . . I am the living bread which came down from heaven: if any man eat of this bread, he shall live for ever: and the bread that I will give is my flesh, which I will give for the life of the world." (John 6:49, 51.) Israel's collective dream of temporal redemption became a spiritual reality in the individual lives of those who believed in the "Bread of Life." The ancient rites and symbols were made real in Christ, and "all things are become new." (2 Cor. 5:17.) Christ himself was the sacrificial lamb of the Passover and the symbolic bread of the sacrament, come to redeem men with his own life.

The blood of Christ also became symbolic of mankind's redemption. The atonement, death, and resurrection of the Lord fulfilled the law of Moses, and the Savior's "great and last sacrifice" put a stop to the ritual "shedding of blood." (See Alma 34:13.) Thus during the Last Supper, shortly before his atoning sacrifice and death, Jesus instituted the symbolic Christian sacrament of bread and wine in remembrance of his body and blood. The Christian Sabbath day was later changed from the last day of the week to the first in commemoration of the Lord's resurrection, and the sacramental remembrance of his sacrifice became a primary purpose of worship services on this day.

WHY DO MOST CHRISTIANS WORSHIP ON SUNDAY?

The steps in the change from Saturday to Sunday as the traditional Christian Sabbath are not completely recorded in the scriptures, but the importance of the first day of the week (Sunday) can be recognized early in the postresurrection narrative. Mary Magdalene went to the sepulchre "the first day of the week" and met the Lord, then ran to tell the disciples afterward. Jesus appeared later to them "the same day at evening, being the first day of the week, when . . . the disciples were assembled." (John 20:1, 19.)

Thomas, one of the twelve apostles, was not present at this first meeting and would not believe that the Lord himself had come. "After eight days" (which brought them again to Sunday[3]), the disciples were assembled again, including Thomas, apparently for a meeting appointed by the Lord. The Lord showed himself a second time and did other sacred things briefly mentioned in the scriptures. (See John 20:26–30.) Because Jesus was resurrected on the first day of the week and met with his gathered disciples both on that day and on the same day a week later, early Christians naturally chose Sunday as a day of worship. Since he ate and drank with them, "renewing the table fellowship that He had shared with them on the night on which He was betrayed,"[4] the sacrament emblems became a natural part of the early Christian worship service. (See Luke 24:41–43; cf. Acts 10:41.)

Bible scholars also report that the day of Pentecost, in which the apostles received the gift and power of the Holy Ghost, "that year fell on the first day of the week."[5] The disciples were already assembled "with one accord in one place" (Acts 2:1) perhaps for a Sabbath type of worship. Some Christian groups believe that Christ's early church "was born as a Lord's Day [Sunday] assembly, whether one thinks of the original gathering of the disciples on the evening of the first Easter or of the subsequent gathering in the upper room at Pentecost when the Spirit was poured out and Christians first preached."[6]

Luke also notes a later occasion in which, "upon the first day of the week, when the disciples came together to break bread, Paul preached unto them." (Acts 20:7.) Paul also refers to the first day of the week when instructing the Corinthians about some monies to be sent to Jerusalem. (See 1 Cor. 16:2.) As one scholar notes, "Since in a later letter (2 Cor. 9:12) he called the collection set aside on this day a *leitourgia,* i.e., a ministration of a sacred character, the choice of the day definitely points to its religious significance. Here then is further evidence that by the middle of the 1st cent. the first day of the week had unique meaning for the Christian community."[7]

Some groups of early Christians held religious celebrations on both Saturday and Sunday, but the first day of the week, Sunday, "the Lord's day" of resurrection, became the exclusive Christian Sabbath by the end of the fifth century. Early Christians found it difficult to worship on either Saturday or Sunday because of the vocational problem of abstaining from work and also because of pagan persecution. Persecution resulted if Christians worshipped on Saturday because they were sometimes confused with the Jews and their day of worship—this became especially dangerous in periods when the Jews were actively persecuted. They were also persecuted for Sunday worship because their loyalty to the Roman Empire was often questioned and their Sunday meetings were misinterpreted as political assemblies. Sunday remained a difficult day on which to hold religious services until Emperor Constantine made a proclamation allowing for rest from work on Sundays in A.D. 321.

Throughout the Middle Ages, Sunday remained the traditional Christian day of rest and worship. Mormons not only continue this tradition, but its validity has also been confirmed in modern revelation: "For verily this is a day appointed unto you to rest from your labors, and to pay thy devotions unto the Most High; . . . on this, the Lord's day, thou shalt offer . . . thy sacraments unto the Most High, confessing thy sins unto thy brethren, and before the Lord." (D&C 59:10, 12.)

In modern times, however, Sunday is losing its significance worldwide as either a day of rest or a time to worship, as more people work and fewer attend church services. Interestingly, most places of employment will still give their employees at least one day off each week, but it is not always Sunday. Humans seem to need one day weekly for a rest from normal labors and work routine. This was particularly demonstrated in the failure of Napoleonic leaders in France who allowed just one day in ten free from work because they wanted to increase productivity. Their change in the ancient weekly routine simply did not succeed, resulting in less productivity and public unrest. People who work too many continuous days or at multiple jobs "burn out," and their productiveness decreases if they do not rest occasionally—preferably weekly. We are better people and workers when we observe the Sabbath.

Having established Sunday as the common Christian Sabbath, we should note that in some non-Christian countries, custom dictates a different day of rest and abstinence from normal labors. In these countries, Latter-day Saints may formally worship on a day other than Sunday. For example, some LDS congregations meet on Friday in Moslem countries and on Saturday in the Jewish state of Israel. These actions have been approved by the living prophets, believing that the devotions of Latter-day Saints in these countries are acceptable to the Lord since the function of the Sabbath predominates over the particular day it is recognized.

WHAT SHOULD WE DO ON THE SABBATH?

Anciently the Lord governed Israel more through specific laws than through general principles, imposing exact restrictions concerning all sorts of activities on the Sabbath day. Under the restored law of the gospel, he governs more through principles rather than specifics, and his followers have more agency and therefore more responsibility to decide their own priorities for the day. Aside from commandments to rest from our labors, to worship the Lord, and to partake of the sacrament on his holy day, Latter-day Saints have no other major scriptural injunctions concerning the Sabbath, and their other Sunday activities are left to their own discretion. (See Ex. 20:8–10; D&C 59:9–13.)

Jesus gave personal examples of some appropriate Sabbath acts, and he also provided some general counsel, affirming that we should do good on the Sabbath day. (See Mark 3:4.) How we observe the Sabbath becomes a good test of whether we are "wise" servants who weekly renew our priorities with the Lord of this earth or "slothful" servants who weakly observe the Sabbath, pursuing instead our own selfish interests or being "compelled in all things." (D&C 58:26.) To recharge our spiritual batteries, four elements—rest, worship, sacramental renewal, and service—should be a part of our weekly Sabbath observance. If practiced, they will lead to a strong spirit of reverence for this weekly holy day.

A DAY OF REST

Modern prophets have given us good counsel and some general guidelines concerning proper Sabbath observance. Concerning the day of rest, President Spencer W. Kimball wrote: "The Sabbath is not a day for indolent lounging about the house or puttering around in the garden, but is a day for ... worship of the Lord, drinking at the fountain of knowledge and instruction, enjoying the family, and finding uplift in music and song."[8] We cease from the routine of normal labor not just to rest, or even to be lazy and waste time, but to rejuvenate ourselves physically and spiritually.

Beyond resting from our physical work, we need to dedicate ourselves to renewed spiritual holiness as we worship God and serve others. We can do this in many ways, beyond just attending church. President Kimball suggested some examples of Sabbath day activities, including "reading the scriptures, visiting the sick, visiting relatives and friends, doing home teaching, working on genealogy records, taking a nap, writing letters to missionaries and servicemen or relatives, preparation for the following week's church lessons, games with the small children, fasting for a purpose, writing devotional poetry, and other worthwhile activities of great variety."[9] Having found restful, appropriate activities, we must be careful that we do not become as the Pharisees and take upon ourselves the role of lawgiver by dictating to others our preferences for Sunday activities. Each family needs to establish its own restful activities for the Sabbath. Appropriately carried out, a restful Sabbath refreshes us in body and soul for the coming week.

A DAY OF WORSHIP

Spiritual refreshment results primarily during periods of worship and religious devotion. Since a major purpose of the Sabbath is to recognize the Lord of this earth and appreciate all the blessings he provides for us, we have a spiritual responsibility each week to worship him and to recommit to live his gospel. The act of worshiping God best takes place in association with others who share our feelings and devotions. Church services enrich the Sabbath as a holy day when we sing hymns, pray, renew vows, and study together.

Typical Sunday Meetinghouse Schedule. Currently, most Latter-day Saints throughout the world travel weekly to their meetinghouse for a three-hour block of meetings. The order of the meetings may vary, but they contain three segments: (1) a sacrament meeting service of seventy minutes, (1) a Sunday School class period (for those twelve and older) or Primary organization meeting (for those three to eleven) of forty minutes, and (3) age-group, organizational, and priesthood assemblies and classes of fifty minutes, with separate sections for Primary-age children, young women (ages twelve to eighteen), Relief Society (adult women), and priesthood holders (young men and adults, twelve and older). The other twenty minutes are used for musical interludes, hymn practice, and breaks between the sessions.

Sunday meetings provide opportunities for partaking of the sacrament, joining in prayer, and singing hymns of religious devotion. Talks and class instruction provide instruction and edification. Social fellowship and spiritual bonding between the Saints also characterize the day.

If for reasons of health, travel, or other serious conflicts, we are unable to attend church services on any given Sunday, we should try to incorporate into that day appropriate spiritual activities—such as scripture reading, gospel study, journal writing, and spiritual discussion. Such activities are not meant as substitutes for attending church, but they may help fill the spiritual void and give spiritual strength. For hospital and nursing home patients, or those housebound people who are unable to attend church and receive the sacrament, arrangements should be made with the local bishop or branch president so that the sacrament can be provided by the priesthood members. Whenever possible, the blessings of the sacrament should be enjoyed weekly by all members of Christ's church.

Other Sunday Meetings. Besides the three-hour block of meetings, additional Sunday activities often take place in a typical LDS meetinghouse. For some adults and older youth in leadership callings, leadership and council meetings are held either before or after the block meetings. Occasionally, special firesides, musical programs, temple preparation classes, and priesthood assemblies are held in the evenings.

In addition, four weekends annually are devoted to larger gatherings of Mormons. Twice a year, the members of an entire stake assemble together for a two-hour session of Sunday stake conference, which replaces the block meetings for that week. A Saturday evening session of stake conference is also held for all adults, and it may be preceded by leadership meetings Saturday afternoon. The first weekends of April and October are reserved for the Church's general conference, with direct video transmission of the conference sessions now made available to most stake centers in North America. (Video- and audiotapes of the general conference sessions are sent to those areas of the Church that are unable to receive the direct broadcasts.)

A Day of Sacramental Covenant Renewal

A major value of the Sunday worship service is the opportunity to renew our covenants with the Lord by partaking of the sacrament.

Through sacrament hymns and prayers, we bring our spirit in tune with the Savior's mission and atoning sacrifice. As he sacrificed body and blood on our behalf, we covenant to take his name upon ourselves and to keep his commandments so we can better serve and sacrifice for others. To assist us in our own lives and in our opportunities to help others, he promises us the constant companionship of the Holy Spirit as we adhere to our promises. The sacrament is a marvelous opportunity to draw near to Christ and to allow him and the Holy Ghost to become a vibrant, spiritual force in our lives. This symbolic act gives purpose to our lives and elevates our existence from mundane weekly burdens.

The Sacrament of the Lord's Supper. The form of the sacrament service consists of two parts, a special sacramental hymn and the actual ordinance. The hymn directs our thoughts toward Christ's atonement and the vows we have made with God, helping to prepare us to partake of the sacrament. The congregation should be especially reverent during the entire ordinance of blessing and passing the sacramental bread and water, which represent the body and blood of Christ — symbols of remembrance for the agony of Gethsemane and the torment of Golgotha that Jesus endured for the redemption of our sins. The sacramental emblems are blessed using prescribed prayers read aloud by priesthood holders. These prayers remind us of what the Son of God has done and suffered for us, and of what we have covenanted with God. Each week we promise to remember Christ, to take his name upon us, and to keep his commandments. In return, we are promised the companionship of the Holy Spirit. (See D&C 20:75–79.)

Our act of partaking of the sacramental symbols brings into focus the offerings of commitment and religious service that we have promised to God. This time of covenant renewal is our promise to live as true Christians and to keep the sacred vows we have made both publicly and privately. Our public vows include the renewal of our baptismal and any temple covenants. Our private vows include personal promises made to God. The sacrament is a sacred ordinance, to be approached with reverence and sincerity. Partaking of the sacrament on a weekly basis provides a regular opportunity to assess our spiritual worthiness and re-evaluate our religious commitment.

A DAY OF SERVICE

Many Sabbath activities furnish opportunities to do good as we give service to others. Indeed, another reason we rest from our vocational labors on the Sabbath is so that we can fully attend to the Lord's work, which is service to others in his kingdom. This can include fulfilling our formal Church callings, which, for some leaders, particularly those in bishoprics and stake presidencies, can involve nearly their entire Sunday. Priesthood and auxiliary leaders provide much valuable service and direction during their Sunday activities and meetings. Teachers, nursery workers, librarians, and others also render valuable aid as they fulfill their callings. In addition, many ward members give important service to other members through home and visiting teaching visits, which may take place on Sunday (as well as the other days of the week).

Some of the most valuable service comes outside of Church callings. Spontaneous visits to the sick and housebound are edifying Sabbath experiences. Writing letters to missionaries and assisting others in gospel study are additional valuable activities. Families are strengthened as family councils and family gatherings are held on Sunday. Scripture reading, gospel discussions, preparations of talks and lessons to be given in church, and other family activities can cultivate a special, reverent spirit of Sabbath devotion within a family. Indeed, one reason the First Presidency consolidated the key Sunday meetings into a single time block was to provide more time for the family on Sunday. They suggested that families participate in gospel study and "other appropriate Sabbath activities, such as strengthening family ties, visiting the sick and homebound, giving service to others, writing personal and family histories, genealogical work, and missionary work."[10]

A DAY OF REVERENCE

The sum of these elements makes the Sabbath into a very special day—a day of reverence. To *revere* is to "treat with deep respect." A spirit of reverence is a feeling of admiration and appreciation. On the Sabbath as we worship the Lord and esteem what he has done for us, we will have a spirit of reverence with us. Conversely, as we cultivate reverence on Sundays, our thoughts will more easily turn to God and his great works in our behalf.

In all respects, the Sabbath day should be a day that is different from others during the week. As the Jewish sages say, "The Sabbath is the queen of the week," and, "Those who both observe the Sabbath and call it an enjoyment will rejoice in the kingdom of God and enjoy the riches of His bounty."[11] Most people spend the majority of their time providing for themselves and their families, and the Sabbath provides them a weekly opportunity to rest from cares and rejuvenate themselves spiritually. The Sabbath is a day to rise above mundane concerns, acknowledge the Lord as the ultimate giver of life, look to the needs of others, and rejoice in the eternal truths that give meaning to our everyday lives.

If we allow our selfish and materialistic concerns to govern our Sundays, we become like a battery with a weakened seam that allows the chemicals to seep out. Such a battery not only loses its power, but it corrodes whatever it touches. If we corrupt the Sabbath, we not only lose our own spiritual powers, but we also weaken the resolve and ability of others to have a proper Sabbath experience. For example, if we insist on shopping on Sunday, we encourage employers to keep their businesses open on the Sabbath, requiring employees to work on what should be a day of rest and worship. Or if we disturb the Sabbath spirit in our families with inappropriate activities, especially those that take us away from Church, we dilute the spiritual energy that should be coming into our family members.

On the other hand, as we set this day apart from the rest of the week and treat it with a special spirit of reverence, we will be physically refreshed, emotionally strengthened, and spiritually renewed. The Lord promises us—as he did ancient Israel—that as we keep the Sabbath holy, we will both inherit special spiritual blessings and be provided with basic physical needs: "Inasmuch as ye do this, the fulness of the earth is yours, the beasts of the field and the fowls of the air, and that which climbeth upon the trees and walketh upon the earth; yea, and the herb, and the good things which come of the earth, whether for food or for raiment, or for houses, or for barns, or for orchards, or for gardens, or for vineyards. . . . And it pleaseth God that he hath given all these things unto man; for unto this end were they made to be used, with judgment, not to excess, neither by extortion. . . . But learn that he who doeth the works of righteousness shall receive his reward, even peace in this world, and eternal life in the world to come." (D&C 59:16–17, 20, 23.)

In conclusion, *Sunday is our SABBATH, a holy day when we should rest from our weekly labors, worship God, renew our sacramental covenants, and serve others in a spirit of reverence.* As we develop a reverential Sabbath spirit with our families and ward members, we are blessed spiritually and temporally. The Sabbath gives us a taste of the heavenly life-style and prepares us for similar celestial pursuits in God's kingdom. A weekly Sabbath observance provides spiritual refreshment and keeps us pointed correctly toward the kingdom of our Heavenly Father.

For further study, refer to the following entries:

TG	BD	EM
Assembly for Worship	Communion	Communion
Church Meetings	Lord's Day	Fast and Testimony Meeting
Reverence	Sabbath	Hymns and Hymnody
Sabbath		Reverence
Sacrament		Sabbath Day
Worship		Sacrament
		Sacrament Meeting
		Sunday
		Worship

CHAPTER 26

THE SANCTITY AND PURITY OF LIFE

In an age of environmental concerns, the advantages of pure air, water, and food are increasingly more obvious. The need for purity extends beyond the external world of our physical bodies, however. It includes the internal recesses of our mind and body and involves the spirit of our soul. Beyond what we breathe, drink, and eat, cleanliness incorporates a variety of mental attributes and sexual practices that influence the body's health and the soul's sanctity. Also, the necessity for pureness extends beyond this life into the future. God's heavenly realms are clean and pure, and he tells us that any who want to live in his presence must have clean hands and a pure heart. (See Ps. 24:4; Matt. 5:8.) Indeed, the prophets repeatedly warn us that no unclean thing can enter into God's kingdom. (See Eph. 5:5; Alma 11:37; 40:26; Moses 6:57.)

Much of God's effort on this earth is directed toward providing and maintaining a pure physical and spiritual environment for us. Many divine commandments address issues of purity, dealing with the sanctity of life, moral cleanliness, and chastity. It is sobering to realize that God has, with few exceptions, given us the power to procreate. Thereby we provide physical tabernacles for his spirit children so that God may achieve his aim "to bring to pass the immortality and eternal life of man." (Moses 1:39.) Not surprisingly, the power of giving life should be carefully guarded and judiciously used. For this reason, God has given us, his creative apprentices, the law of chastity as one of his strictest and most important commandments. The sacredness of the power to create life is a primary reason to study and honor the law of chastity.

In this chapter, we will concentrate on the higher principles surrounding the law of chastity, but we will also touch on the serious consequences of violating this law and the lasting rewards of keeping it.

CHASTITY AS COMMON WISDOM

For generations, the conventional wisdom of many nations and the moral practices of a variety of cultures considered it healthy and proper for young men and women to refrain from premarital sexual relations and to remain faithful to one another in marriage. In Europe and America, these ideas derived from the traditional Judeo-Christian doctrines of marriage being a rite or sacrament ordained by God and of extramarital sex not being condoned by him. In the post-World War II period, however, the religious foundation of public morals greatly eroded, and a drastic corruption of sexual attitudes soon followed. The late 1960s saw the beginning of the "sexual revolution," in which intimate relations between men and women were taken out of their religious context — in fact, out of any moral context at all — and set up as an independent mode of self-expression and gratification. Ironically called the age of the "New Morality," this period appeared to be more a reversion to the old blatant immorality of some ancient, decadent societies.

Despite a flood of public propaganda to the contrary, the experience of people subscribing to new sexual mores eventually confirmed what conventional wisdom had always held — sexual behavior in human beings is much more than an animal instinct for pleasure and must include stable emotional ties to bring long-term satisfaction and fulfillment. Casual sex without emotional ties brings sexually fragmented relationships, since what should be most personal and intimate becomes common and transitory.

Even secular psychologists and therapists now generally accept this view. One Latter-day Saint marriage counselor explained that "if we relate to each other in fragments, at best we miss full relationships. At worst, we manipulate and exploit others for our gratification. Sexual fragmentation can be particularly harmful because it gives powerful physiological rewards which, though illusory, can temporarily persuade us to overlook the serious deficits in the overall relationship. . . . The intense human intimacy that should be enjoyed in and symbolized by sexual union is counterfeited by sensual episodes which suggest — but cannot deliver — acceptance, understanding, and love."[1]

The 1980s, therefore, saw a gradual return toward the traditional commitment of marriage and sexual fidelity between men and women.

As the decade of the 1990s opened, a great majority, over 90 percent, of mental health professionals endorsed the concept of being true to one's spouse.[2] Thus the sexually aware person is torn between a natural instinct for personal gratification and the enticements of the media on the one hand and an inner voice whispering for sexual fidelity and the advice of wise clergy and professionals on the other hand. At least, more people seem to be accepting what the scriptures have taught all along— higher moral values should govern human sexual behavior.

Unfortunately, Western society did not begin to recognize the value of higher moral values until after some tragic societal casualties had occurred. The era of so-called "free sex" came with its own steep price— fragmented families, teenage pregnancies, and a plague of socially transmitted diseases. One of the social casualties of the age of "new morality" has been an astounding divorce rate throughout Western countries. Millions of divorces have left millions of men, women, and their children without the emotional security of strong, permanent family ties. Heavenly Father wants each of his spirit children to be born and reared in a loving, supporting family environment. (See D&C 42:45; 68:25, 28.) However, selfish infidelity seriously handicaps this divine objective. Instead, parents are at odds with each other, marriage bonds are weakened or even severed, parental example is tarnished, adult leadership is fragmented, and confusion and distrust abound. Although infidelity is not the only cause of divorce or family problems, chaos and sorrow often replace the stability and joy that should prevail in a moral family.

Second, though the sexual revolution has now been largely rejected by the generation that initiated it, the fallout of sexual permissiveness prevailed among the succeeding generation. Sexual activity among adolescents reached an all-time high, attended by a soaring incidence of teenage pregnancy and abortion. As reported in the late 1980s: "In America 3,000 adolescents become pregnant each day. A million a year. Four out of five are unmarried. More than half get abortions."[3] Two decades of widespread tampering and experimenting with the wellspring of creation has born its ominous fruit—the random and irresponsible giving and taking of innocent human life.

Third, the seeds of life have become the seeds of death in an equally frightening way through the sexual spread of diseases, particularly Acquired Immune Deficiency Syndrome (AIDS). Lowered moral standards during the sexual revolution led to increased sexual deviancy, which has now spread this deadly and so far incurable disease, initially prevalent among homosexuals and intravenous drug users, into the general population: "AIDS . . . may reach plague proportions. Even now it is claiming innocent victims: newborn babies and recipients of blood transfusions. It is only a matter of time before it becomes widespread among heterosexuals. . . . AIDS should remind us that ours is a hostile world. . . . The more we pass ourselves around, the larger the likelihood of our picking something up. . . . Whether on clinical or moral grounds, it seems clear that promiscuity has its price."[4] Considered prudishness two decades ago, sexual restraint is now heralded not only as good common sense, but also as literally a matter of life and death. Safer than "safe sex,"[5] a virtuous life-style is the best guarantee against sexually transmitted diseases.

OLD VERSUS NEW MORALITY

"Old morality" refers to the Judeo-Christian expectations of the scriptural laws concerning adultery. It is sometimes satirized by highlighting the prudishness of the Victorian era in England. Under the social pressures of the old-morality standards, many who wanted to follow the approved moral behavior found it difficult to determine whether people lived chaste lives out of fear for God's wrath, out of social pressure, or by personal choice. Even among those who claimed to be virtuous, some had hidden affairs and thus lived as hypocrites. After World War I, some public figures, particularly a few movie stars and sports idols, demonstrated their individuality by being unchaste without hiding the fact. People's moral behavior at this time was subject to many conflicting influences.

In the age of the so-called "new morality," sexual preferences and behavior became much more open and free. Initially, much of Western society seemed obsessed with sex. Illicit sexual relations were openly portrayed in books and movies and discussed in magazines and TV shows. Many people rejected moral standards in their quest for personal gratification. However, the shallow emptiness of this life-style soon became apparent as people could not find substance and durability in casual sexual relationships. Searching for more meaningful and permanent values, many rediscovered the traditional principles of fidelity, obligation, and marriage. Under an enlightened moral environment, chastity was seen more as an expression of choice and less as a burdensome obligation—at least until the AIDS epidemic hit and fear became a primary motive for many chaste relationships. As time passes and experiences accumulate, more people are recognizing the wisdom of God's commandments and are encouraging a more virtuous behavior for themselves and their families.[6]

Hopefully, a pattern of increased wisdom leading to more positive behavior will occur in the sexual dimension. This pattern has developed in some health areas, particularly those dealing with tobacco, alcohol, and dangerous drugs. Starting in the late '60s and continuing through the twentieth century, medical research has demonstrated the health risks of smoking and drinking along with the emotional and social ills of alcohol abuse and the street drugs like marijuana, heroin, and crack. Although some people, especially the youth, curiously explore tobacco, alcohol, and drug use, aggressive education programs and government legislation have helped to gradually decrease the percentage of people who smoke, drink, and use dangerous drugs. Much remains to be done, especially concerning the many abuses of alcohol, but the path of wisdom dictates that this pattern should be encouraged.

As similar enlightened wisdom and modified behavior improve the sexual relations of more people, families and cultures throughout the world will be blessed. Granted, people may not be changing their behavior because they recognize the divine wisdom in the scriptural injunctions, but at least they sense the wisdom of these higher moral principles. An even higher level of enlightenment occurs when people appreciate the spiritual values of the law of chastity.

CHASTITY AS A KEY TO SPIRITUAL LIFE

More important than protecting emotional or physical health, the law of chastity affects a person's spiritual status on earth and in eternity. Violating the law of chastity through fornication or adultery is explicitly stated by Alma as the "most abominable above all sins save it be the shedding of innocent blood or denying the Holy Ghost." (Alma 39:5.) By way of definition, fornication is having sexual relations with someone else when you are not married; adultery is having sexual relations with anyone else when you are already married to someone.

The three greatest sins—denial of the Holy Ghost, murder, and adultery—are so serious because they all frustrate God's plan of eternal life for his children, destroying the sanctity of life, both spiritual and physical. To deny the absolute witness of the Holy Ghost devastates the spiritual life of oneself and others by denying known truths and spiritually cutting oneself off from light and truth for all eternity. To murder is to cut short the crucial physical probationary state of a person, immediately thwarting any further chances in the flesh at progression and eternal life. To disregard the law of chastity is to toy with the fountain of physical life for mankind's second estate, tampering with the divinely appointed life-beginning process. All three of these sins demonstrate the sanctity of life and illustrate why God has given important commandments concerning life.

As expressed at the beginning of this chapter, breaking the law of chastity violates the supreme trust God has placed with us to responsibly bring immortal spirits into mortal bodies. Beyond this primary purpose of sexual relations, a positive physical association can help create an emotional and spiritual unity between husband and wife. The secondary purpose of sexuality relates directly to the first, for love and unity between spouses contributes immeasurably to the quality of the family environment in which children are raised. When a commitment to bear and rear children is not central in a sexual relationship, immortal spirits who may be born (on accident) are usually denied the nurturance they need to progress to their full, eternal potential. For this reason, among others, the Lord has expressly commanded that sexual relations be confined to marriage and that children be raised in righteousness, or "the sin be upon the heads of the parents." (D&C 68:25.)

The spiritual effects of immorality are well documented in the scriptures. The seriousness of infidelity, and particularly adultery, might explain Christ's statement where he said that an evil and "adulterous generation seeketh after a sign." (Matt. 12:39; 16:4.) Adulterers are cut off from the Spirit of the Lord, and thus they may seek for supernatural signs as a type of spiritual communication. Joseph Smith said that "whenever you see a man seeking after a sign, you may set it down that he is an adulterous man."[7] In other words, the adulterer, as a sinner, is no longer able to rely upon the Holy Ghost for confirmation of gospel truths, and he or she demands outward manifestations to justify belief.

Of course, since the Lord does not operate in that fashion, the sinner rarely receives his sign. Hence, he self-deceptively justifies his apostasy, reasoning, "After all, wouldn't the Lord show me a sign if the gospel were really true. Since he hasn't, it must not be true, and I should feel no obligation to keep its teachings or commandments." Thus, disobedience to the law of chastity or any other serious sin clouds our perception of truth, and if we do not repent of our immoral behavior, we become corrupt in our beliefs as well as our actions. This warning applies particularly to those who have been taught God's commandments. Believers who commit serious sexual sins must genuinely struggle to regain the companionship of the Holy Spirit so they can be worthy for other blessings promised to the virtuous.

ADD TO YOUR FAITH, VIRTUE

When Peter wrote his epistle to the early Saints, he told them to add virtue to their faith. (See 2 Pet. 1:5.) Faith without virtue would soon languish and die, because without virtue there is no purity. Without purity, there is no moral strength. Without moral strength, there is no spirituality, and without spirituality, there is no salvation in God's kingdom. In short, faith without the works of virtue is dead belief. (See James 2:14, 17, 22.) But faith strengthened through virtuous behavior leads to spirituality and inspired knowledge. (See 2 Pet. 1:8.)

The great sins against life and proper procreation grossly deprive others or ourselves of physical, emotional, or spiritual development. A commitment toward proper moral behavior, on the other hand, can greatly enhance these facets of life. Indeed, only in marriage can a stable hierarchy of enduring physical satisfaction, emotional security, and spiritual unity be experienced through sexual relations.

When sex is viewed as an end in itself for physical gratification, having sex with different partners and experimenting with sexual "techniques" are the surest routes to emotional fragmentation and even sexual dysfunction, since prowess and performance become a preoccupation and source of anxiety. We have no way of knowing the general level of sexual satisfaction in former times when sex was largely monogamous and, thankfully, private. What we can measure *since* the sexual revolution, however, are the reported cases of sexual deviancy and the increased needs for counseling of sexual problems.

Some specialists in "sexual therapy" provide helpful counseling, while others, either through ignorance or shortsightedness, provide suggestions that incorporate no moral values at all. LDS Social Services can recommend discreet, experienced, value-oriented counselors. Some members receive valuable help from their bishops. Others seek their own "cure," learning to appreciate the emotional security of marriage as the basis for sexual satisfaction. Fortunately, many so-called experts on "sexuality" are beginning to recognize that premarital sexual experiences are no guarantee for later, good sexual adjustments in marriage. In fact, the more frequent and transitory the earlier sexual experiences, the more challenging and difficult it becomes to establish a long-lasting intimate relationship.[8]

There is nothing so mysterious about the experience of sex that two young, chaste people cannot sufficiently learn together for themselves in the love and security of marriage. Parents and education can teach the facts of life, but the loving bonds of marriage provide the beneficial context for the actual experience. Mutual marital commitment eliminates the pressure of performance found with "one-night stands." Instead, the couple have their entire married life to grow together in sexual intimacy. The uniqueness, or even "thrill" of this experience, is that their sexual relationship is their own, not shared previously by anyone else. For those who have erred earlier, a genuine, long-term commitment to faithfulness in marriage will lead to a purity in heart and a righteousness in behavior. From this bond of physical and emotional fidelity comes a security and trust in the marriage from which can grow the highest spiritual fulfillment as well.

SPIRITUAL BONDING OF A PROPER, VIRTUOUS RELATIONSHIP

Only those who understand and honor the eternal, procreative purpose of sexual union can know sex as the spiritual experience that it was ordained to be by the Great Creator himself. Sexual relations are a fundamental part of the marriage covenant, which would not be complete without them. To be "one flesh" as husband and wife is a divinely or-dained act that serves as an expression of love as long as it is not abused. As stated in the *Encyclopedia of Mormonism,* "This oneness is as fun-damental a purpose of marital relations as is procreation."[9]

The Lord did not intend that sex be a purely physical act. President Kimball stated that the principal purpose of the union of husband and wife is to bring children into the world. He continued, "Sex experiences were never intended by the Lord to be a mere plaything or merely to satisfy passions and lusts. We know of no directive from the Lord that proper sex experience between husbands and wives need be limited to-tally to the procreation effort, but we find much evidence from Adam until now that no provision was ever made by the Lord for indiscriminate sex."[10] A proper physical union builds emotional and spiritual unity. As one Mormon scholar explained, "Physical intimacy is a blessing to mar-ried couples when it is an expression of their mutual benevolence and commitment to each other's well-being, an affirmation of their striving to be emotionally and spiritually one."[11]

Celestial marriage and its sanctioned sexual relations also symbolize heavenly unity and actualize the purpose of creation: "From the begin-ning of creation God made them male and female. For this cause shall a man leave his father and mother, and cleave to his wife and they twain shall be one flesh: so then they are no more twain, but one flesh. What therefore God hath joined together, let not man put asunder." (Mark 10:6–9.) The Savior speaks symbolically here, since a husband and wife obviously do not literally become one individual upon marriage. Instead, the sexual union of their flesh symbolizes spiritual unity, which can ac-tually be achieved because the God who made them has joined them together eternally. We therefore speak about unity between not two, but three entities. As the husband and wife maintain their bonds of matri-mony and draw closer to each other, they also grow closer to God, becoming more like him.

The unity between husband, wife, and God is actualized in the flesh by the birth of children, who have spirits created by God and bodies created by their earthly parents. This is one way that a man and his wife literally become "one flesh" — through the sexual consummation of their marriage and the procreation of children together with God.

The divine purpose of the law of chastity does not restrict or diminish the physical pleasure of sexual relations, but rather enhances it through added emotional and spiritual dimensions. If we relentlessly crave and pursue purely physical gratification through sex, we live like animals operating on instinct. But by disciplining our spirits to be master over physical desires, we attune ourselves to the Holy Spirit and thereby are able to focus more on the needs of our mates. If our flesh is subdued, the Spirit can enrich and inspire all aspects of our lives.

VIRTUE LEADS TO STRENGTH

The Middle English (*vertu*) and earlier Latin (*virtus*) roots for *virtue* mean strength, that is, having and exhibiting strength and courage. One contemporary meaning in Webster's dictionary states that virtue is having "effective power or force," that is, "efficacy; especially, the ability to heal or strengthen."[12] Pure virtue brings us strength in at least five primary areas of our lives: physical, emotional, mental, moral, and spiritual.

Physically, a chaste and virtuous life by both marriage partners not only avoids the health dangers of AIDS and other diseases, but it also instills patterns of physical self-discipline that carry over into marriage and other social relationships. Self-control by both partners is just as important and yet, ironically, may be more challenging after marriage. Although one is married, one cannot demand or expect the other spouse always to be ready or willing to engage in intimate behavior. Patience developed through sensitivity and mutual consideration becomes a valuable commodity after marriage. Virtuous self-control, patience, and physical integrity also enhance one's human associations outside the marriage. They provide effective barriers against child abuse and workplace indiscretions. They help ensure that private and public behavior remain consistent and harmonious. Virtuous intentions and acts not only encourage a positive, beneficial physical relationship for both partners, they also enrich society.

Sexuality also has important emotional dimensions. As a whole, women tend to be especially sensitive to the emotional values derived from a proper sexual relationship. Sensitive people recognize sex as more than a physical, animal act. They appreciate that mutual respect and pure motives enhance the emotional intimacy. Individuals, especially young people, strengthen their emotional integrity as they take control over their lives and find the courage to avoid peer pressure to engage in pre- or extramarital sex. Emotional power grows as dignity and respect are shared between men and women. A proper sexual relationship conducted by the Lord's standards helps people feel better about themselves and leads to emotional stability and greater self-worth, which, in turn, make them into better family and society members.

Mentally, the importance of pure thoughts is both obvious and subtle. Acts of sexual deviancy, such as rape or child abuse, are almost always (if not always) preceded by "thinking them out" in the aggressor's mind. If any such thoughts of immoral acts were quickly avoided, the possibility for such acts would be blocked. Thus we see the importance of following the modern prophets' advice to avoid movies, videos, music, magazines, photos, and other media with sexually inappropriate or suggestive content. We cannot begin to realize the many subtle influences that improper thoughts can have on the relationships between men and women and between adults and youth. A virtuous person will be one with clean thoughts.

The moral strengths and values of virtue and chastity are very apparent. The most common dictionary meanings for *virtue* emphasize its moral dimensions: a general moral goodness, uprightness, morality, or a good or meritorious moral quality.[13] Living a virtuous life strengthens one's sense of what is right and good in sexual behavior, in business dealings, and in neighborhood and community associations. Virtuous people are committed to the sanctity of life, and they respect God's counsel on how life is to be conceived, protected, and nurtured. They respect their own procreative abilities, the physical sensations, limitations and handicaps of the body, and the intimate feelings of others. They would rather die or suffer themselves than deliberately injure another person. They would no more impose their physical desires on another than beat up a person or steal from another. Their moral values are strong and grow even stronger as they live the law of chastity.

The spiritual strengths of virtue become especially obvious after one has lost them following a transgression against the law of chastity. Moral impurity leads to an immediate loss of the companionship of the Holy Spirit, since he cannot abide in an impure person. (See 1 Cor. 3:16–17; Alma 7:21.) The prophets have always reminded us that the Lord views unchastity as a grievous sin, even the "most abominable above all sins save it be the shedding of innocent blood or denying the Holy Ghost." (Alma 39:5.) One who thinks continuously on physical gratification becomes carnally minded and an enemy to God. (See Mosiah 3:19; 2 Ne. 9:39.)

On the other hand, virtuous behavior leads to spiritual growth (see 2 Pet. 1:5), worthiness to be the Lord's servants in his temple (see Isa. 52:11), and the purity required of all in God's kingdom (see 1 Ne. 10:21). Moroni summarizes ancient prophetic teachings about chastity as he tells us to be wise during our sojourn on earth and to discard uncleanliness. He counsels to avoid consuming our mortality upon our lusts, but instead to seek strength in avoiding temptation so that we can "serve the true and living God." (Morm. 9:28.) A modern prophet has extolled the values of virtue in the following words: "There is nothing more beautiful than virtue. There is no strength that is greater than the strength of virtue. There is no other nobility equal to the nobility of virtue. There is no quality so becoming, no attire so attractive."[14] Virtue brings a variety of strengths into our lives as we obey the law of chastity. Chaste marriage partners are able to expand their interrelationship through the strong bonds of trust, love, and communication.

BUILDING T.L.C. INTO A RELATIONSHIP

Any developing courtship and every effective social relationship, particularly those worthy of the eternities, must develop some "TLC." The initials "TLC" usually stand for "Tender Loving Care," although each initial also represents an essential element in any lasting human affiliation: T = Trust, L = Love, and C = Communication.

TRUST

Trust provides the important foundation in any strong relationship. President McKay often quoted a Scottish poet who said that it is better to be trusted than to be loved. God loves us all with a never-ending, supreme love, but he does not trust us all equally. Staying absolutely true to the law of chastity, that is, never having any sexual relations with anyone other than a marriage partner, solidifies the bonds of trust in a marriage and demonstrates the trustworthiness of a person in other areas of human behavior.

Only those who earn God's trust by obedience to his commandments will be trusted with the choicest blessings of the gospel and the priesthood. Pivotal opportunities for service, temple ordinances, missionary work, or parenthood are entrusted to some as a sacred responsibility. As we are reliable in some things, such as marriage fidelity, then the Lord can bless us in other dimensions of our lives. (See Luke 19:17.) Trustworthiness will enrich our lives if it is the foundation in all our relationships.

LOVE

Love is the bonding power of human relations and should be the glue in every courtship, marriage, family, and social relationship. Although we cannot trust all people, we are commanded to love everyone. Love rather than lust, and affection rather than passion should be the ruling emotions in a strong relationship. The spirit of the law of chastity also requires that we have no lust or sexual yearnings for anyone outside our marriage. (See Matt. 5:27–28.) Betraying this emotional level of fidelity usually precedes the actual physical breaking of the law of chastity.

Love has great power to heal emotional wounds, especially if trust can be built up and open communication encouraged. For instance, one would think that in cases of adultery, the betrayal would completely destroy the love between married couples. However, it is amazing how often the betrayer still professes love for the betrayed, and the betrayed partner will still maintain some love for the betrayer, although trust has been lost. Unless both partners enrich and strengthen their love and trust, their marriage will be almost impossible to salvage. If trust is the foundation of a strong relationship, then love represents the walls and pillars upon which lasting associations are built.

COMMUNICATION

Communication between marriage partners is vitally important.[15] Without communication, each person has to learn everything by himself or herself and has to base decisions on guesswork. No marriage relationship will survive for long without at least some forms of personal communication. Effective communication between a man and woman should include at least three characteristics: it should be open, sincere, and supportive. It should be open so that simple, clear messages can be given and understood. Verbal rather than nonverbal communication is usually more effective in open communication. Sincerity demonstrates the genuineness of a relationship and is usually indicated through the tone of verbal communication and the eye contact of nonverbal communication. Effective communication should build up the other person and enhance mutual rapport; verbal abuse has no place in productive associations. Even negative comments, although based in fact, can be destructive, especially when repeated often. Instead, patience and silence are preferable, with supportive comments being even more preferable.

The messages communicated one to another should reinforce the bonds of trust and love between the individuals. In addition, chaste behavior improves the communication and inspiration channels of both partners with Heavenly Father, who then, through clear promptings of his Holy Spirit, is able to guide the marriage and family. Sensitive, enlightened, and effective communication strengthens any relationship. Inspirational communication is like a door or window that allows valuable blessings and light to enter the association.

By encouraging "TLC" in our marriage, family, and social relations, we include both "tender, loving care" and the essential elements of trust, love, and communication. As we develop our interpersonal associations, we should particularly remember the importance of these principles in our dealings with Heavenly Father. He loves us and knows the very best way for a man and woman to have a meaningful, satisfying, pleasurable, and eternal marriage—by building a pure and loving relationship. We need to trust God when he commands us about chastity. We must follow his directions to attain true marital bliss. His special blessings upon a marriage and family can be like the roof of a strong house—it provides shelter and protection. If a marriage has a strong foundation of trust and faith, solid walls of love, clear windows of communication, and the sheltering roof of the Lord's protection, the winds and rains of earthly disturbances will not bring that relationship down. It is built for the eternities.

In summary, we should remember that *life is sacred, and God has protected procreation through the law of CHASTITY, which teaches self-mastery, enhances physical love, strengthens emotional relationships, and empowers spiritual gifts.* By living pure, chaste lives, we not only keep our bodies in a clean state, but also enrich the moral environment and enhance the joyful experiences of earth life. We purify our souls for richer spiritual experiences now, and we also enhance our preparations for the celestial eternity with our Father in Heaven. The law of chastity and a pure life edifies all Latter-day Saints as they build faithful trust, develop energizing love, maintain open communication with each other, and receive God's divine assistance in their interpersonal relationships. Purity in the physical realm leads to pureness in the emotional, moral, and spiritual dimensions of our existence. Purity increases our effectiveness as we progress on the path toward our celestial future.[16]

For further study, refer to the following entries:

TG	BD	*EM*
Adulterer, Adultery	Adultery	Adultery
Body, Sanctity of		Chastity, Law of
Chastity, Chaste		Homosexuality
Cleanliness		Modesty
Fornication		Pornography
Modesty		Premarital Sex
Purity, Pure		Sex Education
Virtue, Virtuous		Sexuality

CHAPTER 27

SOME WORDS OF WISDOM

Any automobile driver is wise enough to know that one does not put water in the gas tank when the car has run out of gas. However, a few people in some primitive, underdeveloped societies might not be so smart. If they had observed a driver pouring some fluid into the gas tank so the engine could run, they might assume that any liquid, even dirty water, could do the job. A little education and experience would quickly enlighten them as to the wise ways to keep the engine properly fueled so that the quality and length of its performance can be improved.

In a similar vein, our bodies are like engines because they constantly need fuel (food) in order to function. A wise Heavenly Father has known from the beginning the proper ways for humans to feed and care for their physical bodies so that they can function properly for a long period of time. Because of his wisdom and love for his children, Heavenly Father has occasionally directed the prophets with words of counsel and commandment on special health codes. The ancient Israelites were given certain laws of sanitation and were forbidden to eat certain meats, particularly those that would readily spoil or those from possibly diseased animals. God did not tell the people the reasons for these injunctions; he mentioned nothing about bacteria, the dangers of unrefrigerated meats, or other information about why his health commandments were necessary. He simply told the Israelites what they were to do. They then needed to act in faith to gain the benefits of better health and the knowledge that they were doing what the prophets had told them.

A HEALTH CODE FOR TODAY — THE WORD OF WISDOM

God has also shared his wisdom concerning health laws with his prophets in these modern times. People who know little else about Mormons know that we subscribe to a health code that prohibits smoking tobacco and drinking alcohol, coffee, and tea. The Word of Wisdom is one of our best-known hallmarks because, until recently, most people in the Western world regularly used one or more of these substances with little or no negative social stigma. Times truly have changed, however, as the ill physical, mental, and societal effects of tobacco and alcohol, in particular, have been revealed by medical science. Additionally, the dietary practices encouraged by the Word of Wisdom are now confirmed as positive ways to ward off disease and promote better physical and mental health. The Word of Wisdom, however, is more than just good common sense. Increased physical health enlarges our spiritual capacity as well, bringing blessings that endure beyond mortality.

The Word of Wisdom is a revelation given through Joseph Smith the prophet in 1833. He and his wife Emma had been slightly disturbed at the tobacco uses of the brethren in their meetings, particularly the spittoons used with their chewing tobacco. Pondering on the matter, he inquired of the Lord and received the revelation now recorded in Section 89 of the Doctrine and Covenants. Given first as a guideline for the Latter-day Saints, it was enacted by later prophets as a commandment expected of all Church members.

This health code contains two elements of instruction: first, negative prohibitions against certain substances, and second, positive admonitions for special foods. The prohibited substances are alcoholic beverages, tobacco taken into the body in any form, and coffee and tea, particularly when taken hot. The encouraged foods include wholesome herbs, fruits, and vegetables (especially when fresh), meat (to be used sparingly), mild drinks, and above all, the various grains, especially wheat. The revelation concludes with promises of various physical, mental, and spiritual blessings.

MEDICAL SCIENCE CONFIRMS MODERN REVELATION

During the time of Joseph Smith and long afterward, tobacco, coffee, and tea were commonly used by the general populace with few clues that they might be harmful drugs. They had a few medical facts and social observations concerning some dangerous effects of alcohol, but they did not yet know the dangers of smoking or the substances found in coffee or tea. Many generations of Latter-day Saints abstained from them, following the admonitions of the Word of Wisdom as an act of faith and obedience. When pressed by nonmember associates as to why they were abstaining from the prohibited substances in the Word of Wisdom, many Mormons simply had to reply, "We believe this is a commandment from God." They had no scientific knowledge to justify the unorthodox behavior that set them apart from most people of the world.

Only in the 1960s, when the first U.S. Surgeon General's reports appeared, did the health risks of smoking become public knowledge. Indeed, until the 1970s, advertising promoted smoking as sexy and sophisticated, and it enjoyed general acceptance among most people. Since then, however, awareness of the dangers of smoking has steadily increased as more medical proof of its relationship to severe lung and heart disease has surfaced. Along with that, nonsmokers have been more vocal about the annoyance of tobacco smoke and their right to clean air, leading to laws that prohibit smoking in public settings. Current public opinion surveys show that some nonsmokers even contemptuously view smokers as people who lack the self-control to break a foolish, nasty habit.

Nondrinkers hope that drinking alcohol will soon acquire the same social stigma, for its ill effects to individuals and society are even worse than those related to smoking. Not only does alcohol physically damage various body organs, but its intoxicating effects cause more societal problems than any other chemical substance. Alcohol is the number-one cause of absenteeism and decreased productivity among workers. It is directly associated with almost half of all fatal automobile accidents and, along with narcotic drugs, up to 75 percent of all violent crimes.[1] Though the social drinker is not now frowned upon as much as the smoker, educated people are aware of the wasteful and tragic effects of alcohol abuse and no longer consider the nondrinker prudish or unsophisticated. Indeed, they respect those who can abstain from any form of drug dependency or abuse.

Even attitudes toward coffee and tea, traditional food staples for many people, have been changed by medical research. Normally, coffee, tea, and even many soft drinks contain caffeine, an addictive stimulant that upsets body metabolism and weakens the heart. Public awareness of the hazards of stimulants has caused a change in habits and created a demand for decaffeinated coffee, tea, and soft drinks, all of which are now commonplace.

Thus, in the century and a half since the Word of Wisdom was first given, public knowledge and behavior concerning its prohibited substances have improved dramatically. Latter-day Saints can add to their faith the knowledge that God's wisdom exceeds the understanding of mortals. He did not give the Word of Wisdom simply to test the faithful obedience of the Saints, but, as the name implies, to share divine wisdom for a healthy life-style. Reckless is the individual and foolish the Mormon who does not heed the increasing body of knowledge demonstrating the valuable counsel of the Word of Wisdom.

THE RISKS OF ALCOHOL, TOBACCO, COFFEE, AND TEA

If the Word of Wisdom was obeyed by everyone, unnecessary disease and suffering would be avoided, and people would live longer, healthier lives. Many individuals already appreciate that abstaining from alcohol and tobacco is beneficial to the body, and they recognize the societal ills suffered through alcohol and drug abuse. They not only abstain from dangerous substances, but they also educate and encourage others to do the same. Other people may not yet be aware of the many risks associated with the use of the elements prohibited in the Word of Wisdom. The following information is far from exhaustive, but it highlights some major negative effects of these substances, as well as of other dangerous, illegal drugs.

ALCOHOL

The Word of Wisdom prohibits the use of "wine and strong drink." This means that any alcoholic beverage should not be consumed. The effects of alcohol consumption are well-documented. Alcohol abuse afflicts the individual human body and society at large. First, alcohol causes health problems that may lead to death. Most cases of cirrhosis of the liver are caused by alcohol consumption. This disease "is among the ten leading causes of death by disease in the United States."[2] A recent study has linked moderate drinking to increased risk of developing breast cancer in women.[3] Drinking while pregnant can have devastating effects on the unborn child, who can be born with a condition known as fetal alcohol syndrome. This condition has many complications, including mental retardation. A new study has identified a link between drinking while pregnant and lower I.Q. scores of the children born to drinking mothers.[4]

Alcohol abuse also weakens the mind and harms society. The side effects of drinking also impair the nervous system. People under the influence of alcohol lose body coordination and the ability to think clearly. The acts that follow can injure themselves and many others. For example, the problem of drunk driving is an epidemic in many countries. In the United States, almost 40 percent of all automobile accidents are caused by intoxicated drivers. Every twenty-three minutes, someone dies in America as a result of drunk driving.[5] This means that about twenty-five thousand people die yearly in accidents caused by intoxicated drivers.[6] More than five hundred thousand people suffer painful and sometimes permanent injury every year in these accidents, and billions of dollars in economic losses are generated each year as a result.[7]

In addition, alcohol is associated with half of the crimes committed in the United States. It is even more prevalent in violent crimes, such as rape and murder. For example, almost 75 percent of all murders are committed by individuals who have been drinking.[8] Similar disastrous consequences follow alcohol consumption and abuse throughout the world. The addictive nature of alcohol also ruins lives, not only of the individual who is alcohol-dependent, but also of those in the family, or others close to the person. Jobs are lost, families are divided, and society is weakened as alcoholics cease being productive members of society and become dependent upon others for their physical and financial welfare. For all of these reasons, the Word of Wisdom's prohibition of strong drink is clearly justified.

Ironically, the primary products that are distilled to form alcoholic beverages, such as grain, potatoes, grapes, and so on are by themselves healthy, valuable foods. If the amount of these products manufactured into alcohol were processed into food items, many of the hungry masses of the world could be fed. Instead, alcohol destroys lives, devastates families, and weakens the social fiber. Such application is an unwise use of our food resources and a further demonstration that following God's counsel will greatly benefit mankind.

TOBACCO

Another harmful substance prohibited in the Word of Wisdom is tobacco. The most common use of tobacco is cigarette smoking. Cigarette smoke contains more than four thousand chemicals, many of which are toxic or harmful.[9] One of these substances, nicotine, has been recently reported by the surgeon general to be as addictive as cocaine or heroin.[10] Each year, more than three hundred thousand Americans die from diseases caused by cigarette smoking. The United States Department of Health and Human Services has called this problem "the most devastating epidemic of disease and premature death this country has ever experienced."[11] Medical costs associated with these problems total an estimated twenty-three billion dollars per year, and thirty billion more is lost to society due to illness and premature death.[12] Secondhand effects of tobacco are especially harmful to sick or unborn children. Pregnant women who smoke endanger their unborn children through increased risk of miscarriage, stillbirth, preterm births, and low birth weight. After birth, babies of parents who smoke have increased risks of contracting bronchitis and pneumonia.[13]

The Lord's admonition against using tobacco is certainly something that the world would benefit from obeying. Approximately two and a half million people die each year from tobacco use throughout the earth.[14] The Word of Wisdom stands as a prophetic warning of this health disaster in the world.

HOT DRINKS

The Word of Wisdom counsels against drinking "hot drinks," which have been identified by early Church leaders as coffee and tea.[15] "Tea" refers to the standard tea derived from the tea plant, sometimes called black tea or green tea. The Word of Wisdom has not been interpreted as proscribing herbal teas, stating that "all wholesome herbs God hath ordained for the constitution, nature, and use of man."[16] (D&C 89:10.) Coffee refers to drinks derived from the coffee bean.

Since the revelation containing the Word of Wisdom was given, caffeine, acids, and other potentially dangerous substances have been discovered in coffee and tea. The primary chemical in coffee and non-herbal teas that has generated health concerns is caffeine, an alkaloid stimulant. Caffeine has a number of undesirable effects on the body, and most reports on the effects of caffeine done in the last several years have been negative.[17] Caffeine is a cerebral and cardiovascular stimulant that can sometimes be addictive and that causes anxiety, irritability, unsteadiness, insomnia, restlessness, diarrhea, stomach pains, and headaches.[18] A recent study indicates that women who drink more than one cup of coffee per day or ingest an equivalent amount of caffeine from another source, are half as likely to get pregnant.[19] Other studies "have implicated caffeine in a variety of ills, including heart disease, fibrocystic disease, birth defects, miscarriages, cancer, and ulcers."[20] Since caffeine is also found in other food products, such as chocolate and some soft drinks, wisdom would suggest, at most, only limited or moderate consumption of these items.

Of course, caffeine is probably not the only health reason why we should not drink coffee and tea. A recent study has linked coffee drinking to increased risks of developing pancreatic cancer, but caffeine may not be the cause, because tea drinkers do not have this increased risk.[21] Researchers are still finding new ways that tobacco, alcohol, coffee, and tea can be harmful to us. We should not assume that we are presently able to identify all of the harmful substances in alcoholic beverages, tobacco, coffee, and tea, nor should we assume that we understand the full extent of the health problems caused by these items. Maybe with coffee and tea, more than with the other prohibited substances of the Word of Wisdom, Latter-day Saints still need to exercise faithful obedience to God's law without yet knowing all the reasons why. Spiritually, they will always be blessed for obedience, and physically, they will be rewarded in ways yet unknown.

DRUG ABUSE

The abuse of either prescription medications or "street drugs" is not mentioned in the Word of Wisdom, but Church leaders have spoken out against it on many occasions. They have made it clear that drug abuse is not pleasing to the Lord and that it should not be indulged in by any member of the Church. President Kimball warned, "We hope our people will eliminate from their lives all kinds of drugs so far as possible. Too many depend upon drugs as tranquilizers and sleep helps, which is not always necessary. Certainly numerous young people have been damaged or destroyed by the use of marijuana and other deadly drugs. We deplore such."[22]

Cocaine is one such abused and illegal drug in America. Its use has reached epidemic proportions. There are an estimated six million current users in the United States, and Americans spend more than fifty billion dollars each year to purchase it.[23] It has been called "the most addictive substance known to man."[24] Like alcohol and any other drug, it damages both the body and society. Cocaine has a variety of negative health effects on the body. These effects include brain seizures and erratic heartbeat (both of which can kill the victim), psychosis, panic attacks, and depression.[25] Using cocaine while pregnant greatly increases the risk of miscarriage. Babies can be born in an agonizing state of withdrawal that lasts up to four weeks, and they have greater than normal rates of respiratory and kidney problems and sudden infant death syndrome.[26] Undoubtedly, as more research is done and this problem persists, researchers will continue to find more negative effects of cocaine use.

Increases in cocaine trafficking have increased crime rates as well. Homicide rates in America's larger cities are increasing drastically, and police departments put the blame on cocaine.[27] Cocaine addiction can also ruin lives as individuals sacrifice their possessions and their jobs, and leave their families to support their dependency.[28]

The abuse of any drug is not pleasing to the Lord. The effects of so doing are obviously not conducive to good living. Drug abuse also harms an individual's spiritual health. It frequently results in addiction, limiting personal freedom as the individual desperately seeks to feed the habit. Mormons who have become drug addicts need counseling help from Church leaders, such as bishops, and from trained professionals, such as therapists in LDS Social Services, to help them overcome their addiction. All Latter-day Saints should be especially committed to avoiding any drug abuse in their own lives, in keeping with the spirit of the Word of Wisdom. They should also educate, counsel, and encourage others, both within and without the Church, to avoid all dangerous substances. They should also share the positive admonitions of the Word of Wisdom concerning certain wholesome foods.

The Benefits of Healthy Foods

The majority of verses in the Word of Wisdom (D&C 89) go beyond a simple but accurate guide that warns us against harmful substances.

They contain a plan for healthy, moderate eating and drinking habits. The Lord did not intend this counsel to be too difficult for anyone. In verse three, as a part of the introduction to the Word of Wisdom, the Lord states that his counsel is given as "a principle with promise" and it is "adapted to the capacity of the weak, and the weakest of all saints."

After warning against the prohibited substances, the Lord shares positive admonitions about a variety of foods. In verse ten, he states that "all wholesome herbs" are designed to be used by us for food, and some are specifically mentioned in the succeeding verses. Verse eleven contains the admonition to eat fruits and vegetables "in the season," or while they are fresh from the harvest. They are to be used with thanksgiving and prudence, or in other words, wisely and with temperance. Implicitly stated here is a warning against overindulgence and gluttony. This counsel given in 1833 has been verified. Scientific knowledge has since demonstrated the vitamin and mineral value of fresh foods. Also, any food, if taken in excess, can be harmful to the body.

Verses twelve through fifteen contain information about eating meat. The Lord makes it clear that it is perfectly acceptable to eat meat, which he has "ordained for the use of man." But he counsels that meat should be eaten with thanksgiving and that it should be used sparingly. Although fish is not mentioned, the Lord indicates that the meat of beasts and fowls should be especially reserved for "times of winter, or of cold, or famine." (V. 13.) Again in verse fifteen, this advice is repeated, with the addition that the flesh of wild animals is to be used only "in times of famine and excess of hunger." Medical and health specialists have confirmed the wisdom of this counsel. They admonish a limited intake of red meats and warn against the dangers of fats and cholesterol. In addition, large amounts of land and food resources are needed to feed animals marketed for human consumption. Meat, especially red meat, is usually an expensive source of human food.

The use of grains for food as the "staff of life" is the topic of verses fourteen, sixteen, and seventeen. The Lord has ordained all grains for the consumption of man and animals, including domesticated livestock (beasts of the field) and wild birds and animals. Various grains have particular value to man and the different animals. Wheat is singled out as having special use for humans. However, these guidelines are not a rigid rule. Note that Joseph Smith mentioned only those grains that were common to his time and place. Rice and millet are not mentioned, although they are primary food sources for great numbers of people in other areas of the world. The revelation covers this by saying that "all grain is good for the food of man" (v. 16) and may be used "for mild drinks" for humans (v. 17).

The latest nutritional discoveries have confirmed that "we are what we eat," and that the more whole grains and fresh foods we consume in their natural state the better. Processed foods with heavy additives, such as salt, dyes, preservatives, and refined sugar, are now widely known to be nutritionally inferior to their natural counterparts and have contributed to the United States' high cancer rate in the digestive organs. Knowing the nature of man's physical body that he created, the Lord gave counsel over 150 years ago that might be amplified as follows: "Verily I say unto you, all *wholesome* [natural] *herbs* [plants, especially fruits, vegetables, legumes, grains, and so forth] God hath ordained for the constitution, nature, and use of man—every herb *in the season thereof* [fresh] and every *fruit* [including seeds, nuts, and so on] in the season thereof; all these to be used with prudence and thanksgiving." (D&C 89:10–11; italics added.)

Furthermore, while meat has traditionally been at the center of most American dinners, we now know that red meat often contains too much cholesterol and contributes to obesity as well. Many essential proteins found in meat can be taken from other sources both higher in natural fiber and lower in fat, particularly whole grains: "Yea, the *flesh* also of beasts and of the fowls of the air, I, the Lord, have ordained for the use of man with thanksgiving; nevertheless they are *to be used sparingly;* . . . All *grain* is ordained for the use of man and of beasts, *to be the staff of life.*" (89:12, 14; italics added.) From just these few verses of scripture, we can see that all the nutritional knowledge discovered scientifically in the last decades was known in a simplified, accurate format by revelation among the Latter-day Saints for more than one-and-a-half centuries.

Any noble philosophy or movement needs a group of dedicated activists to serve as a vanguard if it is going to succeed throughout the world. Latter-day Saints can help fulfill this role and bring wiser health patterns into the world as they share the principles of the Word of Wisdom. People do not have to believe in God or believe that he has given health instructions to a prophet, Joseph Smith, in order to accept and benefit from the admonitions found in the Word of Wisdom. Its true and valuable principles will bless all families on earth if they will just learn and apply them.

In order to obtain and share these great blessings, we must do more than abstain from alcohol and tobacco. We must be wise and moderate in everything that we eat and drink, according to the instructions given. By implication, we should do everything that we can to take care of our bodies. This is sometimes called the "spirit of the Word of Wisdom," which is simply the logical extension of the admonition in Section 89 to all areas of bodily care. These areas include getting enough sleep, exercising, and avoiding drug dependency and any other habit that is detrimental to our health and well-being.

Other Wise Health Practices

The wealth of wisdom contained in this revelation on diet, however, is not all inclusive. The Lord himself stated that the information was "adapted to the capacity of the weak and the weakest of all saints." (89:3.) For example, regular excrcise, now proven essential for sound health, was not even mentioned. Perhaps this is because weak people have a hard time tolerating exercise. Or, exercise may not have been mentioned because the people of Joseph Smith's time were agricultural and much more physically active. Then, too, the revelation was originally "sent [as] greeting; not by commandment or constraint." (89:2.) Simple compliance with it would have not only pleased the Lord, but also resulted in increased knowledge and other blessings promised at the end of the revelation.

Unfortunately, many Saints in the 1830s and 1840s were not wise enough to follow these revealed health guidelines. Later prophets gave stronger admonitions about observing the Word of Wisdom until 1851, when, under the administration of President Brigham Young, he had the Saints ratify it as a commandment. Similar action was taken again in 1908 under the administration of President Joseph F. Smith and it has been "repeated on several occasions."[29] Compliance with prohibitions concerning tobacco, alcohol, coffee, and tea has become mandatory for receiving a temple recommend, serving as a missionary, or serving in leadership callings. Today, the Word of Wisdom's prohibitions should be easier to follow because they fit more readily into accepted LDS social custom.

The other dietary guidelines concerning the consumption of herbs, fruits, meats, and grains still remain a matter of personal interpretation, adaptability, and accountability. For example, some people may be allergic to corn, cow's milk, or other food products that are healthy for most people. Individuals so affected need to follow the wisdom of medical counsel and modify their food intake accordingly. Thus, their "word of wisdom" may need to be a little different than that practiced by other family members.

Following the basic guidelines will provide the basic nutritional needs for most people. They also need to recognize other physical and mental health needs so they can live a full, productive life. The living and working environment has also changed over the past century, and new health practices should be sought and adapted for individual needs. Some practices to consider could include diet, exercise, and hygiene.

DIETING

Bookstores usually carry a broad selection of cookbooks, which provide menus and encouragement for eating a great variety of foods from all over the world. Ironically, another popular section in most bookstores is a growing collection of diet books, which promote a variety of programs to restrict our food intake. Bodily appetite and human nature being what they are, apparently many of us swing back and forth between indulgence and abstinence. This pattern of self-imposed feast and famine is disruptive to our health and contrary to the essence of the term "diet," which comes from the Greek root *diaitan,* meaning "to lead one's life" or "a regimen or mode of life."

A true diet is not a temporary means to lose weight, but a regular pattern of eating, drinking, and exercise that promotes long-term health. Each individual needs to prescribe a food regimen according to age, body size, activity level, family history, and other variables. Balance, moderation, and discipline are key terms in any diet. Balance provides the essential nutrients (proteins, carbohydrates, vitamins, minerals, and fats) that our body needs to properly function. Moderation in all things encompasses the spirit of the entire Word of Wisdom. Discipline insures that the necessary balance and moderation are maintained. Normal body weight is maintained when a person balances the intake of calories and the expenditure of energy. Healthy body tone is maintained when a person steadily monitors his or her health and avoids the roller-coaster patterns of excess and negligence. When we control our appetites, our spirit has authority over our body, and we are strengthened physically, emotionally, and spiritually.

Exercise

Because of indoor jobs and many modern conveniences, most people do not get as much exercise as their ancestors did when the Word of Wisdom was revealed. Modern technology does allow us more free time than our predecessors had to give back to our bodies what technology took from them—physical exertion and activity. Modern research has confirmed that regular physical exercise benefits the body and mind in many ways. It increases strength and stamina, improves overall health, relieves stress, and helps keep the mind alert. Information about various exercise plans can be found in books and through fitness classes.

The key is to find a plan that works and is enjoyable. Those who have not been physically active should seek their doctor's advice and start with moderation. The general recommendation is to exercise three times a week for thirty to forty-five minutes each session. A total workout program includes stretching movements to maintain joint mobility and flexibility, strengthening exercises to maintain body mass and muscle tone, and cardiovascular activities to maintain heart and lung vitality. Exercising regularly and following general age and fitness guidelines are important. A wise exercise program provides many valuable physical and emotional benefits.[30]

Physical and Dental Hygiene

Good physical and dental hygiene is a basic element of preventive medicine that helps us avoid sickness and disease. Care for the body includes regular bathing and grooming. Safe and sanitary conditions should prevail in the home and at the workplace. Appropriate vaccinations, eye and medical exams, and good health habits will help any person interested in staying healthy. A successful program of dental hygiene strives to prevent dental caries and periodontal disease through regular tooth brushing and flossing, proper eating habits, the use of fluoride or other preventive measures for dental decay, and periodic visits to the dentist. Good hygiene improves body health and enhances our social relations with other people.

Other beneficial health measures could include such items as learning basic first aid and CPR, mastering stress management,[31] encouraging drug prevention and rehabilitation programs, and maintaining positive mental health practices. As we apply the principles of health wisdom learned through inspiration and the study of many interrelated disciplines, we should enjoy longer, healthier lives.

A PRINCIPLE WITH FOUR PROMISES

Though the Word of Wisdom was given specifically to show "the will of God in the *temporal* salvation of all saints in the last days" (D&C 89:2; italics added), it is not just temporal counsel. It is part of the total plan of salvation for the body and spirit, or soul, of man. The body is a physical tabernacle for the spirit. (See 1 Cor. 3:16; D&C 88:15; 93:35.) Although any unbeliever with sound health practices will have better physical health than he would otherwise, a faithful person can enjoy spiritual as well as physical rewards. The physical and spiritual promises of the Word of Wisdom are given to the Saints who not only "remember to keep and do these sayings," but also continue "walking in obedience to the commandments" in general. (D&C 89:18.)

Thus, LDS physical education teacher Bert L. Fairbanks writes: "You can't be healthy if you're in turmoil because of arguments with people close to you. . . . You can't be healthy if you are so worried about worldly problems that you are constantly tense. To be completely healthy, your whole life must be tuned to the Lord's pattern, both temporally and spiritually."[32] The idea of unified physical and spiritual health was also foreshadowed in a revelation received by Joseph Smith just two months before receiving the Word of Wisdom. Note how spiritual and temporal counsel are randomly mixed: "Cease to be idle; cease to be unclean; cease to find fault one with another; cease to sleep longer than is needful; retire to thy bed early, that ye may not be weary; arise early, that your bodies and your minds may be invigorated. And above all things, clothe yourselves with the bond of charity, as with a mantle, which is the bond of perfectness and peace." (D&C 88:124–125.)

To be perfectly sound in body and spirit, then, we must live the gospel of Christ, having "above all things" charity toward our fellowmen. As Mormons purify themselves physically through the Word of Wisdom and spiritually through the pure love of Christ, they are promised four specific blessings: (1) "*health* in their navel and marrow to their bones," (2) "*wisdom* and great treasures of knowledge, even hidden treasures," (3) the *vitality* and ability to "run and not be weary . . . walk and not faint," and (4) the *protection* and assurance that "the destroying angel shall pass by them, as the children of Israel, and not slay them." (D&C 89:18–21; italics added.)

The first blessing of physical *health* has an obvious relationship to keeping the Word of Wisdom. Health not only has temporal value for our present bodies, but it is also promised in the temple endowment as part of our future, resurrected state. When our bodies are healthy, our minds are naturally more capable of receiving *wisdom* — they become more intellectually alert and spiritually more sensitive to the Spirit, which will inspire us in the things we need to do to improve our physical health and spiritual well-being. The third blessing of strength and *vitality* might at first appear to be merely physical, but it includes spiritual powers as well.[33] When we consider an earlier scriptural injunction to "be not weary in well-doing" (D&C 64:33), we realize that we need bodily as well as emotional energy to fulfill the will of God.

Finally, by keeping the Word of Wisdom, we receive physical and spiritual *protection.* Initially, we live healthier, longer lives and greatly reduce the risk of contracting terminal illnesses such as heart disease and cancer. Studies indicate that compliance with the Word of Wisdom increases a person's life expectancy up to seven years.[34] More importantly, we are screened from the false ideologies of men and Satan. Ultimately, Heavenly Father will reward us many times over for our obedience to his words of wise counsel. God's destroying angels, who bring physical death and pronounce spiritual separation into heaven or hell, will pass us by if we are obeying God's commandments when he comes to separate the righteous "wheat" from the wicked "tares." Unfortunately, there are still some Mormons who have not yet demonstrated their readiness and worthiness to receive these promised blessings.

THE WORD OF WISDOM:
A PRINCIPLE OF OBEDIENCE

Some people attempt to rationalize breaking the Word of Wisdom by claiming, "An occasional beer won't hurt me," or by contending that abstaining completely from tobacco, alcohol, coffee, and tea is fanatical. The folly of these excuses should be readily apparent. What right do we have to question the Lord? Ultimately, we should obey the Word of Wisdom not to avoid the negative consequences of its violation, but because it is a commandment of God—not because it seems logical, but because we love the Lord and are willing to do whatever he asks of us. We simply have no right to demand justification for every commandment that we are called upon to obey, even though in this case, an explanation is readily available.

Why should we abstain from all use of tobacco, alcohol, tea, and coffee? It could be because of the addicting nature of these items. One drink opens up the opportunity to become addicted to alcohol. If that first drink is never taken, there is no chance of becoming addicted. But in the end, we obey the Word of Wisdom because we covenant at baptism to obey all of Heavenly Father's commandments.

Some individuals do not see the Word of Wisdom as a serious commandment because they say, "Whether I drink or not has nothing to do with my being a good, decent person." In a general way, this is true. There are many good, honest, loving people in the world who are not members of the Church who smoke and drink. However, these people have not entered into the baptismal covenant. As members of The Church of Jesus Christ of Latter-day Saints, we promised to obey the commandments, including the Word of Wisdom, at baptism. Violating the Lord's health code may not directly affect our "moral goodness," but it does indicate a blatant disregard for keeping our sacred vows. In other words, our integrity is weakened. When one contends that breaking the Word of Wisdom is not a serious sin, that person is not grasping the seriousness of such a position. Because the Word of Wisdom is adapted to the capacity of the "weakest of all Saints," there is no excuse for anyone to violate it.

If we choose to disobey the Word of Wisdom, the physical and spiritual consequences can be serious. We endanger our health as we forfeit the companionship of the Spirit. In addition, we lose the blessings attached to this commandment, and we will not be able to enjoy the blessings of the priesthood and the temple. As we examined the four blessings of health, wisdom, vitality, and protection that the Lord promises to those who live it, we saw that they are not trivial. If the Word of Wisdom was a trivial commandment, the blessings would also be trivial, but they are in fact wonderful and serious.

These promises can serve as incentives to obedience. For example, some Latter-day Saints have called the fourth promise of the Word of Wisdom a special type of "spiritual life insurance." Verse 21 states that the destroying angel will pass by those who live this law. By implication, those found in violation of the Word of Wisdom will have no such promise at the time of the Lord's coming. This could be a significant promise. We should also remember the statement in verse four where the Lord indicates that living the Word of Wisdom will protect the Saints from the plots of evil men. In addition, total abstention from alcohol, tobacco, coffee, and tea sets the Saints apart as a special people. It symbolizes our being set apart from the world. It marks us as a peculiar people, disciples of Christ devoted to living the standards God has set for us, rather than those of the world.

Lastly, we should remember that the Lord does not give trivial and meaningless commandments. Even though in verse three of Section 89, the Lord states that the Word of Wisdom is for the temporal salvation of the Saints, we should remember that the Lord gives no commandments that are not spiritual in nature. (See D&C 29:35.) The spiritual blessings of wisdom and knowledge attest to the fact that living the Word of Wisdom affects more than our physical health. Its blessings are great, and noncompliance for Church members not only takes these blessings from them, but it also deprives them of the blessings and opportunities of the temple, which will ultimately keep them out of God's kingdom. Compliance to the Word of Wisdom not only benefits our physical health, but it also promises us spiritual understanding and divine protection.

In conclusion, *the WORD OF WISDOM provides basic guidelines of eating and drinking that lead to sound health, treasured wisdom, enduring vitality, and divine protection.* This revelation is given to all Saints, even the weakest of them, as a foundation for their physical health to improve both the quality and also the average length of their lives. Obedience to it not only reflects sound medical knowledge, but also indicates faithfulness to God's commandments.

The promises of the Word of Wisdom are temporal and eternal, physical and spiritual. Temporally, they bless us with healthy bodies and spiritual companionship while still in mortality. Eternally, the promises of obedience to this law bless us in our resurrected, celestial state. The principles of the Word of Wisdom reflect God's concern for the physical health of his children, and they enlighten us about the dynamic relationship between the body and spirit. These blessings enhance our conditions of life on earth and improve our potential of a heavenly life in the future. Living the Word of Wisdom can and should be one small step in our pathway of life leading us towards our celestial potential.

For further study, refer to the following entries:

TG	BD	*EM*
Abstain, Abstinence		Alcoholic Beverages
Food		and Alcoholism
Health		Coffee
Word of Wisdom		Doctrine and
		Covenants: Section
		89
		Drugs, Abuse of
		Health, Attitudes
		toward
		Physical Fitness and
		Recreation
		Tea
		Tobacco
		Word of Wisdom

CHAPTER 28

CONTRIBUTING TO GOD'S KINGDOM

One day an unemployed individual received an outstanding job offer with a generous salary, additional benefits, and self-fulfillment opportunities beyond his wildest dreams. Two stipulations accompanied the offer: he would have to relocate to an area noted for its pleasant weather and great natural beauty, and he would be asked, but not required, to contribute one-tenth of his salary to building the local community and assisting those in need. Few people would turn down such an outstanding offer, yet some might accept the offer with both stipulations and then later neglect the promise to share a fraction of their wealth. Indeed, there are many people on this earth who are in a similar situation, who have received great blessings and riches from Heavenly Father but are unwilling to share them with others.

God has placed us on this beautiful earth, surrounded with natural and mineral resources, with fertile soil and adequate climatic conditions to produce enough food, clothing, and shelter for all. But inadequate means of production, transportation, and distribution, along with political manipulations, selfishishness, and unwillingness to share have resulted in an unequal and often unfair distribution of life's natural necessities. To make matters worse, the corrosive and polluting influence of Satan brings wars and destruction that disturb the process even more. This is not how Heavenly Father planned it long ago as we met with him in the premortal councils before we all came to this earth.

Heavenly Father has chosen to remedy these inequities by working from within the heart outward toward society and the world. Rather than impose some all-powerful political-economic system, God chooses to work with the human soul. As each person learns to work and produce commodities or services and then willingly shares them with others, more and more of God's children are benefited. Through his Son, Jesus Christ, our Heavenly Father has also established a body of teachings and an organization to transmit these charitable principles to more and more people. Anciently, the patriarchs and their extended families and then the prophets and the House of Israel transmitted these teachings and practices. Today, the teachings are part of Christ's gospel, and the social structure is The Church of Jesus Christ of Latter-day Saints. God has instituted various programs to help teach his followers how to share their time, talents, and material resources. The most common program of shared resources among God's children through the ages is known as the law of tithing.

TITHING AND CONSECRATION

Like the law of the Sabbath, the law of tithing serves to remind the Saints that the Lord's ways are different from those of man. A capitalistic economy, for example, emphasizes work and free enterprise as means for the individual to accumulate wealth and material goods. Socialistic systems believe that the government rather than individuals should own a nation's resources and control their use. Dictatorships funnel the wealth into the hands of a few while most citizens suffer. In contrast, the Lord's economy discourages the Saints from trying to get ahead of their neighbors, commanding them instead to use their material goods to care for the poor.

Participation in the Church financial and welfare systems remains voluntary, not compulsory. If a Church member cannot provide enough for his or her personal needs, and family or friends also cannot provide enough, then the Church will provide assistance from its available resources. Thus the Lord's plan eliminates the abuses of the common political systems, supports the religious community, and provides for the individual member's needs, all the while respecting the agency and dignity of that person.

By engaging in the Lord's work and by paying tithes and offerings for God's kingdom, we acknowledge that we are not "self-made men" (to use a capitalist phrase), or "selfish pariahs" (to use a socialist phrase); rather we are the Lord's servants. We acknowledge that the riches of the earth are his to share, not ours to take. In return for acknowledging him and caring for the poor, the Lord promises that he will care for our temporal and spiritual needs. This is the covenant and promise of the law of tithing. Further blessings for individuals and greater benefits for society will accrue as more people progress from the law of tithing to the higher law of consecration.

The law of consecration, as revealed to the Prophet Joseph Smith, begins with the individual deeding his property and substance (goods and wealth) to the bishop. (See D&C 42:30–34.) He would then receive back what was necessary for him and his family, and the bishop would retain any excess for the benefit of the Church and other members. Persons in need of assistance could thus receive land, goods, or money from the bishop. Those who build upon their initial grants and gain a surplus, along with those whose circumstances change and who find themselves with an excess of goods, are expected to give what they do not need to the Church. (See D&C 82:15–20.)

The law of consecration was first implemented in Missouri and Ohio during the 1830s with limited success. It was discontinued as the Mormons were expelled from Missouri. Since many early Latter-day Saints were unable to fully live the law, it was withdrawn, and the law of tithing was given in its place. (See heading, D&C 119.) The law of tithing is thus a lesser law, given by the Lord as a test to see if the Saints can keep it and demonstrate their readiness to live higher laws. After Church members live the common law of tithing and contribute one-tenth of their increase, they become ready to live the more perfect law of consecration and share all of their surplus.

Thus, the law of tithing and the law of consecration are separate and distinct, although they embody the same principles: all things belong to God; we should not seek for excessive riches or possessions; we should share with others, whom we esteem as ourselves; as responsible stewards, we should help build Christ's church; and then the Church should have the necessary resources to assist the needy. (See D&C 38:17–27; 51:3; 104:13–18.) Willing obedience to the law of tithing elevates a person's soul by developing a more charitable child of God and follows a pattern set by Abraham almost four thousand years ago.

A BLESSING FOR THE FAITHFUL

The earliest scriptural reference to tithing states that Abraham paid "tithes of all" to the high priest Melchizedek, acknowledging God as "the possessor of heaven and earth." (Gen. 14:20, 22.) When Abraham's grandson, Jacob, later received a dream confirming the promises of the Abrahamic covenant upon his head, he responded with a vow to pay tithes to the Lord: "If God will be with me, and will keep me in this way that I go, and will give me bread to eat, and raiment to put on, so that I come again to my father's house in peace; then shall the Lord be my God: and this stone, which I have set for a pillar, shall be God's house: and of all that thou shalt give me I will surely give the tenth unto thee." (Gen. 28:20–22.) This account teaches that the covenant of tithing was an integral part of the Abrahamic covenant.

That ancient law remains central to membership in the Church to this day. "By this principle," says President Joseph F. Smith, " . . . the loyalty of the people of this Church shall be put to the test. By this principle it shall be known who is for the kingdom of God and who is against it. . . . [Those] who are opposed to this principle . . . cut themselves off from the blessings of Zion."[1] Church members are not excommunicated for failure to pay tithing, but they are encouraged to become full participants in building God's kingdom, for only members who pay a full tithe may receive the ordinances and blessings of the temple, which join our families together for eternity in the lineage of Abraham.[2]

In addition to entitling us to the full spiritual blessings of the gospel, the law of tithing carries with it the promise of temporal security. Just as the Lord covenanted to provide Jacob "bread to eat, and raiment to put on," he promises Latter-day Saints who keep the Sabbath and pay their offerings that "the fullness of the earth is [theirs] . . . ; yea, for food and for raiment . . . to strengthen the body and enliven the soul." (D&C 59:16, 19.)

Notice that the emphasis in both the ancient and modern covenant, even when the "windows of heaven" are opened (Mal. 3:10), is on necessities, not luxuries. In the scriptures, the fullness of the earth pertains to God's natural creations, not the wealth amassed by men. The promise of worldly wealth is not guaranteed with tithing. The promise is one of material necessity and spiritual prosperity. Therefore, Malachi warns the Saints not to be surprised or despair that the wicked prosper. Neither should they complain, saying, "It is vain to serve God: and what profit is it that we have kept his ordinance?" Man's economy, like the rest of man's world, belongs to Satan for a season: "Now we call the proud happy; yea, they that work wickedness are set up; yea they that tempt God are even delivered." (Mal. 3:14.)

The true wealth promised a tithe payer is spiritual in nature, coming from heaven and not earth. God promises that he will open the windows of heaven and "pour you out a blessing, that there shall not be room enough to receive it." (Mal. 3:10.) Special blessings of divine protection are also promised righteous tithe payers who have separated themselves from the wicked in the terrible times preceding the Second Coming. (See Mal. 3:11–18; D&C 64:23.)

Though the basic needs of the righteous are promised through faithful obedience, the poor, the meek, and the righteous will not fully inherit the earth until Christ's second coming. Then the wicked "shall burn as an oven; and all the proud, yea, and all that do wickedly, shall be stubble: and the day that cometh shall burn them up, saith the Lord of hosts, that it shall leave them neither root nor branch." (Mal. 4:1.) Note the imagery in this passage. Instead of receiving the fullness of the earth harvested for the righteous, the wicked will be as dry stubble after the gleaned fields are burned. The Lord uses fire imagery in modern scripture too, condemning those who will not acknowledge the earth as his: "In nothing doth man offend God, or against none is his wrath *kindled,* save those who confess not his hand in all things, and obey his commandments." (D&C 59:21; italics added.)

Thus we see that tithing brings a variety of blessings: it builds faith, demonstrates loyalty to God, promises material security, provides spiritual blessings, and protects against the destruction accompanying Christ's second coming. Note that these blessings are predominantly spiritual in nature, even though the law of tithing appears to be a temporal one.

SACRIFICE BRINGS MULTIPLE BLESSINGS

Once we accept the Lord as the rightful owner and giver of all we possess, the sacrifice he asks of us through tithing seems small indeed. Though we give up ten percent of our increase, we still retain ninety percent for our benefit. Furthermore, even the amount we give to God's kingdom comes back to bless our lives. In this respect, the law of tithing is very much like the law of sacrifice in ancient Israel. Many people have the misconception that in all sacrificial offerings, the entire animal was burned on the altar and transported as smoke and ash to heaven. Actually, there were three major types of sacrifices (the burnt, sin, and peace offerings) and various minor ones in the sacrificial practices under the Mosaic law, only one of which required the whole animal to be burnt on the altar.

The average Israelite offered a complete animal as a burnt offering only a few times at most in his entire life. (See Lev. 1:9; Deut. 33:10.) On the other hand, the frequency of the sin or trespass offering varied greatly according to the faithfulness and righteousness of the individual Israelite. In a sin offering, only the fat and blood of the animal was burnt on the altar, with the priests and their families eating the rest of the flesh.

The most common sacrifice for the average Israelite was the peace or thanksgiving offering, which indicated that the sacrificer was at harmony with God and wished to remain so. In this offering, only the kidneys, internal fat, and some of the blood of the animal was burnt on the altar. (See Lev. 3.) The right front quarter of the animal was separated and dedicated to the Lord to provide food for the Levites and priests. (See Lev. 7:11–34.) Because the Levite tribe had received no land inheritance in the settlement in Canaan, and because their priestly duties did not allow them time to tend fields and large flocks and herds, the burden of providing for them and their families fell to the other tribes. The meat, wine, grain, and other food offerings were the means established by the Lord to provide this sustenance. After the priests took their portion of the peace offering, the remaining three quarters was returned to the giver for his own family's festival meal.

Peace offerings were given during public festivals and at private celebrations. The public feasts included, above all, the three pilgrimage festivals of Passover, Pentecost, and Tabernacles, although the peace offering could be given at any festival. (See Num. 29:39; Ex. 20:24; Deut. 27:7.) The most well-known example of a public thanksgiving offering meal is the annual Jewish Passover dinner. The Last Supper between Jesus Christ and his apostles was also a form of this communal meal. The private celebrations included times of marriage, birth, restored health, abundant crops, or other occasions of thanksgiving, for which a freewill offering could be given. (See Lev. 22:29.) The peace offering marked a feast of conciliation, communion, and thanksgiving with God and his servants. It was an occasion when the bounties and blessings of life were shared with God, his priests, and all the families of Israel.

Like the return of most of the animal that the Israelites received from their peace offerings, most of our tithing money comes back to us in ways that directly and indirectly bless our lives. And the part that does not directly benefit the majority of us advances the kingdom of God, of which we are all a part. Decisions about the spending of these funds are made by the Council on the Disposition of the Tithes, comprised of the members of the First Presidency, the Quorum of the Twelve, and the Presiding Bishopric. This council observes two basic guidelines: "One, the Church will live within its means. . . . Two, a fixed percentage of the income will be set aside to build reserves against what might be called a possible 'rainy day'."[3] From the available funds, these General Authorities of the Church decide where and how the tithing funds should be spent. For our consideration, spending from tithing and general Church funds can be divided into three major portions of approximately two-thirds, one-fourth, and one-tenth.

TWO-THIRDS (DIRECT BENEFITS RECEIVED FROM SACRIFICE AND TITHES)

Similar to the majority of sacrificial meat returned to the giver, about two-thirds of Church contributions are returned directly to the members on a ward and stake level—mostly to build and maintain meetinghouses and to provide local operating budgets. The Church builds an average of three chapels each day throughout the world and continually remodels older buildings as well. The greatest financial assets of the Church are land and physical facilities of the many chapels scattered throughout dozens of nations. Because these buildings are money-consuming rather than income-producing assets, they require tithing to pay for repairs, utilities, custodians, and other upkeep. These physical buildings facilitate the many programs of the Church, providing places to encourage the faith and activity of the Saints, teach gospel doctrines, and stimulate individual and social development. This is possible only because the members of the Church pay tithing.

The basic operating budgets of the stakes and wards also come from tithing funds. Active members thus benefit directly from their contributions through auxiliary programs, instructional materials, and varied social, cultural, and sports activities. Those for whom Church activity is central in their lives could hardly place a monetary value on the blessings of full fellowship in the kingdom and the strengths of learning and growth that our children experience at church. For example, the Primary program for the children, the Scouting program for the boys, and the Young Women's program provide guided, inspirational opportunities for learning, social development, and service. The youth, their families and neighbors, and the whole community are blessed by these programs and the strengths they give to the coming generation. Most of our tithing contributions thus return to our local units where they can bless us directly.

ONE-FOURTH (INDIRECT BENEFITS RECEIVED FROM SACRIFICE AND TITHES)

Equal to the portion of animal sacrifice given to Israel's ancient priests, approximately one-fourth of contributions helps to support smaller, more specialized groups of members: seminary and institute students in the Church Education System, some missionaries, General Authorities, and members who earn wages working as secretaries, translators, office workers, gardeners, maintenance workers, employees, and so on at the Church offices in Salt Lake City and at area headquarters throughout the world.

Many Mormons receive a major tithing benefit from the Church Educational System, which provides some secular learning but mostly religious education for hundreds of thousands of members, mostly in their youth. Besides wages, the CES operation budget includes maintenance of its own university and college campuses, institute facilities (for college and university students at local and private institutions), and many seminary buildings (for secondary school students). Major learning institutions, such as Ricks College and Brigham Young University, are largely subsidized through tithing funds in order to keep the tuition fees reasonable. The continuing education received by hundreds of thousands of members each year strengthens the Church now as well as for the future.

Although individual missionaries are mostly supported from personal and family missionary savings funds, local members and wards and the Church's general missionary fund also provide much-needed help, especially valuable financial support for missionaries from indigent countries. Many unseen costs of missionary work, such as mission offices, mission homes, proselyting materials, pamphlets, and other missionary aids are largely supported through tithing funds. The missionary program benefits the whole Church through increased membership and a spirit of growth and excitement. The testimony and zeal of recent converts are constant sources of spiritual strength for Church members and their local congregations.

Although many members serve as volunteer workers in Church headquarters and area offices, many hired employees are necessary to move the work of God's kingdom along. Tithing money is used to pay secretaries, translators, maintenance workers, and others for their skills so they can provide for themselves and their families. Limited vocational opportunities are also extended to unskilled or vocationally weak workers who find temporary and valuable work experience at Deseret Industries, welfare facilities, and other similar programs. All these recipients of tithing funds and Church wages are like the priests and Levites of ancient times in that they are dedicated full-time workers in the Lord's service who receive their material needs from the tithes and offerings of God's people.

ONE-TENTH (SUBTLE, SACRED BENEFITS RECEIVED FROM SACRIFICE AND TITHES)

Finally, comparable to the small portion actually burned on the ancient sacrificial altar, the last fraction of approximately one-tenth of Church monies is used for special programs that God has directed us to establish in order to provide for the sacred, holy needs of his children. These funds bless the kingdom of God through the construction and maintenance of temples, visitor centers, and other general Church buildings. Vast microfilming programs, genealogy research and library facilities, museums, and the operational costs of these special programs are included in this portion. Outsiders might be critical of the use of such resources, but these sacred programs separate The Church of Jesus Christ of Latter-day Saints from social organizations, government projects, or fraternal orders that care primarily for the material, social, and educational needs of their members. These consecrated funds and programs carry Church members from this world into the spiritual realms of eternity and are, therefore, a truly worthwhile and productive use of financial resources.

So either directly or indirectly, members of the Church benefit from their tithing and offerings. If all members paid a full tithe, tithing alone would cover all the expenses of the Church, and there would be little need for additional missionary, welfare, and other funds. In the past few decades, the increased faithfulness of the Latter-day Saints in the payment of tithes has resulted in the elimination of the major building fund, budget, and priesthood and auxiliary fund projects that were necessary to provide these resources. These needs are now provided from the tithes of the Church. However, one significant financial need remains—caring for the poor.

FAST OFFERINGS FOR THE POOR AND NEEDY

Ancient Israelites had tithes *and* offerings that they brought to the Lord. (See Mal. 3:8.) In addition to tithing, Latter-day Saints are invited to contribute fast offerings, which are used solely to help the poor and needy. Fast offerings have always been kept separate from the general tithing and operating funds of the Church. The prophets of this dispensation have designated one day each month, now usually the first Sunday, as a fast day in compliance with the Lord's command to continue in fasting and prayer.[4] One of the chief purposes of this organized monthly fast is to enable the Saints to contribute the money thus saved to the poor.

This use of fasting to assist the needy is very much in keeping with the admonitions of the great prophet Isaiah, who spoke for the Lord, saying, "Is not this the fast that I have chosen? . . . Is it not to deal thy bread to the hungry, and that thou bring the poor that are cast out to thy house?" (Isa. 58:6–7.) Since fasting is the primary vehicle to care for the poor among us, Church leaders have constantly admonished the Latter-day Saints to be liberal and generous in their fast-offering contributions.

They have also sometimes directed special fasts to assist many people outside the Church in special times of need, such as during famines and droughts in Africa, earthquakes in Armenia, and economic disturbances in Russia. For example, the proceeds from two special fast days in 1985 collected over thirteen million dollars, of which almost nine million dollars was utilized in Africa.[5] Sometimes the Church will cooperate with international relief and service organizations to assist the needy, such as in the joint effort with Rotary International's Polio Plus campaign when the Church purchased polio serum for hundreds of thousands of children. In a similar fashion, local Church leaders have advised special fasts and welfare projects to assist those suffering from regional catastrophes.

Fast offerings are submitted to the local bishop, who has discretionary use of them to assist needy members and others.[6] Surplus funds are forwarded to the stake president on a periodic basis, usually monthly. He can then distribute money to wards that have demands exceeding contributions. Surplus stake fast-offering funds are periodically forwarded to the Church general fast-offering fund, which is only used to help the impoverished. Individuals, including nonmembers, can submit funds for special humanitarian purposes directly to LDS church headquarters in Salt Lake or to the Presiding Bishopric Office of the LDS area headquarters in foreign countries.[7]

One can give generous fast offerings and know that the money is going directly to help the poor. Many operational and overhead needs are contributed through voluntary labor in welfare services, which makes the money even more effective in achieving its noble aims. Thus, while usually ten to twenty percent of money donated to large secular charities is used for operational expenses, less than three percent of fast offerings must be used in that way. Fast offerings, then, remain a pure contribution from the giver, since they are used only to benefit others. Although no member ever knows when unfortunate circumstances might make him the recipient of those sacred funds, he gives to bless others and not for his own benefit. Whatever our circumstances, the Lord fulfills his ancient promise of "bread to eat, and raiment to put on" in modern times through the Church fast offering and welfare system.[8]

The Church program of assisting the needy could become a pattern for the world. President Gordon B. Hinckley observed what would happen "if the principles of fast day and the fast offering were observed throughout the world. The hungry would be fed, the naked clothed, the homeless sheltered. Our burden of taxes would be lightened. . . . A new measure of concern and unselfishness would grow in the hearts of people everywhere. Can anyone doubt the divine wisdom that created this program that has blessed the people of this Church as well as many who are not members of the Church?"[9]

THE SPIRIT OF A HIGHER LAW

Presently, a full tithing is the only monetary commitment required of Church members to enjoy the full blessings of the gospel through the temple endowment and celestial marriage. But tithing, fast offerings, missionary support, and other contributions are within the framework of the higher law of consecration. The full spirit of the law of consecration elevates us to a level of charity and service in which we pledge not just a portion of our wealth and possessions but all that we have and will possess to building the kingdom of God on earth. All endowed Mormons have indicated a willingness to live the law of consecration—the final and highest temple covenant—as it may be asked of them. (See D&C 82:15–20.) The personal covenants made in the temple and the social structure of the Church must someday again be united, for consecration is a celestial law, "and Zion cannot be built up unless it is by the principles of the law of the celestial kingdom; otherwise I cannot receive her unto myself."[10] (D&C 105:5.)

To prepare ourselves to live the higher law of consecration as a community, we can each begin by living the spirit of the law in our tithes and offerings. For example, salaried workers are not explicitly instructed whether to pay tithing on net or gross income, or whether to pay before or after their mandatory deductions, so they must decide what their tithing should be. Self-employed business owners, too, must individually decide for the payment of tithes what constitutes their income, after they have paid their operational expenses. Tithing on the interest or income received from savings funds, stocks and bonds, and other financial investments should also be included. A tithe needs to be a full one-tenth of all our income, but we can be generous in deciding what that income is, sharing with the Lord and his kingdom the material wealth with which he has blessed us.

A spirit of generosity also should influence our contributions to the poor. Concerning fast offerings, President Spencer W. Kimball repeatedly encouraged the Saints to live the spirit of the fast by multiplying their contributions, even up to ten times the amount of their meals, if possible.[11] Many financially established Church members can and do give much more than the estimated cost of meals on fast Sundays, as well as generous contributions to other Church funds beside tithing. On the other hand, there are some poorer members for whom ten percent of their income represents a complete consecration of all their surplus or even a sacrifice of necessities as well. They are like the poor widow of Jesus' day who gave only two mites into the temple treasury, but whom the Lord praised, saying, "This poor widow hath cast more in, than all they which have cast into the treasury: for all they did cast in of their abundance; but she of her want did cast in all that she had, even all her living." (Mark 12:43–44.)

The law of consecration encompasses the highest expectations of the temple endowment because it is the most difficult of all commandments to live: "The law pertaining to material aid is so formulated that the carrying of it out necessitates practices calculated to root out human traits not in harmony with requirements for living in the celestial kingdom and replacing those inharmonious traits with the virtues of character essential to life in that abode."[12] People will naturally state that they need more income before they will admit that they should be giving more to others. The natural human tendency to love riches and use them selfishly must be overcome to inherit the nature of deity: "For if ye are not equal in earthly things ye cannot be equal in obtaining heavenly things; for if you will that I give unto you a place in the celestial world, you must prepare yourselves by doing the things which I have commanded you and required of you." (D&C 78:6–7.)

These verses refer to establishing the first storehouse for the poor, preparatory to making the early Church financially independent through the law of consecration and the "United Order." (D&C 104:48; see also 92:1; 104:1.) The United Order refers to the establishment of cooperative enterprises in Kirtland and Missouri that were later disbanded because of economic difficulties and persecution. During the last quarter of the nineteenth century, Brigham Young also initiated cooperative enterprises under the United Order throughout the Western United States, Canada, and Mexico, some of them involving entire communities. The United Order was seen as a preparatory step to an ideal community based on consecration and stewardship. Although of short life and limited success, the United Orders promoted economic self-sufficiency among inhospitable frontier colonies and fostered group identity and religious commitment among many struggling Mormon communities. Today, as one LDS scholar noted, "The united order experience remains in Mormon historical consciousness as a symbol of the more perfect society that Latter-day Saints believe will one day be achieved."[13]

Living in a Zion society where all things are held in common is a lofty goal, but preparation begins with living the law of tithing and learning to share. We can then catch a vision of its higher principle—to learn to give not only of our wealth, but also of ourselves in building God's kingdom. The greatest gifts of self that we can give are the time and individual talents we possess. Giving of money, hard as it may be, is usually easier than generously giving of our precious personal time and of the energy and abilities we possess.

When we realize that God is the giver of all and that we are all beggars and stewards before him, we understand the foolishness of striving to financially "get ahead" in an attempt to leave our neighbors behind. When we remember that God has given us life itself and the time and opportunities we have on this earth, we learn the wisdom of directing our time and energy toward helping others. When we appreciate that all our good gifts and talents come from above, we more readily use them to bless others. Thus, we learn to share all that we have with others in building God's kingdom.

Saying that we want to help the poor and to build God's kingdom is easy, but the mark of our sincerity comes as we part with the things that are precious to us. Understanding and following the Lord's law of economics are not easy, which seems to say that "charity brings prosperity" (as we share, we are blessed by God) and "greed leads to need" (as we are selfish, we are never satisfied). For most of us, money is a precious commodity, and as we generously share it through our tithes and offerings, we demonstrate that our words of compassion and willingness to serve are genuinely meant. Our time and personal talents are other valuable resources we possess that we can share in building God's kingdom, indicating even further a willingness to live the law of consecration.

In summary, we can say that *paying TITHING prepares us for the law of CONSECRATION, which is God's celestial law of social behavior, inviting us to share our material wealth and possessions and our personal time and talents with others in building and enjoying his glorious kingdom on earth.* We live the spirit of the law of consecration as we apply the principles of stewardship, equality, and charity. When we generously and willingly give of tithes and offerings, we prepare ourselves and Christ's kingdom for the glorious Second Coming, when the King of kings will protect us from destruction, overthrow evil, and welcome us into his marvelous realm.

For further study, refer to the following entries:

TG	BD	*EM*
Consecration	Tithe	Consecration
Sacrifice		Fast Offerings
Tithing		Finances of the Church
		Financial Contributions
		Humanitarian Service
		Sacrifice
		Tithing
		Ward Budget
		Wealth, Attitudes toward

CHAPTER 29

WORK AND WELFARE — PROVIDING FOR ONESELF AND OTHERS

The beehive is the central symbol on the flag and seal of the state of Utah, an emblem from pioneer times representing the hardworking nature of the large Mormon population in that state. If the beehive represents the community, then the people are represented by the many bees, flying in and out of the hive, industriously doing their work. Most people assume that the primary work of the bees is making honey, which they do in such abundance that they can feed themselves and still have a large surplus to be consumed by animals and humans. However, bees have a much more important function than producing honey. Their greatest value is the extensive and essential pollination work they do, particularly with fruit trees, vegetables, and other crops necessary for humans and livestock. Moving from one blossom to another, they transfer pollen from one plant to another, thus fertilizing the seed-producing flowers. Honeybees carry out more cross-pollination than any other insect and are extremely valuable members in our ecological system.

In a similar fashion, one may ask, "What are Latter-day Saints accomplishing with all their industrious work?" An initial response would involve an evaluation of their financial and economic productivity in Utah, the area of their greatest population density. A variety of facts could be brought forth showing the business growth and the solid international reputation of Utah-based firms, such as WordPerfect and Novell. Indeed, the work ethic of the local population (which is over ninety percent LDS) was one reason why *Money Magazine* voted the Provo-Orem area the number-one city in the United States in 1991. For similar reasons, *Fortune Magazine* selected Salt Lake City in 1990 as the best city in the United States for business and labor.

However, as with the honeybees, there are more important but less obvious values in Utah labors, whether performed by Mormons or non-Mormons. The greater LDS values derive from the enrichment that a work ethic provides in the human soul and the lasting effects that work habits carry over into all areas of life. A hardworking person enriches both self and society, but increasingly more people seem to ask, "Why should I work if I don't have to?"

WHY WORK?

Our Heavenly Father and Jesus Christ have shown us by their examples the importance of hard work. "In the beginning God created the heaven and the earth," that is, he was found working for the salvation of humanity. (Gen. 1:1; see also Moses 1:39.) Since God's life is a pattern for us in all things, we should not be surprised that honest labor for the earthly well-being of ourselves and others is a basic spiritual principle of the gospel. Jesus Christ, under the direction of our Father in Heaven, worked to create the heavens and the earth. (See John 1:1–3; Heb. 1:1–2; Eph. 3:9.) Christ, being the Anointed One in the premortal existence, also accomplished much work while on the earth. His example of personal effort and constant concern for the needy provides a role model in our lives and exemplifies the foundation of the Church welfare plan.

Expounding on the creation in modern scripture, the Lord emphasizes that temporal and spiritual salvation are really one and the same: "I say unto you that all things unto me are spiritual, and not at any time have I given unto you a law which was temporal . . . for my commandments are spiritual." (D&C 29:34–35.) We are not commanded to tend to our basic physical and material needs because monetary resources or our choice of careers will matter in the life to come. On the contrary, they will not matter at all. What will matter and remain with us into eternity is the obedience, self-reliance, discipline, and organization we incorporate in our character as we cultivate temporal well-being. Thus our temporal work is preparation for our spiritual inheritance: "If you will that I give unto you a place in the celestial world, you must prepare yourselves by doing the [earthly] things which I have commanded you and required of you." (D&C 78:7.)

Even our first ancestors had to learn to work. When Adam and Eve were driven out of the Garden of Eden, the Lord commanded them: "In the sweat of thy face shalt thou eat bread." (Gen. 3:19.) We likewise are commanded to work, for the Lord commanded his covenant people: "Six days shalt thou labor." (Ex. 20:9.) This command has been repeated in latter days as the Lord has instructed his disciples to not be idle, but to labor with all their might and then to rest from their labors on the Sabbath. (See D&C 42:42; 59:10; 75:3.)

Work is both a divine command and a key to success in life. Like Adam and Eve, we each have to leave paradise or the leisure of our youth and learn to work. Granted, some drudgeries of work can be overcome, but the basic principles of work cannot be violated. Although our many modern labor- and time-saving devices have eliminated much of the physical work required of our ancestors, each of us still must develop the work ethic within ourselves. Learning the habits and enjoying the fruits of work are like most things of lasting value—they take hard, continuous effort. Elder Bruce R. McConkie has stated: "Work is the great basic principle which makes all things possible both in time and in eternity. Men, spirits, angels, and Gods use their physical and mental powers in work. . . . Without work there would be neither existence, creation, redemption, salvation, or temporal necessities for mortal man."[1] The success of God's plan requires his work and our effort. (See Moses 1:39; Matt. 20:1–8; D&C 64:25.) Unlike the quick pleasures advertised by society, work's rewards require time, persistence, and diligence.

LEARNING TO WORK

God has provided us families where we can observe and learn the values of work. Good work attitudes, habits, and skills should first be learned in the home.[2] Elder Joseph B. Wirthlin has taught, "Parents should plant deeply the seed of the work ethic into the hearts and habits of their children. As society has shifted from an agrarian to an urban structure, . . . hard work [has] been neglected. If our young people do not learn to work while in their homes, they likely will be compelled to learn later in a setting where the lesson may be painful."[3] The sooner children learn how to work, the sooner they, their families, and society will be blessed.

Sadly, many people in the world do not want to work. They want the knowledge, gifts, rewards, and privileges of the laborers without putting forth the necessary effort. They want an education but do not want to read, study, and analyze. They want skills without having to learn, practice, or perfect them. They want prestigious jobs, and they envy people in rewarding professions, but they are unwilling to pay the price of apprenticeship, commitment, and effort. Far too many tend to take the course of least resistance, the fastest way to success, and the quickest method for wealth, trying to find substitutes for simple, hard work. The Lord has said that the idler "shall not eat the bread nor wear the garments of the laborer." (D&C 42:42.) If we want to enjoy the great temporal and spiritual blessings of life, we need to learn how to work.

PERSONAL WELFARE PRINCIPLES AND THEIR REWARDS

Through the development of good work habits, one learns the principles of self-discipline, both physical and mental. Such personality traits can then carry over into all aspects of life. They become the foundation in developing and sustaining one's personal welfare. "Personal welfare" and "personal preparedness" are stock phrases used in the Church to describe the individual characteristics necessary to become independent, productive members of society. As people prepare themselves, they become better able to assist in developing family preparedness and alleviating community welfare needs.

Welfare is a combination of health, happiness, and general well-being. The term *welfare* derives from old English and Anglo-Saxon roots meaning "a well journey" or "a good trip." If people are in a state of being or doing well, enjoying health, prosperity, happiness, and spirituality, they will experience a pleasant journey through life. Note that the image of well-being describes people on their way toward some destiny. Welfare becomes the means or the path to this destiny and not the sole object of the trip itself. In other words, preparedness and welfare are not meant to be the end purpose of life; rather, they are aids to assist us and others toward our ultimate destiny.

To reach this destiny, we need to learn how to care for ourselves, our possessions, and others. Six key principles guide us in developing our welfare preparedness: work, self-reliance, consecration, stewardship, love, and service. The first two, work and self-reliance, direct our initial energies toward ourselves as we increase our self-confidence and our capacity to produce. Our personal welfare is enriched as we gain talents, income, and emotional strength. The next two welfare principles, consecration and stewardship, focus our attention upon the wise management of our possessions, property, gifts, and talents.[4] As we develop these resources, we exhibit responsibility and gain respectability in the world, but we then need to use these resources toward helping others. The last two principles, love and service, demonstrate our concern for others as we develop charity. If we are strong in all six basic welfare principles, we strengthen ourselves, improve the world, and assist its inhabitants. In short, we become productive, positive members in society.

THE SPIRITUAL, ETERNAL NATURE OF SELF-SUFFICIENCY

When the modern Church welfare plan (originally called Church security program) was established in 1936, the First Presidency issued this mission statement concerning the program: "Our primary purpose was to set up, in so far as it might be possible, a system under which the curse of idleness would be done away with, the evils of a dole abolished, and independence, industry, thrift and self-respect be once more established amongst our people. The aim of the Church is to help the people to help themselves. Work is to be re-enthroned as the ruling principle of the lives of our Church membership."[5] Though the immediate purpose of this program is for temporal security, notice that none of the primary goals are temporal at all. Instead of planning to help a certain number of people, raise a certain sum of money, or produce a certain amount of goods, the First Presidency's aim was to develop the eternal virtues of "independence, industry, thrift and self-respect," with "work . . . as the ruling principle."

The phenomenal success of the Church's self-sustaining welfare plan is due to its foundation in the correct principle of work, which teaches people to govern themselves temporally and spiritually. In the words of President Joseph F. Smith, "It has always been a cardinal teaching with the Latter-day Saints that a religion which has not the power to save people temporally and make them prosperous and happy here, cannot be depended upon to save them spiritually, to exalt them in the life to come."[6] The mission of the Church welfare program is to help us now in our temporal existence so we can become strong, independent, helpful, and happy members of God's celestial society.

A TEMPORAL PLAN FOR PERSONAL AND FAMILY PREPAREDNESS

With a spiritual underpinning of work to achieve self-reliance and serve others, the modern welfare plan is designed along three levels: "the responsibility for one's economic maintenance rests (1) upon himself, (2) upon his family, and (3) upon the Church, if he is a faithful member thereof."[7]

On the first level, adults are responsible for their own well-being and that of their families. In physical terms, this involves maintaining good health and providing the temporal necessities of the family members. Families are also counseled to live within their financial means and to save a portion of what they earn. Beyond providing basic needs, fathers and mothers also bear the responsibility of preparing their children to serve their fellow men and lead independent, productive lives. To meet these needs, standards in six basic areas of personal and family welfare preparedness have been provided by LDS Church leaders:

1. *Literacy and Education.* The prepared person should be able to read, write, and do basic mathematics. Reading the scriptures and other good written works, attending public schools and availing oneself of other educational opportunities, and using other communication and learning resources should be a high priority for everyone. Parents particularly should use available resources to teach positive learning attitudes and effective educational skills to all family members.

2. *Career Development.* Each qualified head of a household should select a suitable vocation and pursue appropriate professional training. Receiving specific vocational training and higher education (beyond the required minimum education and high school) is especially valuable in our contemporary society. Once in a career track, industrious work, further training, and career advancement will enrich one's professional success. Parents should counsel children to select a career that will satisfy their future family economic needs and provide personal satisfaction.

3. *Financial and Resource Management.* Prudent people establish financial goals, spend money for righteous purposes, avoid debt, preserve economic resources, and save for the future. They learn self-discipline and apply self-restraint in money matters. They pay a full tithing and a

generous fast offering. As they properly budget their money, especially for major purchases, they learn to live within their income and avoid large consumer debt. Where possible, they work for home ownership and a secure retirement plan. A savings plan for emergencies and future needs is an important part of their finances.

Parents should train their children in financial responsibility by providing some regular allowance or other income opportunities and then allowing the children to manage these resources through their own experiences. They should encourage teenagers to develop and use a budget, with savings for missions, education, and other important long-range goals. By using economic resources wisely, the family can avoid much of the stress and friction that otherwise disturbs many people who try to live beyond their practical means.

4. *Home Production and Storage.* Well-prepared individuals and families should seek for some temporal independence by producing basic needs through gardening, cooking, sewing, handicraft, and handyman skills. Families should learn food preservation techniques of home canning, freezing, and drying foods. Where legally allowed, each person or family should store a one-year supply of food, clothing, and, if possible, fuel. Emergency first aid, shelter, bedding, and water supplies should also be maintained. Parents should involve children in the planning and execution of the family storage program, particularly in the selection, inventory, and rotation of the food supplies.

5. *Physical Health.* Sound physical health programs are an essential element of every prepared family. Naturally each family member should obey God's instruction in the Word of Wisdom concerning our bodies.[8] (See D&C 89.) Every member should practice sound principles of nutrition, physical fitness, immunization, home cleanliness, environmental quality and sanitation, accident prevention, dental health, and medical care, especially for young mothers and children. The family should also learn and practice some basic home health skills, such as first-aid, safety, and emergency preparedness. Parents should encourage family members to eat properly, to obtain adequate rest and physical exercise, to have regular physical examinations, and to practice wisdom in all health practices.

6. *Emotional, Social, and Spiritual Strength.* Seasoned, mature people can meet life's challenges with confidence, stability, and commitment.

Each person should build internal strength by learning to love and respect himself or herself through self-mastery and righteous living. Families should learn to love and serve their neighbors and to love God and communicate with him through personal prayer. Parents should teach the children that emotional and social confidence along with spirituality provide an inner strength.

As individuals and families reach these standards for each of the six areas of personal and family preparedness, their temporal welfare will be provided for as they establish a work-ethic pattern that will bless themselves and others.[9]

WHAT TO DO WHEN A CRISIS ARISES

Sometimes people or families are not able to fully provide for their own welfare. When accident, illness, death, or any source of financial hardship strikes a family, the family members should first look to their own resources and then to their extended families for assistance. After the resources of this second level have been exhausted, they may turn to the Church for aid. Whenever possible, those receiving welfare assistance work for what they receive by assisting at various LDS Church or welfare facilities. Cash aid is sometimes provided directly from fast offerings, particularly to help with rent, utility, and medical payments. Food, clothing, and other basic goods are usually provided through storehouses, which are supplied from goods produced by stake and regional welfare projects. The recipient should use his available funds to pay debts and to buy as many family necessities as possible. In addition, LDS Social Services helps members who need personal and family counseling, assistance in adopting children, aid in obtaining employment, and so on.

ACCEPTING AND GIVING ASSISTANCE

Members of the Church are commanded by the Lord to be self-reliant to the extent of their ability. (See D&C 78:13–14.) No righteous, able Latter-day Saint who understands the importance of this principle will voluntarily shift the responsibility for personal or family welfare to someone else. As long as he is able, he will work with his own resources and labor with divine inspiration to help provide himself and his family with the temporal necessities of life. When he or the extended family cannot provide these needs, Church and government assistance will help.

As guided by the Spirit and through applying the welfare principles mentioned earlier, each Church member decides what assistance to accept, be it from the bishop, a governmental agency, or other source. In this way, agency is maintained, while independence, dignity, and self-respect are fostered.

The giving of assistance can always be done on an individual basis by neighbors, home teachers, and visiting teachers who are aware of special needs and who can move directly to resolve them. Church members should be prepared and willing to give of time, talents, and means to the needy in the Church and the community. When greater resources are needed, such as from the priesthood quorums, the ward, or LDS Social Services, the bishop needs to be informed and involved.

WELFARE SERVICES ON THE LOCAL LEVEL

The bishop is responsible for determining who should receive Church help and when and how it should be given. Those eligible for assistance include faithful Church members, part-member families, less-active members who are willing to work for their assistance, and traveling or transient members with emergency problems whose eligibility has been verified by their home bishop. At his discretion, the bishop can provide aid to inactive members and nonmembers with special, temporary needs.

An LDS bishop or branch president has six primary responsibilities for the welfare needs of those living in his unit boundaries: (1) to seek out the poor, needy, and distressed, (2) to meet needs with available resources, (3) to teach welfare principles and explain welfare programs, (4) to administer welfare resources through the ward welfare services committee, (5) to encourage members to give generous fast offerings, and (6) to coordinate needs for Deseret Industries and raise storehouse commodities and funds as requested by regional and area leaders.

A wise bishop relies on much counseling, prayer, and inspiration to resolve the temporal needs of Church members. Other people also provide important help. A valuable local resource to assist the bishop is the ward welfare services committee. This committee is comprised of the bishopric, ward priesthood leaders, and the ward Relief Society presidency. They meet at least monthly to consider the temporal needs of ward members. They become aware of arising needs and keep the bishop informed of the circumstances of needy individuals or families. They then direct their priesthood and Relief Society members in the administration of local resources and manpower to provide assistance.

The bishop also meets regularly with other bishops in the stake in a stake bishops welfare council meeting to receive training in welfare duties, exchange ideas and experiences, study community welfare resources, review fast-offering contributions and use, discuss assistance trends, and evaluate local Church welfare projects.[10] In addition, the bishop should be aware of and use applicable local agencies, such as governmental and United Way offices, which can lend valuable assistance and professional help for his members in need.

CHURCH WELFARE RESOURCES

When the personal or family situation is critical enough that individuals must go "on welfare," they become dependent upon public relief. Some government resources may be available, and depending upon the situation, those in need could apply for them. Other helpful welfare resources are available through the Church. The LDS Church provides a storehouse resource system to help bishops assist needy members. The Church welfare program has six major components: fast offerings, employment assistance, bishops' storehouses, LDS Social Services, Deseret Industries, and welfare service missionaries.

1. *Fast Offerings and Other Welfare Services Resources.* Fast offering and other Church funds are available to help those in need. All Church members in good health are asked to abstain from two meals for one day a month (usually on the first Sunday) and to contribute a fast offering equal to at least the cost of the meals (more when possible). Their donations are used only to assist the poor and needy and not for other Church programs. The bishop directs the distribution of these funds. He is not to make loans to the poor from these funds, but if a recipient is later able to repay assistance, he or she should do so by paying a generous fast offering.[11]

2. *Employment System.* Church members, particularly priesthood quorum leaders, should help the unemployed and the underemployed find good, satisfying jobs. In the meantime, work and service opportunities in the ward, stake, or storehouse resource system facilities are provided members while receiving Church assistance. Local employment special-

ists are also called, and some full-time employment centers and regular employment opportunity newsletters are also provided by the Church. These programs help members find jobs, receive career guidance and direction in vocational rehabilitation, and access job information while coordinating assistance on all levels.

3. *Bishops' Storehouses and Production Projects.* In areas of larger Church membership, bishops' storehouses are maintained, containing food and essential nonfood commodities that bishops can provide for those in need. Some local Church units also operate welfare farms, canneries, and other projects that produce and process quality food and nonfood items for distribution. Church volunteers and welfare recipients provide most of the labor for these projects. Other local units are asked to provide special funds or resources to support various welfare projects.

4. *LDS Social Services.* Various professionals and agencies comprise the LDS Social Services system. They assist ecclesiastical leaders in helping members with critical social and emotional needs. The agencies provide licensed services for unwed parents, adoption procedures, foster homes, and other complex needs. LDS Social Services also provide counseling services through clinics and referred specialists.

5. *Deseret Industries.* Deseret Industries are stores and work centers that recycle clothing, furniture, and other household goods. Located in areas with enough of an LDS population to support them, their primary purpose is fourfold: (a) to provide work opportunities and rehabilitation for unemployable individuals, (b) to provide common household items to the public at a low cost and to bishops for distribution to welfare recipients, (c) to give people an opportunity to share of their means and time to help those in need, and (d) to avoid waste by recycling, refurbishing, and renovating usable goods.

6. *Missionaries with Welfare Services Assignments.* At the request of local priesthood leaders, full-time missionaries with welfare service assignments and local members with specialized callings can be assigned temporarily to special areas to help Church leaders identify needs and provide welfare services. A welfare service missionary makes application and receives a call in the same manner as a proselyting missionary, beginning with a bishop's interview where the prospective missionary might express a desire to serve and use any special talents or professional skills he or she possesses. Welfare service missionaries provide valuable

assistance to the Saints and their neighbors, especially in underdeveloped and depressed areas.

The Church of Jesus Christ of Latter-day Saints not only preaches a concern for the poor and needy, but it also encourages and directs the members in providing help for others. The Church also sets the example as an organization by committing many financial and human resources to these welfare programs. Church humanitarian efforts are sometimes noted in the public press when large contributions or emergency shipments are sent to areas where catastrophic disasters, such as earthquakes, famine, or floods, have afflicted many people.

The validity and value of the guiding principles of the Mormon welfare program are sometimes also noted by government leaders and research foundations. For example, one noted journal suggested that the Church's welfare themes "are ones the secular world would do well to study," stating that the LDS welfare system provides material necessities while focusing on "strengthening the family, teaching a vigorous work ethic and helping the needy to help themselves." It remarked that a sign of the Church's success was that able-bodied people on Church welfare "became independent in an average of about *one hundred days,*" compared "to the federal welfare system in which half of the families . . . will remain on the dole for over *ten years.* The explicit aim of Mormon welfare is to wean people from it. That it succeeds is its greatest achievement."[12]

One editor for the journal suggested five reasons why the Church system is highly successful, especially when compared to government programs: (1) Mormon welfare recipients work at various Church facilities for what they receive, (2) home teachers visit the Church member monthly, helping correct problems before they become critical, (3) local bishops, who are often professionals or business owners, supervise the program, (4) bishops tailor benefits to needs and help the families to budget, and (5) the Church aggressively encourages families to take care of their own members. The article includes a quote from a former Deputy Secretary of the U.S. Health and Human Services agency: "People in need want to be connected to family and community. The Mormon Church recognizes these ordinary human facts."[13]

Although some attention has been directed to the Mormon welfare program, most of its work is done behind the scenes. Like the bees with their unnoticed but valued pollination, the greatest social value of Church welfare usually remains hidden as Latter-day Saints quietly and carefully lend assistance to others, following the principles and guidelines of welfare services.[14]

WOMEN IN THE WORKPLACE

Church welfare principles and the work patterns of families need to adapt to constantly changing social-economic realities. Just a few generations ago, most families lived in rural areas where they farmed or were involved in small family businesses. All family members were expected to work together, and one advantage of larger families was the greater number of available workers. Today, most families live in urban areas where a large family can be a financial liability. To meet the needs and expectations of the family, more and more mothers are entering the workforce as they seek employment outside the home. This naturally puts increased stress upon them and the family. However, by following a few guidelines, these pressures can be lessened.

The family first should counsel together to evaluate financial needs and family priorities. All family members, especially older children and parents, need to work together with a healthy attitude toward work. President David O. McKay gave the following counsel: "Learn to like your work ... [and] say, 'This is my work, my glory, not my doom.' God has blessed us with the privilege of working. When he said, 'Earn thy bread by the sweat of thy brow,' he gave [us] a blessing. Men and women have ... accepted it. Too much leisure is dangerous. Work is a divine gift."[15]

Ideally, the husband's primary work would be in the workplace while the wife's essential efforts would be concentrated in the home. President Benson and other Church leaders have counseled the women of the Church to stay at home with their children if possible. The mother's role in educating, guiding, and nurturing the children is especially critical in contemporary times. Her direction in providing a safe, clean, and loving environment is vital for the whole family, particularly to provide a counterbalance to the weight of evil that children must face today.

Unfortunately, in our present-day society, many women must work outside the home. In such cases, every family member needs to sacrifice and cooperate so that primary family functions and values can be maintained. Such sacrifices should not be required just so the family can keep up with their neighbor's style of living. However, these sacrifices should be expected when there is a real need for the mother to work.

In all families, but especially for those with two working parents, there needs to be a balance of the family work load shared by all family members. Sometimes, children and even husbands erroneously look upon mother almost as a servant/slave, ready and willing to fulfill all their basic needs. For them, mother cooks all their meals, cleans their rooms and makes their beds, picks up after them, chauffeurs them around town, does all the shopping, and is always there to help. Meanwhile, the children feel free to watch TV, play games, be involved in sports and hobbies, and just have fun without learning to work. And in some families, the husband may feel he has a right to relax at home in the evening after his work while also expecting the wife to keep a full family work load in addition to her employment.

In all homes, but especially in those where the mother works outside the home, children need to share responsibility for some of the chores, and the husband can pick up an extra share of duties as well. Too much idleness can cause children to become lazy, selfish, and insensitive. By helping with family responsibilities, family members learn self-discipline, service, and cooperation, and everyone in the family benefits.

The spiritual and emotional needs of the family should always have priority over the monetary values of a supplemental income. Sometimes increased thriftiness and wise budgeting can lessen or eliminate the need for the mother to work, especially while young children are still in the home. After family needs and work load are balanced, then the mother can concentrate on her professional development.

To further help her and her family, she could consider support and involvement with such employment situations as these: *flexible working hours* (or different work schedules for both parents) so that at least one spouse can be home as the children leave for and arrive from school, *child-care facilities* closely associated with and even located at work so she can spend breaks and lunchtime with preschool children, *home work station* opportunities where the employer may set up a computer terminal or other equipment in the home to do all or some of the work there, *job sharing* (splitting a job between two or more people) or permanent part-time work so that the parent has more time to care for family needs, and *contract work* where a person offers services to many people and companies, such as house cleaning, typing, catering, and so on. For working mothers in such situations, hard work is imperative to demonstrate that their productivity, efficiency, and value in the workplace do not diminish but actually increase while family needs and priorities are met.

NOTHING IS FREE

In spite of all the advertising gimmicks, nothing in life is really free. Any goods or services given to someone without cost on their part still require the time and effort of someone else, and the true but hidden cost of the goods or services will be carried by other consumers. As mentioned earlier, productivity and things of greatest value are received only after good, hard work.

We need to ask ourselves not just "What do we do at work?" but also "Why do we work?" Some people work for as much money and as many material possessions as they can acquire for as little effort as possible. They are even willing to cheat and steal to gain more. Other people want to do their fair share in society during their working years. They are willing to give honest work for their wages, and they expect others to do the same. A third category are willing to work as much for others as for themselves, especially for the family and those in need. They develop skills and build themselves and others not just for the present but for the eternities. These three types of differences are illustrated in the following story:

A visitor in a city was passing a construction site and observed three workers near him, all seated on the ground chiseling on some large stone blocks. All three appeared to be doing the same labor. When he asked them, "What are you doing?" one responded, "I'm a laborer earning a few bucks so I can buy some booze and have a party tonight." The second answered, "I'm a stone mason using my labors to build a building and provide wages for my family and my retirement fund." The third replied, "I'm a craftsman helping erect a temple where people can come and worship the Lord in a beautiful setting."

This story illustrates three people doing basically the same work but viewing it with completely different attitudes and a varying sense of pride in their efforts. What is our attitude and pride in our work? Wherever we are working, we can change our attitude, but if we have a hard time taking pride in our work, perhaps we should consider changing our employment, if possible. This is one of the reasons why Church leaders encourage Church members not to be employed in industries where the net effect of the product or activity is negative and destructive to society at large. We should approach our vocation with appreciation for what it can provide us and others.

In conclusion, the Mormon attitude toward work involves four principles: "Work is a universal obligation; work enhances the quality of life on earth; daily work has eternal consequences; and work will continue in the eternities."[16] Latter-day Saints receive multiple blessings as they labor industriously to improve their physical welfare. Indeed, *hard, honest, physical WORK earns self-discipline, self-respect, material rewards, and habits for spiritual growth. The Church WELFARE and social services programs assist individuals after they have tried to help themselves and have used all available family resources.* When developed with understanding and diligence, a strong work ethic blesses many lives. These blessings reach beyond the obvious temporal needs of human beings and enrich us as God's children. Thus, the beehive is not just a Mormon symbol of busy community effort, it represents the sweet lasting fruits derived from honest work.

For further study, refer to the following entries:

TG	BD	*EM*
Almsgiving		Deseret Industries
Needy		Emergency
Offering		Preparedness
Poor		Self-Sufficiency
Welfare		Social Services
Work		Ward Welfare
Work, Value of		Committee
		Welfare
		Welfare Farms
		Welfare Services
		Work, Role of

CHAPTER 30

FAMILIES CAN BE FOREVER

When under attack, some animals develop protective barriers by forming a circle of defense. For example, musk oxen, with their broad shoulders, massive heads, and sharp horns establish an impenetrable, outer perimeter to defend against timber wolves. Only the weak or foolish animals who separate themselves from the herd become vulnerable to the wolf pack. Likewise, pioneer settlers moving across the plains drew their wagons into a circle each night to protect themselves. Similarly, the ancient Israelites formed a large circular community with twelve tribes on the outside and the Levites with the Tabernacle and the Ark of the Covenant on the inside. In these examples, the young and more defenseless individuals stayed inside with whatever else was most valuable.

The family provides the same function as rallying around in a circle — both are natural defense mechanisms. Individuals turn to the family for help in times of confusion and tribulation. The family is often considered to be a miniature reflection of society at large, particularly because the foundation of all human and societal relations originates with the family. In primitive societies, the family was the main social structure that protected family members, bound the community together, and provided most of its productivity. In modern society, families are a source of both weakness and strength. Many societal problems confronting us stem from weak, disturbed family situations. But as society has become more complex, and as some family functions have altered, one primary role of the family has remained—providing a peaceful haven for its members.

THE COMMUNITY VALUE OF FAMILIES

Families should provide more than physical protection; they also need to guard their members against the social and moral evils surrounding them. President David O. McKay stressed this role when he noted that "a child has the right to feel that in his home he has a place of refuge, a place of protection from the dangers and evils of the outside world. Family unity and integrity are necessary to supply this need."[1] The family can offer a peaceful haven as individuals under attack from worldly pressures seek safety. As older, stronger, and more experienced family members give protection, counsel, and aid to other family members in need, the family and society are benefited.

In more complex, modern societies, the family's value becomes less obvious because schooling and employment spread family members outside the home and throughout the community. As family members work in different places of employment, a family role of "working together" becomes minor. Nevertheless, the family's influence in the social structure remains very important because it still establishes much of the emotional, social, moral, and spiritual environment of society.

Families are more than a defense or refuge – they also provide many assets to the community at large. A developed, productive family can be compared to a bustling town or city neighborhood and the local structures that carry out community functions. Like a hotel, motel, or inn, the family home or apartment provides shelter and a place to rest. Like a bank, the family provides financial assistance and resources to its members. Similar to a hospital or clinic, the home is a place for the healing of physical and emotional wounds. Like many bustling shops and stores, the family provides food, clothes, appliances, and other goods. Comparable to a school, the family stimulates the intellectual development while teaching basic communication and social skills. Similar to government offices, the family gives control and direction by providing necessary moral priorities and modes of discipline. Finally, like a church, the family gives spiritual direction to its members. If all these local institutions and family functions are being provided, the whole community profits and each individual enjoys a compatible social environment.

HUMAN RELATIONSHIPS WITHIN THE FAMILY

The Greek philosopher Aristotle recognized several millennia ago that human relationships are based upon three levels of association: pleasure, utility, and esteem. These three levels are most obvious in a couple's relationship. When a man and a woman are attracted to each other, fall in love, and marry, they experience physical pleasure and enjoy the emotional interaction of being together. As their relationship develops, they see the strengths that each brings to their union, and they recognize the utility, or practical value, in their social development. They realize they must work together as a team to foster their relationship and rear a family. As their association matures, they grow in esteem, appreciating more fully the goodness in each other and the value in their association. In other words, partners in a lasting marriage need to be genuine lovers, sincere helpmates, and lasting friends.

These three levels also encompass the children within a family. On the pleasure level, children should be reared in a physical and emotional environment where they are nurtured and loved. On the utility level, the family should meet the children's basic needs, fostering their social and intellectual development and helping them become productive members of society. And on the esteem level, a value system of moral and spiritual principles should teach them that they are children of a loving God who expects them to love and help others. President David O. McKay emphasized these three areas of child development: "Fundamentally, our characters are formed in the home. The family is a divine organization. Man's greatest duty in that family is to rear boys and girls possessing health of body, vigor of mind, and higher even than these, a Christ-like character. Home is the factory where these products are made."[2] Ideally, parents will reinforce these three levels of health, development, and spirituality in their association with their children.

Others, such as relatives, friends, and Church members, can also supplement these relationships. Parents and adult friends need to nourish the body and psyche of children, build their personality and mind, and respect their unique souls and eternal spirits. As children are nurtured, educated, and cherished, they feel love. As they strengthen their relationships with others, especially parents and family members, they value their self-worth. Children raised in such a nurturing environment will almost always become beneficial members of the community.

CHARACTERISTICS OF EFFECTIVE LDS FAMILIES

Good, righteous families do not develop by accident. Much work and inspired effort are required to produce them. An oft-repeated quote from President McKay stresses the priority of rearing a family: "No other success can compensate for failure in the home."[3] Though no single, simple plan has been found for rearing a family, a variety of valuable guidelines have been established. Research by university professors of sociology and organizational behavior has identified several key principles in developing effective families.[4] Additional studies by Parent Teacher Association surveys, family and marriage counselors, and ecclesiastical leaders have provided insights into the characteristics of strong LDS families.[5] Their research findings can be summarized as follows:

1. *Gospel* **commitment** *to the Church and the commandments.* Effective LDS families are committed to the gospel of Jesus Christ, and they are active in the Church as demonstrated by three key barometers: attendance at Church meetings, full payment of tithing, and willingness to accept Church positions. Family prayer, family home evening, and temple attendance are also important patterns in these families. Missions, temple marriage, gospel study, and scripture reading are also emphasized. These religious ideals are not always achieved, but they are encouraged in strong LDS families. In essence, effectual Mormon families feel that their commitment to the gospel is more than verbal — it requires active involvement.

2. *Positive* **environment** *of love, care, and unity.* The motto "Families are forever" is often seen in framed stitchwork and on automobile stickers of LDS families. Conscientious LDS parents recognize that their responsibility goes beyond nourishing and clothing their children; they desire to nurture and rear their children with fostering care. They treat their offspring as precious children of God who have been entrusted to their stewardship. Family members feel a sense of love and belonging — the children especially feel they are wanted, integral members of the family. Family members also try to spend both quantity and quality time together, particularly as parents and older siblings work, talk, teach, study, and play with the younger children. Their support of each other is not always complete since it requires planning, effort, and personal sacrifice, but they strive to provide it because of the importance and eternal nature of the family.

3. *Clear* **communication** *of family expectations, goals, and concerns.* Not only do the parents spend a good deal of time talking with their children, but the children are open and free in their conversations with each other. The talking does not need to be serious or lengthy; it can be

time to just chat and discuss current events and school activities. Individual conversations and group discussions, along with family home evenings and family councils, communicate the high expectations and eternal goals for which the family should be striving. When critical times of decision making arise or as personal problems and concerns develop, family members should feel they can talk freely with each other about feelings, expectations, and goals.

4. *Supportive* **education** *in secular and religious subjects.* Supportive parents consider teaching as one of their most important responsibilities. They take advantage of daily teaching moments and help the children to find answers to their questions about school, secular, and gospel topics. The parents support their children's teachers as they place a high priority on reading, learning, and quality education. To provide the time for this learning, effective LDS families watch less than half as much television as the national average, and they tend to be selective in their television viewing. Thus many home-centered learning hours and opportunities are shared with each other with varying degrees of success.

5. *Affectionate* **reinforcement** *of personal value and successes.* Verbal and physical expressions of love and affection are commonplace in solid LDS families. Family members express praise and approval of each other and their individual and collective accomplishments. Love can be expressed through open signs of affection, such as hugging, or through more subtle means, such as service and help for each other. Other kinds of affection are also important, such as forgiving each other, being patient and willing to accommodate others' schedules and needs, teasing and playing with each other, and exhibiting a sense of humor. In spite of occasional disappointments, each family member generally feels comfortable and welcome in the family, knowing that his or her self-worth and individuality are appreciated.

6. *Strong* **bonding** *and support between parents and children.* The parents have developed a good relationship with each other, and the strengths of their union become a role model for the whole family. This strong bonding requires effort on all three levels of human relationships discussed earlier in this chapter (affection, joint-service as helpmates, and mutual esteem). Although their marriage is not perfect, they are willing to work on improving it through trust, love, and communication. Because they usually are able to work hard together as a team, they are

committed to each other and to their joint expectations for the family. The stability and tone of the parents' relationship reflect directly on the quality of home life and the general well-being of the children.

7. *Firm but fair* **discipline** *for infractions of family rules.* Almost all effective LDS families have few specific rules or long lists of particular requirements, but they do have general family guidelines with high expectations. Among the general rules they usually share are these three: treat each family member with respect, let the parents know where you are going and when you will return, and be honest and dependable. Such guidelines become the family life-style, reinforced both through positive teaching moments (such as individual counseling, family home evenings, and family councils) and through necessary discipline.

The most common form of discipline is through talking and reasoning together. If talking does not produce the desired results, the next line of action is usually withdrawing some privileges, particularly those associated with the type of infraction. Sometimes physical punishment may be administered, such as slapping the hand or spanking, but it is seen as a means of last resort. Some firm control and discipline is required in rearing children, but instead of simply punishing for disobedient behavior, parents should try positive reinforcement, reasoning, rewards, restrictions, and other appropriate means with their children.

8. *Strong* **work** *ethic with industry and honesty.* Learning to work is a desired family value. Almost all successful parents expect their children to work around the house with some household chores. They set examples of industry and teach their children how to work by giving them family responsibilities. While no single method is effective in motivating children to willingly assist in family chores, most will respond as their roles are explained, particularly if they have some choice in which responsibilities they will receive. Older children with heavy school commitments or outside part-time work often do less work in the home, but they are still expected to assist. As they work, they are expected to be honest in their dealings with others and to give diligent labor for their allowance or wages. Mormons usually have a good reputation in their communities for industrious labor and honesty in the workplace.

9. *Family* **identity** *with extended relatives and the community.* A base of support extends beyond the immediate family, and family activities often extend beyond the family into the community. The family interacts

with extended family members through correspondence, visits, and family reunions. Especially in times of need, extended families pull together to help face problems. Those who can do so also join together at times of family celebrations, such as baptisms, missionary farewells and home-comings, marriages, funeral services, and other similar occasions. In addition, these families do not isolate themselves from the world but try to be involved in a variety of activities at work, school, church, and in the community. They often support and help each other in sports, music, Scouting, drama, and other activities. In other words, they reach out to the family first for help and support while demonstrating a willingness to assist and be involved with others, both extended relatives and community members.

10. **Problems** *handled with creativity, sensitivity, and vision.* Effective LDS families are not freed from adversity, health problems, wayward children, financial setbacks, and other difficulties. But rather than dividing or weakening under these afflictions, they combine their resources and energy to solve the problems and to bend with adversity without breaking. As they learn to endure together, they develop empathy for those struggling under trying circumstances. They seek for and respond to advice from others and inspiration from above to meet challenges. They also try to look beyond the immediate difficulties at the long-range priorities and values they must develop. They sense the Lord's help as they exercise their faith, strengthen their patience, and struggle through problems together.

Obviously, no Mormon family is perfect. Although strong LDS families incorporate the principles mentioned above, none of them do them perfectly. Each good family is weaker in some areas than in others and tries to reach these ideals in different ways with varying levels of success. The important thing is that families work together by building upon their strengths and learning to overcome their weaknesses. Following these guidelines will develop committed, loving, and unified LDS families that will not only enrich themselves, but also benefit society.

CHURCH AIDS FOR THE LDS FAMILY

Most of the Church programs and curricula are developed to assist the family with their needs. Home teachers and visiting teachers are assigned to visit each family on a monthly basis and to teach, inspire, and assist the family as needed. Various classes in all age groups emphasize strengthening the family, and they help in this by providing gospel instruction, social interaction, practical learning, and opportunities for spiritual growth. Moral values taught at home are strengthened in various Church meetings and associations.

Spiritual commitment is increased through encouraging service to others, particularly to family members. As family financial crises occur and the immediate and extended family resources are depleted, the Church welfare program and fast offerings are directed to help the family. During times of health problems or hospitalization, Church members often rally to provide meals, child care, transportation, and other needs. During periods of emotional trauma, the bishop and other appropriate leaders (including the professional experts at LDS Social Services) provide counseling, moral support, and other assistance. Undeveloped or unused social skills at home are enriched and expressed though group activities, Church callings, and leadership positions. The full range of Church resources, including the auxiliary organizations and Church periodicals, assist the family to grow and progress together.

INDIVIDUAL ROLES WITHIN THE FAMILY

In marriage, neither the husband nor the wife is more important, and both share in the family responsibilities. As children enter the family, the health and welfare of each family member is of equal importance. In the main, LDS families are patriarchal—the father is expected to assume leadership and to direct the spiritual atmosphere of the family, as well as be the primary provider for the family. Contrary to many societies where the mother assumes the major responsibility for the family's spiritual development, the LDS father should be fully committed to this family priority, though both parents are responsible for teaching their children the gospel, and important decisions are made in tandem.

The mother, as his coequal helpmate, provides her nurturing skills, educational gifts, and other talents to strengthen the whole family. She supports her husband in righteousness while he, in turn, supports her family roles, both of them following the Lord in full obedience and righteousness. As parents, they are commanded to teach their children the gospel principles and to pray and to obey God's commandments. (See D&C 68:25, 28.) They should teach by precept and by example. They should establish a role model of love and respect. Indeed, a husband and wife should join together as one into a unity comparable to Heavenly Father and Jesus Christ, who maintain separate identities and distinctive roles and relationships while working together.

Thus, the key word in parenting is partnership, and no one person acts exclusively in any role. For instance, though one may be called the leader in the home, both parents lead together. Though one may be called the homemaker, both parents function together as homemakers. They operate together. Referring again to the Godhead as an example of unity, we see that one of the roles of the Holy Ghost, who is also called the "Spirit of truth," is to guide men to "all truth." (John 16:13.) At the same time, Jesus Christ himself exemplifies truth as "the way, the truth, and the life." (John 14:6.) Though Christ himself is the Comforter, since he cannot be with us always, the Father sends the Holy Ghost, "another Comforter, that he may abide with [us] for ever." (John 14:16.) This concept of unity, of oneness, which is the goal of husband and wife, is what keeps any family system from being tyrannical, or separatist, or elitist. Keeping this in mind, then, let us examine the primary roles of the members of the traditional LDS family.

ROLES OF A HUSBAND AND FATHER

The father serves as the head of his home and family. His key roles are those of a leader, provider, and role model. He should lead the family through kindness, not force, and with humility, not arrogance. The Prophet Joseph Smith revealed some guiding principles for the husband who desires to be a righteous leader of his family. As a basic premise, a man's power should not be maintained simply because of his position as a husband, father, or priesthood holder. Instead, his influence should generate from the principles of persuasion, long-suffering, gentleness, meekness, love, kindness, knowledge, sincere development, gentle discipline, and faithfulness. (See D&C 121:40–44.) In order to receive the needed spiritual strength and inspiration, he must cultivate the three attributes of charity, faith, and virtue. (See v. 45.) Such leadership and spirituality are far more persuasive than any other kind of leadership.

As a provider, the father earns a living for his family. (See D&C

75:28.) He should assume financial responsibility to provide for the family's material needs, such as the necessary food, housing, clothing, and education, assisted by the other family members as needed. He should also provide encouragement, direction, and supervision to fulfill the family's spiritual needs, such as family prayer, family home evening, gospel study, scripture reading, gospel ordinances, and priesthood blessings.[6] A provident man will prepare and guide the family members as they learn, grow, and serve together.

A righteous man serves as a role model for all the family members, not just his sons. His work, effort, and talents should set an example for the whole family. His faith, testimony, and righteousness should motivate family members toward spirituality. His patience, love, and service should inspire all in the family to do likewise. A wise father will also look to the ultimate example of a righteous father, even our Heavenly Father, to be a role model for him and his own family. Any earthly father who patterns his life after God will be a help and strength for his family.

ROLES OF A WIFE AND MOTHER

Similarly, the main expectations of the wife in an LDS family are to be a mother, teacher, and role model. President David O. McKay said that motherhood is a woman's noblest calling. Motherhood is a sacred partnership with Heavenly Father in bringing his spirit children into the world[7] — a great, creative blessing that only women can enjoy. President McKay also taught that "motherhood is the greatest potential influence either for good or ill in human life. The mother's image is the first that stamps itself on the unwritten page of the young child's mind. It is her caress that first awakens a sense of security; her kiss, the first realization of affection; her sympathy and tenderness, the first assurance that there is love in the world." A mother who successfully nurtures and raises her children "deserves the highest honor that man can give, and the choicest blessings of God."[8]

A mother's greatest service as a teacher does not usually come while helping a child with homework. Family counselors tell us that children experience their most dynamic and important learning within their first few years. Long before the child attends school, a mother should have conveyed the feeling of love, the power of truth, and the value of honesty. A wise mother will teach children the importance of self-worth, diligence, and fair play. Not that she should neglect teaching children to read or do math, but a mother's most important teachings are the ethical and moral values and the spiritual truths of life. Her children can be like the two thousand warriors of Helaman who attributed their greatness to the teachings of their mothers. Their mothers did not teach them how to be successful soldiers; they taught their sons to be faithful, God-fearing, honest, brave, and trustworthy. (See Alma 53:16–23; 56:47–48.) Such women of testimony and conviction are great teachers in Christ's kingdom, both of their own children and other children of God.

Mothers serve also as natural role models in the family. As she provides a pleasant, healthy environment in the home for her husband and children, a mother exemplifies the care and concern we should have for others. As she shares her time and domestic talents in giving the home a taste of heaven on earth, a wife demonstrates the good that can be produced here and now. As she defends the family and community against unrighteousness, a woman shows the importance of vigilance in the cause of truth and right. A righteous daughter of God is a noble example and inspiration for all.

As seen in these brief descriptions, both husband and wife have important, complementary roles in the family. An ideal family needs different but equal partners. As Elder Boyd K. Packer taught, "The separate natures of man and woman were designed by the Father of us all to fulfill the purposes of the gospel plan. . . . Men and women have complementary, not competing, responsibilities. There is difference but not inequity. Intelligence and talent favor both of them."[9]

ROLES OF CHILDREN IN A FAMILY

Children share some responsibility in building happy families. In one of the Ten Commandments, the Lord commanded children to honor their father and mother. (See Ex. 20:12.) The best way to honor someone is to love and respect them. The scriptures also tell children to "obey your parents in the Lord: for this is right." (Eph. 6:1.) Modern Church leaders have admonished children to learn righteous obedience to God's commandments and family guidelines. In addition, they have admonished children to try to cooperate with other family members in sharing family and home duties and to help keep the house or apartment neat, clean, and safe. They can develop responsibility in getting themselves out of bed and to school or work on time. Essentially, they can learn to lend their energy and effort in strengthening the family.[10]

NONTRADITIONAL FAMILIES

As ideal as these father and mother expectations are, the fact is that as many as one-half of LDS families cannot even begin to match the ideal because they are not two-parent families or they are families without children. Some of these are older families where the children have grown up and left on their own, or only one or two older teenagers remain. In other families, one of the parents has either died or left the family. The family members who are left are fairly independent but still lack the companionship, wisdom, and stability of the missing parent. In some cases, families have been started out of wedlock by single parents, some of whom are LDS and others who join the Church. In other cases, couples cannot have children, or they wait many years before a child is born into their home or they adopt a child. There are also many families with children in which one of the parents either is not a member of the Church or is inactive, indifferent, or even antagonistic toward the Church.

These kinds of families find it extremely difficult to develop all the characteristics of effective LDS families mentioned earlier. Single-parent families need especially diligent home and visiting teachers to help provide the missing strengths and role models. Other Church programs, particularly the Scouting and Young Women programs for the youth, and leaders, such as course instructors and advisors, can also be of invaluable help so that all family members can still develop and progress as our Heavenly Father desires.

Another type of incomplete LDS family is apparent in many areas of the world. It is a family without parents during the work hours because both parents are fully employed. The impact of having both parents work is not as strong if the parents can alternate their work schedules so that at least one of them is at home most of the time, or if all the children are in school during most of the working hours (although these "latchkey children" still face some noteworthy challenges). Families with younger children requiring baby-sitting and child care are placed under greater stress, especially if there are no grandparents and extended family members to help fill the void. In any of these situations, close Church members and good neighbors can help bridge some gaps and provide the necessary adult guidance to help out.

Apparently many modern families are reverting back to family patterns common in earlier centuries where both parents were heavily involved in working their farm or small business. The children also started to work at an early age to help the family. Extended family and neighbors were generous to help in times of emergency, and thus the basic family needs were fulfilled. The difference is that the family today is not working together in the fields or small business, but father and mother go their separate directions to work, and the older children may also have part-time jobs. The exception would be a family working together in a family business enterprise. The varied vocations can fracture the family unity unless careful planning and joint effort are achieved.

For such working families, regular family councils with open discussion and careful explanation of family and individual expectations will help moderate the stress and pull the family together. Children not working outside the home can be expected to help more in household responsibilities. All should not be solemn duty and heavy responsibility, however; the parents should insure that the children still have their time for fun with their young peers, and the family should experience their own fun and recreational times together. Hopefully, the time and effects of having both parents work can be lessened so that the family can experience the full advantage of a family environment.

Finally, there are those LDS adults who are unmarried and without any children and thus lack many of the challenges and associations experienced by families. For them, meaningful professional development, full activity and service in the Church (including the Single Adult activities), and interaction with extended family members can provide some of the personal, social, and spiritual benefits of involvement in a full, immediate family.

In all these cases of traditional or nontraditional families, the Church programs are designed to strengthen the individual and the family.[11] Since all families and individuals in the Church are imperfect and face a variety of challenges, families with greater needs should especially emphasize full Church involvement in order to assist each person in the best use of abilities, energy, and resources. In this role, the Church becomes an extended family, providing emotional and spiritual resources otherwise unavailable for a struggling family or individual. With these resources, families large and small, whole and disjointed, can develop strong social and religious bonds while family members strengthen their spirituality. As each family member develops faith and remains obedient to God's commandments, he or she strengthens commitment as a disciple of Christ and renders greater service to the family. Thus, one important goal of life on earth—developing individual spiritual testimony and power—is achieved in spite of less-than-ideal family circumstances.

INDIVIDUAL WORTH AND GROWTH WITHIN THE ETERNAL FAMILY

The family serves not only as a refuge and an institution of learning for children, but also as the prototype of the ideal spiritual environment that exists only in the celestial kingdom. As a small nuclear unit, the family helps us to know and serve a few other individuals who are our spirit brothers and sisters. As an extension of God's family, our earthly family helps us draw nearer to other children of God and, through this involvement, draw nearer to God and become more like him. This experience then expands through our interaction with relatives, neighbors, and others in the Church and community, and we begin to see and appreciate the type of social organization that exists in God's celestial kingdom. As we are righteous and faithful, our families can become eternal units, segments of Heavenly Father's social organization.

The family is the fundamental social unit for people on earth and in God's celestial realms. The blessings of the gospel and the central functions of the Church revolve around the family. As temple marriages and solid family relationships are established on earth, the Holy Spirit promises that families can continue into eternity. As a husband and wife are faithful to their temple marriage and administer their family affairs in unity with the guidelines of the Holy Spirit, "they will continue as co-creators in God's celestial kingdom through the eternities."[12]

As the spirit children of heavenly parents and the physical children of mortal parents, we have an opportunity to emulate the heavenly family environment here on earth, establishing a little "heaven on earth" for our family. The patterns of our family life here and the attitudes and behavior that we develop now will become the patterns of our social interaction and our characters in the future. Thus we need to strengthen our families to achieve our full potential, helping others to do the same. The Church and its programs are to aid the family in its ultimate function—to help each child of God toward his or her ultimate destiny. In other words, the family exists as much to help us as we exist to help the family. Like other areas of service, when we make the family a priority and strengthen it, we will receive much more than we will ever give, becoming more fulfilled and complete children of our heavenly parents.

In summary, *the FAMILY, as a potentially eternal union ordained of God, provides the best environment to learn, grow, develop, and serve in our society; and thus the Church supports the family through various instructions, programs, and activities.* Since, in President McKay's words, "No success can compensate for failure in the home," Latter-day Saints should work diligently to strengthen their families and assist others to do likewise. As they do so, they are best able to protect the family members, perfect themselves and others, and prepare for a celestial community of never-ending love.

For further study, refer to the following entries:

TG	BD	EM
Children	Divorce	Birth Control
Family	Family	Children
Family, Children, Duties of	Marriage	Divorce
Family, Responsibilities toward		Family
		Family Home Evening
Family, Eternal		Family Organizations
Family, Love Within		Fatherhood
Family, Patriarchal		Marriage
Marriage, Marry		Men, Roles of
		Motherhood
		Procreation
		Women, Roles of

NOTES TO PART 4

CHAPTER 24

1. See *EM,* 2:807–10.

2. *AHD,* 1030.

3. Further insights on the law of chastity are discussed in chapter 26.

4. More discussion on the Word of Wisdom is presented in chapter 27.

5. See George Q. Cannon, *Life of Joseph Smith* (Salt Lake City: Deseret Book, 1986), 496.

6. Chapter 2 provides further insights about God the Father.

7. See Spencer W. Kimball, "The False Gods We Worship," *Ensign,* June 1976, pp. 3–6.

8. Further details on this important commandment are found in the next chapter.

9. Chapter 30 teaches us more about the importance of our family relationships.

10. Church leaders have indicated that some abortions are permitted when pregnancy has resulted from incest or rape, when the life and health of the woman are in jeopardy, and when the fetus is known to have severe defects. (See *GHI,* 1989, 11–4.)

11. Chapters 20, 21, and 27 give further suggestions on these positive aspects of our physical, emotional, and mental life.

12. This topic is discussed in more detail in chapter 26.

13. Some further insights on this topic are in chapter 28.

14. See TG, Lying.

15. Review chapter 1 for more reasons why truth is important in our lives.

16. See TG, Covet.

17. Review chapter 10 for more insights on agency.

18. See chapters 16–19 for ideas on the first four principles and ordinances of the gospel.

19. See *MD,* 539.

20. *TPJS,* 255–56.

21. *TPJS,* 332.

22. Truman G. Madsen, *Joseph Smith the Prophet* (Salt Lake City: Bookcraft, 1989), 93.

23. *TPJS,* 256.

24. *GHI,* 1963, preface.

25. "Obedience," *SY,* Dec. 7, 1971, 3–4.

26. See the first two verses of the LDS hymn "Know This, That Every Soul Is Free" (1985, No. 240), which beautifully conveys these same ideas.

27. "Obedience," 4.

CHAPTER 25

1. The Jews retained Saturday as their sabbath, Christians developed the practice of a sabbath on Sunday to commemorate the day of Christ's resurrection, and Moslems have set aside Friday as their sabbath.

2. Judah remained in bondage in Babylon, ironically, for seven decades.

3. Using the Jewish method of reckoning at that time, the count was from Sunday to Sunday, counting the first day (Sunday) as one, the second (Monday) as two, and so on.

4. *ISBE,* 3:158.

5. William Smith, ed., *A Dictionary of the Bible* (London: William Clowes & Sons, 1863), 2:136, "Lord's Day."

6. *ISBE,* 3:159.

7. *ISBE,* 3:158.

8. *FPM,* 270.

9. *FPM,* 270–71; see also "Hold Fast to the Iron Rod" *Ensign,* Nov. 1978, p. 6.

10. *CN,* Feb. 2, 1980, p. 3.

11. Theodor H. Gaster, *Festivals of the Jewish Year* (New York: Morrow Quill Paperbacks, 1978), 272, 283.

CHAPTER 26

1. Victor L. Brown, Jr., *Human Intimacy: Illusion and Reality* (Salt Lake City: Parliament Publishers, 1981), 5–6.

2. See *Professional Psychology: Research and Practice,* June 1988, pp. 290–97.

3. David Van Biema, "What's Gone Wrong with Teen Sex," *People Weekly,* April 13, 1987, p. 111.

4. Andrew Hacker, "Promiscuity and AIDS: Moral or Clinical Issue?" *The Wall Street Journal,* May 21, 1987, p. 28.

5. Ironically, "safe sex" in the 1990s represented sexual activity with any or even many sexual partners, but always with the use of some contraceptive device, whose absolute reliability could not be guaranteed.

6. See John Leo, "The [Sexual] Revolution Is Over," *Time,* April 9, 1984, pp. 74–83.

7. *TPJS,* 157; see also 278.

8. See Ernest Gordon, "The New Case for Chastity," *Reader's Digest,* January 1968, pp. 81–85.

9. *EM,* 3:1306.

10. *TSWK,* 311.

11. *EM* 3:1306.

12. *WNTCD,* 2042.

13. Ibid.

14. Gordon B. Hinckley, "If Thou Art Faithful," *Ensign,* Nov. 1984, p. 91.

15. The value of communication is discussed in chapter 30, a chapter on families.

16. Many concepts of this topic were powerfully addressed in a special message to all Latter-day Saints, "President Kimball Speaks Out on Morality," *Ensign,* Nov. 1980, pp. 94–98.

CHAPTER 27

1. See "UA."

2. Ibid, 6.

3. "Drinking and Breast Cancer," *Newsweek,* May 18, 1987, p. 73.

4. B. Bower, "Drinking While Pregnant Risks Child's I.Q.," *Science News,* Feb. 4, 1989, p. 68.

5. See Testimony of Hon. Byron L. Dorgan (R) North Dakota, in HSIH, 3–4.

6.. "UA," p. 6.

7. See Testimony of Beckie Brown, Chairperson, National Board Legislative Committee, Mothers against Drunk Driving, in HSIH, 71.

8. See "UA," p. 6.

9. *STH,* 1.

10. See Gregory Byrne, "Nicotine Likened to Cocaine, Heroin," *Science* 240 (May 27, 1988): 1143.

11. See *STH,* 1.

12. *STH,* 8.

13. *STH,* 14.

14. See Judith Mackay, "The Tobacco Epidemic Spreads," *World Health,* Oct. 1988, p. 9.

15. See *Times and Seasons* 3:800; *EM,* 1:289, 4:1441.

16. See *EM,* 4:1441.

17. See Laurence Cherry, "Should You Be Worried about Caffeine Risks?" *Glamour,* May 1985, p. 324.

18. See "Spilling the Beans on Caffeine," *Current Health* 2, no. 11 (Jan. 1985): 10.

19. See Jacqueline Rivkin, "A Cup of Infertility?" *American Health* 8 (June 1989): 124.

20. "Spilling the Beans on Caffeine," 11.

21. See "Should You Be Worried about Caffeine Risks?" p. 324.

22. "God Will Not Be Mocked," *Ensign,* Nov. 1974, p. 6.

23. See "Can Cocaine Conquer America?" *Reader's Digest,* Jan. 1987, p. 31.

24. Ibid., 32.

25. See Gina Maranto, "Coke: The Random Killer," *Discover,* March 1985, pp. 16–19.

26. "Can Cocaine Conquer America?" p. 38.

27. See Terry E. Johnson, et al., "Urban Murders: On the Rise," *Newsweek,* Feb. 9, 1987, p. 30.

28. See "Coke: The Random Killer," p. 21.

29. Joseph Fielding Smith, *Answers to Gospel Questions,* 5 vols. (Salt Lake City: Deseret Book Company, 1979), 1:197.

30. One oft-repeated, anonymous admonition states: "When you are physically tired, exercise your mind; when you are mentally tired, exercise your body."

31. See chapter 21 for suggestions on handling stress.

32. Bert L. Fairbanks, *A Principle with Promise* (Salt Lake City: Bookcraft, 1978), 8.

33. The powers of spiritual gifts are elaborated upon in chapter 19.

34. See *EM,* 4:1585.

CHAPTER 28

1. *GD,* 225.

2. See chapter 30 on families for a discussion of this principle.

3. Gordon B. Hinckley, "The State of the Church," *Ensign,* May 1991, pp. 53–54.

4. See chapter 20 for further ideas and suggestions on fasting.

5. Thomas S. Monson, "A Royal Priesthood," *Ensign,* May 1991, p. 48.

6. When a number of wards are located in the same city, one bishop is usually designated to supervise the assistance of the transients and nonmembers in that community.

7. Contributions not submitted directly to an LDS bishop should be sent to the Dispersing Office of the Church, 50 East North Temple Street, Salt Lake City, Utah 84150. A cover letter should accompany the check or money order, especially if the funds are designated for a special purpose.

8. The Church welfare and social services programs are discussed in more detail in the next chapter.

9. Hinckley, "The State of the Church," pp. 52–53.

10. The expectations and prophesied fulfillment of a Zion society are expounded upon in chapter 38.

11. See *TSWK,* 145–46.

12. Albert E. Bowen, *The Church Welfare Plan* (Salt Lake City: Deseret Sunday School Union, 1946), 13.

13. *EM,* 4:1495.

CHAPTER 29

1. *MD,* 847.

2. See *GP,* 169.

3. Joseph B. Wirthlin "Seeds of Renewal," *Ensign,* May 1989, p. 8.

4. Further insights into the law of consecration are found in the preceding chapter.

5. CR, Oct. 1936, 3.

6. Leonard Arrington and Davis Bitton, *The Mormon Experience* (New York: Vintage, 1979), 262.

7. *WSRH*, 1–2.

8. See chapter 32 in this book for an examination of God's health laws.

9. Additional guidelines on these topics are found in *WSRH*.

10. *GHI*, 1989, 2–3.

11. See chapter 28 for a discussion of fast offerings and their uses.

12. Quotations are from the Heritage Foundation's journal *Policy Review* as cited in *The Daily Herald*, Feb. 12, 1992, A1–2; italics added.

13. Ibid.

14. See *Welfare Services Guide for Priesthood Leaders* and *WSRH* for further information on these Church programs.

15. "Man Is That He Might Have Joy," *CN*, Aug. 8, 1951, p. 4.

16. *EM*, 4:1585.

Chapter 30

1. *Pathways to Happiness* (Salt Lake City: Bookcraft, 1957), 119.

2. *True to the Faith* (Salt Lake City: Bookcraft, 1966), 107.

3. *Stepping Stones to an Abundant Life* (Salt Lake City: Deseret Book, 1971), 284.

4. William G. Dyer and Phillip R. Kunz, "Keys to Developing Effective Families," *Ensign*, June 1989, pp. 60–64.

5. For example, see Heidi Swinton, "The Truth behind the Ideal Family," in *This People*, Feb./Mar. 1987, pp. 20–26; William G. Dyer and Phillip R. Kunz, *Effective Mormon Families: How They See Themselves* (Salt Lake City: Deseret Book, 1986).

6. See *GP*, 228–29.

7. See *GP*, 229.

8. *Gospel Ideals* (Salt Lake City: The Improvement Era, 1953), 452–54.

9. "A Tribute to Women," *Ensign*, July 1989, pp. 73–74.

10. *GP*, 230.

11. See *EM* 2:490.

12. *EM*, 2:487.

PART 5

CHRIST'S KINGDOM ON EARTH

CHAPTER 31

VALLEYS OF APOSTASY AND
MOUNTAINS OF RESTORATION

An ideal trip through any Garden-of-Eden countryside should include a leisurely drive over rolling hills and through fertile plains interspersed with forests, lakes, and quaint villages. Any long trip is made more interesting by changes in scenery, especially if the passing countryside has dramatic panoramic views. On the other hand, a trip may seem boring where the scenery remains flat, dull, infertile, and unchanging. Civilizations and personalities are as varied as any topography. Studying humanity and the history of God's dealings with his children on this earth is like traveling through a countryside that constantly changes but repeats certain patterns. Seeing how Heavenly Father has blessed and disciplined our ancestors helps us understand his contemporary efforts in our behalf.

The recorded behavior of mankind likewise presents a changing tapestry of events and personalities. Sometimes so much has happened in short periods that the historian cannot remember and process all that has transpired. When life seems to be a constant maze of change, the natural step is to search for consistency amid the turmoil. In an attempt to understand our past, historians have devised patterns and models of human history, focusing on the factors that shape individuals and nations, including environment, economics, politics, religion, technology, and important leaders, among others. As nations and civilizations have arisen, flourished, and diminished, historians have recognized trends and patterns. They plot the trends using charts, lists, and diagrams to show the key events and links in the flow of history. Their views of the cause and effect of historical trends become stimulating food for thought as students of history look for benchmark events of the past.

Another viewpoint of humanity is seen through the eyes of the prophets, many of whom also wrote history. The historical portions of the scriptures provide an elevated perspective of the past events of mankind. Indeed, one purpose of scriptures is to teach the House of Israel "what great things the Lord hath done for their fathers." (Title page, Book of Mormon.) Instead of seeing history primarily in a horizontal dimension, the prophets often portray events on a vertical axis, measuring the cyclic periods of humility and religiosity and the times of pride and depravity by how close or far they are from God. Within the framework of the restored gospel, the whole history of the world—from Adam to the present—is viewed as one recurring instance of spiritual growth and decline after another. Certain key factors and personalities also seem to be instrumental in this viewpoint. The inspired view of the prophets lets us see the grand scheme of earthly history and the ways our lives fit into it.

GOSPEL DISPENSATIONS THROUGH THE AGES

Throughout history, the Lord has willingly *dispensed* his word to his children to the degree that they are willing to hear it. When a new generation is willing to receive much more spiritual enlightenment and prophetic leadership than their immediate ancestors, then a new *dispensation* has begun. A dispensation is a time period "in which the gospel of Jesus Christ is administered by holy prophets called and ordained by God to deliver his message to the inhabitants of the world."[1] The word "dispensation" derives from the Latin roots *dis + pendere,* meaning "to weigh out in portions." As the gospel truths are weighed and given out in new, significant portions, a new spiritual dispensation begins. This pattern of dispensations beginning and ending can be illustrated by a series of mountain ranges with peaks of varying heights and valleys of various depths. These represent the stages of spiritual enlightenment or apostasy among different world peoples at different times.

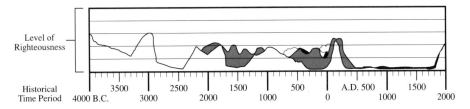

As the mountain ranges of spiritual history show, some peoples and ages have been more willing to accept the truth than others, confirming the word of God to Nephi: "Blessed are those who hearken unto my precepts, and lend an ear unto my counsel, for they shall learn wisdom; for unto him that receiveth I will give more." (2 Ne. 28:30.) Thus, when people receive and apply God's word, they receive more and more — growing and maturing in spiritual power. Conversely, the prophets also warn that "from them that shall say, We have enough, from them shall be taken away even that which they have." (2 Ne. 28:30.) As people reject God's truths, and as the prophets and the priesthood are withdrawn from them, they begin to lose the essential gospel principles and ordinances of salvation. The spiritual blessings and powers are returned to heaven and held in reserve to be restored or "weighed out" again later under divine direction when a new dispensation is founded.

The term *dispensation* appears four times in the Bible, and only in the epistles of Paul. (See 1 Cor. 9:17; Eph. 1:10; 3:2; Col. 1:25.) It is translated from a Greek word, *oikonomia,* describing the administration or stewardship of a household or group. Other English terms deriving from the same Greek root are *ecology, economy,* and *ecumenical.* A dispensation conveys the idea of an extended family or large group working together under centralized leadership. In a gospel dispensation, the prophetic leaders, as dedicated, authorized stewards of the Lord, administer the spiritual affairs of the group. As Moses quickly learned, wise stewards delegate much of the administration and instruction to other diligent workers in the group.[2] (See Ex. 18:25.) As the group loses its cohesiveness, the dispensation comes to an end.

THE SEVEN MAJOR DISPENSATIONS

Due to apostasy and fragmentation, earlier prophetic dispensations declined and weakened until the Lord called new prophets as stewards of restored truth and renewed priesthood power. The mountains outlined in the foreground of the first illustration represent the seven major dispensations of the gospel among the children of Adam and Eve, as recorded in the Old and New Testaments and in modern revelation. The founders of these dispensations were noted patriarchs, prophets, and priesthood leaders. Each dispensation is often identified according to its principal prophet: Adam (see Moses 5:58–59), Enoch (see Moses 6:26–68; 7), Noah (see Moses 8), Abraham (see Gal. 3:6–8, 18; Abr. 2:6–11), Moses (see Ex 3:7–12; D&C 110:11), Jesus Christ and his apostles in the meridian of time (see Matt. 16:18–19; 18:18; D&C 27:12–13; 128:20), and Joseph Smith in the fullness of times (see D&C 112:14–32).

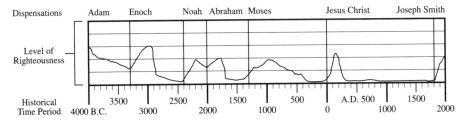

A gospel dispensation typically starts with a selected family or group who receives the charge to take the gospel teachings and priesthood blessings to other specific peoples. (See Abr. 2:11; Matt. 28:19–20.) Correct teachings and practices have rarely been universally disseminated; instead, some peoples have responded to God's directions while most nations have languished in ignorance. Even Jesus Christ's admonition, "Go ye therefore, and teach all nations" (Matt. 28:19), was limited in its fulfillment by where his disciples went in the Roman Empire, and even today, Christians have not yet taken the teachings of the Lord to every nation. Eventually, some ethical teachings of the prophets and some moral values as taught in the scriptures have penetrated most cultures of the earth, but much missionary work remains. Still, the impact of each dispensation has been profound, and several achievements of the earlier ones are worth noting.

1. THE BEGINNING DISPENSATION OF ADAM (C. 4000–3300 B.C.)

Adam and Eve received the commandment to multiply and replenish the earth. (See Gen. 1:28.) They were later given instructions to teach the gospel to their children and to prepare them to receive the saving ordinances. We know from modern revelation that the first man, Adam, received the priesthood, was "caught away by the Spirit of the Lord" to be baptized, and received the Holy Ghost. (Moses 6:64–66.) Thus, the first principles and ordinances of the gospel—faith, repentance, baptism, and the gift of the Holy Ghost—have formed the core of revealed truth from the very first dispensation. From the beginning, however, a major portion of Adam's posterity rejected the gospel and fell into apostasy. (See Moses 5:51–59.) Through Seth's posterity, the gospel was handed down from generation to generation in a patriarchal order.

2. THE EXEMPLARY DISPENSATION OF ENOCH (c. 3300–2900 B.C.)

Among the faithful of Adam's seed was Enoch, who "as he journeyed, the Spirit of God descended out of heaven, and abode upon him." (Moses 6:26.) The Lord called Enoch to preach repentance to those who would listen, and so great was his faith that "the mountains fled, even according to his command; and the rivers of water were turned out of their course; . . . and all nations feared greatly." (Moses 7:13.) In his visions, Enoch beheld the inhabitants of the earth and their history down to the second coming of the Son of Man.

Enoch initiated missionary work and converted many people from throughout the land. He gathered them together into a newly founded city known as the "City of Holiness, even Zion." (Moses 7:19.) He and his people not only lived the first principles and ordinances of the gospel—as did the righteous in Adam's dispensation—but they also formed the ideal political, economic, and social order of a Zion society, "because they were of one heart and one mind, and dwelt in righteousness; and there was no poor among them." (Moses 7:18.) The people of Enoch practiced the law of consecration, having all spiritual and temporal things in common, which is the highest law of the gospel and the culminating covenant of the holy temple. The supreme status of Enoch's Zion is represented by the highest peak in the chart's primary mountain range.

Because the people of Zion lived the order of heaven on earth, they were literally "too good for this world" and were taken from it, closing the dispensation of Enoch: "It came to pass that Zion was not, for God received it up into his own bosom; and from thence went forth the saying, ZION IS FLED." (Moses 7:69.)

3. THE "NEW BEGINNINGS" DISPENSATION OF NOAH (c. 2400–2000 B.C.)

The Lord opened a third dispensation, calling Noah to preach repentance to those whom Zion left behind. "God saw that the wickedness of men had become great in the earth; and every man was lifted up in the imagination of the thoughts of his heart, being only evil continually." (Moses 8:22.) The people tried to kill Noah and would not repent, so Noah and his family (eight people) alone were saved from the great flood that cleansed the earth from apostasy.

Noah's posterity soon spread throughout Asia, Africa, and Europe, where most of them corrupted or forgot the righteous teachings of their fathers. Ham's descendants settled in western Asia and Africa, controlling the rich Nile River civilization of Egypt and the Mediterranean coast of the fertile crescent, from which the idolatrous Canaanites would spring. The seed of Japheth, whose descendants included many of the Gentile nations, settled more into Europe and central Asia. Shem, whose lineage carried on the knowledge of the gospel and the records of the scriptures, settled in southwest Asia, including most areas of the fertile crescent and the Arabian peninsula. (See Gen. 9:18–27; 10.) Most of Shem's seed also apostatized from the truth, especially after their language was confounded at the tower of Babel. (See Gen. 11:6–9.)

4. THE CHOSEN PEOPLE DISPENSATION OF ABRAHAM (c. 2000–1700 b.c.)

Among the descendants of Shem was Abraham, who left the idolatrous city of Ur of Chaldea (near Babylon) where his family had settled. He "sought for the blessings of the fathers, and the right whereunto [he] should be ordained to administer the same." (Abr. 1:2.) Because of Abraham's great faith and righteousness, he received the priesthood from Melchizedek, who had himself received it from his ancestors, all the way back to Adam. (See D&C 84:14–16.) God revealed to Abraham great doctrines of the eternal nature of time, space, matter, and of the eternal existence and nature of intelligences, especially their involvement in the premortal heavenly councils. (See Abr. 3.)

In addition, the Lord entered into a special covenant relation with Abraham and promised him three great blessings: (1) his posterity would be as numerous as the stars in the heavens, (2) they would inherit the land of Canaan (Palestine), and (3) "in [him], and in [his] seed after [him] . . . shall all the families of the earth be blessed, even with the blessings of the Gospel, which are the blessings of salvation, even of life eternal." (Abr. 2:11.) As the Lord's chosen people, Abraham's posterity was to be the light to the world as they increased in numbers and influence. These blessings were deferred for several generations, however, and the sons of Jacob (Israel) settled in Egypt during a great famine, where their posterity mingled with the corrupt Egyptian culture and eventually became captives there. (See Gen. 46:2–3; Ex. 1:8–11.)

5. THE "STEPPING STONE" DISPENSATION OF MOSES (C. 1300–400 B.C.)

After Moses led the children of Israel from bondage in Egypt, he climbed Mount Sinai to receive the Lord's revelations for his dispensation. From Joseph Smith's Inspired Version of the Holy Scriptures (JST), we learn that the first time Moses ascended the mount, he received the fullness of the gospel, as had earlier prophets. Upon returning to camp and finding Israel worshiping an idol, Moses broke the first stone tablets, upon which God's laws were written. Because Israel could not live the higher law of the gospel, the Lord then revealed a lesser law of "carnal commandments" — the law of Moses. (See Ex. 34:1–2, JST.)

Thus, the higher (Melchizedek) priesthood was withheld from most of the Israelite men in Moses' dispensation, leaving the sons of Aaron to officiate in the "preparatory gospel" of the Aaronic priesthood until the time of Christ. (D&C 84:23–27.) Unfortunately, by 400 B.C. the Assyrians and the Babylonians had scattered most of the Israelites, and the last of the Old Testament prophets, Malachi, had finished his time of service. A new period of apostasy and spiritual darkness fell upon Israel.

The dispensations from Adam to Abraham overlapped one another; therefore, the keys of the Melchizedek priesthood passed from one living prophet to the next. (See D&C 84:6–16.) In contrast, for some four hundred years before and after the dispensation of Moses, the children of Israel had no unified, organized priesthood. Throughout the history of the Old Testament, the descendants of Adam and later the House of Israel were encumbered by varying degrees of apostasy. The prophets in the earlier dispensations were often rejected as they called the people to repentance, trying to bring spiritual enlightenment so the people of the world could enjoy gospel and priesthood blessings.

6. THE MERIDIAN OF TIMES DISPENSATION OF JESUS CHRIST (C. A.D. 30–120)

Out of the darkness of apostasy, the light of the dispensation of Jesus Christ shone forth. This dispensation of the meridian of time was heralded by John the Baptist, an Aaronic priest. Christ and his apostles attempted to restore the higher gospel to the Jews, who largely rejected it, as had their Israelite fathers in the wilderness of Sinai. The apostles then preached the gospel to the Gentiles, some of whom accepted it, and the gospel message and baptisms began to spread throughout the Roman Empire. Ideally, Christ's word and church were to have encompassed the known world of that time as the gospel was to be preached "unto the uttermost part of the earth." (Matt. 28:19; Acts 1:8.) However, the early Saints had already begun to apostatize in the apostles' day, and most Gentiles remained in darkness while missionary work faltered, apostles and Church leaders were martyred, and the early church fell into apostasy.

7. THE FULLNESS OF TIMES DISPENSATION OF JOSEPH SMITH (A.D. 1820 through the Millennium)

As the early Christian church became corrupted, the Old World entered into the centuries of the Dark Ages, a period also known as the "Great Apostasy," which continued until the final gospel restoration through the Prophet Joseph Smith in the early 1800s. After God the Father and Jesus Christ appeared to young Joseph in the spring of 1820, other angelic messengers periodically came to the prophet and gave him instruction, the priesthood, and spiritual gifts or keys of this dispensation. He further translated the Book of Mormon from ancient records, and in 1830, he organized The Church of Jesus Christ of Latter-day Saints, the church that Jesus himself had set up during his mortal ministry.[3]

The dispensation of the fullness of times consists of two parts—the time of building Zion and the period of Christ's millennial reign. Zion is built as the gospel spreads throughout the earth, the Saints establish stakes of Zion and build temples, and the Lord's work rolls forth to fill the earth.[4] The Lord himself will usher in the millennial reign as he demonstrates his great powers prior to governing the earth for a thousand years.[5]

TWO NEW WORLD DISPENSATIONS

While the Bible records the seven major gospel dispensations, another scripture witnesses the Lord's doings among some descendants of Shem and Israel in the Americas. The mountains outlined in the middle ground of the first illustration represent the two dispensations in the New World, as recorded in the Book of Mormon: the Jaredites and the Lehi colony.

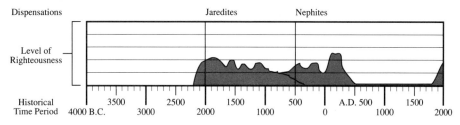

THE ANCIENT COLONY DISPENSATION OF THE JAREDITES (C. 2200–300 B.C.)

After the great flood, even as apostasy prevailed in the Old World, the Lord maintained some blessings of the gospel in the New World, the Americas. When Noah's descendants were confounded and scattered at the Tower of Babel, the Lord preserved a portion of them, led by Jared and his brother, and brought them to the New World. (See Ether 1:33, 40–43.) The Jaredite civilization, with its continuous cycle of righteousness and wickedness, illustrates the value of obeying God. Through it, we also learn the importance of the American continents in God's plans for this earth. (See 2 Ne. 1:7–8; 3 Ne. 20:22; Ether 13:2–8.) Eventually, the same "secret combinations" with Satan and the bloodthirsty oaths and wars that cursed Adam's descendants prior to the flood also destroyed the Jaredite civilization. It came to an end in the lands of North America as a new settlement of Israelites was being established toward the south. (See Ether 11:20–22; 13:19–22; 15:30–33.)

THE NEW WORLD DISPENSATION OF LEHI (C. 600 B.C.–A.D. 400)

Before Jerusalem fell to Babylon, as the dispensation of Moses was rapidly declining, Lehi, a prophet contemporary to Jeremiah, also warned the Jews about their impending judgments and destruction. Lehi's family was joined by others, and they took a copy of most of the scriptural records of the Old Testament, other prophetic teachings, priesthood keys, and additional gifts of the gospel with them. The Lord subsequently led Lehi's family and their associates to the New World. Lehi's more righteous posterity, called the Nephites after one of Lehi's sons, Nephi, recorded their own scriptures and maintained the law of Moses until the dispensation of Christ. When Christ appeared in the New World after his resurrection, he conferred the higher gospel blessings on the people.

Here we reach another pinnacle in religious history, for the Nephites and Lamanites went on to form a perfect society patterned after Enoch's: "They had all things common among them; therefore there were not rich and poor, bond and free, but they were all made free, and partakers of the heavenly gift. . . . And surely there could not be a happier people among all the people who had been created by the hand of God." (4 Ne. 1:3, 16.) But after two hundred years, the society began to disintegrate, "and they began to be divided into classes; and they began to build up churches unto themselves to get gain, and began to deny the true church of Christ." (4 Ne. 1:26.) From this point onward, the Nephites continued to apostatize until they, like the Jaredites before them, were completely destroyed. The Lamanites, a people without prophets and scriptures, remained in a state of apostasy, becoming the ancestors of many of the native Americans.

GOSPEL DISPENSATIONS
AMONG THE TEN TRIBES

Beyond the second mountain range symbolizing the dispensations in the New World lies a third range. To our view, this range is mostly obscured by clouds. These mountains represent the religious history of the lost Ten Tribes of Israel, who were led away to unknown lands by the Lord after the Kingdom of Israel fell to Assyria about 721 B.C. (See 2 Kgs. 17:6; Amos 9:9; 1 Ne. 22:4.)

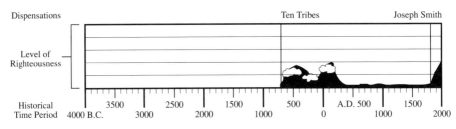

We know little about gospel dispensations among the Ten Tribes, except that the resurrected Christ appeared to them and initiated his own dispensation among them after he visited the Nephites. (See 3 Ne. 15:20; 16:3.) We are also told that eventually a revealed record or scripture will come forth from these ancient people, giving us further details about their spiritual history. (See 2 Ne. 29:13.)

Christ also taught the Nephites that the restoration of the Ten Tribes would be a part of the final restoration of all things in the latter days. (See 3 Ne. 21:26–28.) We can assume, then, that the Ten Tribes have also undergone a "Great Apostasy," coinciding with that in the Old and New Worlds, after Christ's teachings were corrupted and his apostles were rejected by the scattered Israelites and Gentiles.[6]

THE GREAT APOSTASY

Though mankind has suffered through many periods of apostasy, the Great Apostasy marked the first time in history that the entire world labored in spiritual darkness—a period lasting some fourteen hundred years, from A.D. 420 to 1820. Perhaps one reason for this long period of spiritual darkness is that Satan knows the general outline and some key prophecies of God's plan concerning this earth. The father of lies realizes that his reign on earth will draw to a close as the period of "falling away" ends and the Messiah's millennial era is established. (See 2 Thes. 2:3.) The devil desires that all men remain in his power through the bonds of sin and death. Since Satan was unable to foil God's plan by preventing the Savior from fulfilling his mission, his primary course of action has been to perpetuate a world of such wickedness that God's children will never be ready for a kingdom of righteousness.

It is no wonder, then, that Satan has redoubled his efforts after the dispensation of Christ to try to prevent the restoration of all things through Joseph Smith. From the time of Joseph's first vocal prayer in the Sacred Grove in 1820, which resulted in the appearance of the Father and the Son to the young prophet, Satan desperately tried to destroy the young prophet and his work. (See JS–H 1:15–16, 20, 23.) Despite great persecution against the early restored Church, the priesthood keys and saving ordinances were restored and made available to increasing numbers of peoples in many lands, and the Church continues to grow today.

Satan's final recourse, then, is to prevent individuals from accepting the Atonement and the restored gospel. For those who reject these truths, it is as though – in an individual sense – they never were accomplished. Although the gospel is preached in numerous countries, for the most part "darkness covereth the earth, and gross darkness the minds of the people." (D&C 112:23.) Even within the Church, worldliness, false doctrines, and iniquity must be continuously guarded against.[7] As Satan introduces apostate doctrines and incomplete ordinances that will satisfy some and confuse others, he makes finding the truth as difficult as possible for individuals seeking it. He desires that the latter-day church fall into apostasy like the early Christian church did. He also desires that individuals should slide down their own paths of apostasy.

STEPS TO APOSTASY AFFECTING BAPTISM

Since the first and primary ordinance of salvation is baptism, a brief study of the steps of apostasy as they pertain to that ordinance can illustrate the general nature of apostasy so that we can more knowledgeably resist Satan's ambitions. In the early Christian Church, the doctrine of baptism was changed through seven basic steps:

1. *Correctness Practiced.* At first, baptisms were performed in the proper manner (immersion), for the right reason (responsible individuals desiring to covenant with God and to receive forgiveness of sins), and by the correct authority (the true priesthood of God).[8] In other words, the practice, purpose, and power of the ordinance were all correct. The challenge was to maintain this correctness, especially against pressures from erring members within the community.

2. *Exceptions in the Practice.* The form seems to have changed first when exceptions were made for special individual cases (someone old and crippled being baptized in the winter, for example), and so a substitute means, sprinkling instead of immersion, was chosen. Without apostolic or prophetic leadership, these exceptions were granted either by well-meaning but misguided individuals or by arrogant and deceived religious authorities.

3. *The Deviant Form Prevails.* The exception became the rule as the simpler, easier mode became commonplace. Baptisms were not always easy to perform by immersion in the winter or in places where finding or maintaining large bodies of clean water were difficult. Perhaps there may have been a popular demand for sprinkling rather than immersing just as a matter of preference. The earliest Christian churches had bap-

tismal fonts as part of their architectural design, but they were gradually phased out as sprinkling became the standard.

4. *Doctrinal Heresies Develop.* Teachings and other ordinances relating to baptism were later corrupted as justification was sought for the changing practices. Confusion over the nature of the spirit world, the innocence of young children, the teaching of original sin, and a denial of the need for baptisms for the dead also developed. These doctrinal changes resulted in the belief that *all* people, even infants, needed baptism in this life to go to heaven; if it was not performed before their death, they were eternally damned.

5. *Priesthood Authority Is Lost.* The proper priesthood was lost due to the death of the apostles, thus losing the keys to administer the gospel ordinances, such as baptism. The need for priesthood authority was counteracted so that more people, especially in cases of emergencies, could perform the stipulated form of baptism. For example, nurses and emergency room workers in some Christian hospitals are trained to perform baptisms if it appears a patient will die before a priest or minister can arrive. Without a duly authorized legal administration, baptism became an empty rite.

6. *Confusion Abounds.* Whether or not a person needs baptism at all became an issue. To the other extreme, some argued, "Why not recognize any baptism performed by any person as long as the intent is genuine?" The dogma of different Christian churches now ranges across the whole spectrum of possible interpretation. Non-Christians interested in Christianity are even more confused and are uncertain of which course, if any, to take if they want to become Christians.

7. *Corruption and Apostasy Are Complete.* The end result is that baptism becomes uncertain for many people living in Christian countries and meaningless for those in non-Christian areas. When it is performed, especially for an infant, it is often a simple social custom rather than a pure religious rite. When reformation or restoration groups sought to correct these abuses, the apostasy was so entrenched that intense opposition developed and the chaos increased.

Satan has thus succeeded in Christendom to either eliminate baptism altogether, or make it so random and irregular a procedure that people cannot receive a legitimate baptism in the eyes of God. For many centuries, the practice, purpose, and power of the ordinance were completely corrupted. By the time the reforming groups, such as the Baptists, or members of the restored gospel sought to establish more correct practices, the power of the apostasy was so strong that many martyrs gave their lives before the complete, correct ordinance could again be practiced.

These same steps not only characterize the apostasy of large religious communities, such as the Jews after the Old Testament period and the Christians after the New Testament period, but they also typify the path to apostasy that most individuals follow as they leave a true and correct religion:

(1) They feel secure in the *correctness* of their religious beliefs and practices. (2) They make an *exception* for themselves for one of the commandments because of a unique set of circumstances. (3) They *deviate* from more and more of the accepted commandments until their misbehavior becomes standard. (4) They rationalize their own personal behavior or doctrinal interpretations and allow misrepresentations and *heresies* to develop. (5) They become critical of priesthood leaders and other Church members, undermining the authority of the religion, and are often excommunicated, *losing* all *priesthood* blessings. (6) They live in a state of spiritual *confusion,* often not affiliating with any religious denomination. (7) They are in complete *apostasy* — not keeping the commandments, not believing in gospel truths, and not following the Lord's prophets and servants. Indeed, they may actively fight against them.[9]

Lest we become too critical and judgmental of the less active or nonmembers of the Church, we should remember first that any person on the path toward apostasy can stop at any of the steps and turn back toward full activity. Personal apostasy is a spiritual cancer, unpredictably yet continuously destroying the spirituality of a person. But like physical cancer, the sooner it is detected and the sooner steps are taken to counteract it, the easier it is to overcome. The key to full and complete recovery is early recognition and quick personal effort to regain spirituality.[10] We must also remember that people in other Christian denominations who sincerely believe in Christ and have been baptized — though improperly and by one not having authority — will surely have the opportunity to undergo a legitimate baptism. If they cannot be taught and converted to the truth in mortality, that work will be done vicariously for them in holy temples so that they may accept the ordinance in the spirit world.[11]

THE RESTORATION OF THE GOSPEL

To bring back what was lost during each period of apostasy, a "restoration" was necessary. This restoration process usually began when some of God's children on earth desired and prayed for a deliverance from political bondage, intellectual ignorance, or spiritual darkness. God then called and instructed prophets to restore his priesthood authority, gospel teachings, and covenant practices. The period of initial restoration usually took a few years or decades before a strong foundation was laid. The spiritual development then continued through succeeding generations, depending upon the faithfulness of the people and the persistent efforts of later prophets. We are now in the advanced stages of a latter-day restoration that has followed a series of significant steps.

STEPS TO RESTORATION

Just as the early Christian church underwent certain identifiable steps to apostasy, so certain steps can be recognized in the restoration of the gospel. Not surprisingly, we can follow them in the reverse order of the Great Apostasy:

7. *Complete Apostasy.* This period corresponds to the medieval period of the Dark Ages when apostate Christianity ruled the religious life of Europe. All other nations are left to their own devices, and nowhere does any prophet teach gospel truth.

6. *Renaissance, Reformation, and Enlightenment.* Three major movements in history helped bring clarity and understanding into a world of religious darkness: the Renaissance, the Reformation, and the Enlightenment. The Renaissance revival of classical learning and its attendant attitudes of questioning and searching prompted some people to re-evaluate the religious beliefs and practices of the time. The publication and circulation of new ideas stimulated discussion and debate and led to an atmosphere where religious doctrines could be questioned.

The Protestant Reformation in the sixteenth century was the second and most significant step in preparing the world for the gospel restoration to come in the nineteenth century. While Martin Luther and the early reformers did not hold the priesthood or have a complete understanding of true doctrines, the restored Church recognizes them as honorable, inspired men who tried to live biblical teachings to the best of their knowledge and ability. They helped change apostate attitudes and elevate the spirituality of those who followed them from darkness toward the light. A doctrinal statement of the First Presidency describes their efforts as follows: "The great religious leaders of the world such as Mohammed, Confucius, and *the Reformers,* as well as philosophers including Socrates, Plato, and others, received a portion of God's light. Moral truths were given to them by God to enlighten whole nations and to bring a higher level of understanding to individuals."[12] The first New England converts to the restored Church—Protestants from various sects—were products of these earlier movements.

The Enlightenment, an eighteenth-century philosophical movement characterized by rationalism and a spirit of skepticism in religious and political thought, also helped break the bonds of established state religions and prepared people and countries for the gospel restoration. By the time of the Restoration, open religious dialogue and freedom of religion were necessary elements already established in the United States and other western nations.

5. *Restoration of Priesthood Authority.* The Lord next prepared the United States as a place that would allow the Restoration by its guarantee of freedom of religion (even in the face of religious and political bigotry). He sent forth a modern prophet with a witness of God's manifestations, the Book of Mormon with correct doctrines, and priesthood powers with spiritual keys and saving ordinances. (See 3 Ne. 21:4.) This priesthood authority was conferred not by any earthly means, but by the angelic visits of resurrected beings—in particular, John the Baptist and Peter, James, and John—to Joseph Smith and Oliver Cowdery.[13]

4. *True Doctrines Revealed.* From his first clear insights into the Godhead in 1820 and continuing through his life, Joseph Smith received and passed on numerous truths and revelations to the Latter-day Saints. His most profound revelations are recorded in the Doctrine and Covenants and the Pearl of Great Price, with additional inspired insights to be found in collections of his writings and teachings and in the Joseph Smith Translation of the Bible.

3. *Correct Ordinances Restored.* Beginning on May 15, 1829, and es-

pecially after the visitation of Elijah the prophet on April 3, 1836, the full, authorized ordinances of baptism and the temple have been returned to earth. What is sealed on earth is now sealed in heaven. (See Matt. 16:19; 18:18; D&C 124:29; 132:46.) Sealing keys allow complete ordinance work to be done for both those living in the flesh and those living in the spirit world (those who have died) who did not receive this necessary work.[14]

2. *Further Gospel Refinement.* The mantle and keys of the prophet have been handed down through subsequent prophets in this dispensation. Continuous inspiration to teach, direct, and lead the Latter-day Saints motivates the living prophets to adapt Church organization and programs as membership expands throughout the world. The prophetic office also allows them to receive new revelations, such as the one in 1978 on the extension of the priesthood to all worthy men. (See D&C Official Declaration 2.)

1. *The Fullness of Times.* The culmination of this dispensation will occur when Christ brings down his kingdom in heaven to join his Church on earth so they can be united to establish his millennial reign. At this time, his truths, doctrines, ordinances, and priesthood will be universally recognized and available throughout the world. The earth will be a paradise where true spirituality covers the earth and peace and harmony prevail.

Every individual who embraces the restored gospel must undergo a change similar to the historical one just outlined. (7) They must recognize that they are in a state of *spiritual apostasy* or incompleteness. (6) They need to have a humble attitude and a desire to seek out the *light* of truth and goodness. (5) Developing this attitude further, they search for true representatives of God (that is, his missionaries or *priesthood* leaders). (4) They begin to believe in the true *doctrines* of Christ's gospel. (3) They receive saving *ordinances* and spiritual gifts, especially the gift of faith. (2) True faith in the living God naturally leads them to further action and *gospel commitment* as they study the scriptures and follow the admonitions of Christ's authorized servants. (1) Through faithfulness, they qualify for the *fullness* of the temple blessings and the greatest of all spiritual gifts, eternal life — a neverending state of heavenly bliss.

BLESSINGS OF THE RESTORED GOSPEL

The Restoration opened the way for the power of God and his gospel truths to be returned to the earth. As revelations and priesthood authority were "weighed out" in abundance to the Prophet Joseph Smith, a new dispensation began. As God's steward, he received the charge to organize and administer Christ's church on earth. As one of his apostolic successors, President Gordon B. Hinckley, noted, Joseph Smith brought forth six valuable fruits or gifts as he opened this dispensation: a true knowledge of the Godhead, the Book of Mormon and other inspired scriptures, the priesthood of God with its keys and sealing powers, the doctrines of salvation that teach us the eternal purpose of life and provide temporal guidelines, the organization of The Church of Jesus Christ of Latter-day Saints with its profoundly simple financial system of tithing, and a witness and sacrifice of his own life, which he sealed with his blood.[15] Joseph Smith fulfilled his prophetic destiny, ushering in the dispensation that will culminate with the millennial reign of the Savior.

Members of the Church today are able to share in the many blessings provided by the Restoration. They can enjoy blessings of the priesthood, gospel knowledge, revealed scriptures, companionship of the Holy Ghost, temple ordinances, and many other spiritual gifts. As mentioned earlier, Satan is desperately working in his last attempt to thwart God's plans by distracting God's children away from these blessings. As will be discussed in the succeeding chapters, God's priesthood is a mighty power for good as Christ's church rolls forth to fill the earth. The mission of his church is to bring us back into Heavenly Father's celestial presence. Ultimately, blessings of the Restoration will allow us to enjoy Heavenly Father's exalted glory as we rest in his presence. What a contrast that will be from the life of turmoil and strife that mankind has faced on earth over the last six thousand years.

As we look at the changing panorama of human history, we see that God's spiritual dispensations were born on prophetic mountaintops of revelation. They were forged in the deserts of trial and adversity before they began to bear spiritual fruits in the hills of Zion, where the righteous and pure in heart dwelt. Unfortunately, these societies of God's children weakened as the people slid into the valleys of pride, materialism, and idolatry. Eventually, these communities, who were to be a light to the world, fell into darkness and depravity as they became bogged in the swamps of sin. As time passed, Heavenly Father would bring forth new prophets, and the cycle would continue.

To summarize, *GOSPEL DISPENSATIONS are periods of spiritual enlightenment, priesthood keys, and prophetic leadership, usually followed by times of moral decline and worldly corruption. The GREAT APOSTASY concluded the apostolic period of Christ's dispensation, following which, the GOSPEL RESTORATION to Joseph Smith opened this final dispensation of the fullness of times.* The blessings of the restored gospel and priesthood are on the earth to be shared with others as we help prepare the inhabitants of the earth for Christ's millennial reign. As we take advantage of the gospel truths and priesthood blessings available to us today, we should naturally desire to join in fellowship with many others of Christ's followers so we can build his kingdom together.

For further study, refer to the following entries:

TG	BD	EM
Apostasy	Dispensations	Apostasy
Apostasy of the Early Christian Church	Restitution; Restoration	Dispensation of the Fulness of Times
Dispensations		Dispensations of the Gospel
Restoration of the Gospel		First Vision
		Joseph Smith–History
		Restoration of All Things
		Restoration of the Gospel of Jesus Christ
		Visions of Joseph Smith

CHAPTER 32

SHARING GOD'S POWER ON EARTH

Imagine the confusion that would result if you lived in a society where members of the local police force never wore uniforms or carried badges or any form of identification. Soon anybody could claim to be a police officer, and you would not know if he or she were telling the truth, especially if no government agencies could quickly verify if someone was indeed a police officer. In such a setting, what would you do if you were driving, a "police officer" directed you to the curbside, and he ordered you to pay him a fine for some supposed traffic violation? In such a chaotic, uncertain situation, would you pay a traffic fine to this officer, especially if you felt it was unfair?

In order to avoid such anarchy, legal police officers usually wear distinctive uniforms and/or carry badges or other forms of identification. Also, government bodies have passed laws making it illegal to impersonate an officer of the law. They have established criteria to determine if individuals are true, legal public servants of law enforcement agencies. Thus the badge and uniform have become the symbols we usually look for to identify true law enforcement officers.

Just as we might be confused in identifying legal representatives of governmental agencies, we are even more vulnerable in recognizing true representatives of God's spiritual kingdom on earth. While the uniform and badge help us accept the authority of a police officer, we have no such outward, physical symbols that readily establish whether a person is indeed God's true minister or prophet. The power and keys that the Lord gave to Moses and that Jesus gave to the apostles were not recognizable by the clothes, badges, or ID cards that our public servants of today have. The authority of God, as administered through his ecclesiastical servants and by the power of his priesthood, is an inward, spiritual force. It is usually acknowledged through a personal, spiritual witness, which we receive after we have petitioned God or witnessed a manifestation of his power through his servants. One might ask, how can we see the priesthood of God in action today? Or, how can we know if someone is God's true representative?

True prophets and servants of the Lord are not like a police force, but they are authorized to represent him as they administer the affairs of his spiritual kingdom and perform the saving ordinances of the gospel. One way they are recognizable is that they are all ordained priesthood holders who can trace the authority of their priesthood back to the early period of the Church when heavenly messengers conferred priesthood powers upon Joseph Smith and other leaders of the Restoration. Before revealing the fullness of the gospel or organizing a new dispensation through his prophets, the Lord confers upon them his holy priesthood. This priesthood is the power of God given to men to act in his name. Through proper administration within its organizational structure, the priesthood helps build God's kingdom in an orderly way. In order to see how God and his chosen servants act through the priesthood to minister to the Saints, we must first understand what the priesthood is.

PRIESTHOOD IS THE POWER OF GOD

God the Father and Jesus Christ have divine powers far greater than any type of power on earth. They exercise their power in ways that man is not yet able to comprehend. Mankind has gradually progressed from muscle power to mechanical power to electrical power to nuclear power, but other, stronger types of power exist that we do not yet understand or control.

The priesthood of Almighty God is an eternal, all-encompassing power through which God blesses us. Church leaders define *priesthood* as the power and authority of God. It existed with him in the beginning and will exist throughout all eternity. (See D&C 84:17.) By it, "he creates, sustains, governs, redeems, and exalts."[1] Its force was instituted "prior to the foundation of this earth."[2] Likewise, priesthood influence will endure beyond the end of this earth, when all other temporal institutions—both religious and secular—have passed away. God's priesthood encompasses varied powers and forces in the universe.

The Prophet Brigham Young stated, "If anybody wants to know what the Priesthood of the Son of God is, it is the law by which the worlds are, were, and will continue for ever and ever. It is that system which brings worlds into existence and peoples them, gives them their revolutions ... their seasons and times and by which they are rolled up as a scroll, as it were, and go into a higher state of existence."[3] Many of our blessings on earth flow through the priesthood of God. The Prophet Joseph Smith explained that it is "the channel through which all knowledge, doctrine, the plan of salvation and every important matter is revealed from heaven."[4]

For us on this earth, this divine power has always been administered by Jesus Christ. Ancient scriptures imply and modern revelation makes clear that the premortal Messiah was the creator of the world and the author of its salvation: "That by him, and through him, and of him, the worlds are and were created, and the inhabitants thereof are begotten sons and daughters unto God." (D&C 76:24; John 1:3.) Christ, because of his righteousness and the divine faculties granted him by Heavenly Father, received this creative power in premortality when he served in the office of God's great High Priest.[5] (See Heb. 3:1; 5:5–10; 7:14–28.)

In order for us to become God's "begotten sons and daughters" through Christ and to inherit all the Father possesses, we must learn how to fully use the same priesthood promised those in the resurrection of the just: "They are they into whose hands the Father has given all things – they are they who are priests and kings, who have received of his fulness, and of his glory; and are priests of the Most High, after the order of Melchizedek, ... which was after the order of the Only Begotten Son." (D&C 76:55–57; cf. Mosiah 5:7–9.) As soon as we learn how to apply Christ's atoning power, while receiving priesthood blessings and living in righteousness, we develop the power to become like God.

MAN'S USE OF THE POWER OF GOD

To prepare his spiritual children to receive the fullness of his glory in their resurrected state, God gives them the priesthood while they are in their probationary mortal state. God shares priesthood power with worthy male members of the Church, who receive it "by prophecy, and by the laying on of hands" through his authorized servants. (A of F 5;

see also Heb. 5:1, 4.) As Church leaders have instructed us, "The priest-hood enables mortals to act in God's name for the salvation of the human family. Through it they can be authorized to preach the gospel, administer the ordinances of salvation, and govern God's kingdom on earth."[6]

Only through the priesthood are the ordinances of salvation — bap-tism, laying on of hands for the gift of the Holy Ghost, endowment in the temple, and celestial marriage — given to men. Blessings of comfort, healing, and other types of spiritual assistance are also given through the priesthood.[7] A true priesthood ordination can only be conferred from heaven, that is, through heavenly messengers or priesthood bearers hav-ing divine authority. A person cannot seek to take the priesthood unto himself; it must be given him through God's prophets. (See Heb. 5:4.) As stated by the Prophet Joseph Smith, "We believe that a man must be called of God, by prophecy, and by the laying on of hands by those who are in authority, to preach the Gospel and administer in the ordi-nances thereof." (A of F 5.)

Unlike other forms of power available to men that can be used to both bless or harm others, the priesthood of God can be used only for good. For example, nuclear energy can be used as a power source for electricity or destructive bombs. God's power cannot be used for sinful or selfish purposes; it can be used only to bless his righteous children. Whoever is ordained unto the priesthood can only exercise its power to the extent that he fulfills his callings and lives righteously. (See D&C 84:33–41.)

The Prophet Joseph Smith recorded that "the rights of the priesthood are inseparably connected with the powers of heaven, and . . . the powers of heaven cannot be controlled or handled only upon the principles of righteousness." (D&C 121:36.) The Lord also reveals that, although he may confer his priesthood power upon us as his servants, "when we undertake to cover our sins, or to gratify our pride, . . . or to exercise . . . compulsion upon the souls of the children of men, in any degree of unrighteousness, behold, the heavens withdraw themselves . . . and . . . Amen to the priesthood or the authority of that man." (D&C 121:37.) To possess and fully exercise the power of God on earth, priesthood holders must conduct their lives in harmony with his commandments and his righteous will.

Worthy men in the Church may receive this power to perform saving ordinances and to serve others through priesthood blessings and callings. They can also serve through Church callings and service not directly associated with any priesthood office. Righteous women have responsibilities and opportunities for service through motherhood, compassionate service, and Church callings, including leadership positions. Faithful men and women who serve God and others as he has endowed them will both have equal access to the blessings and powers of God. The blessings and ordinances of the priesthood come to Church members according to their faith, through priesthood-bearing fathers, husbands, family members, or ecclesiastical leaders.

In order to have these blessings readily available in the home, women should seek a celestial marriage to a righteous holder of God's high priesthood. Those women who progress to their celestial exaltation will rule and reign in God's kingdom with their husbands, who will serve as Heavenly Father's kings and priests over his many worlds. These women will themselves be queens and priestesses of the Most High God, with great "positions of power, authority, and preferment in eternity."[8]

ORGANIZATION OF THE PRIESTHOOD

God organized the priesthood with order, giving it a definite structure. The priesthood of God is divided into two branches or orders, Melchizedek and Aaronic, and each order contains a variety of offices, such as deacon, teacher, priest, elder, and high priest. Though a man receives various Church and priesthood callings during his lifetime, they remain less important than the priesthood he holds. Elder Bruce R. McConkie explained that "no office adds any power, dignity, or authority to the priesthood. All offices derive their rights . . . and powers from the the priesthood."[9] The differing offices of the priesthood simply indicate administration and responsibility in different areas of stewardship.

THE AARONIC PRIESTHOOD AND ITS OFFICES

When the ancient Israelites failed to observe the gospel laws given by the Lord to Moses, they received a preparatory law of special performances and ordinances along with a lesser priesthood, which was confirmed "upon Aaron and his seed, throughout all their generations." (D&C 84:18.) This priesthood was used to administer outward, physical

ordinances, particularly those characterized by Mosaic ceremonies. Today these ordinances are primarily baptism and the sacrament.

The Aaronic Priesthood continued in a patriarchal order within the
tribe of Levi among the children of Israel until the time of John the
Baptist, who was a priest in the Aaronic order. (See Luke 1:5–25, 57–
80; D&C 84:26–27.) He was the "outstanding bearer of the Aaronic
Priesthood in all history, and was entrusted with its most noble mission" —
to prepare the way for the Savior and baptize him, and to restore the
Aaronic Priesthood to the Prophet Joseph Smith on May 15, 1829.[10] (See
D&C 13.) Thus his ministry operated in three dispensations: he was the
last prophet under the law of Moses, he was the first prophet of the New
Testament, and he restored the Aaronic Priesthood in the dispensation
of the fullness of times.[11] With the keys of the Aaronic Priesthood, Joseph
Smith was empowered to ordain other men and to organize them into
different offices of deacon, teacher, priest, and bishop, and from that
time on, the priesthood has been conferred in the Church without re-
striction to the lineage of Aaron.[12]

Deacon

According to the priesthood organization that the Lord revealed to
Joseph Smith, the first, or lowest, office in the Aaronic Priesthood is that
of a deacon. Deacons are "appointed to watch over the church, to be
standing ministers unto the church." (D&C 84:111.) Beginning at the
age of twelve, they are very limited in the ordinances they can perform.
Deacons generally pass the sacrament among the congregation, act as
ushers, assist in building and grounds clean-up, and perform other tasks
as assigned by the bishopric. To help accomplish the mission of the
Church in an orderly manner, priesthood bearers in some offices are
formed into groups called quorums. In the case of deacons, a group up
to twelve form a separate quorum.

Teacher

Beginning at age fourteen, young men may be called as teachers in
the Aaronic Priesthood. Their duties are similar to those of deacons,
"but neither teachers nor deacons have authority to baptize, administer
the sacrament, or lay on hands." (D&C 20:58.) In the absence of higher
authority, however, the teacher may preside over Church meetings. (See
D&C 20:56.) Teachers assist with preparing the sacrament, serving with
Melchizedek Priesthood holders as home teachers, performing any of

the duties of a deacon, and fulfilling other assignments from the bishopric and priesthood advisors. A group of up to twenty-four teachers form a quorum.

Priest

The office of priest is the highest office that youths will hold in the Aaronic Priesthood, and it is generally bestowed on young men when they reach sixteen years of age. Adult, male converts to the Church are also often initiated into priesthood responsibilities through this office. The duties of priests differ from those of deacons and teachers in that they may perform the first ordinance of salvation—baptism. They may also bless and administer the sacrament and ordain other priests, teachers, and deacons. (See D&C 20:46–48.) A priests quorum contains up to forty-eight people.

Bishop

The presiding office in the Aaronic Priesthood is that of bishop. Bishops are adult men called by stake presidents to preside over the Aaronic Priesthood in their wards. Bishops are called from among the high priests in the ward, or an elder can be ordained a high priest and then called and ordained a bishop. (See D&C 68:15–19.) Any literal descendant of Aaron actually has the right to preside as a bishop if properly called, sustained, and ordained, but since few Jews of Levitical descent have joined the Church, this has not yet become a practice in the Church. As part of the restoration of all things, the office of bishop will one day again be conferred on members of Levitical lineage, as designated by revelation through the president of the Church.[13] (See D&C 84:14–21; 107:13–17.)

Current Church practice requires the stake presidency to nominate a candidate for bishop. The name is forwarded to the Office of the First Presidency at Church headquarters. After the First Presidency and Council of the Twelve Apostles have cleared the name, the stake president is authorized by letter to issue the call. The new bishop is presented to the ward members for their sustaining approval, and he is then ordained and set apart in the calling.

The local administration of the Aaronic Priesthood rests in the hands of the ward bishop. He and his counselors supervise any ordinations and the quorum presidencies, instruction, and activities. The bishop also functions as president of the priests quorum. The offices and affairs of the Aaronic Priesthood for the whole Church are administered through the office of the Presiding Bishopric of the Church.[14] (See D&C 107:15, 68.)

As leader of the Aaronic Priesthood in his ward, the bishop has the primary responsibility for the temporal affairs of the ward and its members. (See D&C 107:68.) Also, as the presiding high priest in his ward, he presides over the ward, administering its programs and counseling the members. He is a "common judge" in Israel with the right to have the gift of discernment for matters of worthiness and fellowship pertaining to his ward members. (See D&C 107:74.) The bishop and his counselors call and set apart all leaders in their Aaronic Priesthood and ward auxiliary callings.

As the lay priesthood leader of the local congregation, the bishop is the most visible and valuable officer of the Church. He is exhorted to be exemplary in his life and diligent in his calling. (See Titus 1:7–9; 1 Tim. 3:1–7.) His three primary functions are to lead the youth, administer the ward, and counsel the members. Indicative of his heavy responsibility, the Church's *General Handbook of Instructions* lists thirty-one primary duties of a bishop, many of which he shares with his two counselors in the bishopric, though he shoulders several on his own.[15] Bishops usually serve for three to five years in their calling.

The most valuable personal association that individual members have with the bishop is developed in moments of fellowship and private interviews. As a spiritual advisor and temporal counselor, the bishop is accessible to every member. Through his ordination and setting apart, he is entitled to a heavenly endowment of the discernment and inspiration necessary to advise the ward members who seek his help.[16] He is indeed the primary shepherd of the local flock of Christ's followers.

THE MELCHIZEDEK PRIESTHOOD AND ITS OFFICES

What is the relationship between the Aaronic and Melchizedek Priesthoods? Although Latter-day Saints commonly speak of two priesthoods, Aaronic and Melchizedek, in actuality there is only one, just as there is "one Lord, one faith, one baptism, one God and Father of all." (Eph. 4:5–6.) The Prophet Joseph Smith confirmed this, saying, "The Melchizedek Priesthood comprehends the Aaronic or Levitical Priesthood, and is the grand head."[17]

The great priesthood of God, however, has been divided into two orders. As noted in the previous chapter, the Aaronic Priesthood was first introduced through Moses because the children of Israel were not spiritually prepared for the fullness of the priesthood. The Aaronic Priesthood is called the lesser priesthood "because it is an appendage to the greater, or the Melchizedek Priesthood, and has power in administering outward ordinances." (D&C 107:13–14.) As one progresses in the offices of the Aaronic Priesthood, all the responsibilities and opportunities of the earlier offices are included in the higher callings. As one receives the Melchizedek Priesthood, all Aaronic Priesthood powers are encompassed within that higher branch of the priesthood, as seen in the following diagram:

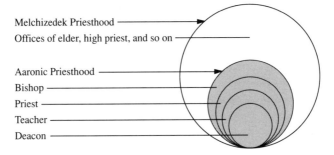

As this illustration demonstrates, higher Aaronic Priesthood offices incorporate the powers of any lesser Aaronic Priesthood office, and any Melchizedek Priesthood office includes all the powers of the Aaronic Priesthood.

The number and magnitude of Melchizedek Priesthood duties are far greater than any in the Aaronic Priesthood, because only the higher priesthood performs all ordinances of salvation and confers many spiritual gifts and blessings. The Melchizedek Priesthood must be present and functional whenever the kingdom of God is upon the earth, regardless of whether that kingdom is organized in a patriarchal order, by tribes, as a congregation, or in an ecclesiastical church structure.[18] This priesthood was first given to Adam; since then, the patriarchs and prophets in every dispensation have had its authority.[19] (See D&C 84:6–17.)

President of the High Priesthood

The Melchizedek Priesthood was restored to the earth in these last days through Peter, James, and John, Christ's chosen apostles of old. As resurrected beings, they came to Joseph Smith in the spring of 1829 and conferred the power and authority of this high priesthood upon him. (See D&C 27:12–13.) Other ancient prophets and angelic messengers restored further priesthood keys and powers to the prophet.[20] Today, the President of The Church of Jesus Christ of Latter-day Saints bears the title "President of the High Priesthood of the Church."[21] This position carries with it all the keys for supervising the priesthood of God on earth, and thus the President directs all the affairs that pertain to the kingdom of God on the earth. He has delegated the local administration of the Melchizedek Priesthood to the stake president.

Stake President

The stake president is the presiding high priest for all the members within the local stake boundaries. Like the bishop who is the president of the priests quorum, the stake president is the president of the high priests quorum. Although not always as visible as the bishop, the stake president has many responsibilities, especially over the spiritual affairs of the members within his stake. He is responsible for fulfilling the mission of the Church and directing all programs, finances, and member discipline for the Church within his stake area.[22]

To help him with this heavy responsibility, each stake president calls two counselors and clerks to help in the stake presidency. He also calls and directs a dozen high priests to serve on a stake high council. Indicative of his heavy responsibility, the *General Handbook of Instructions* lists fourteen areas of primary responsibility and more than twenty-five areas of indirect responsibility, administered through the high council and stake presidency.[23] Called and set apart by the General Authorities of the Church, a stake president usually serves for seven to ten years in his calling. As a part of his administering over the stake, his primary responsibility is to supervise the Melchizedek Priesthood offices and quorums.

The offices of the Melchizedek Priesthood are structured differently than the offices of the Aaronic Priesthood, both in size and relationship to each other. You may remember that the Aaronic Priesthood offices have a definite vertical hierarchy in their relationship to each other, going from deacon up to bishop. Also, their size is somewhat limited, ranging from twelve to twenty-four to forty-eight members. Note that the Aaronic

Priesthood quorums double in size each step upward, in keeping with the vertical hierachy.

On the other hand, the offices of the Melchizedek Priesthood are more in a horizontal relationship to each other. The quorums of the Melchizedek Priesthood are larger in number, and they are usually organized according to geographical ward and stake boundaries. Once a man has received the Melchizedek Priesthood, it really does not matter as much which particular office he holds in that priesthood—with any of them he is eligible to perform most priesthood ordinances, receive a temple endowment, enter into a temple marriage, give priesthood blessings, and share in its power.

Elder

The first and most common office in the Melchizedek Priesthood is that of elder, whose responsibilities include baptizing, laying on of hands for giving the Holy Ghost, conducting Church meetings by the Spirit, healing the sick, preaching the gospel, and carrying out any other duties of the priesthood as needed. (See D&C 20:42–45; 42:43–44; 42:80; 53:3.) A man may be ordained an elder from age eighteen on, so elders are generally younger men in the Melchizedek Priesthood. Some may be preparing to go on missions, although the majority of them are past the primary missionary ages of nineteen to twenty-two years old. Most are married and rearing young families. Up to ninety-six men form an elders quorum, and under the direction of the elders quorum presidency they serve, teach, and fellowship one another. They also assume major responsibilities for home teaching many families in the ward and in assisting the bishopric by caring for the welfare of many ward members.

The term "elder" has a variety of interesting and important meanings beyond identifying the members of the local elders quorum. Actually, the meaning of the term "priesthood" comes from the root word for elder. The word "priest" comes from the Anglo-Saxon *preost* and the Icelandic *prestr,* which in turn derived from the Latin *presbyter* and the Greek *presbyteros,* meaning "an old one," otherwise called a "presbyter" or "elder."[24] Thus, "elder" is the most universal word for identifying a priest of God.

This usage is supported in LDS terminology since the term "elder" is the title given all Melchizedek Priesthood holders regardless of whether they are in the elders quorum.[25] (See D&C 20:38; 1 Pet. 5:1; 2 Jn. 1; 3

Jn. 1.) For example, the apostles of the Church are usually identified as Elder _____, such as Elder Thomas S. Monson or Elder Russell M. Ballard, when they are introduced. Also, all full-time male missionaries of the Church are called elders and have that title printed on their name tags. Some people who first meet a pair of missionaries assume that they share the same first name of Elder, or they wonder how such young people could become elders. After seeing "Elder" on other missionary name tags, they realize that it is a title and not a personal name or a rank of age. If the elders of the Melchizedek Priesthood are true to their office and calling, the term *elder* will be held in high esteem by both members and nonmembers alike.

High Priest

Another common office in the Melchizedek priesthood is that of high priest. From the time of Adam to the present, whenever the fullness of the gospel has been on the earth, there have been high priests to oversee all spiritual affairs of God's kingdom. (See D&C 107:53; Alma 13.) High priests in the latter days are specifically called to minister in spiritual matters, (see D&C 107:18), preach the gospel (see D&C 84:111), and officiate in all other offices of the priesthood when necessary (see D&C 68:19). High priests are organized on a stake level, so no matter how many of them are in a stake, that number constitutes their quorum. Some stakes might have just a few dozen, while older, more established stakes might have a few hundred high priests.

High priests tend to be older men who have been active members of the Church for many years. Usually men will become high priests under one of two circumstances. First, some leadership offices in the Church require that the person be a high priest in order to serve in that office — such as in the bishopric, on a stake high council, or in the stake presidency. Therefore some men will be made high priests so they can serve in those particular callings. Second, as men mature and their children become older, they are brought into the high priests quorum because of the compatible fellowship to be found there. When a man begins to feel awkward or out of place with the younger men in the elders quorum, this usually indicates an appropriate time to be moved into the high priests group in the ward.

Since the high priests quorum is organized on a stake basis, and some stakes can be spread over large areas, the quorum is subdivided into groups, with the high priests of any given ward comprising a separate group. A group leader is called by the stake president, and he and his assistants direct the instruction, fellowship, and home teaching for the group members and their families. The high priests group also assists in the ward as directed by the bishopric, and it usually supervises the temple and genealogy work of ward members. In the main, high priests are sincere, dedicated priesthood holders who exemplify years of service and brotherly kindness.

Other Melchizedek Priesthood Offices

The other offices of the Melchizedek Priesthood—patriarch, seventy, and apostle—are rather limited in number and more universal in the scope of their callings. As indicated in the next chapter, *patriarchs* are called on a stake level to give patriarchal blessings. A stake will usually have only one or two patriarchs serving at any one time. For many patriarchs, as long as their physical, mental, and spiritual health is strong, their service in this calling will last the rest of their natural lives. Thus relatively few men in the Church will ever be called as patriarchs.

The other two Melchizedek Priesthood offices serve in general, central Church leadership positions.[26] *Seventies* serve under the direction of the Quorum of the Twelve Apostles and they have a special call and ordination "to preach the gospel, and to be especial witnesses unto the Gentiles and in all the world—thus differing from other officers in the church in the duties of their calling." (D&C 107:25.) Seventies receive their name from being organized into quorums of seventy men, both in ancient times and modern. (See Ex. 24:1–11; Luke 10:1–24; D&C 107:93–97.) Members of the First Quorum of Seventy are called for a lifetime of service, while members of any other seventies quorum currently serve for approximately five years of full-time service.

The calling of an *apostle* is to be a special witness of Christ in all the world. (See D&C 107:23, 33.) They also serve for their entire lives once they are ordained, and with some of their number serving in the First Presidency, there may be fifteen or more apostles serving at any one time. Apostles serving in the Quorum of the Twelve and in the First Presidency are also sustained as prophets, seers, and revelators.[27] The quorum forms "a Traveling Presiding High Council, to officiate in the name of the Lord, under the direction of the Presidency of the Church, agreeable to the institution of heaven; to build up the church, and regulate all the affairs of the same in all nations." (D&C 107:33.)

The presiding prophet of the Lord administers over all the priesthood offices. He is also the President of The Church of Jesus Christ of Latter-day Saints. He and his counselors are known by the title of "president," which is sometimes considered a special office of leadership. Usually the term *President* refers particularly to the President of the Church, although the title is also applied to stake presidents and to the presidents of any of the priesthood quorums. (See D&C 107:21, 29.) As President of the Church, this prophet, seer, revelator, and apostle holds all the keys of God's kingdom on earth.[28]

CALLING A PERSON TO A PRIESTHOOD OFFICE

Before a young man (aged twelve or older) or an adult male member of the Church receives his first office in the Aaronic or Melchizedek Priesthood, he must receive that priesthood and then be ordained to an office within that priesthood. The initial priesthood ordinance thus consists of two parts: *conferring* the priesthood upon him and *ordaining* him to an office. For example, a youth would have the Aaronic Priesthood conferred upon him, and then he would be ordained to the office of a deacon. Or an adult male would have the Melchizedek Priesthood conferred upon him before being ordained to the office of an elder. Thereafter, when a priesthood holder receives another office within either order of the priesthood, he is simply ordained to that office. For instance, a deacon being ordained a teacher does not need to have the Aaronic Priesthood conferred upon him again.

The bishop and the Aaronic Priesthood advisors assist parents in preparing their young men to receive and honor the priesthood. Together they encourage the young men to be active and worthy and to help them with their priesthood duties. The bishop privately interviews each young man before he is advanced to a new priesthood office.

Along with reviewing the duties of the new office (listed in D&C 20:46–60), the bishop discusses the religious behavior of the young man in order to determine his worthiness. Also he should encourage the youth to (1) pray regularly in private and with his family; (2) honor his parents; (3) speak and act honestly; (4) treat everyone with kindness and respect; (5) be morally clean; (6) refrain from reading, listening to, or viewing pornographic material; (7) pay a full tithing; (8) obey the Word of Wisdom, including abstinence from tobacco, alcoholic drinks, coffee, and tea; (9) refrain from the use of illegal drugs and from the misuse of other substances; (10) refrain from using the name of the Lord in vain, vulgar expressions, and other degrading language; (11) do his duty in the Church and live according to its rules and doctrines; (12) fulfill assignments given him by his quorum presidency; and (13) attend priesthood and sacrament meetings, and participate in other Church meetings and activities.[29]

After the interview, the youth's name is presented in sacrament meeting for the sustaining vote of the ward members. The bishop then directs the priesthood ordinance ceremony and has the ward clerk record the ordination and issue an Aaronic Priesthood ordination certificate to the young man. This procedure is also followed for adult males who are recent converts to the Church, although they may be directly ordained as priests without needing to pass through the offices of deacon and teacher.[30]

Worthy men eighteen and older may become elders. Since Melchizedek Priesthood offices come under the supervision of the stake president, a member of the stake presidency interviews the prospective elder. He asks questions concerning the man's readiness and worthiness to receive the higher priesthood and usually gives instruction concerning the oath and covenant of the priesthood. An oath is a solemn promise, and a covenant is a witnessed act of commitment. A man who receives the priesthood makes a solemn promise to the Lord to righteously magnify that priesthood. The covenant act of commitment is the ordination, which is witnessed by the priesthood holder performing the act and by others.

As the oath and covenant is outlined in Doctrine and Covenants 84:33–42, the Lord presents certain obligations and promised blessings to priesthood holders. They are to receive the priesthood in good faith, with a sincere intent to magnify it by fulfilling all responsibilities associated with the office. Having fulfilled their obligations, Melchizedek Priesthood holders are promised a sanctification "by the Spirit unto the renewing of their bodies." (V. 33.) They become part of "the church and kingdom, and the elect of God." (V. 34.) They receive Heavenly Father's kingdom, and "all" that the Father has will be given them. (See v. 38.) A stern admonition is also given to remain true to the covenant; otherwise, a person who breaks the covenant and deliberately turns away from the priesthood commits an unforgivable sin. (See vv. 41– 42.)

These solemn warnings, promises, and obligations are usually explained and discussed as part of the interview process. After the person's prospective ordination has been cleared by the stake presidency, the high council, and the local stake members, the ordination is supervised by the stake president, who may perform it himself or authorize another Melchizedek Priesthood holder to do it. A similar pattern of interviewing, sustaining, and ordaining is followed later if the man becomes a high priest.

PRIESTHOOD ORGANIZATION AND KEYS

As mentioned earlier, to help accomplish the mission of the Church in an orderly manner, priesthood bearers in their various offices are organized into ecclesiastical groups called quorums. There are the five types of local quorums—deacons, teachers, priests, elders, and high priests—and three quorums that preside over the whole Church—Quorums of the Seventy, the Twelve Apostles, and the First Presidency.[31] (See D&C 107:21–37; 124:125–45.) Bishops and patriarchs are not organized into quorums; they belong to the local quorum of high priests.

Other administrative units such as stake presidencies, stake high councils, bishoprics, and other regional or area groupings of priesthood bearers organized for particular purposes are more correctly identified as councils and not quorums. One simple way to distinguish these two terms is to remember that while all priesthood holders are organized into quorums, the Church members, whether priesthood holders or not, are governed by councils.[32]

Sometimes confusion also arises from misunderstanding about two other terms associated with the priesthood: setting apart and keys of the priesthood. In establishing new leadership in any priesthood quorum, the person performing the ordinance sets apart the new leader and gives the president of the quorum any special keys, or authority, to function in his calling. These keys constitute the distinctive directive powers of presidency.[33] Stake presidents are therefore called and set apart by a General Authority of the Church, who also gives him the keys of presidency over his stake. The stake president may then call and set apart elders quorum presidents and give them the keys of their office because that office comes under the jurisdiction of the stake president and the keys that he holds.

The quorums are not only organized to provide a group for joint instruction and united service, but they also provide a source of rich fellowship and a brotherhood far more valuable and lasting than found in any secular service or fraternal organization. Quorum members who have the vision of their brotherhood willingly care for each other and assist both temporally and spiritually in uplifting and edifying each other.

THE POWER OF GOD THROUGH THE AGES

Because the priesthood is so important and is the power of God that gives validity to all his creations, it always precedes and supersedes gospel dispensations and church organization. The priesthood links between the dispensations verify the authenticity of the new order of God on earth. In the scriptures, we find that the priesthood, not names, titles, or unique callings, is the essential element to establish God's kingdom on earth. The kingdom might be called or organized in any manner, shape, or form, but it always depends upon the inspired leadership of the priesthood holders of God who hold the keys of presidency at that time.

In the example of Abraham, we see the priesthood in use as God's power on this earth. Abraham said, "I sought for mine appointment unto the priesthood according to the appointment of God." (Abr. 1:4.) Thereafter, because Abraham used his priesthood in righteousness, it brought him and his descendants many blessings. Indeed, through the descendants of Abraham, all the families of the earth have been blessed. (See D&C 110:12.) All righteous descendants of Abraham are "lawful heirs" to these blessings and the powers of the priesthood. (See D&C 86:8–11.)

At the time of Moses, a social organization somewhat similar to ours was revealed to the Israelites. Both the Melchizedek and Aaronic Priesthood were on the earth, although the higher was only sparsely used, especially when compared with the numbers of active Melchizedek Priesthood holders today. Anciently, the congregation of Israel was organized into tribes and clans with a prophet, Moses, at its head. Today we have areas and regions administered by modern prophetic leadership. Alongside Moses was his brother Aaron, the presiding High Priest, whose position was analogous to the Presiding Bishop today. The twelve princes of the tribes of Israel, resembling our Council of the Twelve, formed a governing body, aided by seventy elders consisting of older men from all the tribes. Finally, Moses appointed judges or rulers over units of a thousand, a hundred, fifty, and finally ten men. These can easily be likened to stake presidents, bishops, quorum presidents, and perhaps home teachers, who have stewardship over similarly sized groups of men and their families.

In defending the authenticity of the restored church, we often point to the similarities between our modern priesthood organization and that existing in the early apostolic church organized by the mortal Lord himself. We see from many scriptures that the structure was much the same. As Paul said, "Ye are . . . of the household of God; and are built upon the foundation of the apostles and prophets, Jesus Christ himself being the chief corner stone." (Eph. 2:19–20.) Further, Christ "gave some, apostles; and some, prophets; and some, evangelists [patriarchs]; and some, pastors [bishops] and teachers; for the perfecting of the saints." (Eph. 4:11–12.) There was a full ecclesiastical organization of the early church under the Melchizedek Priesthood.

Having the blessings of the priesthood today, all worthy male members of the Church can enjoy the powers of God's priesthood on earth. They can trace the authority of their priesthood office through the individual who gave it to them on back to Joseph Smith, and from Joseph to Peter, James, and John back to Jesus Christ. So every priesthood holder has a direct line of priesthood authority to Christ, who received his power and glory from God, our Heavenly Father.

Indeed, we say that *the PRIESTHOOD is the power and authority to act for God, and with it and through various priesthood councils, Christ's church administers to all members. Worthy men have the Aaronic or Melchizedek Priesthood conferred upon them, are ordained to offices in that priesthood, are organized into quorums, and are set apart and given keys to administer in certain callings.* We recognize that, along with having God's power on earth, righteous use of this priesthood entails many responsibilities. We cannot take for granted the marvelous power given us and expect the priesthood to remain in power in our lives. Like the uniform and badge of a policeman, certain standards of righteousness and displays of service are recognizable emblems of a proper priesthood that remains in full force. As the priesthood is wisely used, both the priesthood bearer and those he serves are richly blessed and strengthened as they journey together on their way toward God's celestial realms.

For further study, refer to the following entries:

TG	BD	*EM*
Priesthood	Aaronic Priesthood	Aaronic Priesthood
Priesthood, Aaronic	Bishop	Deacon, Aaronic
Priesthood, Keys of	Elders	Priesthood
Priesthood, Melchizedek	High Priest	Elder, Melchizedek
Priesthood, Ordination	Melchizedek Priesthood	Priesthood
Priesthood, Power of		High Priest
		Keys of the Priesthood
		Levitical Priesthood
		Melchizedek
		Melchizedek Priesthood
		Oath and Covenant of the Priesthood
		Ordination to the Priesthood
		Priest, Aaronic Priesthood
		Priesthood
		Priesthood Interview
		Priesthood Offices
		Priesthood Quorums
		Teacher, Aaronic Priesthood

CHAPTER 33

GOD'S GOVERNMENT ON EARTH

The creation of any new automobile requires two major stages — planning and production. First, directors, designers, and engineers at an automobile company will struggle to design a new car, with particular emphasis upon its power source — the engine. They know that in any engine, the raw potential power of the fuel must be transformed into energy that can be channeled into productive output so the machine can do its work. Many moving parts are necessary to transfer the power through the engine to the drive train. Good lubricants are also necessary to overcome friction and keep the parts moving smoothly. The engineers design the engine and specify the fuel, lubricants, parts, and servicing necessary to keep it running efficiently. In their design, they also provide mechanical, safety, and aesthetic features so that the end product is an efficient, safe, comfortable means of transportation.

Second, the factory needs to produce the automobile. The purpose of the production phase is to incorporate the design concepts and to profitably manufacture a quality product that customers will want to purchase. So plants and assembly lines are organized, quality controls are established, materials are purchased, and distributing and marketing strategies are developed. Eventually the concept becomes reality as the new car rides the highway.

In a similar process, most of us have experienced occasions when we plan and talk about doing a project and then organize and work (and probably reorganize and revise the work) until we finally get the job done. During the transfer of any expectation into reality, various alternate means must sometimes be provided to transform what was planned into success, especially if the initial plan does not seem to be working. If we are wise, we learn from experience and gradually refine our capacity to

539

transform hopes into reality. For example, a coach spends many hours in training his team for competition. He prepares a game plan and hopes the team will be victorious. Nevertheless, a major part of his coaching effectiveness depends upon his ability to adjust to the changing circumstances and challenges of each game as he coaches the team to a successful season.

God set and followed a similar pattern when he planned for the organization of this earth and the placement of his spirit children upon it, without however having had to fumble through errors and misjudgment. As part of our premortal existence, he designed the truths and ordinances of the gospel to bless many lives. On earth he has also organized a means—the ecclesiastical structure of The Church of Jesus Christ of Latter-day Saints—by which his gospel and power could be delivered for the best benefit of the people. Within that church, the gospel truths and ordinances and the priesthood powers and blessings can be channeled through many active people and programs in such a way that best meets the needs of God's children.

Unfortunately, like workers in a factory who might not produce the highest quality product, members of the church of Jesus Christ are not always successful in fully blessing peoples' lives. Natural friction and resistance occur that impede the smooth transfer of spiritual blessings throughout God's kingdom, especially as new, inexperienced members come into the Church during its rapid expansion to the far corners of the earth. Even worse, the corrosive and polluting influences of the world weaken the Church's effectiveness. God helps compensate for these inadequacies and resistance through the cleansing power of his love, the gospel principles of his Son, Jesus Christ, and the spiritual strength of the Holy Ghost.

UNITY AND STRUCTURE WITHIN THE CHURCH OF CHRIST

Those baptized in Christ's name become members of his church. Baptism serves as a gateway into his spiritual kingdom on earth as well as a cleansing ordinance.[1] Salvation and many other blessings (present and potential) await the faithful members of the Church. However, these spiritual rewards are available only within the religious community as individual members work together, each doing his or her own part to further the Lord's work.

The importance of belonging to the Lord's church is emphasized in the New Testament with these words: "The Lord added to the church daily such as should be saved." (Acts 2:47.) To emphasize the need for unity and order in the early Christian church, the Apostle Paul compared its diverse membership to the various parts of the body. He noted that even though each body member is different and though some body parts are esteemed less than others, each part is essential to the proper functioning of the whole: "Now hath God set the members every one of them in the body, as it hath pleased him. . . . that there should be no schism in the body; but that the members should have the same care one for another." (1 Cor. 12:18–25.) But while all body parts depend on each other, there is a hierarchy of functions, in the Church as well as in the body: "God hath set some in the church, first apostles, secondarily prophets, thirdly teachers, after that . . . helps, [and] governments." (1 Cor. 12:28.)

The latter-day church of Jesus Christ requires the same unity as in the earlier apostolic period. As the membership works together to edify and strengthen one another, the benefits are for the good of the whole. A similar structure and hierarchy is still needed to organize the efforts of the members. Thus the leadership in the Church is structured after the same pattern that existed in Christ's time. Prophets, evangelists (patriarchs), pastors (bishops), and teachers function in their same priesthood offices today. (See Eph. 4:11–14.) Paul repeatedly explained that all the offices and functions of the Church are necessary for the whole structure to be recognized as Christ's church.[2] (See Rom. 12:4–5; 1 Cor. 12.)

While a hierarchy of priesthood leadership continues, an equality of brotherhood and sisterhood is also a hallmark of the church of Christ. These elements are not as contradictory as they might at first appear — the combination of leadership and fellowship promotes the advancement of the Saints as a whole, while preserving a line of authority extending to Christ himself, the head of the Church. Like water coming from heaven to earth, the leadership authority line connects Christ with every bishop and family patriarch to guide the membership. Like water distributed through canals, pipes, and hoses, the fellowship bonding joins every member with each other as they work together to build Christ's kingdom here on earth.

GOD'S SYSTEM OF GOVERNING

The Church of Jesus Christ of Latter-day Saints is an organization structured to meet various needs of the baptized followers of Jesus Christ. The term *church* derives from the Greek *ecclesia,* meaning "an assembly called together." The organized body of believers who have taken upon themselves the name of Jesus Christ through baptism and confirmation are called by their head, Jesus, to work together within the assembly or association of his church and to serve one another.

The current ecclesiastical organization of Jesus Christ is his spiritual kingdom on earth; it has the responsibility to spread his gospel and to prepare all people for his coming millennial reign. The Church thus serves as the Lord's government on earth. A government is a body or system that exercises authority over a group. The concept "to govern" comes from the Greek *kybernan,* meaning "to steer or pilot a ship; to direct or command a group." The church of Jesus Christ serves to steer its members in God's desired direction so his children can strengthen each other within his spiritual kingdom on earth. The Church exercises God's authority over this organized body of Christ's followers as it pilots them safely back to a heavenly realm.

Since the days of Adam, groups of believers in the true and living God have assembled together under the direction of prophets and priesthood leaders to strengthen their spiritual fellowship. God has continually adapted the social structure of his believers to reflect the political systems of the time. In ancient times, this assembly of followers was organized into a patriarchal order, with the primary association being within and between family units. Later in the Old Testament period, the primary social structure was based on the Tribes of Israel and featured a centralized levitical priesthood. This community of believers was commonly called a "congregation" in the Old Testament. In the New Testament period, a fellowship of saints under the direction of priesthood leaders provided the primary assembly for Church members.

As indicated earlier in this chapter, a similar Church organization has been established today for the followers of Jesus Christ. Eventually,

Jesus Christ will come to earth to personally preside over his church after it has joined together with his kingdom from heaven. Indeed, the word *kingdom* is often used in the scriptures to identify God's community of believers, since they are literally God's kingdom on earth.[3]

SOME GOVERNING PRINCIPLES OF CHRIST'S CHURCH

Political scientists have identified five basic elements that are common to all governments: sovereignty, legitimacy, rules of conduct, jurisdiction, and law enforcement.[4] These five elements serve as an outline by which the key governing principles of Christ's Church on earth can be defined and discussed.

SOVEREIGNTY

Sovereignty is the supreme power or authority of a government. In most democratic nations, this sovereign power rests with the people, who then allow the governing body to exercise limited authority. In the church of Jesus Christ, the governing authority must be Jesus Christ himself, or it cannot be his church. To be the Lord's church, it must have his teachings, his laws, his name, and be governed by him through his appointed representatives. (See 3 Ne. 27:1–12; D&C 115:4.)

The foundation for the true power of the Lord's church is laid through the restored priesthood with its keys, revealed scriptures and revelations, and prophetic leadership.[5] Consequently, the same authority, doctrines, and organization established by Jesus Christ in apostolic times have been restored to the earth to constitute the true church of Christ. It operates through his divine authority and under his godly sovereignty.

LEGITIMACY

In the political world, legitimacy is the acceptance by the people of a government's authority to exercise power. In the religious community, after God has empowered his followers as true members of his church, the people must accept the church's legitimacy in order for it to have any lasting effect in their lives.

Indeed, the pattern of the restored church has been to seek legitimacy from both without and within the Church membership. As The Church of Jesus Christ of Latter-day Saints was founded on April 6, 1830, Joseph Smith followed the laws of the state of New York in organizing a legal entity. In a similar fashion, Church leaders seek for legal recognition in all countries where there are members and where they want to send missionaries. They want the members and missionaries to have full legal rights and religious legitimacy in these nations.

Acceptance of authority from within the Church membership is established through the "law of common consent." According to this law, Church members exercise their agency in accepting or rejecting the decisions and directions of Church leaders, who make their decisions after the Lord has given them spiritual confirmation.[6] For example, after a bishop has prepared the annual ward budget or decided on a program of special emphasis for the ward members, he seeks for a spiritual confirmation and then asks the adult members for their sustaining vote before finalizing the plans.

The most common use of sustaining occurs after Church officers are selected through the spirit of revelation by their leaders. These officers must be sustained in their callings by the membership over whom they will exercise authority. This sustaining is usually done in a sacrament meeting or a general assembly of the organization in which they will serve. The presiding officer asks the members to be called into the new offices to stand while their names and positions are presented and the congregation votes. (If any member should oppose a person in a calling, he may, in a private interview, state his reasons, which will be considered by those in authority. It is particularly important to determine whether the negative vote was "based on knowledge that the person presented has been guilty of conduct that should disqualify the person from the position."[7])

As the Lord revealed through the Prophet Joseph Smith, "No person is to be ordained to any office in this church, where there is a regularly organized branch of the same, without the vote of that church." (D&C 20:65.) This sustaining vote by the body of saints is known as the "law of common consent," and it legitimizes the Church leadership in their callings. It also is a sign by those who vote to sustain their leaders that they will support them and take counsel and direction from them. Thus a clear, recognized, and accepted body of leadership is established.

RULES OF CONDUCT

All organizations need basic laws to guide their social structure and to keep life running smoothly for the group and its members. As the Mosaic law and the church of Christ were established in ancient times, the scriptures record some divine expectations for the Lord's followers. For instance, some of the most challenging reading material of the Old Testament is found in the book of Leviticus where the Lord provided quite a few sets of rules for ancient Israel.

The Doctrine and Covenants and the Church's *General Handbook of Instructions* provide similar but more pertinent direction for leaders of the Church today. As an indication of the great diversity of guidelines found in the *General Handbook,* note the titles of its eleven sections: Church Administration; Meetings; Calls and Releases; Ordinations; Ordinances and Blessings; Temples, Marriage, and Family History; Missionary Service; Records and Reports; Finances; Church Discipline; and Church Policies. Approximately one hundred and twenty pages in length and amazingly small for a guidebook directing an organization of over eight million members, the *General Handbook* has been prepared "to guide servants of the Lord in directing the Church and helping to strengthen families."[8]

Further detailed instructions regarding priesthood, auxiliary, and other Church programs are provided in various organizational handbooks, printed guidelines for priesthood leaders, and other administrative publications. Current, up-to-date, and supplemental instructions are given through a periodical *Bulletin* and correspondence sent to local leaders. General Church periodicals, especially the *Ensign* magazine, inform the general membership about changes in Church organization, establishment of new policies, founding of new missions, and other announcements or programs of the Church. All in all, The Church of Jesus Christ of Latter-day Saints diligently strives to keep leaders and members informed about the rules of conduct expected of them.

JURISDICTION

Jurisdiction defines the range of authority that a government or body has. For example, the jurisdiction of a political government extends over the citizens of that entity and the noncitizens who live or travel within its boundaries. The jurisdiction of a church's authority extends only over the members of that given religious community. For example, in the Roman Catholic Church, its leaders govern only other Roman Catholics, and likewise, any disciplinary action or enforcement of religious standards for The Church of Jesus Christ of Latter-day Saints is limited to members of the Church. Thus any one nation or church does not have the right to make and enforce rules or laws for another political or religious group.

The separateness and independence of both political and church groups is a fundamental doctrine of The Church of Jesus Christ of Latter-day Saints as stressed in the eleventh and twelfth Articles of Faith. The eleventh Article of Faith claims our privilege to worship God as we desire and allows all people the same privilege to "worship how, where, or what they may." The twelfth Article of Faith states that we believe in being subject to political rulers and in "obeying, honoring, and sustaining the law" of the nations where we live. We recognize the importance of maintaining jurisdiction over our own members, and we accord other groups the same right.

LAW ENFORCEMENT

The last element of governmental rule comes out of the two previous ones. The concept of enforcement is closely related to the rules of conduct and jurisdiction of a government. Rules are ineffective unless people obey them, and if an organization has little or no jurisdiction to enforce its laws, it loses control and cannot operate. Soon no law or order would exist within such a society.

Religious standards within The Church of Jesus Christ of Latter-day Saints are enforced privately through interviews with local ecclesiastical leaders or through limited, organized disciplinary councils conducted by the bishop or stake president. The purposes of Church discipline are to "(1) save the souls of transgressors; (2) protect the innocent; and (3) safeguard the purity, integrity, and good name of the Church."[9]

Church discipline is handled through one of two ways. First, members are encouraged to be fully active and committed so they can enjoy all the blessings of Church membership, including worthiness to be called into any Church position or to attend the temple, and readiness to have full access to all the Church programs and assistance. Second, if a member's behavior falls below Church standards, certain rights and privileges can be withdrawn, placing members on probation or, if the sins are more serious, withdrawing fellowship and even membership. Thus, in an appropriate, loving manner, obedience to Church laws and God's commandments is developed and maintained among the members of Christ's church.

In summary, all five elements of a sound government or society are found in the Church: sovereignty, legitimacy, rules, jurisdiction, and enforcement. Through the power of God's government on earth, the lives of his children who choose to become active members of the church of his Son, Jesus Christ, are blessed and strengthened.

SOME ORGANIZATIONAL FUNCTIONS OF CHRIST'S CHURCH

After governing principles are set in place, they must be put into practice within the actual structure of a government or church organization. Each nation, church, and religion has certain distinctive characteristics. Five identifying factors can be used to compare different groups or governments: type of government, organizational structure, functioning programs, long-range purpose, and available assets. A study of these five characteristics will distinguish the Mormons from all other religions and Christian denominations.

1. TYPE OF GOVERNMENT

The Church of Jesus Christ of Latter-day Saints is a theocracy. A theocracy is a form of religious government in which appointed leaders receive and interpret God's laws and have his authority in matters pertaining to the organization. The term *theocracy* comes from two Greek words, *theos*, meaning "God," and *kratein*, meaning "to rule." As we indicated in the earlier section on sovereignty, the Lord directs his own church through his appointed servants, be they patriarchs, prophets, priests, or apostles.

Theocracy was God's original earthly government with Adam and the great patriarchs, who served as the Lord's presiding high priest through whom the laws of the Lord were revealed and administered.[10] The ancient House of Israel and the early church of Jesus Christ were also theocracies in that the Lord governed them through his appointed servants: the prophets, priests, and apostles. When the resurrected Messiah comes to personally reign during the millennial era on earth, he will be recognized by all peoples as the King of kings, and a perfect theocracy will govern. (See Rev. 19:16; D&C 38:20–22; 58:20–22.)

2. ORGANIZATIONAL STRUCTURE

When most people compare churches, they often first look at the church organization. The church of Jesus Christ is distinguished by its hierarchy of priesthood councils. The hierarchy of leadership existing in the kingdom of God on earth is patterned after what prevails in the heavens. From the beginning, the affairs of God's kingdom — including the very creation of the world — have been conducted through *councils:* "The Gods said among themselves: . . . We will end our work, which we have counseled; and we will rest . . . from all our work which we have counseled." (Abr. 5:2.) Likewise, the Church today is governed by a series of higher general and lower local councils.

The appointed leader of any one council does not dictate his wishes, nor do the other council members demand the right of "majority rule." They are to arrive at agreement together through discussion and, most importantly, inspiration from God through united prayer.

As quoted earlier from Paul's discussion of the "body of Christ," the highest authority in the Church resides in the apostles whom Christ has called to direct Church affairs. The original council, or quorum of Twelve Apostles, was chosen personally by the Lord during his mortal ministry, and he was the presiding officer. After the resurrection and ascension of Christ, the need for a new presiding authority on earth arose. Peter — the senior apostle — became the presiding officer of the Church, with James and John as his two counselors. (See D&C 7:5–7.)

Presiding Councils of the Church

As the seventh Article of Faith states, "We believe in the same organization that existed in the Primitive Church, namely, apostles, prophets, . . . and so forth." In the latter days, the head of the Church (representing Christ) is the President, again the senior apostle. As President of the High Priesthood of the Church, he presides over the entire Church. (See D&C 107:65–67, 91.) He and two other apostles or righteous high priests form a quorum and constitute the First Presidency of the Church, in whom the supreme authority and keys of the kingdom reside. (See D&C 107:22; 124:126.)

The Twelve Apostles form a quorum "equal in authority and power to the three presidents" (D&C 107:24), but officiating under their direction (D&C 107:33; 112:30). These apostles serve as "special witnesses of the name of Christ in all the world." (D&C 107:23; see also v. 33.) Besides governing the established Church, the Quorum of the Twelve, under direction of the First Presidency, is also called "to open the door by the proclamation of the gospel of Jesus Christ." (D&C 107:35.) Weekly, these two presiding quorums of the Church "meet jointly as the Council of the First Presidency and the Quorum of the Twelve Apostles. Meeting in a room in the Salt Lake Temple, this council discusses and decides all major Church appointments and policy matters."[11] At the death of the President, the First Presidency is automatically dissolved, and the Quorum of the Twelve Apostles becomes the presiding body of the Church until a new president is ordained.

Additional leaders assist the apostles in their callings. The First Quorum of the Seventy holds special authority to help govern the Church together with the Council of the Twelve, but it acts "under the direction of the Twelve . . . in building up the church and regulating all the affairs of the same in all nations." (D&C 107:34; see also vv. 22–30.) Other quorums of Seventy are called as needed to conduct general Church affairs. The temporal affairs of the Church are administered through the Presiding Bishopric, which is also the Presidency of the Aaronic Priesthood of the Church and serves under the direction of the First Presidency. (See D&C 107:15, 68.)

The First Presidency, the Quorum of the Twelve Apostles, and the First Quorum of the Seventy are the standing, presiding councils of the Church. These general priesthood officers of the Church are collectively known as the General Authorities. Their stewardship is Churchwide and they may receive assignments anywhere in the world to administer Christ's kingdom on earth.

Areas of the Church

The worldwide Church is divided into a number of areas, the largest geographical administrative subdivision of the Church. A typical area would consist of two to five hundred thousand saints, organized into dozens of stakes, with a few missions and temples serving the area. An area presidency is composed of three members from the presiding quorums of the Seventy. They "provide spiritual guidance and administrative direction to leaders and members of the Church in their area."[12] They implement the policies and instructions of the presiding councils of the Church and supervise the broad range of Church activities and programs in their area.

Area presidencies will sometimes convene informal councils of regional representatives, stake presidents, and possibly mission presidents in their area in order to provide training and direction. When needed, other councils and lines of leadership are organized as a bridge between the general Church leadership and the local stake and ward units.

Regions of the Church

While the functions of priesthood offices are divinely established, the number and arrangement of officers in the administration of Church affairs can be flexible according to the needs of the members. Hence, Paul made provision in the early Christian Church for various "helps" and "governments." (1 Cor. 12:28.) Because the Church is so large today and is spreading rapidly in many foreign lands, an expanding structure is used to administrate various areas and regions in order to unite them with the whole Church.

Most areas are subdivided into a number of "regions," intermediate geographic units with Regional Representatives called to train, instruct, and advise the local stake leaders as directed by the Quorum of the Twelve through the Area Presidencies.[13] Regions around the world consist of two to six stakes in close geographical proximity. A Regional Representative's primary responsibility is to train stake leaders, which he does "through personal visits, regional council meetings consisting of stake presidencies in the region, stake conferences, or other leadership meetings."[14]

Stakes and Wards of Zion

The fundamental geographic unit of the Church that provides the full Church program to members is a "stake." In ancient Israel, Zion was pictured as a great tent supported by cords securely fastened to stakes. (See Isa. 54:2–7.) In the latter days, segments of Church population and strength are likewise called *stakes*—their presence indicating priesthood strength, membership stability, and Church maturity in the locality. Each stake has an organization patterned after the First Presidency and Council of the Twelve, being governed by a stake presidency of three members and a high council of twelve high priests.

The stakes, in turn, are composed of several *wards* and sometimes smaller *branches,* each having a bishopric (or branch presidency) and a ward (or branch) council. The ward and branch leaders assist the local priesthood quorums and family heads in bringing the blessings of the Church and gospel into the lives of the individual members.

3. FUNCTIONING PROGRAMS

Any viable organization needs to provide strong programs of instruction and leadership training. Through the leadership of the priesthood administration, a variety of local callings and programs are provided to assist the members. Some of these aids are specifically organized to meet special needs or interests of the members, but most of them are structured around different age groups.

Some Church resources assist individual members or nonmembers. For example, on a stake level, two callings deserve particular mention. A stake patriarch is called to give patriarchal blessings to individual, mature members. A patriarchal blessing is a sacred, confidential, and personal blessing of inspiration and direction. It contains an "inspired and prophetic statement of the life mission of the recipient, together with such blessings, cautions, and admonitions as the patriarch may be prompted to give."[15] Also, a stake mission president is called to direct the proselyting efforts of the members and missionaries at a local level. He works together with the full-time mission president and missionaries to preach the gospel to nonmembers living in the stake area.

Other local programs are directed toward special needs and interests. For example, stake and ward music, library, public communications, and auditing personnel are called as needed to assist in their particular areas of expertise, which are often unnoticed by most members. More visible are the efforts of the stake and ward activities leaders and committees as they provide a whole variety of sports, cultural, and social activities for the members. Many of these activities are done on a ward or branch level, but some, such as the sports competition and large-scale cultural productions, are necessarily accomplished on a stake level.

Most of the Church programs are organized for particular age and interest groups and are part of the auxiliary organizations of the Church. Besides the priesthood quorums for the men, the Church also has several major auxiliary groups: the Relief Society for all adult women, the Young

Men's and Young Women's organizations for the youth aged twelve to eighteen, the Primary for younger children, and the Sunday School for members twelve and older. In addition, young adult and special interest programs are organized for single adults and single heads of households.

Relief Society

The Relief Society was formed in 1842, and it has since grown to become the largest women's organization in the world. Twelve years after the organization of the Church, a few women discussed the idea of forming a society to assist workers at the construction of the Nauvoo Temple. When twenty of these women presented their idea to the Prophet Joseph Smith, he said they should be organized "under the priesthood after a pattern of the priesthood." The selected president (Joseph's wife, Emma), two counselors, and a secretary and treasurer were to preside over the society, just as the First Presidency presided over the Church. "The Church was never perfectly organized until the women were thus organized," the Prophet claimed. The leaders of this women's organization work together with priesthood leaders in a "companionship relationship—not inferior or subordinate, but companion, side-by-side."[16]

The duties of that first Relief Society were to administer to the poor, strengthen morality in the community, and support the elders of the Church. While the organization has grown to include millions of women worldwide, the charter is basically unchanged. "As defined for the women of the Church today," says Barbara W. Winder, former General President of the Relief Society, "the mission of the Relief Society is to help women (1) have faith in God and build individual testimonies of the gospel of Jesus Christ, (2) strengthen the families of the Church, (3) give compassionate service, and (4) sustain the priesthood."[17] With the motto "Charity Never Faileth," Relief Society sisters provide sterling examples of compassionate service for Church members and others in their communities.

Young Women's and Young Men's Organizations

Later in Church history, when the Saints were fully established in the Utah territory, and after the initial hardships had passed, young women in the Church began yearning for fashionable clothes like those worn in the East. In 1869, President Brigham Young commissioned Relief Society leaders to form an organization to encourage their daughters in economical and modest dress manufactured locally instead of importing extravagant fashions from other areas. This society became known as the local Retrenchment Association.

The "retrenchment" focus soon expanded to include many areas of "mutual improvement," and then, after a while, the young men were invited to join also. The Young Ladies' and Young Men's Mutual Improvement Associations were organized in the wards in 1875. Besides receiving religious instruction, the teenagers studied history and literature, held debates and dramas, and socialized through dances, picnics, and athletic events. Similar activities still characterize the modern Young Women's and Young Men's organizations as they attend classes on Sunday and participate in various activities during the week, such as game nights, service projects, dances, Scouting camps, sports, homemaking and etiquette demonstrations, and a variety of social and cultural activities.

Primary

In 1878, the need to reach even younger children became apparent, and so Primary Associations were established in wards throughout the areas of Mormon settlements. This organization supplemented the children's early religious training and protected them from worldly influences. Today, small groups of children from three to twelve are taught the basic principles of the gospel in their Primary classes each Sunday and join with larger groups in joint activities that include talks, songs, and stories.

Sunday School

While some adults and a few youth are involved with directing and teaching the Primary-age children, the rest of the members attend age-group classes for religious instruction. Sunday School is the name given the Church auxiliary with the responsibility to instruct members from age twelve upward. Classes for the twelve- to eighteen-year-old youth are coeducational and structured by age. Course instruction focuses on gospel principles and teachings, Church history, scripture study, and the lives and teachings of the modern prophets.

After age eighteen, the adult members can attend a variety of classes, such as Gospel Essentials (primarily for investigators or new members of the Church), Gospel Doctrine (for most adult members), Teacher Development (for prospective or current teachers), Family History (for those interested in help in genealogy and family histories), and Family

Relations (for parents seeking helpful instruction). The curriculum for the most heavily attended course, Gospel Doctrine, is based on a four-year rotation of scripture study, with one year devoted to the Old Testament, one year to the New Testament, one year to the Book of Mormon, and one year to the Doctrine and Covenants (with some emphasis on modern Church history.)

4. LONG-RANGE PURPOSE

Some government bureaucracies, and even a few service clubs and other organizations, continue to exist with minimal effect long after their original purposes have been fulfilled. Having a clear-cut and correct mission statement or declaration of purpose is essential in providing up-to-date, valid reasons for an organization's existence.

The eternal purpose of the church of Jesus Christ is to assist God's children to return in righteousness and purity back into his presence. To focus our attention on more immediate means to achieve this noble purpose, Church leaders have developed a mission statement for the Church with a three-fold emphasis: to preach the gospel to the non-members, to perfect the Saints within the Church, and to redeem the dead through the saving ordinances of the temple.[18] The unique and farsighted mission of the Church distinguishes it as an organization zealously endeavoring to further God's work here on earth and into eternity.

5. AVAILABLE ASSETS

Any effective government, business, or organization needs a variety of personnel and material assets by which it can provide the goods and services its membership needs. By far, the Church's greatest asset is its dedicated members, who work and serve to bring much goodness and righteousness into the lives of many people. As members catch the spirit of the law of consecration, they willingly and anxiously devote their time, money, gifts, and talents to the building of God's kingdom.[19] As they live as true saints and followers of Christ, they become the living beacons of the restored gospel and help bring many into the full fellowship of the Church.[20]

From their childhood, members serve each other closely in the Church organization. The Church programs not only instill gospel principles, but they also prepare people to serve and lead in Christ's kingdom.

The fact that bishops, stake presidents, and other Church leaders are not paid help their motives for service to remain pure. Also, Church callings and offices are rotated frequently to provide many with the opportunity to grow and learn many aspects of leadership and service. Through long-term, deep and personally involved association with each other, members come to feel a kinship with other Saints exceeded only by the natural one in their own families. Thus, in the words of Paul, members "have the same care one for another. And whether one member suffer, all the members suffer with it; or one member be honoured, all the members rejoice with it." (1 Cor. 12:25–26.)

A SCHOOL, A HOSPITAL, OR A MUSEUM FOR THE SAINTS?

In some ways, The Church of Jesus Christ of Latter-day Saints is like a special school of the Lord on earth. The administrators are the presiding councils of the Church, the faculty are the Church leaders and teachers, and the students are the members. However, there is much more cooperation and rotation between the various positions than one finds in a normal school. The principle of common consent and the practice of lay leadership develop a sense of fellowship as member-students become leader-teachers and as leader-teachers always remain member-students. Through teaching, strengthening, and serving one another, all are edified together.

The Church has also been compared to a hospital or clinic where the spiritually ill can go to find the appropriate cure. Like doctors and nurses, divinely called and inspired leaders and teachers bring God's healing powers into our lives so that we can leave the maladies behind us and in turn strengthen ourselves and serve others. Like staff members and volunteer workers who often work behind the scenes, many Church members serve in callings that provide valuable help so that the Church programs can properly function. And like family and friends who visit and support the sick, our brothers and sisters in the gospel give needed help and encouragement. In the Church, each member serves as both "doctor" and "patient" because all have the opportunity to serve and be served. In the end, all of us enjoy greater spiritual health through our association with each other.

Finally, some might claim that the Church is like a museum of holy saints and sacred relics. Granted, the Church of Jesus Christ houses many valuable spiritual gifts and precious priesthood powers, but they are not to be catalogued, mounted, and displayed in sterile showcases. If the Church is like a museum, it is more like a series of dynamic, hands-on exhibits with which people can become actively involved. The gospel truths and ordinances and the priesthood powers and blessings are available for all to study and, more importantly, to take home with them; they are not just stored in the museum's warehouse.

Whether the Church is compared to a school, hospital, or museum, or if it is likened to the development of a new product, such as an engine, the Lord planned and designed his kingdom on earth to provide the greatest possible blessings to his disciples and followers. The Church members who are trying to fulfill his expectations are far from perfect, but, in the main, they are earnestly striving to help and serve one another. Together, they are working diligently to bring spiritual productivity into many peoples' lives.

In conclusion, we recognize that *the CHURCH is an assembly of faithful believers. Although God's kingdom on earth, it is an organization also supported by the law of common consent. Through the Church, the gospel is applied in individual lives as the members strengthen, teach, edify, and serve each other in inspired love and through special programs.* Together the Lord's followers establish a social order for those who have entered a covenant relationship with God. This organization then assists in the perfection of the individuals with the help of the whole group. Thus the members grow spiritually and progress together on their way back toward our Heavenly Father's kingdom.

All Church members are expected to work together with unity and love in this soul-building, heavenly reaching effort. While only a small fraction of the membership will ever rise to positions of high leadership, the highest blessings of the kingdom—eternal life and exaltation—are available to all through compliance with essential ordinances and obedience to the commandments. When this joint effort is accomplished, the Lord promises that "the angels [shall] be crowned with the glory of his [Christ's] might, and the saints shall be filled with his glory, and receive their inheritance and be made equal with him." (D&C 88:107.)

This is the glorious promise awaiting the faithful members of The Church of Jesus Christ of Latter-day Saints—when they and God's angels shall enjoy the Lord's blessings.

For further study, refer to the following entries:

TG	BD	*EM*
Church	Church	Auxiliary
Church Organization	Kingdom of Heaven	Organizations
Common Consent	or Kingdom of God	Bishopric
Kingdom of God on		Callings
Earth		Church of Jesus
		Christ of Latter-day
		Saints, The
		Common Consent
		First Presidency
		General Authorities
		Kingdom of God
		Lay Participation and
		Leadership
		Name of the Church
		Organization of the
		Church
		President of the
		Church
		Primary
		Region, Regional
		Representative
		Relief Society
		Scouting
		Stake
		Sunday School
		Ward
		Ward Organization
		Young Men
		Young Women

CHAPTER 34

A DIVINE MISSION

Business firms and service organizations often develop a statement of purpose, a motto, or a mission declaration. More than a catchy slogan or a commercial jingle, a mission statement defines objectives and gives value to the efforts of the group. This expression of intent is usually printed, circulated, and discussed by the leaders and members of the group. The members then focus and unify their efforts to achieve its stated aims. Families and individuals who desire a fulfilling life also need some personal expectations or a type of "mission statement" to help them achieve success.

Similarly, as God's spirit children work together in The Church of Jesus Christ of Latter-day Saints, they need an understanding of the organization's mission so they can best direct their collective effort in returning to God's presence. Until the 1970s, if members were asked to define the purpose of the Church, they would have given a myriad of good responses and correct answers, but an outsider would have had a hard time determining a single, comprehensive, clear statement of purpose. Today, most active members would express the mission of the Church something like the following: "The threefold mission of The Church of Jesus Christ of Latter-day Saints is to [1] proclaim the gospel to all peoples, [2] perfect the Saints in Christ's church, and [3] perform vicarious ordinances for the eternal spirits of our deceased ancestors and others."

Longtime Mormons sense that although the central purpose of the Church is to help one another, they need to reach out and share the gospel through missionary work and exemplary service, and they also have a responsibility to establish eternal family ties. Through reviewing this threefold mission of the Church, we come to appreciate how united and loving dedication helps Christ's kingdom on earth fulfill its special destiny.

Evolution of the Church's Threefold Mission Statement

The Church's mission has three primary areas of emphasis: sharing the gospel, strengthening one another, and building eternal families. Missionary work, Church service, and temple assignments all find their place in these three all-encompassing objectives. Church leaders starting with Joseph Smith have stressed the importance of these programs, but they were not combined into one concise declaration. For example, since the beginning of the restoration of the gospel, the Church has been dedicated to missionary work. Church programs, from their origin, were encouraged to develop spirituality in each member's life. Furthermore, the prophets have continuously emphasized the importance of redeeming the dead. Indeed, Joseph Smith stated that "the greatest responsibility in this world that God has laid upon us is to seek after our dead."[1]

The Church's mission statement as we now know it was first outlined in a series of statements made by President Spencer W. Kimball. He combined two of the three elements together in a general conference talk delivered on April 1, 1978. He indicated that most Church members were aware of the modern prophets' "intense interest in the missionary work . . . and the appeals we have made in many lands for the rededication to preaching the gospel and . . . the good news of the restoration to the people everywhere. . . . I feel the same sense of urgency about temple work for the dead as I do about missionary work for the living, *since they are basically one and the same.*"[2]

Three years later, again in an April general conference address, President Kimball introduced the threefold mission of the Church for the first time. He said:

My brothers and sisters, as the Brethren of the First Presidency and the Twelve have meditated upon and prayed about the great latter-day work the Lord has given us to do, we are impressed that the mission of the Church is threefold:

1) To proclaim the gospel of the Lord Jesus Christ to every nation, kindred, tongue, and people;

2) To perfect the Saints by preparing them to receive the ordinances of the gospel and by instruction and discipline to gain exaltation;

3) To redeem the dead by performing vicarious ordinances of the gospel for those who have lived on the earth.[3]

Obviously the General Authorities had spent much effort and prayer in preparing this concise but comprehensive statement. Some of their inspiration undoubtedly came from the New Testament and the emphasis given to these same principles by the Savior and his apostles of old.

Concerning the charge to preach the gospel, Jesus instructed Simon Peter to help convert his brethren after he was converted. (See Luke 22:32.) Christ's last instruction to his apostles was to preach the gospel to every nation, kindred, tongue, and people. (See Matt. 28:19–20; Mark 16:15–19.)

The concept of perfecting the saints finds its origin in the admonition of Jesus to his followers to become "perfect, even as your Father which is in heaven is perfect." (Matt 5:48.) Teachings about perfection within the Church are also found in the writings of Paul who told the Ephesians that Christ organized the Church and provided apostles, prophets, and other priesthood leaders "for the perfecting of the saints" so the saints could be unified in faith until each becomes a "perfect man" or woman. (Eph. 4:12–13; see also 2 Cor. 13:11; Col. 4:12.)

The purpose of redeeming the dead, although unfamiliar among other modern Christian denominations, was taught and practiced in early Christianity. Jesus taught that no person can enter the kingdom of God unless he or she is baptized in water and the spirit. (See John 3:5.) Peter declared that "for this cause was the gospel preached also to them that are dead, that they might be judged according to men in the flesh." (1 Pet. 4:6.) Paul also talked about the foundation temple ordinance — baptism for the dead — in his epistle to the Corinthians. (See 1 Cor. 15:29.)

Note that all three of these Church purposes (sharing the gospel, helping one another, and performing salvation ordinances for others) direct us in accomplishing what seems to be Heavenly Father's own "mission statement" as recorded by Moses centuries ago. God the Father stated that his work and glory was "to bring to pass the immortality and eternal life of man." (Moses 1:39.)[4] Mormons actively engaged in fulfilling the Church's threefold mission help bring to pass what God desires.

KEYS RESTORED IN THE LATTER DAYS
FOR THE CHURCH'S MISSION

Essential elements of the Church's mission statement are found in the revelations and angelic manifestations received by the Prophet Joseph Smith in the Kirtland Temple in April 1836. At that time, three prophetic figures from past gospel dispensations returned to earth to impart special keys to the prophet of the restoration. These three ancient prophets were Moses, Elias, and Elijah.

MOSES AND MISSIONARY WORK

After a glorious appearance of the Savior himself, the Prophet Joseph Smith records, "The heavens were again opened unto us; and Moses appeared before us, and committed unto us the keys of the gathering of Israel from the four parts of the earth, and the leading of the ten tribes from the land of the north." (D&C 110:11.)

The keys of divine authorization and priesthood power that the Prophet received from Moses restored authority to perform true missionary work. Moses was the keeper of these keys because he was the ancient prophet who gathered the Israelites out of the wicked world, epitomized by Egypt, the world's greatest empire of that time. Later, wicked Israel was scattered by the Assyrians, Babylonians, Romans, and others among the nations of the earth. However, the Lord promised many prophets that he would remember and gather Israel in the last days.

Moses was the steward for the House of Israel within God's plan. After directing the first gathering of Israel to their promised land, Moses continued through the ages to supervise the later scatterings and the eventual gathering of Israel. He gave the keys for this final gathering to Joseph Smith. Today, authorized missionaries gather the scattered remnants of Israel (as well as willing Gentiles) from nearly every country on earth into the congregations and stakes of Zion. The commission to preach the gospel to every nation and people was reiterated in modern revelation. (See D&C 58:9, 64; 133:7–8, 37.) The promise has been given that all the world will have the opportunity to hear the gospel as this part of the Church's mission is fulfilled.[5]

ELIAS AND THE BLESSINGS OF ABRAHAM

After Moses' visitation, the Prophet Joseph records that "Elias appeared, and committed the dispensation of the gospel of Abraham, saying that in us and our seed all generations after us should be blessed." (D&C 110:12.) The scriptures reveal little about the mortal life and ministry of Elias, but he apparently lived in the days of Abraham and Melchizedek, two role models of faithful and righteous living. Abraham was a noble patriarch, a man of faith and an obedient follower of God. Melchizedek, as his name "king of righteousness" declares, was the king of Salem and an exemplary high priest of God. This man, Elias, committed the keys of the gospel dispensation of Abraham to Joseph Smith.[6]

Moses reviews the dispensation of Abraham in Genesis, enumerating three great blessings promised to Abraham: (1) he would have a numberless posterity, (2) his posterity would be heirs to a certain land, including Palestine and neighboring areas, and (3) through his descendants, all families of the earth would be blessed. (See Gen. 12:1–3; 17:1–7.)

The first and third of these promises were mentioned by Elias as he conferred the keys of Abraham's dispensation upon Joseph Smith—the promise of posterity (or seed) and the blessings of future generations through this posterity. Abraham's descendants among Church members in this dispensation increase their numbers as they rear their families in the gospel, and they bless other families as they share their gifts and efforts in blessing others.

The gospel or "good news" that God gave to Abraham and that Elias restored was the promise that the blessings of truth and the priesthood would come from Abraham's posterity to the whole earth. Abraham records that his seed was called to direct the ministry of the gospel and the priesthood to the nations of the earth. (See Abr. 2:9–11.) The great patriarch's ancient responsibility, then, was to engrain in his children the gospel truths, their covenant relationship with God, and their responsibility to righteous examples. They would thereby continue throughout the ages as a light and example to all other peoples.

In the latter days, too, the fundamental duty of Church members is to rear their children under the Abrahamic covenant—teaching them correct principles, helping them make sacred covenants, and encouraging them to live exemplary lives. In this way, "all generations after us should be blessed," and our seed, as a continuation of Abraham's, will be perpetuated throughout eternity. In addition, as brothers and sisters in the gospel, we are to help one another as we teach, serve, and strengthen fellow Saints through our individual efforts and Church callings. A central principle in the gospel is that by serving others, one can progress closer to perfection. In essence, we help perfect each other.

Mormons strive for perfection, which is made possible by the atonement and power of Jesus Christ, trying to live all of God's commandments as revealed in the Holy Scriptures. They also strive for the companionship of the Holy Ghost as their guide. Modern-day apostles and prophets, as well as personal revelation received from the Holy Ghost, give Church members further direction, knowledge, and encouragement in their ultimate goal of perfection. Elias' keys, then, are being fulfilled as the Saints are involved in perfecting each other.[7]

ELIJAH AND THE SEALING POWERS

Joseph Smith recorded that after Elias delivered his keys, one more angelic visitor appeared to him and Oliver Cowdery in the temple: "Another great and glorious vision burst upon us; for Elijah the prophet, who was taken to heaven without tasting death, stood before us, and said: Behold the time has fully come, which was spoken of by the mouth of Malachi—testifying that he [Elijah] should be sent, before the great and dreadful day of the Lord come—to turn the hearts of the fathers to the children, and the children to the fathers, lest the whole earth be smitten with a curse." (D&C 110:13–15.)

Elijah's latter-day mission, Joseph later wrote, was to "restore the authority and deliver the keys of the Priesthood, in order that all the ordinances may be attended to in righteousness."[8] In other words, Elijah's keys allowed the blessings of the gospel covenants to be enjoyed by all of God's children. The most important key is the power to seal generations of families together through sacred ordinances. If we fail to perform the sealing ordinances for our ancestors in the temple, we are cut off from them, and the Abrahamic covenant is not perpetuated through them to us. Instead of the whole earth being blessed and united through Abraham's seed, it would be cursed, and the chosen seed would be scattered and lost.

In accordance with the third purpose of the Church, Latter-day Saints have built dozens of modern-day temples throughout the world to do work for those who died without a knowledge of the gospel. Baptisms for the dead, washings and anointings, temple endowments, marriages and sealing ceremonies are performed in the temples on behalf of the living and the dead.[9] Latter-day Saints believe that by doing this work, those who accept the gospel on the other side of the veil will be able to receive all the blessings promised to those who are faithful members of Christ's church. This doctrine is an expression of the justice and mercy of God, for he has provided a way that all might have the opportunity to accept or reject the gospel, whether in this life or the next.[10]

Significantly, Elijah, the bearer of the sealing keys, never "tasted death" but was preserved by God to fulfill important missions on the earth that would bless both those living in the flesh and those in the postmortal spirit world.[11] For the Lord there is no barrier between the world of the physically living and the world of those spirits living on after their physical bodies have died. Also, God is able to bridge the past, present, and future generations of his children. He has provided keys so that mortals now living on earth, the spirits of our deceased ancestors, and the souls of those yet unborn will eventually form a continuous family—sealed together through ordinances performed by the living in holy temples.

Physically, without our ancestors, we would not have been born; likewise, the spirits of the unborn depend on us for their future physical bodies. Spiritually, we are indebted to our ancestors for our religious heritage, and we have a responsibility toward future generations to build upon and transmit this religious heritage. So, neither physical nor spiritual life can continue unbroken unless people continue having children and the hearts of different generations turn toward one another.[12]

NURTURING AN OLIVE TREE

The inseparable relationship between spreading the gospel, nurturing members in the Church, and maintaining family ties is beautifully illustrated in the allegory of the vineyard recorded in the fifth and sixth chapters of Jacob in the Book of Mormon. Jacob recites this allegory from the writings of an otherwise unknown prophet Zenos of the Old

Testament period. The allegory is summarized in the following paragraphs, with an historical interpretation written in italics.

Zenos compares the house of Israel to an olive tree that the Lord planted and nourished in the best soil of his vineyard. After a time, despite the Lord's persistent care, the tree began to decay and the main branches started to wither. *(Though settled and preserved in the promised land of Palestine, Israel rejected the word of the Lord until she was nearly destroyed.)* To preserve what he could of the tree, the Lord took some surviving branches and planted them in various places throughout the vineyard. *(Remnants of Israel were scattered throughout the world.)*

In place of the original tree's natural branches, the Lord grafted in branches of wild trees in hope that they might bear good fruit if nourished by strong roots. *(Rejected by Israel, the gospel was given to the Gentiles.)* For a while, the wild branches did bear good fruit, but in time they began to overrun and sap the strength of the roots. *(The early apostolic Christian church flourished among the Gentiles but soon fell into apostasy.)*

Again, to preserve the roots, the Lord cast off the wild branches and again grafted in the original branches. During their absence from the mother tree, these original branches had borne good fruit for a season but later started to bear wild fruit. *(Scattered Israel also received Christ and his gospel, but fell into apostasy. The Lord then started to gather the house of Israel again into the gospel fold.)*

In the end, the Lord will be able to preserve the best of the natural and wild branches. These will bear an abundance of good fruit, which he will gather in and store up against unseasonable weather. *(The Lord gathers and restores Israel to her lands of promise, fulfilling all the ancient covenants. Gentiles who embrace the gospel are numbered among the redeemed house of Israel.)* The rest of the vineyard is burned, and the Lord enjoys his bounteous harvest. *(The Lord destroys the remainder of the wicked world prior to his second coming and glorious millennial reign.)*

In Zenos's extensive allegory, the roots of the natural tree were the only thing that could ultimately produce and preserve good fruit. These roots are the Abrahamic covenant and our ancestral ties to it. We nurture these roots as we perform vicarious ordinances for our deceased ancestors. The natural branches of the olive tree, like our established families in the Church, propagate themselves abundantly, complementing and reinforcing each other while drawing their strength from the roots of faith and righteous tradition. We nourish these branches as we perfect the Saints in the household of faith. The grafted branches that also bear good fruit are converts to the Church from among the Gentiles. We multiply and strengthen these branches as we proclaim the gospel to all peoples.

MISSIONARY WORK TODAY

From this allegory and other scriptures, we know that the gospel of Christ was first preached to the Israelites, who rejected it. Christ's apostles then took the word to the Gentiles. When restored in the latter days, however, the gospel was first preached in the Gentile nations, especially to the scattered remnants of Israel among the Gentiles. (See D&C 109:57–67.) It is only now being taken in force to other more identifiable remnants of the house of Israel, such as the Lamanites. Thus, the prophecy is being fulfilled that says "the last shall be first, and the first shall be last." (1 Ne. 13:42.)

Because of many generations of wickedness, the nation of Israel was broken up into four main parts: the "lost" ten tribes who fled from the Assyrian yoke after their deportation in 721 B.C.; the Book of Mormon exiles (Nephites, Lamanites, and the people of Zarahemla or the so-called Mulekites) who fled Jerusalem around 600 B.C. (their descendants are now usually called Lamanites); the house of Judah (the Jews) who were scattered by the Babylonians (586 B.C.) and the Romans (A.D. 70); and other scattered remnants of Israelites (particularly the house of Ephraim) who mixed in among the Gentiles over the course of many centuries. Except for the Jews, the great majority of the descendants of these ancient Israelite groups lost their distinctive identity. They became "lost" as they mixed in among the nations of the earth and forgot their religious heritage. But they were not hidden to the Lord.

The Lord has used prophets and scriptures to reveal where and how these various remnants of Israel will be gathered back together again into one flock. (See 3 Ne. 15:15–16:20.) Also, the Book of Mormon has revealed the location of the Lamanites in the Americas, and early missionary work quickly began to let these scattered remnants of Ephraim and Manasseh know of their Israelite ancestry. Prophets are also preparing the Ten Tribes for their return since, as prophesied, a remnant of them and their special set of scriptures will come forth in the last days. (See D&C 77:9, 14; 2 Ne. 29:11–14; 3 Ne. 21:26.)

The Lord's Way of Missionary Work

The avowed missionary goal of The Church of Jesus Christ of Latter-day Saints was the same as the rest of Christianity—to take the gospel to every nation, kindred, tongue, and people. In the seventeenth through the nineteenth centuries, most Christian missionary societies concentrated on taking the gospel to the pagan and heathen nations of Africa and Asia. Joseph Smith was definitely inspired in his early missionary decisions because he did not follow this accepted practice of the nineteenth-century Protestant missionary societies. Instead of imitating this proselyting pattern, Joseph Smith received divine inspiration to send the missionaries of the restored gospel to the Christian countries of North America and Europe, where other Christians often rebuked and challenged them to go to the pagans instead. However, the success in the numbers of early converts from other Christian denominations and their migration to the settlements of the Latter-day Saints in the Rocky Mountains provided the nucleus for eventual missionary work in other, non-Christian nations—especially after World War II.

From the 1950s through the 1980s, the Church steadily grew in western Europe, South Africa, and in some nations along the Pacific rim. Stakes were established and temples were built to provide centers of strength. By the mid-1980s, the Church had the organization and numbers of close, strong Church members ready to take the gospel to nations formerly under the communist yoke and into other countries in Africa and parts of Asia that had earlier prohibited our activities. Now, missionary success is rapidly growing in eastern Europe, in a variety of central African nations, and in many Asian countries—all with local government recognition and full Church organizational support readily available. With further growth from Church centers of strength and with the aid of modern media and other helps, Mormons will continue their expansion into the rest of the world until the gospel message is heard by all peoples.

Until the 1970s, the majority of converts to the Church came from Protestant backgrounds. These converts consisted of Gentiles and scattered remnants of Israel living among the nations of North America and northern Europe. Very few Catholics and non-Christians joined the

Church prior to the 1960s. Today, many Protestant converts still join the Church, but many more new members come from Catholic backgrounds, primarily in Central and South America and the Philippines. For example, in the 1980s, consistently eighteen of the top twenty baptizing missions of the Church were in Latin countries every year, with the other two being in the Philippines. The Latin members, usually called Lamanites by the Latter-day Saints, are mainly descendants of the Book of Mormon exiles and are therefore part of the gathering of Israel.

We are also beginning to see increasing numbers of non-Christians join the Church, especially in Japan, Taiwan, Southeast Asia, and some African countries. If this pattern continues, we can soon expect growing numbers of baptisms among the other groups of scattered Israel, such as those descendants of the Ten Tribes living among Moslem or formerly communist peoples. Also, other non-Christians residing in Africa and Asia will come into Christ's church in increasing numbers.

Thus the goal of early Christianity to take the gospel to the whole world will finally be fulfilled as people everywhere will have the opportunity to hear the restored gospel—whether they have heard the message of Christianity from other Christian missionaries or not. The missionary efforts of previous Catholics and Protestants attempted to convert other peoples, and in some cases they made valuable inroads and prepared the way for the restored gospel.

In the eyes of many non-Christians, however, their attempts were often seen as brutal, imperialistic, and self-serving. For example, apostate Christianity of the Middle Ages sent the Crusaders and their weapons to take back the Holy Land from the infidels and to spread Christianity back into that area of the world. They failed and left in their wake a tradition of deceit and manipulation, all in the name of Christianity. In more recent times, traditional Christianity, especially the Protestants, sent missionaries to Asia and Africa, but they had only limited success because they were seen as representatives of the governing European powers. As most African and Asian nations gained independence from European domination, they not only threw off political controls, but also rejected religious influence. However, the message of the restored gospel, especially as it is proclaimed by missionaries sent from the stakes of Zion, is finally reaching more and more of the inhabitants of the earth. Eventually, the message of the restoration will reach every people.

THE MISSIONARY PROGRAM OF THE CHURCH

Mormon missionaries serve on a voluntary, nonpaid, temporary basis. The great majority of missionaries are young men between the ages of nineteen to twenty-six, who customarily serve for two years. A large minority, about one-fifth, of the missionaries are single women, ages twenty-one and older, who usually serve about one-and-a-half years. A smaller minority, about one-tenth, of the missionary force is comprised of older married couples who usually serve for a year or more.

Missionary service is preceded by an interview with the local bishop and the submitting of certain documents, including ID photos, health records, dental forms, and so on. Usually the prospective missionary initiates this process, but the bishop or other Church leaders may initiate the invitation to serve a mission. The bishop evaluates the person's spiritual strengths, commitment to serve, worthiness to represent the Church, social skills, financial resources, and the appropriate timing of missionary service. When the bishop feels the person is ready and worthy to serve, he forwards the recommendation to the stake president, who also interviews the candidate. When the papers and interviews are completed, the stake president submits the recommendation to the Missionary Department of the Church.

The Missionary Department keeps track of all Church missions and their needs for expansion or replacements. In an atmosphere of discussion and prayer, designated members of the Quorum of the Twelve meet weekly with representatives from the Seventies and the Missionary Department to suggest preliminary assignments for each missionary or couple. These recommendations are sent to the First Presidency, who approves or modifies them according to inspiration. After the date for entering a missionary training center is established, a formal letter is sent by the President of the Church to the individual or couple, inviting them to serve in a specific mission.

The prospective missionary usually has from a few weeks to a few months to make final preparations to enter missionary service. The timing depends upon how quickly they are needed in their respective missions and how soon necessary visas and other requirements can be met. Letters from the assigned mission presidents and the Missionary Department inform the missionaries about clothing, health, and other special needs and expectations for the particular areas where they will be serving. On a Sunday shortly before beginning their service, missionaries are almost always invited to speak in their local ward sacrament meetings. Just prior to entering the assigned Missionary Training Center (MTC), each missionary is set apart by his or her stake president, and the mission officially begins.

The first few weeks are spent at one of the Church's Missionary Training Centers, which are established throughout the world. At the MTC, missionaries adjust to missionary life as they study the scriptures, learn methods of teaching the gospel, and attend inspirational meetings and study sessions. Missionaries going to a foreign-language mission also receive intensive language instruction and cultural information and helps. Missionaries going to a foreign mission usually spend two months at the MTC before departing for their field of labor, while missionaries already fluent in the language of their assigned mission usually spend three weeks.

When entering the mission field, new missionaries are welcomed and oriented by the mission president, his wife, and the mission office staff. Mission presidents are typically high priests of late middle age who temporarily leave their professions and serve for three years. A mission president and his wife are both set apart as missionaries and receive special training from the General Authorities before entering the mission field. Dependent children will accompany the parents, but they are not set apart as missionaries, and they continue their schooling and other normal family and social activities, as much as is possible in the area where the parents are serving.

The mission president "trains, counsels, assigns, and gives spiritual support to each missionary, and his wife plays a vital role in training programs and the health, welfare, and safety of each missionary."[13] Together, they nurture and direct the efforts of the one hundred to two hundred and fifty full-time missionaries currently serving in that mission. After three years of intensive, edifying service and involvement with hundreds of missionaries, members, and nonmembers, the mission president and his family return home, and a new president begins his own administration.

The mission president assigns each new missionary and couple to an area where they will serve. New single missionaries are trained by experienced companions, and couples are usually assisted by other experienced couples or local Church leaders. Additional training occurs at weekly district meetings (a missionary district comprises two to five companionships or couples serving in close geographic proximity). Periodic zone conferences and testimony meetings are also held, usually under the direction of the mission president and his assistants (a missionary zone consists of a number of districts). But the most valuable training usually comes from one's companion. A missionary never labors alone; each always has an assigned companion to live, study, and work with as they find, teach, and fellowship people who are searching for the gospel truths and who want to become covenant members of Christ's church by entering the waters of baptism.

Following the principle that one's time and talents as a missionary are dedicated to the Lord, missionaries work very hard in their callings. Typically, they arise early, usually by 6:30 A.M., and spend some time studying and preparing before leaving their apartments for a full eight to eleven hours of missionary-related activities. Part of one weekday, usually known as a "P-Day" (preparation day), is devoted to laundering clothes, cleaning apartments, shopping, writing letters, and meeting other personal needs. Periodically, the mission president changes companions and transfers missionaries to new areas of service. As the months of hard work go by, eternal friendships are established with fellow missionaries and many members in the area. Because missionaries are able to concentrate fully on serving others, most of them later describe their missions as "the best two years" of their lives up to that time.

Missionary work has a long tradition in The Church of Jesus Christ of Latter-day Saints. Except in times of extreme economic or political distress, such as in times of depression or war, large numbers of Latter-day Saints have served full-time missions. In recent decades, more than one-half of one percent of the Church membership is involved in full-time missionary work at any given time. For example, in 1990 over forty thousand full-time missionaries were serving from a Church membership of slightly over seven million people—for a percentage of .57% (or 1.14 missionaries for each two hundred members.) Similar ratios are found in other years: 1970 = .47%; 1975 = .53%; 1980 = .67%; 1985 = .49%. The average for these five measurements is .55% (or 1.1 missionaries serving for each two hundred members.)

This means that at least one of every two hundred Latter-day Saints is deferring schooling, vocation, or retirement in order to serve full-time in missionary service. As they return home, others take their place, and the service cycle continues. Since missionary service is rotated among Church members, many Mormons will have served at least one mission during their lifetimes. Some members will serve two, three, and even more missions, especially in their retirement years. Missionaries receive many social and spiritual rewards from their service, but their greatest satisfaction usually derives from the fact that they are sharing the "good news" of the Lord's teachings with many people. Missionaries are the latest generation of Christ's disciples who are following his admonition to preach his gospel in all the world. (See Matt. 24:14; 28:19.)

As the restored gospel is taught to more and more people throughout the nations, hundreds of thousands of them join the church of Jesus Christ every year. As a result, new branches and wards are organized, and new meetinghouses are dedicated almost on a daily basis. On an average Sunday, one to three new stakes are organized somewhere in the world. As the magnitude of the Church increases, its influence in society grows, and world citizens cannot ignore its presence.

WHAT IS THE WORLD'S VIEW OF THE CHURCH?

Just as convert success has moved from those of Protestant background to the Catholic community and now more into the non-Christian world, a similar evolution is recognizable in the world's changing perception of the Church. The Church was founded in nineteenth-century Protestant New England and shared many practices and cultural traditions with the prominent sects of that day. Like Baptists, we Latter-day Saints baptize by immersion; like Seventh-Day Adventists, we practice a strict health code; like Quakers, we espouse values of self-sufficiency. In fact, the "Mormons" are still commonly grouped with the Protestant sects in many religious textbooks.

As the twentieth century concludes, however, the view is changing. With our continued emphasis on ordinances, revealed doctrine, divine priesthood authority, and a strong hierarchical church structure, Latter-day Saints are now perceived by the world as sharing much in common with Catholic dogma. For example, Mormons and Catholics both share a more traditional family life-style — large families on the East Coast are assumed to be Catholic; in the West they are likely Mormon. In addition, the leaders of both religions repeatedly speak out against abortion and about other moral issues, and they maintain the priesthood and its ecclesiastical callings exclusively for male members.

Another trend has been developing in which people are beginning to identify some church practices with those found among non-Christian religions. For example, the patriarchal family structure of LDS families appears similar to the strong family practices in Islam. The appreciation and reverence for our ancestors and having sacred temples for special worship seem to outsiders to be similar to traditions in some oriental religions. Our peculiar health laws have a similar uniqueness to those practiced by devout Moslems and Jews. And the practice of periodic fasting is found in a variety of non-Christian faiths. Finally, our tolerance toward other religions and our acknowledgment and respect for the truths they contain reflect oriental philosophy more than that of traditional Christianity. In short, as more non-Christians come into the Latter-day Saint fold, they find family practices and religious teachings similar enough to their own that the transition from their culture to that of the kingdom of God on earth is made easier.

The transition from a worldly culture to the spiritual kingdom is nonetheless difficult for many converts. Their families, friends, and peers often ostracize them. They must adjust to new and usually more strict religious and moral expectations. Although the Latter-day Saints are noted for their warm, open, and friendly ways, new members still need time before they feel fully integrated within the congregation. This is particularly true in areas of great missionary success where new converts are brought into young, struggling branches and wards on an almost weekly basis.

This does not mean, however, that a new convert must reject all of his previous culture when joining the Church. Many cultural differences can easily coexist in the worldwide kingdom of God, just as there are differences among the cultures of the Old and New Testaments, the Book of Mormon peoples, and earlier converts in our modern dispensation. Some traditional cultural practices are steeped in pagan idolatry, however, and are antithetical to the gospel and must be given up.

As a simple example, Dr. Arthur Henry King — an English convert

to the Church and a former professor at Brigham Young University—
tells the story of an Asian friend who had joined the Church and later
came to England for a visit. When Dr. King met the man and his wife
at the London train station, he was dismayed to see his friend walking
quickly toward him in greeting, leaving his wife behind struggling with
all of their luggage. Dr. King, in his characteristically straightforward
manner, informed his friend that the docile servitude of Asian wives to
husbands was a tradition not in keeping with noble gospel principles.[14]

When converts join the Church, they must bring their personal background and beliefs into harmony with those of Christ's kingdom on earth.
The threefold mission of the Church becomes the primary means by
which they focus their energy toward building God's kingdom on earth.
Through increasing missionary efforts, all God's children will be given a
chance to hear and accept divine truth. By perfecting the Saints, the
covenant members of Christ's kingdom learn to live together in righteous
harmony, preparing themselves for the heavenly social structure of eternity. By performing temple covenants for the dead, generations of God's
children are linked together in heart and mind, just as they are united
in the loving eyes of the Lord. Thus the blessings of Abraham are made
available to all despite their varied physical and cultural backgrounds,
and the divine social organization of families is established for eternity.

The fulfillment of this threefold mission and the establishment of
this eternal, heavenly kingdom are manifestations of God's power and
orderliness. Things that are not joined together in any kind of order or
system are naturally in a state of disorganization. In the beginning, the
Lord took things that were disorganized (such as intelligences, material
matter, worlds, and so on) and then organized them into a state of order
and purpose. Similarly, he is helping his spirit children develop and
progress from a weak, incomplete, telestial existence toward a glorious
state of eternal order. In the resurrection, God's children will be organized into differing kingdoms, depending upon their actions in this existence.

God's kingdom on earth must likewise follow this organizational
pattern and purpose: "Mine house is a house of order, saith the Lord
God, and not a house of confusion." (D&C 132:8.) We have the opportunity to help God's children achieve their divine potential through the

threefold mission of the church, which unifies our power in this marvelous effort.

In summary, *The Church of Jesus Christ of Latter-day Saints has a threefold MISSION: (1) to proclaim the gospel to all peoples, (2) to perfect the Saints in the household of faith, and (3) to perform vicarious ordinances for the living spirits of the deceased.* The threefold mission of the Church has given guidance, direction, and purpose to Latter-day Saints. God, in his infinite wisdom, has restored his glorious gospel upon the earth to bless the lives of all his children. All three purposes of the Church are part of one great work—to assist our Father in Heaven and his Son, Jesus Christ, in their grand and glorious mission "to bring to pass the immortality and eternal life of man." (Moses 1:39.) Church members working toward fulfilling this mission not only spread the restored gospel abroad, but they also bless others and strengthen themselves, making it possible for more of God's children to progress together on their way back to his kingdom.

For further study, refer to the following entries:

TG	BD	EM
Elias	Elias	Baptism for the Dead
Elijah	Elijah	Elias
Missionary Work		Fellowshipping
Peculiar People		Members
		Missionary,
		Missionary Life
		Missions
		Teaching the Gospel

CHAPTER 35

ONE FOLD — ONE SHEPHERD

Next to physical survival, the need to identify and belong to a loving, supportive group is one of the strongest human needs. A desire for mutually beneficial companionship naturally finds expression in many forms: immediate and extended families, religious denominations, service organizations, professional societies, recreational clubs, political affiliations, nationalities, and races. Even adolescents rebelling against "the establishment" in the name of individualism soon form their own gangs and subcultures. It seems that almost everyone wants to belong to a compatible group.

Belonging to a select group has both requirements and rewards. The most common requirement is a certain allegiance to the association, including a commitment to an expected life-style. The predominant rewards are a sense of identity and positive reinforcement as the mutual purposes of the group are accomplished. To a degree, the rewards of belonging exact the price of conformity because we blend our personality with the assemblage. If this process requires us to drastically change our behavior or does not seem to meet our own needs, we may choose to move on to another group. In fact, since our personalities are so rich and our needs so varied, we are often involved in many groups. Thus people modify their associations throughout their lifetimes in search of the right combination of human interactions.

The gospel of Jesus Christ reminds us that all mankind is bound together in two most fundamental ways—common spiritual parentage from God and our shared physical lineage from Adam and Eve. Since the days of Adam, the Lord has invited us as brothers and sisters to join together with him in several unions—families, church, kingdom, and sometimes even cities and nations. He requires a full gospel commitment

576

of every individual follower. Like a shepherd watching over his flock, he recognizes the strengths of bringing his disciples together as a community of believers. He expects unity among his followers, and in return he promises them great personal and eternal rewards.

Even when some adherents of the gospel kingdom distort the true teachings, practices, or purposes of the Lord's gospel, some good is still accomplished as the imperfect community and its members strive to do things that are right and noble. This is one reason why religious and family traditions have endured for centuries amid the rise and fall of gospel dispensations and the passing of various civilizations and nations.

As we seek to build upon family bonds and grow together in a covenant fellowship, we need to discuss the basic requirements and rewards for discipleship as followers of Jesus Christ. Baptism is the initial requirement for entrance into Christ's church, and the ultimate rewards of salvation and the companionship of the Holy Ghost are promised those who remain faithful in his spiritual kingdom.[1] We will now highlight what is expected of members of his church and review additional blessings flowing from fellowship with other Latter-day Saints.

DISCIPLESHIP

Though the Lord invites "all to come unto him . . . black and white, bond and free" (2 Ne. 26:33), the requirements of discipleship are exacting. The term *disciple* is found frequently in the four gospel accounts of the New Testament. Jesus specifically called twelve special disciples or apostles to help him in his work, and the term was subsequently used to describe all true followers of Christ. Defined as "one who follows or attends upon another for the purpose of learning from him,"[2] a disciple is also identified as "a pupil, follower, or adherent of any teacher or school of . . . learning."[3] Jesus Christ instructs us, as his disciples, that our most noble aim is to perfect ourselves and become like him and our Heavenly Father. He said, "Therefore I would that ye should be perfect even as I, or your Father who is in heaven is perfect." (3 Ne. 12:48; cf. Matt. 5:48.) To become like Christ, we must learn to emulate him and become more than a pupil of his learning—we become a follower of his behavior.

Discipleship requires three steps: motivation, learning, and application; or as Christ calls them: faith, obedience, and righteousness. In order to have the desire to be Christ's disciple, we must first believe in his divinity. Then we must study his teachings and learn to do all that he asks of us. Finally, we must live a life of purity, love, and service as he did. Following these three steps will eventually bring us to where he is — in the heavenly realms in a state of spirituality. Thus, when we become *disciples* of Christ, we learn from him all that we must know, do, and be in order to live with him and God the Father.

Though the pathway is hard, the rewards of discipleship are great. Some are readily apparent, such as the blessing of an ever-increasing testimony, the peace of knowing that what we are doing is right, and the acquisition of spirituality and eternal life. But other rewards are not as easy to perceive — such as new dimensions of understanding, fellowship shared with other Church members, or the sense of fulfilled destiny that accompanies being a disciple. Discipleship with Christ and membership in his church on earth actually prepare us for the heavenly association with Christ and Heavenly Father, where "no unclean thing can dwell." (1 Ne. 10:21.)

FAITH: STRENGTHENING OUR BELIEF IN CHRIST

To the true disciple, Jesus is not merely another great teacher. He was not born just to deliver a message — he is the message: "I am the way, the truth, and the life: no man cometh unto the Father, but by me." (John 14:6.) All people enter into heaven through him, because of his atoning sacrifice and his infinite love. He is the great focal point of the universe, the "light which is in all things, which giveth life to all things, which is the law by which all things are governed, even the power of God." (D&C 88:13.) Every true and good thing is embodied in him.[4]

To follow Christ, a disciple must develop faith in him and remain true to this belief above all else.[5] He or she must also refuse to follow the philosophies of men or to be "conformed to this world" with its patterns of materialistic selfishness. (Rom. 12:2.) A disciple judges all ideas and practices of the world by only one standard, given in great simplicity by Moroni in his closing remarks in the Book of Mormon: "It is given unto you to judge, that ye may know good from evil; and the way to judge is plain, . . . for every thing which inviteth to do good, and to persuade to believe in Christ . . . is of God. But whatsoever thing persuadeth men to do evil, and believe not in Christ, and deny him, and serve not God . . . is of the devil." (Moro. 7:15–17.)

With such a strict standard, we can easily see why the disciples of Christ are usually unpopular with the world, which is full of people who insist on thinking and acting "independently" of any such rigid code. Only when the disciples' testimonies are unshakable will they be able to ignore all other distractions and follow the Savior wholeheartedly.

OBEDIENCE: LEARNING THE DISCIPLINE OF DISCIPLESHIP

Once a person has a strong belief in Christ, the next step is to seek learning from him and to follow his counsel. A commitment to study and achieve requires a great deal of discipline. Indeed, without discipline no one can become a lasting disciple of any great master or school of learning. Discipline is the essence of discipleship, as seen in the common Latin roots of these two words. In English, a *disciple* is a learner, and the word comes from the Latin root *discipere,* meaning "to learn." To discipline oneself is to subject oneself to instruction and training. This term comes from the Latin root *discipulus,* meaning "a learner." Ironically, our contemporary English has almost transposed the original Latin meanings of these terms: the old root *to learn* now means "a learner," while the ancient root for *a learner* now describes the self-control necessary "to learn." Thus, without discipline one cannot be a disciple.

To be a disciple of Christ, we must conform to his standard of moral behavior and obey his spiritual laws. Only those with great discipline are able to do this. Many who will not admit the need for discipline in moral and spiritual behavior at least recognize its value in other fields of human endeavor, such as in the classroom, on the sports field, or in business. As Elder Neal A. Maxwell explains, "Man did not get to the moon with random trajectories and with each astronaut 'doing his own thing.' The price for reaching the moon was obedience to universal law."[6] Likewise, the individual interpretation of the concert pianist and the graceful spontaneity of the ballet dancer are possible only after years of strict technical discipline.

The disciple of Christ must similarly add strict obedience to his belief so that the truth can make him free. (See John 8:32.) In fact, we must first *follow* the example of Christ before we can fully *know* that his doctrine is true. This is another way in which spiritual truth differs from secular knowledge — it is obtainable only through action. "If any man will do his [God's] will," the Savior said, "he shall know of the doctrine, whether it be of God, or whether I speak of myself." (John 7:17.) As we discipline ourselves in keeping Christ's commandments, we earn the companionship of the Holy Ghost, through which we are spiritually reborn and able to overcome bondage to our own earthly ignorance and nature. The Spirit is then able to teach us great hidden truths of the eternities.[7]

RIGHTEOUSNESS: FOLLOWING A PATH TO PERFECTION

As we study and follow Christ's teachings, thereby demonstrating obedience to his commandments, the Holy Spirit enlightens us, and we gradually become more Christlike. We begin to incorporate the divine personality of Christ into our own. Thus, Alma speaks in earnest when he asks, "Have ye received his image in your countenances? Have ye experienced this mighty change in your hearts?" (Alma 5:14.) The spiritually reborn "know that, when he shall appear, [they] shall be like him; for [they] shall see him as he is." (1 Jn. 3:2.) The last step is to become like Christ.

Among the Lord's many titles is "THE LORD OUR RIGHTEOUS-NESS." (Jer. 23:6.) He is also a source and model for our righteousness. In Nephi's great psalm, he calls God "the rock of my righteousness." (2 Ne. 4:35; see also Ps. 4:1.) In becoming like Christ, we must strive to emulate the qualities that he has. Although his attributes and titles are too numerous to mention here,[8] three key qualities characterize Christ's divine nature: purity, love, and service. These three characteristics of Jesus Christ are the basic characteristics of true righteousness.

Jesus' Example of Purity

At first glance, Jesus was simply a carpenter's son from Nazareth. But closer observation reveals a person of absolute purity. Never did he transgress or sin against any law of God. He always sought God's kingdom first as he went about his Father's business. Not once did he seek to acquire worldly wealth. He gave of himself without selfishness or personal ambition. Never did he succumb to the baseness of Satan's world. Without guile or hypocrisy, he brought spiritual power into the lives of others. Pure intent motivated all that he thought, said, and did. And after he had drunk the bitter cup and fulfilled all righteousness in the suffering of his atonement and the glory of his resurrection, he commanded us to follow him since he was then "made perfect." (Heb. 5:8–9; see also 3 Ne. 12:48.)

As we live clean healthy lives, we provide a purer physical tabernacle for our heavenly spirit. As we purge our souls of sin and cleanse ourselves from vanity and pride, we purify our spirit so we can grow spiritually. As pure intent motivates our thoughts, words, and actions, we prepare ourselves to stand in holy places, even in God's celestial realms.[9] (See Ps. 24:3–4.)

Christ's Example of Love

The greatest and most encompassing quality Jesus shows us is his unconditional love for all mankind. His love motivated his atoning sacrifice for our sins. Without his love and atonement, we would be unable to return to our Heavenly Father's presence. All other aspects of the gospel and the commandments hinge on this quality as well. We can only fulfill the necessary requirements to return to the highest realms of the celestial kingdom when we have a love of God and others. Love of God motivates us to return to him, and our love of others increases our capacity to enjoy God's heavenly company.

Any disciple of Christ who develops empathy and sensitivity toward others will experience a special fullness of joy. (See Alma 27:17–19.) Elder Maxwell explains how discipline can foster our capacity to love: "Self-discipline can keep us sensitive to others, whereas hedonism and pleasure-seeking rob us of our capacity to feel and to empathize."[10] Through refinement by the Spirit, sensitivity and empathy can grow to divine love, which is the Savior's ultimate qualification for discipleship: "A new commandment I give unto you, That ye love one another; as I have loved you. . . . By this shall all men know that ye are my disciples, if ye have love one to another." (John 13:34–35.)

When Jesus tells us to love one another, as he has loved us, he encourages us to develop a special type of love that is important for our eternal well-being. Other prophets have described this edifying love as charity, which is "the pure love of Christ, and it endureth forever; and whoso is found possessed of it at the last day, it shall be well with him." (Moro. 7:47.) This passage makes it clear that love is a quality we need in these last days. Through earnest prayer and with God's help, we can obtain this love, as Mormon promised when he said, "Pray unto the

Father with all the energy of heart, that ye may be filled with this love, which he hath bestowed upon all who are true followers of his Son, Jesus Christ." (Moro. 7:48.) After we obtain this love, we manifest it in our works as the Lord did.

The Messiah's Example of Service

Christ manifested his love for us by bearing our sins. We also show love to each other in his Church by our willingness to "bear one another's burdens, . . . mourn with those that mourn; yea, and comfort those that stand in need of comfort." (Mosiah 18:8–9.) When one has a Christlike love, he cannot help but love the people around him and desire to lighten their burdens, whether physical, emotional, or spiritual.

Jesus served people in numerous ways, healing the sick, raising the dead, and providing for their various needs. King Mosiah, who also epitomized service to his people, likewise commanded us to do the same, "I would that ye should impart of your substance to the poor, every man according to that which he hath, such as feeding the hungry, clothing the naked, visiting the sick and administering to their relief, both spiritually and temporally." (Mosiah 4:26.)

One of the ready opportunities that Latter-day Saints have to serve their fellowman comes through membership in the Church. The lay priesthood and leadership of the restored church, upheld by the common consent of members, gives all Saints an opportunity to teach, serve, and support one another. The Church provides many structured opportunities for service through its teachings and programs. In addition, if we are sensitive to the Spirit, we will find many opportunities for service aside from formal Church service. If we keep our lives and service centered around Christ, we will ultimately succeed in helping others. In one of the greatest sermons on discipleship, Jesus calls himself the vine and identifies us as the branches bringing forth the necessary gospel fruits. (See John 15.) With Heavenly Father's nurturing care and Christ's power, we will develop love one for another that will spiritually strengthen everyone it touches. (See John 15:1, 10–16.)

FELLOWSHIP WITH EVERY SAINT

In our introduction, we stated that people may become disillusioned with an organization if it ceases to meet their needs or if they don't feel they make an important contribution to the group. Sometimes a large organization is too large and impersonal; on the other hand, a smaller society might make too many demands on its members. To try to avoid these problems, most Church operations take place in individual branches and wards, usually comprised of a few dozen to several hundred people. In this way, the responsibilities of leadership, teaching, organization, and fellowship are shared, and the differing needs of members can be addressed at a personal level and yet have access to the resources of the greater Church organization.

The LDS community is both large enough to provide wide cultural and human diversity and localized enough to provide ample opportunities for social bonding. As people become involved in an LDS ward, they soon recognize that Latter-day Saints have different personalities and varying levels of testimony, Church activity, and religious behavior. Each member is at different stages of spiritual progression, spiritual understanding, and religious devotion. Members find too that evaluating their own spiritual barometers of faith, obedience, and righteousness is difficult, much less being able to measure them in the lives of others.

Although diversity in the Church may disillusion some and frustrate others, it is actually beneficial. As we observe ourselves and others on the paths of spiritual struggle and progress, we learn the nature of mortality and come to appreciate the helps that a loving Heavenly Father has given us. The diverse gifts of the membership furthermore edify the whole: some may have the gift of faith, others the gift of teaching, others the gift of discernment, others the gift of wisdom, and so on. "To some is given one [gift], and to some is given another, that all may be profited thereby." (D&C 46:12; see vv. 9–27.) In addition, devout and spiritually mature members can help strengthen the spiritual convictions of those who are struggling. We look to this type of faithful, active, and wholesome disciple and say, "If God's celestial kingdom is made up of people like this, I want to be there in such good company."

In our efforts to be perfect even as Christ is perfect, we will find ourselves strong in some areas of discipleship but weak or struggling in others. We may have a solid gospel understanding and doctrinal foundation but still experience times of questioning and concern. We may be active in our Church callings, willing to fulfill their religious obligations but struggling with some particular commitment or commandment. We may be loving, genuine, and helpful while working to overcome some personal weaknesses or character flaws. Comprised of many members, the spiritually maturing group of Saints in LDS wards and branches provide a solid core. Assisting others while receiving strength themselves, the Saints work together to build the human soul.[11]

Some Latter-day Saints with a mixture of good attributes but a variety of minor deficiencies may be involved members who nevertheless feel limited in what they can contribute to the ward or branch. Basically believing, concerned, and decent people, their involvement with the Church may be based more on social contacts and family traditions than on a solid spiritual foundation. Other members at times may experience disappointments in their Church callings or frustration with keeping some commandments. Recent converts, young adults, or individuals who have recently been less active in the Church may feel challenged in their attempt to conform to gospel expectations.

All these members want to build their testimonies, desiring to serve in the Church while developing a more Christlike life, but wanting and needing help to overcome their spiritual deficiencies.[12] In experiencing these frailties, all members learn the necessity of the Atonement and the value of repentance and forgiveness, relying upon the mercies of the Savior. This common, shared experience forges powerful bonds of kinship in the wards and branches of the Church.

Latter-day Saints with weak spiritual convictions, limited Church activity, or inconsistent religious behavior are struggling to maintain their gospel commitment. Sometimes called "less active" members, they usually sense that their faith and life-style are out of harmony with the gospel, and they might feel awkward around other, more active members. They may even feel isolated from the Church and thus not readily seek for full fellowship with other members, especially if they move to a new location where new LDS contacts are not immediately established. Diligent family members, faithful home and visiting teachers, dedicated bishops, and caring friends who take an interest in their spiritual welfare can help such struggling members. On the other hand, if concerned friends, families, missionaries, or other members do not maintain some type of religious contact with them, the less-active members may fall into complete inactivity.[13]

When spiritual weaknesses prevail and one loses the desire to live the gospel, the natural tendency is to completely disassociate oneself from the Church and become inactive. Such a person may keep some belief, but many problems weaken it. Some social and cultural ties may remain, and he or she may attend Church meetings on rare occasions, especially for special religious or family events (such as the blessing of an infant, a missionary farewell, or a Christmas program involving a family member), but the person feels little attachment to the Church or the Saints. Standards of behavior may still fit general social norms, but they will be out of harmony with the commandments of the restored gospel. In essence, this person feels, acts, and lives more like an outsider than like a Latter-day Saint. Unless the hand of God or the concerted efforts of other Church members turns this person around, he or she is well on the path of personal apostasy.[14]

Although few in number, Church members who completely apostatize by committing gross sins, turning against Church leaders, or teaching doctrinal heresies can do immense damage to the Church. They set poor examples to the world and weaken the faith of new or less secure members. If they continue such patterns of wickedness, they soon find themselves outside the Church through the process of excommunication. They are welcome to attend most Church meetings, but because of the seriousness of their offenses, they may not partake of the sacrament, nor are they allowed to give talks or prayers, fill any callings, or contribute financially to the Church. To come back into the Church, they must bring forth fruits of faith and repentance and seek for readmission.

The Church is a God-given vehicle for perfecting the imperfect Saints through instruction, fellowship, support, and love. It will not fail us. Rather we will fail ourselves if we do not become fully involved in God's kingdom on earth. When we strive to lift others, we all become unified and strengthened in Christ's work. As Paul told the Hebrews, "Both he that sanctifieth and they who are sanctified are all of one." (Heb. 2:11.) This "unity is the hallmark of the true Church of Christ. It is felt among our people throughout the world. As we are one, we are his."[15] Thus, we must overcome diversity and weakness and help our fellow Saints to grow if we wish to be true members of Christ's fold.

To help build one another, we are commanded to magnify our callings and responsibilities in the Church, giving of our time, talents, and financial resources to build the kingdom of God. The responsibilities of discipleship are great and require considerable sacrifice, but the rewards of fellowship with the Saints are greater. In the Church, members find a true sense of belonging to an extended family of many brothers and sisters as they prepare for a similar, though far more perfect society in the world to come. Such fellowship brings us together until we indeed become "spiritually begotten" sons and daughters of Christ in his eternal family. (See Mosiah 5:7.) Of course, we should not help and fellowship only those in the Church; Christ reached out to anyone he could. Genuine fellowship with the Saints provides purpose and confidence in building a relationship of trust and friendship with others in the world.

"YE ARE THE LIGHT OF THE WORLD"

We never know how effective the examples of our individual lives can be in spreading the gospel. More than mass media communication or the extensive distribution of literature, our sincere testimonies and devout lives are an open declaration of Christianity in action. The Master told us, "Ye are the light of the world." (Matt. 5:14.) Countless stories are related of people who have seen the righteousness of the Lord's disciples and sought for the same gospel blessings in their lives. Disciples of Christ fulfill his admonition to let their light so shine that others, seeing their good works, will give glory to God. (See Matt. 5:16.)

The best act of service one can perform for another is to give one's most priceless possessions—time and things of eternal value. Parents give this kind of service as they rear their children. As LDS children are brought up in the gospel light, they become the next generation's missionaries, who will perform a different kind of service by sharing the precious religious truths through preaching the gospel to others. A major part of Jesus' own mission on earth was to teach his gospel and help others find their way back to our Father.

A strong desire to share the gospel is the natural consequence of anyone who has been fully converted to the truth. For example, after Alma the Younger and the sons of King Mosiah were themselves converted to the gospel, "they were desirous that salvation should be declared to every creature, for they could not bear that any human soul should perish." (Mosiah 28:3.) So they embarked for the most difficult mission field of their day—preaching among the Lamanites. There they enjoyed great success.

Modern disciples are likewise called to take the gospel "unto all nations, kindreds, tongues and people." (D&C 42:58.) A major portion of missionary work is accomplished by the tens of thousands of full-time missionaries in hundreds of missions throughout the world. Informal missionary work through exemplary members who share gospel teachings with their friends also yields many convert baptisms. Together, members and missionaries bring hundreds of thousands of new members into The Church of Jesus Christ of Latter-day Saints each year. Convert baptisms, coupled with the increase in membership through the baptisms of eight-year-olds in LDS families, make the Church the fastest-growing major religion in the world.

THE ROLLING STONE GAINS IN STRENGTH

Any member of a group or society should hope that the organization he or she belongs to has such value that others would also want to belong to it. A strong, steady growth rate should characterize a dynamic group, especially over the course of time. Such a growth rate is found in The Church of Jesus Christ of Latter-day Saints, symbolized in Nebuchadnezzar's famous dream as a massive stone "cut out without hands," which Daniel prophesied would become "a great mountain, and [fill] the whole earth." (Dan. 2:34–35.)

Starting with six men in 1830, the Church grew to six hundred and seventy thousand by 1930. By 1990, over six hundred and fifty thousand names a year were being added to the Church rolls annually. Of course, a number of names were taken off the Church rolls each year as people died or left the Church, but the rate of those coming in was so much greater than those leaving that the Church grew by five hundred and eighty thousand in 1988 alone.[16]

Even more important than the count of babies and baptisms is the establishment of LDS stakes, which is a sign of genuine Church growth because it indicates Melchizedek priesthood strength, membership stability, and leadership maturity in any given area. For example, enough members come into the Church every two-and-a-half days to fill a stake of three thousand eight hundred members, but the spiritual maturity rate is slower, with a new stake being organized every four days or so.[17]

In first century following the Restoration, the first one hundred stakes were organized over a period of ninety-eight years. After World War I and during the Great Depression, the rate of growth quickened to about one new stake every six to eight months. For example, in the decade surrounding the one hundredth birthday of the Church (from 1926 to 1935), a total of twenty-two new stakes were organized. All of these stakes were formed in the Rocky Mountains alongside the Mormon pioneer colonies from Alberta, Canada, and northern Mexico. After 1950, the rate increased to almost one new stake monthly, with the two hundredth stake being organized in 1952. In the 1960s, usually two new stakes were created each month, with the three hundredth stake being established in 1960, the four hundredth in 1964, and the five hundredth in 1970.[18]

By the late 1980s, however, the Church was growing at a phenomenal pace—up to 126 stakes in a year (1980). For example, in the decade from 1976 to 1985, eight hundred and fifty stakes throughout the world were established.[19] Whereas fifty years earlier, General Authorities were organizing a new stake every six months, they are now creating one every few days. In other words, the restored Church now grows each year as fast as it did in its first century of existence. Furthermore, new stakes are being formed in numerous non-English-speaking countries, with the greatest number of these in Central and South America and a smaller number in the Pacific islands, Asia, Europe, and Africa.

If the rate of growth continues at the same pace, neither accelerating nor decelerating, by the time the Church reaches its two hundredth birthday, over sixty new stakes will be organized each week, or one every few hours. Every country of the world open to missionaries could feasibly add at least one or two new stakes every month. To perform this work, hundreds of General Authorities, including many quorums of Seventies, would be required to organize and set apart the new stake presidencies and to reorganize the increasing numbers of older stake presidencies. In short, what took almost 130 years for the Church to accomplish at the outset of this dispensation would be achieved every few weeks, as over two hundred and seventy new stakes would be created each month.

The stone foreseen by Nebuchadnezzar and Daniel is the restored

church of Jesus Christ. (See D&C 65:2.) It is literally rolling forth —
gaining mass and momentum — to fill the whole earth in preparation for
the second coming of Christ, whose kingdom or Church will replace the
kingdoms and nations of men when he governs during the millennial era.
(See Dan. 2:44–45).[20]

THE REWARDS OF DISCIPLESHIP

As stated earlier, though the pathway is hard to follow at times, the
rewards of latter-day discipleship are great. In addition to the feelings
of kinship and joy in belonging to a strong, growing international church,
three of the most obvious blessings in following Christ are an ever-
increasing testimony, fellowship with the saints, and progress toward
eternal life.

Our testimonies grow as we chase the darkness of ignorance and
apostasy from us and gain more light of truth and understanding within
us. Whatever comes from God is light, and those who receive God's light
and continue in his service will receive more light. Thus, our testimonies
continue to grow as "that light groweth brighter and brighter until the
perfect day." (D&C 50:24.) Christ encourages us as his followers to be
lights to the world, and he admonishes us to avoid hiding our lights under
baskets of fear or uncertainty. (See Matt. 5:14–15.) The sure way to
strengthen our testimonies is to share them with others, and we have
many opportunities to do this as we serve in Christ's church and in our
communities.

Strong fellowship with the Saints develops primarily through living
in righteousness and helping one another. Here again we can be a light
to the world, demonstrating the nature and bonds of true Christian
discipleship. Bible wisdom tells us that "the path of the just is as the
shining light, that shineth more and more unto the perfect day." (Prov.
4:18.) In addition, the bond of love forged in fellowship is a trademark
of Christ's church (see John 13:35), and we benefit from the feelings of
unity and strength that accompany the forging of that love.

Another great blessing of following Christ is one that we do not
always see, but one we may more fully perceive in the future. As Christ
admonishes us to lay up spiritual treasures and to serve God rather than
the world, he tells us to keep our eyes single to God's glory, so that our

"whole body shall be full of light." (Matt. 6:22.) When we come into the light of Christ and follow his precedent, we become baptized members of his Church and are known as his spiritually begotten children. As we rear our own children and serve other brothers and sisters in our Church family, we encourage their spiritual growth. And as we share the light of gospel truths with others, we spread and build Christ's kingdom.

These efforts strengthen us all and solidify the whole Church community. Eventually, our service flows back to us and our families as we are appreciated, loved, taught, and served. In this manner, Christ's church is the vehicle that God has chosen to help his children perfect themselves and others. The full results of our faithful discipleship will become obvious to us as we enjoy celestial light and life with our fellow disciples.

In conclusion, *LATTER-DAY SAINTS become spiritual children and valuable disciples of Christ as they develop faith, adhere to gospel laws, and live righteously while helping others, thus becoming like a shining light (radiating the gospel) and a rolling stone (building his kingdom) that will fill the earth.* Only when we are focused on the light of Christ do we become children of his kingdom. Only when we emulate his example do we become his true disciples. The more we follow the Savior, the more knowledge we gain of him, his doctrine, and his nature. And then, as we become like him, we join with him and Heavenly Father in celestial glory. As followers of Christ, we need to recognize and heed the voice of the Good Shepherd so we can remain in his flock and join our efforts with his until all people on earth become "one fold, and one shepherd." (John 10:16.)

For further study, refer to the following entries:

TG	BD	*EM*
Disciple	Disciple	Discipleship
Example	Saint	Latter-day Saints
Righteousness		(LDS)
Saints		Life-style
		Peculiar People
		Saints
		Unity

CHAPTER 36

RELIGIOUS LIFE IN A MODERN WORLD

Contemporary society has become increasingly complex. To meet the diversified demands of modern life, we must often "wear different hats" while we fulfill varied roles at home and in the community. Within the family, we wear the hats of parent, sibling, and child, and we could also wear hats representing our roles as counselor, cook, dishwasher, gardener, teacher, repair person, and so on. When we pursue vocational ambitions, we wear the hat of employee or student. We may also wear the hat of a soccer coach, amateur artist, neighborhood mechanic, PTA aide, Scout leader, sports fan, homemaker, church volunteer, or any of a dozen other roles.

In fact, we may wear many hats in diverse roles at the same time as we interact with our family, friends, and associates. For example, as we shop for the family (one hat), we might interact with a local Church member working as a sales clerk (another hat). Latter-day Saints not only wear different hats within their professional and Church settings, but they should also wear some important hats within their community and nation. Beyond involvement in local school and community services, Church members throughout the world should be involved citizens of their own country, as much as time and circumstances allow.

God permitted his children on this earth to develop their own different forms of government, as witnessed in the great variety of political systems currently practiced throughout the world. The scriptures do not mandate one form of government over another, but they do record the dangers of some types of rule. For example, the prophet Samuel warned the ancient Israelites about the risks of changing their system of judges into a monarchy. (See 1 Sam. 8:9–18; cf. Mosiah 29.) But the people wanted and received a king, who was selected and set apart by Samuel.

591

(See 1 Sam. 8:19–22; 10:1.) Later during the New Testament period, Jesus told his followers to pay unto the Romans the taxes that were due. (See Matt. 22:17–22.) This counsel disappointed some of Christ's more fanatical, nationalist followers because they wanted Jesus to deliver the Jews from Roman rule. Eventually, Christ will establish his own millennial form of ideal government; in the meantime, we participate in our own national society as good citizens.

Christ's kingdom on earth will not be established by tax revolts, public riots, guerilla warfare, or mass armaments. Instead, his kingdom will be founded on the divine power of his priesthood. Priesthood is the source of God's glorious power, shared with men on this earth, to carry out the plan of salvation. Beyond ordinances and blessings, however, priesthood is also the source of the ultimate, divine form of government. President John Taylor claimed that the priesthood is "the legitimate rule of God, whether in the heavens or on the earth; and it is the only legitimate power that has a right to rule upon the earth; and when the will of God is done on earth as it is in the heavens, no other power will bear rule."[1]

The Prophet Joseph Smith had also previously asserted this view in the tenth Article of Faith, saying "that Zion (the New Jerusalem) will be built upon the American continent; that Christ will reign personally upon the earth." He hastened to add in the twelfth article, however, that until that time, "we believe in being subject to kings, presidents, rulers, and magistrates, in obeying, honoring, and sustaining the law."

Throughout the ages, the saints have struggled to not be of the world though they must live in it. (See John 17:11–16.) In other words, they have tried to live productively in imperfect societies while preparing for the heavenly society. In discussing the fundamental differences between heavenly and earthly governments, we should identify some responsibilities of government, the inspired nature and importance of separation between church and state, and the obligations of members of Christ's true church in their respective countries.

SOME PRIMARY RESPONSIBILITIES OF HUMAN GOVERNMENT

There exists a primary difference between the gospel of Christ and the governments of men. While the Holy Spirit can transform the heart within man to make him an altogether new creature and better citizen, the state can only hope at best to shape outward attitudes and behavior so that people live peacefully together in a well-ordered community. In principle this is a worthy goal of the state that modern scripture approves: "We believe that governments were instituted of God for the benefit of man . . . for the good and safety of society." (D&C 134:1.)

What are some responsibilities that governments have as they strive to provide for the "good and safety of society"? Five priorities come to mind that seem to encompass the primary responsibilities of good government: support for the general *welfare* of the citizens, administration of fair *justice* for all individuals, defense of the rights and *freedom* of the people, encouragement of high *morality* and integrity among the society, and establishment of *peace* in the land.

WELFARE OF THE CITIZENS

Good governments are designed to foster and protect the general welfare of their citizens. More than providing monetary or government assistance for individuals in financial distress, these welfare concerns encompass a broad range of physical, social, and vocational needs. President Joseph Fielding Smith once explained: "You must . . . bear in mind that the temporal and . . . spiritual are blended. They are not separate. One cannot be carried on without the other, so long as we are here in mortality."[2] A good, humane government would recognize that an atmosphere must be provided where health and development can be achieved by its citizens.

Good government helps citizens avoid living the law of the jungle in their daily endeavors. Though they give up some individual freedoms, they gain more freedoms because they are kept from living in anarchy. President N. Eldon Tanner clarified the role of government regulations when he said, "The laws of God and the laws of nature and the laws of the land are made for the benefit of man—for his comfort, enjoyment, safety, and well-being."[3] A good government should not feel obligated to fulfill every human need, but it should develop opportunities so that a person's basic physical and social needs can be met. It will also assist families and others in providing these needs for those incapable of obtaining them for themselves.

JUSTICE FOR ALL INDIVIDUALS

Once a government has enacted legislation to support the general welfare of the people, it must be willing to provide fair and equal treatment for all citizens—be they rich or poor, male or female, leaders or subjects, young or old, healthy or handicapped. It must also be willing to enforce the laws by administering justice to lawbreakers. Justice is an eternal principle, and no nation is truly free without it. The Prophet Joseph Smith said that faith in God includes recognition "of the attribute [of] justice in him; for without the ideal of the existence of the attribute [of] justice in the Deity men could not have confidence sufficient to place themselves under his guidance and direction; for they would be filled with fear and doubt lest the judge of all the earth would not do right."[4]

This principle also applies to the administration of justice within a secular government. If people do not have trust in the administration of justice and the system of judges in a country, they would lack the confidence to place themselves under the laws of the land, and thus the stability of the nation would be eroded. King Mosiah in the Book of Mormon recognized the importance of wise judges in government. He admonished, "Let us appoint judges, to judge this people according to our law; . . . for we will appoint wise men to be judges, [who] will judge this people according to the commandments of God." (Mosiah 29:11.) Likewise, a good government must provide for the election or appointment and support of wise judges who will righteously administer justice.

FREEDOM OF THE PEOPLE

In the premortal existence, we supported Heavenly Father's plan of salvation because we wanted the agency he offered us. The Creator intended for us to be blessed with the ability to freely choose the actions our life would take. Ideally, people in any nation should be free to believe and practice religion, to move to other locations and even leave their country, to work and enjoy recreation where they desire, to speak and write openly and freely, and to learn and study as they desire. We opposed Lucifer's attempt to usurp our options and we prevailed upon God to grant us the gift of freedom. On earth, however, we must struggle to maintain our freedom.

President Ezra Taft Benson has said: "Rights are either God-given as part of the divine plan, or they are granted by government as part of the political plan. If we accept the premise that human rights are granted by government, then we must be willing to accept the corollary that they can be denied by government. I, for one, shall never accept that premise."[5] He also warned the saints that "freedom must be continually guarded as something more priceless than life itself."[6] A good government protects the basic liberties for its citizens so they can be free from abuse and tyranny while in this earth life.

MORALITY AMONG SOCIETY

Throughout the ages our Father in Heaven has expected his children to live honest, moral lives. (See Ex. 20:3–17.) These values and the respect for life and the living are expected of individuals, communities, and whole nations. In a time when the separation of church and state is often interpreted as removing the hand of God from public or government affairs, our society is in danger of moral degradation. President Spencer W. Kimball emphasized the importance of incorporating high moral values in government when he said, "No government can remain strong by ignoring the commandments given to Moses on Mount Sinai."[7]

Clearly, good government must meet high moral and ethical standards itself and then encourage their development among society. Without such inherent goodness, the growth of any nation would falter. Elder David B. Haight has counseled that "the continued survival of a free and open society is dependent upon a high degree of divinely inspired values and moral conduct.... A great need today is for leadership that exemplifies truth, honesty, and decency in both public and private life."[8] Government leaders and citizens must work together to encourage these values in their society.

PEACE IN THE LAND

Ideally, governments should establish peace within their own boundaries and with other nations. The blessings of the gospel rarely flourish under nations that are constantly at war, especially if they are the aggressors. Jesus declared, "Blessed are the peacemakers: for they shall be called the children of God." (Matt. 5:9.)

He later admonished the Latter-day Saints, "Renounce war and proclaim peace, . . . lest I come and smite the whole earth with a curse, and all flesh be consumed before me." (D&C 98:16–17.) Peace, along with law and order, brings stability and predictability among a society. Unfortunately, governments naturally rely on military strength to maintain peace instead of appreciating the peace that can abound in nations where righteous, hard-working, and freedom-loving citizens live. As President Joseph F. Smith taught, "Peace comes only by preparing for peace, through training the people in righteousness and justice, and selecting rulers who respect the righteous will of the people. . . . There is only one thing that can bring peace into the world. It is the adoption of the gospel of Jesus Christ, rightly understood, obeyed and practiced by rulers and people alike."[9]

Isaiah foresaw this formula for peace when he recognized that after the leaders of the peoples would come to the house of the Lord and receive his instruction, they would "beat their swords into plowshares, and their spears into pruninghooks: nation shall not lift up sword against nation, neither shall they learn war any more." (Isa. 2:4.) Lasting peace will come when governments learn to prepare for peace as their leaders and citizens practice the principles of gospel living.[10]

The highest form of noble government seeks peace for its own citizens and works for peace in and among other nations. An ideal government encourages high ethical and moral standards while allowing citizens to make decisions individually and collectively in governing themselves. The call for freedom (political, economic, and religious) should be heard throughout every land. Justice should be administered through fair laws and appropriate order among every society. Such just societies give all children of God good and frequent opportunities to provide for their physical and spiritual welfare. In these cases, they will be blessed regardless of the country in which they live.

Nonetheless, Joseph Smith also said, "It is not our intention . . . to place the law of man on a parallel with the law of heaven; because we do not consider that it is formed in the same wisdom and propriety . . . [It is not] sufficient in itself to bestow anything on man in comparison with the law of heaven, even should it promise it."[11] Even the best of man's ways are not God's ways, explains LDS scholar Hugh Nibley: "The best of human laws leaves every man free to engage in his own pursuit of happiness, without presuming for a moment to tell him where that happiness lies; that is the very thing the laws of God can guarantee."[12]

So, rather than walk after their own knowledge and desires, the righteous submit to government by God, the most just and benevolent of all lawgivers. His laws are based on eternal principles, which alone can properly govern the eternal and divine spirit of man. In addition, faithful followers of the Lord need to live as productive citizens of the world. To guarantee that they and the adherents of other religions have full and equal rights to worship God as they desire, a certain separation must exist between church and state.

SEPARATION OF CHURCH AND STATE

The separation of church and state and the free exercise of religion, as guaranteed by the First Amendment to the U.S. Constitution, laid the earthly foundation for the restoration of the gospel in America in the nineteenth century. For this reason, Joseph Smith praised that great document as "a glorious standard; it is founded in the wisdom of God. . . . It is like a great tree under whose branches men from every clime can be shielded from the burning rays of the sun."[13]

The separation of church and state is inspired wisdom for contemporary governments, since mixing religion with politics in a plural society almost always results in either corruption or persecution of religion. For example, the early Christian church fell into complete apostasy as it was integrated into Roman civil government and as some Catholic emperors sought to impose one set of dogma upon the whole society. Insulating churches from governmental interference helps insure that religion is not corrupted by the machinations of politics. As Joseph Smith revealed, people are only answerable to God and not governments as to the exercise of their religion and their rules and forms of religious devotion. (See D&C 134:4.)

In addition, early Christians, the Jews, some early Latter-day Saints, and adherents of many religious communities have been persecuted by other groups and some governments who claim religious support for their acts of aggression. Religious persecution is often a thinly veiled excuse to gain political power or to plunder personal property. As examples, the expulsion of Jews from Spain and the Mormons from Missouri occurred not because of doctrinal teachings or religious practices. Rather, many Spaniards were jealous of Jewish wealth and influence, and many in Missouri felt threatened by the Church's integration of ecclesiastical

authority, local government, and economics. A church/state separation
helps reduce the possibility and severity of religious persecution. As
Joseph Smith taught, "We do not believe it just to mingle religious
influence with civil government." (D&C 134:9.) We hope eventually to
be part of a theocracy with Christ himself as our supreme ruler. In the
meantime we strive to maintain eternal spiritual values within the political
system we live in.

Besides creating difficulty for churches, mixing religion and politics
without the Lord's personal direction can also produce self-righteousness
and hypocrisy in public affairs. Too often we see that religious attitudes
and even scriptural authority are perfectly acceptable as long as they
back up one's own political platform, but when the opposition uses similar
arguments to support its position, politicians inevitably cry out for separation of church and state. One author wrote in *Time* magazine, "It is,
of course, absurd to tell the church to stay out of politics, if politics is
defined as that universe of activity in which people collectively decide
what the public good is and how to pursue it. The church teaches moral
principles and values, and these inevitably spill over to public affairs,
sometimes into actual policy, like civil rights and nuclear arms. But political partisanship—choosing sides in elections, endorsing or vetoing
candidates—is another matter altogether."[14]

The policy of the LDS Church concerning involvement in politics is
that it may legitimately take a position only on moral issues and on social
and political issues when morality and religious belief are challenged (as
it has on abortion, gambling, and the proposed Equal Rights Amendment). It does not directly align itself with any political party or candidate.
It encourages, however, the individual participation of Church members
in governmental and political issues according to conscience. As an organization, to become an active participant in political partisanship—
which determines the allocation of temporal, secular power—would jeopardize the Church's spiritual integrity and independence.

The separation of church and state applies equally to both entities;
that is, neither church nor state should try to influence the legitimate
power of the other. The civil power of a democratic republic is derived
from the people; the priesthood authority of the true church is bestowed
by God. Man's ways are not God's ways. Just as a government should
not dictate the dealings of a religious society, a religion does not have

the right to try people for property or civil cases unless they concern religious leaders or members who have mismanaged church properties or demonstrated behavior contrary to civil and religious law. (See D&C 134:10.) Religious law and civil law should be administered respectively by the separate bodies of church and state. (See D&C 134:11.)

SOME RESPONSIBILITIES OF CITIZEN-SAINTS

The Prophet Joseph Smith noted that all sectarian religions contain "a little truth mixed with error."[15] The same can be said for all secular governments and political parties, since all promote some good causes and yet may also espouse some that conflict with religion. Because of the importance of governments in our lives and the good they can do, the Church advocates that individual members get involved in providing proper direction to their own governments.

Political participation is a matter of personal conscience: "It is not meet that I should command in all things. . . . Verily I say, men should be anxiously engaged in a good cause, and do many things of their own free will, and bring to pass much righteousness." (D&C 58:26–27.) Almost every general election year, the First Presidency issues a formal statement forbidding the use of Church influence or property for the support of any political party or candidate. At the same time, they encourage members to support the party and candidates of their choice. Latter-day Saints have the privilege and a duty to become educated citizens, to seek for personal inspiration on where and how they can best help their society, and then to vote and participate in government.

In some third-world countries, many citizens think of Mormon missionaries as representatives of "Yankee imperialism." In fact, local Latter-day Saints are sometimes stereotyped as an extension of North American culture and influence. Church leaders throughout the world, however, strive to preserve and encourage local cultural traditions and values that are not antithetical to essential gospel teachings and Church practices. The Church of Jesus Christ of Latter-day Saints is not a Yankee denomination; it is a worldwide church with great racial and cultural diversity.

Just as we earlier asked, "What are some responsibilities that governments have to provide for the good and safety of society?" we should ask ourselves what we as good citizens can do to help our governments. The same five priorities come to mind as major responsibilities of good citizens: the general *welfare* of fellow citizens, the fair administration of *justice*, the *rights and freedom* of the people, the encouragement of *morality* and integrity, and the establishment of *peace*.

GENERAL WELFARE OF FELLOW CITIZENS

Good citizens will help the government by encouraging it to fulfill its duties. In many nations, the citizens can become active participants in the circles of government leadership. They can also make their ideas and concerns known to their leaders, especially those elected by them. The United States was founded on and is still maintained by the voice of the people, and the concerted effort of people with a common objective can and does make a difference. Consider this counsel from former House Majority Leader Jim Wright: "If you are wondering whether or not it is really worthwhile to communicate your views to your own senator or representative in Congress, consider this fact: Others who disagree with you are doing so constantly. . . . Your congressman is one person to whom your opinion definitely is important."[16]

Involvement in the community—that is, assisting our neighbors—is also important. If all citizens would try to help one another rather than assuming that "the government will take care of them," the work load and effectiveness of government agencies would dramatically improve. The best service is done one-on-one, but where we cannot meet others' needs, then the larger church services and state agencies can provide valuable assistance. We should try to remember that true service is only rendered after we demonstrate concern and love for others. As we do our own part in our small corner of the world and then encourage our leaders to do their part, we will often be amazed by the positive effect we will have outside of our own lives.

FAIR ADMINISTRATION OF JUSTICE

Ironically, the seeds for much of the corruption or distortion of justice come from the people themselves when their selfishness or pride motivates them to take advantage of any weaknesses or loopholes in the laws of the land. Such people seek to manipulate, even murder, for personal gain and assume they can get away with something for nothing. They withhold evidence, lie, and cheat. Masters of white collar crime believe that as long as you do not physically hurt someone, deception in order to acquire wealth is acceptable. Racial or sexual bias can cloud judgments, and educational or social-economic discrimination can cause injustices.

All citizens, and especially those who may serve the system of justice, such as police officers, lawyers, judges, jury members, social workers, and so on, need to be vigilant watchmen of society and the legal system to help insure that fair, equal justice prevails for all citizens. Any who abuse their positions of public trust must be held accountable in the efforts to make the world more a paradise than a prison. Futhermore, we need to remember too that any deliberate abuse of the system may avoid detection on earth but will bring the guilty before God's own judgment bar.

RIGHTS AND FREEDOM OF THE PEOPLE

Governments must carefully use the power granted them by their citizens to protect the rights and freedoms of the people. When people give power to a government system, the government receives a sacred trust to use its power for the public benefit. Unfortunately, "we have learned by sad experience that it is the nature and disposition of almost all men, as soon as they get a little authority, as they suppose, they will immediately begin to exercise unrighteous dominion." (D&C 121:39.) Hence, an ideal government should be democratic and representative in nature and include a system of checks and balances to safeguard against unrighteous dominion. (See Mosiah 29:25–29.) One primary duty of good citizenship is to work with the government to insure the rights and freedom of all our fellow citizens.

HIGH ETHICAL AND MORAL VALUES AMONG SOCIETY

Latter-day Saints, as citizens in many lands, should be actively involved in promoting the moral, political, social, and economic values that will create a better society for their families and facilitate the spread of the gospel to those willing to hear it. They are not to force their views upon others, even when they are in influential positions of political power or government, but rather they are to make sure that Mormon views and rights are fairly represented. The Prophet Joseph Smith concurred: "It is our duty to concentrate all our influence to make popular that which is sound and good, and unpopular that which is unsound. 'Tis right, politically, for a man who has influence to use it. . . . From henceforth I will maintain all the influence I can get."[17]

Latter-day Saints should be confident catalysts in uniting all good people to support whatever promotes the public good (honesty, integrity, accountability, frugality, for example) and fight against whatever undermines public values (drunkenness, drug abuse, pornography, leniency toward crime, and so on). We are not of the world but must live in the world. We, therefore, want not only to preserve the privileges of our religion, but also to promote a better social environment for our brothers and sisters outside the faith, with whom we share our nation and our world.

PEACE IN THE LAND AND IN OUR HOMES

Peace in the land often begins with peace in the heart and the home. True peace in the heart and home comes only through righteous living. If all citizens so lived, war and strife would cease to exist. As the prophets testified, when people learn and walk in the ways of the Lord, "nation shall not lift up sword against nation, neither shall they learn war any more." (Isa. 2:4.) Although large-scale "peace marches" and publicity campaigns may move society a little closer to peace, ultimate peace will come only when peoples' attitudes are changed. The quiet work we do with our children and in the neighborhood can be more effective in the long run than joining the masses in a televised parade. Especially as more and more concerned citizens and involved Saints work together, larger and larger communities of people will work together for peace throughout the land.[18]

MORE NATIONS THAN ONE:
THE GOSPEL IN OTHER LANDS

The religious and political freedoms granted by the U.S. Constitution were essential for the restoration of the gospel and the protection of the Saints during early Church history. They continue to provide important security for the formal "base of operations" of The Church of Jesus Christ of Latter-day Saints. The same range of freedoms is not required, however, to successfully preach the gospel in other lands. Converts join and practice the faith in many countries where the Church does not even enjoy public recognition (much less a tax-exempt status). The missions of the Church work as best they can within each nation's culture and political system as missionaries gather the righteous out of the world into stakes of Zion.

In this light, we should remember the early missionary experience of Ammon in contrast to that of the other sons of King Mosiah. They traveled together to work among the hostile, apostate Lamanites, whose armies had often fought against their fellow Nephites. Ammon's brothers immediately set about openly preaching the word among the Lamanites and quickly found themselves in jail. Ammon, on the other hand, first offered himself to King Lamoni as a servant and won the king's confidence by faithfully obeying his commands. Later, through the conversion of both Lamoni and his father, King Limhi, the other sons of Mosiah were freed, and the gospel was spread rapidly among the Lamanites. (See Alma 17–23.) Although missionary success began slowly and under adversity among former enemies, it had lasting success, for "as sure as the Lord liveth . . . as many as were brought to the knowledge of the truth, through the preaching of Ammon and his brethren . . . and were converted unto the Lord, never did fall away." (Alma 23:6.)

Like Ammon of old, LDS couples with unique service assignments and special ambassadors from the First Presidency and the Quorum of the Twelve Apostles travel to foreign lands to initiate special projects and to establish formal relationships with heads of state. In addition to providing educational helps and material assistance, these special representatives establish contacts with government leaders to discuss the rights and freedoms of any Church members living in that nation. Eventually the hope is that the gospel will be securely founded and the Church be recognized as a legal entity throughout the world.

David M. Kennedy, a seasoned diplomat and former U.S. Secretary of the Treasury, was one such special ambassador of the First Presidency. In an essay, "More Nations Than One," Elder Kennedy expressed his views on establishing a world-wide Church under various forms of civil governments: "We now have church members and missionaries living in many countries. Some of these countries have strongly centralized governments, even totalitarian forms of government; some are democracies; some are socialist; some are communist. In terms of the gospel, the prime consideration is the [individual] free agency of man."[19]

In other words, a full range of political freedom is not necessarily required for the exercise of individual conscience in religion. Elder Kennedy continues by listing five expectations and two limitations of any government that will allow religious freedom. As long as the government permits Church members to (1) attend church, (2) get on their knees in prayer, (3) be baptized for the remission of sins, (4) partake of the sacrament of the Lord's supper, and (5) obey the commandments of the Lord; and as long as rulers do not force members to commit crime, or require them to live separately from other family members, a Church member "can live as a Latter-day Saint within that political system."

Individual members can still seek reforms in the system, but they cannot advocate them in the name of the Church or as a right expected for Church members.[20] Just as U.S. members are not allowed to support political parties or candidates in the name of the Church, so members living under other forms of government are not to encourage political reforms or incite rebellion in the name of the Church. Regardless of the political system, the important expectation is that Church members can freely worship according to the dictates of their conscience and the guidelines of the Church.

By the same token, formal recognition of the Church as a legitimate ecclesiastical organization is not always necessary for the gospel to be preached and practiced. Members of the Church, both foreign nationals and native residents, live throughout the world in sometimes unusual circumstances. For example, in Saudi Arabia, a staunch Moslem nation, a fully recognized, fully organized stake of the Church is established, consisting of foreign workers. All Church meetings are held in individual members' homes because if they should demand the right to construct LDS chapels, the resulting political and popular opposition would destroy the Church there. In a similar situation in Egypt, the Church has sought but not yet received formal recognition from the government. Until such recognition is granted, as with the Jewish and Coptic Christian communities, the several branches of the Church are informally organized and free to meet. Since the Church cannot formally buy or rent facilities, individual members must do it. And so the work continues in whatever way it can.

We cannot explain why Heavenly Father places his spirit children in particular nations where they may not enjoy all political freedoms or

Church blessings. The Lord, in his own way and timetable, is changing formerly oppressive governments into opener and freer societies, as was dramatically demonstrated in Eastern Europe in the early 1990s. Ironically, foreign intervention or massive internal revolt did not bring about these changes. Instead, the people, armed with truth and hope made available through worldwide media and international contacts, demanded and received new forms of government. Fortunately, tolerant and far-sighted leaders were on the scene to allow and even encourage these drastic reforms. The people were able to work within the system to bring about change. Concerning the role of truth in bringing about change, Elder Kennedy counsels, "The truth does have a great impact and a good influence on the thinking of people, and with it they are encouraged to improve their lives."[21]

Church members, wherever they are, should daily petition God to open the hearts of government leaders throughout the world so that restrictive policies will change and the doors for missionary work can be opened among all nations. Elder Kennedy counsels that a primary concern of Latter-day Saints "should be whether the teachings of the gospel are allowed to flourish or whether the people are forced to follow immoral or ungodly practices. If the heads of governments allow the people to believe in God and these other fundamental teachings I enumerated, . . . that's all we can ask for."[22]

The safety and security of the Church within any political system is more important than the relative justice of the system itself, for only the gospel can redeem souls for eternity, and all secular governments will someday pass away. "Wherefore, be subject to the powers that be, until he reigns whose right it is to reign, and subdues all enemies under his feet." (D&C 58:22.)

In conclusion, *Latter-day Saints have an obligation to be informed, active CITIZENS of their respective communities and countries where they can worship God, strengthen their families, and serve humanity.* Although they should feel a primary responsibility to assist in building God's kingdom on earth, Mormons should also shoulder appropriate responsibilities within their local and national society. If they are going to "wear different hats" in life, they should wear them well as they continue through life as saints of God and citizens of the world—reaching out to help all our brothers and sisters.

For further study, refer to the following entries:

TG	BD	*EM*
Citizenship		Church and State
		Church in the World
		Civic Duties
		Civil Rights
		Community
		Constitution of the United States of America
		Freedom: Freedom and Government
		Military and the Church
		Politics
		Tolerance
		War and Peace

CHAPTER 37

THE SIGNS OF THE TIMES

Imagine a young married couple, close friends of yours. They have tried for years to have children, and the wife has finally become pregnant. But the very week the baby is due, the husband is unavoidably detained in a foreign land. They ask you to assist her at the time of delivery, and you gladly agree. You become excited as she calls, telling you her labor has begun, and you rush to her side to take her to trained medical personnel. However, you cannot take her place to deliver the child for her; she has to do it herself. Wishing you could do more, you nevertheless give whatever help and assistance you can while waiting for the new infant to come into the world.

In a similar relationship, we will observe and assist mother earth and her inhabitants to bring forth the long-awaited millennial era when the Messiah comes to rule and reign over a world of peace and righteousness. We have been invited to help in preparing ourselves and those in our circle of influence for this glorious era, but we do not actually bring it about—it is an act of God.

God has planned and prepared for the Savior's millennial reign from the very beginning of this earth's history. He knows the day and hour of its arrival, and although he has not shared this information with us, he has revealed promises of its sure coming in these latter days. (See D&C 49:7; cf. Matt. 24:36 and D&C 110:16.) As we study the words of the many prophets who foretold the prophecies and signs of the last days, we come to understand the general framework of what must happen to bring it into existence.[1]

The scriptures reveal guidelines about the major events of the last days and how we should prepare for them. Of all topics dealing with the last days, three stand out with repeated emphasis: repentance, judgment, and signs of the Lord's power. These themes center on the Savior, directing us toward a personal relationship with him and emphasizing his promises for the righteous and the wicked. While the ungodly may be confused and terrified by the events of the last days, the spiritually sensitive who respond to gospel truths and turn to God through repentance enhance their spirituality and anticipate the events surrounding the coming of the Messiah. Indeed, the repentance afforded through Christ's atonement inspires us to live righteously so we, as the "wheat" of Christ's harvest, can separate ourselves from the "tares" of the world in anticipation of mankind's great preliminary judgment. Righteous living qualifies us to be with him at his coming when his great manifestation of power and glory will be seen by all the earth's inhabitants.

We further prepare by knowing "the signs of the times" (Matt. 16:3) as outlined in the scriptures and then learning to recognize them as they occur. The Old Testament, from the first book of Genesis to the last one of Malachi, contains many prophesies concerning the last days. Prophesies dealing with the coming of the Messiah to establish his millennial reign are also found throughout the New Testament, Book of Mormon, and Doctrine and Covenants. Additional volumes of commentary have been written outlining and speculating on the precise nature and order of events preceding the Second Coming. In this chapter, we will discuss how the message of repentance leads to an inevitable polarization between the righteous and the wicked and identify a few specific, major events that must precede the millennial reign of our Lord.

SEPARATING THE WHEAT FROM THE TARES

The repetitious urgency of prophesies concerning the last days serves to remind us that our time for repentance is limited, for when Christ comes again, the earth will be elevated from a worldly telestial state to a more just terrestrial order, and all the wicked will be destroyed. Furthermore, just as each individual must receive baptism by the cleansing immersion of water and the purging fire of the Holy Spirit to be saved, so the earth must undergo a cleansing and purging prior to receiving her Creator when he comes in glory. The ancient apostle, Peter, and the modern prophet, Joseph Smith, both taught that the deluge in the time of Noah was the earth's baptism by water, and that the destruction and burning of the wicked in the last days will be her baptism by fire as a spiritual purging or separation of the righteous and wicked takes place.[2] (See 2 Pet. 2:4–5; 3:5–7.)

In the parable of the wheat and the tares, the Savior himself taught that before the great harvest day of gathering and burning, the righteous and wicked will be intermixed, not easily discernible from each other. As the harvest approaches, however, a great polarization will reveal who is to be gathered in and who is to be burned. (See Matt. 13:24–30.) Christ will direct and empower his servants to spread gospel truths and ordinances among all people as his kingdom spreads abroad. The primary message to the world will be that of repentance. (See D&C 18:6, 10–16, 40–44.)

Many will respond to the gospel invitation and join Christ's church. Others will continue in good, righteous behavior in their respective religions, seeking to live just, decent lives. Still others will be uncertain or indifferent toward religious commitment. Many will follow their selfish desires, and Satan will openly ridicule and persecute what is good. The gulf between the church of the Lamb and the church of the devil will widen and deepen as pressure builds upon people to chose either a way leading to righteousness or a path sliding toward wickedness.

How shall we distinguish the righteous from the wicked? The Savior succinctly answered that when he explained that the disciples of Christ "have love one to another" (John 13:35), but "because iniquity shall abound, the love of many shall wax cold." (Matt. 24:12.) People filled with iniquity no longer have place in their hearts for the influence of the Holy Spirit, which has the capacity to fill them with love for their fellowman.

The Apostle Paul clearly described the frightening state of those who are left to themselves without love and the influence of the Spirit: "Being filled with all unrighteousness, fornication, wickedness, covetousness, maliciousness; full of envy, murder, debate, deceit, malignity; whisperers, backbiters, haters of God, despiteful, proud, boasters, inventors of evil things, disobedient to parents, without understanding, covenantbreakers, without natural affection, implacable, unmerciful: who knowing the judgment of God, that they which commit such things are worthy of death, not only do the same, but have pleasure in them that do them."

(Rom. 1:29–32.) One need only look at a daily newspaper to find nearly every one of these manifestations of love that has waxed cold.

The problem of evil has always existed, but it seems more open and frequent, and people seem to have less feeling toward others. The most telling of the list is perhaps the last item — when people knowingly take pleasure in wickedness. "The fatal symptom of our day," says LDS scholar Hugh Nibley, "is not that men do wrong — they always have — and commit crimes, and even recognize their wrongdoing as foolish and unfortunate, but that they have *no intention of repenting,* while God has told us that the first rule that he has given the human race is that all men everywhere must repent."[3] Since the Book of Mormon is given as a type and fore-shadowing of our day, it is well to remember that gross sin and a lack of remorse for sin were precisely what characterized the Nephite society in the years just prior to its extinction. (See Morm. 2:12–14; 5:16–18; 9:5, 18–23.)

When the weeds, or tares, of the field are large enough to be easily distinguished, they are often so strong that they crowd out the wheat and drastically lessen the field's productivity. In a similar pattern, the wicked in the last days will persecute the righteous and make missionary work more difficult. Latter-day Saints, on the other hand, can counter the power of wickedness by increasing their spiritual power through righteous living and missionary success. As one apostle has instructed us, "The Latter-day Saints in every part of the globe are commanded to gather out from the midst of wickedness, corruption and priestcraft, and every abomination that exists. . . . For what purpose? That we may be separated from the world and its corruptions, which would otherwise work our temporal and spiritual destruction."[4] The wicked will be destroyed by Christ at his second coming when he claims his rightful rule on earth and redeems the righteous. (See D&C 133:50–52.) As we separate ourselves from the wicked world, we prepare for his advent by drawing nearer to God and helping others to do likewise.

JOHN'S SIGNS OF THE TIMES

Though we do not know exactly when the Messiah will come, we do know from the scriptures the sequence of certain events leading up to his great advent, particularly as recorded in the Revelation of John. The importance of this revelation to Mormons is accentuated by Nephi's visions of the last days. (See 1 Ne. 14:18–27; cf. Ether 4:16.) In the New Testament book of Revelation, the Apostle John records events he saw in vision concerning seven seals, or key periods of the earth's history. According to modern revelation, "we are to understand that the first seal contains the things of the first thousand years, and the second also of the second thousand years, and so on until the seventh." (D&C 77:7.) Within this timetable, the first seal began with the fall of Adam and Eve, and we are now nearing the end of the sixth thousand years since then.

THE SIXTH SEAL

The sixth seal is an important time during which three major series of events must take place: the gospel going to all nations, unusual natural events, and special priesthood callings. In the last days, angels will be sent forth who will "have the everlasting gospel to commit to every nation, kindred, tongue, and people." (D&C 77:8; see also v. 10 and Rev. 7:1.) The laborers of this last dispensation have constantly been admonished to share the gospel with others. Through Joseph Smith, the Lord foretold the testifying power of the Latter-day Saints and the significance of their missionary work within the context of the signs recorded by John the Revelator. The members of Christ's church have been called to teach one another and then to warn their neighbors. Elders and missionaries are to preach among the people and warn the nations of God's forthcoming judgment. (See D&C 88:81–92.) Begun in 1830, this process of taking the truths of the everlasting gospel to more and more nations, kindreds, tongues, and peoples is currently taking place at an ever-increasing rate.[5]

The two other major series of events mentioned in relation to the sixth seal have not yet occurred, but must happen before the seventh seal can be opened to usher in the last events before the Second Coming. One series of events deals with natural phenomena on and above this earth, and the other deals with important ceremonies and responsibilities for 144,000 priesthood holders.

As John describes the events of the sixth seal, he mentions a great earthquake such as the world has never seen. Also, he describes great manifestations in the heavens: a darkened sun, a reddish moon, and falling stars. Phenomena in the heavens are rolling together like a scroll while mountains and continents are moving on the earth. (See Rev. 6:12–14; cf. Joel 2:1–11; D&C 88:87.) These occurrences in nature may be related and could originate either on earth or in the heavens.

For example, major shifts along the continental plates may generate earthquakes, volcanic eruptions, and other supernatural events on earth that would cause atmospheric pollution and distortions in the heavens. Or, massive cosmic storms, meteors, or comets may come from outer space and cause major earth tremors and unusual activities in the skies. Some of these unusual phenomena may even be caused by humans as they disrupt nature and shower flaming stars of nuclear missiles upon each other. In any case, these observable events will bring fear into the hearts of many, especially the proud and the wicked, as they seek to hide from the Lord, believing that his coming is imminent. (See Rev. 6:15–17; cf. Isa. 2:10–21; D&C 88:91.)

The other series of events deals with a select group of individuals. John foretells of 144,000 righteous high priests, all of whom have honored the law of chastity, who will receive a special ordinance. (See Rev. 7:3–4; 14:3–4; D&C 77:11.) These 144,000 will be organized into groups or quorums of twelve thousand each according to the twelve tribes of Israel. (See Rev. 7:4–8.) As of the middle of 1992, there were over two hundred and fifty thousand ordained high priests within the Melchizedek Priesthood. It is uncertain, however, how many of them would spiritually qualify for this ordinance and be physically able to fulfill the tasks and callings that await this group when they are called to administer the everlasting gospel throughout the earth. (See D&C 77:11.) Also, it appears that these 144,000 might be gathered from the actual scattered Israelite tribes. (See D&C 77:9.)

Depending upon the earth's population when the Millennium is established, each of these 144,000 high priests could have responsibility for many thousands of people. For example, if the earth population were only three billion, there would be over twenty thousand people for each of the 144,000. In other words, they could be like Regional Representatives today, with responsibility over a number of stakes and the non-members living in that region. With the dramatic change of political and social events in eastern Europe and Asia, perhaps great numbers of converts and priesthood holders in these areas will help supply this body of leaders needed to help the Messiah govern his kingdom on earth. (See D&C 133:18.)

These three signs (the gospel spreading to all nations, the extraordinary natural phenomena, and the special calling of the 144,000 high priests) need to be fulfilled before the end of the sixth thousand years of this earth's temporal history, which should come around the year 2000 A.D. if our calendaring system is accurate. As the gospel is spread among the nations, and when these other signs have been fulfilled, then the way is prepared for the opening of the seventh seal, which will be accompanied by further great signs, including manifestations of God's power and increasing desolations throughout the earth.

THE SEVENTH SEAL

While the events highlighted by John in the sixth thousand years will be occurring at the very end of that time period, the events described in the seventh seal take place shortly after it is opened. After a short period of silence, seven trumpets shall sound forth, announcing seven signs or plagues that will prepare the way before the time of the Savior's coming. (See D&C 77:12.)

As the seventh seal is opened, there is to be silence in heaven for about the space of half an hour. (See Rev. 8:1.) Unfortunately, Joseph Smith did not ask about this verse as he did others in Revelation (see D&C 77), so we do not know if the silence is physical (meaning silence in the atmosphere) or spiritual (referring to a lack of revelation or communication from God). Also, we do not know if the time span refers to our earthly thirty-minute period or, in the ratio of one year with God being like a thousand years on earth, whether it could refer to twenty-one years of our time. This sign is significant enough, though, that those with ears to hear, both physical and spiritual, will be aware of its occurrence.[6] (Cf. D&C 88:95; 38:12.)

In the seventh seal, a time will come when the world as a whole needs to receive further, more dramatic proclamations of God's intentions than during the sixth seal. The Prophet Joseph Smith reveals an important reason why the manifestations in the seventh seal are more severe and intense. He records the Lord's admonition that after the testimonies of the elders and missionaries will come "wrath and indignation upon the people. For after your testimony cometh the testimony of earthquakes, . . . thunderings, . . . lightnings, . . . tempests. . . . And all things shall be in commotion; and surely, men's hearts shall fail them; for fear shall come upon all people." (D&C 88:88–91.) While God's angels sound seven trumpets, representing a series of seven plagues, and send forth the prophesied signs, the fear felt throughout the world will motivate some to seek for truth and understanding and others to pursue selfish ambitions. (See Rev. 8:1–6; D&C 49:23; 88:92.)

THE SEVEN TRUMPETS (PLAGUES)

The first four trumpets or plagues seem to be major physical phenomena that afflict the earth without discriminating between the righteous and wicked. John uses graphic images to describe these events. The first seems to be a major electric/lightning hailstorm that burns up one-third of the trees and grass in the affected area. (See Rev. 8:7.) The second, described by John as a great burning mountain plunging into the sea, seems to be a great meteor that will destroy one-third of the ships and animal life in that sea. (See Rev. 8:8–9.) The third is harder to identify: John calls it "Wormwood," a great star falling from heaven and burning like a lamp, perhaps a comet, which disintegrates and falls upon one-third part of the waters and turns them poisonous and bitter like wormwood. (See Rev. 8:10–11.) Only the effects, and not the cause, of the fourth plague are mentioned as the sun, moon and stars are darkened by one-third. (See Rev. 8:12.) This darkness might be caused by the earlier signs or by other phenomena, such as volcanoes or gigantic dust storms.

Some have speculated that these plagues might even be caused by man as nations send intercontinental missiles descending upon each other with burning, destruction, radiation, and pollution following. In any case, the plagues devastate by one-third wherever they strike, bringing much woe and calamity to the earth.

Besides some obvious similarities with the plagues in Egypt, two patterns similar to how the Lord demonstrated his power in Egypt begin to emerge here. First, the plagues become more severe, and then they begin to afflict only the wicked. In ancient Egypt, the first three plagues (polluted water, an overabundance of frogs, and irritating body lice) afflicted people throughout the country, but starting with the fourth plague (stinging insects), there was a separation between the Hebrews in Goshen and the rest of Egypt. The Hebrews were preserved while the Egyptians suffered the later plagues (livestock disease, festering boils, destructive hail and fire, ravaging locusts, and three days of darkness.) The last of the ten plagues (the death of the firstborn children) only came upon those households, either Egyptian or Israelite, that did not have the blood of a lamb on its doorposts. (See Ex. 8:19–12:13.)

Returning to John's list of plagues, he indicates that the next three woes or plagues are much more severe than the first four. (See Rev. 8:13.) As a distinction between the righteous and the wicked, the fifth plague afflicts only those who do not have the "seal of God in their foreheads," an ordinance or symbol received originally by the 144,000 high priests. (Rev. 9:4; see also 7:3–4.) People without the seal of God will suffer severely when a plague of strange locusts strikes and torments them for five months with the sting or pain like that of a scorpion. (See Rev. 9:1–12.)

The sixth woe also separates the righteous from the wicked, as a great army of "two legions of legions" of cavalry gather for battle while bringing much destruction and death to the world. (See Rev. 9:13–21; 16:14–16.) Since a full Roman legion contained ten thousand soldiers, the King James translators interpreted the phrase as "two ten-thousand ten thousand," or, keeping the same total number, "two hundred thousand thousand." Since actual numbers are not a part of John's record, the phrase "two legions of legions" should probably be translated as "two armies of armies" instead of being seen as representing a specific number, such as two hundred million soldiers.

In the meantime, John completes his special latter-day mission among the Ten Tribes. At this time, two prophets in Jerusalem will seal the heavens, pronounce plagues, and hold enemies at bay for three-and-one-half years, after which they will be martyred. Their bodies will lie in the streets for three days before they will be resurrected as a great earthquake hits the Holy City. (See Rev. 10:1–11:13; D&C 77:13–15.)

The seventh and final woe highlights the great conflict between the forces of evil and good, with seven powerful punishments, depicted as seven vials of judgment, befalling the wicked who refuse to repent. (See Rev. 16.) The signs and events culminate with the desecration of the temple in Jerusalem, the battle of Armageddon, and the glorious appearance of the resurrected Christ on the Mount of Olives. (See Rev.

11:15–19:21.) Satan and his hosts will then be cast into the depths of hell's pit as the millennial reign of a thousand years of peace and righteousness on earth is ushered in. (See Rev. 20.) It is unknown how quickly these events will follow in succession after the seventh seal is opened, though if the second coming of Christ is anything like the signs and events surrounding his appearance in the Americas, they could transpire within just a few years.

THE MODEL OF THIRD NEPHI

The events recorded in Helaman and Third Nephi serve as a useful model for comparison. From the preaching of Samuel the Lamanite, the Nephites knew how many years they had in which to prepare before signs would be given of the birth of the Savior. Only a few repented, however, and prepared themselves for the long-awaited event. In the meantime, the unrepentant made plans to kill all these believers if the sign of the Savior's birth did not come to pass in the appointed year. However, the promised sign was fulfilled, and a day, a night, and a day passed without darkness. Thereafter all the people repented, and lived righteously, but only for a short period. The majority returned to wickedness within a few years. By the time of Christ's crucifixion and resurrection, all the people had demonstrated their righteousness or wickedness, and they were ready to be judged. Thus, the sign of his death was a signal for their preservation or their destruction. (See Hel. 14–16; 3 Ne. 1–8.)

Likewise, many who witness prophesied signs in the last days will be unprepared when the Savior comes. Some will confuse the timing of world events within the sixth and seventh seals of John's revelation. Particularly as the earthquakes at the end of the sixth seal come forth, many will think the Lord's judgment is coming. (See Rev. 6:16–17.) For example, some evangelical Christians anticipate Christ's second coming with the year 2000. The opening of the seventh seal will mark the intensification of tumultuous events and prophesied signs—so much so that many will think the end of days has arrived. But when the years pass without his arrival, they will quickly revert to their former ways, and the people will separate themselves toward goodness or evil.

The righteous will continue their faithful watchfulness and call others to repentance. (See D&C 88:68; cf. Luke 17:20–36; Matt. 24; JS–M.) The wicked will not repent before the Second Coming, saying "that Christ delayeth his coming." (D&C 45:26.) Others may say that the Messiah "comes not at all" as they seek to justify their gross behavior. John saw such types in vision, describing many people who witnessed the signs but "neither repented . . . of their murders, nor of their sorceries, nor of their fornication, nor of their thefts." (Rev. 9:21.) Like the Nephites before, many will return with vigor to their wickedness after the initial scare.

Thus, the church of the devil will continue to grow in power and opposition to the church of the Lamb until the telestial world is completely destroyed and replaced by the terrestrial world of the Millennium. Though the signs preceding the Second Coming will have been abundantly manifest, Jesus will surprise many like "a thief in the night" when he returns in power and glory, destroying the wicked so only those of at least a terrestrial nature will be allowed to live on the millennial earth.

THE SECOND COMINGS OF CHRIST

Before the final appearance of Christ at the end of the world's telestial state, he will make major appearances in his temple and among two select groups—one near the New Jerusalem in the New World and another near the Old Jerusalem in the Old World.

APPEARANCE AT THE TEMPLE

One significant appearance of the Lord in the last days was foretold by both Malachi and Joseph Smith. They prophesied that the Lord will "suddenly come to his temple." (Mal. 3:1; D&C 36:8.) This prophecy may have already been fulfilled when Jesus Christ appeared to Joseph Smith and Oliver in the Kirtland Temple on April 3, 1836. (See D&C 110.) Or perhaps it will be fulfilled just prior to the Lord's appearance to the whole world by a visit to either the temple in Jackson County, Missouri, or the one in Jerusalem, Israel.

Under Christ's direction, faithful saints will build on the American continent a righteous city called the New Jerusalem, located in Independence, Missouri. (See D&C 57:1–5; 84:2–5; 124:44–54.)[7] The holy city of Jerusalem will also be restored with a temple before the Second Coming. The Prophet Joseph Smith taught, "Judah must return, Jerusalem must be rebuilt, and the temple, . . . and all this must be done before the Son of Man will make His appearance."[8] Jerusalem will be sanctified with a temple of the Lord in the last days. (See Zech. 2:12; D&C 77:15.)[9] The sudden appearance of the Lord to his temple in either Jackson County or Jerusalem could easily accompany important prophesied events near both areas.

APPEARANCE AT ADAM-ONDI-AHMAN

In another event, Christ and all the great prophets of the seven dispensations will gather at Adam-ondi-Ahman, the site where Adam anciently gathered his posterity to bless them before he died. (See D&C 107:53–57.) Through modern revelation we know that Adam-ondi-Ahman, which originally was near the Garden of Eden, is located in Daviess County, Missouri. (See D&C 116.) There will be a significant latter-day reunion or conference at this place when a select assemblage of Latter-day Saints will join these resurrected leaders.[10] At this great gathering, the modern prophets will return their priesthood keys to the apostles and prophets from whom they received the keys. The ancient prophets, in turn, will return the keys to their predecessors until all keys are delivered to Adam himself. Adam, as the Ancient of Days, will then restore the keys to Christ, who will use them to personally establish his kingdom here on earth as it is in heaven.[11] (See Dan. 7:9–14.)

APPEARANCE AT JERUSALEM

Christ's other and more spectacular series of appearances will be in eastern Jerusalem on the Mount of Olives. In a revelation to Zechariah concerning the Second Coming, the Lord says, "I will gather all nations against Jerusalem to battle." (Zech. 14:2.) As the great army of Armageddon descends from the north under the leadership of Gog of Magog, half of Jerusalem will be conquered, and its inhabitants will be cut off from an escape to the more populated areas of the western coastal plains. Then an earthquake will divide the Mount of Olives to create a valley passageway. (See Zech. 14:1–7; Ezek. 38; Matt. 24.)

As the people flee east into this valley, the Savior will meet them there. The Lord described this scene: "Then shall the Jews look upon me and say: What are these wounds in thine hands and in thy feet? Then shall they know that I am . . . Jesus that was crucified." (D&C 45:51–52.)

After twenty centuries, the Jews, as a people, will finally accept their true Lord when he delivers them from their enemies at Armageddon.

Elder Bruce R. McConkie has commented upon the words of the ancient prophet Zechariah to describe the effect of this visitation: "Then comes this gladsome word: 'In that day there shall be a fountain opened to the house of David and to the inhabitants of Jerusalem for sin and for uncleanness.' They shall be baptized and receive the Holy Ghost! . . . And thus cometh the day of the conversion of the Jews. It is a millennial day, a day after the destruction of the wicked, a day when those who remain shall seek the Lord and find his gospel. And, for that matter, so shall it be with reference to the gathering and triumph of all Israel."[12] The Prophet Joseph also revealed some details about this appearance of the resurrected Lord upon the Mount of Olives, when the Messiah will return to the place of his ascension centuries earlier as he descends out of the clouds, clothed with power and great glory. (See D&C 45:43–44.) Thus, before the world as a whole knows that Jesus has returned to the earth, the Jews in Jerusalem will recognize and accept their Messiah, who will then utterly destroy their enemies and all the wicked upon the earth.

His Glorious Appearance — The Second Coming

Christ and his angelic forces will then go out from Jerusalem and destroy the enemy army, leaving so many dead that it will take seven months to bury them all. For seven years afterward, the inhabitants of the land will use fuel from the instruments of war to light their homes, cook their meals, and for other purposes. (See Ezek. 39:9–14.)

In the meantime, the most glorious and spectacular appearance of the resurrected Lord will take place. The Messiah will circle the earth in a manifestation of power and glory so that all will know that he has come to establish his millennial reign throughout the earth. Those still left on the earth will be good, honorable, and just people, who will be preserved as the Messiah establishes his heaven-like kingdom here.

As Christ appears in glory to the remaining inhabitants of the earth, no one will doubt that the Savior has come again. As Isaiah promised, he will come from the east in robes stained red, representing both his atoning sacrifice and his terrible destruction of the wicked. (See Isa. 63.) The angel's trump will sound "to all people, both in heaven and in earth, and that are under the earth—for every ear shall hear it, and every knee shall bow, and every tongue shall confess, while they hear the sound of the trump, saying: Fear God, and give glory to him . . . forever and ever." (D&C 88:104.) Just as among the Nephites after Christ's appearance, missionary work will accelerate after the Second Coming since it will meet no more opposition. Similar to the pattern of building an ideal Zion society as recorded in Third Nephi, within a few years his kingdom will spread throughout all the inhabitants. At this time "shall the heathen nations be redeemed," for "Satan shall be bound, that he shall have no place in the hearts of the children of men." (D&C 45:54–55.)

Before the Second Coming of the Lord in full glory, the righteous will be watching for the prophesied signs and be aware of their fulfillment. The Lord's preliminary appearances before the Second Coming will be to the righteous in special assemblies or under unusual circumstances, and these earlier comings certainly will not find their way into the major evening news broadcasts or the front page of the world's newspapers. To the unprepared, the increasing signs of physical phenomena and social disorder will seem as intensifications of what has happened in other chaotic times, until the Savior comes in the brightness of his glory.

PREPARED LABORERS NEEDED
TO THE LAST HOUR

The Lord has spent centuries preparing the world for his glorious coming, and it has been promised by nearly all the prophets, ancient and modern. To be ready, we need to set our temporal affairs in order through food storage, emergency preparedness, elimination of debt, and so on. But even more important is the need for spiritual preparation. Whether our spirits are living in bodies on the earth, or without bodies in the spirit world, or as resurrected beings is not as important as the spiritual state of our righteousness and preparedness. Our inner lamps must be lit and have oil in reserve like those of the five wise virgins. (See Matt. 25:1–13.) The valiant, both on earth and in the spirit world, will have the great blessing of being laborers for the last time in the Lord's vineyard: "The field is white already to harvest; therefore, whoso desireth to reap, let him thrust in his sickle with his might, and reap while the day lasts, that he may treasure up for his soul everlasting salvation in the kingdom of God." (D&C 6:3; cf. D&C 88:51–61, 70–73.)

But lest we put too much importance upon being on the earth as it enters its millennial era, we should ask ourselves: "Which is more important for me personally – the first or the second coming of the Savior?" For us as children of God, the first coming is infinitely more important because without the atonement and resurrection that Christ brought about with his first coming, nothing would be worth living for, and we could never enjoy a glorious celestial world here or anywhere else. The events near the end of the first coming of Christ, particularly the last few hours of his mortality and the opening of his resurrection ministry, transcend any other event that has happened on this earth before or afterward. Although the terms B.C. and A.D. of the common Christian calendar refer to the years before or after the birth of Jesus, the events of his atonement and resurrection are the true "meridian of time" against which all things will be measured and to which all God's children look for their individual redemption from spiritual and physical death.

The first coming of Christ, with its spiritual and heavenly rewards, is more significant for us personally. However, as far as the general history of this earth is concerned, the events surrounding the Second Coming will be more splendid and exciting because of the mighty signs that precede the earth's elevation from an evil, telestial existence to a paradisiacal, terrestrial order.

THE FULFILLMENT OF GOD'S PROMISES

Why do we have so many prophesies about repentance, judgment, and signs of God's power surrounding this particular period of time immediately preceding the Second Coming? One response is that Heavenly Father wants to teach, warn, and edify us while demonstrating his capacity to plan and fulfill his good and eternal plan.

In teaching us, there is a need for repetition because the more we read or hear certain prophecies, the more we should understand them. As we are more aware of the prophecies, we should then appreciate the importance of key events as they transpire. Also, prophecies are a warning to us that as the earth is elevated to a millennial glory, we must be at a certain spiritual level to be worthy to remain on the earth. All need to be warned as to what is required of them so that they may repent and be ready to receive their judgment and reward—either preservation in a millennial world for the righteous or a removal from the face of the earth for the wicked. In addition, while the trials and tribulations of the last days may test our faith and righteousness, the promised signs give us hope to persevere through the difficult times.

Ultimately, the pattern of early prophecy (as recorded by the ancient writers) and later fulfillment (as witnessed in these last days) demonstrates God's ability to plan and then to complete promises that affect this earth and its inhabitants. The completion of an earth cycle with an establishment of a paradisiacal world is the pinnacle of world history. Of the many things that our Heavenly Father, Christ, and others have prepared and anticipated through the ages, this promised new world gives us a utopia for which we can yearn and work. Our Heavenly Father talked about these times in the premortal councils, revealing to us the beginning from the end as he outlined his plan. Thus, key signs and promises of the last days have been revealed from the beginning as various prophets through the ages recorded many events that must precede the millennial era. The fulfillment of God's plan verifies his premortal perspective and his universal power.

Of course, some major conflicts will occur before all is prepared for the Messiah's advent. Satan will disperse confusion and seek control because he does not want to lose his dominion. The proud and the selfish will perpetuate their evil deeds, causing many to suffer before the wicked experience their own agony and destruction. (See Isa. 27:7.) An increasing gulf between the church of the Lamb and the great and abominable church, or the church of the devil, will open up, creating stress, suffering, and anguish for many. Turmoil, earthquakes, wars and rumors of wars, fear, sickness, tests of faith, oppression, and challenges to God's authority will spread across the land. Knowing this, God has forewarned us about these challenges leading to the Millennium.

Heavenly Father wants us to be more than casual observers as a new paradise is born on earth under the direction of his Son. With the Lord's direction and power, we can assist in bringing about these marvelous prophecies. Like the pregnant friend in labor and in need of our support, many of God's children need our assistance in fulfilling his promises. Different from the personal, private relationship we develop with the

Savior through the Atonement, the Lord's efforts in the last days require our public involvement as workers in the vineyard, missionaries in the field, and servants in the kingdom. Our help is needed as he calls for more and more to assist, even in the last hours. Those who have partaken of the personal redemption offered by Christ feel an obligation and excitement in assisting in the preparations for his second coming.

Indeed, *in these last days, a widening gulf is separating the righteous from the wicked as the Lord Jesus Christ expects continued obedience to his commandments (in spite of worldly pressures and persecution), and as he sends prophesied SIGNS OF THE TIMES prior to his coming in power and glory.* Every person should hear the gospel call to repentance before the Millennium begins.

As the Messiah comes to rule over the earth, he will not separate us according to *where* we are (in New Jerusalem or Old Jerusalem or elsewhere; in mortality or the postmortal spirit world or somewhere as a resurrected being). Instead, it will be *how* we are (our level of spirituality, commitment, and righteousness) that will determine whether we view the events of his great and dreadful day from a vantage point of peace and joy or from a position of fear and anxiety. Especially for those of us who appreciate what Christ did in Gethsemane, at Golgotha, and in the garden tomb, we naturally look forward to the signs of his imminent return. We want others to join with us as we share the ushering in of his glorious reign, when the whole world will finally recognize and accept him as the Lord of lords and the King of kings.

For further study, refer to the following entries:

TG	BD	*EM*
Jesus Christ, Second Coming	Abomination of Desolation	Armageddon
Last Days	Armageddon	Great and Abominable Church
Millennium, Preparing a People for	Revelation of John	Jesus Christ, Second Coming
Signs	Tares	Last Days
World, End of		Signs of the Times

CHAPTER 38

ZION'S MILLENNIAL PARADISE ON EARTH

Most religions contain the hope of some ultimate heavenly realm where an eternal state of joy and blessedness will exist. A few also anticipate a golden age when ideal conditions will prevail on this earth. The idea of an ideal earthly era is particularly attractive since many people want a taste of heaven on earth. History and literature reveal that humans have an inherent longing for a utopian society, known by such names as Paradise, Shangri-la, Bali Hai, or Nirvana. Perhaps such hopes are rooted in the early biblical account recorded by Moses of Adam and Eve living in such a paradise. Many readers of Genesis have yearned to go back in time to join our first earthly ancestors in their paradisiacal Garden of Eden. But since such trips back in time are impossible, we search elsewhere for our utopia.

Recognizing that an ideal state does not yet exist on earth, we hope that it can be created in the near future. Although secular literature expresses some utopian ideas, the scriptures contain the divine promises of such a time when the whole earth will become a millennial paradise. Studying the prophecies, we join the prophets and apostles in looking forward to a time when the earth will be restored to a paradisiacal glory — a time when God's children will live long lives filled with abundance, harmony, peace, and love.

HOPES FOR A MILLENNIAL ERA

Many ancient prophets looked forward to the latter periods of this earth's history, especially its messianic era when the Savior will reign for a thousand years. Indeed, the blessings of his righteous rule are a recurrent topic in the scriptures, from the first to the last books of the

Bible—from Genesis, which promises a time when every family of the earth will be blessed (Gen. 12:3; 28:14), to the book of Revelation, which prophesies concerning the last days and the Messiah's millennial glory.

Interestingly, the actual terms *millennium* or *millennial* do not appear in the Bible. The concept derives from the writings of John the Beloved in Revelation 20, especially verse 4, where the thousand-year reign of Christ is prophesied. The term *millennium* is mentioned twice in the Doctrine and Covenants, and that volume of scripture and the Book of Mormon provide helpful additional prophecies concerning the last days and the Lord's righteous reign. All these scriptures indicate that prophets through the ages, including those of our own dispensation, have foreseen this epic period of the earth's history.

Why do we have so many prophecies dealing with this particular period of time? Some passages give hope to mortals struggling in the challenges of a wicked world and wondering if peace will ever rule on earth. Through repeated emphasis of the events leading up to the Millennium, people looking for a better day understand and appreciate its importance and reality. In addition, the scriptures challenge the readers to personally prepare for the time when the earth will be elevated to its terrestrial state, a time of millennial glory when people, in order to qualify to be on the earth at that time, will have to live at a certain spiritual level.

Although readers in all generations have been motivated to greater spiritual commitment by anticipating this paradise on earth, the prophecies have special significance to those who will help usher in the Millennium. They give the signs of the times and provide insight about the preparations and requirements for such a paradise. The scriptures highlight how the ushering in of the millennial era will be one of the most spectacular events in the history of the world, an occurrence that our Heavenly Father, Christ, and others have been preparing for since the fall of Adam and Eve.

WHY A MILLENNIAL ERA?

The purposes of the Millennium are at least fivefold. First, the establishment of a promised millennial era demonstrates that God the Father has a plan for his children and that he can bring it into fulfillment in spite of opposition. The occurrence of the Millennium will vindicate his knowledge, vision, goodness, and power.

Second, the millennial reign verifies Jesus as the true Christ or Messiah for all mankind. Eventually, every knee will bow and every tongue confess that he is the Lord of this earth.

Third, this peaceful epoch gives the Holy Ghost opportunity to seal all declarations of faith and the saving ordinances, including those of the temple, with his Holy Spirit of promise. He will be free to spread truth and knowledge among all the children of God.

Fourth, the thousand-year period provides each child of God a full, equitable, and just opportunity to learn truth, choose allegiance, and receive ordinances — in short, to prepare themselves for God's final judgment. Thus every person will receive, justly, that eternal resurrected state commensurate to his or her true desires, capacities, and worthiness.

Finally, the Millennium gives mother earth an opportunity to rest as corruption, pollution, and abuse will cease and the earth's paradisiacal glory will return. Plants, animals, and humans will live in peace and harmony as all forms of life enjoy a latter "garden of Eden" throughout the world.

CHRIST PREPARES HIS DISCIPLES PRIOR TO HIS SECOND COMING

Naturally, many prophesied signs of the times and essential preparations for Christ's reign must precede his coming in power and glory. In many ways, his efforts with the Latter-day Saints will mirror his labors among the early saints during his ministry after his resurrection. After his resurrection, Jesus appeared to several groups of his disciples and to others of scattered Israel on at least two continents during the course of many weeks. He gave instructions, initiated ordinances, and prepared his apostles and disciples to lead his church. He then ascended to heaven, and his disciples were told by an angel that in a like manner he would return to the earth. Shortly before his second coming with its dramatic signs, and prior to revealing himself to the whole earth, Jesus Christ will visit select groups of his followers and segments of the House of Israel. He will come suddenly to his temple and appear both in Missouri of the New World and at Jerusalem of the Old World.[1]

In addition to receiving the keys of his kingdom and revealing himself to the remnants of Israel, Jesus will undoubtedly give important instruction and training to his followers and the leaders of his kingdom. (Cf. 3 Ne. 11–26.) He will prepare his disciples for all that is to follow when he establishes his millennial reign. Ultimately, Jesus will circle the earth in a manifestation of power and glory so that everybody remaining on the face of the land will know that he has come. The survivors of the tribulations and judgments will be elevated to a terrestrial order of life and will know that Jesus reigns as Lord and King over the whole earth. Missionary work will progress like never before, and within a few years, his kingdom will spread throughout all the inhabitants of the earth. (See 4 Ne. 1:1–5.)

THE NATURE OF MILLENNIAL LIFE

Many scriptural passages prophesy of key signs and events that precede the Millennium, but relatively few tell what life will be like in that golden era. They do indicate, however, that there will be major physical, social, and religious differences from present life on earth. Careful readers of the scriptures recognize that major physiological changes will take place as the earth is transformed back into its paradisiacal order. They also understand that political peace and social stability will dominate during the millennial era and that a strong Christian community will spread throughout the world. They watch for any movement toward the fulfillment of these prophecies and wish that they could witness more of them. But some positive experiences are already available that provide a taste of what millennial life might be like.

As Latter-day Saints travel throughout the world, and as their families relocate to new areas, they take comfort in knowing that wherever they go, other members of the Church are usually close by. The gospel and the church of Jesus Christ are available as a source of stability and strength in an often-troubled world. While waiting for the redemption of the world at the Savior's second coming, the association with the Church is often the closest experience to what life will be like during the Millennium. The Church of Jesus Christ of Latter-day Saints is already the kingdom of God on earth, and when all its telestial members, or "tares," have been "weeded out," it will be prepared to have the kingdom of God come from heaven to join with it.

The scriptures contain at least three models from earlier dispensations that help us understand the nature of the forthcoming Millennium, when "Christ will reign personally upon the earth" and "the earth will be renewed and receive its paradisiacal glory." (A of F 10.) The paradisiacal glory of the earth in its natural, physical state will parallel Eden, the garden of paradise; the millennial political and social order will compare with Zion, the city of Enoch; the personal reign of Christ will mirror his postresurrection righteous community established at Bountiful, the Nephite utopia founded in the temple courtyards.

A RETURN TO EDEN

The natural, physical conditions of millennial life. One outstanding feature of the original paradise in Eden was that there was no death: Adam and Eve were immortal (though not perfected) beings. To achieve a similar state during the Millennium, the reign of Christ will commence with the resurrection of all the righteous who have died since his own resurrection. (See D&C 63:49.) From that time forward, everyone will be instantaneously resurrected when they reach the end of their mortality. (See Isa. 65:20; D&C 45:58.) There will be neither death nor the sorrow of separation through death as we know it: "In that day an infant shall not die until he is old; . . . and when he dies he shall not sleep, that is to say in the earth, but shall be changed in the twinkling of an eye, and shall be caught up, and his rest shall be glorious." (D&C 101:30–31.) Disease, illness, physical and mental handicaps, and other restrictive elements of physical life will be overcome so that all can live a long, productive life.

Also as in Eden, the plant and animal kingdoms will be elevated above their telestial state. The land will return to the pristine condition it had before being cursed to bring forth thorns and thistles, briars and noxious weeds. (See Gen. 3:18.) Springs and streams will burst forth in the deserts to provide life-sustaining waters in previously barren and unproductive regions. (See Isa. 35:7.) Many rugged mountains and steep valleys will be transformed into land areas more accessible for human occupation and agricultural pursuits. (See Isa. 40:4; 55:13; D&C 63:21.) The harshness of the climates will be moderated, and the devastation of catastrophic weather phenomena will be abated so that seasonal and weather varieties can exist without destroying lives and crops. The soil of the earth will produce abundant grains, fruits, and vegetables for human consumption, instead of being devoured by insects and animals or lost, destroyed, or wasted before people can consume them. (See Isa. 41:19; 55:13; 65:17–19.)

As in the beginning, the whole face of the earth will be a delightful garden, with the major land surfaces joined together instead of separated by oceans.[2] (See D&C 133:23–24.) The transfiguration of the earth will be so radical and complete, that it will be "a new earth." (Isa. 65:17.) Animals of the earth will live together in harmony as the natural cycle of predator and prey will be broken: "In that day the enmity . . . of beasts, yea, the enmity of all flesh, shall cease from before my face." (D&C 101:26.) Instead of animals eating animals, they will eat straw and other natural by-products of plant life. (See Isa. 11:6–7; 65:25; Hosea 2:18.) Thus, a harmonious relationship will exist on earth between nature, animals, and humans.

PEACE AND PROSPERITY IN ZION

The millennial social and political conditions. As equally miraculous as the new harmonious physical nature of the earth will be the new peaceful social and political order established during the Millennium. The physical, national, and ideological demarcations that now divide mankind will be swept away, and all people will be united under one kingdom and one king, the Lord Jesus Christ: "Ye shall have no laws but my laws when I come, for I am your lawgiver, and what can stay my hand?" (D&C 38:22.) A theocratic kingdom will supplant all the governments of men as the Lord's kingdom will reign supreme. (See Dan. 2:44; D&C 38:22; 45:59.) His kingdom will be free of war and bloodshed as nations will not battle against nations and people will not fight against people. (See Micah 4:3; Isa. 26:15; 27:6.) Social peace and political stability will prevail over the whole earth as all humanity will be one large community under the sovereignty of Jesus Christ.

This community will comprise a Zion society, named after the ancient city of Enoch "because they were of one heart and one mind, and dwelt in righteousness; and there was no poor among them." (Moses 7:18.) The Book of Mormon record states that the Nephites living after the advent of Christ lived a similar order and "had all things common among them." (3 Ne. 26:19.) Both these ancient societies lived the law of consecration, a practice of shared abundance, which is actually a celestial law.

While the exact conditions of economic life during the Millennium are uncertain, we are assured that, as with the ancient Zion societies, there will be no "rich and poor, bond and free." (4 Ne. 1:3.) The division between the "haves" and the "have nots" will no longer exist, for each man will share his abundance, and all will receive according to their needs and just wants. (See D&C 82:14–19.) Work and labor will be amply rewarded as all will enjoy the fruits of their own labor: "They shall build houses, and inhabit them; and they shall plant vineyards, and eat the fruit of them. They shall not build, and another inhabit; they shall not plant, and another eat: ... and mine elect shall long enjoy the work of their hands. They shall not labour in vain." (Isa. 65:21–23.)

After war and contention between the Book of Mormon peoples had ended, the members of their Zion society were able to attend to their daily labors in the full hope of enjoying its fruit. They rebuilt their cities that had been destroyed and reared their families in peace and prosperity: "They were married, and given in marriage, and were blessed according to the multitude of the promises which the Lord had made unto them." (4 Ne. 1:11.) The same sense of security will also prevail during the Millennium when civil and ecclesiastical authority are one.

Furthermore, the abundance and fair distribution of goods under a single government will enable people to concentrate more on education and learning and to devote more time and attention to edifying one another. This they will do without the hindrances we now have in a telestial world. Knowledge and scientific understanding will quickly expand among all peoples. (See Acts 3:21; D&C 101:32–34; 121:28–32.) The learning and communication process will be quickened because all people will speak the same language. (See Zeph. 3:9.)

Note that some conditions and experiences of earth life will be the same during the Millennium as they are today. As in essential stages within our second estate, people will be born, grow, and develop into adulthood. They will eat and drink, wear clothing, gain an education, build and live in homes, work the soil and harvest the fruits of the earth, develop social and family relations, learn to give service, and experience the myriad of opportunities essential for a full, productive earthlife.

Full religious freedom will prevail during the Millennium. Just as Latter-day Saints today feel a sense of comradery and trust with the "goodly and just" people of the earth, the Saints, other devout Christians, and the adherents of other religions will enjoy being good neighbors and fellow citizens. No vile, evil people of a selfish, telestial nature will be on the earth; only those who are honorable people striving to live productive lives will live during the millennial era. However, since all will not yet be celestial people, differences in personality will exist, and disagreements will still arise. These types of problems will be present during the Millennium, but they should not disrupt the overall peace that will reign.

The ideal role model for society will be in the New Jerusalem, the Holy City of Zion that will flourish in Jackson County as a capital of the Lord's righteous kingdom. Those who follow righteousness and truth will gather together from the four corners of the earth. Enoch's ancient city of Zion will join with them as Christ's ideal social and political reign of a thousand years is established. (See Moses 7:62–65.) Together with a new natural environment, there will be a new social order on the paradisiacal earth.

RIGHTEOUSNESS IN BOUNTIFUL

The millennial moral and spiritual conditions. While Christ reigns as the Lord of lords, the current conflicts between religions and contrasting philosophies will end. New scriptures will be brought forth, and the true doctrines of the Messiah will be taught throughout the land. (See 2 Ne. 30:15–18; Isa. 11:9.) No atheists will be on the earth because every knee will bow and all tongues confess Christ to be the Lord of this earth. (See Isa. 45:23; Rom. 14:11; Philip. 2:10; D&C 88:104.) Although some differences of opinion and varied patterns of human behavior will still exist, knowledge of the supreme sovereign and his expectations will be universal.

The closest any people have ever come to such a complete political, social, and religious unity were the Nephites after the resurrected Lord had appeared and preached to them: "The people were all converted unto the Lord, upon all the face of the land, both Nephites and Lamanites, and there were no contentions and disputations among them, and every man did deal justly one with another." (4 Ne. 1:2.) A review of the nature of this ideal society reveals many similarities with what the prophets have said millennial society will be like.

Like among the Book of Mormon peoples, all people living on earth during the Millennium will have the opportunity to become members of Christ's church. (See 4 Ne. 1:1–2.) People living at the beginning of the Millennium will include those of a terrestrial nature, "who are honorable men of the earth, who were blinded by the craftiness of men." (D&C 76:75.) Missionary work will be easier in the Lord's kingdom, so that every person will hear the gospel message: "The earth shall be full of the knowledge of the Lord, as the waters cover the sea." (Isa. 11:9; see also Hab. 2:14.) Many, if not all people will be converted to the truth.

One reason truth will prevail is that the great liar and deceiver, Satan, will be bound by the power of God and the righteousness of the people. God's power will send the devil to his own spiritual prison where the wicked suffer. (See Rev. 20:1–7; D&C 43:31.) The righteousness of the people on earth will allow Satan no influence on the face of the earth during the Millennium. (See D&C 45:55.) Children born during the Millennium will not be subject to sin, for "Satan shall not have power to tempt any man." (D&C 101:28.) Therefore, the children "shall grow up without sin unto salvation." (D&C 45:58.) Though God had not formally bound Satan during the Nephites' golden age as he will during the Millennium, the Nephites were so righteous that Satan could not get hold on their hearts: "There was no contention among all the people, in all the land; but there were mighty miracles wrought among the disciples of Jesus." (4 Ne. 1:13.)

Through their faith and the people's righteousness, the Nephite apostles were able to "heal the sick, and raise the dead, and cause the lame to walk, and the blind to receive their sight, and the deaf to hear; and all manner of miracles did they work among the children of men." (4 Ne. 1:5.) As mentioned earlier, disease and premature death will be unheard of during the Millennium: "There shall be no more thence an infant of days, nor an old man that hath not filled his days: for the child shall not die, but shall live to be an hundred years old; but the sinner living to be an hundred years old, shall be accursed." (Isa. 65:20, JST.) In other words, nobody will die prematurely—all will live to a ripe full age; to die at a hundred years of age would be considered to have died as a child, or in one's youth.

People can still be righteous or sinful because after they reach the age of accountability, they can commit sins of their own free will and choice—Satan will not be tempting them to do so. They can then choose to either accept Christ's atoning sacrifice or suffer for their own sins. One interpretation of the last part of this verse is that those who accept Christ's atonement will enjoy a long life followed by instantaneous resurrection. On the other hand, the terrestrial beings who will not accept the Savior must pay for their sins—however minor—during mortality since they too will be resurrected without experiencing the postmortal spirit world. Thus the "sinner" will find the last years of a long life to be a curse, rather than a blessing.

One major purpose of the millennial era will be to complete God's plan of salvation for all his children. As we discussed in earlier chapters, the time must come when all people must be taught the gospel and have the opportunity to enter into Christ's church. Vicarious baptisms and other temple ordinances for these individuals must be completed. Thus during the Millennium, temples of the Lord will cover the earth, and worthy saints will be able to perform all the required ordinances of salvation. Genealogy and temple work will be one of the primary activities of Latter-day Saints during this era.[3] To facilitate this work, mortals will be able to associate and communicate with postmortal spirits not yet resurrected.[4] A sense of fulfillment and divine destiny will encompass this temple work as mortals work in God's vineyard prior to the end of this temporal earth.

The end of this earth will be similar to the latter history of the Book of Mormon peoples. After nearly two centuries of unprecedented peace, the Nephites' terrestrial society began to disintegrate into a telestial one. People once again divided into different nations, social classes, and churches. (See 4 Ne. 1:20, 26.) Similarly, as the Millennium draws to a close, Satan will be loosed, men will again deny God, and the righteous and wicked will square off for their final confrontation. (See D&C 29:22–23; 88:110–14.) Ultimately the earth will be purified and exalted to an eternal, celestial state where only the righteous can visit or dwell. (See D&C 88:18–19.)

Many books, songs, and poems have been written about utopias, golden ages on this earth, where prosperity abounds, death is not feared, peace prevails, justice rules, and righteousness is the behavioral norm. Mere humans cannot create this perfect world, but with the help of God, the scriptures promise that it will eventually be established. The Lord Jesus Christ will return and establish his perfect kingdom on this world. Evil, wars, and hatred will be removed, while righteousness, tranquility, and serenity will prevail. Satan will be bound for a season so that the children of God on earth can be left to choose and to act without his lies, distortions, and interferences.

In summary, *as Christ's kingdom in heaven joins his church and kingdom on earth, he will begin a glorious MILLENNIAL REIGN as Lord of lords and King of kings—fulfilling Heavenly Father's plan, verifying his administration as the true Messiah, enabling the Holy Ghost to seal all sacred ordinances, allowing all Heavenly Father's children opportunity to prepare themselves for God's final judgment, and giving mother earth an opportunity to rest.* When the Messiah comes, it really will not matter where we are at that moment—living as mortals on earth, as spirits in the postmortal spirit world, or as resurrected beings. What will count is our state of righteousness, for if we are righteous, we will be among those welcoming in his millennial reign.

Only the righteous will accompany the Savior at that glorious moment. In order to become righteous and pure, we must take advantage of his atoning sacrifice. Thus, for us, what he did in Gethsemane, at Golgotha, and from the garden tomb is much more important than when, where, and how he comes to earth to rule as King of kings. But we should look forward to witnessing the ushering in of his glorious reign when the world will finally recognize and accept him as the Lord of all lords and King of all kings.

In the meantime, we have a unique opportunity to be instruments in the fulfillment of his prophecies and the preparations for his return. We are the servants in the vineyard who are called forth in the last hours of the day. (See Jacob 5:70–72; D&C 33:3; 39:17–22.) We are those going out to gather the seeds of righteousness among the scattered souls of the earth. (See D&C 86:1–7; 101:65.) We are the servants of God, the wise maidens with our trimmed and filled lamps, the children of the prophets in the day of Christ's harvest. (See Matt. 25:1–13; D&C 45:56–57.) May we do our part by staying on the path of righteousness and serving God with our whole soul and all of our gifts, time, and talents. Then we can join Heavenly Father and our Savior in the way of eternal life.

For further study, refer to the following entries:

TG	BD	EM
Day of the Lord	Zion	Armageddon
Earth, Cleansing of		Kingdom of God on
Earth, Renewal of		Earth
Jesus Christ, King		Millennium
Jesus Christ,		New Heaven and
Millennial Reign		New Earth
Jesus Christ, Second		New Jerusalem
Coming		Second Coming of
Millennium		Jesus Christ
		Zion

NOTES TO PART 5

CHAPTER 31

1. *EM*, 1:387.

2. See chapter 30 for further ideas on the principles of stewardship.

3. The unique roles of a prophet of the Lord are discussed in chapter 7. Further discussion on the special contributions of the Prophet Joseph Smith are found later in this chapter.

4. The divine mission of The Church of Jesus Christ of Latter-day Saints is presented in chapter 34. The effort of Latter-day Saints in furthering the Lord's work is discussed in chapter 35.

5. Further discussion on the signs of the times before the millennial era and the major characteristics of the Millennium are presented in chapters 37 and 38.

6. This spiritual dark age began about A.D. 100 in the early Christian church and A.D. 200 in America. (See 4 Ne. 1:24–25.) The last known prophet of Christ's dispensation was Moroni, A.D. 421. (See Moro. 10:1.)

7. Chapter 12 reviews how sin and wickedness come into our lives.

8. See chapter 18 for a discussion of the ordinance of baptism.

9. See pages 187–93 in this book for a more detailed discussion of the pattern of personal apostasy.

10. See chapter 17 on repentance.

11. This ordinance work for the deceased is discussed in chapter 23.

12. "God's Love for All Mankind," declaration of the First Presidency, Feb. 15, 1978; italics added.

13. The priesthood, including its restoration, is discussed in the next chapter.

14. Chapter 23 presents further insights into the ordinances and sealing powers of the temple.

15. From notes taken at his opening address, Joseph Smith Symposium, Feb. 22, 1992, Brigham Young University.

CHAPTER 32

1. *MPLH*, 1.

2. *TPJS*, 167.

3. *DBY*, 130.

4. *TPJS,* 166–67.

5. See chapter 3 for a discussion of the roles and work of Jesus Christ.

6. *MPLH,* 1.

7. A full discussion of ordinances and other priesthood blessings is found in Chapter 22.

8. *MD,* 594; see also John Taylor, *The Gospel Kingdom,* comp. G. Homer Durham (Salt Lake City: Bookcraft, 1943), 221–22, 229.

9. *MD,* 595.

10. BD, 714.

11. See BD, 715.

12. See BD, 600.

13. Ibid.

14. See *GHI,* 1989, 1–1.

15. Ibid., 1–3 to 1–4.

16. Ibid., 11–2.

17. *TPJS,* 166.

18. See BD, 730.

19. See *TPJS,* 180–81.

20. See BD, 730–31.

21. See *GHI,* 1989, 1–1.

22. See *MD,* 763.

23. See *GHI,* 1989, 1–1 to 1–3.

24. *WNTCD,* 1428.

25. See *MD,* 215.

26. These offices as they constitute the three presiding councils of the Church are also discussed in the following chapter.

27. See chapter 7 for further details on the distinctive roles of prophets, seers, revelators, and apostles.

28. See BD, 731; chapter 7 in this book.

29. See *GHI,* 1989, 4–1.

30. Ibid.

31. See *EM,* 3:1144–46.

32. The function of Church councils is presented in the next chapter.

33. See *MD,* 410.

CHAPTER 33

1. See chapter 18 for further values of the baptismal ordinance.

2. See BD, "Church," 645.

3. Ibid.; see also chapter 38 for more insights into the millennial reign of Jesus Christ.

4. *World Book Encyclopedia* (Chicago: Scott Fetzer Co., 1987), 8:272.

5. See chapters 7, 8, and 32 for further insights on prophets, the scriptures, and the priesthood.

6. See *MD,* 149.

7. *GHI,* 1989, 3–2.

8. Ibid., Foreword.

9. Ibid., 10–1.

10. See *MD*, 789.

11. *EM*, 1:327.

12. *EM*, 1:65.

13. See *GHI*, 1989, 1–1.

14. *EM*, 3:1198.

15. *MD*, 558; see also chapter 22.

16. *EM*, 3:1199–200.

17. *Learn of Me: Relief Society Course of Study, 1987* (Salt Lake City: The Church of Jesus Christ of Latter-day Saints, 1986), 4.

18. This three-fold mission of the Church is discussed in more detail in the next chapter.

19. See chapter 28 for a discussion of financial donations to the Church.

20. See chapters 34 and 35 for a discussion of missionary work and discipleship.

Chapter 34

1. *TPJS*, 356.

2. "The True Way of Life and Salvation," *Ensign,* May 1978, p. 4; italics added.

3. "A Report of Stewardship," *Ensign,* May 1981, p. 5.

4. This passage has purportedly been quoted more often by General Authorities at general conference than any other single verse of scripture.

5. More highlights on the missionary program of the Church will be given later in this chapter.

6. See BD, 663.

7. Our specific responsibilities as Latter-day Saints are discussed in chapters 33 and 35.

8. *TPJS*, 172.

9. See chapter 23 for an examination of the temple, its purposes, and uses.

10. See chapter 14 for a discussion of the period after death and before resurrection.

11. See BD, 664.

12. More details about the eternal family and temple covenants are presented in chapters 23 and 30.

13. *EM*, 2:915.

14. Related in an informal gathering of BYU students, Provo, Fall 1983.

Chapter 35

1. See chapter 15 for the rewards of salvation, chapter 18 for an examination of baptism, and chapter 19 for the gift and companionship of the Holy Ghost.

2. *Oxford English Dictionary* (Oxford: Clarendon Press, 1989), 4:733.

3. *WNTCD*, 520.

4. Chapters 3 and 13 explain more about the attributes of Christ and the power of his atonement.

5. Refer to chapter 16 for further insights on the gift and power of faith.

6. *TC,* 22.

7. Chapters 20 and 24 provide further insights into why and how we can strengthen our spirituality through obedience to God's commandments. Chapters 4 and 19 highlight the teaching and testifying roles of the Holy Ghost.

8. Titles used in the scriptures to describe Christ are listed at the end of chapter 3. Insights about the Messiah's redeeming role in God's plan are highlighted in chapters 13–15.

9. Chapter 26 reviews other blessings that result from living a pure life.

10. *TC,* 24.

11. Further insights on the roles and values of Church fellowship are in chapter 33.

12. Chapter 20 provides a variety of suggestions for improving one's spiritual health.

13. Chapter 17 outlines the steps of repentance that can help any struggling Saint to find the way back into full gospel commitment and Church fellowship.

14. Chapter 12 covers the warning signs and dangers of falling into the path of sin.

15. Gordon B. Hinckley, "Except Ye Are One," *Ensign,* Nov. 1983, p. 5.

16. *CA,* 334–35.

17. See "Our Solemn Responsibilities," and "Church Membership Passes Eight Million," *Ensign,* Nov. 1991, pp. 49, 105.

18. *CA,* 185–96.

19. *CA,* 203–19.

20. More ideas on the signs and preparations for the Millennium are found in chapters 37 and 38.

CHAPTER 36

1. *JD,* 5:187.

2. *GD,* 208.

3. "Obeying the Right Voice," *Ensign,* Nov. 1977, p. 43.

4. *LF,* 7:13.

5. *SY 1986–87,* 39.

6. CR, April 1953, 40.

7. CR, Oct. 1976, 7.

8. "Ethics and Honesty," *Ensign,* Nov. 1987, p. 15.

9. "The Great War," *IE,* Sep. 1914, pp. 1074–75.

10. The preliminary steps and conditions of millennial peace are discussed in chapters 37 and 38.

11. *TPJS,* 50.

12. "BP," 287–88.

13. *TPJS,* 147.

14. Charles Krauthammer, "Rectifying the Border," *Time,* Sep. 24, 1984, pp. 79–80.

15. *TPJS,* 316.

16. *You and Your Congressman* (New York: G. P. Putnam, 1976), 200, 206.

17. *HC,* 5:286.

18. Excellent comments on the values and responsibilities of good citizenship are found in *TETB,* 569–706.

19. "More Nations Than One," in *The Expanding Church* (Salt Lake City: Deseret Book, 1978), 70.

20. Ibid.

21. Ibid., 71.

22. Ibid., 75.

Chapter 37

1. The major purposes of the Millennium are discussed in detail in the next chapter.

2. See *TPJS,* 12; *MD,* 289.

3. "BP," 297; italics added.

4. Orson Pratt, in *JD,* 12:303.

5. See chapters 34 and 35 for further facts of missionary success and Church growth.

6. See also TG, Silence.

7. See *EM,* "New Jerusalem," 3:1009–10.

8. *HC,* 5:337.

9. See also *HC,* 4:456; *EM,* "Jerusalem," 2:722–23.

10. See *TPJS,* 157.

11. See *MD,* 492–93, 500, 694; *DS,* 3:13; *NWAF,* 640.

12. *MM,* 230–31.

Chapter 38

1. The second coming of Jesus Christ is discussed in the previous chapter.

2. See *Man: His Origin and Destiny* (Salt Lake City: Deseret Book, 1954), 380–97.

3. See *JD,* 15:138; *MM,* 608; *DS,* 2:251–52.

4. See *HC,* 5:212; *TPJS,* 268.

SUMMARY OF PRINCIPLES AND PRACTICES OF THE RESTORED GOSPEL

The Members of the Godhead and Our Relationship to Them

1. TRUTH is an accurate understanding of physical, moral, and spiritual reality that God imparts through the ages to bless his children, bringing them freedom.

2. GOD OUR HOLY FATHER is an immortal, perfect being whose infinite wisdom, supreme power, and active love offer us immortality and the possibility of eternal life with him.

3. JESUS is the firstborn, literal, and perfect son of Heavenly Father, and he is also our holy, elder brother who became the chief advocate and administrator of God's plan, serving as the father of his gospel and our salvation. Indeed, he is the Lord of this earth!

4. The HOLY GHOST is a spirit personage who serves as a revelator of truth, a witness of God's work, and a comforter for the human soul.

5. PRAYER is the communication gift between God and mortals through which we praise Deity, give thanks, confess weaknesses, petition needs, and express devotion to our Heavenly Father in the name of Jesus Christ.

6. REVELATION encompasses a variety of means chosen by God to communicate divine truth and his will to his prophets and his children — without it, the true gospel and church could not exist on earth. TESTIMONY is our spiritual witness of divine truths.

7. PROPHETS are called through divine authority and revelation to represent the Godhead, and they are often endowed as seers, revelators, and apostles as they speak for God and build Christ's kingdom on earth.

8. SCRIPTURES are pearls of divine wisdom and gems of sacred writing that record God the Father's plans and works, teach his commandments and covenants, inspire expressions of his truths through great literature and profound doctrine, verify his prophecies and promises, and testify of him and his Son.

God's Plan of Salvation

9. In our first estate, we existed as primal INTELLIGENCES until our

Heavenly Father provided us with spirit bodies, thus allowing us new dimensions of organization, experience, and progression.

10. The divine gift of AGENCY is an eternal principle that permeates our relationship with the Almighty, and it requires identity, knowledge, freedom of choices, action, law, efficacy, and preservation to be in full operation.

11. EARTH LIFE is a probationary state that separates us from God's presence and provides us with a physical body. Mortality provides an opportunity to discover the physical world, to serve others in new dimensions of unselfishness, and to increase our spiritual stature.

12. SIN develops when we pervert truth and goodness by disobeying God's commandments, rationalizing our wickedness, criticizing God's works and servants, then becoming despondent, even antagonistic.

13. JESUS of Nazareth lived a sinless life, taught eternal values, and became the PERFECT WAY—showing all people the path toward happiness, holiness, and exaltation; his ATONEMENT satisfied both the demands of justice and the expectations of mercy, bringing salvation to God's children.

14. AFTER DEATH, we continue learning truth, deciding moral and spiritual issues, and serving others in a postmortal spirit world, where we either enjoy peace with the righteous in restful paradise or suffer torment with the wicked in the hell of spirit prison.

15. RESURRECTION and the FINAL JUDGMENT are gateways into eternity whereby God's children enter into one of his many kingdoms, the joy and glory of which depend upon how they have lived and proven faithful.

Basic Principles, Ordinances, and Blessings of the Gospel

16. FAITH is an assurance of unseen truths, a feeling of confidence in God, and a principle of action centered in Christ, which provides us a hope of divine promises, a motivation toward righteous living, and a catalyst that generates spiritual life.

17. REPENTANCE means both feeling genuine sorrow for our sins and turning our hearts toward God. It is a process involving recognition of our transgressions, sincere remorse, renunciation of wickedness, a firm resolve to become more godlike, restitution to those we have wronged, and reconciliation through forgiveness (and a willingness to forgive)—qualifying us for a release from our burdens through Christ's atonement.

18. BAPTISM is a symbolic ordinance of cleansing and new life, and it is also the covenant gateway into Christ's church and God's celestial kingdom.

19. The GIFT OF THE HOLY GHOST is shared among God's children as the Holy Ghost confirms our membership in Christ's church, as his power and gifts transform us spiritually, and, as a God, he sanctifies our souls preparatory to receiving celestial glory.

20. We need to regularly strengthen our SPIRITUAL HEALTH through daily activities like prayer (along with occasional fasting), scripture and gospel study, service to others, and personal development in one or more of the financial and vocational, physical, emotional, social, intellectual, moral, and spiritual areas of our lives.

21. PERSONAL GROWTH through wise, consistent patterns of character development, preparation of value-oriented goals, and commitment to cooperative success will lead to self-fulfillment and individual perfection and help us progress toward our personal destiny.

22. A variety of BLESSINGS (or GIFTS) edify the Saints through their righteousness; and various sacred priesthood ORDINANCES magnify the Saints through God's power.

23. Latter-day Saints, like the ancient Israelites, are a covenant people who worship in TEMPLES, where they learn about their relationship with God, make sacred commitments, receive key directions about returning to God's presence, and do ordinance work for their deceased relatives.

The Lord's Commandments for Obedience and Blessing

24. Out of God's love for us, he gives us diverse COMMANDMENTS and makes OBEDIENCE to him the first law of the gospel; as we learn to obey him and to serve others because of love (more so than logic or fear), we receive multiple timely blessings.

25. Sunday is our SABBATH, a holy day when we should rest from our weekly labors, worship God, renew our sacramental covenants, and serve others in a spirit of reverence.

26. Life is sacred, and God has protected procreation through the law of CHASTITY, which teaches self-mastery, enhances physical love, strengthens emotional relationships, and empowers spiritual gifts.

27. The WORD OF WISDOM provides basic guidelines of eating and drinking that lead to sound health, treasured wisdom, enduring vitality, and divine protection.

28. Paying TITHING prepares us for the law of CONSECRATION, which is God's celestial law of social behavior, inviting us to share our material wealth and possessions and our personal time and talents with others in building and enjoying his glorious kingdom on earth.

29. Hard, honest, physical WORK earns self-discipline, self-respect, material rewards, and habits for spiritual growth. The Church WELFARE and social services programs assist individuals after they have tried to help themselves and have used all available family resources.

30. The FAMILY, as a potentially eternal union ordained of God, provides the best environment to learn, grow, develop, and serve in our society; and thus the Church supports the family through various instructions, programs, and activities.

Christ's Kingdom on Earth

31. GOSPEL DISPENSATIONS are periods of spiritual enlightenment, priesthood keys, and prophetic leadership, usually followed by times of moral decline and worldly corruption. The GREAT APOSTASY concluded the apostolic period of Christ's dispensation, following which, the GOSPEL RES-

TORATION to Joseph Smith opened this final dispensation of the fullness of times.

32. The PRIESTHOOD is the power and authority to act for God, and with it and through various priesthood councils, Christ's church administers to all members. Worthy men have the Aaronic or Melchizedek Priesthood conferred upon them, are ordained to offices in that priesthood, are organized into quorums, and are set apart and given keys to administer in certain callings.

33. The CHURCH is an assembly of faithful believers. Although God's kingdom on earth, it is an organization also supported by the law of common consent. Through the Church, the gospel is applied in individual lives as the members strengthen, teach, edify, and serve each other in inspired love and through special programs.

34. The Church of Jesus Christ of Latter-day Saints has a threefold MISSION: (1) to proclaim the gospel to all peoples, (2) to perfect the Saints in the household of faith, and (3) to perform vicarious ordinances for the living spirits of the deceased.

35. LATTER-DAY SAINTS become spiritual children and valuable disciples of Christ as they develop faith, adhere to gospel laws, and live righteously while helping others, thus becoming like a shining light (radiating the gospel) and a rolling stone (building his kingdom) that will fill the earth.

36. Latter-day Saints have an obligation to be informed, active CITIZENS of their respective communities and countries where they can worship God, strengthen their families, and serve humanity.

37. In these last days, a widening gulf is separating the righteous from the wicked as the Lord Jesus Christ expects continued obedience to his commandments (in spite of worldly pressures and persecution), and as he sends prophesied SIGNS OF THE TIMES prior to his coming in power and glory.

38. As Christ's kingdom in heaven joins his church and kingdom on earth, he will begin a glorious MILLENNIAL REIGN as Lord of lords and King of kings—fulfilling Heavenly Father's plan, verifying his administration as the true Messiah, enabling the Holy Ghost to seal all sacred ordinances, allowing all Heavenly Father's children opportunity to prepare themselves for God's final judgment, and giving mother earth an opportunity to rest.

SUBJECT GUIDE

Aaronic Priesthood
  Melchizedek Priesthood,
    relationship with, 527–28
  organization, 524–27
Abraham
  blessings of Abraham, 562–63
  dispensation, Abrahamic, 506–7,
    536
Accountability, 159–60, 269–70
Activity in Church, 583–86
Adam
  Dispensation, Adamic, 504–5
  Fall of Adam, 183–87
Adam-ondi-Ahman, Lord's
  appearance at, 618
Administering to sick, 352–55
Adultery, 389, 418–20
Adversity, purposes of, 173–74
Agency. *See also* Freedom
  accountability, agency involves,
    159–60, 212
  efficacy of agency, 160–62
  elements essential to choice, 156–
    63, 210–11
  freedom, 155
  growth depends on agency, 165–
    66
  obedience, relationship of, to
    agency, 160, 397–99
  plan of salvation requires agency,
    148, 165–66
  preservation of agency is
    guaranteed, 162–63
  Satan's attempts to undermine
    agency, 163–65

Agnosticism, 27
Alcohol, adverse effects of, 432–33
Angels, 85–86
Apathy, 28
Apostasy
  baptism, steps of apostasy
    affecting, 512–14
  Great Apostasy, 511–12, 515–16
  personal apostasy, 187–93, 585
  recurring times of apostasy, 502–4
  steps of individual apostasy, 514–
    15
Apostles, 110–11, 532–33, 548–49
Areas of Church, 549–50
Assets, Church, 554–55
Atheism, 26–27, 29
Atonement of Christ, 208–9, 212–16
Authority. *See* Priesthood

Baptism
  apostasy, steps of, affecting
    baptism, 512–14
  authority to perform ordinance,
    293–94, 295
  counterfeit baptism, 296
  covenants of baptism, 291–92
  gate to celestial life, 292
  immersion, baptism by, 283
  Jesus' baptism, 292–93
  preparing for baptism, 294–95
  procedures of baptism, 295–96
  purposes of baptism, 281–82
  salvation, ordinance of, 285–87,
    346–47
  symbolism, 282–85

Preparation for Second Coming, 620–21, 626–27

President
area presidency, 550–51
high priesthood, president of, 528–29, 533, 548
mission president, 570
stake president, 529–30
stake mission president, 551

Presiding councils of Church, 548–49

Priest, 526

Priesthood
authority, God's, 520–21
blessings given through priesthood, 92–93, 286, 349–58
callings to priesthood offices, 523, 533–35
history of priesthood, 536–38
keys, priesthood, 535–36, 561–64
loss of priesthood, 513
oath and covenant of the priesthood, 534–35
ordination to priesthood, 347–48
organization of Aaronic Priesthood, 524–27
organization of Melchizedek Priesthood, 527–33
power, God's, 521–22
restoration of priesthood, 516, 525, 561–64
symbols of authority, 520
use of priesthood, man's, 522–24

Primary, 553

Principles
eternal principles, 382–83
governing Church, principles of, 543–47

Prison, spirit, 222–25

Problem solving, 341–42, 484

Proclaiming gospel. See Missionary work

Programs, Church, 551–54

Progression
action required for development, 334–35
agency required for progression, 165–66
capacity for progression, 152
challenges in personal development, 330–31, 338–42
measuring development, 337
mortality as necessary step in progression, 180
motivation to develop oneself, 335–36
passage through estates, 145, 149, 167–68, 225–26
perception of truth, progression in, 15–17
sin, progression of, 187–93
steps in personal development, 331–38

Promises, God's, fulfillment of, 621–23

Prophecy
gift of prophecy available to all, 105–6
Millennium, prophecies of, 624–25
spirit of prophecy, 104–5

Prophets
apostles, 110–11, 532–33, 548–59
dispensations, prophets establish, 502–3
mouthpieces of God, 101–3
prayers of prophets, 68–69
preparation of prophets for callings, 111–12
priesthood, prophets operate through, 520–21
revelation through prophets, 29–30, 86–87, 109–10
seers, 106–9
true prophets, test of, 103–5

Prosperity during Millennium, 629–31

Purity, 414, 425, 580–81. See also Chastity, law of

Quorums, priesthood, 525–26, 530–33, 535–36, 548–49

Records, 92, 235

Social Services, 472
Sovereignty of Church, 543
Spirit of God. *See* Holy Ghost
Spirit of man
  bodies organized to house spirits,
    145–47
  death, condition of spirits after,
    217–27
  matter, spirit as, 141
  paradise, spirit, 220–23
  prison, spirit, 222–25
  world, spirit, 219–20
Spirituality
  change of heart, 299–300
  nourishing spiritual health, 313
  refining spiritual life, 177–79
Stake president, 529–30
Stakes, 550–51
State, separation of church and,
  597–99
Stealing, commandment against,
  389
Stress, 339–41
Structure of Church
  unity, structure based on, 540–42
  organization, 547–51
  programs, 551–54
Suffering
  atheists' arguments regarding
    suffering, 26
  purposes for adversity, 173–74
  spirit prison, suffering in, 222–23
  unrepentant, suffering of, 279
Sunday School, 553–54
Sustaining, 554
Symbolism
  ordinances, 282–85, 365–66
  temple structure, 360–63
Synergy, 336–37

Talents, expanding, 175–76
Tares, parable of wheat and, 608–
  10
Tea, 434–35
Teacher, 525–26
Teaching, gift of, 306–7
Telestial glory, 239–41

Temple
  appearance of Lord at temple,
    617–18
  "halfway station" between heaven
    and earth, 359–60
  Millennium, temple work during,
    633
  ordinances, temple, 348–49, 364–
    69, 633
  symbolism, structure of, in
    temple, 360–63
  vicarious work, 370–71
  worship in temple, 93–94
  worthiness to attend temple, 364,
    369–70
Ten Commandments, 386–90
Ten Tribes of Israel, dispensations
  among, 510–11
Terrestrial glory, 241–42
Testimony
  bearing testimony, 93
  gift of Spirit, testimony is, 304–5
  seeking testimony, 97–99, 255
  weakening of testimony, 99–100
Theocracy, 547–48
Third Nephi as model for last days,
  616–17
Tithing
  blessings accompanying payment
    of tithes, 449–51
  disbursement of tithes, 453–56
  law of tithing, 448–49
  preparation for law of
    consecration, tithing is, 458–60
Tobacco, adverse effects of, 434
Tongues, gift of, 308
Trials, purpose for, 173–74
Trumpets, seven, 614–16
Trust, 425–26
Truth
  applying truth, 19–20
  faith in truth, 253
  freedom through truth, 21–22,
    206
  Jesus as truth, 205–6
  moral truth, 11–12
  past, present, and future,
    knowledge of, 17–19

ISBN 0-87579-649-4
SKU 2329357
$21.95